BLUE-EYED CHILD OF FORTUNE

12.50

BLUE-EYED CHILD OF FORTUNE

The Civil War Letters of
COL. ROBERT GOULD SHAW

Edited by

RUSSELL DUNCAN

AVON BOOKS ◆ NEW YORK

Frontispiece: Robert Gould Shaw, May 1863. Boston Athenaeum

AVON BOOKS
A division of
The Hearst Corporation
1350 Avenue of the Americas
New York, New York 10019

Copyright © 1992 by the University of Georgia Press
Published by arrangement with the University of Georgia Press
Library of Congress Catalog Card Number: 91-46644
ISBN: 0-380-72168-6

The University of Georgia edition contains the following Library of Congress Cataloging in Publication Data:
Shaw, Robert Gould, 1837–1863.
  Blue-eyed child of fortune: the Civil War letters of Colonel Robert Gould Shaw/edited by Russell Duncan.
    p. cm.
Includes bibliographical references and index.
1. Shaw, Robert Gould, 1837-1863–Correspondence. 2. United States. Army. Massachusetts Infantry Regiment, 54th(1863-1865)–History 3. United States–History–Civil War, 1861-1865–Personal narratives. 4. Massachusetts–History–Civil War, 1861-1865–Personal narratives. 5. United States–History–Civil War, 1861-1865–Participation, Afro-American. 6. Massachusetts—History–Civil War, 1861-1865– Participation, Afro-American. 7. Soldiers–United States–Correspondence. 8. Soldiers–Massachusetts–Correspondence. I. Duncan, Russell. II. Title.
E513.5 54th.S53   1992
973.7'81'092–dc20
[B]   91-46644
                                                         CIP

First Avon Books Trade Printing: February 1994

AVON TRADEMARK REG. U.S. PAT. OFF. AND IN OTHER COUNTRIES, MARCA REGISTRADA, HECHO EN U.S.A.

Printed in the U.S.A.

OPM 10 9 8 7 6 5 4 3 2 1

For Holly

". . . everything softened and made unreal by distance, poor

little Robert Shaw erected into a great symbol of deeper

things than he ever realized himself."

—William James to Henry James, Jr.

June 5, 1897

CONTENTS

In the fall of 1856, two great American educations glanced across one another. Robert Gould Shaw was a freshman at Harvard, Henry Brooks Adams a junior. As there were only 382 students at the college, the two must have met, although there is no record that either made much of an impression on the other. The upperclassman, traveling far, went on to record the better part of his eighty-year struggle with knowing himself and his world in one of the classics of our literature, *The Education of Henry Adams*. The freshman, who only remained in college for two-and-a-half years—but long enough to read Thucydides on war—was dead and thrown in a trench dug in Carolina sand when he was twenty-six. Shaw's was an education for a short life.

Henry Adams's education has instructed generations of his countrymen and women in our twentieth century. It contains a famous apostrophe on the evils of slavery; Adams learned that you could reach the seat of the nation's greatness, George Washington's Mt. Vernon, only over the dusty rutted roads of slavery. But America's slavery was but one of the world's failings he so perceptively recorded in the vast breadth of the *Education*. Adams told his fellow European Americans nothing of the people who had been slaves.

In 1856, although his parents were far more ardent antislavery people than were Adams's, Shaw could have told us even less about African Americans than his fellow student. When he died at Fort Wagner on July 18, 1863, he had taught all Americans a lesson of incalculable value, one that for long years languished, but has never been forgotten. Like any teacher who is honest, his command of his subject was less than perfect, as his letters show. But he was groping to know the black men who had enlisted in the Fifty-fourth Massachusetts, a regiment of freeborn Northern Negroes organized by Governor John A. Andrew after President Lincoln signed the Emancipation Proclamation on January 1, 1863. Shaw, at his mother and father's urging, reluctantly accepted the regiment's colonelcy aware that he was ignorant of the men he would be leading. Much as did Shaw, white America still gropes to know; we can learn from his life and his death.

The pupils, of course, taught the teacher. The men recruited into the regiment had to take only one look to know that their world-traveled young Harvard lord had a lot to learn. Black citizens who had long been eager for black men to be allowed to fight in the Civil War participated actively in the organization of the regiment; late in January (before the training camp at Readville was open) Shaw wrote his mother: "At the meeting Richard Hallowell said it would please the coloured population to have some influential darkey on the committee and cousin John told him he would like to take in a nigger and turn him (H[allowell].) out, which naturally caused some merriment." This was the level of discourse in which Shaw began to learn, but, in the same letter, he added: "Some of the influential coloured men I have met [perhaps the first he had met] please me very much. They are really so gentlemanlike and dignified."

In March, as the recruits were training, Shaw reported, "My regiment is making pretty good headway. We have nearly 150 men in camp, and they come in pretty fast. There are several among them, who have been well drilled, & who are acting sergeants. They drill their squads with a good deal of snap, and I think we shall have some good soldiers. Thirty four came up from New Bedford this afternoon, and marched with a drum & fife creating the greatest enthusiasm among the rest. We have them examined," he continued, "sworn in, washed & uniformed as soon as they arrive—and when they get into their buttons they feel about as good as a man can." He was amused—and fascinated—by the black sergeants; as they "explain the drill to the men . . . they use words long enough for a Doctor of Divinity."

Later that month, recalling conditions he had observed during his earlier service with the Army of the Potomac, he noted that the "company from New Bedford are a very fine body of men, and out of forty, only two cannot read and write. Their barracks are in better order, and more cleanly, than the quarters of any volunteer regiment I have seen in this country." As he was overcoming one set of prejudices, another specialty of Protestant Boston revealed itself: "Everything goes on prosperously. The intelligence of the men is a great surprise to me. They learn all the details of guard duty and Camp service, infinitely more readily than the Irish I have had under my command."

Shaw encountered considerable scorn from other white men engaged in the war, and was pleased when his men proved it to be misplaced: "The mustering-officer, who was here to-day, is a Virginian, and has always thought it was a great joke to try to make soldiers of 'niggers'; but he told me to-day, that he had never mustered in so fine a set of men, though about twenty thousand had passed through his hands since September last. The sceptics need only come out here now, to be converted."

On May 28, 1863, the Fifty-fourth Massachusetts, trained and ready, marched through the streets of Boston to the wharf and the ship that would carry them south to the islands off the Georgia and South Carolina coasts that had been in Union hands since the fall of 1861. There were snide comments from the gentlemen of the Somerset Club and catcalls from many along the streets, but none of that mattered as the black men marched past leaders of the antislavery movement and ordinary citizens, men and women, black and white, cheering from sidewalks, balconies, and the governor's reviewing stand. Four days later, on board ship as they passed Cape Hatteras, Shaw reflected on the day: "The more I think of the passage of the Fifty-fourth through Boston, the more wonderful it seems to me. Just remember our own doubts and fears, and other people's sneering and pitying remarks, when we began last winter, and then look at the perfect triumph of last Thursday. . . . Every one I saw, from the Governor's staff (who have always given us rather the cold shoulder) down, had nothing but words of praise for us. Truly, I ought to be thankful for all my happiness, and my success in life so far; and if the raising of coloured troops prove such a benefit to the country, and to the blacks, as many people think it will, I shall thank God a thousand times that I was led to take my share in it."

Shaw's life was to last only a little over a month longer, but by the time he and hundreds of those proud soldiers who marched and fought with him fell in the terrible, failed assault on Fort Wagner, guarding the port of Charleston, they had come a long way toward knowing each other. And dead together in their common grave they still instruct.

Russell Duncan has given us a rich portrait—virtually a biography—of Robert Gould Shaw as his introduction to this scrupulously edited collection of Shaw's letters home. Duncan's Shaw is a vastly different man from the one played by Matthew Broderick in the film *Glory*, that excellent fictional account of the Fifty-fourth that did so much to awaken Americans to knowledge of the critical participation of African Americans in their own liberation. But the Robert Gould Shaw of *Blue-Eyed Child of Fortune* is more interesting for that difference. His reach to know his men is full of the indirections, inconsistencies, and even blindness that have characterized the stumbling efforts of so many Americans to grasp the simple, obvious realities of the lives of other Americans.

The other America that Shaw sought to understand, to change, was an America in which people lived as slaves. Today's other America is the dwelling place of people, many of whom are descendants of those slaves, who are living with the poverty and despair of our cities. They live surrounded by people who, rich, privileged, and unknowing, fear and scorn them. Like the soldiers of the Fifty-fourth, these Americans are due the understanding that Shaw sought more than a century ago. That we can reach a solution to our present immense social problems without recourse to the violence to which Shaw's generation turned is devoutly to be wished. A crucial beginning surely lies in the simple, difficult business of knowing each other.

The sculptor Augustus Saint-Gaudens took Shaw's learning a brilliant step farther when, for his great monument to Shaw and the Fifty-fourth on the Boston Common, he made each of the men marching into battle a separate individual, with distinctive physical features, committed to a common purpose. In "For the Union Dead," Robert Lowell, a generation ago, tried to make his Boston—his America—look at those men and learn. Too few have.

Henry Adams, teaching much, taught that an education is never complete. Robert Gould Shaw, studying his fellow soldiers, did not live to more than glimpse completion of his lesson. But his letters—cluttered as they are with all the other things of his life—are an invitation for Americans to learn about one another. *Blue-Eyed Child of Fortune* is an education for America.

—William S. McFeely

PREFACE

Robert Gould Shaw was merely a competent officer, but he was not an ordinary soldier. Coming from great wealth and advantage, Shaw stood among the high profile regiments of the war: Seventh New York National Guard, Second Massachusetts Infantry, and Fifty-fourth Massachusetts (Colored) Infantry. The Seventh distinguished itself by being the first regiment to arrive in Washington after Lincoln's call for troops. The Second was Boston's own and many Brahmin sons officered its men. The Fifty-fourth, the vanguard unit that became the most watched regiment of the war, filled its ranks with the cream of the Northern black population. Shaw joined to fight for the North, to do his duty, and to prove his courage and manhood. In that, he was a very average soldier. His letters home reveal his self-reflection on the meaning of the war and the constant widening of the gap between his expectations and the actualities of the conflict.

Shaw's letters convey the change wrought by battlefield casualties, camp life, commitment, and homesickness upon the sensibilities of youth. His soldiering experience was as common as it was distinctive. He joined to win a quick war, but committed to fight to the end. He "saw the elephant" at Cedar Mountain, Antietam, and Fort Wagner, made wearying marches, and spent days in tedious boredom awaiting orders to the front, orders to anywhere. Like others, he wanted wounds—and got them. The adrenaline of life and death on the field of battle brought Shaw closer to his comrades in a male world than he had ever been to his classmates at Harvard or to his boyhood companions. This universe of maleness helped him to pull at the strings of his female-dominated family, and helped him mature even though he had not been able to break free of his mother's dominance by the time of his death. In that sense, Shaw never got past his mother; the monument on Boston Common is much more representative of her ambition than of his.

Shaw's letters enwrap his background in the antislavery community and convey his wrenching struggle within and without to make sense of a war among brothers. Shaw's upper-class education and influential family inform his letters, written in what may be the most eloquent prose any soldier wrote home during any war.

Military and social historians and readers will learn from Shaw's descriptive insights into camp conditions and battle manuevers. His letters are open and trustworthy. After his father published excerpts from his August 12, 1862, letter home in the aftermath of the battle of Cedar Mountain, Shaw warned, "I can't write what I want to, if my letters are to be put in the papers" (October 5, 1862, collected herein). Shaw's family kept subsequent correspondence private until after his death. In return, they received honest accounts of his experiences and sincere expressions of his thoughts. His letters are a celebration of life in an environment of death.

The pathway of Shaw's experience in the war is a microcosm of the conflict. Within a week of Fort Sumter he marched into Washington and swore before Lincoln that he would fight for the Union. Three months later, after training at Brook Farm and upon singing "John Brown's Body" as he strode into Harper's Ferry, Shaw began to reflect that the war was about more than nationhood. After his friends and fellows began to die, Shaw grew into a competent officer and into a man who hoped that the higher goal of freedom could be achieved by a Northern victory.

Cedar Mountain brought the destructive war to Shaw in the form of Stonewall Jackson's assault and victory. Positioned in a wheatfield, Shaw's Second Infantry lost sixteen of its twenty-three officers killed or wounded. Before Shaw came fully to grips with the suffering that resulted from this Virginia battle, he fought through a bloodier slaughter in a Maryland cornfield along meandering Antietam creek. With more officers dead and the regiment at half strength, Shaw knew firsthand the costs of war.

The preliminary, then the actual, Emancipation Proclamation replaced Union with Freedom, and thereby lifted the Civil War to a moral plane that makes it worth studying and teaching. Black men enlisted as soldiers to end slavery and to prove themselves capable of citizenship. When Shaw accepted the colonelcy of the North's first black regiment and led it past the ditches and abattis up onto the parapets of Fort Wagner, part of the Charleston Harbor defenses, he gave us an education: in race relations, in strength of character, and in the meaning of freedom. His letters home transcend his time to give meaning to our own.

I owe many people a great deal. They helped me unearth evidence, rethink conclusions, marry nouns to verbs, reunite infinitives, explore repositories, devise research strategies, and live my life while I relived Shaw's. While I cannot possibly repay—or rename—all of those who gave me much, I do appreciate their patience with my bungling style, continual questioning, and interrupting impatience.

Every author who has published with the University of Georgia Press knows the pleasure of working with its staff. In the book's earliest stage—two weeks after the premier of the movie *Glory*—editor Malcolm Call talked with me about my ideas for a book and encouraged me to move quickly on the project. Malcolm remained the book's warmest supporter during the two-year period of research and writing. He is all the things an editor should be: hardnosed, available, and amiable. Karen Orchard offered timely enthusiasm and questions to push me along, just as she had done on two previous collaborations. Matt Brook shepherded the book through the rough stages, added expert advice on style, and made sure the manuscript went to a good copyeditor. Michael Senecal did the copyediting and deciphered my peculiar, non-conforming bibliographical notations into standard form.

The community of John Carroll University aided my work in many ways. Among my colleagues in the history department who read sections and offered criticism, I want to thank Marian Morton, David Robson, Bob Kolesar, Jim Krukones, Mary Kay Howard, Francesco Cesareo, Roger Purdy, Harry Lupold, and Bill Ulrich. Mary McGeary helped me with the technical details of reproducing the manuscript and gave up an entire Saturday to convert my word-processor files to the required format. Computer whiz extraordinaire Ken Brownlie became the sine qua non of the conversion. Fred Travis, Sally Wertheim, and Lou Pecek provided monies from funding sources—and a very fast printer—to enhance my research time. Wilhelm Bartsch and Pam Waldschmidt translated Shaw's passages and letters from German and French, respectively, into English. A very gifted student, Mary Beth Fraser, searched diligently for many of the notes that supplement this work.

Even though the library at John Carroll University is small, the staff's professionalism (and many computers) turned its interlibrary loan office and reference desk into a considerable research facility. Thanks especially to Nevin Mayer, Caron Knapp, Ruth Reider, and Mary Kay Sweeney. Chuck Zarobila expertly photographed several of the illustrations that complement this book.

Several archivists at the manuscript repositories I visited were particularly helpful. Denny Beach of Houghton Library spent many hours helping me locate evidence and getting me through the necessary paperwork of what seemed endless requisitions. At the Massachusetts Historical Society photo archivist Chris Steele and research librarian Virginia Smith guided me through the collections. The Boston Athenaeum's Sally Pierce was extremely helpful as was the staff in the manuscript room of the Boston Public Library.

In New York, Carlotta Defillo and Sarah Clark worked overtime in the materials of the Staten Island Historical Society. Everyone at the Staten Island Institute of Arts and Sciences, but especially Hugh Powell and Cathy Meyer, professionally sifted materials for information. The archivists in the rare-book room of the New York Public Library aided my search.

Mike Meier, Mike Musick, Gary Morgan, and Rick Peuser are experts in the military records of the National Archives who, while overworked, generously gave of their time. Randy Hackenberg and Richard Sommers of the U.S. Army Military History Institute at Carlisle Barracks, Pennsylvania, expeditiously found photographs and manuscripts. At the Old Dartmouth Historical Society and Whaling Museum in New Bedford, Richard Kugler and Virginia Adams pointed me toward valuable sources. Ernestina Furtado and Paul Cyr spent long hours uncovering bundled documents at the New Bedford Free Public Library.

Pat Givens of Waban, Massachusetts, and David Johnson of Greenwich, Connecticut—both friends of friends—graciously allowed me the open reign and free use of their homes so that I might do long-term research in Boston and New York City. Their generosity made this project possible and enjoyable.

Joseph T. Glatthaar, C. Peter Ripley, and James M. McPherson offered professional judgments on the value and quality of Shaw's letters and on my editing and writing abilities. None of them will be absolutely pleased to see that I did not include all of their proposals, but those I did adopt greatly strengthened the work and brought order from confusion in more than a few places. Any errors or omissions that remain are entirely my own.

At various times when my confidence sagged, many close friends stepped in to read and make comments on the manuscript. Mary and John Sedney, Pat Bloem, and David Klooster carefully massaged my ego while they beat up my prose. They saved me from a few grievous errors and helped me evaluate and reevaluate Shaw's letters over dinner, around campfires, and in backyard visitations. Bill and Mary McFeely interchanged ideas, fed me, helped me dig in the sand, and swam gracefully in a Walden-like pond still unfound by the multitude. Bill encouraged me in ways that go beyond the pages of this book. Christopher Phillips, who is the second-best one-on-one historian basketball player ever to put up a jump shot, challenged all my conclusions in many conversations that stretched into overtime. Doug White corrected a factual error of importance.

Emory Thomas's advice and friendship have supported my efforts for the past decade (since 1982) in all areas of Clio's discipline. His friendship lets me take advantage of him more than I should. More than once he has intervened for me with the unfailing words, "I guarantee it!" I miss the softball games and the Rock Glen porch talks.

Joan Creekmore Stringer, Betty Freeman McCurry, Asben Alpha McCurry,

Mary Ella King Freeman, and John Wesley Freeman sustained me in kindnesses for which I can only thank them, but never repay otherwise.

Holly McCurry Duncan and Bonnie Katherine Duncan continue to provide me with pleasure and support in ways only they know. I cannot be certain of what they have sacrificed to allow me weeks of days and nights in the wombs of faraway libraries or behind the keyboard in my basement study. Holly fretted over the title, helped me past my tendency for melodrama, and corrected many sets of proofs. Holly and Bonnie gave freely of their opinions and openly of themselves whenever I looked up from the dazzling sand of Shaw's lifetime to the brighter beaches of our own.

In 1864, Sarah Shaw compiled the Civil War letters written by her son Robert, edited them, and had them published for members of the family and close friends. That volume, *Letters: RGS*, exists today only in the rare book rooms of a handful of libraries and in private collections. The most accessible copies are at the Houghton Library, Harvard University; the Boston Public Library; the Massachusetts Historical Society; and the New York Public Library. In 1876 a collection of Shaw's juvenalia was also published as *Letters: RGS*. I used these letters to inform the biographical sketch, but they are not collected herein.

The Houghton Library has the largest and by far the best collection of Shaw manuscripts although many of the original letters which served as the source for *Letters: RGS* have been lost or are unavailable. Additional letters can be found in the T. Lyman III and Robert Gould Shaw II collections at the Massachusetts Historical Society and in the Shaw Family Letters collection of the New York Public Library. The letters from the printed collection and from the four manuscript sources form the present volume, *Blue-Eyed Child of Fortune*. The collection and repository for each missive is noted in the top right-hand corner of the letter, as follows:

[HL]   Robert Gould Shaw Papers, Houghton Library, Harvard
         University
[LYM]   T. Lyman III Collection, Massachusetts Historical Society
[MHS]   Robert Gould Shaw II Collection, Massachusetts Historical
         Society
[NYPL]   Shaw Family (Personal Miscellaneous), Rare Books and Manu-
         scripts Division, The New York Public Library, Astor, Lenox and
         Tilden Foundations
[RGS]   *Letters: RGS*. Cambridge: Harvard University Press, 1864.

Sarah Shaw took liberties in editing her son's letters for publication. In the salutation, capitals replaced lowercase letters and colons replaced commas. In the body of the text, commas appeared where none had existed. Robert rarely misspelled words, but the few he did get wrong were corrected. Sarah also split long passages into paragraphs or divided run-on sentences to facilitate reading. Those are minor changes. She deleted the names of several individuals who might have been embarrassed or angry by what her son wrote about them. She was especially sensitive when her son criticized specific clergymen. Sarah also removed sentences and whole paragraphs from her son's letters to his wife Annie. Many of those comments were much too personal to be reproduced for family gossip in 1864, or probably even in 1992. There is a possibility that Annie may have deleted those portions she found too sensitive before allowing Sarah to read the letters in the first place.

More troubling than these minor deletions was Sarah's exorcism of some of Robert's more overt prejudicial remarks toward blacks. Because Robert is important to history only because of his position atop the North's first black regiment, any remark he made concerning black soldiers or people is important. While I found just three such deletions when I compared the manuscript letters to the printed ones, they gave me pause. In only one case, did her deletion change the meaning of Robert's sentence and mislead. The other two simply removed information that reflected negatively upon coastal blacks and upon Robert's attitude toward them. Naturally, when I had a choice between a manuscript and the printed letter, I used the manuscript and noted the difference from the printed letter. There are numerous examples of Robert's attitudes in the letters without those deleted by a longtime abolitionist and proud parent. It should be noted that while conscious about slights toward blacks, Sarah does not seem to have been at all sensitive to Robert's bias against the Irish, a bias she shared.

Robert wrote well and clearly. For the most part, his original letters have been nicely preserved. Manuscript letters are herein printed in their entirety and have been returned to the punctuation, abbreviations, and spelling used by the writer. Misspelled words are not followed by the editorial [sic]. Instead, notes following each letter correct the spelling of proper names and provide information, and I hope amusement, for the reader. There is an exception. His consistent misspelling of "beleived" seemed particularly worrisome for the modern reader and has been replaced by "believed." Inkspots, age, or other factors, such as scribbling over the text, made a few words illegible. Those are clearly marked with brackets and contain an explanation of how much was lost, i.e. [two words illegible].

The letters selected from *Letters: RGS* are printed as they were in 1864 with one exception. Robert used commas after the salutation instead of colons in the manuscript letters and I added those back confidently to the printed ones. Elsewhere, with no available proof, even if with a high suspicion that the spelling or punctuation differed, the letters appear as they were edited by

Sarah. With one exception, Sarah did allow us to know that material had been removed by placing ellipses for the reader's benefit. Those have been retained in this volume.

Beyond this limited tampering with what Robert wrote, Sarah and I have let him speak for himself. His prose is often eloquent, always articulate, intensely informative, amusing, heartwrenching, and provocative more than a century after he described himself in letters to his family and friends. As interlopers to words never meant for us to ponder, we can enjoy him and gain insight into his times and into ours.

ABBREVIATIONS IN NOTES

BPL	Boston Public Library
CMSR	Compiled Military Service Records, National Archives
DAB	*Dictionary of American Biography*
FGS	Francis George Shaw
HL	Houghton Library, Harvard University
MHS	Massachusetts Historical Society
NA	National Archives
NBFPL	New Bedford Free Public Library
NYHS	New York Historical Society
NYPL	New York Public Library
NYDT	*New York Daily Tribune*
NYT	*New York Times*
OR	*The War of the Rebellion: A Compilation of the Official Records of the Union and Confederate Armies*
RGS	Robert Gould Shaw
SBS	Sarah Blake Shaw
SIHS	Staten Island Historical Society
SIIAS	Staten Island Institute of Arts and Sciences
WVU	West Virginia University

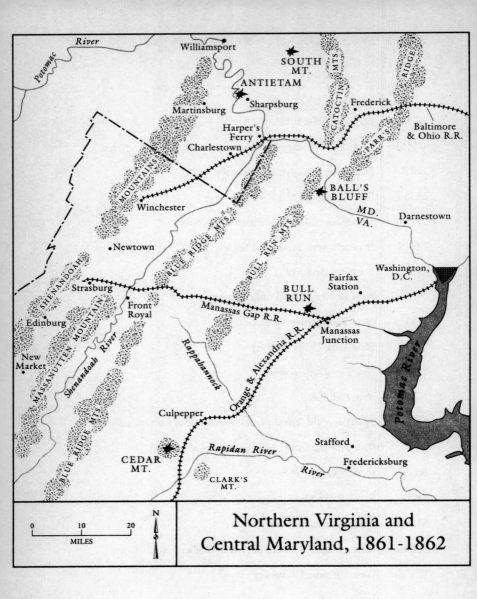

Northern Virginia and
Central Maryland, 1861-1862

BLUE-EYED CHILD OF FORTUNE

Robert Gould Shaw

A BIOGRAPHICAL ESSAY

On the Boston Common, Robert Gould Shaw rides his horse in step with his regiment marching Southward forever with straight backs, forward eyes, and long strides. In Augustus Saint-Gaudens's greatest sculpture, Shaw, white, and his men, black—and all bronze—recall that eight and twentieth day of May in 1863 when one thousand men strode with swaying steps and swinging flags through the streets of Boston and into glory. The drummer boys tapped out the beat and the men's lusty voices sang out their vow that while John Brown's body might be a-mouldering in the grave, they would carry forward his vision of black men redeeming themselves from 250 years of slavery. In their right hands and on their right shoulders gleamed a thousand Enfield rifles that had been supplied them from an armory they had not had to break open to obtain.[1]

The largest crowd in the city's history assembled on Essex and Beacon streets, leaned from balconies, waved from windows, ran out to touch or praise, and surrounded the reviewing stands around the State House and in the Common to cheer and gape at the pride of abolitionist Boston. Hundreds of wives and sweethearts smiled and fretted over their men. Frederick Douglass, a formidable man in stature, stood even taller and bigger as he watched his eldest son, Lewis, march past. Douglass surely recalled his own words as he saw each black soldier with "an eagle on his button and a musket on his shoulder" and was sure that this would earn them "the right to citizenship in the United States." William Lloyd Garrison wept openly as he rested against a bust of John Brown at Wendell Phillips's home overlooking the parade route. Pacifist John Greenleaf Whittier, who attended the parade of no other unit for fear that doing so would encourage and give "a new impulse to war," could not keep away from the line of march. Runaway Georgia slave Thomas Sims, who had been dragged back to slavery in 1851 under the authority of the Fugitive Slave Act, to be sold downriver to Mississippi, and finally freed in 1863 to return to Boston, trembled with satisfaction as he watched armed black men tread over the same ground where he had been chained and returned to bondage. The family of Colonel Shaw, commander of the Fifty-fourth Massachusetts Infantry, watched and hugged each other as their son, brother, and husband saluted them by briefly stopping his horse and raising his sword to his lips in front of the house at 44 Beacon Street. When this day passed, they would see his youthful figure again only when the statue found its place on the Common in 1897.[2]

Sixty years before the unveiling, Shaw was born into one of the nation's richest families. He had all the advantages of the fortunate—the easy life, famous friends, the best schools, finest clothes, widest travels, ripest food, and richest drink the world could offer. Yet, he died with sand in his mouth and sword in hand face down among the sons of the unfortunate and despised.

Shaw never attained the scholarly insight of his father, the reform conviction of his mother and sisters, or the business acumen of his grandfathers and uncles. He did not join the army in 1861 to fight for the Union or to free the slaves, but simply to do his duty. He did want to avenge the name of his country and to revenge what he considered years of bullying by Southern slaveholders. He did not particularly care if the South was forced back into the Union; he had merely grown tired of the atmosphere of sectional tension that pervaded his daily life. Shaw craved a nation freed from this disorderly opprobrium so that he could get on with the pleasures of living. Eight hundred days of war barely changed his outlook before it spilt his lifeblood into the sand of South Carolina. Friends and family, poets and philosophers, Northerners and Southerners, and blacks and whites eventually would praise him and make him a martyr to a cause he neither fully understood nor dedicated himself to.

Born in Boston on October 10, 1837, Shaw attended the kindergarten of "Miss Mary Peabody." He played with older sister Anna and younger sisters Susanna, Josephine, and Ellen in the homes of his many uncles and aunts. His father, Francis George Shaw, was the eldest of eleven children, and his mother, Sarah Blake Sturgis Shaw, stood eighth in a brood of twelve. Robert's eighty-five first cousins afforded him plenty of playmates. The children of his parents' friends were willing confederates when the Shaws visited. George and Willie Garrison often played with Robert in the home and yard of their father, the abolitionist editor of the *Liberator*, William Lloyd Garrison. In Garrison's home, Robert no doubt heard his parents discuss the immorality of slavery. Years after the editor died, his sons remembered the Shaws among "the original abolitionists."[3]

Robert's grandfathers, Robert Gould Shaw and Nathaniel Russell Sturgis, made millions of dollars in the West India and China importing trades of their fathers. The first Robert Shaw was Boston's wealthiest merchant, operating a dry goods store, an auction and commission house, and real estate business worth $1.5 million in 1852. As Shaws intermarried with Sturgises and others, the variously named companies of Russell and Sturgis, Russell and Company, and Sturgis, Shaw and Company opened offices in Boston, Manila, Canton, and New York City and made or increased the fortunes of many relatives, including the families Cabot, Forbes, Russell, Parkman, Hunnewell, and Lodge.[4]

In 1841, thirty-two-year-old Francis Shaw, Robert's father, retired from his business as a merchant and part-time lawyer and moved his family to West Roxbury, Massachusetts, to be near the newly established commune of Brook Farm. In this noncommercial world, he devoted the rest of his life to literary pursuits, family, and philanthropy. He translated many literary and historical works into English, including George Sand's *Consuelo* (1848) and Heinrich Zschokke's *History of Switzerland* (1855).[5]

Francis Shaw allied himself with those who wanted to raise the lot of the working class. He rejected the idea that the overall advancement of society required some people to be poor. He also scoffed at the notion that poverty was a permanent condition and refused to believe in a hierarchy of races. The responsibility to better the world must be shouldered. One of his closest friends recalled that Shaw "believed too much in man to accept the state of things as the will of God." Shaw believed in, translated, and published the socialist views of Mathieu Briancourt's *The Organization of Labor and Association* (1847) and Felix Cantagrel's *The Children of the Phalanstery* (1848). To give wider audience to the ideals of a happier social order, he put into English Charles Pellarin's *The Life of Charles Fourier* (1848). Many of Shaw's translations first appeared in the Brook Farm paper the *Harbinger*.[6]

Later, he wrote "A Piece of Land," which reformer Henry George included in his famous work *Social Problems* (1883)—a book dedicated to Shaw. Shaw cast "A Piece of Land" as a morality play with three characters: Labor, Capital, and Landowner. Labor leased Capital's spade to plant a potato crop for market on common land. At harvest time, Labor paid for his use of the spade with interest in the form of a share of the crop. All was fine and good as Capital and Labor became partners. Labor rose and prospered. Then, the villain Landowner stepped in, put up fences, and charged Labor exorbitant prices, which soon drove Labor and his family into the ruin of the poorhouse. All society suffered from the greed of Landowner. The play expounded the tenets of free-labor ideology as well as George's repugnance at the power that went with the ownership of land. Shaw promoted fairness to all groups and worried over what the inequities of class and race portended for the future.[7]

The Shaws did not join fully in the communal lifestyle at Brook Farm, but they associated weekly with many of that group of intellectuals and reformers, including Ralph Waldo Emerson, Nathaniel Hawthorne, and Margaret Fuller. Francis and his wife's brother-in-law George Russell, who had retired at age thirty-five and also lived in West Roxbury, had helped finance the start-up costs of Brook Farm. They continued to provide monetary support until the experiment ended in 1847. Unitarians made up a large number of the communalists and came under the direct influence of ministers William Channing and Theodore Parker. Parker had a small country church near Brook Farm where he preached abolitionism, rational thinking, open-mindedness, and human uplift. He told his congregation that man had to expand beyond "self-culture" not only to improve the individual but also to rid the nation of social problems and injustice to better the entire "house." The Shaws regularly attended Parker's services and counted him among their close friends.[8]

Robert attended school in West Roxbury and was influenced by the humanitarianism of the Brook Farm intellectuals. His father and mother were devoted to the antislavery cause, and the boy knew not only William Lloyd Garrison but also other friends of the family, including Harriet Beecher Stowe. Sarah Shaw's closest friend and lifelong correspondent was Lydia Maria Child. Child began writing in favor of abolition in 1833 with "An Appeal in Favour of that Class of Americans called Africans," and from 1840 to 1844 she and her husband David coedited the *Anti-Slavery Standard*. Her widely published 1859 edition of letters between John Brown and Virginia governor Henry Wise fueled the controversy over slavery, helped make Brown a martyr, and provided a strongly worded argument that the North was under the heel of the Southern aristocracy and "Slave Power." Child and Sarah Shaw attended classes together at Brook Farm and kept each other strong in the face of those who wanted the abolitionists to keep quiet.[9]

Shaw's parents joined Child in the American Anti-Slavery Society in 1838, and by 1842 Francis was working with the Boston Vigilance Committee to help runaway slaves to freedom. That same year, he joined with Wendell Phillips and five others to head a petition drive asking Congress for the immediate abolition of slavery and the slave trade in the District of Columbia. The petition called this request "a question of justice" and asked that no new states be admitted to the Union whose constitutions tolerated slavery. In 1851, Vigilance Committee members unsuccessfully tried to rescue Thomas Sims from the slave catchers; their failure only increased their conviction to oppose the Fugitive Slave Law.[10]

The abolitionists clung to each other for the support necessary to carry on with their convictions. One of Francis Shaw's best friends, Sydney Howard Gay, who edited the *Anti-Slavery Standard* before becoming managing editor of the *New York Tribune* in 1862, observed that this small group of reformers seemed "to the outside world a set of pestilent fanatics . . . [but were] among themselves the most charming circle of cultivated men and women that it has ever been my lot to know." The Shaws consistently devoted their time, money, and influence to gain freedom for slaves. One neighbor said of Francis, "He was a man among ten thousand. Born to wealth, he treated his wealth very largely as a trust for the use and benefit of suffering mankind. To every good cause he lent his sympathy, his advocacy, and his material support." [11]

With the decline of Brook Farm and with his wife's failing eyesight, Shaw moved the family to Staten Island to be near the nation's premier eye specialist, Samuel MacKenzie Elliott. The family settled in the north end town of West New Brighton, a literary neighborhood of Unitarians, free-soilers, and abolitionists. The Shaws often took the ferry to Brooklyn to attend the church of Henry Ward Beecher and were instrumental in establishing a Unitarian church on Staten Island. The island was a sparsely settled rural area of fourteen thousand residents, and Robert, age nine, found the island a wonder to be explored. On the North Shore, farmland interplayed with dense woods near the mouth of the Kills, where a deep ravine extended inland and accepted the ebb and flow of the tide. Robert picked ripe blackberries and explored this mysterious terrain with his sisters. To secure his education, Sarah placed him in the private school of "Herr Marschalk." [12]

When the time came for Robert to advance to more challenging studies, his uncle Coolidge Shaw miraculously talked Francis and Sarah into sending the boy to the preparatory school of St. John's College in Fordham, New York. Coolidge had forsaken material goods to join the Jesuits and felt that a Catholic schooling would be good for his nephew. Robert's first letter to his mother in June 1850 revealed his response to being away from home, to the workload, and to the discipline: "I wish you hadn't sent me here . . . for I hate it like everything." In September, Robert continued his litany ("I hate Fordham") and added a note about his professor: "My old Teacher scolded me to-day because I didn't do something he didn't tell me to do, and I hate him." He confided that his homesickness embarrassed him when he cried in front of his classmates. There is no evidence that he was punished by "Father Regnier, the one who whips the boys," but he ran away twice and told his parents in October, "I'd rather do anything than stay here." Nevertheless, he remained at Fordham for the entire semester, studying French, Spanish, Latin and Greek and continuing his violin lessons. While Robert attended school, his parents planned an extended tour of Europe for the entire family. In January 1851, they said goodbye to Fordham forever and sailed from New York.[13]

For the next five years, Robert studied, developed a "wanderlust" he never lost, and lived through those particularly difficult years between the ages of thirteen and eighteen. Beginning in October, he attended the boarding school of Monsieur and Madame Roulet in Neuchâtel, Switzerland. He could hardly have found a more beautiful setting. Neuchâtel sits on the western edge of a lake cradled by the Jura Mountains in the western part of the country near the border with France. Shaw looked southward from his corner room up the valley to the magnificent, tall, rounded, snow-covered form of Mont Blanc. His southeastern vista brought the Alpine peaks of the Jungfrau and Eiger pressing into his window. In summer, orchestras played in the town park and grapes grew spectacularly big and sugar rich to be turned into the wine Shaw learned to love. Still, Shaw missed his parents. While pleased that "M. and Mme. Roulet are very kind . . . ," he still felt he had been "left" and wrote, "I hate to be here. I keep thinking what you are all doing." Shaw would never outgrow his need to be with his family or his special love for his mother, who remained his faithful confidant until his death. He did, however, learn to like Mr. Roulet as a friend and came to enjoy Neuchâtel.[14]

Roulet administered a rigorous curriculum. Weekly, Shaw studied geometry, algebra, chemistry, and geology as well as six languages—though he concentrated on French and German. He took parts in student theater productions and kept up his lessons in violin and piano. In good weather, Roulet took the students on tours in France and Switzerland, teaching as he went. Roulet emphasized nurturing the students, but he could lose his temper. As Shaw told his mother, "Roulet hardly ever gets mad about the lessons, but only when we break some of the rules, or are impolite. But when he does get angry he's just like the wolf." Still, Shaw never saw the master punish anyone; rather, "he only scolds." Shaw did resent having to explain where and when and why every time he wanted to go for a walk or take a horseback ride or visit town. After a year of explanations, Shaw remarked, "I shall be very glad to have more freedom when I leave here."[15]

During his two years at Neuchâtel, Shaw struggled to define himself and the world around him. He had grown up among ardent abolitionists; now he began to evaluate whether he could live up to the level of his parents' dedication to social reform. His self-search coincided with the release of Harriet Beecher Stowe's *Uncle Tom's Cabin* (1852), which Shaw read and reread. He perused newspaper articles about Southern slavery and Northern compliance with the Fugitive Slave Law and reported, "I didn't know there were a great many free blacks in our slaveholding States." He questioned his parents about comparative statistics concerning numbers of blacks and whites in the South. In many of his letters Shaw fished for his parents' opinions by mentioning *Uncle Tom* or slavery. His mother wrote him that Mrs. Stowe was the sister of Henry Ward Beecher, the minister in Brooklyn that she liked so much, and that Stowe had written the novel "as a matter of conscience, after the passage of the 'Fugitive Slave Law.'" Shaw responded that he hoped Russians would read the novel and that it "will help them to set their slaves free." He questioned whether the royalists in Rome would ban the book because of its republican principles. Still, in a worldly teenage reflection, he resigned himself to the status quo and rationalized, "I don't see how one man could do much against slavery." Earlier, he made his position clear, "I don't want to become reformer, Apostle, or anything of that kind." Yet, when Stowe's *The Key to Uncle Tom's Cabin* (1853) was published Shaw pored through it for the "facts" of slavery.[16]

Shaw also questioned religion. He never forgave the Jesuits for his experience at Fordham. After he received a letter from one of his St. John's teacher-priests who feared for his education at Roulet's and expressed hope that Robert would go to school in Italy, Shaw scoffed: "He meant that he's afraid I won't be converted to Catholicism, because he hopes I'd be left in the clutches of the Jesuits at Rome, and would become Catholic right off." On the other hand, Shaw did his best to hide his Unitarian upbringing from everyone, because to mention it "would only bring up discussions and conversations which would be very stupid and tiresome." When Roulet tried to convince Shaw that he should take religion classes and attend church regularly, Shaw angrily wrote his parents that it was not Roulet's business if he were "good or bad" and that those students who do go are not "any better than me and that's what I told them." Shaw, who would never devote himself to a church or to a religion as his parents did, did attend protestant worship services of several denominations.[17]

Shaw also began to look at career goals. He did not want to be a reformer, which was the occupation—or rather calling—of both his parents, but what did he want? Education surely, but where? His father had gone to Harvard, so that became the likely choice. He mentioned Harvard to his parents in one sentence and in the next probably caused them a little concern by announcing,

"I think I should like to go to West Point." His parents probably laughed at and worried about this; with their son's loathing of discipline and authority, the army seemed the least likely place for him to succeed and as far from their pacific concerns as any institution could be. After Sarah wrote him of her disapproval with his military leanings, Shaw insisted, "I think I should like it, and what else can I do? I can't think of any thing else, for I don't want to be a Merchant, or Doctor, or Minister, or any thing like that." In his early teens, Shaw still had plenty of time to reconsider his prospects.[18]

During the summer of 1853, Shaw traveled with Roulet throughout Switzerland and said goodbye to him as school began again in September. He spent the next ten months with his family at their rented house in Sorrento on the Amalfi peninsula south of Naples. The family also toured Rome, Florence, and Heidelberg. In Sorrento, Shaw met English actress Frances "Fanny" Kemble, an abolitionist who had been married to Pierce Butler, the wealthiest slaveowner along Georgia's rice coast. Kemble held the Shaws spellbound with stories about her firsthand experiences among the slaves and certainly must have answered questions from Shaw, as he compared what she knew with what he had read in *Uncle Tom's Cabin*. A decade after they sat among the grapevines of Sorrento, Shaw would find himself on the very plantation Kemble described to him.[19]

After celebrating the Fourth of July with his parents and sisters, Shaw, accompanied by his father, traveled north to Hanover, Germany, where they secured him "two rooms—a parlour and a bed-room" in the home of Herr and Frau Eisendecher and their two daughters. Robert continued his education in Hanover for the next two years by hiring private tutors to further his classical education. He remained concerned about slavery and about his own future but spent most of his time pursuing pleasure. After all, he had not yet turned sixteen, his parents were far away, no Jesuit watched his every move, and Monsieur Roulet was in Switzerland demanding explanations from other boys. Independent for the first time, Shaw made his own schedule and used his own house key to let himself in or out whenever he chose. Recognizing his relative lack of homesickness, Shaw wrote his mother of "how big inside I've got since I've been here. I'm at least five years older than when I came."[20]

His mother probably wondered how "big" he had gotten when she read in his letter of November 5: "I have no taste for anything excepting amusing myself!" He had spent all his money and, in a statement that must have seemed arrogant to Sarah, said, "You mention my becoming a merchant, but that is entirely out of the question. I had rather be a chimney-sweep." Eight months later, Sarah read, "I hope that when I come home I shall be as much at liberty as I am now for after having had my own way as much as if I were of age for two years it would be nasty to be a child again. It's very unwillingly that I *ask* you to let me do anything because that's submission, but I haven't enough money to do it otherwise."[21]

Despite his boasts and threats, Shaw managed to give time to his studies, from 9 A.M. to 2 P.M. daily, with an occasional late afternoon class. Most nights he was in place for the 7 P.M. curtain at the theater, opera, or concert. He loved literature and music. Shakespeare enchanted him, and he saw "A Midsummer Night's Dream" eight times and "Hamlet" twice. Shaw attended many performances of operatic and symphonic pieces, among them "The Barber of Seville," "Figaro's Marriage," "The Magic Flute," "Don Giovanni," "Othello," "William Tell," and several of Beethoven's works.[22]

He became a regular at parties. At a "fancy-ball" in February 1855, Shaw shaved his blond beard and dressed as a woman. He had reached his full height of five feet five inches, was slim, and had delicate features. He looked much like his sisters Anna and Josephine. He "made such fools" of his friends, none of whom recognized him until he spoke. At the party he drank too much champagne. The next night, he attended a ball that started at 7 P.M. and ended at 6 A.M. and left him feeling "rather seedy . . . as it's almost impossible not to drink a good deal, because there is so much good wine here." As he got bolder with his freedom, he took a trip to Norway with two other students from Hanover, only informing his parents of it once he returned. Not surprisingly, he wrote his parents, "My purse is getting hollow cheeks again." When his mother counseled him against "sprees," Shaw countered that he was enjoying his youth. When his mother wrote of his spendthrift ways, Shaw insisted, "I have not been very extravagant" and told his father, "I think Mother's letter is a bit *too* strong." Actually his mother had miscalculated his expenses by 120 English pounds and felt she had to apologize. Shaw replied to his mother, "I won't be too hard upon you . . . your excuse is ample satisfaction."[23]

In the midst of his pleasure, Shaw turned his attention away from slavery. He did mention the formation of a new abolitionist society in New York. He took notice of a *Tribune* account of a slave being burned alive in Alabama and commented, "I didn't think that this . . . would happen again." Beyond those brief mentions, which may have been included to pacify his mother, Shaw does not appear to have thought much about abolition. There is no mention of the Kansas-Nebraska Act or of the sensational stories about "Bleeding Kansas." Shaw's letters are filled to overflowing with tales of travels to Berlin, Paris, and Norway, party escapades, crushes on women, and despair that he is not "growing any more." His mother could take some consolation in

Shaw's confession that there were fifteen English girls boarding in Hanover and because they went to church every Sunday, Shaw wrote, "I am beginning to go too."[24]

Besides his growing curiosity for women and drink, the only real emotion in Shaw's European letters to his family came bursting forth on December 11, 1855. At a tea party, Shaw met a man who "railed against America." Shaw admitted, "I *did* get very angry to-night. I can't help wishing for war between America and some European country, and that I were in the navy, so that I might cut some of their heads open. . . . I *must* hate them when they talk so about us; and the worst of it is, that they don't say anything against the real abuse, Slavery, but begin on some little insignificant thing. . . . They generally talk of the Know-nothings and the bullying of emigrants. But whatever anybody says about America here commonly puts me in a wax."[25]

Shaw maintained this strong sense of national patriotism throughout his short life. As the years to Civil War wound down, Shaw increasingly felt that the Slave Power soiled the fabric of an otherwise great nation. When war came, he was primed to take revenge on the South for the abuse he wrote about on December 11, 1855. To him, the South was the transgressor, not the North. If it took the end of slavery to redeem the honor of America, and to end the embarrassment Northerners felt to be in the same union with an anachronistic system, then Shaw stood for that. If the North could avenge itself in battle against the South, then let her go with or without slavery intact, and leave the North as a separate nation, now more honorable for the fight, then Shaw stood for that. He never really felt the immorality of slavery the way the abolitionists did; he was never quite an abolitionist. His gripe with the Jesuits, Monsieur Roulet, his parents, and those who spoke against America certainly revolved around his struggle to become his own person, but it was more than that. When a priest disciplined, Roulet questioned, his parents scolded, or a foreigner opposed him, Shaw bristled and sought to right these "unfair" attacks on his honor. He demanded atonement. He would join the navy if he could "cut some of their heads open" and thus stop the offensive words coming from mouths of those who blasphemed his America. In 1861, he joined the army to do just that to Southerners. He would hope that slavery would fall, but he did not enlist to fight for that goal.

Even while he told them of his parties and travels and shared his feelings about girls, Shaw reassured his parents that his studies progressed well. He had decided on Harvard and thought that he would have no trouble passing the entrance examinations in the fall of 1856. He hoped he might be able to enter as a junior, but certainly would enter no lower than with sophomore standing. To help him, his parents suggested that he might want a tutor to push him through an intensive study during the summer before he took the examinations. Shaw acquiesced and told them, "Engage the Crammer by all means, and I'll work like a steam-engine when I get home." [26]

Shaw returned to Staten Island in May 1856 to much excitement. The Shaws had a new $80,000 house on Bard Avenue in Elliotville. At least eight servants tended to the cooking, cleaning, driving, and gardening. Shaw met George William Curtis, a Brook Farmer who was well known as one of the country's top orators and writers and who edited *Putnam's Monthly*. Curtis and Anna Shaw were engaged and would marry that fall. In politics, Shaw's father had been a vehement free-soiler and now contributed to the Republican party's first campaign. He had just returned from the Republican National Convention, where he helped nominate John C. Frémont for president. Curtis made many speeches on behalf of the candidate. Frémont set up his New York campaign headquarters on Staten Island and attended the Shaw-Curtis wedding. At the same time, abolitionists were busy with lectures and weekly meetings at the neighboring house of Sydney Howard Gay, which became a refuge for runaway slaves. Prominent visitors to Gay's home included Whittier, James Russell Lowell, Garrison, Phillips, Angelina and Sarah Grimké, Robert Purvis, and Lucretia Mott. Meanwhile, Shaw spent long hours under the tutelage of the "Crammer," Francis C. Barlow, who had been educated at Brook Farm and graduated from Harvard as valedictorian; he became a general in the Civil War and the husband of Shaw's youngest sister, Ellen.[27]

Shaw passed the Harvard entrance examination, which he rated as "very easy." Yet he could only enter as a freshman. Spoiled by his elaborate European education, he immediately found everything "horridly stupid here and just like a school." The freedom of Hanover did not repeat itself in American classrooms; he had "to ask when I want to go anywhere." By October, he discovered that he had not prepared well for Harvard's academic demands and threatened to leave school to "go into a store" if "at the end of the year I stand very low." He got his worst grades in mathematics and history. His dislike of discipline and his intellectual shortcomings brought the pronouncement, "I hate Cambridge." He considered transferring to Columbia or New York University, but did not. Shaw stayed in school but never pulled himself academically into the top half of his class. He may have taken some consolation in the faculty's overall displeasure with the Class of 1860 when he reported that the faculty felt "we are the laziest class they have had for a long while." [28]

Shaw excelled at extracurricular activities. He enjoyed playing "foot-ball," but with fifty to seventy men on a team all engaged at once, he was beaten up regularly by bigger players. He wrote that he had learned to keep "among fellows of my own size on the outskirts." His height made him feel inferior; asked to be one of four groomsmen in a wedding in 1858, Shaw wrote his mother, "I don't want to a bit. . . . The other three are all six feet tall." He quit football to participate in activities he felt better about. In his second year, Shaw joined a boat club and participated in rowing races with other clubs. He took boxing lessons. He played the violin well enough to join a musical group, the Pierians, who played twice a week. He was always inclined toward music and now wished often for musical talent. Undoubtedly, Shaw enjoyed the after-performance social hour of ale, cheese, and crackers. He joined all eight societies sponsored by the university, even though the last to accept him was the Hasty Pudding Club, a theatrical organization. His best friend at Harvard was cousin Harry Russell, who combined ability and popularity to get elected president of many of the societies. Shaw roomed with Harvard's football and rowing champion, Caspar Crowninshield. Perhaps these relationships strengthened his spirits and helped him with his height complex.[29]

During the time Shaw studied and played at Harvard, Boston and Cambridge buzzed constantly with abolitionist activities. Shaw was a visitor in the home of James Russell Lowell. He "escaped" school on the weekends by getting a pass to see his "guardian," cousin Harry's father George Russell, in West Roxbury. Every Sunday Russell took him to Theodore Parker's church, where they heard Parker preach brilliantly against slavery, and, on one occasion, heard Wendell Phillips preach in Parker's place. "I liked him very much," Shaw told his mother. Fanny Kemble visited Boston in March 1857 and Shaw went to hear her read several times. But the constant whirr against slavery tired Shaw, and he lashed out at Kemble, whom Bostonians talked about constantly. He discussed Hinton Rowan Helper's antislavery—and antiblack—polemic, *Impending Crisis* (1857), with a friend who argued that Helper was too poor himself to be able to evaluate slavery fairly and not hold a "grudge against slaveholders."[30]

Even if Shaw could have avoided the issue at Cambridge, his parents constantly exposed the moral issue in their letters. After Frémont's failure in 1856, a despondent Sarah wrote that she would never live to see "truth & justice prevail in this land." Robert responded that the Republicans would do well in the next election and added, "I can't help hoping that there will be a disunion sometime. . . . Slavery is the only fault in America and we get just as much blame for it as the Southerners, and besides, the disgrace of all their shameful actions." Shaw wanted to rid his nation of slavery but showed little interest in the people who were slaves. The barrage of antislavery voices led Shaw to complain and defend himself to his mother in March 1858: "Because I don't talk and think Slavery all the time, and because I get tired . . . of hearing nothing else, you say I don't feel with you, when I do."[31]

The Panic of 1857 hit both the Shaws and the Curtises hard. Francis Shaw's investments suffered, and his income was diminished as much as half. *Putnam's Magazine* failed, and George William Curtis, a partner, owed huge debts that took him a decade to repay. As Shaw watched these woes, he began to think of alternatives to a business career. He had always enjoyed the outdoors and thought of going into agriculture with a friend, Henry Vezin of Philadelphia, whom he met in Hanover. Shaw was still considering a "farming project" in the fall of 1858 when his uncles persuaded him to work in their mercantile office in New York. Uncle George Russell in West Roxbury adamantly pushed Shaw "to leave college and not let this opportunity go." Whether Shaw's parents encouraged their brothers to dissuade Shaw from the idea of farming is not known, but they did not stand in the way of his decision. Shaw withdrew from Harvard in March 1859, moved into his old room on Staten Island, and entered his uncle's firm, Henry P. Sturgis and Company, in New York City.[32]

Initially, Shaw gloried in his life with his family at Staten Island. He took long rides with his sisters and discussed events with Curtis and his parents. He still entertained ideas of farming with Vezin, but settled into his duties as a clerk in his uncle's mercantile business and counting room. Shaw expected to pay his dues to the company by working in China sometime in the next three years, but he hoped he would get to spend a summer in England, Germany, and Norway before he went. In July, he wrote Vezin, "I expect to do well. I like business very much." By September his tune had changed: "I am a slave now." Shaw did not enjoy the import business and was heartily bored with the long hours and day-to-day drudgery of inventory. He complained to his mother that he had a "hankering after something more 'juicy.'" He leaned on his parents for support, and when they took his sisters Josephine and Ellen on a cruise to Havana and Nassau in the spring of 1861, Shaw doubted that he had any talent for business and fought depression. He lacked confidence in his managerial abilities and talked with one of the partners, Chandler Robbins, about his concerns. Robbins told him that he just needed more experience and if he stuck with it he would find himself able to succeed at business.[33]

Shaw had been excited about the 1860 presidential contest. George Curtis chaired Staten Island's Republican party and had been to the national nominating convention in Chicago, where he supported the more radical candidate, William H. Seward of New York. After Abraham Lincoln won the nomination, Curtis campaigned for the railsplitter. Shaw also voted for Lincoln and was excited when the election prompted the rapid secession of the lower South. In tune with the feeling of the times, he joined an exclusive militia regiment, the Seventh New York National Guard. He drilled twice a week and talked about what he would do if and when the South made trouble. He did not have long to wait. Writing his mother on March 29, Shaw told her of the "great state of excitement about Fort Sumter. First it was to be evacuated, then re-enforced." After South Carolinians fired upon the fort and caused its surrender, Lincoln called for troops to march to the capital. Shaw's Seventh was among the first to respond.[34]

On April 16, the day following Lincoln's call, Marshall Lefferts, commanding the Seventh, notified Governor Edwin Morgan that the regiment stood "ready to march forthwith." Two days later orders came; the regiment would depart the following afternoon at 4 P.M. with a march down Broadway. With Shaw's father in the Bahamas, Sydney Gay took over the parental role. Gay wrote a note to his wife on April 19: "I saw Theodore Winthrop and Bob [Shaw] off today. The former looked very grave. The latter sent thee this (his boyish photograph) with his love." Shaw had had time to write short letters to his parents, sister Susanna, and George Curtis. He hugged Anna, put on his gray uniform with its starch-white crossbelts, and gladly marched away from his business office to take his place in the excitement of the hour.[35]

The hour turned into four years of war. But the men of the Seventh were a long way from realizing that fact. They had only agreed to serve thirty days even though Lincoln had called for ninety-day volunteers. It is interesting that the "Darling Seventh," which included the sons of New York society who had wanted to prove themselves and their class to be patriotic, would arrive in and depart from Washington before there was much danger to their lives or fortunes. After the Seventh disbanded and many of its members returned to civilian life, Shaw remained a soldier. He quickly gained an officer's commission in the newly organizing Second Massachusetts Infantry. He would fight with that regiment until he made an even bigger commitment. While he never found himself in the worlds of scholars, reformers, or businessmen, this short, blond, small-boned, blue-eyed youth discovered himself among the living and dead soldiers of war. A boy who could not adapt to the discipline in civilian circles became a good soldier who followed orders and expected the same from others. He could be counted on when bullets flew and Rebels yelled. Twice wounded, he proved himself in the grim battle of Antietam in September 1862. He wrote hundreds of letters home, and they are significantly absent of homesick whining. Shaw stood up to be counted, and he intended to see the war to conclusion or death. Then he finally got "big inside" and courageous enough to do the bravest thing he ever did, accepting the command of the North's first regiment of black soldiers, the Fifty-fourth. He became a reformer, whether he liked it or not.

But Shaw had a difficult road to travel and many friends to make and to bury before he grew confident enough to do the thing that brought him a monument on Boston Common and the poems of the Lowells. First he campaigned with an army that could not find a commander until Ulysses S. Grant grabbed the reins; by then Shaw had passed to the ages. Shaw marched in the mud, fought and killed men he neither knew nor hated, slept among the dead, defeated dysentery, married a woman before either of them were quite ready, and tried to maintain a sense of who he was in relation to his mother.

During his twenty months in the Second Massachusetts, Shaw learned about the love that grows from depending on others for life. Parents, sisters, cousins, childhood and college friends were held dear, but that was not the same affection as that which a soldier reveals to a comrade on the field of battle, around the campfires of an army, or in the tents of a regiment. With fear, hate, and love so near each other that one easily turned into another, a soldier felt all three at once. Afraid to be injured or killed or called a coward, a man could take another's life and convince himself that he hated him, all the while admiring him by knowing that he felt and acted the same way. When the battles ended, friends frantically searched one for the other, but they also did what could be done for those they had just been trying to kill. Killing one moment, trying to save the next, hating then consoling the enemy in acts of tremendous violence interspersed with tender mercies, Shaw felt these emotions, and he brought them to bear on his fellow officers. He knew that his friends in the Second were dearer to him than any he had made before. He depended on them, and they on him, for life and honor. They shared experiences that no one who had not been with them could imagine. And even if someone could imagine, Shaw and his comrades knew that only they really understood how they felt for each other because of the mingling of three very different yet similar emotions into an inseparable unity in a time of great stress.

Shaw wanted promotion and his letters can be read to suggest that an ever-higher rank stood paramount in his mind. He did advance from a second lieutenancy to a captaincy, but those promotions were based more on the deaths of senior officers than on Shaw's abilities. He was a good officer, but not a spectacular one. When those who knew him spoke of him, they emphasized his loyalty, gentleness, and obedience, not his military acumen. Shaw had chances to advance in rank by changing regiments or accepting staff positions with general officers. He told himself he wanted a higher commission and watched for opportunities, but when decision time arrived he stayed in the Second. During the first year of the war, Shaw would have transferred to obtain a higher rank. But after the Second lost men in battles, and feelings of loyalty settled around him and his friends, only something extraordinary could pry him away from the regiment.[36]

He entered the war with the naïveté of his generation. Not only would the war be short, but he reassured his mother, and himself, that "there is not much more danger in war than in peace at least for the officers. There are comparatively few men killed." A few days later one of Shaw's childhood friends, Theodore Winthrop, fell dead at the Battle of Big Bethel. Before Shaw met his own fate in July 1863, he endured the pain of losing close Harvard friends at Cedar and South Mountains, Antietam, and Gettysburg. Still, the deaths only wound around Shaw like ropes of determination to see the war to victory. He was fighting for what he considered his manhood, a manhood wrapped up with the nation's honor. Eighteen days after Fort Sumter, he said it was great to be in Washington "bullying the Southerners." Four months later, Shaw ruminated openly: "I sincerely hope the war will not finish without a good, fair battle, as we should never hear the end of Bull Run." Fighting not for slavery or even union, Shaw fought solely, at first, for honor and bragging rights.[37]

He adapted quickly to the roving camp life of armies in the field. He enjoyed sights he had never seen and was quite the tourist in letters telling of scenery, weather, and oddities in a "wish you were here" tone. His letters home detail his experiences in the South. John Brown's engine house in Harper's Ferry, jail in Charlestown, and legal correspondence from supporters and detractors, interested Shaw greatly. He enjoyed rummaging through the private letters and personal property of Southerners, particularly women, in homes or offices where he boarded or broke into. Whenever he was near a town and far from the enemy, Shaw would take the opportunity to attend balls, or stay late at parties. He danced and socialized with women at every turn during the Second's campaigns through Maryland and Virginia. He drank wine and smoked cigars with his new civilian companions and his "old" military friends. After the years of scholarly and business worlds where he felt ill cast, Shaw had returned, in many ways, to the merrymaking of his Hanover years. One year after he marched off to war, he exulted in his good fortune: "What a blessing that we happened to be born in this century and country!"[38]

For the first time in his life, Shaw had to deal with men of all classes. Growing up in the worlds of the educated and rich at Brook Farm, Fordham, Neuchâtel, Hanover, Harvard, and in the business circles of New York City, Shaw had few dealings with the less fortunate. But as an officer, he could no longer avoid them. He had always enjoyed the power of money, and now he held the power of rank. He came to believe that "discipline is wonderful" and stated that "without it a soldier is not a soldier." He was quick to criticize any man or unit that did not meet his standards of order. He directed his deepest criticism toward the Irish, whom Shaw distinguished from "Americans," and his letters consistently berated their abilities as soldiers. Undoubtedly these feelings had grown as he watched the Irish stand strongly with the Democratic party and against the abolitionists. Here again, Shaw was unforgiving.[39]

In keeping with his "us against them" mind-set, Shaw laughed at or scorned many of the Southerners he met. He ridiculed them as stupid. The especially ignorant ones were always those who challenged the North's supremacy or castigated Northern troops. One girl in Frederick, Maryland, told Shaw: "I like a *nigger* better than a Massachusetts soldier." Shaw labeled Secessionists in Edinburg, Virginia, "a nasty, dirty, ignorant race." In another letter, Shaw wrote about a "screaming, swearing, bawling, & blubbering" family whose mother was "not ladylike." He said that the common people did not even know what the war was about.[40]

The life of an officer differed greatly from that of an enlisted man. Of course the pay differed. Privates got thirteen dollars a month, plus a three-and-a-half-dollar clothing allowance. Second Lt. Shaw received $150, "part of two months pay." Officers also had servants to attend to their cooking, set up their tents, clean their clothes, and run their errands. Whenever the opportunity existed, Shaw and his friends had their servants secure room and board for them in private homes near the camp ground of the regiment. They ate and slept far better than their lower-ranked, lower-class soldiers. Shaw liked to eat and sleep in what he called "a Christian and reasonable manner" in contrast to "the rest [who] dine in the woods."[41]

Battles interfered with the gaiety of tourism, parties, and camp. In March 1862, the Second had a small bloodletting, and Shaw wrote home that he now knew "what war really is." But he also showed how he had become one with war. He was getting used to "terrible sights" and felt that he had spent all his "life among dead & wounded men." Even while knowing that each battle meant widows, orphans, and countless suffering, Shaw craved the experience of battle. He felt cheated of the honor and glory he desired and feared the war would end before the Second had "seen the elephant"—a soldier's phrase for battle. He worried for naught. The Second was severely tested at Cedar Mountain and Antietam. Saddened by the deaths of friends, Shaw never lost his enthusiasm for the fight, not even after he was assigned as the officer for the dead. In that job, Shaw supervised the removal of bodies from the field, packed them in charcoal, and sent them off to be placed into metallic coffins for shipment to loved ones in the North. He did admit that it was a "fearful thing" to see two hundred men dead who had been alive moments before; but in his next sentence, Shaw hoped to see Rebels "hacked to little pieces."[42]

While experiencing the love-hate relationship of the battlefield, Shaw lost his heart to a woman. He met Annie Haggerty in the months before the war when his sister Susanna arranged a small party for the opera. That night Shaw decided that one day Annie would be his "young woman." Annie came from a wealthy family with a summer house in the Berkshire Mountains at Lenox, Massachusetts. Her father, Ogden Haggerty, inherited and made a fortune in the auction and commission house, Haggerty and Company, in New York City. Shaw saw Annie only a few times, but after he went away to fight he began to miss her. In August 1861, he asked Susanna to send him a picture of Annie, but adolescently implored, "I don't want you to get it from her." He began to write Annie and arranged to see her when he got the chance to leave his regiment to visit Staten Island. By November 23, 1862, he confided to her, "I felt wicked when I told you I wanted to see you even more than Mother." He probably proposed to her in that same letter. After she accepted, they kept the engagement a secret from everyone but their parents and Susanna, until February. While Shaw dreamed about Annie he continued with the daily activities of war.[43]

Shaw's letters tell remarkably little about the institution of slavery and his thoughts about it. He knew the war was about slavery and wrote of the "crime of slavery," but offered little else. In his first mention of the institution after arriving in the South, Shaw told his mother that the slaves in Charlestown, Virginia, seemed "well cared for but they are evidently glad to see us." His descriptions of "the delighted darkies" and his regular use of the term "nigger" revealed his prejudices. Yet, while most Union officers ignored the preliminary Emancipation Proclamation in their letters home, Shaw took notice of it. He thought it was of little value militarily, but after the war, "it will be a great thing." As for the wrong of slavery, Shaw wrote that it belonged "entirely to another people." He happily stood with the side that was freeing the slaves, but his attitude was based more on honor than egalitarianism. He was an early supporter of the use of blacks as soldiers. Believing that white soldiers would at first complain but then get used to the idea of having blacks in the ranks, Shaw thought blacks would make "a fine army after a little drill, and could certainly be kept under better discipline than our independent Yankees."[44]

From the beginning of the war a few voices called for the inclusion of blacks into the military. The most persistent urging came from Frederick Douglass. He determined that military service for blacks was a revolutionary move that should herald both freedom for the slaves and citizenship rights for all African Americans. Three weeks after Lincoln's call for troops, Douglass suggested, "Let the slaves and free colored people be called into service, and formed into a liberating army, to march into the South and raise the banner of emancipation among the slaves." In the same call, Douglass objected, "Until the nation shall repent of this weakness and folly, until they shall make the cause of their country the cause of freedom, until they shall strike down slavery, the source and center of this gigantic rebellion, they don't deserve the support of a single sable arm." In Missouri, Maj. Gen. John Frémont had freed the slaves on August 30, 1861, but Lincoln quickly vetoed that. Next Maj. Gen. David Hunter's emancipation order of May 9, 1862, declared that "slavery and martial law in a free country are altogether incompatible," and all former slaves in his command, the Department of the South, "are therefore declared forever free." After hearing of Hunter's decree, Francis Shaw wrote to Garrison, "Has not the President used a very sharp knife, in Genl Hunter's hands, to cut the knot." Three days after Shaw wrote his letter, Lincoln revoked Hunter's proclamation.[45]

Lincoln continued to worry what northern slaveholding whites and their allies would do if he complied with the calls for emancipation from Douglass, Frémont, and Hunter. But in late 1862, with the war going badly, recruitment falling off, casualties mounting, and the threat of aid to the Confederacy by England or France still alive, Lincoln had to act. With the victory at Antietam, he issued the preliminary Emancipation Proclamation as a warning of what was to come if the South did not lay down its arms. Additionally, this preliminary proclamation gave him time to judge Northern reaction. Many still held that this was "a white man's war." Lincoln received letters of support from abolitionist groups and from lone voices who agreed in the need for black enlistment. From Massachusetts came a letter from the Republican electors of 1860 telling Lincoln they had "happily certified" his election two years ago and now "congratulate you upon your having begun the greatest act in American history, the emancipation . . ." of the slaves. They ended the letter with a call "to let blacks fight for us."[46]

Republicans knew that Lincoln had stepped onto precarious political ground. Ten days before the Emancipation Proclamation would take effect, Massachusetts congressman Charles Sedgwick wrote high-powered industrialist and Shaw's cousin John Forbes, "Be ready to shout Hallelujah on the morning of 1st January, and let the President know that he is to have sympathy and support. By all means, put him up to practical measures to make it a success. Tell him the world will pardon his crimes, and his stories even, if he only makes the proclamation a success, and that if he fails he will be gibbeted in history as a great, long-legged, awkward, country pettifogger, without brains or backbone." Lincoln did have backbone and historical savvy. Once he announced the Emancipation Proclamation and authorized the raising of black regiments, the war turned. Moral suasion had failed to free the slaves; now the sons of slaves would free themselves and guarantee a Union victory.[47]

Before the war ended, 178,975 African Americans, one-twelfth of all the soldiers for the Union, joined the armed forces of the North. They fought in 145 infantry regiments, 7 cavalry groups, 13 artillery units, and 1 engineering batallion. At least 60 of these 166 units fought on the battlefield; the others performed garrison duty. Black sailors had been enlisted since the war began and by war's end made up one-fourth of the navy's ranks. Black men who had been born free joined with black men who had run away from slavery or had been freed by Union armies to strike a blow for the destruction of slavery. The most amazing single statistic is that approximately 34,000 of 46,150 (74%) free Northern blacks of military age, 18 to 45, fought for their country. Nearly 37,000 Northern and Southern black soldiers died from wounds or disease.[48]

Among the regiments raised in the North, the Fifty-fourth Massachusetts Infantry led the way. Massachusetts governor John A. Andrew, who strongly advocated using blacks in the military, had helped form and lead the Free Soil and Republican parties in Massachusetts. He was elected governor in 1860 and served five one-year terms beginning on January 2, 1861. An abolitionist, Andrew wanted to prove that black men would fight—which would in turn prove that they were men and thus entitled to be free citizens. He also thought that black enlistment would take the pressure off his state to meet its enlistment quotas. If Lincoln failed to let blacks fight, Andrew would have to fill quotas with factory workers, a thought loathed by business interests in this most industrialized state in the Union. Thus businessmen supported the Emancipation Proclamation out of self-interest as well as the conviction that it was the moral and egalitarian thing to do. The *New York Times* argued against raising black troops simply to prove blacks would fight or for the purpose of "loosing an ethnological knot," but supported their use for "its immediate effects . . . on the fortunes of war." Andrew sent his friend John Forbes to Washington in early January to lobby for the inclusion of blacks in the army. On January 22, Forbes reported the good news that "our Rulers . . . seem at last open to the necessity of using the *negro* for our own salvation first and secondly for his own." Four days later, Secretary of War Edwin M. Stanton authorized Andrew to raise regiments which "may include persons of African descent, organized into special corps."[49]

Andrew understood the importance of making the venture a success, and he staked his reputation and career upon his conviction that blacks would fight and fight well. After all, there were many who hoped the experiment would fail and some who were sure it would. The latter gave several reasons: a rebellion by whites should be put down by whites; blacks would not enlist; blacks were too cowardly to fight and would run when faced with white Southerners; blacks were not intelligent enough to learn drill; blacks with guns would return to the savage instincts of the jungle; Southerners would become more determined to keep up the fight; white soldiers would not serve alongside black soldiers; blacks would demoralize white soldiers. Andrew determined to prove the error in these objections. Frederick Douglass too was countering these racist notions and trying to persuade uncertain Northern whites. In a speech in New York on February 6, Douglass gave witness that "the colored man only waits for admission into the service of his country. . . . They are ready to rally under the stars and stripes at the first tap of the drum. Give them a chance; stop calling them 'niggers,' and call them soldiers." Andrew agreed.[50]

Because of the political delicacy of the situation, Andrew carefully selected white officers who had proven themselves in battle and who came from powerful and respected families with antislavery convictions secure enough to deflect the criticism and pressure of accepting such a position. Also, the costs of raising a regiment were enormous and could be offset with private contributions; sons of wealthy families with good connections would ease the strain. Andrew again turned for help to Forbes, who responded with two names. He recommended Capt. Norwood Penrose Hallowell of the Twentieth Massachusetts Infantry, and Shaw, by then a captain in the Second Massachusetts. Both candidates had been in the war since the beginning and had stood the test of many battles, including the war's bloodiest day at Antietam. Hallowell's father, Morris, was a wealthy Philadelphia merchant, Quaker, and longtime abolitionist who used his resources to establish a hospital for recuperating soldiers. Forbes favored Hallowell, telling the governor, "He is a born leader . . . he has *convictions*." Andrew knew Morris Hallowell, but he also knew the Shaws. After listening to Forbes about the strengths and weaknesses of each, Andrew opted for the one with the better family connections. He decided to write Francis Shaw to inform him of his decision to ask Robert to take command of the new regiment. That move not only showed political shrewdness, it indicated that Forbes and Andrew were not certain Robert measured up to the difficult task that lay ahead. One way to strengthen the hand that offered the commission was to apply pressure through a family long committed to ending slavery.[51]

Francis and Sarah Shaw read and then joyfully reread the governor's letter explaining his choice of Robert to head the country's first regiment of Northern black soldiers. Andrew flattered and appealed, spoke of his own "deep conviction," and made it impossible for them to deny him their son. He called this "the most important corps" yet organized, "a model for all future colored regiments" whose "success or . . . failure will go far to elevate or depress the estimation in which the character of the colored Americans will be held throughout the world." To command this vanguard unit, Andrew wanted a gentleman "of the highest tone and honor" from the "circles of educated, anti-slavery society." Andrew counseled that antislavery groups had the most at stake in the unit, next to blacks themselves.[52]

Abolitionists had been ridiculed for years as fanatic dreamers; now they had the chance to prove they had been right all along. The governor offered a challenge to the family's honor when he admonished that if Shaw could not "enter upon it [leadership of a black regiment] with a full sense of its importance, with an earnest determination for its success" and with family encouragement, then he should not take it. He brought out their competitive fire by telling them of others who wanted the position. He sealed their support by asking them as "ardent, faithful, and true Republicans and friends of liberty" who "have always contributed to the strength and healing of our generation" to demonstrate those qualities again. Significantly, Andrew had not sent the offer directly to Shaw, but had enclosed it in a separate envelope with this letter to Francis. Andrew was still unsure of the strength of Shaw's commitment to abolition; otherwise he would have corresponded directly, man to man, not man through father to son. The governor asked his friend to forward the offer to Shaw knowing that the son would have a hard time refusing the father. Andrew closed by pleading, "If in any way, by suggestion or otherwise, you can aid the purpose . . . of this letter" you will have my "heartiest gratitude."[53]

Francis left immediately to carry the governor's letter to his son in the Army of the Potomac's winter camp at Stafford Court House, Virginia, where the army had camped since its repulse from Fredericksburg in December. Shaw found his son, took him to a quiet spot, and gave him Andrew's letter. The fact that the governor had placed his confidence in the father's ability to persuade can be seen in the letter to the son. Andrew felt no need to flatter or elucidate the arguments to Shaw:

Captain,

I am about to organize in Massachusetts a Colored Regiment as part of the volunteer quota of this State—the commissioned officers to be white men. I have today written your Father expressing to him my sense of the importance of this undertaking, and requesting him to forward to you this letter, in which I offer to you the Commission of Colonel over it. The Lieutenant Colonelcy I have offered to Captain Hallowell of the Twentieth Massachusetts Regiment. It is important to the organization of this regiment that I should receive your reply to this offer at the earliest day consistent with your ability to arrive at a deliberate conclusion on the subject.

Respectfully and very truly yours,
John A. Andrew

Andrew might have expected that Francis would personally carry the letter to Shaw, but just in case he did not, the governor made certain that Shaw knew that his parents had been informed. Psychologically, this would make the parents partners in the offer and make it difficult for a son to refuse.[54]

But Shaw did refuse. His father tried not to pressure him, but his presence surely indicated his feelings. Shaw had been through a lot with his regiment, and seen many of his friends die near him. He was loyal to their memory and to the men who remained to fight on future fields. He discussed the offer with his close friend and tentmate Charles Morse, who wondered with him whether the position might be ridiculed, doubted that blacks would enlist, and questioned the fighting ability of black troops. Morse felt so strongly about the Second that he told Shaw he would never leave it.[55]

Shaw sought the opinions of other officers, most of whom hated to see him leave the regiment. Some of them reminded him that he had just declined a good position with the Second Massachusetts Cavalry, a unit being formed under his sister Josephine's fiancé, Charles Russell Lowell. The two fellow officers who could have provided Shaw the most support, Morris Copeland and James Savage, were no longer around to help him decide. Shaw's best friends from the Second, his cousin Harry Russell, Copeland, Savage, Morse, Greely Curtis, and Dr. Lincoln Stone, all held antislavery views, but only Copeland and Savage were ardent abolitionists. Months before Andrew's offer, Copeland had talked with Savage and Shaw about starting a black regiment not only to "sever the connection between master and slave, but . . . aid the race in its own regeneration." Savage agreed to join such a unit. Copeland had taken Shaw with him to Washington in May 1862 to ask permission of Secretary of

War Stanton to raise a regiment of black soldiers. With Copeland in the lead and before the Second had been in a major battle, Shaw had agreed to transfer to this unit. But the plan was rejected. After Copeland published an open letter in a Boston paper asking Stanton to reconsider, Stanton forced him out of the army on grounds of insubordination. It is more than likely that when Governor Andrew first considered those he wanted to head the Fifty-fourth, Copeland stood at the top of the list.[56]

Savage, who was described by Second Massachusetts captain Richard Cary as "quite prominent among the rabid republicans" and as "one of those who came out to whip the rebels [and] free all the niggers . . . ," died in October 1862 from wounds received at Cedar Mountain. After Savage's death, Shaw remembered that "Jim's purity, conscientiousness and manliness were well known. . . . The best we can have for a friend is, that he may resemble James Savage." Savage had publicly stated that only to raise a black regiment would he leave the Second. Maybe Shaw would have accepted readily had Copeland and Savage been there to offer support, but they were not.[57]

Shaw pondered and fretted, and the next morning he wrote his refusal. He told his father, "I would take it, if I thought myself equal to the responsibility of such a position." Shaw's father accepted the letter and, leaving to make the heavyhearted journey to Boston, sent word to Sarah that Robert had refused. In Virginia, Shaw continued to ponder his decision. He may have thought of his words to his mother the previous fall, after she accused him of "degenerating sadly from the principles" by which he was raised. He had responded that he was just "an ordinary mortal." It is highly probable that Francis Shaw hand delivered a letter Sarah wrote on January 31, 1863, to Robert. Sarah praised Governor Andrew's offer, then elevated the pressure: "Well! I feel as if God had called you up to a holy work. You helped him at a crisis when the most important question is to be solved that has been asked since the world began. I know the task is arduous . . . but it is God's work." Incredulously, Sarah closed by writing, "If you decide no after prayer and thought, I shall feel that you did entirely right." Shaw believed in abolitionism, but it was his mother's life work. He felt guilty over his lack of commitment. In November 1862, Shaw wrote Annie Haggerty of his great love for his mother and of "the sacrifices she has made for me, and for which I can never repay her." The day he rejected the governor, he also rejected his mother. Shaw wrote Annie of his decision and told her, "Mother will think I am shirking my duty." Always cognizant of duty and honor and thinking of his mother's reaction, Shaw agonized over what he had done.[58]

Two days later, Francis Shaw received a telegram that made him proud. His son had changed his mind and was telling him to destroy the letter. He followed his son's instructions to telegraph Governor Andrew that he accepted the commission. Whether or not the pressure he felt from home, from the memory of his dead friends, from his antislavery sympathy, or from a chance to be near mother and Annie while he recruited in Boston had the most influence on his action cannot be known; perhaps they all pushed and helped him to be courageous.[59]

Years later, philosopher William James, an acquaintance of Shaw's, recalled Shaw's special sense of duty. James spoke of the "manly virtues" of courage, battle instinct, and willingness to sacrifice one's "life-blood" on the fields of war. James said most men had this kind of "common and gregarious" courage. But what Shaw did when he left the Second, James continued, showed a higher courage—the "lonely courage" it took to drop "his warm commission in the glorious Second" to lead black troops. James hailed Shaw's courage in leaving a regiment so correct "socially" to throw himself into "this new negro-soldier venture, [where] loneliness was certain, ridicule inevitable, failure possible; and Shaw was only twenty-five."[60]

Governor Andrew got the bad news before he got the good. After Francis telegraphed Sarah, Sarah wrote the governor, told him of Robert's answer, and lamented, "This decision has caused me the bitterest disappointment I have ever experienced." Had her son accepted, "It would have been the proudest moment of my life and I could have died satisfied that I had not lived in vain. . . . I have shed bitter tears over his refusal." She did not have long to ache. On hearing that Robert changed his mind, she wrote him of her "deep and holy joy" that he had been "willing to take up the cross." She thanked him: "God rewards a hundred-fold every good aspiration of his children. . . . Now I feel ready to die, for I see you willing to give y[ou]r support to the cause of truth that is lying crushed and bleeding." For his part, Andrew worried a bit over Shaw and tried to get him to accept the lieutenant colonelcy. If Shaw accepted this change, Andrew would then give the colonelcy to Hallowell, who had had no misgivings and had responded immediately and was on his way to Boston to begin recruiting. But Shaw held on to the original offer, took the colonelcy, and soon proved to Andrew the correctness of his trust.[61]

In addition to the praise of his mother and the governor he received for taking the position, Shaw received accolades from many sources. Before he made the trip to Boston, Shaw rode with Charles Morse to talk with their friend Greely Curtis, now with the First Massachusetts Cavalry. Curtis lived with another of Shaw's friends who had joined the Second at its formation,

Henry Lee Higginson. Higginson recalled that what Shaw told them was "great news, indeed a real event in all our lives; for we all knew how much Robert cared for his own regiment, . . . how fond he was of his old comrades, and how contrary to his wishes this move was." Curtis and Higginson told Shaw they were proud of him and approved his decision. On February 12, Shaw received a letter from an officer he barely knew but who had been talking with Morse. He admired Shaw: "Rest assured you have done a good thing. I could not myself do what you and Hallowell have done, and so I respect it the more." This officer went on to tell him it was natural to be scared, and that one day history will "justify your course" and "all will confess that you were right, and wonder how the world could have been so wrong." Bolstered by this welcome support, and believing that most officers favored arming blacks, Shaw arrived in Boston on February 15 and threw himself into the job.[62]

Governor Andrew left very little to chance for his "design and hope to make this a model regiment." Even before Shaw arrived, Andrew named a special "black committee" to advise, recruit, and raise money. Andrew knew that if blacks failed to pick up the gauntlet and volunteer, whites would further stereotype them as cowardly. Even before she heard that her brother would head the regiment, Shaw's sister Anna wrote her cousin Mimi and worried, "I wonder if they will enlist. They would have a year ago but I have heard that a good many have felt very indignant at being excluded & say that they will not go now. I hope that is not so." Writing to his mother on February 4, Charles Russell Lowell feared that "the blacks here [in Boston] are too comfortable to do anything more than talk about freedom." But Shaw's appointment and Andrew's committee changed Lowell's assessment: "I think it very good of Shaw (who is not at all a fanatic) to undertake the thing. . . . You see this is likely to be a success, if any black regiment can be a success." Many prominent blacks did speak out against enlistment. They were angry that the unit would have no black officers and that the government had turned to them to fight when they were not allowed to vote or hold office in most Northern states. Andrew told the committee to get to work and "awaken interest" among the black community. On February 17, at a war meeting at the Joy Street Baptist Church, a crowd of black Bostonians heard speakers who implored them to join the army. Wendell Phillips, whom many recognized as a longtime friend of equality, acknowledged the injustice of not being able to have black officers, but asked, "If you cannot have a whole loaf, will you not take a slice? That is the great question for you to decide." Soon, many decided to grasp the slice; they would try for more later.[63]

Andrew named George L. Stearns to head the committee on recruiting.

Stearns was a wealthy manufacturer of lead pipe from Medford, Massachusetts, who became an active abolitionist after he married a niece of Lydia Maria Child. Unitarian in belief, Stearns wore an imposing chest-length brown beard that made him look like an Old Testament Moses. He never flinched in his conviction that slavery should be destroyed at any cost. He sent rifles to the free-soilers of Kansas in the 1850s. As a member of the "Secret Six," he financed John Brown's raid on Harper's Ferry in 1859. Historian William S. McFeely summed up Stearns's interest in the Fifty-fourth as "making good on his mentor's promise of raising an insurrection." Other members of the committee included the ubiquitous John Forbes, who had met with Brown but had not helped him financially; Norwood Hallowell's brother Richard, from Boston; James B. Congdon, a prominent merchant of New Bedford; businessmen Amos Adams Lawrence, William I. Bowditch, and LeBaron Russell of Boston; Willard Phillips of Salem; and Francis Shaw.[64]

All of these members were active in raising money and helping recruiters. They paid for scores of advertisements in many newspapers. One such ad of February 16 in Boston papers called: "TO COLORED MEN! Wanted – Good men for the 54th Regiment of Massachusetts Volunteers, of African descent, Col. Robert G. Shaw. . . . All necessary information can be obtained at the Office corner of Cambridge and North Russell streets. Lieut. J. W. M. Appleton, Recruiting Officer." Another focused upon honor: "Colored Men Attention! Colored Men, Rally around the Flag of Freedom and evince that you are not inferior in Courage and Patriotism to White Men. An opportunity is now being afforded to Colored Men to prove their Manhood and Loyalty by enlisting in the 54th Regiment. . . ." By February 13, the committee circulated a "Subscription Paper" which asked for help in establishing the new regiment. The paper ran a middle course of not mentioning black freedom or moral arguments. Instead, it focused on the belief—albeit prejudicial—that blacks had an advantage when fighting "in a Southern climate." The paper reminded readers that black soldiers would "reduce the number" of white replacements required to bolster dwindling armies. Most members of the committee opened the drive by pledging themselves to five hundred dollars each. Abolitionist leader Gerrit Smith of New York added five hundred more, and the "friends of F.G. Shaw" gave fourteen hundred dollars. In the end almost every abolitionist in Boston had anted up between twenty and five hundred dollars.[65]

While his comrades worried about money, Stearns took to the road to do most of the leg work in raising the regiment. He established a central recruiting office in Buffalo, New York and successfully implored black leaders to hold recruiting meetings. He told them the state legislature had appropriated funds to remunerate recruiters two dollars for each recruit, and would pay each recruit a fifty-dollar bounty for enlisting, after the regiment mustered into service. The committee would absorb the transportation costs to camp, and then, if the enlistee were rejected by the surgeon there, would pay return costs. The state would give eight dollars a month to families left behind. Local communities would probably contribute enlistment bonuses and additional bounties. The men would be paid thirteen dollars a month, the same as white privates. Now was the time to help themselves and their race and to support old John Brown. While many black leaders had initially spoken out against the regiment, most now changed their minds to join with those who argued that they must pick up the gauntlet or forever lose their chance. The recruiters who threw themselves behind the Fifty-fourth included many of the leaders of mid-nineteenth-century black America: William Wells Brown, Charles Lenox Remond, Martin R. Delany, John Jones, Robert Purvis, O. S. B. Wall, Henry Highland Garnet, and John Mercer Langston. First Stearns went to Rochester to ask his friend Frederick Douglass for the help he knew Douglass would give. Three weeks before this, the great orator told an audience, "The paper proclamation must now be made iron, lead, and fire, by the prompt employment of the negro's arm in the contest." Douglass proved his support by enrolling sons Lewis and Charles into the regiment and issuing, in the March issue of *Douglass's Monthly*, the famous editorial "Men of Color to Arms." Then this most famous of black leaders canvassed western New York to encourage black men to fight. In all, Douglass sent over one hundred men into the regiment.[66]

While Stearns worked his way through the Midwest and Canada seeking help and enrolling men, Shaw selected officers. Shaw's work was considerably easier than Stearns's because Shaw had more applications than positions and because the governor and Norwood Hallowell had already made some key selections. Of the original twenty-nine officers appointed, fourteen came from three-year regiments, eight from nine-month units, and one from the militia. The others came from civilian jobs. Most of them had been enlisted men; only six had prior service as officers. As third in command, with the rank of major, Governor Andrew named Norwood Hallowell's brother, Lt. Edward Needles Hallowell of the Twentieth Massachusetts, whom Forbes recommended as "a tip top man, a regular Negrophile."[67]

Other abolition-minded men were selected for the officer corps. John W. M. Appleton of Boston had served some garrison duty in Boston harbor until his discharge in 1862. Then he was stirred by what he called the "Glorious

Proclamation of our President." In January, Appleton applied for a commission to serve with Col. Thomas W. Higginson, who was recruiting a regiment from among the runaway and freed slaves in South Carolina. Appleton told Higginson, "The two great problems that demand our attention in connection with the freedom of the slave are Firstly will the freedman work for his living? Secondly will he fight for his liberty? I believe that he will do both and I desire to assist him to do the latter." Notably, George Stearns recommended him to Higginson in a letter of January 20. Higginson gave Appleton a commission, but Appleton had already accepted another with the Fifty-fourth and was recruiting in Cambridge for what became Company A.[68]

Handsome William H. Simpkins, a clerk from West Roxbury who was serving as a sergeant in the Forty-fourth Massachusetts, became the captain of Company K. A thoughtful man, Simpkins related his reason for joining the enterprise: "This is no hasty conclusion, no blind leap of an enthusiast, but the result of much hard thinking. It will not be at first, and probably not for a long time, an agreeable position, for many reasons too evident to state. . . . Then this is nothing but an experiment after all; but it is an experiment that I think it is high time we should try." Twenty-three-year-old Simpkins would die near Shaw on the rampart at Fort Wagner five months later.[69]

By the end of March, Shaw had added his selections to those already commissioned. Wilkie James, the younger brother of William and Henry James, had learned from his parents that "slavery was a monstrous wrong, its destruction worthy of a man's best effort, even unto the laying down of life." He and his buddy Cabot Russel, both of the Forty-fourth Massachusetts, were quickly accepted by Shaw. James remembered that many of the men of the Forty-fourth gave them "sharp rebukes" for joining into this "crazy scheme." Russel gleefully hoped for "the power of darkness" to help win the war. James suffered severe wounds and Russel died at Fort Wagner. In addition to Simpkins, James, and Russel, Shaw raided the Forty-fourth for Charles Tucker, Willard Howard, Henry Littlefield, Edward Jones, and George Pope. Not only were they available, but they already knew each other—a situation that would strengthen their commitment to each other and speed the training of the regiment. One of the officers remembered "that we were selected to try a most important experiment, an experiment which must not fail." Shaw did not pull men from his old regiment, the Second, probably out of loyalty to the unit. However, he did persuade his close friend, Dr. Lincoln Stone, to transfer to the Fifty-fourth to inspect all the recruits to guarantee their overall state of health and physical aptitude.[70]

Shaw would organize and drill the regiment at Camp Meigs, located in

Readville, just southwest of Boston on the Boston and Providence railroad. Norwood Hallowell opened the camp on February 21 by reporting to the commandant, Brig. Gen. R. A. Peirce. While Hallowell took charge at the facility, Stearns, Douglass and others continued to look for men. Recruiter John Mercer Langston scoured Ohio, Indiana, and Illinois, and sent to Camp Meigs several hundred "of the very best young colored men" who understood "the dignity, responsibility and danger of their position." One Xenia, Ohio, mother told Langston she worried for her son, but was proud to see him fight because "liberty is better than life." Her son died at Fort Wagner. James Caldwell, the grandson of Sojourner Truth, came from Battle Creek, Michigan. Among the early enlistments, three fugitive slaves and three emancipated slaves joined the group of fourteen from egalitarian Oberlin, Ohio. Lewis and Charles Douglass arrived in camp in late March with fifty men from western New York. Their father accompanied them to Readville. Stephen A. Swails, thirty and married, quit his job as a canal boatman in Elmira, New York, to join the army. He would be promoted to become the regiment's first black lieutenant in January 1865.[71]

By February 18, Lt. James W. Grace had recruited twenty-seven men in New Bedford. Among the first to join was a former slave from Virginia, William H. Carney. Carney had been born in Norfolk in 1840, the son of William Carney and Ann Dean. Their owner's will freed them in 1854. Two years later, the family left Virginia, having chosen New Bedford over Pennsylvania because, as Carney put it, "The black man was *not secure* on the soil where the Declaration of Independence was written." Strong and brave, William Carney would become the first African American to win the Medal of Honor. Effervescent, highly literate, twenty-six-year-old seaman James H. Gooding also cast his lot with the Fifty-fourth. Gooding wrote weekly letters to the *New Bedford Mercury* to keep the home folks apprised of the unit's activities. Gooding died on July 19, 1864, after spending five months as a prisoner of war at Andersonville, Georgia. In the middle of March, a recruiting rally in the city induced others to join. Thomas Dawes Eliot, the U.S. Congressman representing New Bedford, told the gathering, "This is a war between the principles of slave labor and free labor. . . . They say you have not the courage to fight, that you are not manly enough. They lie! and you will prove it to them." Twenty-four-year-old Wesley Furlong, who had been a steward, appeared at the meeting in a uniform with sergeant's stripes on his sleeves. He told his neighbors, "The black man must put down this war." Furlong wanted to be remembered as one "who fought for the liberty of his race and to prove himself a man." Grace did his job well enough in New Bedford, and a few days after the meeting the town's company, Company C, had eighty members.[72]

Most recruits arrived by train to the Readville station and marched or walked the four hundred yards to Camp Meigs. After reporting to the officer of the day, the men went through a rigorous physical examination with Dr. Stone. For most of them, this was their second physical. In order to save the costs of transporting unsuitable men both ways, contract physicians examined recruits in the town where they signed enlistment papers. Even with this screening, Dr. Stone turned many away. Regimental Adjutant Wilkie James thought that enough men had been rejected to make another full regiment. On March 23, James Gooding of Company C wrote home that 132 of 500 men had been rejected by Stone. William Schouler, the adjutant general of Massachusetts, recorded that every third man had failed. Whatever the number, those who passed were quickly made to look like soldiers. Norwood Hallowell described the change: "Upon arrival they were marched to the neighboring pond, disrobed, washed and uniformed. Their old clothes were burnt. The transformation was quite wonderful. The recruit was very much pleased with the uniform. He straightened up, grew inches taller, lifted not shuffled, his feet, began at once to try, and to try hard, to take the position of the soldier." Every day, Shaw oversaw the repetition of this process as new recruits arrived. As a result of Shaw's instructions to Stone to maintain high standards, the regiment was healthier and stayed that way because chronic sufferers had been rejected. Still, men caught colds and a few died of bronchitis, pneumonia, and smallpox.[73]

When completed the regiment occupied ten wooden barracks, each housing one hundred men. There was a separate officers' barracks and a cook house. Hallowell ran the camp until Shaw took over in early March. Beginning the daily schedule, reveille woke the men at 5:30 and they formed for roll call. Shaw ordered the officers to "see that the men stand at attention while in the ranks." After roll call, the men cleaned the barracks, aired their bedding, and dressed for breakfast at 7:00. Half an hour later, Stone held sick call and the men took in their bedding and prepared the barracks for inspection. The regiment reformed at 8:00 to begin drill instruction. For the first weeks of camp, snow stood deep on the ground and prevented full regimental and company drills, so Shaw ordered the men drilled by squads inside empty barracks. He instructed his officers: "Particular attention should be paid to the soldierly bearing of the men, and their steadiness in the ranks." After the snow melted, Shaw moved outdoors and drilled the men five hours per day. Daily, with an order specifying "no excuses," corporals and sergeants took special instruction on drill and tactics from senior captain Alfred S. Hartwell. Long marches with full packs to build up the men's endurance took up some of the days. With lunch, supper, and inspections, the men had little time for anything else. Tattoo sounded to put men into bed at 8:00 P.M. Taps at 8:30 meant lights out and no talking.[74]

Shaw did what he could to insure the comfort of his men. Recruits who came in too late to see Stone and visit the pond still found, in the words of Gooding, "a nice warm fire and a good supper." First Lt. John Ritchie, the regimental quartermaster, kept up with the supply needs of the men. Two days before camp opened, Ritchie requisitioned and received the "necessaries" for one hundred men: one hundred woolen blankets, rubber blankets, bedsacks, overcoats, uniform coats, sack coats, pants, pairs of shoes; and two hundred shirts, pairs of underwear, and pairs of socks. The day camp opened, he had twenty-five cords of wood ready to warm the barracks. Every week, Ritchie received similar items from General Peirce, plus badges of rank, drums, fifes, kettles, mess packs, flannel shirts, forage caps, haversacks, canteens, three wall tents, 522 shelter tents, and four hospital tents. As the governor's "model" regiment, the men were well supplied and cared for by the state. However, they drilled through the winter with old muskets, having to wait until one thousand Enfield rifles became available in May.[75]

Shaw knew the stakes were high. Any misstep would be used to embarrass those who already were being ridiculed for believing that blacks would fight. Just after accepting the colonelcy, Shaw wrote his fiancée: "what I have to do is to prove that a negro can be made a good soldier." He would impose the strict discipline he had seen while in the Second. He believed strongly that most enlisted men acted in excess unless restrained by the educated and civilized officer ranks. Often Shaw wrote of the superiority of strictly managed regiments over those with lax standards. He was sure that a soldier's behavior in battle "depends almost entirely on the discipline." Shaw admired Gen. George B. McClellan for turning his disorderly recruits of 1861 into a professional army by 1862, and he sought to emulate "Little Mac." But Shaw also believed he had different material than did McClellan. Shaw was a paternalist, not at all sure that the detractors were incorrect about black abilities. Still he could not show those reservations to his men or to outsiders. He understood that in these early stages, appearances meant everything. Shaw insisted that all company commanders personally inspect every soldier who wanted to leave the base to insure that that man was "neatly dressed in his uniform & in fine weather with his boots blacked."[76]

Yet, in an effort to prevent ridicule and instill discipline, Shaw went too far. For a minor disturbance, Shaw put the offenders in the guard house, chains, and worse. When men quarreled with officers, Shaw threatened them with death. He forced some men to stand on barrels for hours. Others were gagged and had their hands and feet bound with their arms stretched around heavy sticks. Even the officers were not exempt. Captain Appleton complained to his wife about the "very stringent discipline. In fact I have never known a Regiment where the officers were under as strict discipline as the 54th." Undoubtedly too, Shaw's tough demands made his officers stricter on the men. These methods were all commonly used punishments during the war. Norwood Hallowell recalled that Shaw punished in accord with what white soldiers received "in all well-disciplined regiments." He labeled Shaw's technique "the method of coercion, and it was successful." However, the records are incomplete as to exactly the punishments inflicted, and they were harsh enough that camp commandant Peirce called them "contrary" to what the army permitted. Peirce ordered Shaw to stop all "severe and unusual punishments not laid down by regulations." Shaw was overbearing, but appearances were good. And as to punishment, one witness reported, "The guard house is seldom occupied." With the regiment's high profile, a full prison would only be a target for abuse by those who already defamed the Fifty-fourth. Shaw knew that once winter turned to spring, many visitors would come to see the regiment; he must instill order before that happened.[77]

The Fifty-fourth had the pick of the Northern black population. In the middle of April, fifty recruits from Buffalo, Cincinnati, and Detroit took a train to New York and transferred to a steamer bound for Boston. An observer claimed that they all could "read and write" and made "an excellent appearance." At one regimental muster, a newspaperman noted that "408 . . . signed their names in a good and clear hand." Many of the men came from large cities where they had had more opportunities to attend school and where daily jobs required reading. Black recruiting sergeant A. M. Green helped enlist one hundred men from Philadelphia into Company B. In camp many took reading lessons offered by volunteer teachers. The men increased their dedication to each other through play. After drill, the men sang, played instruments, and danced in the barracks. Often they picked sides for football. They took pride in themselves and in their mission and tried to get others to join them. Corporal Gooding made a plea to black women to "drive all these young loungers [who have not joined us] off to the war, and if they don't go, say, 'I'm no more gal of thine.'" Attending to their spiritual needs, black preachers William Jackson and William Grimes, both of New Bedford, competed for congregations and held prayer services in the barracks each evening. The Reverend Mr. Jackson performed at least eight marriage services at the camp. Everyone looked forward to mail call, when letters or packages poured in from wives and brothers, girlfriends and parents, and various benevolent groups.[78]

Still, as in every regiment, some felt they had made a mistake by joining, a few believed they had been disciplined unfairly, and others were overcome by homesickness or news of trouble at home. Some of the married men had endangered their families' already tenuous economic positions by sacrificing to fight against slavery; bad news from home caused discontent and desertion. Some men had trouble getting along in the closeness of barracks life, others fought with their comrades, and a few could stay no longer. Deserters were a fact of life among Civil War armies, but they presented a special problem among this vanguard black regiment because of the belief that blacks were cowards.[79]

Shaw ordered his officers to round up the slackers. Captain Appleton remembered going on several expeditions to capture those absent without leave. Once, he and Lieutenant Russel found two men in Dedham "and after a little fracas . . . marched them back over the road ironed together. Cabot Russel and I arm in arm, together behind them. Cabot quoting Shakespeare." One snowy night Appleton tracked down eighteen-year-old Charles Draper, whom he found after climbing up a water pipe and looking into a window of a house in Boston. When Appleton called for Draper, "two stout negroes" obstructed him. The captain recalled, "I put my foot in the opening and pointed a pistol at the men . . . they gave way." He found the private under a pile of clothing. Draper would desert again, this time successfully, in April 1864. Another time, Appleton found two of his men in a room with two women. After a scuffle over his pistol, Appleton marched the men to the train station for return to Readville.[80]

Besides the problem of desertion, two scandals received some attention. Word reached the governor that the Reverend Mr. Jackson and other clergymen had induced soldiers to get married to white women, "some of them worthless characters," just to get the fee from the men. In turn, the women were induced by false promises "that they could draw the State Aid." In fact, Massachusetts would not pay aid to women who married soldiers, if the men had married after enlisting. While the accusations were probably true in some cases, Jackson, who, on March 10, 1863, became the army's first official black chaplain, adamantly maintained his innocence: "I have never married any white and colored people together on this ground. Neither have I persuaded any persons to get married for the sake of getting the state aid, or bounty." The other scandal happened after the men were paid the fifty-dollar bounty for enlisting. James Gooding said that most men sent the money home, but peddlers "are reaping a rich harvest" by selling jewelry at inflated prices and four-dollar boots for twice that. Norwood Hallowell called these reports "greatly exaggerated." Shaw had ordered that no peddlers be allowed among the men. He told the men to send their money home or put it into a bank. Hallowell admitted that even with these precautions some men had been deceived. Fortunately, these scandals caused only minor flaps and truly were insignificant.[81]

Shaw left the Second with reservations about the competence of black men to become soldiers. Always sensitive to criticism, he determined to prove that he had made the right choice. His early letters from Readville to his friends show that he still had misgivings as he referred to the black recruits as "niggers" and "darkeys"—terms he avoided in his letters to his mother. Shaw made some racist remarks based upon stereotypes of physical character-istics. He joked to others about the men's poor language. Yet, near the end of March, Shaw admitted himself "perfectly astonished at the general intelli-gence these darkeys display." Never before around African Americans, Shaw changed through contact with them. He still held himself above blacks and formally addressed them, but he began to respect their abilities in camp. Soon, Shaw became attached to his men and defended them strongly against outside abuse. He had been forced by their actions to question, then conquer, his own misconceptions. They proved their intelligence, commitment to order, pluck, and adaptability to military life. As Shaw changed, he won the respect of his men. Recruiter William Wells Brown, a black man, and Corporal Gooding both wrote of the love the men held for their colonel. Shaw still wondered what they might do when they reached the battlefield, but he finally stopped calling them niggers.[82]

With the regiment half filled, Shaw was proud but worried. Secretary of War Stanton wanted Governor Andrew to send the available men to North Carolina to join with the contraband regiment being assembled there under Col. Edward Wild. Shaw protested that "the moral effect on the people at home, of seeing a well-armed, well-drilled, and well-disciplined regiment march, will be lost entirely." He said that they had not yet been supplied with rifles, so no one knew how to use them. That being the case, the men would look foolish in front of white troops in the South. Shaw knew that "it is of much importance to make a favourable impression on the white soldiers from the very beginning." Shaw told Andrew that the regiment would soon be full and should not be sent away piecemeal. If the governor complied with Stanton, Shaw would resign his commission and let Hallowell assume command. The next day Andrew answered that Shaw had an extra month to get the regiment ready.[83]

By April 6, Shaw felt confident enough to invite the public to watch the regiment's first dress parade. It was a huge success. Thereafter, Camp Meigs welcomed thousands of well-wishers, scoffers, and curious spectators who came to see the black soldiers. Hallowell remembered that "thousands of strangers" changed their minds after only one visit. Gooding spoke of the "crowds of visitors daily, drawn, no doubt, by the great reputation the regiment is gaining by competency in drill." William Lloyd Garrison and Wendell Phillips regularly took the train to Readville to admire the regiment. Politicians, looking for press opportunities, came to see firsthand how black men looked in blue uniforms. Here was a regiment to be proud of. Gooding gave all the credit to Shaw, "whose quick eye detects anything in a moment out of keeping with order or military discipline."[84]

On May 6, the week before the regiment was filled, Governor Andrew escorted Secretary of the Treasury Salmon P. Chase to see the troops Lincoln had authorized. A soldier remembered this as "a grand gala day" with much cheering and "military spirit." Certainly the feeling of the men improved that day when the quartermaster distributed into each set of eager hands a .577 caliber Enfield rifle. The soldiers promised to "make good use of them." Thoroughly impressed by the unit's abilities, a correspondent for the *Springfield Republican* reported: "Here was a regiment of a thousand men . . . with rather an uncommon amount of muscle. . . . They marched well, they wheeled well, they stood well, they handled their guns well, and there was about their whole array an air of completeness, and order, and *morale*, such as I have not seen surpassed in any white regiment." The men knew what they were about. They were proud of themselves and took special pride in the designation of the unit as the Fifty-fourth Massachusetts and not the First Colored Infantry. After the War Department established the U.S. Colored Troops, the men of the Fifty-fourth, and those of the soon-to-be raised Fifty-fifth, along with the later organized Twenty-ninth Connecticut, were the only three Northern black infantry regiments to keep their original designations. It set them apart, and they knew it. They believed all Northern black men would be proud to join them. As Gooding noticed some "strong able-bodied" black men among the visitors, he wondered, "Why are you not here?"[85]

Shaw was not in camp when Secretary Chase visited; the colonel was on his honeymoon. Since announcing his engagement to Annie Haggerty just days after he accepted command of the Fifty-fourth, Shaw had divided his time between organizing the regiment and courting his fiancée. He absented himself often from the rigors of training to travel to New York or Lenox to be with her. Shaw's mother began to worry that Annie distracted her son from his obligation to the regiment. Sarah told Shaw that he should put off the marriage until after he had devoted himself fully to the Fifty-fourth. But she had deeper objections. Sarah had the motherly love for Robert that one might expect, but she also had always been her son's closest confidant. In that role, she spoke to him as a voice of conscience—and he listened. He always worried what his mother would think. He admired her strength and personal confidence—something he and his father lacked. Sarah had always had his deepest love and his earnest ear. When she worried what Annie would do to their relationship, Shaw insisted that he had not abandoned her "entirely for Annie, as you seem to think." Jealous, Sarah hated to lose him to another woman. To her, Robert was more than a son. Since his acceptance of the regimental command, he was her John Brown and she would fight the war vicariously through her son's body. Long committed to moral perfectionism and uplift, Sarah couched her son's work in terms of God's mission: "I see you willing to give y[ou]r support to the cause of truth that is lying crushed and bleeding, I believe the time to be the fulfillment of the Prophecies, & that we are beholding the Second Advent of Christ. . . . I do not fear the lions in y[ou]r path." Sarah raised her son on principles of abolition; now, she believed God had chosen him to strike a blow against the evil slave system. She could not let him get married without expressing her disapproval. Then, Annie's father and mother joined the chorus that perhaps the timing of the wedding was wrong and should be postponed.[86]

Shaw answered that the wedding would be held while he was in camp. He swore never to "neglect my duty" because of marriage. He told his mother that he might never return from this assignment and that he wanted to be married in case that happened. Shaw did not explain why he felt that way, but the reasons were the same ones that drive people to the altar during every war. After seeing the horrors of battle deaths, Shaw worried more for his own life. Young men often feel invincible, but Shaw had to realize that men much stronger, much "better," than he had been killed right beside him many times. Perhaps Shaw wanted someone to love who was not in danger of an unfriendly bullet—someone beautiful and caring who would write him love letters to comfort him. Philosopher J. Glenn Gray has written that war uproots soldiers from home and community and places them unnaturally in a world of violent men. The rush to the altar in wartime is a grasp for order, moorings, home.[87]

Shaw might have feared that if not now, when?—maybe Annie would not wait for him. Marriage meant the future because of hopes and plans that had to be made and accomplished; it meant that he could not die yet since there was too much to do. Perhaps Shaw feared that he had not checked off "marriage" on the list of life experiences. Maybe he worried that his seed would not be passed to another generation; he was an only son in a nineteenth-century world where it was important to keep the family name, the line, alive. Whatever the reason, he would not be turned away this time. He had taken the regiment for his mother; he would take Annie for himself.

In mid March, Shaw went to Lenox, picked up his bride-to-be, and took her to Mrs. Crehore's boarding house, only a half-mile from camp. Every evening Shaw rode to see her, stayed in the room he occupied beside hers, and got up to be in place for reveille. Shaw spent many happy evenings sitting at Mrs. Crehore's with Annie and with his sister Josephine and her fiancé, Charles Russell Lowell, who both boarded there.[88]

Bowing to their children's wishes, the families of Annie and Robert gave their assent to the marriage. They assembled in the Protestant Episcopal Church of the Ascension on Fifth Avenue in New York City on May 2 for the ceremony. The couple took a train to the summer home of the Haggertys in Lenox, where they spent four happy days before the worst happened. On May 6, the day Andrew took Secretary Chase to see the regiment, Hallowell telegraphed Shaw that he must return to camp because the governor had ordered the unit to leave on the 20th. The couple spent two more days in Lenox, then returned to Boston on May 9. The next day they were back at Mrs. Crehore's, where they stayed until the regiment actually left Boston on May 28. In preparation for that spectacle, another ceremony was in order.[89]

Nearly two thousand members of Boston's black community and a vast group of others gathered at Readville on May 18 for the presentation of flags to the regiment. While many black Bostonians had initially discouraged their young men from joining the army, the community soon swung around with encouragement, food, clothing, and sons. In all, 40 percent of black Bostonians of military age joined the Fifty-fourth or, later, the Fifty-fifth. Now they had come to Readville to see for themselves. Among them stood all the prominent Boston abolitionists as well as Frederick Douglass and members of Shaw's family. The regiment formed a hollow square around the speaker's platform. Governor Andrew presented the colors and left little doubt of the pressure that rested upon the men's shoulders for the vindication of a race, and of himself. Andrew recognized that his reputation as a man and a politician would "stand or fall" with the action of this regiment. The entire abolitionist community hoped with him that these men would not let them down. Andrew put the burden of mankind upon them: "I know not . . . when, in all human history, to any given thousand men in arms there has been committed a work at once so proud, so precious, so full of hope and glory as the work committed to you." He told Shaw and the officers that he had a "confidence which knows no hesitation or doubt" that they would do their duty. After receiving the four flags and the governor's admonition that the unit must succeed, Shaw responded that his men knew "the importance of the undertaking." He hoped for "an opportunity to show that you have not made a mistake in intrusting the honor of the State to a colored regiment." Shaw and his men had ten days to ponder the events of this day before they would leave the barracks of Massachusetts for the tents of South Carolina.[90]

The crowd lining the parade route in Boston on May 28 welcomed the steady breeze as they stood under a cloudless sky in summerlike weather. Many purchased a remembrance of the day, a "Souvenir of the Massachusetts Fifty-Fourth," from which they read a quote from Byron: "Who would be free, themselves must strike the blow." Finally, down the street came a large contingent of policemen leading mounted riders, two bands, a drum corps, and—what everyone had awaited—the men of the North's first black regiment. The sight of a thousand dark-skinned soldiers in arms marching behind the Stars and Stripes led one admiring reporter to gasp: "Can we believe our own eyes and ears? Is this Boston? Is it America?" Runaway slave Harriet Jacobs, whose *Incidents in the Life of a Slave Girl* (1861) illuminated the special horrors female slaves faced, was there to applaud the regiment, and recalled: "How my heart swelled with the thought that my poor oppressed race were to strike a blow for Freedom! Were at last allowed to help in breaking the chains." Shaw's mother looked upon her son, astride an ebony horse, and wondered aloud, in nearly the same words she would write to him the next day, "What have I done, that God has been so good to me!" One week later, she wrote her friend John Cairnes, a leading English abolitionist and author of *The Slave Power* (1862): "If I never see him again, I shall feel that he has not lived in vain." Amos Adams Lawrence of the black committee told his wife that nothing like this had been seen before and at the head of it all came Shaw, "riding out front, as handsome as a picture. Everybody cheered him; the girls threw flowers at him." Another observer noted that this was "no parade" but a march led by a "boyish" commander with "only a simple air of determined devotion to duty." John Greenleaf Whittier remembered thinking that Shaw seemed as "beautiful and awful as an angel of God come down to lead the host of freedom to victory."[91]

Of course, not everyone came to praise the regiment. The Democrats of Boston's fashionable Somerset Club hissed the regiment as it passed their windows. Many of Boston's Irish felt that emancipation and the raising of black regiments threatened their tenuous position by enabling blacks to compete for the low-paying jobs they occupied. For weeks, the *Boston Pilot*, an organ of the Irish community, had alternately spread fear of black equality and ridiculed the idea that blacks would fight as men. In perhaps the most spirited attack, one critic wrote:

> They are as fit to be soldiers of this country, as their abettors are to be its statesmen. One Southern regiment of white men would put twenty regiments of them to flight in half an hour. *Twenty thousand negroes on the march would be smelled ten miles distant*. No scouts need ever to be sent out to discover such warriors. There is not an American living that should not blush at the plan of making such a race the defenders of the national fame and power.

Lt. Wilkie James remembered the "rankest sort" of prejudice and groans as the regiment wound through the streets of Boston. Overall, though, the police and the unit's supporters far outnumbered the detractors.[92]

The regiment halted on Boston Common for an hour-long review and to hear speeches in its honor. Then, Shaw dismissed the unit to meet with well-wishers and to say goodbyes. Capt. John Appleton remembered the "blessings, shouts & some tears—strangers clasped our hands and blessed us." After this short respite, Shaw ordered assembly. The men reformed, marched to Battery Wharf, and boarded the brand-new transport steamer *DeMolay*. Shaw had not yet informed the men of their destination, and rumors spread quickly. Once aboard the ship, Captain Appleton wrote his wife: "I tell you a secret that I think we are going to Newbern but maybe not." Later that day, he penned her that he had guessed wrong. The Fifty-fourth had orders to report to Maj. Gen. David Hunter, commander of the Department of the South, headquartered at Hilton Head, South Carolina. Hunter requested Governor Andrew to send him the regiment and he would put them to good service alongside white soldiers and with the units of freed slaves that had been organized under Thomas W. Higginson and James Montgomery. Hunter swore himself a friend of black troops, testified that "the prejudices of certain of our white soldiers and officers . . . are softening or fading out," and promised to use these "intelligent colored men from the North" to subdue the Rebels. Andrew had already been advocating this very arrangement with the secretary of war, once pleading with Stanton: "I pray you to send the 54th to So. Carolina, where, under Genl. Hunter, negro troops will be appreciated and allowed a place in . . . active war." By the middle of May, Stanton decided to grant Andrew's request.[93]

Frederick Douglass joined Massachusetts adjutant general William Schouler and a few friends aboard the *DeMolay* as it made its way out of Boston Harbor. Once clear of the sound, Douglass bade farewell to his son Lewis, spoke with those he had recruited, and undoubtedly told others to do their duty. Shaw and the officers were already talking with a captain from Colonel Higginson's staff, who accompanied them to explain conditions and procedures under General Hunter. After a while, Douglass and the other guests climbed aboard another boat and returned to Boston. Schouler remembered all the hopes he felt as "the large vessel with its precious cargo" sailed into the night. So much rested on the conduct of this unit. The men, the officers, and Shaw knew the whole white and black world watched their every action. They had to be better than "good"; they had to be perfect.[94]

The trip to Hilton Head took one week. It was unremarkable. Some men attempted to liven up the voyage by drinking liquor smuggled aboard in direct violation of Shaw's orders. When the officers attempted to take the drink from intoxicated soldiers, some fighting erupted. In an ugly incident, one soldier stabbed another in the face with a bayonet. Once, Shaw ordered a *DeMolay* crewman lashed to the ship's rigging for stealing from a soldier. Dr. Stone treated seven men for illness and many more for seasickness. The one fatality was Major Hallowell's horse, whose burial the men made into a ceremony consigning the body to the sea. Mostly, the voyage offered little entertainment. The men talked of loved ones left behind, wondered if and when they would get a chance to fight, and sang away the monotony. On the fifth day out, they steamed past Charleston, saw the blockading fleet and the top of Fort Sumter, and were amazed at the fury of a thunderstorm. Everyone quickly tired of water and sky and close quarters and longed to get to dry land.[95]

The *DeMolay* arrived at Hilton Head on June 3, and Shaw reported directly to General Hunter. Hunter inspected the regiment, found it "excellent," and ordered it to Port Royal Island, where Col. W. W. Davis would assign a campground. As the ship steamed upriver twelve miles to Beaufort, Shaw and his men saw, most of them for the first time, visions of the Old South. Captain Appleton described the scene: "We saw . . . the mansions and the long rows of Negro houses, here and there, also groups of Red and yellow dressed mammys. . . . We ran from side to side of the ship to see the different plantations." The Fifty-fourth arrived at Beaufort and met another group of black soldiers, the contraband regiment of Col. James Montgomery, the Second South Carolina, which had just returned from its raid up the Combahee River, where it burned property and transported 725 slaves to freedom. The men and officers no doubt looked upon each other with curiosity and wondered about their differences. After spending one more night aboard the steamer, the Fifty-fourth set up camp in what had been an old cottonfield. The only enemies were the insects and snakes the men found everywhere. At least one rattlesnake died to make room for the tents. Appleton told his wife that "sand flies, midges, mosquitoes, stinging ants, little red ticks, . . . leave very little of us."[96]

Shaw wrote to Governor Andrew informing him of the arrival in South Carolina. He mentioned Montgomery and said he did not admire his "Indian style of fighting." Shaw complained that he had hoped for better service for the regiment: "bushwacking seems pretty small potatoes." Montgomery had learned his fighting style in Kansas, when as an intimate of John Brown, he spread fire and brimstone among the proslavery settlers. Shaw would have much to say later about Montgomery's methods. Still worrying over what others thought and feeling insecure, Shaw wrote of his relief that most of the officers at Beaufort had treated him well even though many of them seemed "rather coppery."[97]

On the day the regiment set up camp, Shaw met Col. Thomas W. Higginson, the only prominent abolitionist to command black soldiers during the war. Higginson had formed his regiment, the First South Carolina Volunteers, with ex-slaves from the nearby plantations. Higginson later recalled this meeting with Shaw, and wrote that Shaw "asked only sensible questions" about the performance of black troops and declared the "matter of [their] courage to be settled." Yet, Shaw still wondered how his men would do in a firefight and told Higginson that perhaps it would be good to put them "between two fires" so that battle-proven men at their backs would prevent them from running in the face of the enemy. White rookie soldiers commonly ran during their first fight, but in this case, Shaw feared that if his men turned to escape, Northern whites would seize on the example to "prove" black inferiority and persuade the government to withdraw its commitment to black regiments. At the least, any cowardice by the Fifty-fourth would create trouble and suspicion with white units who would then fear to fight beside them. More than that, Shaw was still struggling with his own racism and would not exorcise fully his belief in inferiority until his men proved themselves in front of the Confederate army.[98]

Two days later, Hunter ordered the regiment to Hilton Head. From there, the Fifty-fourth went directly to St. Simons Island, Georgia, seventy-five miles to the south, to join with Montgomery's Second. The Fifty-fourth arrived at St. Simons on June 9 after a stormy trip over rough seas. John Appleton noted their proximity to Jekyll Island, where in 1858 Charles Lamar's infamous ship *Wanderer* unloaded a cargo of 409 Africans. Since the U.S. Constitution specifically prohibited the importation of slaves after 1808, authorities had seized the ship and prosecuted Lamar. Even though Lamar escaped conviction, his action increased sectional tension. Appleton confidently remarked, "I think no more will be landed there for some time." Montgomery too knew of Lamar's action, and it further incensed him. He had sworn to make the slaveholders suffer for their sins against humanity. The afternoon after Shaw put his men into camp on an abandoned plantation, Montgomery invited him to go on a raid. Shaw left a camp guard and quickly boarded his men onto transports to join the expedition. He had been anxious to get his men into action; he would not let this opportunity slip past.[99]

Shaw got more and also less than he wanted. Montgomery directed the force of three transports and one gunboat up the Altamaha River to the seaport town of Darien. Georgia's second leading port, Darien actively engaged in supplying cotton, rice, turpentine, and timber to the world market. Montgomery claimed that the town was a rendezvous point for blockade runners, and—something he considered more heinous—the prewar home of some of the South's richest slaveowners. At the time Montgomery and Shaw arrived, the townspeople had removed themselves further inland for safer haven. After a noontime shelling of the town, the men landed to no opposition. Shaw followed Montgomery's example, assembled his men in the streets, then detailed men to gather supplies. One officer recalled Shaw's order: "Captain Appleton, take twenty men from the right of your company, break into the houses on this street, take out anything that can be made useful in camp." The men did as they were told. Lt. James Grace of the New Bedford company later wrote to General Peirce at Readville to describe the loot: "I wish you could see my tent all furnished with rosewood and black walnut furniture, looking glasses, pictures, some very fine ones. Some of our officers got very nice carpets."[100]

While participating willingly in the plunder, Shaw was indignant when Montgomery gave orders to burn the town. Shaw believed the action unjustified and disgraceful, and said he could have assented to it only if they had met Rebel resistance. He wrote to Annie about his "dishonour" in the "dirty piece of business" which he called "wanton destruction" and he feared the possible negative publicity this would heap upon black soldiers. In camp he had been careful to enforce strict discipline, now his efforts would go for naught if this action hurt public opinion, which was far from decided about black soldiers. Charles Lowell wrote his fiancée, Josephine Shaw, that Shaw "must be peculiarly disturbed" about what had happened. Lowell, a friend of the Fifty-fourth, explained that "instead of improving the negro character and educating him for a civilized independence, we are re-developing all his savage instincts." Writing the War Department to complain against using blacks to destroy property, Lowell warned that if this continued, "no first-rate officers" would join black regiments. He explained that the end result would not be "an army of disciplined blacks, . . . [but] a horde of savages." Obviously, if Lowell ascribed to the argument of latent violence within black bodies, others, less committed to the end of slavery, would see the worst.[101]

North and South, newspapers carried the story. Confederate papers and Northern detractors of black troops naturally berated the action and said "told you so." An article in the *Savannah News* was widely reprinted. Among other epithets, that paper called the Fifty-fourth "accursed Yankee vandals," "wretches," and "cowardly Yankee negro thieves." In a book found in Darien, private Stewart Woods, a twenty-seven-year-old laborer from Carlisle, Pennsylvania, had written his name, his regiment, and the names of his officers, including Shaw. Because of that graffiti, which was actually a message of pride from a free-black soldier to black and white Southern readers, many began to blame Shaw for torching civilian property. The men of the Fifty-fourth knew that the opposition press objected to the raid by "nigger guerillas" upon Darien. The raid and the negative response put even more pressure on the men and Shaw to redeem themselves at the earliest opportunity.[102]

Others rallied to defend the act. Frederick Douglass insisted that the Confederate Congress and President Jefferson Davis must be made to understand that their unjust actions declaring white officers be put to death and black soldiers to be sold into slavery would not be tolerated. Douglass said if burnings were necessary to force the Rebels to adhere to "rules of civilized warfare" then let the torch be applied. The *Boston Commonwealth* called the action "divine justice" against "those who have so long traded in human bodies and souls" and deemed it retaliation for what Confederate navy commerce raiders were doing to Union shipping. At the same time, the *Commonwealth* warned that this hurt the Fifty-fourth, which had won "prestige" that would soon be "wasted." Shaw could agree with this paper's admonition that blacks already suffered from a "vast accumulation of undeserved odium" and must therefore "be employed only in the strictest duties of war." White soldiers could set fires with impunity; black soldiers would fan the flames of racial hatred if they struck a single spark. Shaw knew this and resented Montgomery for casting a shadow over his honor and his men's reputation. He reported to Governor Andrew that the raid "disgusted" him, and claimed his men "superior" to the contraband regiments and worthy of better service.[103]

Shaw also wrote a letter to Hunter's adjutant, Lt. Col. Charles Halpine, and complained about the "barbarous" burning of the town. Montgomery had told Shaw that he had his orders from Hunter. Now Shaw wanted to know if Hunter had indeed issued such instructions. Shaw said that if Hunter deemed future actions necessary, he would do it, but he did not like it. It turned out that Montgomery had been acting on his commander's orders. Shaw, hoping that Hunter would change his policy, got better than that. Lincoln too had been reading the papers and felt aggrieved over Hunter's scorched-earth policy. Lincoln knew his political life marched with the public opinion of black troops, so he replaced Hunter with a less vindictive general.[104]

On St. Simons, Shaw assured his men that they would have better duty and told them they must be ready to prove their detractors wrong. Shaw's old stereotypes of blacks as savages resurfaced as he thought about what had transpired in Darien. Fighting against his racism while determining to keep his men in line, Shaw ordered that any soldier who discharged his rifle without supervision or who became a "nuisance" would be "severely punished." He warned that if the men slept on duty or deserted, he would have them shot. Initially, because of the heat, the regiment drilled four hours a day, from five to seven in the morning and from four to six every afternoon. Later, to keep the men busy, or perhaps unhappy with what he saw or feared, Shaw ordered an extra drill from eight to ten. Company sergeants met daily to recite lessons and tactics. Every day, Shaw inspected his men and equipment. After one unsatisfactory review, Shaw chastized five of the ten companies for the unpolished condition of their rifles. Every evening before dinner, Shaw reviewed the regiment in a formal dress parade. He enforced Taps at 9:30 P.M. There is no evidence to support a conjecture that soldiers in the regiment now behaved differently than they had at Readville or that participation with the contraband regiment had diminished their soldierly bearing. Fearing a loss of discipline, Shaw made his men pay for his insecurity with increased drill.[105]

Everything was not hardship and maneuver. The island presented a beautiful stage for military pageantry. As described by Wilkie James, it was "a perfect paradise . . . with its wealth of tropical beauty. . . . The live oak and the magnolia, the orange, the lemon and the palmetto, the citron, the fig-tree and the yellow jessamine attained apparent perfection." Mission walls built by the Spanish and the tabby construction of James Oglethorpe's Fort Frederica whispered the romantic military history of the island to a new generation of soldiers. Appleton concentrated his descriptions on the two alligators that were killed in camp and the snakes to be found everywhere. Gooding admitted, "To tell the honest truth, our boys out on picket look sharper for snakes than they do for rebels." The men ate well on the cattle deserted by a Rebel owner and on turtle eggs dug from the beach. They bathed in seawater and rinsed in the rains that swept the island. Some soldiers spruced up their tents with furniture pulled from Darien mansions. Most of each day, they spent searching for shade in which to sleep or write letters.[106]

Shaw situated himself in the absent owner's home and added to its furnishings with accent pieces from Darien. He spent his time writing letters and studying manuals on military tactics. Perhaps the increased drill he put the men through was more for his preparation than theirs; not a captain obeying orders, he was a colonel giving them. Besides attending to the regiment, Shaw basked in the loveliness of the island and took time to visit some of the plantations he had heard Fanny Kemble describe during the summer in Sorrento. Coincidentally, Kemble's *Journal of a Residence on a Georgian Plantation*, published in May 1863, allowed abolitionists to read about what Shaw was seeing firsthand. The plantation homes of T. Butler King, James E. Couper, and Pierce Butler provided a contrast to the slave cabins that stood nearby. Shaw's letters reveal the excitement of a tourist tempered by the realization that the glory of his surroundings rested on the ingloriousness of slavery. Shaw talked with some of the Butler slaves who were still on the plantation. Many of them fondly recalled Kemble. Shaw found them "faithful creatures" and affirmed his antislavery convictions that every abandoned plantation "is a harbinger of freedom to the slaves." Still, Shaw obviously did not think of all blacks as men.[107]

While he toured and drilled, Shaw pined for a standup battle instead of raids or sequestration from white troops and main arenas of battle. He soon got his wish. The regiment returned to Hilton Head on June 25 to support the coming assault upon Charleston. Shaw settled the regiment on St. Helena Island and waited for action. During this period, most of Shaw's letters deal with Colonel Montgomery, a man he greatly respected but did not understand. Shaw admired Montgomery's dedication and envied his clear vision of vengeance and mission. Besides the Darien raid, Shaw watched Montgomery shoot a man for disorderly conduct and execute a soldier for desertion. Undoubtedly, Shaw respected Montgomery for his adherence to discipline. But Shaw believed that Montgomery's troops were inferior to his own because they were made up of contrabands from the plantations who had "never had the pluck to run away" before the war started. Shaw's letters reveal this lack of vision and his belief that southern blacks were "perfectly childlike." He admired Montgomery for leading these troops but he felt his northern men were better; certainly, his disdain for the South affected his analysis. Additionally, as an extension of abolitionist thought that freedom uplifted and made better men, Shaw had to believe his men were better soldiers because of their prewar experiences in the North. Constantly doubting his own abilities and worried about his men, he sought comparisons to deal with his insecurity.[108]

He missed his mother and his wife. He found female companionship in the northern schoolteachers who came to Port Royal to teach the freed people. In particular, he enjoyed socializing with Charlotte Forten of Philadelphia, the only black teacher on St. Helena. Forten grew up in a prominent family of abolitionists, attended an integrated school in Salem, Massachusetts, and went to Beaufort in October 1862. She met Shaw on July 2 and spent much time with him until the regiment moved to the front on July 8. Shaw's four-day letter to his mother dated July 3–6 indicated his infatuation for Forten. Forten was equally taken with Shaw and wrote of him in her journal:

> I am perfectly charmed with Col. S. He seems to me in every way one of the most delightful persons I have ever met. There is something girlish about him, and yet I never saw anyone more manly. To me he seems a perfectly lovable person. And there is something so exquisite about him. . . . We had a pleasant talk on the moonlit piazza.

They attended the Independence Day celebration together and visited again the next day. On July 6, Forten again confessed to her journal:

> I am more than ever charmed with the noble little Col. What purity, what nobleness of soul, what exquisite gentleness in that beautiful face! As I look at it I think "The bravest are the tenderest." I can imagine what he must be to his mother. . . . Yesterday . . . leaning against our carriage and speaking of mother, so lovingly, so tenderly. He said he wished she c'ld be there. If the reg[iment] were going to be stationed there for some time he sh'ld send for her. . . . I do think he is a wonderfully lovable person. To-night, he helped me on my horse, and after carefully arranging

the folds of my riding skirt, said, so kindly, "Goodbye. If I don't see you again down here I hope to see you at our house." But I hope I shall have the pleasure of seeing him many times even down here.

Obviously, Forten and Shaw were entranced with each other. For Shaw, being so far from home, and questioning himself and his men, this admiring, caressing woman gave him impossibly much when he had gotten accustomed to so little. Before their relationship could develop further, matters of war intervened.[109]

Shaw fretted over being left behind when the other troops, white troops, moved to support the activities around Charleston. On July 6, he wrote to Gen. George C. Strong, the brigade commander in charge of the Fifty-fourth. Shaw expressed his disappointment at not being part of the campaign. He flattered Strong and requested "better service than mere guerilla warfare." Shaw understood that to elevate the popular opinion of black troops it was paramount "that the colored soldiers should be associated as much as possible with the white troops, in order that they may have other witnesses besides their own officers to what they are capable of doing." Strong liked Shaw and would honor the request if possible. But for now, the Fifty-fourth had other orders.[110]

On July 8 the regiment was ordered to James Island. The men were excited. After their employment on raids, perhaps they were finally going to participate in an action alongside white regiments. Maybe they would even get the chance to use the Enfields they had fired only in target practice. With thoughts of Darien and the renewed criticism of black troops that came with the burning there, the men wanted more than ever to prove that they could fight as well as white men. Some were upset that they would have to stay behind as camp guards and for other detail duty. Of those going, many worried if they could stand the test of battle. They thought they could and determined to fight to the finish but they were afraid nonetheless.

The officers also reflected the tension of the moment. A week before, there had been an awful rumor that the government had decided to arm black troops with pikes instead of rifles. Some of the officers and men were angry and some talked of quitting if that happened. Shaw wrote home that "pikes against Minie balls is not fair play—especially in the hands of negroes whose great pride lies in being a soldier like white men." He added, in another missive, "They might as well go back eighteen centuries as three, and give us bows and arrows." While John Brown had wanted to distribute pikes during his crusade, Shaw had seen too many modern battles to support that kind of insanity. But Captain Appleton coolly told the officers: "I came out to prove that colored men could fight and I would go into action armed with pick-axes if ordered." The rumor passed. Now that they would keep their rifles, Appleton itched to fight and the men wanted to prove they could handle the guns. With relief and hope for more, Shaw had his officers load the seven companies—about seven hundred men—aboard two transport ships bound for James Island.[111]

Gen. Quincy A. Gillmore, who had replaced Hunter as commander of the Department of the South, had won fame as an artillerist by forcing the sur-render of Fort Pulaski on Tybee Island near Savannah. He planned to re-duce the forts and batteries that protected Charleston Harbor, to seize Fort Sumter, and to conquer the city where the rebellion began. Troops on James Island would divert attention from the real assault against Morris Island's Fort Wagner, which protected the guns defending the harbor at Cummings Point. On July 11, after a heavy bombardment of Wagner, Gillmore's infantry as-saulted the position and was repulsed, incurring heavy losses. That afternoon, after waiting aboard ship at anchor for two days, the Fifty-fourth landed on James Island. Shaw thought that Gillmore would now begin siege operations against Wagner; but he thought wrong.[112]

While Gillmore made plans to renew the attack, Shaw put his men into camp. He hoped for but did not expect any action now that Gillmore's as-sault had failed. Shaw's pickets were on duty beside white soldiers from other regiments. At least that was a beginning. Capt. Cabot Russel informed his father that "the men behave exceedingly well on picket, of which we have been having a large dose." Still, Russel wrote that "their spirits are super." At dawn on July 16, a nine-hundred-man Rebel force struck the Federals. Russel's company and two others—about 250 men—of the Fifty-fourth stubbornly held their ground and retreated in good order while the Union forces rallied. Still, the Confederates pushed them back until the Union troops found pro-tection under the artillery of their gunboats. They prepared for a last stand that never came. The Confederates broke off the attack and left the field.[113]

Shaw could barely restrain his excitement. His men had fought well in co-ordination with white soldiers against white Confederates. He had wanted to prove that black men could fight, and they had stood the test well. Cap-tain Russel, whose life was saved by Pvt. Preston Williams, explained simply: "My men did nobly." Captain Appleton wrote that the men's "stubborn cour-age filled the officers with joy." Gen. Alfred H. Terry, in charge of the Union division on James Island of which the Fifty-fourth was a part, praised the regiment and told Shaw that the best disciplined white regiments could have done no better. The soldiers of the Tenth Connecticut Infantry, camped next to the Fifty-fourth, were convinced by what they saw. One of their men wrote his wife: "But for the bravery of . . . the Massachusetts Fifty-fourth (colored), our whole regiment would have been captured. . . . They fought like heroes." The Tenth congratulated the Fifty-fourth and, in the words of Captain Appleton, "These first praises of white men made the dusky cheeks burn." Shaw called the fight "a fortunate day . . . for me and for us all, excepting some poor fellows who were killed and wounded." Shaw seemed to think the sacrifice of fourteen killed, eighteen wounded, and thirteen missing a small price to pay for the proof and praises he received. The casualties *were* small compared with what he had seen in Virginia. He wanted to write another letter full of details of the battle, but he did not have time for that. To save his outnumbered troops on James Island against further attack and to bolster his forces on Morris Island for another assault against Fort Wagner, Gillmore ordered Terry's division to join him.[114]

Withdrawing just a few hours after the battle on July 16, the Fifty-fourth made a difficult night march through the mud flats between James and Cole islands. Engineers laid wooden planks and the men marched single file over them for nearly eight hours. A moonless night and a relentless thunderstorm with lightning flashing all around made things worse as the planks got slippery and men fell into the marsh. Shaw said he never had such "an extraordinary walk." Across Cole Island, the regiment reached its transport rendezvous point exhausted, dirty, famished, and parched. "The sun and sand are dazzling and roasting us," Shaw wrote. As for the lack of food, "It seems like old times in the army of the Potomac." The men slept all day on the beach, searched for shelter from the sun, and watched for the steamers that would take them closer to Gillmore.[115]

At an hour before midnight on July 17 the regiment boarded the transport *General Hunter*. The loading took five hours and was delayed by another thunderstorm. The steamer ferried them to Folly's Island, which they marched up, waited on the beach, looked upon the distant forts Sumter and Wagner, then boarded another transport to cross the five-hundred-yard-wide inlet to Morris Island. The march up Morris took two hours. Shaw reported to General Strong's headquarters.[116]

Strong told Shaw that Gillmore had ordered another infantry assault upon Wagner later that evening. Strong's brigade would lead. He probably did not tell Shaw of General Truman Seymour's comment to Gillmore when the attack plan had been formulated: "Well I guess we will let Strong put those d——d negroes from Massachusetts in the advance, we may as well get rid of them, one time as another." Federal artillery, monitors, and floating batteries had been pumping shells into Wagner since noon. The fort's defenders must be dead, wounded, or demoralized. It was almost six in the evening. The attack would come at dusk—two hours away. Shaw and his men looked "worn and weary." Strong had become friends with Shaw in the tents at St. Helena and admired the soft-spoken young man with the heavy load to bear. He told Shaw that the James Island fight gave the regiment credibility. Strong offered Shaw what Wilkie James later called "the grand chance . . . the one chance which above all others seemed essential!" Strong held out "opportunity." He asked Shaw if he wanted the Fifty-fourth to lead the charge. Shaw could have declined. His men were more than a little tired and hungry. But Shaw knew that the key to Charleston lay at the end of the beach. If black men could storm the fort and open the door to the birthplace of the rebellion, the symbolism would be enormous. His duty was never clearer. Since that day at Readville, when the first black civilian put on a soldier's uniform and Shaw began to instruct a regiment, this had been the goal. The chance for the sons of slaves to show that they would fight and thus to vindicate those who supported them suddenly reached out its hand to Shaw. His answer was yes.[117]

Even while Shaw believed that he would die in the battle forthcoming, he overcame that fear to do his duty. He never felt comfortable in the Fifty-fourth and always considered himself a part of the Second. Maybe the responsibility was too much. Colonel Higginson remembered that when he met Shaw at Beaufort, Shaw had a "watchful anxiety in his look." Higginson believed that Shaw felt the destiny of a race upon his shoulders. On July 13, Shaw had written Annie that he would probably be a major in the Second had he stayed: "As regards my own pleasure, I had rather have that place than any other in the army." Of course, that admission came after news of more friends killed, this time at Gettysburg. Also, the fight on James Island had not yet happened. Shaw had committed himself to the Fifty-fourth, but he missed the days when he had close friends around him and less on the line. On July 15, Shaw confided to Hallowell his fear of dying and said that if a fight came, "I trust God will give me strength to do my duty." Just hours before saying yes to Strong, a melancholy Shaw sat on the transport between Folly and Morris Island, and told Hallowell, "If I could only live a few weeks longer with my wife, and be at home a little while, I might die happy, but it cannot be. I do not believe I will live through our next fight." Still, Shaw hid his fear from the other officers and men.[118]

Shaw took his men to the front, through or past the thirteen white regiments that would support the Fifty-fourth in the assault. Many white soldiers cheered the men they had come to respect. At six hundred yards from the fort, Shaw ordered his men to form two lines of battle, fix bayonets, and lie down on the sand. The men exchanged letters, shook hands with each other, reminded others who to write in case they were killed or captured, and told friends which pocket held letters for whom. Shaw gave some letters and papers to Edward Pierce and asked him to make sure his father got them if anything happened. Shaw walked up and down among the men, smoked a cigar, and talked with them in a most friendly way. Corporal Gooding of Company C remembered that he had never seen Shaw so informal with the soldiers. Shaw sat with this group and that, reminded them that nothing like what they were about to do had been done before, and warned them that the world was watching. With lips compressed and with a slight twitch at the corner of his mouth, Shaw challenged the men to "take the fort or die there." They swore to try.[119]

The bombardment stopped at seven o'clock. Thirty minutes later, Strong made a short speech to the men and ordered Shaw to advance. With a final admonition to "prove yourselves men," Shaw positioned himself in front and ordered, "forward." Years later, one soldier remembered that the regiment fought hard because Shaw was in front, not behind. They marched ahead until the batteries of Wagner and Sumter opened up on them about two hundred yards from the fort. Shaw ordered "double quick" and the regiment surged across the beach. At eighty yards the seventeen hundred Confederate defenders, who had been barely hurt by the nine-thousand-shell bombardment, opened up with grape shot and cannister. Lieutenant Grace said later: "Our men fell like grass before a sickle." The men waded kneedeep through seawater, crossed a moat, tore through abatis, and climbed up the sloping sand walls of Wagner as rifle fire blazed against them.[120]

With a small group of men, Shaw somehow made it to the top of the parapet before an enemy bullet killed him and dropped his body into the fort. Those near him remembered his last words differently, but they agreed that Shaw had waved his sword and urged his men forward. Nearly half the regiment succeeded in pushing its way inside Wagner. The men held their ground on the wall for almost an hour before being forced to withdraw. The Confederates lost 174 men. Of the 600 men of the Fifty-fourth who charged the fort, 272 were killed, wounded, or captured. Additional casualties from the white regiments that followed brought Union losses to 1,515. Confederate gravediggers buried eight hundred Union soldiers in the sand in front of the fort the morning after the battle. Showing the contempt Southern whites held for the "principle line of the Abolitionists"—white officers leading black soldiers—the fort's commander, Gen. Johnson Hagood, ordered Shaw thrown into a ditch with his men. The diggers made a trench, dropped Shaw's body within it, threw the bodies of twenty of his men on top of him, and shoveled them over with sand. Morris Island lived up to its earlier name. Old maps showed it as "Coffin Land." [121]

Obviously, the assault was ill-conceived and, if judged on a military basis or on the loss of lives, a failure. If judged by its scale as compared to other battles of the war, it would attract little notice. But the charge upon Wagner changed things. Blacks had proven themselves as fighting men and vindicated their sponsors, the abolitionists. By year's end, sixty black regiments were being organized, and they would not be used simply to dig fortifications, handle baggage, and cook food for white soldiers. They would be allowed to fight.

The propaganda effect of Wagner was enormous. The *New York Tribune* reported that the battle would be to black Americans what Bunker Hill was to white Americans. The influential *Atlantic Monthly* declared: "Through the cannon smoke of that dark night the manhood of the colored race shines before many eyes that would not see." The *Boston Commonwealth* tied the charge to John Brown by printing that the bodies of the men were "mouldering in the ground" and quoted a white soldier at Wagner as saying, "We don't know any black men here, they're all soldiers." The *Richmond County Gazette*, Staten Island's paper, quoted another white soldier at Morris Island in support of black troops and against those who still wanted only whites to fight: "We know men from monkeys. . . . If you have any blue or green men that can work and fight, send them along." The Northern population that accepted putting blacks into uniforms as a test, now acknowledged that black men could fight and kill like white men. In 1935, historian W. E. B. Du Bois wrote about the change that the black soldier wrought on white minds: "How extraordinary . . . in the minds of most people . . . only murder makes men. The slave pleaded; he was humble; he protected the women of the South, and the world ignored him. The slave killed white men; and behold, he was a man." [122]

The men of the Fifty-fourth were proud of what they had done and determined to do more. Just after the fight, several remarked that they would continue until "the last brother breaks his chains." Some said, "If all our people get their freedom, we can afford to die." Pvt. Francis Myers, a twenty-three-year-old laborer from Paterson, New Jersey, who was wounded in the attack, expressed best what many felt: "Oh, I thank God so much for the privilege." The men justified the expectations of their officers and convinced all but the most sceptical critics of their bravery. Instead of being objects to which things happened, these men had been actors who changed their times. And they wanted more. Two weeks after Wagner, Sgt. Albanus Fisher declared: "I still feel more Eager for the struggle than I ever yet have, for I now wish to have Revenge for our galant Curnel." Like others before them, once blood spilled around them, black soldiers got more determined to continue to the finish. The men participated in the siege which brought the fall of Wagner on September 6, 1863, then continued to serve their country for the remainder of the war. They always remembered the "little colonel" who sacrificed his life for a promise of better lives for black people. In the hospital at Beaufort, one of Shaw's men told Charlotte Forten, "He was one of the very best men in the world." [123]

Shaw's family grieved their loss but were consoled by the many letters that mourned with them or glorified their son. Charles Lowell interpreted Robert's death as "a perfect ending. I see now that the best Colonel of the best black regiment had to die, it was a sacrifice we owed,—and how could it have been paid more gloriously?" Lowell told Harry Sturgis Russell that Shaw had died "for a cause greater than any National one." Edward Pierce forwarded Shaw's last letters. Pierce told Shaw's parents, "With the opening of the war, your son gave himself to his country, and he has now laid down his life for a race." Lydia Maria Child comforted Sarah Shaw with the thought that Shaw had "died nobly in the defence of great principles, and has gone to join the glorious army of martyrs." Sarah already believed that. Later, Francis Shaw became convinced too, and he wrote his old friend William Lloyd Garrison, "We do thank God that our darling . . . was chosen, among so many equals, to be the martyred hero of the downtrodden of our land." [124]

When Francis and Sarah heard the news that Shaw was "buried with his niggers," Francis immediately wrote to Pierce that they could hope for "no holier place" for Shaw's body. Three days later, Francis sent more explicit instructions to regimental surgeon Dr. Lincoln Stone: "We mourn over our own loss & that of the Regt, but find nothing else to regret in Rob's life, death or burial. We would not have his body removed from where it lies surrounded by his brave & devoted soldiers, if we could accomplish it by a word. Please to bear this in mind & also, let it be known, so that, even in case there should be an opportunity, his remains may *not* be disturbed." Francis also wrote to General Gillmore and told him: "You will forbid the desecration of my son's grave." Because of the father's plea, when Fort Wagner fell to Union arms one month later, the grave remained undisturbed. Undoubtedly, this noble sentiment by Shaw's parents led to even higher praise for Shaw and the regiment. The burial symbolized the brotherhood of man.[125]

In fact, all the circumstances surrounding Shaw, his family, the abolitionist movement, the raising of the regiment, his youth, his marriage just eighty days before his death, his acceptance of an unpopular command, the sacrifice of life for human freedom, the death upon a parapet of a fort protecting Charleston, the burial and sneer—"with his niggers"—the comparison with John Brown, and his parents' response to it all, made him larger than life. Eleven days after the storming of Wagner, Charles Sumner recognized that Shaw's "death will be sacred in history and art."[126]

New England's poets, writers, and editors—many of them friends or relatives of the Shaws—also recognized what Sumner knew. They began to write verses to Northern idealism and the fallen hero. Shaw's death symbolized their expressed moral conscience and they were quick to explain that to others. By so doing, they helped make Shaw one of the Civil War's most celebrated legends. Since his death, at least forty poems have been written to eulogize him, and he has become more monument than man. Ralph Waldo Emerson wrote: "So nigh is grandeur to our dust, So near to God is man, When Duty whispers low, *Thou must*, The youth replies, *I can*." Six months after Wagner, James Russell Lowell penned "Memoriae Positum: R.G.S., 1863": "Brave, good, and true, I see him stand before me now. . . . Right in the van, On the rampart's slippery swell With heart that beat a charge, he fell Foeward, as fits a man." A century after Lowell wrote his elegy, another Lowell composed "For the Union Dead": "He is out of bounds now. He rejoices in man's lovely peculiar power to choose life and die—when he leads his black soldiers to death, he cannot bend his back." The latter Lowell compared the moral degeneration of modern Boston with the unselfish sacrifice of Shaw.[127]

And so there is the monument on Boston Common. Shaw rides in step with his men. An angel of the Lord glides over them. The bronze breathes and challenges viewers to remember the American creed. Shaw deserved the monument for his steadfastness to honor even though he never had the clear-eyed crusader's vision, commitment to abolition, faith in moral uplift, or deep-thinking ability of some in the antislavery movement. What Shaw had was courage and loyalty. He was responsible enough to give black troops a fair trial. He did his duty to his men, his mother, and himself.

Fortunate in birth and in war, Shaw grew stronger and developed a richer personal character after he accepted an unwanted position at the head of a black regiment and struggled with his own preconceptions of black inferiority. The men of the Fifty-fourth lifted him to a higher plane and educated him even as their efforts caused others to reexamine their own prejudices. William James explained the meaning of their sacrifice and of Shaw's when he looked upon the monument in 1897: "There they march, warm-blooded champions of a better day for man. There on horseback among them, in his very habit as he lived, sits the blue-eyed child of fortune."[128]

NOTES

1. Among his many works, sculptor Augustus Saint-Gaudens created exquisite statues of Abraham Lincoln, William Tecumseh Sherman, and David Farragut. In molding Shaw and the men of the Fifty-fourth, Saint-Gaudens hired many models and crafted forty heads before deciding on the twenty-one that stand in clear relief in the monument. Richard Benson, *Lay This Laurel: An Album on the Saint-Gaudens Memorial on Boston Common Honoring Black and White Men Together Who Served the Union Cause with Robert Gould Shaw and Died With Him July 18, 1863* (New York: Eakins, 1973); for an excellent look at the Shaw monument as seen through the eyes of the artist, see Homer Saint-Gaudens, ed., *The Reminiscences of Augustus Saint-Gaudens* (New York: Century, 1913).

2. *Douglass' Monthly* (Aug. 1863), quoted in James M. McPherson, *Battle Cry of Freedom: The Civil War Era* (Oxford: Oxford University Press, 1988), p. 564, for Sims see p. 83; Whittier quote from John B. Pickard, ed.,*The Letters of John Greenleaf Whittier* (Cambridge, Mass.: Harvard University Press, 1975), vol. 3, p. 362.

3. Robert T. Teamoh, *Sketch of the Life and Death of Colonel Robert Gould Shaw* (Boston: Boston Globe, 1904); Marion W. Smith, *Beacon Hill's Colonel Robert Gould Shaw* (New York: Carlton Press, 1986), pp. 491–92; Roger Faxton Sturgis, *Edward Sturgis of Yarmouth, Mass., 1613–1695, and His Descendants* (Boston: Stanhope, 1914), pp. 50–54; W. P. Garrison and F. J. Garrison, *William Lloyd Garrison, 1805–1879: The Story of His Life* (New York: Century, 1889), vol. 3, pp. 79–80.

4. Robert Gould Shaw (1776–1853) and Nathaniel Russell Sturgis (1779–1856). Shaw was one of only eighteen men in Massachusetts worth over one million dollars in 1852. Sturgis, *Edward Sturgis*, pp. 50–51; Cleveland Amory, *The Proper Bostonians* (New York: E. P. Dutton, 1947), pp. 20, 49, 209; Abner Forbes and J. W. Greene, *The Rich Men of Massachusetts* (Boston: Fetridge, 1852), p. 61; Mary C. Crawford, *Famous Families of Massachusetts* (Boston: Little, Brown, 1930), vol. 1, p. 242, vol. 2, p. 163; Lawrence Leder, *The Bold Brahmins: New England's War Against Slavery, 1831–1863* (New York: E. P. Dutton, 1961), p. 110.

5. Forbes and Greene, *Rich Men*, p. 194; Richard M. Bayles, ed., *History of Richmond County (Staten Island) New York From Its Discovery to the Present Time* (New York: L. E. Preston, 1887), pp. 572–74.

6. Bayles, *History of Richmond County*, p. 572; newspaper clipping from *Boston Transcript*, May 29, 1897, in Fifty-fourth Massachusetts Infantry Regiment Papers, MHS; Shaw's friend quoted in *Richmond County Gazette*, Nov. 18 (2:1–2), 1882 [page and column numbers are indicated within parentheses]; Lindsay Swift, *Brook Farm: Its Members, Scholars, and Visitors* (New York: Macmillan, 1900), p. 257; Francis George

Shaw, trans., *The Children of the Phalanstery: A Familiar Dialogue on Education*, by Felix Cantegrel (New York: W. H. Graham, 1848), p. 6, expressed the danger of capitalism to future generations: "All things are bound together in nature, and if your social order engenders evil and infinite suffering for men and for women of all ranks and all conditions . . . so it is with children"; Francis George Shaw, trans., *The Life of Charles Fourier*, by Charles Pellarin (New York: W. H. Graham, 1848).

7. Francis George Shaw, "A Piece of Land," in Henry George, *Social Problems* (New York: J. W. Lovell, 1883), pp. 298–304.

8. Article from *Sewanee Review* 39 (Apr.–June 1931): 131–42, in Robert Gould Shaw Collection, HL; Swift, *Brook Farm*, pp. 19–25; Brook Farm participant Nathaniel Hawthorne remembered Shaw's monetary contributions as crucial but insisted his kindness was more important than money. Thomas Woodson, Neal Smith, and Norman H. Pearson, *Nathaniel Hawthorne: The Letters, 1843–1853* (Columbus: Ohio State University Press, 1985), pp. 201, 238, 251; FGS to George Ripley, Feb. 1845, Dana Collection, MHS; George William Curtis, *From the Easy Chair* (New York: Harper, 1892), vol. 3, pp. 14–15; George W. Cooke, *Unitarianism in America: A History of Its Origin and Development* (Boston: American Unitarian Association, 1902), pp. 353–57, 382, 399, 428; George M. Frederickson, *The Inner Civil War: Northern Intellectuals and the Crisis of the Union* (New York: Harper & Row, 1965), p. 13.

9. Teamoh, *Sketch of Shaw*, p. 11; Milton Meltzer and Patricia Holland, eds., *Lydia Maria Child: Selected Letters, 1817–1880* (Amherst: University of Massachusetts Press, 1982), pp. 85, 324–27; Lydia Maria Child, "Correspondence between Lydia Maria Child and Gov. Wise and Mrs. Mason of Virginia" (Boston: American Anti-Slavery Society, 1860), reprinted in *Anti-Slavery Tracts* (Westport, Conn.: Greenwood Press, 1970); for the best of Child's letters to the Shaws, see Lydia Maria Child to FGS, June 2, 1854, Oct. 27, 1856, and Dec. 22, 1859, Sarah Blake Sturgis Shaw Papers, HL.

10. FGS, Wendell Phillips, et al., to Hon. Rufus Choate, Feb. 1, 1842, William Lloyd Garrison Papers, BPL; Walter M. Merrill and Louis Ruchames, eds., *The Letters of William Lloyd Garrison* (Cambridge, Mass.: Harvard University Press, 1979), vol. 4, pp. 334–35.

11. Gay quoted in Peter Burchard, *One Gallant Rush: Robert Gould Shaw and His Brave Black Regiment* (New York: St. Martin's Press, 1965), p. 6; William R. Stewart, *The Philanthropic Work of Josephine Shaw Lowell* (New York: Macmillan, 1911), pp. 1–3, quote by a neighbor (Joseph Choate), p. 3.

12. Vernon B. Hampton, *Staten Island's Claim to Fame* (Staten Island: Richmond Borough, 1925), p. 165; SBS to RGS, Dec. 6, 1852, Shaw Collection, HL; Charles W. Leng and William T. Davis, *Staten Island and Its People: A History, 1609–1929* (New York: Lewis Historical Publishing Co., 1929), vol. 1, pp. 253–54; Franklin B. Hough, comp., *Census of the State of New York for 1855* (Albany: Van Benthysen, 1857), p. xxxiii; Charles G. Hine and William T. Davis, *Legends, Stories and Folklore of Old Staten Island* (New York: Staten Island Historical Society, 1925), pp. 26, 31, 36–37, 63, 64; Teamoh, *Sketch of Shaw*, pp. 11–12.

13. RGS to SBS, June 3, 1850, Sept. 7, 17, and 29, 1850, and Oct. 3, 1850, RGS to FGS, Nov. 30, 1850, Robert Gould Shaw, *Letters: RGS* (New York: Collins, 1876), pp. 3–6, 8, 10; Burchard, *One Gallant Rush*, p. 8.

14. RGS to FGS, Oct. 13, 1851, and July 7, 1853, RGS to SBS, [Oct. 13], 1851, *Letters: RGS* (1876), pp. 13–15, 39.

15. RGS to SBS, Nov. 13, 1851, Feb. 28, 1852, Mar. 13, 1853, Apr. 14, 1853, and June 2, 1853, *Letters: RGS* (1876), pp. 16–17, 22, 32, 33, 35.

16. RGS to SBS, [n.d.], 1851, Jan. 3, 1852, Mar. 13, 1853, Apr. 14, 1853, and June 12, 1853, RGS to SBS and FGS, Apr. 24, 1853, RGS to FGS, July 13, 1853, *Letters: RGS* (1876), pp. 15, 18, 34, 36, 40; SBS to RGS, Dec. 6, 1852, Shaw Collection, HL; Shaw probably was not as touched by *The Key to Uncle Tom's Cabin* as Frederick Douglass, who asserted, "There has not been an exposure of slavery so terrible"; in Harriet Beecher Stowe, *The Key to Uncle Tom's Cabin* (Boston: Jewett, 1853; reprint ed., New York: Arno Press, 1968), p. ii.

17. RGS to SBS, [n.d.] 1851, and Jan. 3, 1852, RGS to SBS and FGS, Mar. 21, 1852, *Letters: RGS* (1876), pp. 15–16, 19, 23–24.

18. RGS to SBS, [n.d.] 1851, and Feb. 6, 1853, *Letters: RGS* (1876), pp. 16, 30.

19. Ibid., p. 46n; RGS to Annie [Kneeland Haggerty Shaw], June 9, 1863, Robert Gould Shaw, *Letters: RGS* (Cambridge, Mass.: Harvard University Press, 1864), p. 299.

20. RGS to SBS, July 19, 1854, *Letters: RGS* (1876), pp. 46, 47.

21. RGS to SBS, Oct. 8, 1854, Nov. 5 and 23, 1854, and July 16, 1855, Shaw Collection, HL.

22. RGS to SBS, Nov. 23 and 27, 1854, Sept. 30, 1855, Oct. 7, 1855, and Jan. 30, 1856, *Letters: RGS* (1876), pp. 59, 77, 79.

23. RGS to SBS, Feb. 27, 1855, and Apr. 9, 1856, *Letters: RGS* (1876), pp. 63, 108; RGS to SBS, Oct. 28, 1855, and Dec. 26, 1855, RGS to FGS, Mar. 5, 1856, Shaw Collection, HL.

24. RGS to SBS, July 1, 1855, Dec. 31, 1855, Jan. 30, 1856, and Feb. 26, 1856, *Letters: RGS* (1876), pp. 66, 94, 98, 101.

25. RGS to SBS, Dec. 11, 1855, *Letters: RGS* (1876), p. 86.

26. RGS to SBS, Apr. 9, 1856, Shaw Collection, HL; RGS to SBS, Oct. 14, 1855, and Apr. 9, 1856, *Letters: RGS* (1876), pp. 80, 108.

27. RGS to FGS, Nov. 7, 1855, RGS to SBS, Feb. 20, 1856, and Mar. 15, 1856, *Letters: RGS* (1876), pp. 83, 101, 105; Elliotville became West New Brighton in 1866, with Francis Shaw as one of its four trustees. Leng and Davis, *Staten Island*, p. 271, and H. F. Walling, "Map of Staten Island, 1859," SIHS; U.S. Census, Eighth Census (1860), N.Y., Richmond County, Castleton, p. 152; Hine and Davis, *Legends*, pp. 54, 65–66, 77, 79; Hampton, *Staten Island's Claim*, pp. 23–24, 74; J. J. Clute, *Annals of Staten Island From Its Discovery to the Present Time* (New York: Charles Vogt, 1877), pp. 294–95; the Shaws leased pew number 57 in the Unitarian church for two hundred dollars a year. Curtis Collection, SIIAS.

28. RGS to SBS, Aug. 29, 1856, and Dec. 2, 1857, Shaw Collection, HL; RGS to

SBS, Sept. 30, 1856, Apr. [n.d.], 1857, and Dec. 2, 1857, *Letters: RGS* (1876), pp. 113, 121, 138; Thomas W. Higginson, *Harvard Memorial Biographies* (Cambridge, Mass.: Sever & Francis, 1867), vol. 2, p. 172.

29. RGS to SBS, Sept. 5, 1856, Oct. 7, 1856, Mar. 29, 1857, Apr. 22, 29, and [n.d.], 1857, May 11, 1857, June 3 and 22, 1857, Oct. [n.d.], 1857, Sept. 9, 1858, and Nov. [n.d.], 1858, Shaw Collection, HL; Walter R. Spalding, *Music at Harvard: A Historical Record of Men and Events* (New York: Coward-McCann, 1935), pp. 71–74.

30. RGS to SBS, Mar. 14 and 29, 1857, Apr. [n.d.], 1857, and May 23, 1858, Shaw Collection, HL. Helper's book called for the South's poor whites to unite against the slaveholders, because slavery gave them an advantage that harmed nonslaveholders.

31. RGS to SBS, Nov. 18, 1856, and Mar. 19, 1858, Shaw Collection, HL.

32. RGS to SBS, Sept. 20, 1857, Oct. 31, 1857, Sept. 9, 1858, and Dec. 1 and 9, 1858, RGS to FGS, Mar. 24, 1858, Shaw Collection, HL.

33. RGS to Heinrich [Henry Vezin], July 24, 1859, and Sept. 16, 1859, RGS to SBS, Mar. 29, 1861, Shaw Collection, HL; RGS to SBS, Nov. 18, 1860, *Letters: RGS* (1876), p. 157.

34. RGS to SBS, Mar. 29, 1861, Shaw Collection, HL.

35. William Swinton, *History of the Seventh Regiment National Guard, State of New York During the War of the Rebellion* (New York: Dillingham, 1886), pp. 24–36; Emmons Clark, *History of the Seventh Regiment of New York, 1806–1889* (New York: Published by the author, 1890), vol. 1, pp. 473–74; Theodore Winthrop lived on Staten Island with his sister. Gay quoted in Hine and Davis, *Legends*, p. 83; Ernest A. McKay, *The Civil War and New York City* (Syracuse: Syracuse University Press, 1990), pp. 67–68.

36. RGS to FGS, May 12, 1861, RGS to Effie [Josephine Shaw], Nov. 21, 1862, RGS to Annie [Kneeland Haggerty], Nov. 23 and 28, 1862, RGS to SBS, June 9, 1861, Nov. 17, 1862, and Dec. 1, 1862, collected herein.

37. RGS to SBS, June 9 and 16, 1861, and Sept. 5, 1861, collected herein.

38. RGS to Effie [Josephine Shaw], July 31, 1861, Dec. 8, 1861, and Jan. 15, 1862, RGS to SBS, July 18 and 21, 1861, and Apr. 19, 1862, collected herein.

39. RGS to SBS, May 25, 1861, Aug. 30, 1861, Mar. 14, 1862, and Sept. 25, 1862, collected herein.

40. RGS to Effie [Josephine Shaw], Jan. 15, 1862, RGS to SBS, Feb. 16, Apr. 11 and 19, and Sept. 25, 1862, collected herein.

41. RGS to Anna [Shaw Curtis], Sept. 23, 1861, RGS to FGS, Oct. 13, 1861, RGS to Effie [Josephine Shaw], July 31, 1861, Dec. 8, 1861, Jan. 15, 1862, and Feb. 9, 1862, collected herein.

42. RGS to SBS, Mar. 28, 1862, May 9, 1862, and Aug. 12, 1862, RGS to Annie [Russell Agassiz], Aug. 13, 1862, collected herein.

43. RGS to Annie [Kneeland Haggerty], Nov. 23, 1862, RGS to Mimi [Elizabeth Russell Lyman], Feb. 20, 1863, RGS to Sue [Susanna Shaw], Aug. 15 and Sept. 17, 1861, RGS to SBS, Dec. 1, 1862, collected herein; obituary of Ogden Haggerty, *NYT*,

Sept. 1 (4:7), 1875; Anna [Shaw Curtis] to Mimi, Feb. 16, 1863, Lyman Family Papers, 1785–1956, Reel 13, No. 14.2, MHS.

44. RGS to SBS, July 18 and 21, 1861, Sept. 25, 1862, Oct. 5, 1862, RGS to Mr. [Sydney] Gay, Aug. 6, 1861, RGS to FGS, Aug. 3 and Nov. 13, 1862, RGS to Effie [Josephine Shaw], Jan. 25 and Nov. 21, 1862, collected herein.

45. *Douglass' Monthly* (May 1861), quoted in Dudley T. Cornish, "To Be Recognized as Men: The Practical Utility of History," *Military Review* 58 (Feb. 1978): 46; FGS to William Lloyd Garrison, May 16, 1862, William Lloyd Garrison Papers, BPL.

46. "U.S. Electors to Abraham Lincoln," Dec. 24, 1862, in Sarah Forbes Hughes, ed., *Letters and Recollections of John Murray Forbes* (Boston: Houghton Mifflin, 1899), vol. 1, pp. 344–46.

47. Charles B. Sedgwick to J. M. Forbes, Dec. 22, 1862, in Hughes, *John Murray Forbes*, vol. 1, pp. 347–48.

48. William F. Fox, *Regimental Losses in the American Civil War, 1861–1865* (Albany, N.Y.: Albany Publishing Co., 1889), p. 53; Ira Berlin, Joseph P. Reidy, and Leslie S. Rowland, eds., *Freedom: A Documentary History of Emancipation, 1861–1867*, series II: *The Black Military Experience* (Cambridge, Eng.: Cambridge University Press, 1982), p. 12; Martin Binkin and Mark J. Eitelberg, *Blacks and the Military* (Washington, D.C.: Brookings Institution, 1982), pp. 14–15.

49. Richard H. Abbott, "Massachusetts and the Recruitment of Southern Negroes, 1863–1865," *Civil War History* 14 (Sept. 1968): 197–98; J. M. Forbes to Governor Andrew, Jan. 22, 1863, John Albion Andrew Papers, MHS; *NYT*, Jan. 9, 1863, quoted in Cornish, *The Sable Arm*, pp. 96–97; *Annual Report of the Adjutant-General of the Commonwealth of Massachusetts . . . for the Year Ending Dec. 31, 1863* (Boston: Wright & Potter, 1864), pp. 54–55.

50. William Schouler, *A History of Massachusetts in the Civil War* (Boston: E. P. Dutton, 1868), vol. 1, pp. 407–8; *NYT*, June 6 (4:2), 1863; Phineas C. Headley, *Massachusetts in the Rebellion* (Boston: Walker, Fuller, 1866), p. 449; Douglass's speech quoted in John W. Blassingame, ed., *The Frederick Douglass Papers* (New Haven: Yale University Press, 1985), vol. 3, pp. 566–67.

51. Hughes, *John Murray Forbes*, vol. 2, p. 67; J. M. Forbes to Governor Andrew, Jan. 30, 1863, newspaper clipping of obituary of Morris Hallowell, June 17, 1880, Norwood P. Hallowell Papers and Scrapbooks, 1764–1914, MHS.

52. John A. Andrew to FGS, Jan. 30, 1863, J. A. Andrew Papers, MHS. Also printed in full in Luis F. Emilio, *A Brave Black Regiment: History of the Fifty-Fourth Regiment of Massachusetts Volunteer Infantry, 1863–1865* (Boston: Boston Book Co., 1891; reprint ed., New York: Arno Press, 1969), pp. 3–5.

53. John A. Andrew to FGS, Jan. 30, 1863, J. A. Andrew Papers, MHS.

54. Ibid., John A. Andrew to Capt. Robert Gould Shaw, Jan. 30, 1863; Higginson, *Harvard Memorial Biographies*, vol. 2, p. 189.

55. Charles Morse to [?], Feb. 8, 1863, Charles F. Morse, *Letters Written During the Civil War, 1861–1865* (Boston: Privately printed, 1898), pp. 119–21. In July 1863,

Morse had the opportunity to take a colonelcy in a black regiment, but he refused. See his letters, pp. 142–43.

56. RGS to SBS, Aug. 8, 1861, RGS to FGS, May 19, 1861, collected herein; after Copeland's dismissal, Andrew tried to intervene on his behalf, and probably first thought of him for the colonelcy. About the same time Shaw accepted the position, Andrew wrote Senator Sumner, asking, "What is Decided about Copeland. . . ." See Andrew to Sumner, Feb. 9, 1863, in Berlin, *Black Military Experience*, p. 337; RGS file, CMSR, George L. Andrews Papers, United States Military History Institute.

57. Richard Cary to Helen [Cary], Oct. 16, 1861, and Jan. 16, 1862, Richard Cary Papers, MHS; Henry Lee Higginson, *The Soldier's Book* (Boston: Privately printed, 1890), no page numbers [Savage section]; Higginson, *Harvard Memorial Biographies*, vol. 1, pp. 305–26, Shaw's comment on Savage, p. 326.

58. Higginson, *Harvard Memorial Biographies*, vol. 2, p. 189; RGS to SBS, Oct. 14, 1862, RGS to Annie [Kneeland Haggerty], Nov. 23, 1862, and Feb. 4, 1863, collected herein; SBS to RGS, Jan. 31, 1863, quoted in Robert Shaw Sturgis Whitman, "The 'Glory' Letters," *Berkshire (Mass.) Eagle*, Feb. 2 (6:2), 1990. Whitman's grandfather, Robert Sturgis, was a first cousin of Robert Gould Shaw.

59. RGS to FGS, Feb. 6, 1863, in Teamoh, *Sketch of Shaw*, p. 16.

60. Oration by William James in *The Monument to Robert Gould Shaw: Its Inception, Completion and Unveiling, 1865–1897* (Boston: Houghton Mifflin, 1897), pp. 77–85.

61. SBS's letter to Governor Andrew quoted in Burchard, *One Gallant Rush*, p. 73; SBS to RGS, Feb. 6, 1863, Shaw Collection, HL; Governor Andrew to FGS, Feb. 6, 1863, two telegrams in Hallowell Papers, MHS; John A. Andrew to RGS, Feb. 7, 1863, and John A. Andrew to E. M. Stanton, Feb. 9, 1863, Andrew Papers, MHS.

62. Higginson, *Four Addresses*, p. 90; *Memorial: RGS*, p. 6; John A. Andrew to James B. Congdon, Feb. 9, 1863, Soldier's Fund Committee, Scrapbook, James Bunker Congdon, NBFPL; Anna [Shaw Curtis] to Mimi [Elizabeth Russell Lyman], Feb. 16, 1863, Lyman Family Papers, MHS.

63. Anna [Shaw Curtis] to Mimi [Elizabeth Russell Lyman], Feb. 1, 1863, Lyman Family Papers, MHS; Charles Lowell to Mother, Feb. 4 and 9, 1863, Charles Lowell to H. L. Higginson, Feb. 15, 1863, in Edward W. Emerson, *Life and Letters of Charles Russell Lowell* (Boston: Houghton Mifflin, 1907), pp. 233, 235–36; newspaper clipping, *Boston Herald*, Feb. 17, 1863, in Hallowell Papers, MHS.

64. Charles E. Heller, "George Luther Stearns," *Civil War Times Illustrated* 13 (July 1974): 20–28; William S. McFeely, *Frederick Douglass* (New York: W. W. Norton, 1990), p. 223; *Boston Commonwealth*, Feb. 22 (3:3), 1863; newspaper clipping of *Boston Transcript*, Feb. 17, 1863, in Hallowell Papers, MHS.

65. Advertisements from newspaper clippings in Hallowell Papers and Scrapbooks, MHS; *Boston Daily Journal*, Feb. 14 (2:4), 1863; Subscription Paper, Feb. 13, 1863, Scrapbook, Soldier's Fund Committee, NBFPL. The committee expanded and eventually had about one hundred members.

66. At least one newspaper reporter put Forbes in charge of the committee: "It

is curious to see a meeting of the Committee on the Enlistment of Colored Troops. John M. Forbes is its chairman, a man of headlong energy, longtime an abolitionist, and more than any other man the confidential adviser and helper of Governor Andrew." Hughes, *John Murray Forbes*, vol. 1, p. 10; *Boston Commonwealth*, Apr. 10 (2:2–3), 1863; RGS to James B. Congdon, Mar. 17, 1863, Scrapbook, Soldier's Fund Committee, NBFPL; Henry Greenleaf Pearson, *The Life of John A. Andrew, Governor of Massachusetts, 1861–1865* (Boston: Houghton Mifflin, 1904), vol. 2, p. 82; Berlin, *Black Military Experience*, pp. 93, 98, 101–2; *National Anti-Slavery Standard*, Feb. 14 (1:5, 3:1), 1863; McFeely, *Frederick Douglass*, p. 48; David W. Blight, *Frederick Douglass' Civil War: Keeping Faith in Jubilee* (Baton Rouge: Louisiana State University Press, 1989), p. 158.

67. Telegram, J. A. Andrew to N. P. Hallowell, Hallowell Papers, MHS; Teamoh, *Sketch of Shaw*, pp. 17–18; J. M. Forbes to J. A. Andrew, Feb. 2, 1863, Andrew Papers, MHS.

68. J. W. M. Appleton to Col. T. W. Higginson, Jan. [n.d.], 1863, George L. Stearns to Col. T. W. Higginson, Jan. 20, 1863, Memoir of J. W. M. Appleton, Letterbook, J. W. M. Appleton Papers, 1861–1913, WVU.

69. Simpkins quoted in Burchard, *One Gallant Rush*, p. 78; William H. Simpkins file, CMSR.

70. Garth W. James, "The Assault upon Fort Wagner," *War Papers read before the Commandery of the State of Wisconsin, Military Order of the Loyal Legion of the U.S.* (Milwaukee: Burdick, Armitage & Allen, 1891), pp. 9–10; Cabot [Russel] to Father, Mar. 8, 1863, Cabot Jackson Russell Papers, 1859–1865, NYPL; RGS to John A. Andrew, Apr. 8, 1863, Shaw Collection, HL; RGS to Col. [Francis L.] Lee, Apr. 9, 1863, in William A. Gladstone, *United States Colored Troops, 1863–1867* (Gettysburg, Pa.: Thomas Publications, 1990), p. 35; Appleton Scrapbook, pp. 3–4, WVU; William Nutt, a first sergeant in the Second, was the only man to be commissioned in the Fifty-fourth from that regiment. Emilio, *A Brave Black Regiment*, p. 337.

71. Emilio, *A Brave Black Regiment*, pp. 19, 373; John M. Langston, *From Virginia Plantation to the National Capital* (Hartford, Conn.: American Publishing Co., 1894; reprint ed., New York: Johnson Reprint Corp., 1968), pp. 200, 203; newspaper clipping from *Oberlin News*, Hallowell Papers, MHS; *National Anti-Slavery Standard*, Apr. 25 (3:2), 1863, May 2 (3:2), 1863.

72. *New Bedford Daily Mercury*, Feb. 18 (2:2), 20 (2:2), 1863, Mar. 9 (2:2), 11 (2:2), 1863; William H. Carney to Col. M. S. Littlefield, Oct. 16, 1863, newspaper clipping, Hallowell Papers, MHS; James H. Gooding file, CMSR; Emilio, *A Brave Black Regiment*, pp. 349, 350. Virginia Adams has compiled the letters of James Gooding into *On the Altar of Freedom: A Black Soldier's Civil War Letters from the Front* (Amherst: University of Massachusetts Press, 1991).

73. James, "Assault upon Fort Wagner," p. 13; *New Bedford Mercury*, Mar. 24 (2:3), 1863; *Annual Report of the Adjutant-General of Massachusetts*, p. 13; Norwood P. Hallowell, *The Negro as a Soldier in the War of the Rebellion* (Boston: Little, Brown, 1897),

p. 9; newspaper clipping, "54th Mass at Readville," in Hallowell Papers, MHS; Emilio, *Brave Black Regiment*, pp. 22–23; Virginia M. Adams, ed., *On the Altar of Freedom: A Black Soldier's Civil War Letters from the Front* (Amherst: University of Massachusetts Press, 1991), p. 8; First Lt. Cabot Russel wrote his father that the men "have begun to die all ready" because of lung inflammation from close quarters and indoor drill. Cabot [Russel] to Father, Mar. 23, 1863, Russell Papers, NYPL.

74. Newspaper clipping, "54th Mass. at Readville," in Hallowell Papers, MHS; General Order No. 1, HQ 54th Mass., Camp Meigs, Readville, Mar. 5, 1863, by command of Robert G. Shaw, Capt Cmdg 54th, and General Order No. 5, Records of the Adjutant General's Office, Record Group 94, Bound Record Books, 54th Massachusetts Infantry (Colored), Order Book, NA; General Order No. 12, Special Order Book, Camp Meigs Papers, NBFPL; *New Bedford Mercury*, Mar. 24 (3:2), 1863; Appleton Scrapbook, p. 6, WVU.

75. *New Bedford Mercury*, Mar. 8 (2:3), 1863; Requisition for the 54th Massachusetts, Feb. 19, 24, and 27, 1863, Mar. 4 and 5, 1863, Apr. 6, 21, and 22, 1863, and May 6, 11, and 22, 1863, Camp Meigs Papers, NBFPL.

76. RGS to Annie [Kneeland Haggerty], Feb. 8, 1863; RGS to FGS, Aug. 29, 1862, collected herein.

77. Hallowell, *Negro as a Soldier*, p. 9; Appleton Scrapbook, p. 3, WVU; *New Bedford Mercury*, Apr. 6 (2:3), 1863; General Order No. 9, Brig-Gen R. A. Peirce, Mar. 26, 1863, Bound Record Books, 54th Mass., Record Group 94, NA; Dale's report quoted in Smith, *Beacon Hill's*, p. 403; newspaper clipping, "54th Mass at Readville," in Hallowell Papers, MHS.

78. *National Anti-Slavery Standard*, Apr. 4 (3:1), 11 (3:4), 18 (3:4–5), 1863; two newspaper clippings in Hallowell Papers, one dated Apr. 4, 1863, the other undated, MHS; *New Bedford Mercury*, Mar. 24 (2:3), 30 (2:3), 31 (2:3), 1863, Apr. 6 (2:3), 13 (2:3), 21 (2:3), 1863; James M. McPherson, *The Struggle for Equality: Abolitionists and the Negro in the Civil War and Reconstruction* (Princeton: Princeton University Press, 1964), p. 206; Edwin S. Redkey, "Black Chaplains in the Union Army," *Civil War History* 33 (Dec. 1987): 332.

79. Lewis Jackson wrote his wife that the men were having trouble getting along in the Readville barracks. McFeely, *Frederick Douglass*, p. 224. Joseph T. Glatthaar, *Forged in Battle: The Civil War Alliance of Black Soldiers and White Officers* (New York: Free Press, 1990), p. 61. Grimes was a pastor of the African Methodist Episcopal Church and Jackson the preacher at the Salem Baptist Church. Adams, *On the Altar of Freedom*, pp. 6, 8.

80. Appleton Scrapbook, pp. 4–5, WVU; *New Bedford Mercury*, Mar. 24 (2:3), 1863.

81. William Schouler to John A. Andrew, June 19, 1863, and N. P. Hallowell to John Andrew, June 20, 1863, in Requisitions Book, Camp Meigs Papers, NBFPL; *Record of the Service of the Fifty-Fifth Regiment of Massachusetts Volunteer Infantry* (Cambridge, Mass.: John Wilson & Son, 1868), vol. 2, p. 101; William Jackson to Brig Gen R A

Peirce, June 19, 1863, Special Order Book, Camp Meigs Papers, NBFPL; *New Bedford Mercury*, May 26 (2:2), 1863.

82. RGS to Charley Morse, Feb. 21 and Mar. 4, 1863, R. G. Shaw II Collection, MHS; RGS to Mimi [Elizabeth Russell Lyman], Feb. 20, 1863, T. Lyman III Collection, MHS; RGS to A. A. Lawrence, Mar. 25, 1863, A. A. Lawrence Collection, MHS; newspaper clipping, Aug. 16, 1863, in Hallowell Papers, MHS; Lydia Maria Child to Willie Haskins, Apr. 30, 1863, in Meltzer and Holland, *Lydia Maria Child*, p. 427; William Wells Brown, *The Negro in the American Rebellion: His Heroism and His Fidelity* (New York: Lee & Shepard, 1867), pp. 203–4; *National Anti-Slavery Standard*, Aug. 8 (2:4), 1863; *New Bedford Mercury*, Aug. 29 (2:2), 1863; for the best discussion of the change black soldiers wrought upon white officers, see Glatthaar, *Forged in Battle*, especially pp. x–12, 79–108.

83. Newspaper clipping, *New Bedford Standard*, Apr. 8, 1863, in Scrapbook, Soldiers' Fund Committee, NBFPL; *New Bedford Mercury*, Apr. 6 (2:3), 1863; RGS to Governor [John A.] Andrew, Apr. 6, 1863, Miscellaneous Bound, MHS.

84. Hallowell, *Negro as a Soldier*, p. 10; *New Bedford Mercury*, Apr. 27 (2:3), 1863, May 6 (2:3), 26 (2:2), 1863; Garrison, *William Lloyd Garrison*, vol. 4, p. 79.

85. *New Bedford Mercury*, May 6 (2:3), 11 (2:4), 1863; newspaper clipping from *Springfield Republican* in *Memorial: RGS*, p. 18; Charles Lowell to Effie [Josephine] Shaw, May 27, 1863, in Emerson, *Life and Letters of C. R. Lowell*, p. 248.

86. RGS to Annie [Kneeland Haggerty], Mar. 3, 1863, RGS to SBS, Feb. 20, 1863, Mar. 17, 1863, and Apr. 1, 1863, RGS to FGS, Apr. 3, 1863, SBS to RGS, Feb. 6, 1863, Sarah Blake Shaw Papers, HL.

87. RGS to SBS, Apr. 1, 1863, collected herein; J. Glenn Gray, *The Warriors: Reflections on Men in Battle* (New York: Harper & Row, 1970), p. 62.

88. RGS to SBS, Mar. 25 and 27, 1863, and Apr. 14, 1863; RGS to FGS, Mar. 30, 1863, collected herein.

89. RGS to SBS, Apr. 8, 1863; RGS to Charley [Morse], May 3, 1863; RGS to Sue [Susanna Shaw Minturn], May 7, 1863, collected herein; *Trow's New York City Directory for the Year 1863*, p. 14; RGS to Mrs. Robert Gould Shaw, May 9, 1863, RGS to Ogden Haggerty, May 8, 1863, Robert Gould Shaw, Military and Personal Telegrams, NYHS.

90. James Oliver Horton and Lois E. Horton, *Black Bostonians: Family Life and Community Struggle in the Antebellum North* (New York: Holmes & Meier, 1979), p. 127; *National Anti-Slavery Standard*, May 23 (3:5), 1863; *Boston Commonwealth*, May 22 (2:2–4), 1863; Emilio, *Brave Black Regiment*, pp. 25–30.

91. *National Anti-Slavery Standard*, June 6 (3:3), 1863; "Souvenir of the Massachusetts Fifty-Fourth (Colored) Regiment" (Boston: 1863), p. 1; reporter quoted from *Commonwealth*, June 5 (2:1), 1863; Jacobs quoted by Lydia Maria Child in *Memorial: RGS*, p. 168; SBS quoted from Shelby Foote, *The Civil War: A Narrative* (New York: Random House, 1963), vol. 2, p. 697; SBS to J. E. Cairnes, June 4, 1863, in Weinberg, *John Elliot Cairnes*, p. 164; SBS to RGS, May 31, 1863, Shaw Collection, HL; A. A. Lawrence to Sarah A. Lawrence, May 28, 1863, Amos Adams Lawrence Papers, HL;

Robert Rantoul, "A Reminiscence of War Times," in Garrison, *William Lloyd Garrison*, vol. 4, p. 80; Pickard, *Letters of Whittier*, vol. 3, p. 362.

92. Hallowell, *Negro as a Soldier*, p. 7; "Souvenir," p. 7; James, "Assault upon Fort Wagner," pp. 13–14.

93. *New Bedford Mercury*, May 29 (2:3), 1863; John Appleton to Mary [Appleton], May 28, 1863, two letters, Appleton Papers, WVU; Maj-Gen David Hunter to Gov [John A.] Andrew, May 4, 1863, and J. A. Andrew to E. M. Stanton, Apr. 1, 1863, in "The Negro in the Military Service of the United States, 1607–1889," Records of the Adjutant General's Office, Record Group 94, NA; *NYT*, May 17 (3:3), 1863.

94. John [Appleton] to Mary [Appleton], May 29, 1863, Appleton Scrapbook, p. 9, WVU; Schouler, *History of Massachusetts in the Civil War*, pp. 409–10; Emilio, *Brave Black Regiment*, p. 33.

95. John [Appleton] to Mary [Appleton], May 29, 1863, Appleton Scrapbook, pp. 8–9, 11–12. James Gooding reported that one man jumped overboard on the first night at sea, *New Bedford Mercury*, June 19 (2:3), 1863. RGS to John Andrew, June 5, 1863, in *Annual Report of the Adjutant-General of the Commonwealth of Massachusetts... for the Year Ending Dec. 31, 1863* (Boston: Wright & Potter, 1864), p. 58.

96. Maj-Gen David Hunter to Col Shaw, June 3, 1863, "Special Orders," Department of the South, Record Group 393, NA; Maj-Gen [David] Hunter to E. M. Stanton, June 3, 1863, and Maj-Gen [David] Hunter to John Andrew, June 3, 1863, *The War of the Rebellion: A Compilation of the Official Records of the Union and Confederate Armies* [hereafter cited as *OR*], ser. I, vol. 14, pp. 462–63; *Report of Adjutant-General, 1863*, p. 900; John [Appleton] to Mary [Appleton], June 5 and 7, 1863, Appleton Scrapbook, pp. 13–17.

97. RGS to John Andrew, June 5, 1863, *Report of Adjutant-General, 1863*, p. 58.

98. Thomas W. Higginson, *Army Life in a Black Regiment* (1869; reprint ed., New York: W. W. Norton, 1984), p. 216.

99. Maj-Gen [David] Hunter to Col W. H. Davis, June 6, 1863, "Registers of Letters Sent," Dept. of the South, Record Group 393, NA; Appleton Scrapbook, p. 20; Morning Reports of June 9 and 10, Bound Volumes, 54th Mass. Inf. (Colored), Records of the Adjutant General's Office, Record Group 94, NA.

100. Appleton Scrapbook, pp. 22–23; Report of Capt. W. G. Thomson, June 13, 1863, and Report of Capt. W. A. Lane, June 19, 1863, *OR* I:14, pp. 318–19; newspaper clipping, June 16, 1863, in Hallowell Papers, MHS; E. Merton Coulter, "Robert Gould Shaw and the Burning of Darien, Georgia," *Civil War History* 5 (Oct. 1959): 363–65; J. W. Grace to Gen. Peirce, June 14, 1863, Camp Meigs Papers, NBFPL.

101. John [Appleton] to Mary [Appleton], June 11, 1863, Appleton Scrapbook, p. 24; RGS to Annie [Kneeland Haggerty Shaw], June 9, 1863, collected herein; Charles Lowell to Effie [Josephine] Shaw, June 20, 1863, and Charles Lowell to William Whiting, June 26, 1863, in Emerson, *Life and Letters of Lowell*, pp. 261–62, 265–67.

102. *Savannah News*, June 16, 1863, quoted in *Boston Commonwealth*, July 3 (4:3),

1863; newspaper clipping, *NYDT*, June 24, 1863, in Hallowell Papers, MHDS; Emilio, *Brave Black Regiment*, p. 383; newspaper clipping, *New Bedford Mercury*, July 8, 1863, in Scrapbook of James Bunker Congdon, Soldiers' Fund Committee, NBFPL.

103. Frederick Douglass, "The Burning of Darien," newspaper clipping in Hallowell Papers, MHS; *Boston Commonwealth*, July 3 (2:3, 3:3–4), 1863; RGS to Governor [John A.] Andrew, June 14, 1863, *Annual Report of Adjutant-General, 1863*, p. 59.

104. Emilio, *A Brave Black Regiment*, pp. 43–44; Burchard, *One Gallant Rush*, pp. 110–11; James, "Assault upon Fort Wagner," p. 15; *OR*, I:28.

105. Special Order No. 13, June 13, 1863, Special Order No. 16, June 16, 1863, Special Order No. 19, June 19, 1863, and Daily Call Order, June 28, 1863, Bound Volumes, 54th Mass, Record Group 94, NA; Cabot [Russel] to Father, June 14 and 21, 1863, Russell Papers, NYPL; J. W. Grace to Gen [R. A.] Peirce, June 14, 1863, Camp Meigs Papers, NBFPL; Appleton Scrapbook, June 18 and 22, 1863, pp. 26–27.

106. James, "Assault upon Fort Wagner," p. 15. Appleton Scrapbook, June 18, 1863, p. 27; Gooding quoted from *New Bedford Mercury*, June 30 (2:3), 1863; J. W. Grace to [R. A.] Peirce, June 14, 1863, Camp Meigs Papers, NBFPL; RGS to Effie [Josephine Shaw], June 15, 1863, collected herein.

107. RGS to Annie [Kneeland Haggerty Shaw], June 9–13, 1863, RGS to SBS, June 13, 1863, collected herein.

108. RGS to Annie [Kneeland Haggerty Shaw], June 26, 1863, RGS to SBS, June 28, 1863, RGS to Charley [Morse], July 3, 1863, RGS to Mary Forbes, June 7, 1862, collected herein.

109. Ray Allen Billington, ed., *The Journal of Charlotte L. Forten* (New York: Dryden Press, 1953), pp. 10–16, 25, 191–93; Dorothy Sterling, ed., *We Are Your Sisters: Black Women in the Nineteenth Century* (New York: W. W. Norton, 1984), pp. 279–82.

110. RGS to George C. Strong, July 6, 1863, quoted in Smith, *Beacon Hill's*, p. 441.

111. RGS to Governor [John A.] Andrew, July 2, 1863, in Emilio, *A Brave Black Regiment*, pp. 47–48; Appleton quoted in *Commonwealth*, July 24 (3:2), 1863.

112. Emilio, *A Brave Black Regiment*, pp. 51–52; the best source for details on Gillmore's operation against Charleston is *OR*, I:28.

113. Emilio, *A Brave Black Regiment*, pp. 53–63; Cabot [Russel] to Father, July 14, 1863, Russell Papers, NYPL; *NYDT*, July 27 (1:1), 1863; *New Bedford Mercury*, Aug. 8 (2:3), 1863.

114. RGS to Annie [Kneeland Haggerty Shaw], July 15, 1863, collected herein. In the excitement of the fight, Shaw probably misdated this letter—should be July 16; Cabot [Russel] to Father, July 18, 1863, Russell Papers, NYPL; Appleton letterbook, WVU; soldier in Tenth Connecticut quoted in Glatthaar, *Forged in Battle*, p. 136; Bowen, *Massachusetts in the War*, p. 674.

115. RGS to Annie [Kneeland Haggerty Shaw], July 17, 1863; Appleton letterbook, WVU; Morning Reports, July 16 and 17, 1863, Regimental Order Book, 54th Massa-

chusetts, Bound Volumes, *Records of the Adjutant General's Office*, Record Group 94, NA; Emilio, *A Brave Black Regiment*, pp. 63–65.

116. Emilio, *A Brave Black Regiment*, pp. 65–68.

117. Appleton Papers, WVU; *NYDT*, July 27 (1:2–4), 1863; Seymour quoted in the Testimony of Nathaniel Paige, in Berlin, *Black Military Experience*, p. 534; *OR*, I:28, pt. 1, p. 362; Edward L. Pierce described the regiment as "worn and weary," *National Anti-Slavery Standard*, Aug. 8 (1:5–6), 1863; James, "Assault upon Fort Wagner," p. 20.

118. *Memorial: RGS*, p. 151, Hallowell quoted on pp. 165–66; Burchard, *One Gallant Rush*, pp. 34–35; Emilio, *A Brave Black Regiment*, p. 67.

119. Pierce recalled his last meeting with Shaw: "I parted with Colonel Shaw as he rode to join his regiment. As he was leaving, he turned back and gave me his letters and other papers, telling me to keep them and forward them to his father if anything occurred," Higginson, "Soldier's Book"; Emilio, *A Brave Black Regiment*, pp. 73–78; Luis F. Emilio, "The Assault on Fort Wagner" (Boston: Rand Avery, 1887), pp. 8–9; J. W. M. Appleton, "That Night at Fort Wagner," *Putnam's Magazine* 19 (July 1869): 13; Appleton letterbook, WVU; Gooding letter in *New Bedford Mercury*, Aug. 29 (2:2), 1863.

120. *NYDT*, July 31 (3:4–5), 1863; *New Bedford Mercury*, Aug. 29 (2:2), 1863; a black soldier's remembrance in Josephine Lowell to Annie [Kneeland Haggerty] Shaw, July 9, 1882, Stewart, *Philanthropic Works*, pp. 63–64; Grace quoted from *New Bedford Standard*, July 29 (2:2), 1863; *Charleston Daily Courier*, July 20 (1:3–5), 1863; Robert C. Gilchrist, *The Confederate Defence of Morris Island, Charleston Harbor* (Charleston: News & Courier, 1884), p. 18; James, "Assault Upon Fort Wagner," pp. 21–22.

121. *National Anti-Slavery Standard*, Aug. 8 (1:5–6), 1863; *OR*, I:28, pt. 1, pp. 210, 279; Testimony of Nathaniel Page, in Berlin, *Black Military Experience*, p. 535; Johnson Hagood, *Memoirs of the War of Secession* (Columbia, S.C.: The State Company, 1910), vol. 1, pp. 142–43; newspaper clipping no. 594 in Hallowell Papers, MHS; letter of John Luck in Higginson, "Soldier's Book," no page numbers.

122. *Atlantic Monthly* quoted from Lader, *Bold Brahmins*, p. 290; Anna Mary Wells, *Dear Preceptor: The Life and Times of Thomas Wentworth Higginson* (Boston: Houghton Mifflin, 1963), p. 180; *Boston Commonwealth*, July 31 (3:1), 1863; *Richmond County Gazette*, Aug. 19 (2:5), 1863; W. E. B. Du Bois, *Black Reconstruction in America: An Essay toward a History of the Part Which Black Folk Played in the Attempt to Reconstruct Democracy in America, 1860–1890* (New York: Atheneum, 1935), p. 110.

123. *National Anti-Slavery Standard*, Aug. 1 (3:5), 1863; Emilio, *A Brave Black Regiment*, pp. 105–27, 386; A. S. Fisher to My Dear Aflicted Captin [George Pope], July 31, 1863, Albanus S. Fisher Papers, Gettysburg College; Surgeon Stone to Governor Andrew, July 24, 1863, in *Annual Report of the Adjutant General of Massachusetts for 1863*, pp. 59–61; Billington, ed., *Journal of Charlotte L.*, pp. 193–96.

124. Charles Lowell to Effie [Josephine] Shaw, July 28, 1863, and Charles Lowell to Harry Russell, July 26, 1863, in Emerson, *Life and Letters of Charles Russell Lowell*, pp. 285, 288; Edward L. Pierce to SBS and FGS, July 22, 1863, in *Memorial: RGS*, p. 54; Meltzer and Holland, *Lydia Maria Child*, p. 433.

125. FGS to Edward L. Pierce, July 31, 1863, FGS to Dr. Stone, Aug. 3, 1863, Francis George Shaw Letters, HL.

126. Charles Sumner to E. L. Pierce, July 29, 1863, in Edward L. Pierce, *Memoirs and Letters of Charles Sumner* (Boston: Roberts Brothers, 1877–1893), vol. 4, p. 142.

127. Allen Flint, "Black Response to Colonel Shaw," *Phylon* 45 (Fall 1984): pp. 210–19; Steven Gould Axelrod, "Colonel Shaw in American Poetry: 'For the Union Dead' and its Precursors," *American Quarterly* 24 (Oct. 1972): 523–37, Emerson quoted from p. 525; J. R. Lowell manuscript, "Memoriae Positum: R.G.S., 1863," in Robert Gould Shaw Collection, HL; Robert Lowell, *Life Studies and For the Union Dead* (New York: Noonday Press, 1971), pp. 70–72.

128. Oration of William James, May 31, 1897, quoted from Hallowell Papers, MHS.

CHAPTER I

"*G*oodbye the drum is beating"

The election of Abraham Lincoln in 1860 was more than Southern white leaders could tolerate. After years of acrimonious compromise over whether the nation would embrace slave or free labor in the expanding western lands, many, North and South, understood that the results of the late presidential election would intensify the momentous question of what to do about slavery in a land whose creed emphasized freedom and human liberty. Many people sighed with relief that, whatever was to come, the issue would be settled once and for all.

South Carolina accelerated the movement toward war when its state legislature voted to secede from the Union on December 20, 1860. By February 1, 1861, Mississippi, Florida, Alabama, Georgia, Louisiana, and Texas had also voted themselves out of the Union. On February 4, a convention of the seceded states opened in Montgomery, Alabama, to form what would become the Confederate States of America. Jefferson Davis became interim president of the new nation on February 18, fourteen days before Lincoln took his own oath of office. The two presidents' inaugural addresses demonstrated the commitment each held toward secession and union. Davis reminded Northerners of "the American idea that governments rest on the consent of the governed"; Lincoln responded to Southerners that the Union was "perpetual" and warned, "in your hands, my dissatisfied fellow countrymen, and not in mine, is the momentous issue of civil war."

As tensions increased, American men and boys raced to join militia units. In New York City, Robert Gould Shaw enlisted in the unit of high society, the Seventh New York National Guard. While he drilled in the armory and worked in the counting house of his uncle's mercantile office, Shaw wrote to his family, who were vacationing in the Caribbean, of the "great state of excitement about Fort Sumter. First it was to be evacuated, then re-inforced." On April 5, Shaw wrote to his sister Susanna that he had been a disunionist for about two years, but now wanted "to see the Southern States either brought back by force, or else recognized as independent." He joined other Americans in hoping that Lincoln would act with firmness and finally confront the issue that had divided the country since its inception. One week later, Fort Sumter fell. Lincoln called for 75,000 men to put down the insurrection, and Virginia, Arkansas, North Carolina, and Tennessee quickly joined the Confederacy. The war had started.

Private Shaw's Seventh Regiment became the first unit to reach the capital after Lincoln's call for troops. It was a time for bragging, adventure, and adjustment to military life.

New York   [RGS]
April 5, 1861
My Dear Susie,

I didn't write you[1] last week because George and (I believe) Anna did.[2] You probably had letters from Nassau by the same mails which brought them to us.[3] They must have written to you direct, as they sent nothing to us for you.

I have just come from Boston, where I went to escort Aunt Cora, who came here to see Mimi off; so I haven't seen any of the Staten-Islanders for some days.[4] I had a note from George to-day, dated 3d inst., in which he says that Anna is well, and that there has been "no re-inforcement as yet."[5]

The day before yesterday, I went to call on Annie Agassiz at Cambridge, and had a most pleasant visit.[6] I sat with her and Ida (who looks as nice as ever) for some time, and then we went over to the Museum to see Alex.[7] It is a splendid collection they have there, and Alex. seems to be in the right place. He has the principal care of it, you know. Harry is staying at Uncle Howland's, where he is comfortable, though he seems a little lonely, as the family in Boston is so small now.[8]

We have very exciting news to-day from the South. It is now almost certain that Mr. Lincoln is going to re-inforce the United States forts, and in that case the Southerners will surely resist. All the vessels in the Navy are being got ready for sea, and several sail from here to-day. Lincoln has kept his own counsel so well hitherto that the newspapers have not been able to get at anything, and have consequently been filled with the most contradictory rumors. But, now that all the important appointments have been made, and the State elections, &c. are over, it is the universal belief that *something* decisive is to be done.

Every other man has a different opinion as to what will be the consequences. Some think it will drive all the Border States into the Southern Confederacy, and that we shall all be ruined; and others say it will encourage the Union part in the South to make itself heard. For my part, I want to see the Southern States either brought back by force, or else recognized as independent; and, as Lincoln cannot do as he likes, but must abide by the Constitution, I don't see what he can do but collect the revenue and re-take, by force of arms, the United States property which they have stolen.[9] As for making concessions, it is only patching the affair up for a year or two, when it would break out worse than ever. At any rate, we should have this same row over again at every Presidential election; and if we gave them an inch, they would be sure to want thousands of ells, as is proved by their history and ours for the last 50 years. Indeed, they would not be content with anything less than a total change of public opinion throughout the North on the subject of slavery, and that, of course, they can't have. In the mean time, they tar and feather, hang, drown, and burn our citizens who are travelling there, attending to their own business and troubling no one. I have been a Disunionist for two years; but, as there seems to be no way of making a peaceable separation without giving up everything, I am glad, for the credit of the country, that they will probably act now with some firmness. A great many people say they are ashamed of their country, but I feel proud that we have at last taken such a long step forward as to turn out the pro-slavery government which has been disgracing us so long;—and they begin to grumble now about the present Administration being no stronger than the last, when it has had barely one month to make thousands of appointments, put money into its empty treasury, and extricate almost every department from the infernal state of confusion in which it was left by the rascals that have been in power for the last four years. That sort of work can't be done by steam; nor could Lincoln and his Cabinet do everything at once, even if they had machines to make Ambassadors, Postmasters, Collectors of ports, &c., besides besieging forts, building ships, recruiting the army, and picking out officers who won't turn traitors, as many have done.

I had a long talk with Mr. Robbins the other day, and the result was, that I think I shall stay.[10] He seemed to think I was getting along very well indeed; and, as my only reason for dissatisfaction was the idea that I should never be much of a business-man, it made me feel much better. As I have come to the end of the paper, and have a great deal to do this morning, I will come to a close myself, and, hoping to hear from you soon, and to see you soon after, am, with much love,

Your affectionate brother,
Robert G. Shaw

P.S.—The next time I write, I will try to give you a little more variety in the way of news.

1. Shaw's sister Susanna (1839–1926).

2. Shaw's older sister Anna (1836–1923) married writer, publisher, and lecturer George William Curtis (1824–92) in 1856. They lived next to the Shaws on Staten Island.

3. Shaw's parents and his two youngest sisters, Josephine (1843–1905) and Ellen (1846–1936), were vacationing in Havana and Nassau. R. W. Weston to D. Weston, Feb. 19, 1861, Weston Sister Papers, BPL; RGS to FGS, Mar. 28, 1861, Robert Gould Shaw Collection, HL.

4. Aunt Cora is unidentified. Mimi is Shaw's first cousin Elizabeth Russell Lyman, the older sister of Henry Sturgis Russell [see note 8]. Marion W. Smith, *Beacon Hill's Colonel Robert Gould Shaw* (New York: Carlton Press, 1986), p. 491.

5. George Curtis's "re-inforcement" is a reference to Anna's pregnancy.

6. Annie Russell Agassiz (1840–73), sister of Harry and Mimi Russell.

7. Ida Agassiz. Her brother Alexander Emanuel Agassiz (1835–1910) married Annie Russell in 1860 and lived with Alex's father, Swiss naturalist and Harvard professor Louis Agassiz. Mary C.

Crawford, *Famous Families of Massachusetts* (Boston: Little, Brown, 1930), vol. 1, pp. 224–29.

8. Henry Sturgis Russell (1838–1905) was one of Shaw's first cousins on his father's side. He entered Harvard with Shaw in 1856. Russell worked in a mercantile firm in Boston until Apr. 20, 1861, when he served in the Fourth Battalion, Massachusetts Volunteer Militia, at Fort Independence in Boston Harbor. Elizabeth C. Putnam, comp., *Memoirs of the War of '61: Colonel Charles Russell Lowell, Friends and Cousins* (Boston: G. H. Ellis, 1920), pp. 38–41; Smith, *Beacon Hill's*, p. 491; *Harvard College: Report of the Class of 1860, 1860–1866* (Cambridge, Mass.: John Wilson & Sons, 1866), pp. 44–45.

9. The only forts in Confederate territory that were still under Union control were two in the Florida Keys, Fort Pickens in Pensacola Bay, and Fort Sumter in Charleston Harbor.

10. In early 1859, Chandler Robbins became a partner of Shaw's maternal uncle Henry Parkman Sturgis (1806–69) in the mercantile firm of H. P. Sturgis and Company, 73 South Street, New

York City. This was the firm Shaw joined after leaving Harvard in March 1859. *Trow's New York City Directory for the Year Ending May 1, 1861* (New York: John F. Trow, 1860), p. 724; *Letters: RGS* (Cam-bridge, Mass.: Harvard University Press, 1876), p. 150; Roger Faxton Sturgis, *Edward Sturgis of Yarmouth, Mass., 1613–1695, and His Descendants* (Boston: Stanhope, 1914), pp. 51–52.

North Shore S.I. [Staten Island]   [HL]
Thursday, April 18, 1861
Dearest Mother,

You will probably know when you get this, that the only piece of bad news to greet you when you arrive is that of my departure with the 7th Regt. for Washington.[1]

It is very hard to go off without bidding you goodbye, and the only thing that upsets me, in the least, is the thought of how you will feel when you find me so unexpectedly gone. But I know, dearest Mother, that you wouldn't have me stay, when it is so clearly my duty to go. If I could get permission to wait, it would be impossible to say when I could get off, as no one knows what may happen in Maryland or Virginia in the course of a day or two.[2] And then if I go at all I feel as if I ought to go with my Company. It would be the greatest comfort to me to know that you think I have been right in not waiting for your return, under the circumstances. I won't say there is no selfishness in this, for I feel that it would be very hard to start off alone, after saying goodbye to you & the girls; but if this were the only reason I should certainly wait.

We all feel that if we can get into Washington, before Virginia begins to make trouble, we shall not have much fighting. We expect to get there on Saturday. The Massachusetts men passed through N.York this morning.[3] We start tomorrow, (Friday) at 3 P.M. Won't it be grand to meet the men from all the States, East and West, down there, ready to fight for the country, as the old fellows did in the Revolution?

I came down this morning to see Anna before I go. She and the new baby look finely as well as old Frankie.[4]

Please give ever so much love to Effie & Nellie.[5] I feel perfectly certain I shall come back safe, and see you all before many weeks. Our Col. tells us we are only going to Washington for the present & shall be sent back to New York as soon as troops from the more distant States can arrive.[6] I feel as if I were not going on anything but an ordinary journey. I can't help crying a little though when I think of Father & you & the girls. Don't be too anxious about me, dearest Mother. I shall write to you almost every day if possible. Please be careful of your health. May God bless you all. When we are all at home together again, may peace & happiness be restored to the Country. The war has already done us good, in making the North so united.

Goodbye, Dear Mother.

Ever your loving son,
Robert G. Shaw

1. Shaw had joined the Seventh Regiment, New York National Guard shortly after the election of Lincoln. The Seventh organized on Apr. 17, 1861, with 991 men, drilled in the armory, and marched down Broadway two days later to ovations from the largest crowd ever assembled until that time. The *New York Times* reported that as for New York, the Seventh had "all its best blood in it." Shaw was one of eighty privates in Company F who carried with him one day's rations, "one blanket, . . . suitable underclothing, an extra pair of boots, . . . knife, fork, spoon, tin cup, and plate, body belt, cap pouch." Frederick H. Dyer, *Compendium of the War of the Rebellion* (Des Moines, 1908; reprint ed., New York: T. Yoseloff, 1959), vol. 1, p. 187; Emmons Clark, *History of the Seventh Regiment of New York, 1806–1889* (New York: Published by the author, 1890), vol. 1, pp. 473–74; *NYT*, Apr. 18 (1:1–5), 19 (4:3), 20 (1:4–5),

1861; *NYDT*, Apr. 17 (8:2), 19 (8:4), 20 (5:4, 5:6, 8:1–2), 1861.

2. Many feared for the safety of the nation's capital because of its geographical enclosure by the slaveholding states of Maryland and Virginia.

3. The Sixth Massachusetts Infantry was the first of many units to converge upon Washington after the bombardment of Fort Sumter.

4. Francis ("Frankie") George Curtis (1857–1936) was Anna's first child. Elizabeth Burrill Curtis (1861–1914) was born on Apr. 15, 1861. Curtis folder, SIHS; Charles W. Leng and William T. Davis, *Staten Island and Its People: A History, 1609–1929* (New York: Lewis, 1930), vol. 2, p. 254; Roger Faxton Sturgis, *Edward Sturgis*, p. 57.

5. Effie and Nellie are Shaw's sisters Josephine and Ellen.

6. Col. Marshall Lefferts. The Seventh mustered out of service in New York on June 3, 1861. Dyer, *Compendium*, p. 187.

New York [RGS]
April 18, 1861
Dear Susie,

You mustn't be made anxious or uneasy by what I am going to tell you. The President has called for 75,000 men, and the Seventh Regiment is ordered to Washington for its protection, with a great many men from Massachusetts and other States.[1] You will be astonished at my going off before Mother gets home; and it makes me cry whenever I think of it, though no one but Biddy has seen me.[2] You mustn't think, dear Sue, that any of us are going to be killed; for they are collecting such a force there that an attack would be insane,—that is, unless the Southerners can get their army up in an almost impossibly short space of time.

We go off to-morrow, and Father and Mother will be back three days after. If I *could* wait, I would; but if I don't go now, it is hardly probable I could go at all, and I know Mother wouldn't have me stay at home at such a time. I can only write a few words now, but you shall hear from Washington.

Please send this photograph to Mrs. Haggerty, and tell her why I can't write her a note.[3] I want to send her one like yours, but they are not ready yet.

Give my love to Uncle Russell and Aunt Julia.[4] We shall probably be in New York again by the time you get back.

With much love, dearest Sue,

Your loving brother,
R. G. Shaw

1. On Monday Apr. 15, 1861, in response to Lincoln's call for 75,000 men, Governor Morgan of New York called for 25,000 volunteers. The Seventh received its marching orders on Apr. 18. *NYDT*, Apr. 15 (4:2), 19 (8:4), 20 (5:4), 1861.

2. Biddy is probably Shaw's sister Anna Curtis.

3. Shaw's future mother-in-law Elizabeth Kneeland Haggerty of Lenox, Massachusetts, and New York City. Robert T. Teamoh, *Sketch of the Life and Death of Colonel Robert Gould Shaw* (Boston: Boston Globe, 1904), p. 19.

4. Russell Sturgis (1805–87) married on June 4, 1846 for the third time to Julia O. Boit (?–1888). In 1833, Sturgis entered the family business and engaged in the mercantile and China trading company of Russell & Sturgis. Later, he was a member of Russell and Company as well as a senior partner in the London banking firm, Baring Brothers. Sturgis, *Edward Sturgis*, pp. 50–51.

Philadelphia 9 1/2 A.M.   [HL]
Saturday Apr 20/61
Dear Mother,

I have written you one short note this morning, but am afraid it won't go, so I send another. We have been here since two o'cl. this morning & as soon as we hear that there is no trouble in Baltimore we shall go on. If there is a chance of our passage through Maryland being resisted we shall probably go by water.[1] Everyone has treated us with the greatest hospitality & enthusiasm so far.

Goodbye the drum is beating. I will write from Washington. Don't know what road we take yet. Your loving son,

R. G. Shaw

1. On Apr. 19, 1861, a prosecession mob in Baltimore tried to prevent the passage of the Sixth Massachusetts Infantry on to Washington. Northern editors played up the fact that the attack had taken place on the anniversary of the battles of Lexington and Concord. In this first bloodshed of the war, Union losses were four killed and thirty-nine wounded. The mob lost twelve killed and dozens wounded. *NYDT*, Apr. 20 (5:1), 1861; Patricia L. Faust, ed., *Historical Times Illustrated Encyclopedia of the Civil War* (New York: Oxford University Press, 1970), p. 37.

Annapolis   [RGS]
Tuesday, April 23, 1861
Dear Father and Mother,

I should have dated my note yesterday "Off Annapolis." Last night at 6 o'clock we landed here, and have been quartered in the Naval School, where we are very comfortable indeed.[1] The officers keep their plans to themselves; so we don't know how long we shall be here. They say the road to Washington is full of Secessionists, and the students have been in readiness for an attack for two or three days. About 800 Massachusetts men are here too; so, with them and the students,—making nearly 2,000 men,—we can drive off any who venture to make an attack on us here. We expect two or three more New York Regiments here by water shortly. It is very pleasant staying here, as it is a beautiful place; but the uncertainty of our future movements is worrying. I hope, unless the Colonel ascertains that the enemy is at Washington, as some think, that we shall start very soon. If they have possession of the city, of course such a small force as ours could do no good outside of it. We have had no papers, so we know nothing of what is going on; but I, for one, do not believe the South Carolina army has got to the Capital quite yet.

We came from Philadelphia in the steamer Boston, and, though some complained very much of the accommodations, they were no worse than I have had many a time before. I have had enough sleep and enough food, and am in excellent health in every way. I only hope you are all as well as I am. There are a few sick ones. Sam Curtis is well.[2] John Irving was engaged the evening before we started; another man was married a week before; and one told me his first baby was two days old when he left: so some felt blue at coming away.[3]

We didn't leave Philadelphia, until 2 P.M. on Saturday, and have had beautiful weather both on board the boat and since. If it had been rough when we were at sea, we should have had a fearful time, as we were piled together like pigs on the two upper decks and in the lower cabins, filling the boat perfectly full. Our food was not very satisfactory, as the rations we had with us were pretty old, and the meat furnished on board was very horsey. We were short of water at last. When we arrived, we found the Massachusetts men in a large steamer run aground by the pilot, whom they immediately put in irons and wanted to kill. He is a Secessionist. They had been trying to get off for three days. Our boat got them off at last. General Butler, their commander, is an energetic, cursing and swearing old fellow.[4] As soon as they got ashore, he sent a company into the town, took possession of the railroad depot, and set his men to work laying down the rails which have been torn up by the Secessionists. He says "he'll be damned if he's going to be stopped by a lot of Maryland men." There is an old fellow among them with ten sons, all shoemakers, who say they have had no work for so long they are going to lick those chaps into buying their shoes. More than half their men were without water for two days, and had only two crackers per diem for some time, on board their boat. They are in all sorts of uniforms, and drill in the funniest way. All fishermen from Marblehead and shoemakers from Lynn, they seem itching for a fight, and look upon the men here with about as much respect as we would accord to a toad.

This is a lovely place, and the weather is magnificent. We had a parade this morning, and the Middies had one in the afternoon. All the evening our band has been playing under the trees. We hear the national airs, and look at the stars and stripes, with new emotions in an enemy's country. There are about 120 Midshipmen at the School, 20 or 30 Southerners having resigned. The youngest class is kept aboard the "Constitution" school-ship, and the others live here.[5] They are all dressed in dark navy-cloth, well-fitting jackets and trousers, with pistol and sword in their belt. The dress sets off their figures very well, and they give the impression of a remarkably fine-looking body of young men. The healthy life they lead develops them finely; and they *all* look like gentlemen, which is partly the favorable effect of the dress, I suppose, but I have seen some very handsome and fine faces.

We had a large guard all night, for fear of being surprised, but I don't believe any one will attempt that.

There are rumors that we start for Washington to-morrow, and I think they have some foundation. The man who takes this letter is one of our company, who is afraid he won't be able to stand the march. I shall ask him to write on the outside of this whether anything new has turned up before he leaves (in the boat which brought us); for I am afraid, if I don't close it to-night, I shan't have a chance to see him to-morrow morning. If we go, it will be as early as 3 o'clock, A.M.

Good-bye dearest Father and Mother. Best love to all. Please send Harry $5, which I forgot to enclose to him before I left.[6] I wrote about a dozen letters. Send love to Susie.[7] Perhaps you have not got back from Nassau, after all; wouldn't that be funny? Isn't the baby a fine one? And aren't we fortunate to have a girl?[8]

I took my clothes off to-day for the first time, and had a splendid bath. Good-bye again. I hope you are all well.

Ever your loving son,
Robert G. Shaw

P.S. The mails are stopped here. Have you received my note from Philadelphia and from on board steamer "Boston"? The men are in good spirits; the stay here has freshened us all. Hope to see "Old Abe" soon. We write under difficulties, there are so many of us,—991 men of our regiment.

1. Annapolis is home to the United States Naval Academy. The officers and midshipmen of the Academy relocated on May 9, 1861, to a more secure location at Newport, Rhode Island. Faust, *Encyclopedia*, p. 521.

2. Samuel Bridgham Curtis (1834–87) was half-brother of Shaw's brother-in-law George William Curtis. He enlisted as a member of the Seventh New York National Guard and marched to war with Shaw. Curtis folder, SIHS.

3. John Irving is unidentified.

4. Brig. Gen. Benjamin Franklin Butler (1818–93) commanded the Eighth Massachusetts Militia until his appointment as major general of U.S. Volunteers on May 16, 1861. Butler was a political general who later served in the U.S. Congress (1866–75) and as governor of Massachusetts (1883–84). The Eighth Massachusetts had arrived in New York the day the Seventh New York departed, and the two regiments "raced" to Washington. Butler lost when the pilot of the steamer *Maryland* ran aground near Annapolis. Mark M. Boatner, III, *The Civil War Dictionary* (New York: David McKay, 1959), p. 109; *NYDT*, Apr. 20 (6:6), 1861.

5. The USS *Constitution*, dubbed "Old Ironsides" in the War of 1812, is still the most famous ship in U.S. history.

6. Henry Sturgis Russell.

7. Susanna Shaw.

8. Elizabeth Burrill Curtis.

April 26, 1861, House of Representatives

Dearest Mother,

I wrote to Father yesterday, just after our arrival, to let you know that we got here safely. I am very anxious to get a letter from some of you, to hear how you all are. I got a real nice, kind note from Mr. Tweedy to-day, dated New York, April 22; but he hadn't seen any one from the Island.[1] I know some one must have written, but no mails have come from New York for some time. Perhaps, though, you have waited to get my address. I hope all that I have written has reached you.

Just after closing my last, at Annapolis, our Company got orders to fill their water-canteens, and be ready to receive three days' rations, as we were to start at 4 o'clock next morning. We turned in to get a little sleep, but had hardly got our blankets about us when all the drums in the Regiment began to beat, and our officers came rushing in and bundled us all out on to the parade-ground. All the Middies and every man of our Regiment turned out ready for a fight, and the four howitzers were hauled up and down the brick walks like mad. It didn't take long to get us all ready, as every one had his belt and accoutrements on. The sentinels had seen sky-rockets, and heard guns in the bay and all along shore, and we thought we were going to be attacked by a large force, but it turned out to be the eleven steamers with New York and Rhode Island troops; so, after standing for some time under arms, we returned to our quarters in the recitation rooms all over the buildings. It was a most exciting time, being called up so suddenly, and standing still expecting every moment to see troops landing along the shore. By this time it was nearly midnight, and the rations were ready; so we had to fall into line to receive and pack them in our provision-boxes. This took as much as an hour for our Company, and some didn't lie down until 2 o'clock. I slept soundly enough, I assure you, until we were again aroused at 4, and, having everything in readiness, were soon out on the Green. We then found that Company 2 and Company 6 (ours) were to start for the Junction (Station between Baltimore and Washington) as advanced guard, and the others were to follow at about 9 A.M. We considered this a great honor, and stepped off through the town for the Railroad depot in good spirits, waking up all the people as we went. At the depot we found the Massachusetts Company which had taken possession.[2] There was one old engine out of order, and half a dozen cars. One man had stepped up the night before, and said he could put it in order, because he had helped build it. It came from New England, of course. Another one jumped on when it was mended, got up the steam, and in a little while we were ready to start; so we packed our knapsacks into one car and started off in the other. The Massachusetts boys had been laying the track, where it was torn up for about a mile ahead, during the night,—having in the mean time had nothing to eat, to which they appeared to have got accustomed, for they were almost famished on board their steamer, and some of them actually drank salt water.

When we had gone about a mile by rail we had to get out, as the track was torn up in many places. We left our knapsacks on the train, which went back for the luggage of the rest of our men, while we trudged forward under a fearfully hot sun, with muskets loaded and cartridge-boxes full, ready for a brush at any moment. We had scouts and skirmishers all around and about us, for we had been positively assured that we should be attacked by a large body of cavalry. Not a shot was fired, however; and, though we stopped several couples of mounted men, they were released again. We saw principally only women and negroes, which made the reports of the body of men being assembled somewhere on the road seem true. We marched slowly along, pushing our howitzers on two baggage-cars, and stopping again and again to lay rails and make repairs on the roads. At length, about 2 o'clock, we came to a halt, and waited for the main body to come up, working meantime on a bridge which had been completely broken down, helped all the while by the Massachusetts boys, with whom we divided our rations, gaining thereby their enthusiastic admiration. Neither they nor we could have got through without each other's assistance; for tho' they did a great deal of the labor, our officers directed the building of the bridge, &c., and we fed them out of our knapsacks. They arrived at Washington a day after us, and we all (being off duty) rushed out and cheered them; and they never let us go by now without clapping and hurrahing. They are rough fellows, but of the best kind. The feeling of affection that has sprung up between us is really beautiful! One of them was accidentally shot, and will lose his leg; so we got up a subscription which will set him up for some time.[3]

When the rest of our men had got up to where we stopped, and we had all rested and taken a nip at our crackers and beef, (six crackers and three pieces dried beef for three days!) we started off again, our two Companies still in advance as scouts; but we had to wait until after 6 o'clock, P.M., before the bridge was mended. In the meanwhile we had some very nice singing, patriotic songs being preferred, and at last got our howitzers over the bridge, and trudged along under a clear sky and splendid moon. But 4 hours' sleep the night before, and 4 or 6 hours a night since we left New York, had not been sufficient to keep up our strength. However, we went on and on as before, stopping every half-hour and starting again, pushing and pulling on our old baggage-cars, sometimes up some very steep grades. Gradually, as time wore on, the men began to lie down every time we stopped, in larger and larger numbers, until at last every one who was not at work was catching a sort of a nap by the roadside. We had scouts out, as I said before, so that we should have been warned in time of any enemy; but I don't believe it would have been possible to keep the men on their feet unless there had been an enemy really in sight. We actually fell asleep standing up, and scores of the men would drop their pieces and just catch *themselves* as they were toppling over. We went through all sorts of defiles, where the Marylanders might have pounced upon us with great advantage; but though we had good evidence of their being about, from fresh tracks and newly torn-up rails, they took good care to keep well out of our way. The Annapolis men were perfectly certain we should be cut to pieces. I suppose they were frightened by our numbers, and by the fact of there being 7,000 troops on board the steamers at Annapolis. We went into a good many farm-houses along the road, and were treated very well. We paid for everything we got, which pleased the people amazingly; for they had expected, so they told me, to be robbed and bullied. We hear now, that other regiments, which have come through since, have behaved in a very different manner, shooting pigs and chickens, and taking forcible possession of what they wanted. I don't know how much of the report is true,—not much, I think; but the people couldn't expect much else after trying to run us off the track on the very edge of a high precipice.

At daybreak, 4 1/2, we came to a halt about two miles from the Junction, perfectly overcome with sleep, shivering with cold, and a good many of us grumbling in quite a mutinous way. We built a dozen large fires,—for the night air had gone through and through us, we had moved so slowly,—and stood about them, cogitating on the gloomy prospect before us. Provisions all gone,—a good chance of having to march to Washington, twenty miles farther, as we heard no train had come up to the Junction for us,—and the expectation of being attacked in a little while, before we could get any rest. Our officers told us we should have to fight then, if ever. But some of us ventured off, being well armed, and got breakfast at a farm-house near. The lady of the house was a real pretty, nice woman, and, though she seemed frightened at first, was soon reassured, and furnished us hoe-cake, pork, bread and butter, potatoes, coffee, tea, and milk in abundance. This worked a wonderful change in us, and we took an entirely new view of life. I really seemed to myself to be another man, and was ready to start for Washington at a minute's notice. Getting back to the camp, we found a party had been up to the Junction, found a train ready for us, and the coast clear. The men were lying about the road and field in the most ridiculous positions, having fallen asleep where they dropped, and the air was filled with snorings in every key and of every variety. In a little while we fell into line, marched two miles farther, got on to the train, and whirled on to Washington. The nodding and snoring went briskly on for an hour in the cars, and then we all turned out for a parade just as we were, covered with dust, and with our blankets slung over our shoulders. Our knapsacks came on after us in another train. We parted with the "National Rifles," a Washington Company that had gone up to the Junction to meet us, and then marched straight up to the White House and through the grounds, where "Old Abe" and family stood at the doors and saw us go by. We then were distributed at the different hotels in companies, and had our first regular meal since we left New York. That evening we marched up to the Capitol, and were quartered in the House of Representatives, where we each have a desk, and easy-chair to sleep in, but generally prefer the floor and our blankets, as the last eight days' experience has accustomed us to hard beds. The Capitol is a magnificent building, and the men all take the greatest pains not to harm anything.[4] Jeff Davis shan't get it without trouble.[5] Troops from New England are quartered all over it, but we have the best place. My desk is on the Republican side of the House, and has Mr. Thos. D. Eliot's name on it, who, I believe, is a Massachusetts man.[6] Charles Sedgwick's is next to me.[7] We have a great deal of fun here, but I have no doubt we are the best-behaved Congress that has been in session for a good while, though we *were* waked up this morning by cockcrows, cats, dogs, and cows all howling together.[8] They give us our liberty about the building and grounds, but don't let us out very often, and then only a few at a time. The lights are put out at 10 P.M., and the drums beat about 5 A.M. Those who are not waked up by the latter are soon aroused by the racket and rumpus.

April 27.—Yesterday afternoon at 3 o'clock we had a grand parade, and were all sworn into the service of the United States government. It was a very impressive scene, as we all held up our hands and repeated the oath together after the magistrate.[9] We are Uncle Sam's men now for the next thirty days. "Old Abe" stood out in front of us, looking as pleasant and kind as possible, and, when we presented arms, took off his hat in the most awkward way, putting it on again with his hand on the back part of the rim, country fashion. A boy came by with a pail of water for us, and the President took a great swig from it as it passed. I couldn't help thinking of the immense responsibility he has on his shoulders, as he stood there laughing and talking. I have seen many uglier men.[10] We drill every morning in companies, and parade every afternoon. While we are stationed here, we take our meals at the hotels, but shall soon go into camp, and have to take care of our own cooking. We consider ourselves pretty well off for common soldiers in the United States service, but we have to pay a good deal extra for our good fare. We have collected about $800 for the Massachusetts men, and bought them a great pile of provisions; $200 or $300 will be given to the lame one, I believe.[11]

I am longing to hear from you, dearest Mother, and hope a letter will come soon. A good many men have heard from home. Address Co. 6, Seventh Regiment, care Quartermaster Winchester, Washington, D.C.[12] Give my best love to Father and all the girls. Sam Curtis sends his love, and wants me to say that there are no desks where he is quartered, and so wished some one would tell his mother that is why he can't write long letters. He has to scribble with his pencil on a knapsack.[13]

The Winthrops are both well, and send kind regards.[14] This has been written in a great hurry, and at odd times, as we have much less time than I thought we should. They keep us trotting pretty steadily. Please tell Susie I am well. Indeed, I am in splendid condition, though we have seen some unusually hard service. That march of twenty-four hours, with no former rest to help us, was really something extraordinary. At least, every one seems to think so. The men bore it finely. Mr. Robbins gave me a fine revolver when I left.[15] I hope George and Anna and the children are well. I am afraid I shan't have time to write to any of them. Give my best love to all. I shall see you again soon. You can imagine how I look forward to the time, though, if they want us for a longer time than the thirty days, I shall vote to stay.[16] It would be very hard for some, though, whose families are dependent upon them. Goodbye. Remember me to all friends. I have a great deal more to write, but have confined myself to giving an account of our doings, as I thought that would interest you most. Did you receive my note asking you to send Harry $5?[17] Some men from New York have joined us since we got here; but I am glad I didn't wait, as it was so uncertain.

> Ever, dearest Mother,
> Your loving Son

P.S. Love to Father, and did he find things generally in order that he left me to attend to?

1. Ephraim Tweedy of Staten Island. The Shaws and the Tweedys enjoyed a long-term friendship. *Letters: RGS* (1876), pp. 46, 50.

2. After the riot in Baltimore, the Sixth Massachusetts moved out to secure this strategic railroad junction.

3. Lieutenant Merrick of the Sixth

Massachusetts had his leg amputated after the accident. *NYT*, May 1 (1:5), 2 (1:4), 1861.

4. The Capitol dome was under construction in 1861.

5. Confederate president Jefferson Davis (1808–89). Having served in the U.S. House (1845–46), the Senate (1847–51, 1857–61), and as secretary of war (1853–57), Davis was very familiar with the Capitol. Colleen McGuiness and Maria J. Sayers, eds., *American Leaders, 1789–1987: A Biographical Summary* (Washington, D.C.: Congressional Quarterly, 1987), p. 123.

6. Thomas Dawes Eliot (1808–70), Boston lawyer, served in the U.S. House as a Whig (1854–55) and as a Republican (1859–69). He strongly advocated the extension of equal rights to black Americans. Ibid., p. 137.

7. Charles Baldwin Sedgwick (1815–83), New York Republican, U.S. Congress (1859–63). Ibid., p. 284.

8. Shaw is probably referring particularly to the decade of acrimonious Congresses that met since the Compromise of 1850 established a Fugitive Slave Law most heinous to Northern abolitionists.

9. The Seventh took the oath of allegiance in Capitol Square. Private Theodore Winthrop recalled the ceremony: "We raised our right hands, and clause by clause, repeated the solemn obligation in the name of God, to be faithful soldiers to our country. . . . We were thrilled and solemnized . . . [in] the fundamental belief that our system was

worthy of support." *Atlantic Monthly* 8 (July 1861): 108–9.

10. Republicans and Democrats could agree upon one thing, if nothing else, that Lincoln was the ugliest man in America.

11. The *Times* reported that the Seventh gave four hundred dollars to the Sixth Massachusetts to defray expenses after the Baltimore riot and gave four hundred dollars to the wounded Lieutenant Merrick. *NYT*, May 1 (1:5), 2 (1:4), 1861.

12. Locke W. Winchester. William Swinton, *History of the Seventh Regiment National Guard, State of New York During the War of the Rebellion* (New York: Dillingham, 1886), pp. 152, 156.

13. Samuel Bridgham Curtis.

14. Brothers Theodore Winthrop (1828–61) and William W. Winthrop (1831–?) lived with their sister, Mrs. Templeton Johnson, near the Shaws on Staten Island. Theodore wrote the novels *Cecil Dreeme* and *John Brent* and was a contributor to the *Atlantic Monthly*. William was a fellow private of Shaw's in Company F (6th Company). Leng and Davis, *Staten Island and Its People*, vol. 1, p. 278, vol. 2, p. 811; Swinton, *History of the Seventh*, pp. 152, 156.

15. Chandler Robbins.

16. The first troops to respond to Lincoln's call were known as "thirty-day men." The Seventh did not stay in active service and returned to New York in late May 1861.

17. Henry Sturgis Russell.

Washington, D.C.
April 29, 1861
Dear Mother,

Your and Effie's letters came yesterday, and I was glad enough to get them, I can tell you. To-day, Ed. Delafield came up from the steamer, and brought me Father's note, with the money, for which I was very much obliged, and glad it was in gold.[1] I find a great deal of difficulty in getting bank-notes changed. We are still quietly staying in the House of Representatives, and, yesterday being Sunday, had a good deal of time; so I wrote a lot of notes, which I sent by Jewett.[2] If you see Mr. Tweedy, won't you say I was very much obliged to him for his note?[3] It was the first one I received, and was very cheering. And please give my love to Mr. and Mrs. Gay, and say his note gave me the first news of your safe arrival at home.[4] I didn't see the bearer.

There has been no excitement here, excepting the arrival of troops,— among them, 160 men to our Regiment. As soon as all our camp equipage gets here, we shall be stationed either on Georgetown Heights or Capitol Hill,—none of the men know which.

We had a sermon yesterday from our Chaplain, Mr. Weston, of New York, and part was very affecting, as he spoke very feelingly of our friends and families at home.[5] There was a good deal of blowing of noses and wiping of eyes.

This Capitol is one of the finest buildings I ever saw. I don't believe Davis will get it without some little trouble. We had the greatest fun treating the Massachusetts men. We got them all in a circle, and then carried round meat, bread, cheese, and beer, and fed every one well. It was a jolly kind of a party. Harry will send you some photographs of me, two of which I wish you would put into the enclosed notes to M. Roulet and Mme. Unger, and forward to destination.[6] Another I should like to have sent in an envelope to Wilhelm Melhuus, Drammen, Norway.[7] The Winthrops and Sam are well.[8] Theodore W. got the key of the House of Representatives post-office last night, and we went in there and slept quietly. I am still in good order, and shall get the things you recommend if I can. I have not seen anything of Washington yet, as they only let a very few men out at a time. Give my love to all. I shall write to Effie soon.

Your loving son,
Robt G. Shaw

1. Probably Edward Delafield, son of Staten Island cement manufacturer Rufus K. Delafield. Edward was twenty- two years old in 1860. U.S. Department of Commerce, Bureau of the Census, Eighth Census (1860), Richmond

County, New York, Castleton, p. 126.

2. Orville D. Jewett (1838–?) worked as a clerk in a white-lead company in New York and lived near Shaw on Staten Island. Ibid., p. 166; *Trow's NYC Directory for 1863*, p. 441.

3. Ephraim Tweedy.

4. Sydney Howard Gay (1814–88) and Elizabeth Neall Gay. Sydney edited the *National Anti-Slavery Standard* (1843–57), then joined the *New York Daily Tribune* and became its managing editor in May 1862. Leng and Davis, *Staten Island*, vol. 1, pp. 254, 276; James Brewer Stewart, *Holy Warriors: The Abolitionists and American Slavery* (New York: Hill & Wang, 1976), p. 184.

5. The Reverend Sullivan H. Weston, Episcopalian. William J. Roehrenbeck, *The Regiment That Saved the Capital* (New York: A. S. Barnes, 1961), pp. 84–85; Swinton, *History of the Seventh*, p. 142.

6. Shaw attended the private school of Monsieur and Madame Roulet in Neuchâtel, Switzerland, from Sept. 1851 to Aug. 1853. From July 1854 until Apr. 1856, Shaw attended school in Hanover, Germany. He spent his last few weeks there in the home of Madame Unger. Shaw claimed that he was not in love with Madame Unger's daughter, but admitted: "The Lord only knows what might happen if I stayed here a year longer, until she budded; for she is a very nice girl . . . rather good looking, too, and lively." Shaw, *Letters: RGS* (1876), pp. 14–46, 106, quoted pp. 107–8.

7. In an 1855 letter, Shaw mentions, but does not name, a Norwegian he met in Hanover and visited on a trip that stopped in Drammen that year. This is probably Wilhelm Melhuus. *Letters: RGS* (1876), p. 89.

8. Theodore and William Winthrop. Samuel Bridgham Curtis.

Washington D.C.   [HL]
April 30/61
Dear Effie,

Your very welcome letter reached me safely as you have probably already heard. I was very glad you wrote and told me of Mother's being so well. What a nice place Nassau will be to run down to in winter when she is not well. I wish you would write me an account of what you did there and how you had such a nice time. You know I haven't heard anything about it yet. Didn't you find things looking nicely at Staten Island? I never liked the house & place so much as the day I went down to pack up my things. My feelings were rather too much for me when I thought of your all being back there in two days & finding my room empty. Before I forget it, as I have every time I have written, let me ask you to get Father to send me an India Rubber blanket which I left on account of its weight. I shall want it when we go into camp. If the

Expressman got my things from the Oriental as I ordered, it will be at home. If I could have a lighter one I should like it better.[1] Do you know whether Mimi & Theodore arrived safely out? & whether Harry has been ordered to any where yet?[2] I have really enjoyed this trip very much—as much as any fishing or shooting excursion. We have had hard work, but the exercise & fresh air make me feel finely and we have been quartered in some beautiful places. The grounds at Annapolis Naval Academy are something on the style of the Cambridge College yard & the officers & Professors live in nice old fashioned houses with gardens. We landed there a little before dusk and it was a most picturesque sight to see the men lying about on the grass with arms stacked & knapsacks piled in long rows and also when we halted one morning just at day break on the way from Annapolis & built 12 or 20 large fires by the road side. I was on guard in the Capitol last night, so today was a holiday for me & I am going out to see the town. I walked up and down one of the corridors from 8 till 11 P.M. & then was relieved until 3 A.M. when I had to go on for two hours more. I rather enjoyed it, as I didn't feel sleepy at all & had plenty to think of, besides stopping suspicious individuals in citizens' dress & remonstrating with the men when they made a noise after 10 o'cl. There are a great many regiments quartered here and some of them rather unruly.

"Stah ich in finstrer Mitternacht
So einsam auf der stillen Wacht"

occurred to my mind very often.[3] I never used to think I should have an opportunity to apply the words to myself. The sunrise was magnificent.

Our life here reminds me all the time of the soldiers we used to see in such crowds in Italy.[4] The Reveille beats at 5 1/2 A.M. and at 6 1/2 we march in companies to breakfast, often going double-quick through the town which gives us a good appetite. When we get back Roll is called & at 9 1/2 we have company drill, then nothing to do (unless when on guard duty) until dinner time, 1 o'cl, & ten of each company can get passes to go out of the grounds. At 3 1/2 or 4 we have a full parade of the whole regt. We march down again to supper at six. Retreat beats at sunset & every one who comes in after that without special permission from the colonel is put in the Guard-house. These are the regulations of the U.S. Army. Tattoo sounds at 10 & every one has to turn in as soon as the Roll is called. The lights are all turned down—the sentinels walk up & down between the rows of sleepers. There is a heavy guard kept up all about the grounds so that not a soul can get in or out without being seen. We have permission to go all over the grounds and it is very pleasant to go out & lie under the trees in fine weather. All the rest of Washington with exception of White House grounds & some other public buildings is a pretty poor place.

We don't know where Davis' army is. They think at Richmond—but there seems to be no fear of attack as there are so many men here.[5] Yesterday when we were on parade we heard guns over on the Virginia side and began to think the fight was en train, but it turned out to be flying artillery at target practice.

I am sure I hope there will be no occasion to use your flannel shirts &c but if we are going to fight I should like to have it begin soon, so that we may know what it is.

This morning I have received a note from Cousin Sarah Forbes, Annie Agassiz & Mr. Robbins.[6] Please ask Father to send me a Tribune now & then.[7]

Almost every day I meet another familiar face in the street here. Yesterday I saw Frank Barlow who is in the engineer corps of the 12th Regt. N.Y.[8] The papers say this morning that the ports of Virginia & North Carolina are to be blockaded. Lincoln knows what he is about. No one would have suspected, who saw him reviewing us, holding his two little boys by the hand that he had so much to think of.[9] When he laughs he doubles himself up something as Theodore Lyman does.[10] He talked a good deal with our officers & seemed to be in good spirits. Mrs. L. was there but I couldn't see her face distinctly.[11] Doesn't it seem odd to have every man, woman & child in the North ranged on one side? Was there ever so much enthusiasm seen in the country? Of course it will die out somewhat in time but still it will do a great deal of good. It is a pleasant feeling to be here bullying the Southerners.[12] They looked so [one word illegible] & helpless along the streets at Annapolis. I hope Mother will take care of herself & not get ill again. Is Anna up yet?[13] Give my love to her & George & to Nellie, Mother & Father.[14] All our friends here are well— the W's & Sam Curtis.[15] Write to me when you can. I often wonder what you are all doing at home. The great time for thinking as I said above is when we are on guard duty. Don't let yourself be persuaded to go any where as a nurse if there is a fight—as you say, you are not old enough. We received some white cap covers today from New York but I had one already made here and fitted to my head. They [two words illegible] hanging down behind. Some of the men have had great boxes full of dainties sent by well meaning friends but in our small quarters we have little room for extra luggage & when we move it will be very embarrassing. I have nothing to write about but ourselves & myself & have given you a good deal of it in all my letters. The best feeling prevails among the troops here. Sprague's men from Rhode Island look well dressed in felt hats & blouses with grey trousers, a very serviceable uniform.[16]

Our grey things look as well as the day we started and our men are decidedly the neatest and natiest looking in the town. Give my love to Frankie.[17]

Ever dear Effie,
Your loving Brother,
Robert G. Shaw

1. Shaw is probably referring to Oriental Hall, a popular meeting place at Port Richmond, Staten Island. Leng and Davis, *Staten Island*, vol. 1, p. 277.

2. In 1858, Mimi married Theodore Lyman (1833–97), who served in the U.S. House of Representatives (1883–85). McGuiness and Sayers, *American Leaders*, p. 217; Smith, *Beacon Hill's*, p. 491, Mary C. Crawford, *Famous Families*, vol. 2, p. 255.

3. Translated as: I stood in dark midnight completely alone on silent watch.

4. Shaw spent ten months with his family in Sorrento, Rome, and Florence, in Italy, and Heidelberg, Germany, from Sept. 1853 to July 1854. Shaw, *Letters: RGS* (1876), p. 46.

5. Beauregard's army was in Charleston and there was the nucleus of an army in Richmond. Correspondence and etc., Apr. 27, 1861, *The War of the Rebellion: A Compilation of the Official Records of the Union and Confederate Armies*, ser. I, vol. 2, pp. 771–800 [hereafter cited as *OR*, Series:Volume].

6. Sarah Swain Hathaway Forbes (1813–99).

7. Horace Greeley's *New York Daily Tribune*.

8. Francis Channing Barlow (1834–96) graduated first in his class at Harvard in 1855 and tutored Shaw on Staten Island in preparation for the 1856 Harvard entrance examinations. Barlow was practicing law in New York City and writing for the *Tribune*, in 1861, when he volunteered as a private in the Twelfth New York Infantry. Faust, *Encyclopedia*, p. 39.

9. Thomas "Tad" Lincoln (1853–71) and William "Willie" Wallace Lincoln (1850–62). Mark E. Neely, *The Abraham Lincoln Encyclopedia* (New York: McGraw-Hill, 1982), pp. 188–89.

10. Theodore Lyman graduated from Harvard in 1855. Son of former Boston mayor Theodore Lyman (1792–1849), Lyman served as an aide to General Meade throughout the war. Boatner, *Dictionary*, pp. 496–97.

11. Mary Todd Lincoln (1818–82). For the best study of Mrs. Lincoln, see Jean H. Baker, *Mary Todd Lincoln: A Biography* (New York: W. W. Norton, 1987).

12. For years there had been in the North a feeling that a "Slave Power Conspiracy" ruled the country in favor of the South. The Shaws and their closest friends subscribed to this theory. Many also felt that now that the North and West had asserted themselves with the election of Lincoln, Southerners had seceded when they no longer "ruled."

13. Anna Shaw Curtis.

14. George William Curtis, Ellen Shaw, George Francis Shaw, and Sarah

Blake Sturgis Shaw.

15. Theodore and William Winthrop. Samuel Bridgham Curtis.

16. William Sprague (1830–1915), a Cranston, Rhode Island, textile manufacturer and son-in-law of Secretary of the Treasury Salmon P. Chase, served as governor of Rhode Island (1860–63) and as U.S. senator (1863–75). Governor Sprague was one of the first to respond to Lincoln's call for troops. He personally financed and raised the First Regiment of the Rhode Island Volunteer Infantry and transported them by steamer from New York to Annapolis before marching them into camp at "Camp Sprague" near Washington, D.C. During the war, Sprague served as aide to Brigadier General Ambrose Burnside. *NYDT*, Apr. 22, 1861 (7:5); Faust, *Encyclopedia*, p. 709; McGuiness and Sayers, *American Leaders*, pp. 104, 395.

17. Shaw's three-year-old nephew, Francis George Curtis. U.S. Census, 1860, N.Y., Richmond Co., Castleton, p. 150.

Washington D.C.   [HL]
May 2, 1861
Dear Mother,

Yesterday I received yours of 27 Apr & Father's of 29 same and was very glad to find from the latter that you had at least got my letters from Annapolis & from here.

I have received all yours & had one from Annie Agassiz & one from Cousin Sarah Forbes. I wrote to Effie day before yesterday.

We received notice yesterday that we were to leave our present quarters and go into camp today at 3 P.M. Our engineer corps went off last night to lay out the camp & pitch the tents at a place called Meridian Hill, about two miles to the East of the White House. They say it is a beautiful place and we are all glad to get out into the fresh air, though it is a little cold just now for the 2d May. I am much obliged for the things you are going to send me and hope I shall be able to see the Dr. I have been able to get almost everything I wanted here but my needle & thread have disappeared so the new ones will be welcome. There are a great many men who think apparently, that when they lose their own things they are justified in laying hands on those of other people, so we have to keep a watch over such small articles as soap, brushes, &c. I bought some woolen socks, drawers &c. before I left New York & am well furnished in that respect. A good many men are troubled with dysentery &c. but I am & have been perfectly well all the time, probably because I have been very careful.

On Tuesday a fellow named King, son of Pres. of Columbia College, asked me to go with him to see Mr. Seward, so we got leave to go out for the afternoon & walked up to the War Department.[1] King knew him very well & we had a little talk with him. He gave the impression of being a pretty sly old fellow & really didn't look as if he could have written those great speeches.[2] I didn't have time to tell him I was related to George though I wanted to.[3]

We told him we should like very much to see Mr. Lincoln so he gave us a note to him & off we trotted to make a call. After waiting a few moments in the antechamber we were shown into a room where Mr. Lincoln was sitting at a desk perfectly covered with letters & papers of every description. He got up & shook hands with us both in the most cordial way, asked us to be seated & seemed quite glad to have us come. It is really too bad to call him one of the ugliest men in the country for I have seldom seen a pleasanter or more kind-hearted looking one and he has certainly a very striking face. It is easy to see why he is so popular with all who come in contact with him. His voice is very pleasant and though to be sure we were there a very few moments, I didn't hear anything like Western twang or slang in him. He gives you the impression of being a gentleman. I told him I had heard of his son at Cambridge & we talked a little about our Regt. & the others stationed in the city, some of which he said they were trying to put in good trim as fast as possible.[4] Though you can't judge of a man in a five minute conversation, we were very much pleased with what we did see of him. We got rather ahead of the rest of the Regt., as none of the others have seen him, and thought we had done a pretty good afternoon's work in calling on the President & Secretary of State both.

I wish I could see something more of Mr. Seward for knowing how much there is in his head, I should like to hear him talk. He seemed a very kind old gentleman, but not so cordial as Mr. Lincoln & not nearly so firm & decided. Don't think that my admiration of Mr. Seward is diminished in the slightest by having seen him, for if he were the most disagreeable & insignificant looking man I ever saw it wouldn't change what we *know* about him.[5] At first sight I don't believe any one would think him a great man and that is why I want to see him again. I am going to get my photograph taken here today to send you. I shall try to have my belts, knapsack & musket just as we came into Washington but perhaps it will be too much trouble to bring them all down from the Capitol which is some way off & they don't like to have the pieces taken away excepting when we turn out. Father & Effie both say you are very well. I am glad the Nassau trip did you so much good. I hope Bridget is better than she was.[6] How glad I shall be to see you all dear Mother when our time is out—but if the war goes on much longer I don't believe I shall feel like staying at home. The Winthrops have me to say again that they were well. Ned Delafield went off last night with the Engineers & was very well.[7]

The Country about here looks beautifully. I suppose Staten I[sland] begins to too. We hear nothing reliable about Davis & his army but no one seems to expect a fight in this vicinity. Did you know those Mass. men were killed on the Anniversary of the battle of Lexington? We saw the cars at Phila. which they were in. The windows & doors were all broken to bits.[8] That Regt. is here, but is not the same one that came with us. I wish I knew whether Harry is ordered off.[9] Annie's letter was of 18th April.[10] Mr. Robbins has written twice, enclosing several letters, one from Mr. Fisher asking me to collect rent from Mr. Arnold.[11] Has Mrs. Wood got the House?[12] They say that the letters sent by our Regt. alone have averaged 1000 per day. Mr. Macy of Adams Express has forwarded all letters to us free of charge and those which have come by them are the only ones which have not been delayed.[13] This is the reason I didn't get yours sooner & that of 27 Apr. But now the way is clear and everything will go through safely. We have yesterday's New York papers but they cost 10 & 15 cents.

> With much love to all,
> Ever your loving son,
> Robert G. Shaw

Sam Curtis is still in good order. I shall see him again tonight when we get up to the camp. Please give my love to Mrs. Curtis when you see her.[14] I was very sorry I forgot to call for Mr. Thorpe's letter to you, when you were away.[15] I heard Mr. Simms was coming here soon, if so, I will try and go and see him.[16]

1. Private Rufus King, son of Charles King, president of Columbia College, New York.

2. William Henry Seward (1801–72), former governor of New York (1839–43) and U.S. senator (1849–61), was U.S. secretary of state in the administrations of Lincoln and Andrew Johnson. Seward was a founder of the Republican party and its favorite to win the 1860 nomination for president, but his radical antislavery stance lost to Lincoln's moderation on the third ballot at the Chicago Convention. His "Higher Law" speech in 1850 chastised the 1850 Fugitive Slave Act, and his "Irrepressible Conflict" speech in 1858 forecast the Civil War.

Faust, *Encyclopedia*, pp. 668–69.

3. Shaw's brother-in-law George W. Curtis was active in Republican party politics and had been a campaigner for John C. Frémont in 1856 and Seward in 1860. Curtis attended the 1860 Republican Convention in Chicago.

4. Robert Todd Lincoln (1843–1926) entered Harvard in 1860. Neely, *Lincoln Encyclopedia*, p. 184.

5. Seward was a favorite among abolitionists for his antislavery speeches. In September 1850, Seward had tried unsuccessfully to abolish slavery in the District of Columbia.

6. Shaw's parents had two servants named Bridget: twenty-nine-year-old

Irish chambermaid Bridget Divine and twenty-two-year-old Irish waitress Bridget Kennedy. Shaw is probably referring to Divine. U.S. Census, 1860, N.Y., Richmond Co., Castleton, p. 152.

7. Ned is possibly Edward Delafield of Shaw's Apr. 29, 1861, letter to Sarah Shaw, collected herein.

8. Reference to the Sixth Massachusetts and the Baltimore riot of April 19, 1861.

9. Harry S. Russell would be mustered into the Second Massachusetts Infantry on May 25, 1861, the same day Shaw joined that regiment. Harry Sturgis Russell file, Compiled Military Service Records, Records of the Adjutant General's Office, Record Group 94, National Archives [hereafter CMSR].

10. Annie Russell Agassiz.

11. Chandler Robbins of New York City. Mr. Arnold is unidentified.

12. Mrs. Wood is unidentified. Many families of Woods lived on Staten Island.

13. Mr. Macy is otherwise unidentified. The Adams Express Company operated its main New York office at 59 Broadway. *Trow's NYC Directory for 1861*, p. 24.

14. Julia Bowen Bridgham Curtis was the second wife of George Curtis (1796–1856); they wed in 1834. Her sons were Samuel Bridgham Curtis and Joseph Bridgham Curtis (1836–62). George Curtis married in 1821 his first wife, Mary Elizabeth Burrill Curtis, mother to George William Curtis, the author and brother-in-law of Shaw. Curtis folder, SIHS.

15. Probably Charles G. Thorpe of Staten Island. Charles G. Hine and William T. Davis, *Legends, Stories and Folklore of Old Staten Island* (New York: Staten Island Historical Society, 1925), p. 77.

16. Mr. Simms is unidentified.

"Virtue's Bower" (our tent) [HL]
Stone's Farm, Meridian Hill, Washington D.C.[1]
May 4 1861
Dear Father,

Yesterday I wrote Mother a short note by Henry Vezin.[2] They tell us now that there is a great quantity of preserved meats among the Regt. Stores so I don't believe we shall need much of those. Please send 2 lbs. green seal smoking tobacco to be got from H. G. Beach & Co., 71 Pine St. and some cakes of Oronoco Tobacco which is milder than the others & which is for myself.[3] Also a box of mild Havanas. We are six men in a tent so everything that comes is common property. Some preserved vegetables I think would be good—and the tea—not much of the latter as no one seems to drink it but I. You might put some oranges, nuts &c in the box. Men bring us milk & eggs every morning so it will be more convenient to send the money to buy them with than to send those things themselves.

The money goes pretty fast as everything is dear. We have had to buy some mattresses, as we were allowed only 3 for 6 men.—& a good many other things with which to make ourselves comfortable. It has been raining hard for two days but our tents are perfectly dry and I have slept better here than anywhere since we left, for we have never had any mattresses before. The poor devils on guard all night have to suffer. Fortunately I have escaped that hitherto and it is clearing off now so I don't care how soon I am put on. The cold weather here is extraordinary at this season. The first night out, some of the men suffered a good deal but yesterday we got a quantity of woolen jackets sent by Mr. Aspinwall which have been of immense service.[4] He & Mr. Macy ought to have the thanks of every man of us & of all our relations.[5] We hear the 79th is not coming so we shan't see the Dr.[6] I am sorry for it.

I really don't like to ask you to send me any more money, but if we had nothing but what the Gov't furnished we should fare very poorly. I suppose they know we can afford to take part care of ourselves so they don't give us much or if they do, we have seen only some poor coffee & not very good ham. I don't know where it came from. I have tonight nothing but necessaries.

Last evening I went out to tea at George Wilson's tent & had a very pleasant evening.[7] We talked a good deal about home & you would be amused at the rush, when the arrival of mail is announced.

Ellsworth's men came day before yesterday & have our old quarters.[8] Men come pouring in every day both to Washington & Annapolis. There was a letter in the Times about our march which I should think would make people laugh.[9] We are encamped on the road to Harper's Ferry. There seems to be little fear of an attack from any quarter. We can't tell what will happen in the next 3 weeks but it certainly looks as if we will not have much fighting. I am sorry we are not going to stay 3 mos. with the other troops from Rhode I. & Mass. though I want to see you all very much too. Please send some solidified coffee. Did you get the letters I sent by Jewett?[10] I hope you will let me know if any one of the family is ill. I promise to do the same by you, if anything befalls me. The W's send regards. They have done me a great many kindnesses & I hope I shall have a chance to be of some service to them. Theodore lent me his India Rubber cloak last night. He is stationed in a house & assured me he didn't need it. He is very much obliged to Mother for the bananas & hopes to taste some of them when he gets home. It is rather hard writing on a knapsack, so excuse the looks of this. Remember me to the Wards & Depeysters & Johnsons & Sickles & especially to Mrs. Staples who was one of the last I saw & with whom I had a consoling talk as I was coming away.[11]

Ever your loving son,
Robert G. Shaw

P.S. I wrote you a letter in pencil last night which I didn't intend to send this morning, but I hear some one picked it up & sent it to the P.O. so you will get both.

1. An *Atlantic Monthly* correspondent reported that the Seventh set up its headquarters and camp in "the villa and farm of Dr. Stone, two miles due north of Willard's Hotel." Stone's Farm was officially named Camp Cameron, after the Secretary of War. *Atlantic Monthly* 18 (July 1861): 110; Roehrenbeck, *The Regiment That Saved The Capital*, p. 145.

2. Henry Vezin, a fellow student with Shaw in Hanover, Germany, and traveling companion on Shaw's 1855 trip to Norway, was from Philadelphia. *Letters: RGS* (1876), pp. 100, 143, 146, 152–56.

3. H. G. Beach and Company, tobacconists, of New York City. *Trow's NYC Directory for 1863*.

4. William H. Aspinwall (1807–75), of the New York City mercantile firm Howland and Aspinwall, lived on Staten Island. He was a pioneer in the California trade. In 1846, the *New York Sun* listed his wealth at $400,000; by 1855, he had nearly $4 million. He donated worsted-wool jackets, thereafter known as "Aspinwalls," to the Seventh Regiment. *Dictionary of American Biography*, vol. 1, p. 396; *Atlantic Monthly* 8 (Aug. 1861): 243–44; Leng and Davis, *Staten Island*, vol. 2, p. 854; Ernest A. McKay, *The Civil War and New York City* (Syracuse: Syracuse University Press, 1990), pp. 23, 69, 100.

5. Mr. Macy worked at the New York City Adams Express office.

6. The Seventy-ninth New York Infantry, the "Highlanders," were not mustered into service until May 29, 1861. Dyer, *Compendium*, vol. 1, p. 19.

7. George Wilson is unidentified.

8. Col. Elmer Ephraim Ellsworth (1837–61) commanded the "Fire Zouaves"—a unit composed entirely of New York firemen. An infuriated Southern sympathizer, James T. Jackson, murdered him in Alexandria, Virginia, on May 24, 1861, after Ellsworth cut down a Rebel flag from the Marshall House Hotel. Lincoln ordered that Ellsworth's body lie in state in the White House. *Harper's Weekly*, May 11, 1861, p. 1, June 8, 1861, p. 5; *Atlantic Monthly* 8 (July 1861): 119–25; Faust, *Encyclopedia*, p. 240; Boatner, *Dictionary*, p. 431.

9. Private Fitz James O'Brien wrote of the Seventh's passage from New York to Washington: "We are here. . . . Dandies, who were the pride of club windows, were not above brown paper parcels. . . . Delmonico, calm and serene, superintended sandwiches. . . . Fellows who would at Delmonico's have sent back a turban de volaille aux truffes because the truffes were tough, here cheerfully took their places in file between decks, tin plates and tin cups in hand, in order to get an insufficient piece of beef and a vision of coffee." *NYT*, May 2 (2:1), 1861.

10. Orville D. Jewett of Staten Island.

11. All of these families lived on Staten Island. The Shaws had two sets of friends named Ward: Mr. and Mrs. George Cabot Ward, who lived near the Sydney Howard Gays, and George Atkinson Ward, a member of

the Unitarian church. Frederick Agustus Depeyster and his wife, Jan, lived at Sailor's Snug Harbor. Mrs. William T. Johnson, sister of Theodore and William Winthrop, lived with her husband at West New Brighton. Mrs. Sickles is unidentified. John Staples and his wife Elizabeth, with whom Sarah Shaw maintained a close relationship, lived on the Shore Road. Hine and Davis, *Legends*, pp. 28, 34, 46, 70, 83–85; Leng and Davis, *Staten Island*, p. 494; for the Depeysters, see U.S. Census, 1860, N.Y., Richmond Co., Castleton, p. 108.

Camp Cameron [HL]
Washington D.C.
May 10/61
Dearest Mother,

Your letter of 6 May & Father's of 7 came night before last and yesterday I got another one from him of May 8. All the packages have also come safely to hand—Milk, tea, guava jelly & yours with needle & thread &c. The last will be very useful to me as well as the bag they were in. I do take great care of my diet but have such an appetite that I eat a good deal. I must have dropped a piece of the strip of newspaper you sent in opening the letter for I couldn't find the beginning of the article. I bought some woolen socks before I left N. York. My feet have not troubled me for a moment. Balmoral shoes are the best things I have ever had to walk in. You can have them loose in the foot & prevent them from chafing by lacing them as tightly as you please. I am glad of what you say about my enlisting for the war, though I was certain before that you would think I was right in wanting to. But I certainly shouldn't act entirely without regard to you, as you say, both on your account & because no one else can give me better advice. As you will see from what I wrote Father day before yesterday I don't want to go without a commission though I would do so without any hesitation if there were a lack of men. I shouldn't have thought of the [regular] army if I hadn't seen the want of discipline in volunteer companies & the difficulty the officers have in enforcing it. That though would, no doubt, be different after they had been for some time in service & discovered that the Government was in the war to back up the officers. Still it is likely the volunteers will see more service & be the most prominent in the war. But after the fighting is over they won't have anything to do while a man in the army can resign or keep his commission as he chooses.

I believe I haven't told you yet of our departure from the Capitol. After the engineers left we got our things all ready to start the next morning. When the time came to fall in, I was one of the first ready so our orderly sergeant asked me & 3 others of the company to go & report to one of the officers for about 10 minutes guard duty, while the luggage was being taken out of the quarters & then to fall in & march up with the regiment. But as luck would have it, we weren't relieved for as much as an hour, the regiment in the meantime marching off. Then we were ordered to lay down our muskets & they furnished us with brooms & set us to work sweeping out the House of Representatives. We were about 25 from all the companies & such a dust as we raised you never saw. There was an astonishing amount of filth there & it took us as much as two hours to scatter it about, so that it seemed to me to look much worse than before. We left it so & had the satisfaction of going up to the camp in omnibuses instead of marching as the others did. I went all over the Capitol when we were there & read the names on the desks in the Senate Chamber with much interest. Mr Sumner & Mr. Hale sit together & J. Davis sat not far off, I think.[1] I supposed Sumner occupies the same place now as when Brooks assaulted him.[2]

Since the fine weather began we have had quite a merry time up here. We have to turn out [at] 5 o'cl. every morning for roll call. Then we put up the bedding & get ready for breakfast which we had to cook the first week ourselves. Now they furnish us with the substantial part, & we make coffee & tea & anything else we want or plutot can get in eggs, toast, &c. Two of the men in our tent are excellent cooks. At 9 1/2 we have company drill which lasts from one to two hours & is pretty hard work on hot days. At 12 A.M. [noon] the drums sound for "Roast beef" which is usually an Irish Stew or something of that kind but always well cooked. At 5 1/2 P.M. we have regimental parade & have been reviewed by General Mansfield, Mr. Cameron & Major Anderson.[3] Yesterday we had no one but Col. Lefferts.[4] The short leave of absence they give us now makes it hardly worth while to go in town unless to get a bath which we do as often as possible, that is, about once a week. We can't get away oftener unless for some very urgent reason.

Susie and I will get home at about the same time if nothing happens to prevent. Shan't we be glad to see her again?

Don't you think I had better wait until I am unwell before I take to the flannel? For if I wore it all the time perhaps it would be of no service. Though we go home in two weeks a good many will come back, for they are going to get up a volunteer corps from among the members.

I must close rather abruptly for the mail goes very soon. Love to all again.

Always affectionately,
Your loving Son,
Robert G. Shaw

Our band plays really beautifully & they give us some 3 times a day [two words illegible] doings up quite a large crowd.

1. Charles Sumner (1811–74) of Massachusetts was one of the most out-spoken antislavery Republicans in the U.S. Senate (1851–74). New Hamp-shire's John Parker Hale (1806–73) sat in the Senate (1847–53, 1855–65). Mississippi's Jefferson Davis was then president of the Confederate States of America. McGuiness and Sayers, *American Leaders*, pp. 165, 304.

2. On May 19 and 20, 1856, Senator Sumner gave an impassioned two-day speech on "The Crime Against Kansas" in which he castigated proslavery "Border Ruffians" and talked about the "rape of virgin territory." Sumner personally blamed Senator Andrew But-ler of South Carolina for choosing the "harlot, slavery" as a mistress. Butler's nephew, U.S. representative Preston Brooks, took offense to this slur on his family's honor, and took revenge on May 22 by caning Sumner unconscious as he worked at his desk in the Senate chamber. Sumner was unable to return permanently to his desk until Dec. 1859; his vacant chair served as a rallying symbol against the brutality of slavery. During its stay in Washington, the Sixth

Massachusetts occupied the Senate chamber and symbolically avenged the assault on Sumner. For a whimsical look at the seat of government as a military camp, see *Atlantic Monthly* 8 (July 1861): 105–18.

3. Joseph King Fenno Mansfield (1803–62) had a long army career that began with his graduation from West Point in 1822. On Apr. 28, 1861, he became commander of the Department of Washington, D.C. His commission as a brigadier general dated from May 18, 1861. Pennsylvanian Simon Cameron (1799–1889) served many terms in the U.S. Senate (1845–49, 1857–61, 1867–77) and was Lincoln's secretary of war until 1862, when, charged with corrup-tion in army contracts, he became U.S. minister to Russia. Maj. Robert Ander-son (1805–71) gained the first notoriety of the war with his defense against the Rebel bombardment at Fort Sumter on Apr. 12, 1861. Faust, *Encyclopedia*, pp. 14–15, 107, 473; McGuiness and Sayers, *American Leaders*, p. 98.

4. Col. Marshall Lefferts commanded the Seventh New York.

Washington   [RGS]
May 12, 1861
Dear Father,

Your two notes of 11th inst. enclosing George's and Mother's, came to hand this afternoon. I shall leave on Tuesday, and am glad to get the commission.[1] Nevertheless I don't want to give up the regular army, if I can get in there. Charley Lowell has got a commission by his own exertion, and without any recommendations.[2] I am sure I should be successful, with letters from some of your and George's friends,—and perhaps without, for Lowell is going to write and see what he can do, and Barlow may be able to help me in some way.[3] I should like to get into the cavalry. They are signing up a light brigade. If I can get it, I shall resign from Colonel Gordon's regiment, though it will be a pity to lose the chance of being with Harry.[4] Don't you think, though, I am right? Volunteers have almost always been badly treated and much neglected, you know, in our wars. You remember in what a condition they came back from Mexico. Don't think I am not pleased with what I have got, for it is second best. I shall see you on Tuesday or Wednesday.

Your loving son,
Robt G. Shaw

1. Shaw received his commissioning letter from the Second Massachusetts Infantry on May 10, 1861, and was mustered into his new regiment on May 28 as a second lieutenant. *Memorial: RGS* (Cambridge, Mass.: Harvard University Press, 1864), p. 34.

2. Charles Russell Lowell (1835–64), grandson of the founder of the first power loom cotton mill in the United States, had graduated Harvard at the top of his class in 1854. He worked for Russell and Company in New York City and the Mt. Savage Iron Works in Cumberland, Maryland—both companies headed by John Murray Forbes. On May 14, 1861, he was commissioned a captain in the Third (renumbered the Sixth) U.S. Cavalry. In 1863, Lowell married Shaw's sister Josephine. According to his biographer, Lowell was "slight in frame and stature, with commanding intellect and fine taste, a lover of classics and versed in philosophy." Edward W. Emerson, *Life and Letters of Charles Russell Lowell* (Boston: Houghton Mifflin, 1907), p. 69; Thomas W. Higginson, *Harvard Memorial Biographies* (Cambridge, Mass.: Sever & Francis, 1867), vol. 1, pp. 275–304; Sarah Forbes Hughes, ed., *Letters and Recollections of John Murray Forbes* (Boston: Houghton Mifflin, 1899), vol. 1, p. 147; Smith, *Beacon Hill's*, 415–20.

3. Francis Channing Barlow.

4. Col. George Henry Gordon (1823–86), graduated from West Point in 1846 and served in the Mexican War, raised and commanded the Second Massachusetts. Boatner, *Dictionary*, p. 347; James L. Bowen, *Massachusetts in the War, 1861–1865* (Springfield, Mass.: Bryan, 1889), pp. 113, 931.

CHAPTER 2

"*The road through the woods*"

The war had certainly not ended during the thirty-day enlistment period of the Seventh New York. Private Shaw decided that there was as much of a reason to stay in the army as there had been to come out in the first place. Commissioned a second lieutenant in the newly formed Second Massachusetts Infantry, Shaw found the life of an officer much different from that of a common soldier: "We have cots to sleep on, much better fare, and servants in abundance from among the men." He signed on for three years. The new regiment formed and trained at Camp Andrew near West Roxbury, Massachusetts, site of the Brook Farm experiment.

As regiments formed into brigades and brigades joined into armies, both sides jockeyed for position. Then came bloodshed. The Union's first combat casualty, Colonel Elmer Ellsworth, killed on May 24 trying to remove a Confederate flag from a hotel in Alexandria, Virginia, followed by the death of Shaw's friend Theodore Winthrop and nineteen others at Big Bethel, Virginia, on June 10, brought fears of many deaths and long war home to thousands of families. The war was young and the young had begun to die.

May 19, 1861

Dear Mother,

Your note was handed me a few minutes ago by Uncle Henry.[1] I managed to come over here to dinner, as Lawrence Motley (First Lieutenant) came out to camp to-day.[2] I was very comfortable coming on, as I went into the sleeping-car, where there are plenty of blankets, and slept soundly. My cold is much better, but I am somewhat hoarse from talking and giving orders. Brown's Troches are curing it. We have 45 men now, but hope to get 100. We may not start for two months, as there will be much drilling necessary to get the men into working order. As the regiment is accepted for three years, they will not want to start until they are fully equipped, and well drilled.[3] Everything is apparently managed with great care. Blankets and mattresses are plenty, meals good and regular. The physician is a very good one, and the men are kept clean and comfortable. They have to wash all over every week, and keep their quarters well aired and clean. It is very odd to be at Brook Farm.[4] The cottage is the only one of the old houses that remains. There is a new house on the site of the "Hive," and these two are the only ones now standing.[5] Most of the men (perhaps 500) are in tents, but our two companies are, for the present, in barracks close to the new house, where we are quartered. I shall do all I can, when we go off, to keep up the health of my men, and make them comfortable.

I am so sorry you feel so about me. But it can't be helped, I suppose, as long as I am away. You must recollect that there is no danger of my being ill, or otherwise made away with, until we march, which will not be for six weeks at the earliest; so try to feel easy until then, at least. I assure you I am not very careless about myself. I knew I should not suffer from cold coming on here, for those cars are always too warm for me, and I had quite a thick coat on.

There is a great difference between the life of a private and that of an officer, I find. We have cots to sleep on, much better fare, and servants in abundance from among the men. When we get our company full, I shall have more liberty, for then the other officers will be at the camp. Now the Captain and First Lieutenant are recruiting and attending to business, in town.[6] I was snapped up yesterday by Captain Tucker for a moment after I got to the Colonel's office, much to Uncle Jim's disgust, and had to stay all day in a desolate-looking unfurnished hall with the men, and at 6 o'clock go out to the camp without any luggage.[7] There are a great many old acquaintances of mine at the camp, and I had a very pleasant time last night.

I have just written to Father, and sent the letter to town, but this will be too late for to-day's mail. Good-bye, with much love to all. I will write soon again.

Your loving son,
Robt G. Shaw

1. Henry Parkman Sturgis founded the trading company of Russell and Sturgis of Manila, the Philippines. Roger Faxton Sturgis, *Edward Sturgis of Yarmouth, Mass., 1613–1695, and His Descendants* (Boston: Stanhope, 1914), pp. 51–52.

2. T. Lawrence Motley (1834–?) was mustered in as a first lieutenant, Second Massachusetts Infantry Regiment, on May 28, 1861. *Record of Massachusetts Volunteers, 1861–1865* (Boston: Wright & Potter, 1870), vol. 1, p. 28.

3. The Second Massachusetts Infantry, organized eight days after Lincoln called for three-year volunteers, went into training at Camp Andrew, Brook Farm, West Roxbury, Massachusetts, on May 11, 1861. Dyer, *Compendium*, vol. 1, p. 157; James L. Bowen, *Massachusetts in the War, 1861–1865* (Springfield, Mass.: Bryan, 1889), p. 113; *OR*, III:1, pp. 78–79, 111–12.

4. Officially named the Brook Farm Institute of Agriculture and Education, this transcendentalist community lasted just six years, 1841–47. The fact that it existed at all is due in large part to the generous financial support of Francis George Shaw and his brothers-in-law, Henry P. Sturgis and George Russell, who contributed $1,500 each to get it started. In 1845, F. G. Shaw gave Ripley $2,500 more to keep it going. Lindsay Swift, *Brook Farm: Its Members, Scholars, and Visitors* (New York: Macmillan, 1911), pp. 19–25.

5. The "Hive" was a farmhouse with two rooms on each side of a main hall-way. The "Hive" quickly became an assembly hall, described as "the heart of the community." Ibid., p. 27.

6. Capt. J. Parker Whitney and First Lt. Charles R. Mudge. Bowen, *Massachusetts in the War*, p. 114.

7. Capt. Francis H. Tucker and Col. George H. Gordon. Uncle Jim is Shaw's maternal uncle James Sturgis (1822–88), a merchant and lifelong resident of Boston. *Record of Mass. Vols.*, p. 28; Sturgis, *Edward Sturgis*, p. 53.

Camp Andrew[1]   [RGS]
May 21, 1861
Dear Father,

I forgot to ask you to send my revolver. If you have not fired it off, you might send it with the charges in it, as there are no caps on it. Everything sent by "Express" will be brought out here if addressed "Gordon's Regiment, Camp Andrew, West Roxbury."[2] If my box has not come from Washington, I shall have to get another set of things to go with the revolver, as they are all in there. The case is on the table in my room. We are full of work. The air here is fine, and my cold is almost gone. We have pitched our company's tents behind where the Pilgrim house stood.[3] Every day I see something which recalls the "Community" days. Give my love, and write as often as possible. I dreamt last night that this regiment was sworn into service for forty-seven years!

Your loving son,
Robert G. Shaw

1. Camp Andrew was named for John Albion Andrew (1818–67), governor of Massachusetts (1861–66). McGuiness and Sayers, *American Leaders*, p. 373.

2. The Adams Express Company was the prime shipper of freight by private means during the Civil War.

3. The Pilgrim House was actually two houses with a common back wall that had been originally occupied by two families before being converted into the Brook Farm community laundry, tailor shop, and newspaper office. Swift, *Brook Farm*, pp. 32–33.

Camp Andrew   [HL]
25 May 1861
Dear Mother,

Your note telling me of Susie's arrival was received day before yesterday and succeeded in surprising me very much. Since then I have got one from Susie herself enclosed in Father's of 22d inst. I am very glad to hear that she is so well & in such good spirits. Please say to her that I shan't be able to answer her note very soon as I am really busy almost every moment of the time. I never knew before what it was to be busy. My Captain & 1st Lieut. have not been here excepting sometimes in the evening since I came which leaves me a good deal of responsibility.[1] On the whole I think I had rather have them away than here, as I have got the men into a track from which they are usually turned when any one else is in command.

Annie Agassiz was out here on Wednesday & gave me a needle & thread &c case & also a flannel band.[2] The next day she sent me 2 flannel shirts, 2 prs. woolen stockings & 2 hdkchfs which came from Mrs. H. G. Otis who represents some Society or other.[3] The trunk you sent arrived safely day before yesterday & I am now well provided with everything I want.

Annie said she would write to you that same day so I suppose you have heard from her. She is looking very well & seems very much improved (not only in looks) every time I see her.

All the officers here are, as far as I can judge, very gentleman-like men, and

I think just the sort I shall like to associate with. Of course some will begin to show their black streaks in the course of time. A good many I have known well before. Sam Quincy is not a fascinating creature. He is Captain & has a company of fine looking men from Lenox & vicinity.[4] His lieutenant, Sedgewick, got almost all of them. We have a good many Irishmen in our company who were very hard to manage at first, but they are getting toned down by degrees.[5] We are filling up with Americans & yesterday got 16 everyone of whom was above the average both in height & muscle. Some of them are really immense. Every man is examined by the physician & we have turned away at least 25 or 30.

We have a great deal of fun with the sentinels at night for they very seldom can remember the form of challenge & the Irishmen seem sometimes utterly unable to learn or understand anything.

When more than one man approaches a sentry he must say: "Halt! advance one & give the countersign!" So one man said: "Advance one & give the counterfeit." Another "Advance & give the consignment." Another "advance one & count ten." And night before last when I was officer of the guard a sentry challenged Greely Curtis & said: "Coom forrad & give an account of yersilf!"[6]

I suppose there are as many as 20 different stories of the kind, some of which are very funny & true too, I think.

I have met many of the old inhabitants from Spring Street & they all seem very glad to see me.[7] Moses Cass never drinks anything now, they tell me, and is a very respectable member of society.[8] Mr. Guild thought I was Colonel of the regiment & said some one told him so.[9]

The road through the woods from here is just as it used to be & I found some quartz in the same place we got it 13 or 14 years ago to strike sparks from.

I am very much obliged for all the things you put in the trunk & don't know what there is left in the box from Washington excepting straps & cartridge box which I shall not want. Shall I send you your little carpet bag? I can furnish myself with any little things I may want. Mr Robbins paid me $177.50 before I left, part of which he said was due, but to which I didn't think I had any claim.[10] I hope you will not change your mind about coming on & bringing Susie. I want to see her very much. I had a note from Uncle Robert yesterday acknowledging receipt of my photograph.[11] He says they will be at home soon. I don't know yet what size trunk I shall want. I should like to have the daily Tribune for one month.

Best love to all. Both our Col. & Lieut. Col. are West Point men. The latter graduated higher than anyone else ever did.[12] I hear Uncle William wants to come home to fight.[13]

Your loving son,
Robert G. Shaw

P.S. Do you take any exercise. I hope you do. Harry and I are both well. I like what I am doing now better than anything I have tried hitherto. Tell father that our commissions are sure as we have all been appointed by Govnor & the Regiment was organized before the 22 year old order came out.[14]

1. Captain Whitney and First Lieutenant Mudge.

2. One of seven children, Annie Agassiz was the daughter of Shaw's paternal aunt Sarah Parkman Shaw Russell (1811–?) and uncle George Robert Russell, who lived nearby at West Roxbury. While in training at Camp Andrew, Shaw frequently visited the Russell household for entertainment and to seek the advice of Uncle George. George had been influential in Shaw's decision to leave Harvard in his junior year to take a position in Henry Sturgis's business in New York City. Smith, *Beacon Hill's*, p. 491; Shaw, *Letters: RGS* (1864), pp. 141, 143, 148.

3. Eliza Henderson Boardman Otis (1796–1873), daughter of wealthy Boston merchant and China trader William H. Boardman, married Harrison Gray Otis, Jr. (1765–1827). A philanthropist, Mrs. Otis headed Evans House, a home and hospital for Boston's Civil War soldiers. She devoted her time, labor, and influence to get her neighbors to donate food, clothing, and money to soldiers. As an example to others, she gave $50,000 to the U.S. Sanitary Commission in 1861. Crawford, *Famous Families*, vol. 2, pp. 250–52; William

Schouler, *A History of Massachusetts in the Civil War* (Boston: E. P. Dutton, 1868), vol. 2, pp. 651–54.

4. Samuel Miller Quincy (1833–87) graduated from Harvard in 1852. In 1863, Quincy volunteered as a lieutenant colonel in the Seventy-third U.S. Colored Troops. Boatner, *Dictionary*, p. 676.

5. William Dwight Sedgwick (1831–62) of Lenox, Massachusetts, graduated from Harvard in 1851. His family was closely acquainted with the English actress Fanny Kemble. *Record of Mass. Vols.*, p. 28.

6. Greely Stevenson Curtis (1830–97) attended the Lawrence Scientific School in Boston but failed to graduate with his class in 1851 because of eye trouble. Before the Civil War, Curtis worked as an engineer for a California gold-mining company and on projects in Canada and Boston. He was an architect in Boston when he enrolled in the Second Massachusetts on May 11, 1861. Two weeks later, Curtis received his commission as the captain of Company B. Crawford, *Famous Families*, vol. 2, pp. 171–72; Greely S. Curtis file, CMSR; Bowen, *Massachusetts in the War*, p. 114; Boatner, *Dictionary*, p. 214.

7. Spring Street in Boston is north of the Charles River Basin and one mile and a half east of Harvard.

8. Moses Cass is unidentified.

9. Mr. Guild is unidentified.

10. Shaw worked directly under Chandler Robbins, a partner in the New York City firm of Sturgis and Company.

11. Robert Shaw Sturgis (1824–76), the youngest of twelve children of Shaw's maternal grandparents, Nathaniel Russell Sturgis (1779–1856) and Susan Parkman Sturgis (?–1827), worked in the family's China trading business, Russell and Company, before marrying, retiring, and resettling in Philadelphia in 1858. Sturgis, *Edward Sturgis*, pp. 50, 53–54.

12. Col. George H. Gordon graduated from the U.S. Military Academy at West Point in 1846 ranked 43d in a class of 59. Five years later, Lt. Col. George L. Andrews finished first of 42. *Record of Mass. Vols.*, pp. 27–28; Boatner, *Dictionary*, pp. 19, 347.

13. Col. William Batchelder Greene (1819–78), of Haverhill, Massachusetts, a Brook Farmer, Unitarian minister, and abolitionist, was married to Shaw's paternal aunt Anna Blake Shaw Greene (1817–?). Smith, *Beacon Hill's*, p. 491; *National Cyclopedia of American Biography* (New York: James T. White, 1897), vol. 7, pp. 526–27.

14. On May 22, 1861, Simon Cameron issued orders to state governors that no one over twenty-two years of age should be appointed a lieutenant, no one over thirty a captain, no one over thirty-five a major, no one over forty a lieutenant colonel, and no one over forty-five a colonel, with exceptions for West Pointers or for those with proven military service or knowledge. Simon Cameron to Andrew G. Curtin [and all other governors], May 22, 1861, *OR*, III:1, pp. 227–28.

Camp Andrew [HL]
June 9, 1861
Dear Mother,

I didn't receive your letter of the 3d Inst. until yesterday and got Father's of 7th at the same time. Effie's, which he addressed to 20 State St. has not yet made its appearance.

It appears that the Office there has been closed within a day or two so everything will have to be sent here in future.

I think you had better send me the portfolio & handkerchiefs as we shall probably have very little time in New York, if we go through there at all as I wrote Father last week. It is very hard, to think of going away for so long and now I see it was better for all hands to go as I did before, without saying goodbye. Father says you felt badly when you got my letter to him speaking of our possible early departure, but that you nevertheless would not want me to stay at home. I think of how many people have been in this same situation without the consolation of knowing that they are suffering for a good cause,

& of the Frenchmen & Germans who have to serve whether they will or not.[1] And just think how many young men here are doing just what I am & how many Mothers & Fathers & sisters will feel just as badly as you will. It is a great satisfaction to me to know that you really would not have me stay at home and I hope you will not feel differently as long as this war lasts. Shan't you feel yourself that you had much better not come on here whether we pass through New York or not? After all when you look at it coolly there is not much more danger in war than in peace at least for officers. There are comparatively few men who are killed. By far the greater number die of diseases, contracted by dirt & neglect of all laws of health & those are things which we escape.[2] I can't help pitying some of our privates who are nice respectable men & who have to be treated just like the rest.

A great many of them want to go and see their relations & we have to refuse them lest all the rest should count to go too. It seems too bad when I put myself in their position. Most of them find soldiering very different work from what they expected, but having been sworn in, they seem resigned to the hard work & army rations. This Regt is going to be very different from most volunteer corps. If the commission which has been sent me is in the Infantry I hope I may be able to accept it & stay here, but I don't believe that is allowed. Miss Felton whom has just been in Washington heard from Charles Lowell that I had a commission in the cavalry.[3] That will be too tempting to refuse. I wish now I had put in for something more than 2d Lieut. and why didn't I think of applying to Mr. Sumner?[4] Through him Charley Lowell has got a Captaincy. But I think he is the cleverest young man I know & will do well in any position. I hope Father will be able to send me some particulars about this pretty soon, as I don't like to retain my place here so long as to cause any inconvenience by resigning.

I have [a] leave of absence for Tuesday and am going to drive Annie Agassiz over to Milton. I heard today that Cousins John & Sarah would get back tomorrow so I expect to find Effie over there.[5]

They say he has been fitting out ships for Government at his own expense & has about as much influence at Washington as any man. Is it true?[6] We have had a beautiful day today and a great many people out here. I am enjoying myself as much as ever. The drilling begins to show now & the men look very well. They are remarkably well disciplined for the short time we have been here.

Lieut. Col. Andrews visited the Guard tents last night or rather this morning at 1 o'cl. & was at Roll Call again at 4 3/4 A.M. He keeps one eye open all the time, I believe.

I will write soon again. The report today is that this Regiment will be the 4th & not the 2d to go, but no one knows anything about it. If I go to Washington I shall see you soon. I will answer Susie's letter before long.

Your loving son,
Robert G. Shaw

P.S. Uncle William has been here & is to be Major of some regiment.[7] Tell Father I had heard of his trouble with Uncle George had been made up.[8] I mean Uncle William's. I know a good many men who have tried to get commissions in this regt. & failed & many more who have tried for the army with the same result & here I have both.

1. France and Germany already had conscription laws. The Civil War saw the first draft laws in American history. On Apr. 16, 1862, the Confederacy authorized a draft of all men ages eighteen to thirty-five to serve a three-year hitch; the Union passed a draft law in March 1863 for men from twenty to forty-five years old. James M. McPherson, *Battle Cry of Freedom: The Civil War Era* (New York: Oxford University Press, 1988), pp. 430–31, 600–605.

2. Twice as many men died of disease during the war than were killed in battle. Ibid., pp. 485–86.

3. Miss Felton is unidentified. Charles Russell Lowell was nephew of the famous poet and abolitionist James Russell Lowell.

4. Senator Charles Sumner.

5. Shaw's first cousin Annie Russell Agassiz. John Murray Forbes (1813–98) and Sarah Swain Hathaway Forbes married in 1834 and settled in Milton, Massachusetts. One of the richest men in Massachusetts, worth $300,000 in 1852, Forbes made his money as a partner in the Boston-China trading operations of Russell and Company, before purchasing and building railroads and manufacturing iron. In 1859, Forbes had a most interesting visitor to his Milton home, whom he described: "Captain [John] Brown was a grim, farmer-like looking man, with a long gray beard and glittering, gray blue eyes which seemed to me to have a little touch of insanity about them." Forbes did not help finance Brown's raid on Harper's Ferry. He described himself as "not good enough to be an abolitionist. . . . I am essentially a conservative . . . and have been anti-slavery more because Slavery is anti-republican, anti-peace, anti-material progress, anti-civilization than upon the higher and purer ground that it is wicked and unjust to the slave! I have no special love for the African any more than for the low-class Irish, but don't want to see either imposed upon." During the Civil War, Governor John Andrew depended on Forbes to help keep the state on a war footing. Annie and Shaw were close friends with the Forbes's six children, especially Mollie, and twins Alice (1838–1929) and Ellen (1838–60). *Dictionary of American Biography*, vol. 3, pp. 506–8; Abner Forbes and J. W. Greene, *The Rich Men of Massachusetts* (Boston: Fetridge, 1852), p. 188;

Hughes, *John Murray Forbes*, vol. 1, pp. 110, 185, Forbes quote from p. 18; second Forbes quote in Edith E. Ware, *Political Opinion in Massachusetts During the Civil War and Reconstruction* (New York: Columbia University Press, 1916), p. 107; Smith, *Beacon Hill's*, pp. 415–16; Crawford, *Famous Families*, pp. 297–303.

6. Forbes used his wealth and influence to aid the Northern war effort. Perhaps his most spectacular assignment for the Department of the Navy was his

1863 trip to England to try to purchase the infamous "Laird rams" being built for the Confederacy. *DAB*, vol. 3, p. 507.

7. William Batchelder Greene commanded the Fourteenth Massachusetts Infantry, then the First Massachusetts Heavy Artillery before resigning on October 11, 1862. *National Cyclopedia*, vol. 7, p. 526.

8. George Robert Russell of West Roxbury.

Camp Andrew   [RGS]
June 16, 1861
Dearest Mother,

I meant to have written you a long letter to-day, but we have been almost as busy as on week-days, for we had a grand inspection of arms and quarters and everything else. After dinner I was so tired I had to take a nap, and then went to church. Effie came down in the afternoon, and stayed to see evening parade. We hear now that we shall not go this week, but I place no reliance on the reports we hear. I have thought a great deal about poor Winthrop.[1] I think that, if he had expected it, he would not have been sorry, excepting for the sake of his family. Some remarks I heard him make in Washington led me to think so. I find that thinking continually of the possibility of getting hit accustoms one so to the idea, that it doesn't seem so bad, after all. I was very much obliged for the books, writing-case, &c., which you sent, and am very glad you thought of the lock of your hair.

I have a pretty good chance to be promoted before we leave, as some of the officers above me are ill. Colonel Gordon has taken occasion several times to say he hoped I should stay, and told me not to decide in a hurry, as there was plenty of time.[2] Give my love to all, and thank Sue for the writing-case. Friday is Class-Day, and I shall try to get over to Cambridge with Effie, and Mollie Forbes.[3]

Your loving son,
Robert G. Shaw

1. Theodore Winthrop was the first of Shaw's friends to be killed in the war.

Winthrop graduated from Yale in 1848, became a writer and lawyer in New

York, and campaigned for Frémont in 1856. Theodore's June 7, 1861, *Atlantic Monthly* article is the best primary source for details on the departure of the Seventh New York Militia and its "adventure" to save the capital. Three days after his article appeared, in which he had declared of the march down Broadway: "It was worth a life that march," Theodore Winthrop was killed at the Battle of Big Bethel. *Atlantic*

Monthly 7 (June 1861): 745, 8 (Aug. 1861): 242–51; Theodore Winthrop file, CMSR.

2. Shaw's father had been trying to obtain a higher commission for his son. RGS to FGS, June 14, 1861, RGS Collection, Houghton Library, Harvard University.

3. Mollie Forbes, daughter of Sarah and John Murray Forbes.

CHAPTER 3

"John Brown's prison"

For many Americans of Shaw's era and for some later historians, the Civil War started not in Charleston Harbor on April 12, 1861, but in the Virginia river town of Harper's Ferry on October 16, 1859. At Harper's Ferry, an unremarkable place except for the U.S. Arsenal located there, John Brown led an "army" of twenty-one liberators on a plan to seize the arsenal and distribute the weapons to black Virginians. This slave army would roar through the South killing slaveholders, freeing humans from bondage, and growing larger with new recruits from the plantations. Brown envisioned an atonement of the nation's sins as Jehovah used him, a new Joshua, to slay the sinners and free the innocent. Brown's plan failed, but his effort increased tensions between the sections as Southern fears of slave rebellions soared and Northern voices to end slavery grew to fever pitch.

Shaw's circle of friends led those who supported Brown. Unitarian leader Theodore Parker christened Brown "a saint"; Lydia Maria Child's open letters to Brown and Virginia governor Henry Wise escalated the verbal war; Ralph Waldo Emerson claimed that Brown made "the gallows as glorious as the cross." In 1861, the Second Massachusetts Infantry camped at Harper's Ferry. Lieutenant Shaw visited the engine house where Brown made his last stand and ultimately surrendered to U.S. Army colonel Robert E. Lee. Shaw also toured the jail cell in Charlestown that confined Brown until the gallows swung his body into martyrdom. Obviously inspired by what he saw, Shaw wrote home that the government should "call on all the blacks in the country to come and enlist in our army!"

While Shaw reckoned with the ghost of John Brown and the reasons Northern soldiers marched upon Southern soils, the first major battle of the war was being fought at Manassas Junction on the banks of a stream called Bull Run. Forty miles south of Harper's Ferry, the armies of Joseph E. Johnston and Pierre Gustave Toutant Beauregard met those of Irvin McDowell in a fight that many thought would end the war. The Southern victory sent panic throughout Washington and brought the realization that the conflict would be a long one. Lincoln replaced McDowell with George Brinton McClellan.

Shaw wished that he had been in the battle but for the time being he suffered from a "wound" that for many soldiers proved more fatal than bullets—dysentery.

Martinsburg, Va.   [HL]
July 13, 1861
My dear Mother,

We arrived here last night some time before dark and we encamped just outside the town towards the South East. There are camps on every side of us and on every side of the city. About 25000 men in all, they say, but I don't know how near the truth the estimate is.

We landed at Elizabethport Tuesday evening after seeing you all on board the Flora passing Staten Island, and came on as far as Hagerstown by rail. I was very glad we saw each other as our boat passed you in the Kills. You saw me on the paddle-box didn't you?[1]

I had a pretty comfortable time the first night in the cars as I slept in a baggage car on some straw and didn't wake up at all—but the next day & night I was on guard and had to keep awake to look out for the prisoners. It was very hard keeping my eyes open as I couldn't walk about. If I hadn't been afraid of falling off the platform I should have gone to sleep in spite of myself.

We got out of the cars just in front of the town & marched in at 5 A.M. There we were quartered in three churches and started off again for the Potomac at 3 1/2 P.M. The people in Hagerstown seem very loyal now because a Connecticut regiment is quartered there, but we were told that a little while ago there were a good many secessionists among them. All through Pennsylvania everyone was glad to see us & at the last place, near the border, we were furnished with bread at midnight by some people who brought it to the cars.

From Hagerstown we marched 6 miles to Williamsport on the Potomac and pitched our tents close to the river. The next morning we forded the river about 7 o'clock and started for Martinsburg which is about 13 miles. The Officers had an easy time of it but the men's accoutrements are so heavy that a good many had to give up and be taken into the wagons.[2] Fortunately it was quite cool and pleasant.

It was a very pretty sight to see the men & baggage trains fording the river. We passed a place where there had been a little battle between the Pennsylvanians under Patterson and Johnson's men and rested in a grove where the latter had been encamped for a good while.[3] We saw nothing of the enemy though they say here that some of them were supposed to be about. In one of the houses on the road I saw an empty box addressed to Genl Johnson, & another one marked "Candles Newton, Mass." both of which were found in his camp.[4] The people were very friendly but had hardly anything to eat because the troops passing through had bought or taken everything. We saw very few negroes & the crops looked pretty good—i.e. the wheat. Martinsburg is in the blue ridge and the country is beautiful and very healthy. They thought we were regulars as we came through this town because the men had their knapsacks on & the uniform is very similar.

The difference in discipline between our men & most of the others here is remarkable. They seem to do just as they please & go about wherever they want to.

I was very glad indeed I saw you all in New York as you looked so healthy & strong. I hope you don't lie awake much dear Mother thinking of me, & that you will try not to be ill again. I know the parting is harder for those who stay at home than for us, for we have so much to do that we can't think long of anything but our [work]. If you send a photograph of me to Mrs. Haggerty, as you said, why don't you send one of the old ones instead of one in uniform as the latter looked all boiled out?[5]

They say the Rebels are not very far from us, but are still retreating. Genl McClellan is said to have captured Gov. Wise & his men, owing to one third of the latter's troops having refused to fight.[6] It is impossible to know the truth of the rumours we hear. We may move forward shortly, but can't tell. I will let you know of our movements. I suppose a letter addressed to this Regt (2d Mass.), Genl Patterson's division, Martinsburg, Va. will reach me. I hope so at any rate as I want to hear from you. Best love to Father & all.

Always your loving son,
Robert G. Shaw

Please tell Mr. and Mrs. Gay I was very sorry not to have seen them in New

York.[7] Provisions are very scarce and are brought from Pennsylvania for our troops I believe.

1. "Kills" are channels of water; in this case, the streams around Staten Island. On Aug. 9, 1861, Josephine Shaw wrote into her diary: "Our last sight of Rob was from the *Flora*, he was standing on the paddlebox of the *Kill van Kull* waving his handkerchief to us." William R. Stewart, *The Philanthropic Work of Josephine Shaw Lowell* (New York: Macmillan, 1911), p. 14.

2. Officers had supply wagons and servants to transport their necessities; enlisted men carried what they could.

3. Robert Patterson (1792–1881) and Joseph Eggleston Johnston (1807–91). Patterson was a banker and owner of thirty cotton mills in Pennsylvania and a sugar plantation in Louisiana. He also loved the uniform, taking to it in the War of 1812, the Mexican War, and the Civil War. Johnston was a career soldier who graduated from West Point in 1829 and held rank as a brigadier general when the Civil War began. Johnston resigned his commission and accepted a like post in the Confederate army on May 14, 1861. On July 2 and 3, 1861, Brig. Gen. Robert Patterson chased Johnston through Martinsburg and won a small skirmish at Falling Waters. Johnston would redeem this defeat by slipping away from Patter-son to join in the Confederate victory at the battle of First Manassas on July 21. E. B. Long, *The Civil War Day By Day: An Almanac, 1861–1865* (New York: Da Capo, 1971), pp. 90, 97–99; Faust, *Encyclopedia*, pp. 400, 562.

4. Probably from the molds of Edmund Jackson, who manufactured soap and candles in Newton.

5. Mrs. Ogden Haggerty of Lenox, Massachusetts, and New York City.

6. Gen. George Brinton McClellan (1826–85) graduated from West Point in 1846 and participated in the Mexican War. In 1857, he resigned from the army and worked as an engineer on Ohio railroad projects. After Fort Sumter, McClellan offered his services and was appointed major general, Department of the Ohio. Virginian Henry Alexander Wise (1806–76) served in the U.S. Congress (1833–44), as U.S. minister to Brazil (1844–47), and as governor of Virginia (1856–60). On July 11–13, 1861, McClellan won instant fame with victories in western Virginia at Rich Mountain and Corrick's Ford; but he did not capture Brig. Gen. Wise. Long, *Civil War Day By Day*, pp. 93–94; Faust, *Encyclopedia*, pp. 185, 456, 633, 839.

7. Sydney and Elizabeth Gay.

Charlestown, Va.   [HL]

July 18, 1861

Dear Mother,

We left Martinsburg the day after I wrote to you and got as far as Bunker Hill where we stayed that night and the next day.

Yesterday we started, as we thought, for Winchester, but came here. We have just had orders to cook two days rations & march again leaving our luggage here. I haven't the slightest idea where we are going to.

We expected a fight at Bunker Hill but the last of the enemy left 20 minutes before we arrived.[1] The country is very beautiful—covered with open woods. McClellan as you know has been very successful & we may be going to join him or we may be going to Harper's Ferry. I saw John Brown's prison this morning & the place where he was executed.[2] The slaves here seem well cared for but they are evidently glad to see us.

Major Doubleday is with this army & I was introduced to him.[3] He said he knew George & that he had a great respect for him.[4] 60 of his men were in Fort Sumter. Chas Goddard is his Company Surgeon.[5]

I will write again as soon as I can.

Ever your loving son,
Robert G. Shaw

1. On July 15 Patterson's men skirmished with Confederate cavalry at Bunker Hill, but the fight was so small it went unnoticed by many in the division, including Shaw. Long, *Civil War Day By Day*, p. 95.

2. John Brown (1800–59), militant abolitionist and leader among Kansas free-soilers, became a martyr to Northern abolitionists and a trigger for the Civil War. Brown was tried in Charlestown, held in jail from Oct. 18 to Dec. 2, 1859, then hanged for crimes against the state of Virginia. Stephen B. Oates, *To Purge This Land With Blood: A Biography of John Brown* (New York: Harper & Row, 1970), pp. 307–52.

3. Abner Doubleday (1819–93), a career soldier, graduated from West Point in 1842. He fired the first shot in defense of Fort Sumter on Apr. 12, 1861. Doubleday is best known for founding the American game of baseball. Faust, *Encyclopedia*, p. 224.

4. George William Curtis.

5. Charles Goddard is unidentified.

Harper's Ferry   [HL]
July 21, 1861
Dear Mother,

You have probably received my former letters but we haven't had the good fortune to receive a single mail.

We left Charlestown the day I wrote to you from there & our regiment came alone to Harper's Ferry & took possession. You know what a beautiful place it is and our tents are pitched among the trees around the house of the Superin[ten]dent of the Armory. We look right down upon the Shenandoah river and altogether it is the prettiest encampment we have had. The U.S. Works are all in ruins; but they were destroyed here by our troops while at Martinsburg the rebels did the business. There we saw 55 of the largest sized locomotives burned so as to be useless and all set up in a row and a beautiful bridge destroyed too.[1]

Yesterday I went on a foraging expedition with the Quartermaster taking 25 or 30 men for guard.[2] We squeezed a man who had secession proclivities & got two excellent horses at our own price & gave him a draft on the government.[3] While the Qtmaster went with 3 wagons to look for corn, Lt. Bangs & I took 3 others to the house of a Mr. Lucas former member of Congress & now with the rebels at Winchester.[4] We loaded our wagons with hay & the delighted darkies treated all our 25 men to pork & hoe cake while Bangs & I went up to the big house to get our dinner. There were only two black women there & they gave us a good luncheon. When the Qtermaster came up we took 4 great draught horses out of a cart they were drawing & 4 lighter ones from a drove in the pasture. We then got into the windows of the main house which was locked up & searched every where for arms &c. The only articles of interest we found were a pair of Miss Virginia Lucas' boots & some wine (not good at all) so we left with our train for the house of another rich secesher. When we got back Col. Gordon made the Quartermaster return all Lucas' horses because the owner had not been there to receive drafts for them. One was a beautiful little mare which the darkeys told us was the aforesaid Miss Virginia's own saddle horse. I was opposed to taking her (the mare) but the Qmstr said he must have her for himself.

There are a great many fine places between here & Charlestown but the houses generally seem shabby inside. All these gentlemen seem to breed a great many fine horses. We opened some papers which we thought might have useful information & one proved to be a letter from Virginia to her brother in which she constantly alluded to the Goths thereby meaning our humble selves.[5] I wonder what she would have called us if she could have seen us stamping round her house which they left two days before & eating & smoking pipes on the front piazza. The women said she was very fine-looking and as good as anyone that had slaves. She certainly wears small boots. The men were perfectly delighted with our proceedings & said they wished we would take all the horses & all the crops & asked if anyone would prevent them from running away. We told them a secessionist's slaves could go where they pleased without hindrance from Northern armies. There was an old Scotch overseer who looked as if he would like to cut all our throats but he managed to be very polite and humble.[6]

We were out all day & I never had a better time in my life, especially as we (the officers) were on horseback & galloped about to our hearts' content. Some of our wagon horses go finely under the saddle. Coming back half the men were mounted but having neither saddles nor bridles they didn't make much of a show.

I was going to write some more but am ordered out to dress with the Company so goodbye & much love to all. I long to hear whether you are all well. Our fight at Bunker Hill was so small that I didn't know anything of it until I saw the New York Tribune.[7]

Ever your loving son,
Robert G. Shaw

1. Joseph E. Johnston's Confederates destroyed the trains as they retreated through Martinsburg on June 15. Long, *Civil War Day By Day*, p. 85.

2. Robert Morris Copeland (1830–74) joined the Second Massachusetts as quartermaster and first lieutenant on May 28, 1861. Copeland took with him a private servant, J. D. Francis—described in army records as "Black, 5' 6'"—for whom he got government subsistence. Copeland's pay voucher for the two month period, July 1–Aug. 31, 1861, reveals the difference in a first lieutenant's pay and that of an enlisted man, who made $13 a month plus $3.50 for clothing. For that period, Copeland received: pay $152.52, subsistence $93.00, forage $22.40, and clothing $5.00, for a total of $272.92. R. Morris Copeland file, CMSR.

3. Congress permitted commanders in the field to grant regimental quartermasters the authority to conscript provisions from civilians in order to maintain the necessary supplies for an army on the march. When supplies were seized in this manner, the quartermaster issued the previous owner a draft on the government—at the government's price.

4. First Lt. George P. Bangs. Virginia Democrat William Lucas (1800–77) served two terms in the U.S. House of Representatives (1839–41, 1843–45). *Record of Mass. Vols.*, p. 28; McGuiness and Sayers, *American Leaders*, p. 216.

5. The Goths were a Teutonic people who swept South from the area of the Baltic Sea, briefly allied with Attila, king of the Huns, and, later, under Theodoric, became rulers of Italy. Justinian overthrew the Goths in 555 A.D. The word "Goths" came to stand for all who were considered barbarians.

6. The Scottish overseer is unidentified.

7. *NYDT*, July 18 (5:5), 1861, reported that on Monday, July 15, Union troops at Bunker Hill had "a slight skirmish with a troop of Rebel Cavalry, routing them, arresting two."

July 23, 1861

Dear Mother,

Soon after my last to you, Genl Patterson moved up here with the whole army; so we had to leave our shady camp & pitch our tents in another field which is far from being so pleasant.

Today we have heard of the fight at Mannassas Gap & expect to be ordered away at any moment.[1]

We felt sheepish enough before at coming here out of Johnson's reach, instead of attacking him at Winchester, but feel worse now since we have heard that he had reinforced the Confederates at Mannassas & probably was the means of their gaining the day.[2]

It is true that 19 regiments here have served out their time & must be discharged so that Patterson could not have gone far into the interior, but it seems as if he might have tried Winchester, at least until the N.Y. & Phila papers came.

I hope there is as much exaggeration about Mannassas as there was about the fight at Bunker Hill of which we knew nothing.

No one has had letters from home yet & we suppose our mail has been detained.

I think the licking will do us good. All well.

Ever your afftc son

Robt G. Shaw

If we move today I will write as soon as I can.

1. The first major battle of the war, First Manassas (First Bull Run), took place on July 21 between the forces of Irvin McDowell and Confederates under P. G. T. Beauregard and Joseph Johnston. Even though casualties were relatively even, the Northern stampede back across the thirty miles to Washington gave the Rebels a victory and woke the nation to the reality that this would be no short contest.

2. Shaw means Joseph Eggleston Johnston. For the failure to hold Johnston in the Shenandoah Valley, Gen. Winfield Scott relieved Patterson of his command.

July 30, 1861

My dear Susie,

Mother says that you and Effie have written to me, but I have not yet received the letters. As you will have seen from what I have written Father and Mother, we are still in perfect ignorance as to where we are to be sent, and what we shall have to do. Hitherto we have been part of quite a large army, but now all the others have gone over the river; and we are very glad of it, for the discipline of our regiment has been very much hurt by contact with the three months' militiamen, who are allowed a great deal of liberty. However, it is the best regiment I have seen yet, and I hope we shall be able to continue as well as we have begun. We are now all in a lump in the only remaining building of the Arsenal and Armory,—the men on the ground-floor, and the officers just above them. The railroad bridge and as many as fifteen large buildings are burnt half down to the ground, and everything about the place looks as if a set of barbarians had been through here. We use the engine-house which John Brown took possession of, for a guard-house; and there are three or four loop-holes which he made to fire through, and marks of musket-balls on the walls inside.[1] It seems to be the worst place he could have chosen to defend against an attack; for when the doors are shut, it is like a brick box, as all the windows are high up, and his loop-holes are so small that they give no range at all to the men firing through them.

We have a parade as often as possible; and, as the band passes along, playing often the same airs it did at Camp Andrew, we imagine we can see the skirts and hats opposite us: but, alas! after the officers march up to salute the Colonel, the dream is dispelled, for nothing remains for us but to return to our quarters. And after supper,—which meal, like the others, has not been very palatable for some time,—we have a little music, and get very glum talking about the evenings at Brook Farm, when we had some partners to dance with and talk to. For my part, though, I still enjoy myself and feel well, but wish we could have a chance to do something. The excitement which used to be occasioned by a report that the enemy was near has entirely disappeared now. We have slept on the bare ground for several nights, and, if it hadn't been for India-rubber blankets, I believe we should all have suffered a good deal from the dampness, and the men would probably have been ill. I hope I shall get your letters soon, as I have received all Mother's and Father's. I wish I had something interesting to write you; perhaps I shall, if the Secessionists come to this place again. We hear nothing of them yet, though we have had a good many reports, which have proved to be false. Love to Anna, George, and Frankie. I wish you would send me the small photographs of all the family, which are in my room; and, if there are any missing, please make me a present of them, if you have them. I wrote Mother a short note this morning, when I thought I shouldn't have time to write any more.

Your loving brother,
Robert G. Shaw

1. Brown, with seven followers and eleven prisoners, made his last stand in the engine house at Harper's Ferry. Oates, *Purge*, pp. 295–300.

Washington County, Maryland   [RGS, HL]
July 31, 1861
My dear Effie,

Both your letters have reached me safely; the first came from Martinsburg to-day, and the other I received yesterday. As you will perceive from the date, we have left Harper's Ferry, and are now encamped on the hills just opposite our former place. I wrote to Mother and Susie day before yesterday, and dated the letters 30th instead of 29th. I had just closed them, when our company got orders to cross the river, to join some artillery which was to be posted in the woods on this side. So we gathered our traps together, and waded across. About two hours after, six other companies came, and we all pitched our tents here. Harry's company was left in the Arsenal at Harper's Ferry, so I can't give him your message for the present.[1] They are to look out for, and give warning of, any advance of the enemy. Having learnt by experience that, at every change of camp, there comes a temporary cessation of officers' meals, I put my man on guard in a little house we found, as soon as we got over, at the same time engaging board there for four. The man kept all the other servants out; and the consequence is, that our mess (Greely Curtis, Morse, Robeson, and I) take our meals and siestas in a Christian and reasonable manner, while the rest dine in the woods, and, at first, had nothing at all.[2] It may seem stingy to keep every one else out, but, at Bunker's Hill, we fasted all day because we didn't take the precaution to put a guard over our dinner. The camp servants are an unscrupulous set of rascals, and swear that everything they can lay hands on was ordered, long before, for their masters. Our landlady's name is Mrs. Buckle, and her cooking is an improvement on that of our servants, who happen to be very deficient in that line.[3] Mudge has been ill a good deal of the time since we left, so I have had command of the company, which is a great deal better for me than being Lieutenant.[4] Your letter of the 21st would have amused a Secessionist a good deal, as it was written when you thought we had gained the day at Bull Run; and everything you said, if applied to the other side, would be perfectly [continued from HL fragment] correct, but, under the present circumstances, reads wrong.

I am sorry to say I have seen very little of Harry lately as since my change to Company F our tents are far apart. Greely Curtis and Charles Morse, I see a great deal of & I like them both more & more every day. Our two companies have been sent off on picket guard & other duty several times together; so we have been thrown into company a great deal besides being close together in line. Choate & Bangs & Cary, Motley, Higginson, Mudge, Robeson, Savage & indeed all the officers in the Regt. excepting one scalliwag, from Salem named Hill are real nice fellows & some of them very superior men, in my opinion.[5]

I am very glad indeed to hear that Mother is so well and hope I shan't ever get any other account of her while I am away. Please tell her I have received all her letters, the last one (July 28) yesterday. It is very fortunate you mentioned the quarter orange mark on her ankle, as I may stay away so long that on my [return] I shan't recognize her, and, in that case, she will only have to take off her stocking to prove her identity. "Then you are my long lost Mother &c."

If you see Miss Higginson again please tell her that her brother is in good health.[6] I believe it was Father though, who wrote me that she had not heard from her brother since we left N.Y., & not you.

Miss Virginia Lucas is 22 & very pretty.[7] I didn't forget to inquire into particulars. I saw Mrs. Lewis Washington yesterday, a very large, red faced woman, who was probably handsome once.[8] Our horses have been feeding on her or rather his hay for some time past.

There is a nice old fellow living close to our camp who reminds me of cousin John Forbes. He got acquainted with John Brown when the latter first came here under pretense of settling, and they became great friends. When he heard of the fight over at the Ferry, he went across to find out about it, & was perfectly astonished to find that his friend (whose name here was Smith) was the leader of it.[9] He says he has seldom known such an intelligent man. Give my best love to all. Anna & George & Frankie. I am glad the baby has a jointless thumb.

Ever dear Effie, Your loving Brother

1. First Lt. Henry Sturgis Russell, second in command of Company G, Second Massachusetts Infantry. Bowen, *Massachusetts in the War*, p. 114.

2. Captain Greely Stevenson Curtis of Boston, First Lt. Charles Fessenden

Morse (1839–1926) of Roxbury, and Second Lt. Thomas Rodman Robeson (1840–63) of New Bedford. Shaw knew Morse and Robeson at Harvard. According to Charles Morse, the mess also included Capt. Charles R. Mudge (1839–63) of New York City. *Record of Mass. Vols.*, p. 28; Charles F. Morse, *Letters Written During the Civil War, 1861–1865* (Boston: Privately printed, 1898), p. 12.

3. Mrs. Buckle is unidentified. Charles Morse wrote home on July 31 that Shaw had arranged for rooms and meals with Mrs. Buckle in a "very neat little farmhouse quite near our camp." On the first night, Mrs. Buckle's dinner for the group included tea, broiled chicken, applesauce, bread, and molasses. Morse wrote that the meal was so good, they had been living and eating there ever since. Morse, *Letters*, p. 13.

4. Charles Redington Mudge was a Harvard classmate and close friend of Shaw's in the Hasty Pudding, Glee, and rowing clubs. In the spring of 1861, he quit his job at Victoria Mills, New York, to join the Second Massachusetts as a first lieutenant on May 25, 1861. Mudge

gained promotion to captain on July 8, 1861. Higginson, *Harvard Memorial Biographies*, vol. 2, pp. 142–52; Harvard College, *Class of 1860*, p. 34.

5. Second Lt. Rufus Choate (1834–66), First Lt. George P. Bangs, Capt. Richard D. Cary (1836–62), First Lt. T. Lawrence Motley (1834–?), First Lt. Henry Lee Higginson (1834–1919), and Capt. James Savage, Jr. (1832–62). "Scalliwag" Edwin R. Hill (1827–?) was mustered in as a first lieutenant on May 28, 1861. He resigned on Nov. 29, 1861. *Record of Mass. Vols.*, pp. 28, 29.

6. Mary Lee Higginson (1838–?), sister of Henry Lee Higginson. Crawford, *Famous Families*, vol. 1, p. 265.

7. Ten days before he wrote this letter, Shaw had "explored" Miss Lucas's belongings. See letter of July 21, 1861, included herein.

8. Mrs. Lewis Washington is unidentified.

9. John Brown arrived in Harper's Ferry on July 3, 1859, to familiarize himself with the town's layout. He took the alias "Isaac Smith" and the cover of a New York cattle buyer. Oates, *Purge*, pp. 275, 298.

Maryland Heights [RGS]
Aug. 6, 1861
Dear Mr. Gay:[1]

Mr. McDaniel went away from here to-day, and I meant to have given him a great many messages for you, but his sudden departure prevented [it]; so I thought I would write you a note.[2] I was sorry not to see you in New York when we went through there. Mr. McD. may tell you that our regiment is in a very discontented state, for he told me and other officers that he heard that such was the case. It is true that our men have been made rather sulky by conversation with other volunteer regiments, who tell them "they would be d——-d if they would submit to the discipline" we have been trying to keep up since we came here; and at one time we had very bad rations, which made them complain very much. It is just as hard to keep one regiment under strict discipline, among a number of undisciplined ones, as it is for a man not to be corrupted by bad company. We are entirely satisfied with the men so far, though, and I hope the report Mr. McD. spoke of, will not spread without a better foundation to stand on. What makes me say so much of this is, the fear that it may get to the ears of our friends, and make them uneasy. I must say I shouldn't blame the men if they did make a row about their pay; for we have been in the United States service for nearly three months, and haven't touched anything yet. Please give my best love to Mrs. Gay and the children, and remember me to Mr. Dana.[3] I am sorry I can't go down there with you this summer, as I expected. I am more fortunate than a good many others, though, for, besides doing my duty, I am having a good time. Isn't it extraordinary that the Government won't make use of the instrument that would finish the war sooner than anything else,—viz. the slaves? I have no doubt they could give more information about the enemy than any one else, and that there would be nothing easier than to have a line of spies right into their camp. What a lick it would be at them, to call on all the blacks in the country to come and enlist in our army! They would probably make a fine army after a little drill, and could certainly be kept under better discipline than our independent Yankees. General Banks is reported to have said that this must be a war of extermination, or that we shall have to make an inglorious peace.[4] It does not seem as if it need be so, if the Government would only make use of all its opportunities.

This is an answer to the note you wrote me at Washington when I was in the Seventh.

With much affection,
Yours truly,
Robert G. Shaw

1. Sydney Howard Gay of Staten Island.
2. Perhaps this is lawyer William V. McDaniel of 8 Pine Street, New York City. *Trow's NYC Directory, 1863*, p. 546.
3. Charles Anderson Dana (1819–97) had been associated with the Shaws at Brook Farm. A reformer, Mr. Dana was managing editor of Horace Greeley's

New York Daily Tribune. DAB, vol. 3, pp. 49–51; F. B. Sanborn, *Recollections of Seventy Years* (Boston: Gorham Press, 1909), vol. 2, p. 325; Boatner, *Dictionary*, p. 221.
4. Nathaniel Prentiss Banks (1816– 94) of Massachusetts, one of the Union's prominent political generals, had been a U.S. Representative (1853–57), Speaker

of the House (1856), and governor
of Massachusetts (1858–61). Lincoln

appointed Banks a major general on
May 16, 1861. Faust, *Encyclopedia*, p. 38.

Maryland Heights
Aug. 8, 1861
Dear Mother,

I am afraid you have been longer without hearing from me than usual, for I hardly think my letter of 6th inst. got to the mail soon enough. As you say, it is very bad for us all to sleep on the bare ground, but I think our India-rubber and woollen blankets prevent us from feeling the bad effects of it. Now we are under huts made of branches, which are a complete protection from dew and night-air, but don't keep out the rain much. We have had two thunder-showers since our tents were sent off, and had to wrap everything up in India-rubber, put on our coats, and wait patiently for it to pass over.

Everything was taken away, because we are the outposts of the army, and are not to be encumbered with luggage. We hear that General McClellan will make a great change in the army.[1] I hope he will, for, from the little I have seen, I think it needs it sadly.

The other day I was sent down with my company to guard the ferry and ford, over the Potomac. While there, the Fifth Connecticut came in, and a great many of the men wandered off and got drunk.[2] Some of their officers were really not ashamed to ask me to send their own men to their quarters, and to lock the unruly ones up in our guard-house! In fact, before long, the whole management of the regiment seemed to devolve upon us, and one of our sergeants broke his knuckles knocking men down, and had his arm in a sling several days after. If officers are to have no more command over their men than these gentlemen did, we might as well be without them. The same night, I had a nice ride with some United States cavalry. About seventy of them were going up the river, and a company of Indiana men, about a mile above us, would not let them go by, saying their orders were to allow no one to pass. It was very important they should get out, so the officer in command wanted me to go up with him, and talk to the Indiana captain, and he furnished me with a horse for the purpose. All the way up and back, I wished I could always be on horseback, instead of trotting about on my own legs. After a good deal of blarney, the Indiana man agreed to let him through, and we rode back to my station, where we had left the detachment. It was then after midnight, and the officer told me he had started from his camp, two miles back, just after dusk, and had been talking and reasoning with sentinels ever since! You can see from this how carelessly orders are given, when our own men can't get out for picket duty. But everything seems to be getting straightened under Banks, and since the three months' men have gone.

Mr. Copeland (Quartermaster) told me he had had a long talk with General Banks about making use of the negroes against the Secessionists. I thought it was a waste of breath, but we hear to-day that Banks has offered him a place on his staff, which shows that he thinks a good deal of his opinion.[3] Copeland's sole subject of thought, now, seems to be slavery, and he is always fuming and raging about it.

Your loving son,
Robert G. Shaw

P.S. I am ashamed to have so many of my photographs "toted" about.

1. McClellan's victory at Rich Mountain on July 13 combined with McDowell's loss at First Bull Run on July 21 led Lincoln to replace McDowell with McClellan as commander of the Union's main army in the East, which would soon be named the Army of the Potomac. McPherson, *Battle Cry*, p. 348.

2. Organized at Hartford on July 26, 1861, the Fifth Connecticut Infantry was assigned to George H. Thomas's Brigade, Banks's Division, Army of the Shenandoah. Dyer, *Compendium*, vol. 1, p. 114.

3. Robert Morris Copeland of Roxbury, Massachusetts, graduated from Harvard in 1851 and joined the Second Massachusetts at its organization in May 1861. Copeland became dedicated to the cause of using blacks as soldiers. He joined Banks's staff as an aide-de-camp even before the reassignment became official on Oct. 15. One month later, Banks promoted him to major and assistant adjutant general. Copeland file, CMSR; "Descriptive Book. Companies E-K," Records of the Adjutant General's Office, Record Group 94, Bound Record Books, Second Massachusetts Infantry; *Record of Mass. Vols.*, p. 28; Brown, *Harvard University in the War*, p. 49.

Maryland Heights   [RGS]
Aug. 10, 1861
Dear Father,

Since I last wrote, I have been suffering under a slight attack of dysentery, and am staying at a house near our bivouac. I attribute it to having caught cold one night, when I was off on guard at some distance from here, and, my man having forgot my blankets, I fell asleep with nothing over me. Though I am afraid Mother will be apt to think I am seriously ill, I think you will both be better pleased to have me tell you, when anything is the matter with me, than to have me say nothing about it. This time it is really nothing serious, and I am much better than I was yesterday. Several of our officers have been laid up with this, since we came here. I have just received yours of 9th inst. I will send you at least a line or two every day until I am well. Love to all.

Your loving son,
Robert G. Shaw

Maryland Heights [RGS]
Aug. 13, 1861
Dear Father,

I have nothing to write you to-day, excepting that I am getting better. I shall stay in the house until I get entirely well, and, with a little care, I think I shall escape it in [the] future. One of our officers has been laid up with it, ever since we left Martinsburg, but has just returned to duty.

We are all very much disgusted at the law lately passed, which provides that vacancies among volunteer officers shall be filled by an election in the company.[1] The very reason that, in most volunteer regiments, the officers have so little control over their men, is because they owe their places to them. It upsets the line of promotion with us entirely, and I believe that, in the end, it will be found to be a mistake. If every officer, so elected, were obliged by law to pass an examination, then it would do well enough, but they are not. If the captain of a company is killed, they can vote a private into his place, and he needn't be examined, unless some one reports to the Board that it is necessary.

There was some expectation of an attack last night, but morning came without anything unusual having occurred. I don't believe they will ever make one, unless they have a good chance of getting and holding Baltimore.

Every one seems impressed with General Banks' ability. The last eight days have been very stupid for me, as I lie on the bed all day, and have absolutely nothing to do. There are no books to be had here. Love to Mother.

Your loving son,
Robert G. Shaw

1. It was commonly believed that volunteer units selected their own lieutenants and captains, who in turn selected the majors, lieutenant colonel, and colonel; this rarely happened. Usually, when a governor authorized the raising of a regiment, the man responsible for recruiting became the unit's colonel, and the recruiters selected by him became the officers. Advertisements,

which tried to induce men to enlist, most often named the new unit being formed, its colonel, and officers. In May, Congress had given governors the authority to name officers. On Aug. 3, 1861, the War Department ordered that when vacancies opened in volunteer units "an election shall be called by the colonel of the regiment to fill such vacancies; and the men of each company shall vote in their respective companies for all officers as high as captain." Challenging that order, Governor Andrew queried Senators Charles Sumner and Henry Wilson on Aug. 3, 1861: "Can it be intended by Congress, that volunteers in the field shall fill vacancies by election? Where is to be the source of discipline, when every candidate is seeking personal favor from the men?" War Department General Orders No. 15 and 49, May 4 and August 3, 1861, *OR*, III: 152–54, 383; Bell I. Wiley, *The Life of Billy Yank: The Common Soldier of the Union* (Baton Rouge: Louisiana State University Press, 1952), p. 24; Andrew quoted from Schouler, *Mass. in the Rebellion*, vol. 1, pp. 226–27.

Maryland Heights [RGS]
Aug. 15, 1861
My dear Sue,

Yours of 1st August came a good while ago, as I suppose Father has told you. For the last ten days I have been laid up, and have had a pretty stupid time. The house I have been staying at is built of logs, has two rooms on the ground-floor, and (I suppose) one up-stairs, and is inhabited by a Mrs. Buckle, four children, a fat black woman, and myself and man. We two sleep in the dining-room, I on a bed, and he on the floor. Where the rest are stowed, I don't know; but, as I hear strange sounds overhead at night, and deep breathing and snorting, as of a fat pig, in the kitchen, I think Aunt Betty, the black woman, is in the latter uncomfortable hole, and the rest above. Six of our friends come down here to dinner every day, which rather breaks the monotony of my existence.[1] Two days of this week, some of them spent all their time here, as there was no drilling on account of rain. Mrs. B. is very neat and clean, and cooks me nice rice puddings, and Aunt Betty brings me flowers, and washes my clothes, for all of which I am very grateful, but still wish I could go back to the regiment, especially as I feel perfectly well, and, indeed, am so; but the Doctor says I had better lie perfectly quiet for a few days longer, and make sure of it.

From the hill which we are on, there is a very magnificent view across the river into Virginia, which is a most beautiful State, and the sunsets which we have here are really finer than ours. The last two days have been so cold as to make it very uncomfortable, and, when sitting still, we had to put on our overcoats. Up at the camp, they couldn't keep warm in the night, and I was chilly, though in the house. To-day the weather is beautiful,—neither warm nor cold. I myself have not suffered from the heat at all, and we have had no mosquitoes, or rather not enough to trouble us. I sent for the netting on account of the flies in this house, which trouble me very much.

Phil. Schuyler is fortunate in being in the regular service.[2] I see more clearly, every day, that the volunteer system is a perfectly rotten one, at least as it is organized in this country; and Congress, instead of trying to put the whole of us under real military regulations, makes us more and more militia-like.[3] They seem to be transformed into a set of muttonheads, as soon as they begin to legislate on military matters.

It makes me perfectly ashamed to have my photographs "toted" round as they are; and the idea of there being twenty-four in the house, and all Mother's friends having from four to six apiece, is rather strong. I shouldn't care, if they were all kept at home. Please tell Annie H., when you write, to tell her mother that I had nothing to do with sending them so many.[4] By the by, if you have, or know where to get, a photograph of the former, you might send it with the rest which are coming to me: of course I don't want you to get it from her. I don't want to hurt Mother's feelings by my remarks about the photographs, but some of the persons they are sent to can't care for them; and, as they of course don't want to say so, they have to take them whether they will or no.

Aunt Betty just sent her boy to the spring, and told him, if he dirtied his clothes, she would beat him. On his way back, he got into a quarrel with some other boys, soiled his clothes, and broke the jug; so he is now being pounded. Mrs. Buckle has seized the opportunity, under cover of the noise, to hammer her boy for some reason; and as the howling is too much for the head and nerves of a convalescent, I must stop.

Give my love to all the family. I shall write to Effie and Nellie soon. It must be good for Mother to go about as much as she does.

Your loving brother,
Robert G. Shaw

1. Mrs. Buckle had provided room and board for Shaw since late July. Aunt Betty is unidentified. See Shaw's letter of July 31.

2. Philip Schuyler (1836–1906), of an old New York family related to Alexander Hamilton, marched down Broadway in April as a fellow member with Shaw in Company F, Seventh New York Militia. Schuyler would become a brigadier general and, after the war, one of New York's leading philanthropists

and sportsmen. Philip Schuyler, Letters to his parents, 1863–64, NYHS; "Roll of Company 6, 7th Regiment NG," Major Philip Schuyler, Misc. MS., NYHS; *NYT*, Nov. 30 (3:1), 1906.

3. Reference to allowing volunteers to elect their officers.

4. Shaw's future bride, Annie Kneeland Haggerty of Lenox, Massachusetts, and New York City.

CHAPTER 4

"A regular old jog trot camp life"

After the First Battle of Bull Run, Northern armies in the Eastern Theater put more effort into training and discipline than into searching out and fighting Southern armies. George B. McClellan worked hard to transform raw recruits into competent soldiers. Lieutenant Shaw admired "Little Mac's" abilities and, in his letters home, assessed the worth of volunteers, officers, and men. Shaw eagerly compared himself and his regiment with any in the army. Worried about bragging rights, Shaw hoped that "the war will not end without a good, fair battle, as we should never hear the end of Bull Run."

As eastern armies drilled, the nation turned its attention to events beyond the Mississippi River. On August 10, in the West's first major battle, impetuous Brig. Gen. Nathaniel Lyon was killed and his army defeated at Wilson's Creek, Missouri. Northern morale suffered as Union armies lost the first two big battles of the war.

In the weeks that followed, Maj. Gen. John C. Frémont declared martial law in St. Louis and ordered the confiscation of the property of Missouri residents who fought against the Union. Further, Frémont proclaimed freedom for all slaves belonging to the insurrectionists. Shaw and his parents praised the general and hoped his emancipation order would "not be interfered with by the

Government." But Lincoln revoked the proclamation and later cashiered the general.

In Maryland, Lieutenant Shaw adapted to camp life and formed new friendships. He attended a church service with ten thousand soldiers and ten preachers. He found himself better suited to soldiering than to office work and wrote happily: "Isn't it a strange sort of life for us to be living who never expected to be anything but merchants & lawyers three months ago?" While Shaw enjoyed himself, his parents and sisters vacationed in fashionable northern watering holes. They provided comfort to Shaw with photographs, letters, and material accoutrements not provided by the U.S. Army or the state of Massachusetts. In his own evaluation, Shaw lived "a regular old jog trot camp life."

Camp near Darnestown   [HL, RGS]
Aug. 30, 1861
Dear Mother,
We started from Georgetown with our company, one from Col. Webster's Regt and one from the 2d Pennsylvania, at about eight o'cl. day before yesterday morning and made a march of about 18 miles halting at 3 o'cl. P.M.[1] We pitched our tents in a beautiful grove beside the road. Major Dwight of our Regt was in command and he rather astonished the Pennsylvanians & the 12th Mass. by gagging & tying them to trees whenever they were unruly.[2] Before we got back they began to behave more like soldiers than at first. That evening we took supper at the house of a gentleman who owns a large farm near there (Rockville, Md.). He seemed to be very well off and has never been farther from home than Alexandria, on one side and Hyattstown on the other. He lives in a place which belonged to his grandfather, has a very good library and seemed from his conversation to be a great reader, especially of history as he kept comparing circumstances in our war with those of Napoleon and the beginning of last century. He mentioned several instances of panic like that at Bull Run. All his clothes and those of his family were spun and made in his own house. He is an enthusiastic Union man and begged us to stop and see him if we ever came that way again.[3]

The next day (yesterday) we got away at 6 A.M. and at half past eight o'cl. after having marched eight miles we suddenly met the head of the Column moving down in the opposite direction. So we halted & waited for our regts which didn't come up until 3 P.M. owing to detention of wagons &c which couldn't get along as it was raining hard & the country is very hilly & roads slippery. We marched back a little way but soon turned off and came down here towards the Potomac which is a few miles from us now. Our company had their wagons, with tents, provisions, &c but all the others had to go supperless & sleep on the wet ground for the wagon train didn't get here until this morning.

Today I got yours and Father's letters of 22, 23d and 27th Aug. with several papers. I think some must have gone astray as I never have received any from Father speaking of the appointments of volunteer officers, though I did get two pamphlets containing the enactments of Congress on the subject & which set us right on some points about which we had been misinformed.

I saw a letter in the Tribune of 27 inst. from Mr. Olmsted speaking of the duties of captains and how seldom they were properly attended to.[4] Like everyone else who writes about it he pitched into the Captains but never said a word about the government having appointed 3000 officers without requiring them to pass any examination, and everyone of whom may be, for all the govt knows, as unfit for his place as the most ignorant private in the ranks. And as for moral character, I know that some men have commissions in the army who have kept gambling saloons, rum holes & other disreputable houses for years—men much worse than the Meads, whom Father ejected from the house in Boston opposite the Howard Athenaeum.[5] Certainly the Govt is to blame for such things for it is natural for a man to take a good position when it is offered & they often think themselves competent when they are not. As to our regiment, we are getting more & more pleased with it and taking everything into consideration the discipline is wonderful. Thank Heaven *we* weren't elected by our men—when men are all good perhaps it will do to make the army democratic but until then I am certain it is a great mistake. But in spite of the ridiculous, rotten volunteer system, the army in and about Washington has improved greatly. All the men are kept in camp and even officers are not allowed to go about without passes unless they can give good evidence of having some business to attend to. One of our sergeants who was taken by the patrol in town said he passed the night in the Guard house with two Captains.

It seems as if McClellan were doing wonders and the influence extends to our division too, for all the regiments have improved very much in respect of discipline. We are never troubled as formerly by stragglers from the regiments encamped near us.[6] Copeland, who is on Banks' staff, says he is a real genial, kind-hearted man, and always ready to do disagreeable work himself & spare his officers. They are all attached to him.[7]

You don't know how queer it is to see by your letters how much you think of the war, & the danger &c. When it hardly ever enters our heads to think of an enemy being near any more than it did at Camp Andrew. It doesn't even make us go out of our tents when we here [hear] cannon or musketry in the neighbourhood which often happens as they go out for practice. Harry & the others say the same of their letters. We get much more credit for being soldiers than we should think ourselves entitled to if our friends didn't think we were devoting ourselves. Harry is very much obliged to Father for

[manuscript pages missing; continued from RGS]

his kind offers. The gaiters I kept myself, as I hadn't sent for any others. Tell Effie I should like to have her write every week, if she will not expect immediate answers, and indeed, in that case, every day, but otherwise not so often. I am much obliged to Susie for the photograph of Annie and Clem.[8] It is an excellent one. When are the rest coming on? So Uncle Jim is going to live in New York at last! Oh! why didn't he do it before?[9] Please ask him to remember me kindly to Mr. Robbins as soon as he writes, and say I hope he will be successful out there. I don't believe he will like the East, this time, as much as he did, though he always wanted to go back.

The other evening, walking along Georgetown Heights, all the houses being open from top to bottom, I could hear the people inside, having a nice time round the tea-table, and I couldn't help wishing, for a while, to be inside our own house among you all; but, as much as I want to see you, dear Mother, it would really be hard to get me to go home until the war is over, or my term out. And it is the same with all our officers. It would be so hard to go away again! It was a great relief to us all to get away from New York, and through the last adieux.

Isn't it humiliating to have Russell's letter read all over England? I think, for my part, though, it agrees pretty well with all other accounts. I read the two articles from the "Star" and "News" which you sent. I have not seen the "Times." The latter has managed to change the friendly feeling that has existed between England and the United States the last few years.[10]

I meant to have written to George to-day, but I have to go on guard, so I shan't have time.[11] Give my best love to him and all the rest. It will soon be two months since we left Camp Andrew. The time passes very quickly. We hear nothing of what the Rebels are doing, but of course they must know something about it at head-quarters. Every one seems to think that the next great battle will be ours, and indeed the Government seems to have set to work in real earnest.

Ever your loving son,
Robert G. Shaw

1. Col. Fletcher Webster (1813–62), son of nineteen-year Massachusetts Senator and two-time U.S. secretary of state Daniel Webster (1782–1852), raised the Twelfth Massachusetts Infantry in Boston in Apr.–June 1861. Webster led the Twelfth to Harper's Ferry on July 27, then to Darnestown, where it remained until Dec. 1861. The Second Pennsylvania Reserves Infantry organized in Philadelphia in May 1861 and had been in Darnestown only one or two days at the time of this letter. *Harper's Weekly*, Aug. 3, 1861, pp. 4, 6; Higginson, *Harvard Memorial Biographies*, vol. 1, pp. 20–25; Dyer, *Compendium*, vol. 1, p. 158, vol. 3, p. 1577.

2. Wilder Dwight (1833–62) of Springfield, Massachusetts, educated at Phillips Exeter Academy and Harvard (1853), practiced law before the war in Cambridge. Dwight helped George Gordon raise the Second and gained a major's commission for it. He brought two civilian servants and three horses with him when he enlisted. "Massachusetts Infantry, 2nd Regiment. Letters from the Army: A Scrapbook," p. 58, BPL; Elizabeth Dwight, ed., *Life and Letters of Wilder Dwight, Lieut-Col, 2nd Mass Inf Vols* (Boston: Ticknor & Fields, 1868), pp. 1, 44; Wilder Dwight file, CMSR.

3. Wilder Dwight also wrote of this encounter, identifying Mr. Desellum as an "ardent Union lover." Dwight, *Life and Letters of Wilder Dwight*, p. 87.

4. Frederick Law Olmsted (1822–1903) lived on Staten Island. He gained fame as a landscape architect for his progressive planning of urban parks, especially Central Park in New York City in 1857. His article, "The Right Man in the Right Place," argued that captains need to know little of military knowledge or drill, but must be good administrators who attend to their men's food, clothing, and sanitary needs. *NYDT*, Aug. 27 (6:4–5), 1861; Leng and Davis, *Staten Island*, vol. 1, p. 252; Laura Wood Roper, "Frederick Law Olmsted in the 'Literary Republic,'" *Journal of American History* 39 (Dec. 1952): 461, 469.

5. The Meads are unidentified.

6. McClellan turned a gaggle of raw recruits into effective soldiers. He demanded discipline, did not tolerate stragglers, and tightened examination procedures for officers. Whatever the Army of the Potomac became later was due in part to McClellan's superb abilities as an organizer.

7. Not only the officers loved "Little Mac"; soldiers in the Union army cheered for McClellan as they would do for no other commander. They recognized that they owed their abilities as soldiers to him.

8. Clemence Haggerty, sister of Annie.

9. James Sturgis probably never relocated from his Boston home to New York City. Sturgis, *Edward Sturgis*, p. 53.

10. William Howard Russell headed the *Times* (London) war bureau in Washington, D.C. His descriptions of the Northern soldiers' lack of professionalism and full flight from First Bull Run were widely reprinted in U.S. papers. Embarrassed and infuriated Northerners, an embittered Edwin Stanton, and a president that would not support Russell caused him to leave the United States

one year later. He never wrote again for the *Times* about American affairs. *The History of* The Times: *The Tradition Established, 1841–1884* (New York: Macmillan, 1939), pp. 363–76. Russell collected his memoirs of the war in *My Diary North and South* (London, 1863).

11. George William Curtis.

Camp near Darnestown [HL]
September 3 1861
Dear Father,

Your letter of the 21st Augt from Baltimore came to hand day before yesterday. We have received no news of recent date for some time from home.

Yesterday Harry and I got 24 hours leave of absence & drove over to Frederick. We went to the Seminary & saw Uncle Coolidge's portrait & grave. He has on a Jesuit's dress & the miniature I think has a cassock with buttons down the front. They treated us very well and got permission for us to visit the convent which was very interesting. The nuns, who never go out, and the pupils too, though they cleared the way for us with precipitation, were inquisitive enough to peek out of the windows as we went along the gallery.[1]

It is 25 miles from here to Frederick and we worked hard to get there for it was necessary for one of us to beat the horse with a slat almost without intermission to keep him in a trot while the other drove. There is talk of our moving tomorrow & I will leave this open so that I can give you the latest news.

Sept 4/61 It is nearly 4 P.M. and we have had no orders to march yet, so we shall certainly not go today. When we do make a movement it will only be towards Washington they say.

I have just got a note from Effie at Newport dated Aug 25. I don't know what is detaining our mails. An officer from one regiment was sent to Washington today to try to get them for the whole division. We are at work drilling now every day and the whole regiment being together it seems like old times again. We are, as a general thing, in good health and our men in excellent spirits. Rations are good and plenty and things go on much more systematically than formerly. We have always been in the habit of selling extra rations, as they do in the regular army, & every company has a fund from which they draw when the Captain thinks proper to let them. In this way they can get a great many things not furnished them by Govt. A great many men, besides their $13 a month, get $10 or $12 from their town which makes about as much as they could earn at home. Think of a soldier in Europe getting as much as that! It is only the married men who get the bounty.[2] I hope you hear from me more regularly than I have from you lately. We have got permission to use the old stamps for the present in this division.

Dearest love to Mother & the girls. I wrote her a long letter a few days ago. Harry & I are well.

Your loving son
Robert G. Shaw

1. Joseph Coolidge Shaw (1821–51) received theology training at St. Joseph's Seminary in Fordham, New York (1848–50), and entered the Jesuit Novitiate at Frederick, Maryland, in 1850. Coolidge read widely, amassing a personal library of 1,200 volumes on theology and nearly 600 on other subjects. He was instrumental in convincing his older brother, Francis George Shaw, to send young Robert to Fordham in 1850. Coolidge died at the Novitiate.

Walter Meagher, ed., *A Proper Bostonian, Priest, Jesuit: Diary of Fr. Joseph Coolidge Shaw, S.J.* (Boston: Published by the author, 1965), pp. x, 23, 77–78.

2. To stimulate enlistment, Northern states and localities gave men monetary enticements to join up. Bounties varied from city to city, helped communities make their quotas, and supported the families left behind when the men marched off to war. Faust, *Encyclopedia*, pp. 72–73.

Camp near Darnestown   [HL]
Sept. 5, 1861
Dearest Mother,

Your two notes of 28 & 30 Augt came from Washington with our mail yesterday and I am glad you have received all mine. I think I have got all you have written now, though they came rather irregularly.

Day before yesterday we were ordered to be ready to march at a moment's notice, but nothing came of it. The cooks' fires were going all night, and the whole neighbourhood was illuminated by them.

There are half a dozen regiments within sight of us and so many little fires have a peculiar effect in the dark night.

You had better continue to send your letters to Washington as we can't tell when we shall move nor where we shall go to. Isn't it a strange sort of life for us to be living who never expected to be anything but merchants & lawyers three months ago? Every little while I feel astonished at my being here, especially when waked up at midnight and started off—not one of us knowing where we are going.

Fremont's proclamation has made a stir. I hope he will not be interfered with by the Government and that the other Generals will follow his example.[1]

We hear today that the Union men in North Carolina are beginning to take heart and have got a good many men together.[2] If it is so, we shall probably have similar news from some of the other states soon.

Please tell Father that I am much obliged for the present of my debts to him and also for his offer to make an application for the regular army for me. I feel very well satisfied for the present where I am and don't want to leave the regiment until it has been into an action of some kind. It looks very much from our drawing nearer & nearer to Washington, as if we were to be held in reserve, when McClellan makes an attack. In that case we shall not see anything of the fight, I suppose, unless our troops are in danger of being beaten, which is not probable. Can you imagine anything worse than our losing another battle? And the Confederates will fight hard of course as a defeat would be death to them. I sincerely hope the war will not finish without a good, fair battle, as we should never hear the end of Bull Run. And after all, a great many of the men on both sides, who are killed, are better out of the world than in it, though of course some of them are a great loss. This is not a very charitable sentiment but don't you think it is true?

Our band has been playing tonight & though the music is not very fine it makes me think of going to concerts again with you some time. You will have a good chance for that, now Aunt Katie is going to be in New York.[3]

I often think of the house & you all sitting on the porch looking across the lawn & Anna & George & the children & Tib walking over from their house.[4] It is hard to realize that Theodore Winthrop is not there too, in the summer evenings.[5]

I shall not need any more clothing as we wear the same things all the year round. If it is unusually cold, we have only to put on another flannel shirt.

It is after tattoo & I must turn in, in a few moments.[6]

Harry received Father's note enclosing one from Uncle George. We were very sorry to hear about poor Aunt Susan.[7]

I got Harry's note which you sent and feel quite sure I mentioned it in one of mine to you or Father—probably never received. Good-night dear Mother.

> Your loving son,
> Robert G. Shaw

1. John Charles Frémont (1813–90) explored the American West, agitated for taking California from Mexico, became one of California's first two U.S. senators (1850–51), and campaigned in 1856 as the Republican party's first presidential candidate. On May 14, 1861, Lincoln appointed him as one of only four major generals and gave him command in the West. Early on, Frémont recognized that

the war for Union should be turned into a war to end slavery. On Aug. 30, he issued a Proclamation of Emancipation which proclaimed martial law, confiscated all enemy property, and freed all slaves in Missouri. This was too fast for Lincoln, who worried about keeping loyal slaveholding states in the Union. On Sept. 2, Lincoln overrode and rescinded Frémont's proclamation. Abolitionists, including the Shaws, railed at Lincoln's veto. Boston editor William Lloyd Garrison announced that Lincoln might stand "six feet four inches high" but he was still a "dwarf in the mind." Perhaps Staten Island resident-poet James Russell Lowell put it best: "How many times are we to save Kentucky and lose our self respect?" Allan Nevins, *Frémont: The West's Greatest Adventurer* (New York: Harper & Bros., 1928), pp. 561–74; *NYDT*, Sept. 2 (4:6), 17 (7:2), 1861; Garrison quoted in Stewart, *Holy Warriors*, p. 181; Lowell quoted in Dudley T. Cornish, *The Sable Arm: Negro Troops in the Union Army, 1861–1865*

(New York: Longmans, 1956), p. 14.

2. While many North Carolinians fought for the Union, the first regiment of North Carolina Volunteers, Union, did not organize until June 27, 1862. All in all, seven regiments from the state—three white, four black—fought for the North. Dyer, *Compendium*, pp. 1471–72.

3. Mary Catherine Townsend Sturgis (?–1887) married Sarah Shaw's brother James in 1845. Sturgis, *Edward Sturgis*, p. 53.

4. Shaw's parents lived next to their daughter Anna and son-in-law George William Curtis; in fact, they built the Curtis's house as a present in 1859. "Tib" was Anna's dog. George W. Curtis to (C. E.) Norton, Mar. 2 and Sept. 18, 1859, Curtis Collection, SIIAS; *Atlantic Monthly* 8 (Aug. 1861): 247.

5. Winthrop was killed at the Battle of Big Bethel on June 10, 1861.

6. Harry's father, George R. Russell.

7. Susan Parkman Sturgis Parkman (1818–69). Sturgis, *Edward Sturgis*, p. 52.

Camp Darnestown Md.   [HL]
Sept 11 1861
Dear Effie,

Your letter of the 1st Septr. came in one from Mother the other day. I am glad to hear you had a pleasant time at Newport & also that you were going to Naushon, where you of course, enjoyed yourself. Harry and I took occasion to wax melancholy over past, and hopeful over future pleasant times, on hearing of your being about to make a cruise in the Azalea and a visit to Naushon.¹ Every little while we have a talk about future prospects, and fancy ourselves, walking about on shady lawns, sitting on piazzas after dinner with a mild cigar, riding, rowing, & sitting in chairs, in all of which visions, the prominent objects, & without which there would be no attraction, are muslin skirts, jemmy straw hats, white cuff, collars &c &c. But we both think more

& oftener of the time when we shall see our Mothers & sisters again than of anything else & pray that we shall find you all well & happy as when we came away. Do you want Mimi's & Annie's photograph particularly?[2] I thought you had some already. If you do, you can have them, unless Mother has already sent them to me, as I requested.

I heard a curious story about our Colour-bearer the other day. He was colour-bearer for a Russian Regt in the Crimea & was taken prisoner by some English Soldiers.[3] When he enlisted in this regiment, he found that one of his captors was in the same Company that he was put into. If it is true it is a more extraordinary coincidence than the fact of Mr. Pickwick's being put into prison on St. Valentine's day.[4]

Our camp here is a very nice one and when we leave I shall remember it with satisfaction as it is the first time since we got to Harper's Ferry that we have been all together and every one has been perfectly satisfied and in good humour. In the same field with us are the Webster Regt & the 12th Indiana.[5] On a hill opposite are the headquarters of Genl Banks, which our sentries are instructed to watch continually during the night, as a Roman Candle sent up from there is the signal to strike tents & march. So we keep two days rations always ready & never lie down to sleep without thinking of the possibility of being waked up in the middle of the night, by the long roll.

A few days ago we had a little excitement in Col. Webster's Regt.[6] One of our men was sentenced by Court-Martial to be tied to a tree for a certain time each day for three days. On the first day the whole Webster mob turned out hooting & howling & groaning our Officer of the day & Lieut. of the Guard. Whereupon Col. Gordon, who was in command of the Brigade, Genl Abercrombie being in Washington, sent over & had a good many of them arrested, and also put their Officer of the day under arrest for not making efforts to stop the row.[7] Tying to a tree can be made a very painful process, but as it is usually done, it is only very disagreeable as the man is kept in a constrained

"*The way they treat volunteers who come here to fight the battles of their country.*"

position embracing the trunk.[8] I found a drawing something like the following on a table in the tent where the Court-martial had been sitting. It represents the man as tied to a branch by the thumbs about 15 feet from the earth which would be fearful torture.

It was gratifying to us that our men kept perfectly quiet while the others were kicking up such a rumpus.

We frequently hear of our being called "stuck up" by Officers of other Mass. Regt but they are certainly not backward in making our acquaintance when we give them a chance. They imagine we are of the Beacon St. crowd & look down on them & there are a good many common men among them.[9] It is P.M. & raining very hard & no signs of fair weather—our tents are perfectly dry. Good night. Love to all. I suppose you are just going to bed too & Father is reading under the gas-lamp in the corner of the sofa, or playing a game of billiards with Mr. Gay.[10]

Your loving Brother

Give my love to Frankie. I ought to say after this story about Col. Webster's men, that his regiment is considered by many to be the best in the division and is really a very fine one. Their discipline is not so good as ours though & we consider that of more importance than drill. Please don't repeat any remarks I may make about Mass. regiments where they can come to Massachusetts or Boston ears as they would certainly come back here. So be careful.

1. Josephine went to Naushon on Sept. 4, 1861, with four young women and three men, including her sister Ellen and her father. Located thirty miles from the southern point of Rhode Island, Naushon Island, seven miles long and a mile and a half wide, divides Buzzard's Bay from Vineyard Sound. John Murray Forbes purchased the island jointly with W. W. Swain, his wife's uncle, in 1843. By 1857, Forbes owned it outright and was calling it a "Paradise for children young and old." Charles Russell Lowell described Naushon as "the finest island on the whole Atlantic coast,—horses *ad libitum*,—guns enough for a regiment,—and a squadron of sail-boats. The house is filled with a constantly changing crowd of visitors,—who are always the best people in the country." Henry G. Pearson, *An American Railroad Builder: John Murray Forbes* (Boston: Houghton Mifflin, 1911), p. 12; Hughes, *John Murray Forbes*, vol. 1, pp. 16–17, Forbes quoted from p. 23; Emerson,

Charles Russell Lowell, p. 163; Stewart, *Philanthropic Works*, p. 18.

2. Shaw's first cousins and Harry Russell's sisters, Elizabeth Russell Lyman and Anna Russell Agassiz. Marion W. Smith, *Beacon Hill's Colonel Robert Gould Shaw* (New York: Carlton Press, 1986), p. 491.

3. The Crimean War (1853–56) started when Russian czar Nicholas I tried to expand his empire into regions of the Ottoman Empire. Britain, France, and Sardinia, fearing that Russian imperialism would threaten their interests in the Middle East, backed Turkey. After losses on both sides approached 200,000 men, Russia withdrew its claim to the region and removed its warships from the Black Sea. The "colour-bearer" was Sergeant Lundy. Charles F. Morse to [?], Morse, *Letters Written*, p. 97.

4. Shaw is referring to the leading character in Charles Dickens's works of the same name. There were many publications of the *Pickwick Papers*; the

first editions published in the United States were *The Posthumous Papers of the Pickwick Club* (New York: W. H. Colyer, 1838; Philadelphia: Cary, Lea, & Blanchard, 1838).

5. Fletcher Webster's Twelfth Massachusetts. The Twelfth Indiana Infantry Regiment organized in Indianapolis in May 1861. Dyer, *Compendium*, vol. 1, p. 134.

6. In the printed version, *Letters: RGS* (1864), this and the next two paragraphs criticizing the Twelfth Massachusetts were excluded. Shaw's mother probably followed the wishes of her son's postscript that these remarks were sensitive.

7. John Joseph Abercrombie (1798–1877) was promoted to brigadier general on Aug. 31, 1861, and subsequently commanded the Second Brigade, Banks' Division, Army of the Potomac until

Mar. 1862. Boatner, *Dictionary*, pp. 1–2; Everett W. Pattison, "Some Reminiscences of Army Life," *War Papers and Personal Reminiscences, 1861–1865* (St. Louis: Becktold, 1892), pp. 252–53.

8. Punishments for enlisted men varied by each commander's leniency or sadism. Common punishments included the guard house, extra duty, suspension by the thumbs with the entire body pulled off the ground, tying to a barrel, and gagging.

9. Boston's Beacon Street was the residential hub for the wealthiest of the city's wealthy. Shaw's Aunt Mary lived at 44 Beacon Street, near the State House.

10. Sydney Howard Gay, Quaker, abolitionist, editor, Staten Island neighbor, and longtime friend of Francis George Shaw. Leng and Davis, *Staten Island*, vol. 1, p. 254.

Near Darnestown, Md.   [RGS]
Sept. 17, 1861
Dear Susie,

Your note written at Mrs. Blatchford's came safely, as I mentioned in a letter to Effie a few days ago.[1] Since then, I have received one from Father, just after his return from Naushon, and two from Mother, of 10th and 13th inst.,— all of them to-day. Our mail doesn't come every day from Washington, so the letters collect there. As you see from the date of this, we have not moved yet, though we are told continually that we shall start in a few hours; but the rumours have proved to be only rumours so often, th[a]t they make little impression. Some day, though, and probably at short notice, we shall have to bundle off very fast, and, I hope, cross the river. Have you seen the "Punch" that has the illustrations, songs, &c. about Bull Run?[2] Mr. Hughes' article, which I read to-day, is consoling.[3]

A Boston paper, which we got to-day says, "We hope General Banks will discover that the men of Colonel Gordon's Regiment are treated much too severely by their officers."[4] That sort of thing is rather amusing, as General

Banks can look out of his tent straight down into the centre of our camp, and rides through it, besides, almost every afternoon. I wish we had the editors of half the papers in our ranks. They all make a great fuss about want of discipline, and then publish the letters and complaints against officers from men, many of whom can't possibly be brought to a sense of their duty without punishment, and who then consider themselves unjustly treated. You can't conceive how much harm such articles do. Men growl, and get impertinent and mutinous, the consequence of which is, of course, more frequent and more severe punishment. I have not the slightest doubt the compassion of the papers and public, for imaginary wrongs, often works the discontented ones up to the rebellious point.

Won't it be disgusting if Fremont is superseded?—the only man who has really shown that he knew what he was about. Who could replace him? Mother talks a good deal about his proclamation in her last. How she must feel after what Lincoln wrote him on the subject![5] It is really too bad to think of. The only thing I have thought about lately, as *very* desirable (if I were older, and had some experience), is a place on General Fremont's staff. As soon as we have had a fight, if it looks as if the war were going to be a long one, I think I shall try to get into the regular army,—i.e: if I get out with both legs. You will probably be back from Newport by the time you receive this. I hope you have had a nice time there. I forgot to mention that I received Effie's letter from Naushon, giving an enthusiastic account of her visit, which was what we should expect, of course. Please tell Mother that I *should* like Bob's and Sallie's photographs, as they would please Harry very much, as he has none of his family with him, and I like to have them myself.[6] Mimi's came safely in Mother's last letter. You don't seem very prompt in having yours taken and sent, though I asked for them long ago. I don't accuse *you* particularly, but all of you! Please tell Mother I have not heard Frankie's remark about Bull Run, and should like to very much; also, that I did not see ——— ——— when I was in Boston, at all.[7] Excuse impertinence, but I should like to implore you, Effie, and Nellie, not to be curious as to who the individual is. I don't suppose it will torture you much, but it might some people, you know.

Do you ever see Colonel Raasloff?[8] I tried to find him out in Washington, but had not time to look him up. There was to have been a grand review of General Banks' Division to-day by General McClellan, but he didn't come, for some reason. The Twentieth Massachusetts passed within a few miles of here, on their way to Poolesville.[9] A good many of our officers went over to see them, but I was on guard, and couldn't go. They were all well. Our reveille is to be twenty minutes after sunrise in future, which gives us more than an hour longer than we have had hitherto, and tattoo is a half-hour earlier. General McClellan made these changes. Give my love to all at home. We are all well. Harry has a full beard, which is not so becoming, I think, as moustache alone. You would hardly know him. I always think of you when I write, as your writing-case is brought out every time, and is a most convenient one.

Always with much love,
Your affectionate brother,
Robert G. Shaw

1. Mrs. Blatchford is unidentified.

2. The ultraconservative London political-humor magazine *Punch* derided the Union's chances of beating the Confederacy. Commenting on First Bull Run, *Punch* carried a poem (to the tune of "Yankee Doodle"): "Yankee Doodle, near Bull's Run, Met his adversary; First he thought the fight he'd won; Fact proved quite contrary. Panic-struck he fled, with speed of lightning glib with unction Of slippery grease, in full stampede, From famed Manassas Junction. . . ." A cartoon depicted Yankees in full flight, but insisting while they ran that next they "gwine to take Canada." *Punch*, Aug. 17, 1861, pp. 4–5.

3. Mr. Hughes's article is unidentified.

4. The Boston paper is unidentified.

5. Lincoln removed Frémont on Nov. 2, 1861, and replaced him with Maj. Gen. David Hunter. On Nov. 19, the Department of the West was reorganized into the Department of Kansas, headed by Hunter, and the Department of Missouri, commanded by Henry W. Halleck. Nevins, *Frémont*, vol. 2, pp. 615–23; Dyer, *Compendium*, vol. 1, p. 255.

6. Probably Harry's brother and sister, Robert Shaw Russell and Sarah Shaw Russell. Smith, *Beacon Hill's*, p. 491.

7. Frankie Curtis, son of George and Anna Shaw Curtis. The unmentioned person is Annie Kneeland Haggerty. Shaw was falling in love with Miss Haggerty and tried to keep it a secret from everyone other than his mother and father.

8. Colonel Raasloff is unidentified.

9. The Twentieth Regiment, Massachusetts Infantry organized at Camp Meigs, Readville, Massachusetts, on Sept. 4, 1861. Many of Shaw's closest acquaintances and Harvard classmates served in the Twentieth. Dyer, *Compendium*, vol. 1, p. 158.

Near Darnestown, Md. [HL]
Sept 23/61
My dear Anna,

I was very glad to get your letter yesterday morning, with the photographs, for which I thank you very much. I should have written to you myself before, if I hadn't considered all my letters as addressed to the whole family.

Harry thinks the photograph of you is an excellent one, but I must say I don't like it so much as some you have had, particularly the one with Frankie in your lap. That one is connected in my mind with my visit to Niagara with George, as he had it constantly by him.[1]

Yesterday was Sunday, and I got leave of absence for the day, to go and visit Col. Lee's (the 20th Mass.) regiment which is encamped about 12 miles from us.[2] A very fat man, named Brown, went with me in an old one seated covered wagon, which we hired from a farmer in this neighborhood.[3] The horse was one of the most wretched of his race, and had a harness that was on its very last legs, being fastened in many places with twine. These places proved to be the strongest parts of the harness, for they held out very well, while one of the traces snapped in the middle where it had seemed perfectly sound. We patched it together with the cheek rein & finally arrived at our destination, but what with anxiety about the harness, whipping the horse, & being jammed against the side of the wagon by Brown, who weighs about 180 & is outstandingly broad, I was exhausted. I found a good many friends & acquaintances there—Harry Sturgis, Wendell Holmes, Jim Lowell & many other Cambridge fellows.[4] Caspar Crowninshield had gone off that very day with his Company so unfortunately I missed him.[5] Harry S. seems to me very much improved and I believe this work is going to do him an immense amount of good. I was really surprized at the change in him, the interest he takes in his company, & the appreciation he shows of the responsibility of his position. He feels badly about his Father being alone, and tears really came into his eyes when he spoke of him. I haven't been so much pleased with Henry Sturgis since he came home from Europe.[6] He talked a good deal about Mother & was very sorry he hadn't seen her in New York. His uniform is very becoming to him.

Coming home it was dark and we had a hard time picking out the road which was in a frightful state. I couldn't stand having Brown joined over on to my body every few minutes, so I sat in his lap and drove, which was very comfortable for me, though he complained bitterly after the moon came up of sitting in the dark, for the night was very fine & the country which is full [of] great trees & open spaces was beautiful by moonlight. As the cape of my overcoat filled the front of the wagon completely he didn't enjoy the scenery at all. We arrived safely at home without any breakages.

We are living a regular old jog trot camp life here and it really seems as if we should never go.

The reveille beats at 6 o'clock—at seven the Breakfast-call, or as it is called "Peas on the Trencher" is beaten. Then we have nothing to do until 9 when we march out for company drill, which has become rather tedious now. At

10 1/2 comes the recall from Drill & then we lie round until 1 P.M. dinner time. Sometimes we lie about talking, or reading, and sometimes there is work to do in the company: drawing rations, giving out clothes & shoes &c, examining the cooking. But very frequently we find occupation in overseeing the drill of men who are awkward and can't keep up with the rest—or who are punished with extra drill for talking & unsteadiness in the ranks & other peccadilloes. At 1 o'cl. "Roast Beef" is beaten, which is the call for dinner. Now the rations are very good and in great plenty but we have seen the times (& shall probably see them again) when it seemed bitter irony to mention "Roast Beef" unless hard bread can go by that name.

We (the officers) have a steward who provides our meals for us, so that we all mess together—which is very pleasant. We very often send down to our respective Companies though for some [of] their spare soup, baked beans, or stew. They have learned to cook very well now.

After dinner we have time to lie round, & smoke, read or sleep—and at 3 turn out for battalion drill which we always like as the colonel keeps us spinning about at the "double quick" in great style. At 4 1/2 we march in again & polish up everything for dress-parade at 5. After that the day's work is over and we have supper. The evenings which are getting long now, we usually spend in each other's tents & manage to have a good deal of fun in one way and another. There have been several packages of books sent on to different fellows lately, and they are all devoured in turn with great avidity. I am now reading Mr. Kapp's life of Baron Steuben, but have hardly got into it yet.[7] At 8 1/2 we have tattoo and at 9 taps after which no lights nor talking is allowed in the men's tents but the officers are not interfered with unless they make a noise. We ought really to have our lights out too at 9 I believe.

The days & weeks pass very quickly tho' they never vary excepting when we go on guard, which is not a pleasant variety.

When I began this, I intended to have written to George too, but this is so long and it is getting so late, I must put it off as I have before several times. I am very glad you are all so well. Give all the family lots of love. I hope your doe & jackass will thrive morally & physically. How's Filo getting on?[8] Tell Mother to excuse my not having written to her for so long. I had so many letters from the girls to answer and Nellie is still neglected. Has George ever heard anything of Mr. McLean, our little Scotch friend?[9]

I think I shall have to send for a Buffalo robe. Some of our officers have them and they will be great when the real cold weather comes. Even now they are not a bad thing.

Good night dear Anna

Ever your loving Brother,
Robert G. Shaw

I wish I had some interesting news to tell you, but I so seldom go out of the camp I never hear or see anything. I have only been out twice. If I had had a good horse yesterday I should have gone down to the River where Caspar C. was & from where you can see the Rebel camps & batteries. There has been some firing across the river and 300 men went down from the 20th while I was there.

1. In Nov. 1860, Shaw and several members of his family attended the Chicago wedding of Annie Russell to Alexander Agassiz. Returning from the wedding, Shaw accompanied his brother-in-law George William Curtis to Buffalo, New York, where the latter gave one of his many lyceum speeches. Shaw visited Niagara Falls, calling it "the greatest sight I ever saw." Commenting on George, Shaw wrote: "G. keeps his daguerreotype of Anna and Frankie by him, and now and then takes it out, or rather very often. He looks at it with a very *attendri* air, as you may imagine. It is great to see how he keeps up his honeymoon." Shaw, *Letters: RGS* (1876), pp. 157–58.

2. William Raymond Lee (1804–91) was a railroad superintendent in Roxbury, Massachusetts, before the war. On July 21, 1861, Governor John Andrew named Lee to organize and command the Twentieth Massachusetts Infantry. Boatner, *Dictionary*, p. 478.

3. Second Lt. Robert B. Brown (1840–?). For a more thorough description of Brown, see Shaw's letter to Effie, Nov. 21, 1862, included here; "Descriptive Book. Companies A-E," Records of the Adjutant General's Office, Record Group 94, Bound Record Books,

Second Massachusetts Infantry, NA; *Record of Mass. Vols.*, pp. 28–29.

4. Shaw's first cousin Second Lt. Henry Howard Sturgis (1838–81), of Boston, son of Henry P. Sturgis and his first wife, Mary Georgianna Howard Sturgis (?–1850). First Lt. Oliver Wendell Holmes, Jr. (1841–1935) served with the New England Guards and the Twelfth Massachusetts Infantry before being commissioned in the Twentieth. First Lt. James Jackson Lowell (1837–62), brother of Shaw's future brother-in-law, Col. Charles Russell Lowell. Shaw was at Harvard with Jim Lowell and Holmes. Sturgis, *Edward Sturgis*, pp. 51–52; Putnam, *Memoirs of the War of '61*, pp. 45–48; Ferris Grenslet, *The Lowells and Their Seven Worlds* (Boston: Houghton Mifflin, 1946), p. 422; Mark DeWolfe Howe, ed., *Touched With Fire: Civil War Letters and Diary of Oliver Wendell Holmes, Jr., 1861–1864* (Cambridge, Mass.: Harvard University Press, 1946), pp. 3, 4.

5. Caspar Crowninshield (1837?–97) shared a room with Shaw when both were students at Harvard. Shaw admired Caspar's athletic and scholarly abilities, which far surpassed his own. Crowninshield had worked in Boston until joining the Twentieth Massachusetts on

July 10, 1861, as a captain. *Letters: RGS*, pp. 110, 125, 130, 140, 149; Boatner, *Dictionary*, p. 211; Harvard College, *Report of the Class of 1860*, p. 19; for Crowninshield's Civil War correspondence, see the Crowninshield-Magnus Papers, MHS.

6. Harry is Henry Sturgis. Henry's father had married for a second time in 1851 to Elizabeth Orne Paine (?–1911) and was not really "alone." Sturgis, *Edward Sturgis*, p. 52.

7. Friedrich Kapp (1824–84), *The Life of Frederick William von Steuben, Major General in the Revolutionary Army* (New York: Mason Brothers, 1859).

8. Filo is unidentified.

9. During their train trip in Nov. 1860, Shaw and George Curtis met Mr. McLean, "a little Scotchman going shooting on the prairies. He had a very broad brogue, and the most good-natured, jolly face in the world." *Letters: RGS* (1876), pp. 157–58.

Near Darnestown
Sept. 26, 1861
Dear Nellie,

[RGS]

It seems a very great while since I received your note. It was when we were on Maryland Heights, opposite Harper's Ferry, and before Father's visit. We were then having a very uncomfortable time, living in huts, and getting wet very often; but for the last five weeks we have been as comfortable as if we were at home. To-day is set apart by Mr. Lincoln for Fast and thanksgiving, and, instead of letting us stay comfortably at home, we are going to march two or three miles to hear somebody preach!

We have been to church, and come back dusty, thirsty, and hungry. The services were in a field three miles away, and there were about ten regiments present, beside a good deal of artillery. It was very hot, and, though the men kept very quiet, we could hear very little, which was, perhaps, a disadvantage, and perhaps not. *Our* Chaplain delivered the sermon, but as many as ten others had a shy at us, each in his turn.[1] There were two Massachusetts regiments there, and, as usual they were the best-equipped, best-behaved, and most soldierly-looking men on the ground. The difference between them and all others that I have seen is really extraordinary. The Thirteenth Massachuset[t]s looks better than any other. Their Colonel (Leonard) lets the men go where they want to, and puts them on their honour to obey all the rules.[2] They say it works well, and they have only one man in the guard-tent.

I have just received a letter from Henry Vezin, in which he says he has got a commission as Lieutenant of Engineers, and is on General Blenker's staff, near Washington.[3] He offered himself at first as a non-commissioned officer, until he could show he knew something, and fortunately they discovered how much he had studied and learnt of his profession. Did you enjoy yourself as much at Naushon as Effie did? Harry has just got a letter from Will Forbes, giving a full history of everything that happened while he was down there.[4] It is one of the best letters I ever saw, as it tells all the details and particulars of his visit, and a great many funny anecdotes. Many people don't tell little things in their letters, because they think them stupid; but, in my opinion, that is just what makes a letter interesting.

When are you going to send me your photographs? The sooner the better, as we may go away from here at any time, and then it will be hard to get anything by Express, i.e. if we move nearer the Potomac. Will you please ask Father to get me a good buffalo-robe, and send it as soon as possible, charging the amount to me? Tell Mother I shall write to her soon. I thought I would finish up my other correspondence, as some letters had been waiting a long time to be answered.

I don't remember if I asked Anna to tell Sue that I saw a young man named ——— ——— the other day. If I didn't, won't you mention it to her? He is a Lieutenant in the ———, and I have no doubt his fate will interest Susie.[5] He has not grown any since she saw him, but looks somewhat older, and has some vestige of a whisker. I think he may still be called a great ass.

I haven't heard from any of you for a good while, but hope to get a letter soon, and to hear that you are all well.

Ever your loving brother,
Robert G. Shaw

1. Alonzo H. Quint (1828–96), of West Roxbury, enlisted as chaplain in June 1861 and resigned on May 25, 1864. *Record of Mass. Vols.*, p. 847.

2. Thirty-six-year-old Samuel H. Leonard was commissioned colonel of the Thirteenth Massachusetts Infantry at its inception on July 16, 1861. Leonard was wounded at Gettysburg on July 1, 1863. Samuel H. Leonard file, CMSR.

3. Louis Blenker (1812–63), born in Germany, fled the 1848 German Revolution to immigrate to New York City. He commanded the Eighth New York, a brigade composed of German immigrants,

at First Bull Run. He was promoted to the rank of brigadier general on Aug. 9, 1861. Faust, *Encyclopedia*, p. 67.

4. William Hathaway Forbes (1840–97), oldest son of John Murray Forbes, left Harvard in 1860 to work in his father's company. After the war, Will married Ralph Waldo Emerson's daughter, Edith, and was president of the Bell Telephone Company. Gay Wilson Allen, *Waldo Emerson: A Biography* (New York: Viking, 1981), p. 629; Francis Henry Brown, "Roll of Students of Harvard University who served in the Army or Navy of the United States

During the War of the Rebellion" (Cambridge, Mass.: Welch, Bigelow, 1866), p. 23.

5. The lieutenant and his unit are unidentified.

Near Darnestown [RGS]
Sept. 30, 1861
Dear Father,

I received yesterday, by mail, yours of 21st and 24th, Effie's of 22d, and Uncle Jim's from Boston.[1] General Banks has taken Harry for temporary Aide.[2] His Assistant Adjutant-General has gone to Massachusetts, to take command of a cavalry regiment, and they have sent no one from Washington to replace him. Some army officer will come ultimately, I suppose. Though Harry expects to come back, this will, of course, give him a lift; for General Banks will like him, without any doubt, and will be glad to help him along. He got the place through Copeland's recommendation.[3] Some staff-officers about here ride pretty poor horses, but they have given Harry a beauty.

I wish you would send me a few books. We have read everything in the camp, and anything new would be very acceptable. There is an edition of Shakespeare published by Phillips & Sampson, in which each play is in a separate pamphlet.[4] The print is large. A half-dozen would be good to have. I don't care which plays you send. If there is any difficulty in getting them, don't trouble yourself about it. I really don't know what else to ask for, but should like a few books of poetry, and some essays, such as Bacon's, Macaulay's, Lamb's, &c., &c.[5] I mention these so as not to trouble you with choosing, but I don't care about your sticking to the programme. Love to Mother. I shall write soon again. We have a review of the whole Division this afternoon, for which I must get ready.

Your loving son,
Robert G. Shaw

1. Uncle James Sturgis.

2. Henry Sturgis Russell was detached as an aide to Banks on Oct. 1, 1861. Henry S. Russell file, CMSR.

3. Robert Morris Copeland, formerly of the Second, now on Banks's staff.

4. Boston publishers, Phillips and Sampson, reproduced many of Shakespeare's works in the 1850s. Among them were editions for young people and for use by actors in plays—any of these could have been large-print volumes.

5. Sir Francis Bacon (1561–1626), essayist, historian, scientist; Thomas Babington Macaulay (1800–59), historian, essayist; and Charles Lamb

(1775–1834), essayist, poet, novelist. Frank N. Magill, *Cyclopedia of World Authors* (Englewood Cliffs, N.J.: Salem Press, 1974), vol. 1, pp. 103–5, vol. 2, pp. 1020–22, 1111.

Darnestown [RGS]

Oct. 6, 1861

Dear Mother,

Yesterday came a note from Father, of 4th, one from Susie, at Newport, and one from Effie, both the later enclosing photographs. I received Bob's and Sallie's the other day from you, and sent them up to Harry at head-quarters. Effie's is as good a portrait as I ever saw, and the others I like very well. I am much obliged to the girls for sending them, and wish I had yours and Father's. I am afraid, though, you will never consent to have one taken again. Father says he sent the buffalo-robe, and I suppose it will arrive in time. What a pleasant visit Susie seems to be having in Newport! Her recent hard work at the Sanitary probably makes her enjoy her vacation more than she would otherwise.[1] I wrote to Father to send some books, but I don't want you to take any trouble about them. Anything readable will do.

Our Lieutenant-Colonel (Andrews) has been appointed Assistant Adjutant-General to General Banks.[2] I don't know whether he will accept it or not. If he does, I shall not feel so much reluctance to leave the regiment, if I can better myself by it, as I should have heretofore. He will be a great loss to us. He has taken more interest in making the regiment a good one, and worked harder, than any one.

Susie said Mrs. Haggerty was expecting a letter which I was going to write her. If so, I shall not delay. (*Annie conducts all her mother's correspondence,— doesn't she?*)[3]

When I went to bed last night, I hadn't had any sleep for forty hours!— the longest pull I ever had, but by my own fault, for, after coming off guard, instead of going to sleep I rode ten miles, over to Poolesville. The horse was not an easy one, and twenty miles of him made me so tired that I actually didn't feel sleepy after I got back. I heard a report over there that Fort Sumter was taken, but didn't believe it, of course.

Oct. 7. There is a little German book called "Soldatenleben im Frieden," which I should like to have sent with the other books. It is somewhere in my room.[4] There is a report that we shan't stay here much longer. A battery belonging to our Brigade has gone back to Harper's Ferry to protect the bridge, which is to be rebuilt. From what I said above about leaving this regiment, you may think I have had some thoughts of it, but it is not so. If Colonel Andrews stays, I shall certainly not give up my present position, even for a better or more pleasant one. If I ever *do* think of it, I will let you know, of course.

Ever, dear Mother, your loving son,
Robert G. Shaw

1. The U.S. Sanitary Commission, a private organization, mobilized in June 1861 and soon had over seven thousand branches nationwide. The Sanitary Commission was the largest voluntary organization of the Civil War. It provided medicine, clothing, food, and nursing care to wounded and sick Union soldiers as well as helping desti-tute families whose men had enlisted. Faust, *Encyclopedia*, p. 656.

2. Lt. Col. George L. Andrews.

3. Annie Kneeland Haggerty.

4. Probably Friedrich Wilhelm Hack-lander, *Das Soldatenleben im Frieden* [The Life of Soldiers in Peacetime] (Stuttgart: C. Krabbe, 1855; reprint ed., 1890).

Darnestown, Md.   [HL]
Oct. 8/61
My dear George,

At last, after many weeks of "intending," I begin my note to you. I don't think I have written to you since I was at Albany after our little journey to Buffalo & Toronto—which I have often thought of lately, and wondered what has become of the "Haig of Bummerside."[1]

We are still lying idle at Darnestown and wish we could go back to our old occupation of guarding fords & ferries & living without tents, rather than stay here any longer. General Banks seems to be rather set aside and I don't believe he will get a chance for the present of showing what he can do. Probably McClellan prefers putting the West Point men forward. They won't even give Banks an army officer on his staff, since Capt. Williams went away.[2] When *will* the time come for making an advance? This is the month we have been looking forward to.

It has been very warm lately, but last night there was a change. It blew and rained very hard, and we lay trembling in our tents, fearing each moment the guys and pins would give way. About midnight I found I couldn't be still without first having a look at them. So out I went in the pouring rain & hammered at the pins & tightened the ropes & fussed about for nearly an hour, inside & out.

A week ago coming down to my tent to go to bed I found it streaming like a banner from the rear-pole & its contents drenched with rain. It took about as much trouble & as many men to set it right again, as it would to furl the mainsail of a large ship. Tents are very pleasant when the weather is fine—but in the rainy season—[illegible].

Give my love to Frank and tell him, I was much obliged to him for his letter, which came safely enclosed in Effie's. How beautiful the Island must look now—the trees beginning to change their colour and I suppose the weather is just right for riding & walking. What a difference between October 1860 and Oct 1861 in America—and where will we all be next year at this time? Perhaps Jefferson Davis will be in New York—though it is not probable. I am prepared not to be surprised at anything though—and feel persuaded too that if England, France & all the world should declare war against us, we should still come out right in the end. Your photograph and Frank's are very good, but Anna's I don't like much.

One which Effie sent me of herself is splendid—and looks more like her every *day*. It is odd how a portrait grows upon you—Susie's and Nellie's which I didn't like at first, begin to seem very good.

When do you begin your lecturing again? And what is the name of your new lecture?[3]

Give my love to Anna, Frank & the baby.

Your afftc Brother,
Robert G. Shaw

1. The Scotsman, Mr. McLean.

2. Thirty-three-year-old Milo M. Williams joined the army as a captain in the Fourth Massachusetts Infantry on Apr. 22, 1861, before serving on Banks's staff. Milo M. Williams file, CMSR.

3. Curtis, a well-known writer of travel books who published regularly in *Harper's Weekly*, *Harper's Monthly*, *Putnam's*, and the *Atlantic Monthly*, was a regular on the lyceum speaking tour.

His orations blended literary criticism and overt patriotism with a reformer's zeal and thrust for politics, abolition, women's rights, and, later, civil service reform. In 1861–62, Curtis lectured mainly against slavery. *DAB*, vol. 2, pp. 614–16; Gordon Milne, *George William Curtis and the Genteel Tradition* (Bloomington: Indiana University Press, 1956), pp. 34–76, 90–119, 253.

Oct. 13, 1861

Dear Father,

Enclosed are $150 in United States Treasury notes, part of two months' pay, which I wish you would take care of for me; and please send me a memorandum of what remains to my account after you have paid for the various things you have got for me, and the clothes Uncle Howland has ordered in Boston.[1] He will send you the bill when they are finished. I received a note from Anna, enclosing photographs of her and the baby, for which please thank her; also, your last, and one from Effie, and one from Nellie.

Last night we had another terrible storm; heavy rain and cold wind. Being on guard, I had the full benefit of it. I really felt ashamed when I turned out the reliefs, and made them march off, for it seemed as if no one had a right to make a man walk his beat for two hours in such weather. There was no grumbling, though, and they all seemed very well satisfied. It will be strange if the winter doesn't come harder to the Rebel army than to our New-Englanders. Most of our officers have had the earth dug out inside their tents four or five feet deep, and built fireplaces inside, with chimneys running through the ground to the back. A small wood-fire warms the tent completely, and makes as cheerful a little sitting-room as one can desire. This alone would, I think, make it easy to winter in the field with little or no suffering from [the] cold. I don't know where the idea came from, but Greely Curtis introduced it, and I have seen it nowhere else.[2]

Your loving son,
R. G. Shaw

1. Gardner Howland Shaw (1819–67). Smith, *Beacon Hill's*, p. 491.

2. Greely Stevenson Curtis was

Shaw's best friend in the Second Massachusetts.

CHAPTER 5

"*Ladies with petticoats about*"

Union armies had accomplished little by the end of 1861. At Ball's Bluff, Virginia, Confederate troops surprised and routed the Federals. Many of Shaw's friends, including future Supreme Court Justice Oliver Wendell Holmes, Jr., suffered wounds, death, or capture. In Southern elections, Rebel victories helped elect Jefferson Davis to a six-year term as president of the Confederacy.

With his regiment in winter quarters near Frederick, Maryland, Lieutenant Shaw lived through unhealthy conditions and camping in the snow. As Thanksgiving gave way to Christmas, the first mass desertions from the army required him to serve on a court-martial board. But Shaw also enjoyed life in the city and spent many evenings dancing at night-long parties. After five months of living with men, he took advantage of the companionship of women. Shaw also entertained his mother and father and others who took the opportunity to visit while the army lay idle in camp. Even while he made merry, Shaw reckoned: "We shall have much more soldiering to do than we expected when we started."

Conrad's Ferry
Oct. 22, 1861

Dearest Mother,

We marched all night, and arrived here this morning in a pouring rain. So, instead of resting, we had to stand up until 2 P.M., as there are no buildings in the neighbourhood. We have pitched our tents now. All along the road, we met men of the Fifteenth Massachusetts, who told us their regiment had crossed, been surprised by a superior force, and very much cut up.[1] A good many of them were in their shirts, having thrown off their clothes to swim. We thought they exaggerated the story, but imagine how we felt, on arriving here, to find that not only the Fifteenth, but the Twentieth, in which we have so many friends, had suffered terribly, and especially the officers.[2] Willie Putnam was wounded, and probably cannot recover.[3] Jim Lowell, his cousin (First Lieutenant of same company), is wounded, I don't know how badly, and Schmidt (their Captain) also.[4] John Putnam has lost an arm.[5] Poor Wendell Holmes has a ball through the leg, and one through the lungs.[6] All these were taken down to the hospital at Poolesville, this morning, in a canal-boat. Willie Putnam sent for Henry Higginson when he heard we had arrived, and Henry says he lay on his cot, and talked as calmly about the fight as if he were in perfect health, though he knows he has little chance of living.[7] Henry Sturgis carried him down to the river after he was hit. Colonel Lee and Major Revere are also missing.[8] Of the Fifteenth, there are only three or four of the company officers left, the rest killed and missing. Many will probably turn up. Caspar, whom Curtis saw, says the men behaved splendidly, and the officers evidently exposed themselves recklessly, and they must have had their wits about them, for they remember all the circumstances of the fight, and speak about it with wonderful calmness.[9] General Baker, of the California regiment, was killed.[10] The first body of men that went over were sent to surprise a camp by night. They arrived only at daylight, and, being discovered, a large body of troops came down from Leesburg; and as we only had one boat to send over reinforcements, they could not be furnished with men enough, and were overwhelmed. The California Brigade, the Tammany Regiment, and the two others were sent over piecemeal, which did no good at all.[11] So the general engagement was brought on by accident, and the leaders are the ones who blundered, as usual. Imagine having only one boat, which would hold at most thirty-five or forty men, and no means of retreat! Caspar was one of the last to leave, and he swam the river. Holmes and Putnam were hit while lifting up a wounded officer. It is a terrible thing, but we must get used to it. I was afraid you might think we had been in this engagement, if I didn't write. Our Major sent a telegraph to the contrary to the Boston papers. I will write again as soon as we move.

Your loving Son

1. The Fifteenth Massachusetts Infantry organized at Worcester, mustered into service on June 12, 1861, and served in Gordon's Division, Army of the Potomac. Dyer, *Compendium*, vol. 1, p. 158.

2. The Battle of Ball's Bluff took place on the steep and heavily wooded south bank of the Potomac River near Leesburg, Virginia, on October 20, 1861, between two evenly matched armies. The Rebels caught the Yankees on top of the bluff and many Union soldiers drowned trying to escape. Union casualties numbered 49 killed, 158 wounded, 714 missing; the Confederates lost 36 killed, 117 wounded, 2 missing. Long, *Civil War Day By Day*, pp. 129–30.

3. Second Lt. William Lowell Putnam (1840–61) graduated from Harvard in 1861 and helped raise the Nineteenth Massachusetts, but joined the Twentieth Massachusetts on July 10, 1861. Putnam hoped the war would do more than restore the Union. In a letter of Oct. 15, Putnam explained: "He who said that 'A century of civil war is better than a day of slavery' was right. God grant that every river in this land of ours may run with blood, and every city be laid in ashes rather than this war should come to an end without the utter destruction of every vestige of this curse so monstrous. Human being never drew sword in a better cause than ours. . . . I know full well that all is not yet as it should be,

and that a union man and an abolitionist do not mean the same thing." Brown, *Harvard University in the War*, pp. 348–49; Putnam, *Memoirs of the War*, pp. 49–53; Martin B. Duberman, ed., "A New England Soldier's Last Letter," *Civil War History* 9 (Sept. 1963): 325–27.

4. Captain Schmidt is unidentified. James Jackson Lowell recovered from his wound at Ball's Bluff to be mortally wounded eight months later at Glendale. Oliver Wendell Holmes, Jr., caught the precariousness of life in battle when he talked about his last goodbye to Lowell: "I looked down the line at Glendale. The officers were at the head of their companies. The advance was beginning. We caught each other's eye and saluted. When next I looked, he was gone." Lowell died July 4, 1862. Howe, *Touched With Fire*, p. 56.

5. Twenty-six-year-old Capt. John C. Putnam lost his right arm in the battle. From May 1862 to June 1863, Putnam served as a recruiting officer in Boston. He was discharged on Sept. 9, 1863. John C. Putnam file, CMSR.

6. Besides these wounds, Holmes attracted bullets at Antietam on Sept. 17, 1862, and at Fredericksburg on May 3, 1863. Oliver Wendell Holmes, Jr., file, CMSR.

7. Putnam had been struck in the abdomen. He died later that day. Henry Lee Higginson joined the Second in May 1861 and transferred to the First

Massachusetts Cavalry in Oct. 1861. After the war he entered the banking business and founded the Boston Symphony Orchestra. Richard Cary to Helen [Cary], Oct. 25, 1861, Richard Cary Papers, 1861–62, MHS; *DAB*, vol. 5, pp. 12–13.

8. Col. William Raymond Lee of Roxbury, Massachusetts, commanded the Twentieth since its organization in July 1861. He was taken prisoner at Ball's Bluff. Maj. Paul Joseph Revere (1832–63) of Boston and his brother Edward Hutchinson Revere (1827–62), an assistant surgeon with the Twentieth, were grandsons of colonial patriot Paul Revere. Major Revere was captured and taken with Colonel Lee to Libby Prison in Richmond. George A. Bruce, *The Twentieth Regiment of Massachusetts Volunteer Infantry, 1861–1865* (Boston: Houghton Mifflin, 1906), pp. 445, 459; Higginson, *Harvard Memorial Biographies*, vol. 1, pp. 204–17.

9. Caspar Crowninshield and Greely Curtis.

10. Edward Dickinson Baker (1811–61) was born in England, immigrated to the United States, and settled in Illinois.

He served two terms in the U.S. House of Representatives (1845–47, 1849–51), participated in the Mexican War, became a U.S. senator from Oregon (1860–61), and was practicing law in San Francisco when the war began. Baker accepted a colonelcy in the Seventy-first Pennsylvania, which was called the "First California" to honor him. Baker had a powerful friend, Abraham Lincoln, who named his second son after Baker and named Baker a major general of U.S. Volunteers on Sept. 21, 1861—a post Baker had neither declined nor accepted at the time of his death. Lincoln attended Baker's funeral in Washington, D.C., on Oct. 24. McGuiness and Sayers, *American Leaders*, p. 68; Boatner, *Dictionary*, p. 39; Faust, *Encyclopedia*, p. 34; Long, *Civil War Day By Day*, p. 131.

11. The Forty-second New York Infantry, nicknamed the Tammany Regiment, fought in thirty-six battles, lost nearly one hundred killed and six hundred wounded or missing during the Civil War. McKay, *Civil War and New York City*, pp. 76–77.

Near Muddy Branch, Md. [HL]
November 5, 1861
Dearest Mother,

Your note of the 2nd enclosing that from Mrs. Holmes was received tonight.[1] I am very glad indeed that the news I wrote of Wendell proved useful, especially as it was almost by chance that I wrote just at that time, for I was about falling asleep when I thought it might do no good unless I sent the note that morning. I am much obliged to her for her kind wishes. The note is enclosed as you may want it. I wrote to James Lowell & also to Captain

Schmidt and asked them to make their home at our house, and they were both as grateful to you for your kind invitation as anyone could be, but are both going home. Wendell Holmes has gone to the Hallowells at Philadelphia to stay and I wrote him a note asking him to pay you a visit if convenient.[2] I have no doubt he will like to go very much, after a while, as he needs change of air. I got a letter from George, with yours, for which please thank him—and one the other day from Uncle Jim.[3]

I am longing to hear about the naval expedition and whether it suffered from the late storm.[4]

We heard this afternoon that there is probability of our going into winter quarters in Frederick or Baltimore. There is a rumour to the effect that this division will not be kept together during the winter. In that case, some of us may form part of another expedition or be sent to the West. There can certainly be no move in winter excepting by the Mississippi or the Atlantic—and in that way the seat of war may yet be changed before spring. I do hope we shan't be entirely inactive but that they will continue to keep the fleet at work.

Harry is probably coming back in a few days as Col. Gordon told the General he was needed in the regiment. It is true in a measure, but it is rather hard for him to have possible advantages interfered with in that way.

I sent you a letter to send to Mrs. Haggerty, but didn't leave it open because I thought you would break the seal if you cared particularly about reading it. Leaving it open would have been an invitation to look at it which it was certainly not worth.

George says you are all looking wonderfully well and I hope I shall be able to judge of it for myself some time during the winter—if we don't go down South.

I am very well now. The other night I got chilled through and lay by for a day or two, but am all right again now. The air here is cold and bracing.

Ever dearest Mother
Your loving son,
Robert G. Shaw

1. Amelia Lee Jackson Holmes (1818–87). Marian Rossiter Small, *Oliver Wendell Holmes* (New York: Twayne, 1962), pp. 49, 145.

2. Norwood Penrose Hallowell (1839–1914) knew Holmes at Harvard and joined him in the Fourth Massachusetts Volunteer Militia at Fort Independence in Apr. 1861 before accepting active duty with the Twentieth. Norwood's father, Morris L. Hallowell, a Quaker, lived in Philadelphia, where he opened his home as a hospital during the war. Brown, *Harvard University in the*

War, pp. 167, 168.

3. George William Curtis and James Sturgis.

4. The largest federal naval expedition that had ever assembled—seventy-seven ships and 12,000 men under the command of Admiral Samuel F. du Pont—was rocked by heavy winds near Cape Hatteras, North Carolina, on Oct. 29 and Nov. 1. On Nov. 7, du Pont forced his way into Port Royal Sound and landed the army on South Carolina soil, thereby establishing a naval base in Confederate territory from which the Union would operate throughout the war. Long, *Civil War Day By Day*, pp. 132, 134, 136.

Near Muddy Branch [RGS]
Nov. 11, 1861
Dear Mother,

Yours of the 6th was received last night, together with the stockings and band from Mrs. Cushing.[1] Please thank her very much for them. The band will be very useful, and I should like two or three more, as you suggest. I like Fremont's address to his army exceedingly, especially his not hinting in any way that any injustice had been done him.[2] As you say, it is perfectly simple and dignified.

We are in the worst camp we have ever had. It is in a hollow, where the dampness collects, and, as we have had a great deal of rain lately, it has been a perfect bog. There are more ailings among the men than we ever had before. We expect to change to-day or to-morrow, and get a more wholesome place. I have been reading an article in the Atlantic,—"Health in Camp," by Miss Martineau, in which she says the Sardinians suffered very much in the Crimea from disease, because they lived underground. This is just our experience, for we began by digging out the earth inside our tents when the cold weather first came, and, though it was warmer, the dampness was very unwholesome. The article has a great many good things, but one can see that it is written by a person who has had no personal experience in the thing.[3]

We are still in the dark as to the fate in store for us this winter, and I confess I am getting rather impatient to know. Please tell Father that three caps have been ordered, for which he will pay with my money,—one by Harry, with bugle; one by Mr. Mudge for me, size 7, with bugle; and one by me, size 7 1/8, without bugle.[4] If Warnock sends me one without bugle, I shall send it back.[5]

Your loving Son

1. Probably ninety-one-year-old Sarah Cushing, who lived with the Shaw's Staten Island neighbor George A. Ward. Eighth Census (1860), Population, N.Y., Richmond Co., Castleton, p. 63.

2. Frémont made his farewell speech to his army on Nov. 3, when Maj. Gen. David Hunter took active command in the West.

3. Harriet Martineau (1802–76) wrote that "The Sardinians suffered . . . from their way of making their huts. They excavated a space, to the depth of three or four feet, and used the earth they threw out to embank the walls raised upon the edge of the excavation. This provided warmth in winter and coolness in hot weather; but the interior was damp and ill-ventilated; and as soon as there was any collection of refuse within, cholera and fever broke out." *Atlantic Monthly* 8 (Nov. 1861): 571–80; *Dictionary of National Biography* (Oxford: Oxford University Press, 1950), vol. 12, pp. 1194–99.

4. Mr. Mudge is probably the father of Capt. Charles Redington Mudge of New York City, a classmate of Shaw's at Harvard. Harvard College, *Report of Class of 1860*, pp. 34–35.

5. Joseph and Robert Warnock made hats and military goods at 519 Broadway, New York City. *Trow's NYC Directory, 1863*, p. 907.

Near Muddy Branch   [RGS]
Nov. 15, 1861
Dear Susie,

I was very glad to get your letter, as I hadn't heard from you for so long. Indeed, I have never been told that you were not still at Newport. To tell the truth, my letters tell me much less about home than I should like to hear, because the writers, I presume, think more about the war than anything else. The subject gets a good airing here every day, as there is little else to talk about. What you say of Mrs. Gay is indeed news to me.[1] I am very glad to hear that they are to have an increase of population in the house. We have never had any supplies from the "Sanitary Commission." I fancy they go generally to the "General Hospital." All the articles we draw come from the Government. Do you make clothes for well men? If you do, I hope the drawers and shirts are of good gray flannel. Our first issue from Massachusetts were excellent, like everything we get from there, but those we get from [the] Government we don't think much of. Our men will be much pleased to get the mittens, though a great many of them buy gloves of the sutler, who sells almost everything that was ever invented in the way of clothing and pies. The latter, though, are going to be banished, as they are unwholesome.

We have had a cold, rainy, and intensely uncomfortable day, but I have a nice little stone fireplace in my tent, with a pretty high chimney outside, which makes it draw finely, and keeps the tent warm and dry. In this camp, mine happens to be one of the successful fireplaces (they often smoke), so that I have had company all day. We have been, from reveille until tattoo, talking and reading, and having quite a nice time. Stephen Perkins, Rufus Choate, and Captain Savage were the guests.[2] The latter is one of the best men I have ever known, and, at the same time, he is one of the best officers, and a real brave fellow. One of the rarest articles to be found is a pure-minded man, and Savage is as much so as any woman. Though I have seen him every day for five months, I didn't get to know him well until six weeks ago.

Give my love to Mary Parkman, if she is still at Anna's.[3] Hoping to hear from you soon again.

Your loving brother,
Robert G. Shaw

1. Elizabeth Neall Gay of Staten Island.

2. First Lt. Stephen George Perkins (1835–62), of Boston, graduated from Harvard in 1856. Later, Charles Francis Adams remembered: "Stephen was perhaps the closest of my friends. The choicest mind I ever knew." Second Lt. Rufus Choate and Capt. James Savage. Before the war, Savage had been close friends with Wilder Dwight and Greely Curtis. Putnam, *Memoirs of the War of*

'61, pp. 19–25.

3. Shaw was related to the Parkmans through his mother's grandfather, Samuel Parkman (1751–1824). Additionally, his father's father, Robert Gould Shaw, married Elizabeth Willard Parkman, a daughter of Samuel Parkman, thereby entwining and confusing the family tree. Shaw had several relatives named Mary Parkman. This is probably Mary Eliot Parkman. Smith, *Beacon Hill's*, pp. 494, 495, 497.

Seneca Md.   [HL]
November 20, 1861
Dear Mother,

I mentioned in a note to Father a few days ago that I had received yours of the 13th inst.

My chief piece of news for this mail is that Harry has come back to the regiment and though I should be very sorry if he lost any advantage in the shape of promotion by it, I am heartily glad to have him here.[1] He and I have a tent together now, and live happily together. This week, since he came back has been the pleasantest I have had for a long while, and we both look forward, every day, to our evening together with great pleasure. The fireplace in the tent is the greatest comfort and we sit talking or reading as if at home. Our talks are endless, for we always find something to chat about. If he goes back again (Copeland wants him very much) I shall be infernally lonely. He appears to have made a good many friends at headquarters for the other members of the staff, as well as Genl Banks were very sorry to have him go.

Tomorrow is Thanksgiving day in Massachusetts and it is to be celebrated in all the Mass. Regiments. The country round about has been depopulated of geese and turkeys and the amount of plum-pudding preparing for consumption in this regiment is astounding. Of turkeys & geese there are about 30 to a company, I should think. There will be no drills, and as no one reported sick by the surgeon is to have any of the dinner, we shall have a healthy set of men tomorrow. But if half the battalion can turn out the next day, we shall be surprized.

Speaking of sickness—we have never had so much of it as now. We changed our camp a short time ago, because the first one was said to be in an unwholesome place, but this, though an improvement, is both damp and without protection from the storms, which are sometimes very violent. Our Lieut. Col., Capt Savage, & Capt Mudge & the adjutant are sick in bed in neighbouring houses—and two lieutenants are also laid up.[2] They seem to have a sort of intermittent fever and it prevails among the men too. Other regiments are in a much healthier state, probably because they are all a good way from the river, while we are near it. Motley is one of the invalids, but is much better lately.[3] Rufus Choate has got leave to go home to recruit. We shall miss him very much at our Thanksgiving dinner for he is the witty man of the regiment—and at the same time a nice, sweet-tempered fellow, who never uses his wit to make fun of or hurt the feelings of any one.

Tell Effie that the mittens will be most welcome and I hope they will arrive safely.

The first two caps which Father sent have arrived safely, and the third is probably in Washington waiting an opportunity of pursuing its journey. The reason I got chilled as I mentioned to you sometime ago, was I think because I was so fatigued. It didn't last more than a day or two & I had no fever. I am in a continual state of surprise at being well when so many of the officers & men are laid up.

Our brigade (Genl Abercrombie) was reviewed & inspected yesterday, which makes us hope that something is on foot for us. We are to be furnished with everything wanting, to put us in good marching order again.[4] If we don't go off I think there will be no difficulty in my seeing you *somewhere* in the course of the winter. Let us hope so at any rate.

                                        Ever your loving son

1. Harry Russell had been detached temporarily to Banks's staff since Oct. 1. Russell file, CMSR.

2. Lt. Col. George L. Andrews. First Lt. Charles Wheaton, Jr., was the regimental adjutant. Bowen, *Mass. in the*

War, p. 113.

3. First Lt. T. Lawrence Motley. *Record of Mass. Vols*, p. 28.

4. John Joseph Abercrombie commanded the Second Brigade.

Camp near Seneca [RGS]
Nov. 23, 1861
Dear Father,

Your letter of the 15th, with Mother's and Effie's of 17th and 18th, were received day before yesterday. I don't know why yours was so long on the way. I will try to let you know, if we are ordered off, in time for you to come down. I hope you won't think of letting Mother come here, unless we get into the neighbourhood of some city. I believe there is some chance of our moving to Frederick, as this part of the country is supposed to be unwholesome. In that case, you could get a comfortable place to stay, and we could see a great deal of each other. I don't think now we shall go into winter quarters, but will keep our tents until we are wanted, which may be at any time. I will do my best to keep you informed of where we are likely to go, and when. We had a fine time on Thanksgiving Day. The men enjoyed themselves very much. In the morning we had divine service, after which there was a turkey-shoot; and at 12 1/2 P.M. the men had their dinner. Besides all the turkeys and geese, they had nearly twelve hundred pounds of plum-pudding![1] In our company they got themselves up as good a dinner as any one could desire. It cost only $31, which came out of the company fund. In the evening the band played for them, and they had a good dance. The officers' dinner was at 5 o'clock, and we enjoyed ourselves very much. Our mess-tent was gorgeously lighted with candles, bayonets serving for candlesticks, and the dinner was excellent.

Men are deserting very fast from the New York regiments about here. They have very little discipline in them, as a general thing.

Give my love to Mother, and say that Mrs. Cushing's bands are very comfortable indeed.

Your loving son,
Robert G. Shaw

1. Regimental Chaplain Alonzo Quint wrote a newspaper article enumerating the Thanksgiving dinner of the regiment: 94 turkeys weighing 973 pounds,

76 geese (666 lb.), 73 chickens (176 lb.), plum pudding (1,179 lb.), and more. Massachusetts Infantry, 2nd Regiment,

Letters from the Army: A Scrapbook, p. 11, BPL.

Camp near Seneca Md. [HL]
Nov. 25 1861 3 A.M.

Dear Mother,

This is my night for Guard, and I have been thinking that you may have waked up at some time during the night and thought of me.

We are no doubt often awake and thinking of each other at the same time. We had a very unpromising evening, for it snowed pretty hard for some time—but that stopped and left the earth in just the proper condition to be converted into slosh, mud & mire. It is now clear again and everything is still excepting the Potomac, which never stops rolling & roaring. It doesn't seem as if it can have been flowing as long as the Nile, or the Rhine, or the Tiber, but if everything else *is* new in America, our lakes, rivers & forests are as old as any one's. I have had quite a good time tonight, as the prisoners have behaved well & needed no punishment, and the Guard are asleep and quiet. Often the latter sit round the fire and talk till you get perfectly sick of hearing them and wish every one of their Yankee noses were cut off. Instead of getting accustomed to the Yankee twang it becomes more and more disagreeable to me, and everytime I hear a "What saaaay?" (every two minutes) I want to go out & kick them all round.

As I wrote Father the other day, dear Mother, I shall give you the most reliable news I can get about our movements. If we go into Virginia, we shall probably start at a moment's notice. It is useless to try to get a furlough now too, unless for sickness. An officer in this division wanted to go home to see his wife during her confinement & they wouldn't let him go.

Do you understand why no reinforcements go to Beaufort?[1] They may be getting ready, but if they had had them to send five days after the news of the landing, I should think it would have been wiser. If we do have any trouble with England (and it seems to be an even chance) the Government will probably wake up. I hope then that they will oblige the whole army, if possible, to remain in the field, and draft as many more as they want. It would be fair to use the citizens for the safety of the country, even against their will. Perhaps all Europe will be drawn into this before it is finished.[2]

The sergeant of the Guard tonight, who has been to sea several times before the mast, told me that he had never led such a hard life as this. I was surprised for I had more exaggerated notions of the hardships of a sailor's life. We have certainly had a pretty easy time as yet.

It has cleared off cold and it is freezing quite hard. We have had a little ice every night for some time past. My best love to yourself & all the rest.

Your loving son,
Robert G. Shaw

1. The Union had a strong position established at Beaufort, South Carolina, which Confederates never really threatened after it was seized on Nov. 9. For the rest of the war, the Union navy and army used it as a staging base for actions along the South Atlantic coastline. Here also the North instituted its first experiment in converting freed slaves into free people. For the best account of that experiment, see Willie Lee Rose, *Rehearsal for Reconstruction: The Port Royal Experiment* (London & New York: Oxford University Press, 1964).

2. Shaw is probably referring to the saber rattling on both sides of the Atlantic between the United States and Britain over the *Trent* affair. On Nov. 8, the USS *San Jacinto* stopped and boarded the British ship *Trent* and arrested James Mason and John Slidell, Confederate commissioners bound for Europe to seek recognition for the Confederacy from England and France. In the weeks that followed, the British demanded an official apology and dispatched warships to North America.

Camp Hicks near Frederick Md
December 8 1861

[HL, RGS]

My dear Effie,

Your weekly & welcome letter came yesterday. I look for it regularly now and shall be much disappointed the first time it misses, if such a thing can be imagined after your long & faithful regularity. I didn't have time to write again from Seneca, before we left, as I said I should, for the order to march came at 12 1/2 A.M. We got off early in the morning. It was tout ce qu'il y a de plus unpleasant to be waked up at Midnight, the weather icy cold, to wake up in their turn the cooks, & see about rations.[1] We had a good two days march, for the cold weather kept us going. The roads didn't soften even at noon.

The day after we arrived it changed and we have had almost an Indian summer for 5 days, during which time we have made ourselves comfortable & can defy Jack Frost when he comes again.

Yesterday I went into Frederick to see Capt Mudge who has been ill for about 3 weeks. I found him much better & was coming out, not having any acquaintances to visit when I fell in with Copeland & it turned out to be a fortunate rencontre for me. He took me to a house where I was presented to two young ladies & we shortly sallied forth all together & after picking up Mrs. Copeland, another lady & Capt Savage, we repaired to a bowling alley where we had a perfectly jolly time all the afternoon.[2] We then took a walk, after which we went home to the house of the afore-mentioned young ladies, & took tea. In the evening there was a great deal of playing on the piano & chorus singing, in which latter we all howled, & made as much noise as we could. I can't describe to you my sensations at sitting once more in a nice parlor & seeing real ladies with petticoats about. I had hardly realized before that for 5 months we had been living like gypsies & seeing only men. I had really not spoken to a lady since we left New York. These two are daughters of Genl Shriver, a Union man here, who was very active in helping break up the Maryland legislature 2 months ago.[3] One of them is a very nice girl indeed, I should think, if one can judge on so short an acquaintance. She sings very well too.

Today I have been in a heavenly humour from dawn until the present moment 10 1/2 P.M. In the first place the day has been lovely. Then every man in my company was clean de cap a pie on Sunday morning inspection.[4] Then the band played some beautiful music at service & the parson preached a good sermon. Then we have cleaned away all the rubbish & underbrush from the camp & everything looks clean & neat. Then our stove & other furniture has come out & the tent is very comfortable. After this we had an A-1 dress-parade & finally I find [I] have not got to go off on picket guard tomorrow as I had expected. What effect yesterday's pleasures had on my spirits, or in what degree they contributed to making me feel happy today, I don't know, but dissipation usually produces the contrary result, you know. For instance, namely: My servant, whom I sent in town to get some articles of luxury enjoyed himself also, but is today in the depths of despair. He allowed himself to partake too freely of the intoxicating cup, was arrested by the Provost Guard for riotous conduct & knocked in the eye with the butt of a musket—after which process, he tells me, he knew nothing for two hours, which is highly probable as he was fast approaching that condition before. He was released today and is now suffering acute mental agony because I have put him back in the ranks & he will have to stand guard & drill besides carrying his knapsack on the march. The effect which his Katzenjammer, his black eye, and his mental prostration, united, produced on the expression of his countenance is very ridiculous—though I suppose I ought to pity him.[5]

I have asked Father to bring you three girls when Mother & he come to Frederick, and though

[last page missing; continued from RGS]

It is getting late, and I must stop. The mittens are splendid. Please thank all the ladies who are at work on the others. Best love to Susie and Nellie.

Ever your affectionate brother,
R. G. S.

1. Literally, "all the more there is."
2. Wife of Robert Morris Copeland. The other woman is unidentified.
3. Gen. Edward Shriver, leader of Maryland's Union party, was instrumental in preventing the meeting of the Maryland secession legislature in Frederick on Sept. 17, 1861. T. J. C. Williams and Folger McKinsey, *History of Frederick County, Maryland* (Baltimore: Regional Publishing Co., 1967), vol. 1, pp. 365, 371–72. For information on the arrest of secessionist members of the Maryland legislature, see "Correspondence Between S. Teackle Wallis, Esq., of Baltimore, and the Hon. John Sherman of the U.S. Senate" (Baltimore: N.p., 1863).
4. Literally, "from head to foot."
5. A *Katzenjammer* is a hangover.

Camp Hicks, near Frederick   [RGS]
Dec. 14, 1861
Dear Father,

I have left you without news of me for a week this time, but hope you haven't imagined I was dead or ill. Your note of 11th came to hand, as also Effie's last. I was very sorry to hear you were not coming down this week, though you will probably find us still here in January. Alex. and Annie think of coming about Christmas.[1] Harry is Captain now; his commission has not yet come, but will be along soon. We hear that Colonel Gordon is likely to be made Brigadier. There is not a man in the regiment, I believe, who will not be very sorry not to go into action under him. As far as we can judge, he is a man who would be cool and clear-headed in a fight. He has, besides, the affection of the men, and, when he takes hold, can make them do what he chooses. It is my opinion that every officer will be heartily sorry to lose Colonel Gordon. We are having a comfortable time here. The weather continues fine, but no doubt we shall have to pay for it in time. Captain Tucker goes to-morrow. Harry will have his company.[2] I went up to a place called Newmarket, to stop liquor, the other day. An old gentleman there told me there was no doubt that the slaves in this State would be emancipated if the question were to be decided to-morrow by vote of the people. I was rather astonished at this, but he said there were many men who, like him, would never own a slave, though well able to buy them. Give my love to all. I shall write to Mother soon. The shirts and drawers are very satisfactory. I hope the other mittens will come soon. Thank Effie, for Harry and me, for the mittens she sent to *us*.

> Your affectionate son,
> Robert G. Shaw

1. Alexander and Annie Agassiz.
2. Capt. Francis H. Tucker resigned his commission on Dec. 12, 1861, and opened a vacancy for Harry Russell. *Record of Mass. Vols.*, p. 28.

Guard-Tent Second Massachusetts   [RGS]
Camp Hicks, near Frederick, Md., 3 1/2 o'clock, A.M.
Dec. 25, 1861
Dearest Mother,

It is Christmas morning, and I hope it will be a happy and merry one for you all, though, it looks so stormy for our poor country, one can hardly be in a merry humour.

I should be very sorry to have a war with England, even if we had a fine army, instead of a pack of politicians for officers, with their constituents for rank and file; and all the more so, of course, thinking that we shall have to take many "whoppings" before we are worth much. War isn't declared yet, but doesn't it look very much like it to every one at home?[1] Here, we have made up our minds that we shall have much more soldiering to do than we expected when we started. I think we may as well consider ourselves settled for life, if we are to have a war with England!

My Christmas Eve has been very much like many other eves during the last six months. On the whole, I have passed quite a pleasant night, though what our men call the "fore-part" of it was principally occupied in taking care of two drunken men (one of them with a broken pate), and in tying a sober one to a tree. After this was over, I did a good deal of reading, and, towards 1 o'clock, A.M., had some toast and hot coffee,—having previously invited my Sergeant to take a nap, so that I might not be troubled by hungry eyes, and made to feel mean, for there wasn't enough to give any away. The drummer (who, with the Sergeant of the Guard, for some reason which I never discovered, sits and sleeps in the officers' tent) kept groaning in his sleep; and I couldn't help imagining that his groan always came in just as I took a bite of toast, or a large gulp of coffee. This diminished my enjoyment; and when he suddenly said, "*Martha! there isn't any breakfast*," I was certain that my proceedings were influencing his dreams!

It began to snow about midnight, and I suppose no one ever had a better chance of seeing "Santa Claus"; but, as I had my stockings on, he probably thought it not worth his while to come down to the guard-tent. I didn't see any of the guard's stockings pinned up outside their tent, and indeed it is contrary to army regulations for them to divest themselves of any part of their clothing during the twenty-four hours.

Please ask Father to bring me a pocket-revolver, if he can get it, when he comes,—one small enough to carry in the breast-pocket. Also, tell the girls that Harry would be very much obliged if they would send him seventy or eighty pairs of mittens. I heard him say he would like to have some. The men were all glad to get them, though, as usual, they didn't express their thanks.[2] They get so many things that they are spoilt, and think they have a right to all these extras. Thirteen dollars per month, with board, lodging, and clothes, is more than nine men out of ten could make at home. Poor soldiers! poor *drumsticks*! But this is not the sort of language for me to use, who am supposed to stand in the light of half mother to the men of my company. I should like about fifteen more pairs mittens; and some *warm* flannel shirts and drawers would be very useful, if there are any spare ones. "Uncle Sam's" are miserable things. "Merry Christmas" and love to all, dear Mother. I suppose Sue is at Mrs. Schuyler's.[3] I am so glad she is coming with you next month! Alex. and Annie will be here next week.

Your loving son,
Robert G. Shaw

1. On Dec. 26, to calm tensions between Washington and London, Lincoln acceded to British demands and released Mason and Slidell. With the settling of the *Trent* affair, chances of English intervention and war became increasingly remote.

2. Josephine sent forty-two pairs of mittens to Shaw in mid December. Josephine's Diary, Dec. 16, 1861, in Stewart, *Philanthropic Work*, p. 22.

3. The Schuylers lived on Staten Island.

Cantonment Hicks   [HL, RGS]
Jany 15 1862
My dear Effie,

I have, I believe three letters from you unanswered, the last received day before yesterday in which you relate your encounter with, and defeat by the invidious fog. I hope he relented at last and that you have got away.

I proceeded immediately after receipt of yours to inspect my cheeks and

I don't think you w'd find them much less flabby than formerly. Indeed Mother's account of my corpulency must have been a little exaggerated for I don't perceive much increase my-self.

I returned yesterday noon from the Monocacy bridge, between here and Frederick where I was on guard for 24 hours, and where I should have had a very pleasant time if it hadn't been for three brats who tormented me. I stayed in a house near the bridge, and thought at first that the landlady was a very pretty & pleasant woman, but the bad behaviour of the above-mentioned children soon brought out some little characteristics which were, to say the least, not ladylike. She got very much enraged and said to the nurse: "Hang you you black imp, I'll knock your black head off"—and to the children "Get out of this or I'll smack your jaws!" and made use of many other similar expressions. At night instead of putting the children to bed, the plan was, to get them asleep down stairs & then carry them up. Of course this was a tedious process & involved much screaming, swearing, bawling & blubbering. Three times it was tried & three times they waked up on the way upstairs. After the third failure the noise was something terrible—all the three children screamed at the top of their lungs. Mrs. Waters cussed & swore at the black girl. The black girl cried and actually said it wasn't her fault. Mr. Waters consoled himself & vainly tried to amuse the children by vigorously playing upon the most infernal old fiddle that ever was manufactured and beating time very hard with his cowhide boots.[1] I sat with a smile on my face, but despair in my heart trying to concentrate my ideas sufficiently to understand "Halleck's Elements of Military Art & Science."[2] May I be preserved in [the] future from such scenes as these! I didn't bargain for anything of the kind when I joined the regiment.

We have had a large ball in Frederick since Father & Mother went away.[3] It was given by a gentleman who has a fine large house a little way out of town and we went over in an omnibus from here. There were about 100 ladies & 300 gentlemen & some of the latter had to do a good deal of "standing round." I enjoyed myself very much though and danced nearly all the time. None of the Frederick ladies dance round dances, but there were a good many officer's wives & daughters who don't object to it.

One lady from Philadelphia, a

[last page missing; continued from RGS]

Jewess,—was a beautiful dancer, but the rest were not of the best. This Jewess is the wife of a Captain here, who went home on furlough the other day, and ran off with her. She is very silly, and tells every one about it. Two or three days after she left home, her parents had a great funeral ceremony, and buried her carefully! Frederick seems to be full of pretty and nice girls, and the officers who live in town are having a very gay time. The ball didn't end so pleasantly as it began, for the host, very rashly, had a large quantity of liquor taken up into the gentlemen's dressing-room, and those who didn't dance, or couldn't get partners, consequently got very drunk. The result of it was, a general scrimmage between some Secession civilians and some officers. It was rather startling for some of the ladies, but the natives didn't seem to think anything of it. The combatants were finally pacified, without having done any damage. The house was beautifully decorated with banners; and outside there were transparencies, on which were to be seen compliments to General Banks, sentiments of loyalty, &c., and quotations from Union speeches.

Of course I enjoyed Father's and Mother's visit very much. I never saw her looking better, or in better spirits. I was very sorry none of you could come with them. I fully expected to see Susie, and was very much disappointed. Mr. Trayer, an acquaintance that Mother made in my tent, went home raving about her, as I heard from Shelton, who was stationed at his house.[4] He thought she was the most beautiful, intelligent, and industrious lady (she was knitting a mitten) he had ever seen. Shelton told him and his family that she was a good specimen of Northern ladies; whereat they wondered,—and with good reason.

Dan has this moment arrived.[5] I have no doubt he will make a good officer, for he is a manly fellow, and will probably do his duty to the best of his power. I am really very glad he has come at last. Give my love to Mrs. Oakey and the young ladies when you see them.[6] Excuse blots in this letter: I am sitting in the guard-tent, and as it is snowing, raining, and hailing, and I have to go out every little while, everything is dampish and dirtyish. Give my love to Aunt Mary and Loulie.[7] I hope you will have a nice time in Boston (as you will, of course), and that you will be back by the time I get home. That will be in three weeks, perhaps, if my application is not refused.

Always your loving brother,
Robert G. Shaw

1. The Waters are unidentified.

2. Henry W. Halleck (1815–72) was a West Point graduate, lawyer and engineer. His *Elements of Military Art and Science* (1846), with revisions, was the standard military textbook used for training officers in staff duties and Napoleonic tactics.

3. Francis and Sarah Shaw visited their son in Frederick, Maryland, in early January. Richard Cary to Helen [Cary], Jan. 5, 1862, Cary Papers, MHS.

4. Mr. Trayer is unidentified. Second Lt. Eugene E. Shelton of Boston joined the regiment on Nov. 1, 1861. *Record of Mass. Vols.*, p. 29.

5. Second Lt. Daniel A. Oakey (1839–?) was mustered on Nov. 30, 1861. *Record of Mass. Vols.*, p. 29.

6. Sarah Williams Sullivan Oakey, husband William Forbes Oakey, and children lived near the Shaws on Staten Island. Stewart, *Philanthropic Works*, pp.

11, 32.

7. Mary Louisa Sturgis married Shaw's paternal uncle Robert Gould Shaw, Jr. (1815–53). She lived with daughter Mary Louisa (Loulie) Shaw at 44 Beacon Street, Boston. Smith, *Beacon Hill's*, pp. 127, 133, 491.

Frederick Md.   [HL]
February 9 1862

My dear Effie,

I have received two letters from you since I last wrote and I admire your constancy in writing so regularly.

Susie is in Washington & I have just telegraphed to Cousin John to know if he can't go home this way and make us a short visit.[1] I can't possibly go away, so if they don't come to Frederick I shan't see Susie at all. That would be too bad when we are so near together. Today, for the first time, I think, for five weeks the weather is fine—but it looks as if it were going to cloud over again in a little while.

I have very pleasant lodgings here in a family consisting of a very queer old party, named Delaplane, and his wife.[2] The latter has a most wonderful appetite and an extraordinary love of good dinners, the result of which is, that we live remarkably well. Capt Savage & Dr. Stone of the 2 Mass. live here too, but will soon be going back to the regt.[3] I am afraid I shall be rather lonely then. We have two rooms adjoining each other, one of which has a large open fire-place, which is very comfortable & cozy. I go round to the Court-Martial about 10 o'cl. A.M. and we usually get through at 2 P.M. so that I have a good deal of time to myself. I find though, that camp is the best place for me. I am always in good spirits out there—probably because it is such a wholesome life. As soon as I can get a horse, I shall have a much pleasanter time here, for I have much difficulty in getting about now—especially out to camp where I want to go quite often.

Mills has arrived here and I was sorry it wasn't somebody whom I wanted to see more.[4] Not that I don't like *him*, but when I see other people coming down here with so little trouble, I always wish it was some of "my folks."

Your treatment of James Jackson struck me as being very brutal.[5] I can imagine the poor devil's feelings, while a lot of girls were laughing at him. I am improving my spare time in learning to write with my left hand. I may lose my right you know and then I should have to wait a long time before I could write you myself, unless I learn now.[6]

Thank Aunt Mary for the few lines she wrote in one of your letters. Give my love to her & to Loulie.

There have been a good many balls & parties here and at some of them I have had a very nice time. The ladies here don't dance round dances and if it hadn't been for officers' families we should have had quadrilles until 5 in the morning, for they invariably keep it up until as late as that.

I think you ought to have held out about round dances after Susie's good example.

Your loving brother,
Robert G. Shaw

1. John Murray Forbes.

2. Probably, Theodore Crist Delaplaine (1810–?), who owned the Monocacy Flour Mill, and his wife Hannah Wilcoxon Delaplaine. *History of Frederick County Maryland* (Baltimore: L. R. Titsworth, 1910), vol. 2, p. 1036.

3. Capt. James Savage, Jr., a Boston abolitionist, became one of Shaw's closest friends. Dr. Lincoln R. Stone (1833–?), of Salem, was mustered into the regiment as an assistant surgeon with the rank of first lieutenant in May 1861. Stone brought with him, and received government subsistence for, one servant and two horses. Henry Lee Higginson scrapbook, "The Soldier's Book," HL, section on Savage; James Savage, Jr., and

Lincoln R. Stone files, CMSR.

4. Probably Shaw's second cousin Charles James Mills (1841–65) of Boston, who graduated from Harvard in 1860. Higginson, *Harvard Memorial Biographies*, vol. 2, pp. 133–41; Smith, *Beacon Hill's*, p. 366.

5. James Jackson is unidentified. Perhaps he is the "invidious fog" Shaw mentioned in his Jan. 15 letter to Effie.

6. Worried that they might lose the use of their writing hand, many soldiers worked on their ambidexterity. Oliver Wendell Holmes, Jr., mentioned that after he was wounded at Antietam on Sept. 17, 1862, he had to write with his opposite hand. Howe, *Touched With Fire*, pp. 67–68.

Frederick, Md.   [RGS]
Feb. 16, 1862
Dear Mother,

Yesterday I went up to have my photograph taken, but it was so dark that it had to be put off. To-day, being Sunday, I can't go, though it is a beautiful day. Susie is coming up here to-morrow with Mrs. Hooper and Annie, and will stay until Wednesday afternoon.[1] I was afraid she would have to go home without my seeing her. I am still in Frederick, and there is no probability of my rejoining the regiment until a forward movement is made. We have a great many cases on hand, and new ones coming every day, several of them commissioned officers. Frederick is quite a pleasant little city, and I have made a good many agreeable acquaintances. The other evening, Savage and I went to call on a Mrs. ———, who is the prettiest woman in the town. She got up a nice little supper, and we ate, drank, and played whist with her and her sister until 11 o'clock.[2] On Wednesday I went to church with a young lady from Baltimore, and was rather astonished, when I got there, to find myself and the sexton the only men in the building! It was full of ladies, though; and, as we sat facing the congregation, I had a fine view. I was much confused by finding twelve little orphan girls who sat on the front seat, in enormous hoods, staring at me every time I looked up. The sermons that I have heard are pretty poor, though, to be sure, I have only been to one church, and that Episcopal.

How do you feel about the good news from the South and West? All I want or wish this week is to hear that Fort Donelson and Savannah are taken.[3] Next week I should like to have Burnside take Norfolk.[4] I am very much afraid, though, that we shan't have such a run of luck as that. Some of the Secession people here were enraged at the news. I heard one girl say to another, when I was standing near them in the street, "I like a *nigger* better than a Massachusetts soldier!" This same young person turns up her nose, and makes faces, whenever she meets us riding or walking. Most of the Secession ladies, though, have good enough manners to refrain from any such demonstrations. Love to Father, Anna, and Nellie.

Ever your loving son,
Robert G. Shaw

1. Perhaps Shaw is referring to Ellen Sturgis Hooper, wife of Boston physician Robert William Hooper and friend of his parents. Stewart, *Philanthropic Works*, p. 24; Ward Thoron, ed., *The Letters of Mrs. Henry Adams* (Boston: Little, Brown, 1936), p. xiii.

2. Whist was a popular card game in nineteenth-century America.

3. On Feb. 6, Union naval forces under Adm. Andrew Foote forced the surrender of Fort Henry on the Cumberland River in Tennessee. At nearly the same time Shaw penned this letter, Gen. Ulysses S. Grant was demanding the "unconditional and immediate surrender" of Fort Donelson on the Tennessee River. Grant had earned a sobriquet and a promotion to major general. The Union gained control of Kentucky and Tennessee. In the South, Federals won the battle for Roanoke Island, North

Carolina, on Feb. 8. Savannah did not fall to the North until Sherman captured it on Dec. 21, 1864. Long, *Civil War Day By Day*, pp. 167, 168, and 171–72.

4. Ambrose Everett Burnside (1824–81) was the victor at Roanoke Island.

Increasing naval pressure and the defeat of the ironclad *Virginia* by the *Monitor* off Hampton Roads in March led to the Confederate abandonment of Norfolk in May 1862. Faust, *Encyclopedia*, p. 97.

CHAPTER 6

"What war really is"

As winter melted into spring in 1862, Federal troops made major advances. In the West, a nova exploded upon the scene in the form of Ulysses S. Grant's victories at Shiloh and Forts Donelson and Henry. In the East, McClellan launched his peninsular campaign against Richmond. Off Hampton Roads, two ironclads, the *Monitor* and the *Merrimack*, dueled to a draw.

While he enjoyed the beauty of Virginia, Lieutenant Shaw passed the first anniversary of the war and of his enlistment. He had little time to rest as the army of General Nathaniel Banks marched and countermarched between Winchester, Strasburg, and New Market in pursuit of Stonewall Jackson— the South's new star. Up and down the Shenandoah Valley, Shaw encountered fugitive slaves, Secessionists, and "terrible sights." As Jackson's army inflicted casualties on Union soldiers, Shaw wrote of the horrible inadequacy of field hospitals. He praised the Northern enlisted men but noted that many of them were "thieves" and "drunkards." Itching for a chance to fight and celebrating his military life, he rejoiced: "What a blessing that we happened to be born in this century and country!"

Charlestown, Va.
March 3, 1862
Dear Mother,

We are still in Charlestown, but expect to go away to-night or to-morrow morning. A good many prisoners and contrabands have been brought in, and the general impression seems to be that the Rebels will evacuate Winchester. We (of this Division) seem destined never to have a fight with them.

The Hon. Andrew Hunter's office, where several of us have had our quarters, has yielded a rich crop.[1] You remember that he was prosecuting attorney in John Brown's case.[2] We have found piles of letters and papers about it. The testimony and confessions of different members of his company. Letters from Governor Wise, President Buchanan, Mrs. Child, and from people in all parts of the country, some interceding for Brown, and some hoping and praying that he would be executed without delay.[3] There is one from a detective who went to Montreal after Dr. Howe, saw him at the hotel, but didn't like to do anything about getting hold of him.[4] Another, from an anonymous correspondent in New York, says that Sanborn and T. W. Higginson were the principals in the plot; and another tells a long story about Brigham Young, and says that *he* was at the bottom of the whole thing.[5] This last is very funny. There is a roster of Brown's company, and Hazlett's commission as Captain, signed by John Brown himself.[6] There are also as many as a hundred scraps of paper covered with the finest possible writing, which appear to be notes of sermons. They are dated in Kansas, Iowa, &c., and must have been taken from the prisoners. Enclosed is one of these scraps, which I send as a curiosity in spelling. They are hard to read, and when deciphered, unintelligible in a great measure, as they seem to be the relation of dreams, and all sorts of strange fancies. One letter from New York says that Mr. Bryant should be summoned as a witness, and that all the newspaper correspondents here, at that time, even those of the "Herald," were wild and bitter Abolitionists.[7] The Mormon letter says that Gerritt Smith is probably a relation of the Prophet Joe.[8]

It may seem to some people that we should not have touched Mr. Hunter's papers, but I don't think there is anything wrong in it. He is in the Virginia Secession Legislature, and was one of the early Rebels. Our men and we are obliged to pay for everything we use, and we are not to blame for making good our opportunities to examine the papers of such a traitor as he is. We might bring something important to light. It is really astonishing that, after having been here, in the nest of traitors, for four days, no property has been destroyed, and nothing been stolen excepting a few chickens.

Last night, our company was sent out about a mile and a half from town with a battery. We built ten huts of rails and cornstalks, and were as comfortable as possible, with fires blazing, when we were ordered back, because Colonel Gordon complained that too many of his companies were out. So we had to march home through the snow and darkness, and when we got here we couldn't find any quarters. At last we got the men into a garret, where it was very uncomfortable,—and this was the unfortunate result of the Colonel's doing us a favour.

The people here have had no gold nor silver, and no salt, sugar, tea, or coffee since last summer. A great many of them, perhaps all, think that our forces were repulsed from Fort Donelson, and really know nothing about our recent successes. They don't want to take United States notes, because they say we shall have to move back again soon. They are obliged to take that or nothing though. Captain Strother (Porte Crayon) is on General Banks' staff. He is a native of Virginia, and a nephew of our Mr. Hunter, and was here during the John Brown troubles.[9] He showed us the room in the jail where he drew John Brown and his men. He says they might easily have escaped, if they hadn't been all broken down. I was looking at the wall, which Cook tried to get over, this morning, and wonder why he didn't succeed.[10]

When we move, we go to Berryville, I believe, about eight miles on the way to Winchester. I hope Father and Susie got home safely, and that her indisposition didn't last long. I have just received another letter from Effie at Milton Hill.[11] I often reproach myself for not answering her more regularly; she has been so constant in writing to me. Give my love to all.

Ever your loving son,
Robert G. Shaw

1. Among the "several," Charles Morse bunked in Hunter's office. His letters home similarly describe the correspondence concerning Brown. Morse, *Letters Written*, p. 40.

2. Andrew Hunter (1804–88) practiced law in Harper's Ferry, then Charlestown, and served in the Virginia legislature before and during the Civil War. Oswald Garrison Villard, *John Brown, 1800–1859: A Biography Fifty Years After* (Boston: Houghton Mifflin, 1910; reprint ed., New York: Knopf, 1943), p. 645.

3. Lydia Maria Child (1802–80) early on joined the antislavery movement and became one of its most persistent and eloquent advocates.

4. Dr. Samuel Gridley Howe (1801–76), of Boston, wanted to perfect American society. After graduating from Harvard Medical School in 1824, Howe helped pioneer training for the blind, moved for educational and prison

reform, and wrote for abolition from his position as editor of the Boston *Commonwealth*. Howe married Julia Ward (1819–1910), who later gained fame for writing "Battle Hymn of the Republic." Howe raised money in 1854 to buy rifles for the free-soilers in Kansas before joining others in the "Secret Six" who financed John Brown's raid. After Brown failed at Harper's Ferry, Howe fled to Canada to avoid prosecution. Howe's participation in different reform movements is best delineated in his daughter's two-volume compilation of his papers. Laura E. Richards, ed., *Letters and Journals of Samuel Gridley Howe* (Boston: D. Estes, 1909).

5. Frank Benjamin Sanborn (1831–1917) and Thomas Wentworth Higginson (1823–1911) joined Howe in supporting Brown's raid on Harper's Ferry. Brigham Young (1801–77) grew up in Vermont. After settling in Merndon, New York, in 1829, he converted from methodism to Mormonism. His ability as an evangelist thrust him upward in the church hierarchy. After the 1844 lynching of the sect's founder, Joseph Smith, in Nauvoo, Illinois, Young became leader of the church. Due to the growing animosity against Mormons, he organized and led five thousand followers to the territory of Utah in 1846–47. His public support of polygamy from his office as territorial governor of Utah opened him to many false charges, including, apparently, the charge that he supported John Brown. *DAB*, vol. 7, pp. 326–27.

6. Pennsylvanian Albert Hazlett had not been in the engine house where John Brown made his last stand. Hazlett escaped Virginia only to be captured in Pennsylvania. A Virginia court tried Hazlett for his part in the raid, convicted and hanged him. W. E. B. Du Bois, *John Brown* (Philadelphia: Jacobs, 1909; reprint ed., New York: International Publishers, 1962), pp. 334–36.

7. William Cullen Bryant (1794–1878), best known for his poetry, was the longtime publisher of the *Evening Post*, a newspaper increasingly dedicated to fighting slavery. Bryant threw his editorial energies to Frémont and Lincoln. With the war, Bryant demanded that the South be forced to surrender to Union and abolition. *DAB*, vol. 2, pp. 200–205.

8. Gerritt Smith (1797–1874), a wealthy New Yorker, stood tall among the abolitionists. He helped finance John Brown's raid and gave money liberally to promote reform. He was among the first to subscribe to the raising of black soldiers. Joseph Smith (1805–44) had revelations that God called him to bring Christ's church to the world. Smith believed an angel gave him golden plates inscribed with God's word. Smith translated them into the Book of Mormon and founded the Church of Jesus Christ of Latter-Day Saints in 1830.

9. David Hunter Strother (1816–88) served as a staff officer for a succession of Union generals, including McClellan, Banks, Pope, and Hunter. Under the pen name "Porte Crayon" he regularly contributed pen and ink sketches to *Harper's*. Boatner, *Dictionary*, p. 812.

10. John E. Cook was a veteran of "Bleeding Kansas." Cook lived in Lawrence when John Brown recruited him to take part in the raid on Harper's Ferry.

Cook escaped the capture of Brown, but was later captured and hanged for crimes against Virginia. Du Bois, *John Brown*, pp. 219–20, 336; Oates, *To Purge This Land With Blood*, pp. 218–19.

11. Effie was at Milton Hill, the home of cousin and close friend Alice H. Forbes.

Charlestown Va.   [HL]

Mch 9 62

My dear Effie,

I received your note of March 2, last night, and think it is full time for me to write to you, as I have three letters from you unanswered. As you know, we have had possession of this town for nearly ten days, and a wretched hole it is. I don't know what it was in its palmy days, but now the inhabitants are the most avaricious, grasping set of people I ever saw. They expected when we came that we should burn the town, but finding that their property is respected & no harm done them, they have become very impertinent and exacting & think it a great hardship to have our men quartered in the un-occupied parts of their houses. Genl Banks has issued strict orders against the men's taking any private property & I don't believe the inhabitants have lost anything since the first day. On that day several companies of the 2 Mass were attacked by a large body of pigs, turkeys, chickens & ducks, and as some of those secession animals & fowls met their death in the affray, it was no sin to eat them. One of our company was also assailed in broad day light by a fine cambric shirt, whereupon he gave battle & fortunately came off victorious, taking his enemy prisoner.

Last week all the troops in town were sent into camp with the exception of 4 companies who remain here as Provost Guard. One of these is ours and we have part of a large house on the main street for ourselves & men. When we first took possession the old hag who owns the house was very glad to have us as protection against stragglers, but now there are no more in town she wants to get rid of us & says we are ruining everything. We have not hurt a single article of furniture or anything else in the house and when we go off I shall try to have one of the Indiana Companies put in here so that she may perceive how lucky she was to have had a quiet set of New Englanders instead of Western men.

Night before last there was a great alarm and a Maryland (Union) regiment fired into a body of our own cavalry killing three horses & one man. It was a very unfortunate thing and it doesn't seem to be decided, who was most to blame—the Marylanders or the Michigan Cavalry.

Is Col. Lee's daughter, Lizzie Lee, the one who used to live near Uncle Jim's on the plain?[1] If you see George Perry to speak to him, will you please congratulate him for me, on getting back.[2] I have not heard a word from home since we left Frederick. Give my love to the Forbes if you are still there &, if not, write it—& tell Mollie I am much obliged for her postscript which I will shortly answer.[3]

We don't expect to be here long. I shall write before we go, to some one at home, & afterwards, when I have a chance.

> Always dear Effie,
> Your loving brother,
> Robert G. Shaw

1. Probably Elizabeth Lee, daughter of Colonel Henry Lee of Twentieth Massachusetts. Crawford, *Famous Families*, vol. 2, p. 284.

2. First Lt. George B. Perry of the Twentieth Massachusetts spent time as a prisoner of war in Libby Prison, Richmond. Paroled on Oct. 24, 1861, Perry never fully recovered from the malaria he contracted in prison. On Sept. 30, 1862, the army recognized Perry's disability and discharged him. George B. Perry file, CMSR.

3. Cousin Mollie Forbes.

Camp, near Winchester, Va.   [RGS]
March 14, 1862
Dearest Mother,

It is some days since I have written. We left Charlestown the very night of the day I wrote to Effie. I have just received yours containing Nellie's photograph, which I think is the prettiest picture I ever saw. Ask Susie to send me one of hers. Don't direct to the War Department any more. If you address to Banks' Division it will always come. We left Charlestown at about 11 P.M. last Monday, and marched to Berryville, where we bivouacked. Our waggons with the tents were left behind, as we started off in a great hurry to reinforce Colonel Gorman, who had advanced towards Winchester.[1] It was pretty cold, but after all, I like sleeping out of doors when it doesn't rain. We stayed at Berryville all the next day, and got our tents in the evening. The next afternoon we were started off again in a great hurry, for it was reported that General Hamilton, who had got into Winchester, was taken prisoner with all his men by the force under Jackson.[2] Before we had marched three miles it was discovered to be a false rumour, but we kept on, and arrived here about midnight. We had another night in the open air, and got tents again next day. The weather was very fine, and we had a bright moonlight all the way. I never saw anything more picturesque than some of our bivouacs in the groves on this road. The trees are very fine, and look beautifully in the moonlight with the smoke of forty or fifty fires curling among them. An artist would find many opportunities for his pencil.

To-day I went into Winchester, being curious to see the town which we longed for so much last summer. It is rather a tumble-down place, with some good houses, and a great many trees, which must make it very pretty in summer. We have to pay enormous prices for everything. It is rather too bad that the men should be cheated of their pay by this, but the poor Rebels, you know, must be protected in their rights. They are a pack of rascals, and are treated too well.

I saw the Thirteenth Massachusetts march by to-day, and watched every file, but didn't see a bad face among them; most of them were handsome.[3] I don't believe such a body of good-looking, respectable, healthy men could be seen in any other country in the world, unless they were carefully picked. With the Irish left out, the other New England regiments are of as good material as the Thirteenth.

We heard to-day, from a citizen, that after the battle of "Bull Run," some Northern skulls were sold here at $10 apiece; also that many officers had spurs made of our men's bones.[4] I don't know whether to believe these things or not. There seem to be more Union people here than at Charlestown.

Stephen Perkins asked for some Virginia cigars to-day in a shop, and the man gave him some which he said were the *natives*, and which he had bought himself in Richmond.[5] On opening the package we found each bundle marked "Manufactured by A. Radden, Saugus, Mass." The shopkeeper was much astonished at it, and assured us he had got them in Richmond two weeks ago. If they go to Massachusetts for cigars, no wonder they don't succeed very well with other manufactures. I am glad you think Fremont has come out so well. I have seen no report of his defence.[6]

It is more than a fortnight since I have heard from you. Your letter of to-day has been two weeks coming. Will you send me a photograph-book; my collection is becoming quite large. Please ask Father to pay Alfred Chandler $1.50, which I owe him for express.[7] We shall probably make another advance soon. I hope very soon, as it is not a very glorious thing to have allowed Jackson to get away so easily.[8] There was a skirmish about five miles out to-day, and the Third Wisconsin took about thirty prisoners.[9] I hope you are still as well as Susie said you were.

Ever, dear Mother, your loving son,
Robert G. Shaw

1. Perhaps Willis Arnold Gorman (1816–76), a journeyman politician from Kentucky who served as an Indiana congressman (1849–53) and governor of Minnesota Territory (1853–57). At the start of the Civil War, he led the First Minnesota Volunteers. *DAB*, vol. 4, pp. 435–36.

2. Charles Smith Hamilton (1822–91), of Western, New York, graduated from West Point in 1843, fought in the Mexican War, and formed a flour company before the war. He recruited and led the Third Wisconsin Infantry before being promoted to brigadier general in the fall of 1861 and sent to the Shenandoah Valley. *DAB*, vol. 4, pp. 183–84. Thomas Jonathan Jackson (1824–63), already nicknamed "Stonewall" for his actions at First Manassas, added to his hero status in Mar.–June 1862 in the Shenandoah Valley by successfully thwarting capture by three Union armies.

3. The Thirteenth Regiment Massachusetts Infantry organized at Fort Independence on June 16, 1861. In Mar. 1862 it was part of Banks's V Corps. Dyer, *Compendium*, vol. 1, p. 158.

4. The selling of skulls is unconfirmed and most likely was a rumor.

5. First Lt. Stephen George Perkins.

6. Frémont had been removed from command in Missouri for issuing his emancipation proclamation and for fortifying St. Louis while his armies lost battles at Springfield, Lexington, and Wilson's Creek. In early Mar. 1862, Northern papers carried his defense of his actions. On Mar. 29, Lincoln named him to command the Mountain Department in Western Virginia. Nevins, *Frémont*, vol. 2, p. 635.

7. Alfred Chandler is unidentified.

8. Jackson had 4,600 men; Banks had 17,000.

9. The Third Wisconsin Infantry organized at Fort Du Lac on June 19, 1861. In Mar. 1862, it formed part of the Third Brigade, First Division, of Banks's V Corps. Dyer, *Compendium*, vol. 1, p. 328.

Winchester   [RGS]
March 24, 1862
Dear Father,

There has been a fight three miles from here, and we returned from *Snickersville* to-night.[1] *We* are too late, as usual, and don't know whether we go back towards Centreville to-morrow or not. There was not a general on the field yesterday, as Shields was wounded in a skirmish the day before.[2] Copeland was out there, and they say, though he had no command, he rushed round the field and made himself very useful. General Banks arrived from Washington this morning, and is off with all Shields' Division in pursuit. Harry would be much obliged if you would drop a line to Annie, and tell her we were not in the fight.[3] There were two hundred prisoners brought in here to-day, and over four hundred wounded. One of the latter recognized Crowninshield of our regiment as a classmate at Cambridge.[4] I will write as soon as I find out where we are going.

Love to Mother.

Your affectionate son,
Robt G. Shaw

1. In the First Battle of Kerns-town, Virginia, Stonewall Jackson sent 4,200 men against the Union's 9,000. Although the battle was a tactical defeat for Jackson, Lincoln worried about Harper's Ferry and the back door to Washington. This small battle yielded strategic results for the South as Lincoln diverted Banks's and McDowell's armies from supporting McClellan's Peninsular Campaign against Richmond. The Shenandoah Valley Campaign had officially begun. Shelby Foote, *The Civil War: A Narrative* (New York: Random House, 1958), vol. 1, pp. 270–72; McPherson, *Battle Cry*, p. 425.

2. James Shields (1810–79) was a prominent political general. Born in Ire-land, Shields immigrated to the United States in 1826, served in the Black Hawk and Mexican wars, and became a justice in the Illinois Supreme Court. Shields served as U.S. senator from Illinois (1849–55) and from Minnesota (1858–61). Even though he had once challenged Lincoln to a duel, Lincoln appointed him as a brigadier general on Aug. 19, 1861. Faust, *Encyclopedia*, pp. 683–84; McGuiness and Sayers, *American Leaders*, p. 288.

3. Harry Russell and sister Annie.

4. Second Lt. Francis Welch Crownin-shield (1843–66) of Boston left Harvard in Dec. 1861 to join the Second Massachusetts. Higginson, *Harvard Memorial Biographies*, vol. 2, pp. 433–37.

Near Strasberg Va   [HL]
March 28 1862
Dearest Mother,

Your letter from Phila was received day before yesterday just after we arrived at this place.

I wrote to Father from Winchester telling him that we had been stopped on our way to Centreville in consequence of the fight at the former place. We had got as far as the Shenandoah and were to cross it on the second day, but were delayed by the breaking of the bridge. In the meantime news of Jackson's advance came & we hurried back—Arrived at Winchester we found that the enemy had been driven back & the town was full of prisoners & of the wounded of both armies.[1] Our surgeons Drs. Leland & Stone went immediately to work and, the medical director says, did more good than all the Ohio & Pennsylvania surgeons together who had been in attendance until then.[2]

They had actually left the majority of the wounded men on the bare floors of the hotels & public buildings without even straw to lie upon.

I went into the Court-house where Dr. Leland was, and out of about 40, there were very few who were not seriously wounded. In the entry there were about 20 dead men laid out, with the capes of their overcoats folded over their faces. We looked at a good many faces to see if there might not by chance be some college-acquaintance among them. It was strange to see the dead & wounded Ohio men & Virginians lying there side by side.

Harry and Morse went out to look at the battlefield & said the dead men were lying about every where in all positions.[3] Most of them were shot through the head. From all accounts it was a sharp little fight.

The people along the road tell us that Jackson lost about 1000 killed, wounded & missing, which is the same estimate made by us. We lost about 300 they tell us.[4] I don't know whether you will like to hear about these things or not for they are horrible to see or to think of—but such scenes show us, more than anything else, what war really is. I was surprized to see that the men even who had the worst wounds didn't seem to suffer much. There's no need of going into an account of my feelings—as you can imagine what they were. It is astonishing though, how soon one gets accustomed to terrible sights. The second time I went to the Hospital I found myself looking about, as if I had lived all my life among dead & wounded men. Of course you don't lose your feeling of pity for the sufferers.

There is one thing about which every man who has been in a battle seems to be pretty sure & that is that he doesn't want to go into another if he can avoid it. I have no doubt though that this feeling wears off after a man has had more experience in fighting.

The day after I wrote from Winchester I thought I had better telegraph to Father that we had not been in the fight and I hope he received it. That same evening at 6 o'cl we marched from there, & bivouacked by the road side at 1 A.M. At 7 A.M. we started again & came to Strasburg & stayed that day & night just the other side of the town. Yesterday morning we were suddenly startled by the "Long Roll" & were marched off in a great hurry through the town & about two miles to the South West. Here it was discovered that it was again a false alarm and we halted. Our wagons with tents came up in about two hours, the tents were pitched and here we are still waiting for something to turn up. What you wrote about the fine, intelligent faces of our men is, I think, borne out by their conduct in these battles all over the country—for if you could see what officers most regiments are afflicted with, you would be convinced that all the praises & glory should be given to the privates. I consider that it is the pure bravery & intelligence of our people that are winning our battles. It would be an absurdity to talk about discipline under such officers as we have, if the men weren't so good of their own free will.

The Western men, though they are rough & not nearly so steady nor so respectable as our Yankees, are as a general thing, fine, honest, intelligent men. There is an Ohio Regt here, in which a man six feet tall, comes about the middle of the company.[5] You know they are placed in the ranks according to size.

Indeed physically as well as morally, I believe we have the finest army in the world. Nevertheless a well disciplined European army would give us a terrible whopping because of our poor officers. Another wonderful thing is the soberness of the men. Though we can't claim much merit for that in Virginia, as the Rebels have destroyed all the distilleries in this part of the State & probably every where.

Last Sunday as we were waiting for the bridge to be repaired at Snickersville, a dozen of us listened to a sermon, which was a real sermon. We were lying in the sun on the side of a hill & 4 or 5 negroes who had come up in their Sunday clothes to see the soldiers passed along. Among them was a white man with two little curly headed boys—all these as handsome people as you would find. Harry said "That's a white slave" so we called to him & asked what his trade was. "Nothing Sir," said he, "but working in the field under another man." There he stood there in front of us & talked for two hours, as eloquently as any educated man I know. The simplicity of his language made it all the more impressive. He said he had nine children all whiter than the two boys with him. Some one asked if any of them were ever sold. He said no— & that often when he looked round at his children sitting about him, he thought of other Fathers & Mothers crying for theirs he felt how kind God had been to him. "Yes" he said ["]taking away my children from me would be the same as if a man should tear out my heart," and he thrust his hand inside his vest "and throw it down & stomp on it."

I asked him if his Father had lived on the same plantation that he did, for he said he was born there. I guessed what the answer would be. And he said his Master was his Father & that it had often been a bitter pill to swallow when he had been badly treated by him to think that it was so. He said it was "like having a forked stick in him."[6]

I should have taken this man for a well to do mechanic and a remarkably intelligent one too—but he couldn't read. Bangs gave him advice about getting North where he wanted to go very much, he said on account of his children—who was Savage's friend in Phila?[7] Was it Forney?[8] If this reaches

you before you leave there give my love to Uncle Robert & Susie.[9] Tell Father
that by chance Chandler did just right in sending my shoes to Strasburg. They
have not yet arrived. Love to Nellie.

Ever your loving son

1. Banks's army had been on its way
to support McClellan when Lincoln
ordered it back to the valley.

2. Francis Leland of Milford, Massa-
chusetts, served with the Second in 1862.
Record of Mass Vols., p. 28. Lincoln R.
Stone was one of Shaw's best friends.

3. Harry Russell and Charles F.
Morse.

4. Actually, Jackson lost 718 as follows: 80 killed, 375 wounded, and 263
captured or missing. Union casualties
totaled 590: 118 killed, 450 wounded, 22
missing. Long, *Civil War Day By Day*,
p. 188.

5. The Eighth Ohio Infantry organized at Camp Denison in June 1861 and
made up the part of Shields's Division
that bore the brunt of Jackson's attack at
Kernstown. Dyer, *Compendium*, vol. 1,
p. 205.

6. In his 1845 autobiography,
Frederick Douglass demonstrated the
falsehood of the proslavery argument
that used the Bible to prove that Ham
and the sons of Ham, who were black,
would forever be slaves. Douglass
pointed at all mulattoes, of which he
was one, and remarked that these were
the sons of *white* men. James Savage
also remembered sitting at that bridge
with Shaw talking with "One man
(almost as white as I). . . ." James Savage to My Dearest ———, Mar. 30,
1862, in Higginson, *Harvard Memorial
Biographies*, vol. 2, pp. 320–21.

7. George P. Bangs of Boston.

8. Probably John Wien Forney (1817–
81), a Philadelphia and Washington
journalist and editor. He founded the
Washington Chronicle in 1861. *DAB*,
vol. 3, pp. 526–27.

9. Robert Shaw Sturgis married
Susan Boit (?–1900) and retired from
the family firm of Russell and Company
in 1858. Sturgis, *Sturgis*, pp. 53–54.

Near Edinburg, Va.   [RGS]
April 5, 1862
My Dear Nellie,

Your letter, which I received long ago, has never been answered. I get so
many from all the family, that it is almost impossible to answer them all, and
I often wonder that they continue to arrive so regularly, when I give so little
encouragement.

We left our camp just south of Strasburg the first of this month, and
marched fifteen miles to this place. The Second Massachusetts has no reason
to complain of being held back, for we have been in the advance ever since we
left Harper's Ferry. We should have been in the Winchester affair, if we had

started for Centreville six hours later than we did. On the march up here, five companies were deployed as skirmishers, and we did nothing all day but climb fences and jump brooks. We seldom halted, and it was astonishing to see how the excitement of firing now and then at the enemy's rear-guard made the men forget the heat of the day and the weight of their knapsacks. One of our men was slightly wounded by a rifle-ball, and a Pennsylvanian was killed by a shell. These were the only mishaps on our side, though a good many shell fell near us. But these were not nearly so dangerous for us, as for the troops in our rear who were marching *en masse*. I know now how a shell sounds flying through the air, and that it is an exceedingly unpleasant sound. It is a moment of great anxiety from the time you see the smoke issuing from the cannon, until you see where the shot falls. It was amusing to see the men duck involuntarily at first. They soon found, however, that they had often been in much greater peril on Boston Common on 4th July.

The burning bridges all along the road looked like war. Day before yesterday, our company was sent down to guard the Ford across Stony Creek, and there we had some excitement, for at daybreak the Rebels brought up a battery, and threw a few shell at us. I was asleep at the time, having been on my feet all night, and knew nothing about it until I waked up; but two fell so near Mudge and Fox, that it threw the gravel over them.[1] We are doing nothing now, as has been our custom for eight months. Don't believe what the papers say of showers of shell being thrown at us; if there were more than twenty in ninety-six hours, they were so far off that we neither saw nor heard them.

There have been two mails since we arrived here, but I have not received anything from home. I hope you are all well. Tell Mother I should have written a line the day I arrived, if I had had any idea that such accounts of the movement, as I have since seen would appear in the papers. But, in reality, nothing happened that seemed calculated to make you anxious, and I have been very busy on outpost and other duty.

Tell Father he was very right in what he said of our venturing imprudently beyond our lines. Cogswell and Mudge did so the other day, and were fired at from behind a house; Cogswell came very near getting a hole through his coat.[2]

Does any one at home know anything of McClellan's doings?[3] We hear nothing about him here, as the papers are silent. If Father knows anything about his movements, I wish he would write me something of them.

I had a letter from Effie just before she left Boston; also one from Mother, of about the same date, and another from Sue. Give my love to them all. I suppose you are all together again now, and I wish often enough I could be at home for a little while too. Though I really do enjoy this life, I find myself so often thinking, "Oh, why did I go for a sodger?" that I don't believe I shall want to leave home again, when the war is over. If I had nobody to care for me, or rather if I cared for nobody at home, I shouldn't ask for anything better than this. Some of the regular officers I have met are melancholy objects. Living on the frontier for years together, and supporting their families on Lieutenants' and Captains' pay, until they are forty or fifty years old, and dying, so to speak, in rags, isn't a cheerful prospect. When we are lying in camp, we are apt to get discontented, and wish for a wound in the little finger of the left hand, to enable us to go home and recruit, but every one seems to be cheerful when there is anything doing.

Your loving brother,
Robert G. Shaw

1. Capt. Charles Redington Mudge and Second Lt. John A. Fox.

2. William Cogswell (1839–?) of Salem, Massachusetts, graduated from Harvard Law School in 1860 and joined the Second as a captain in May 1861. Brown, "Roll of Students," p. 44; *Record of Mass Vols.*, pp. 27–28.

3. McClellan, upset that Lincoln had diverted troops to the Shenandoah, moved his 100,000 men slowly up the peninsula toward Richmond. On Apr. 5, McClellan began a siege of Yorktown instead of attacking the 15,000 Confederate defenders. Emory Thomas, "The Peninsular Campaign," in *The Image of War: 1861–1865*, vol. 2: *The Guns of '62* (Garden City, N.Y.: Doubleday, 1982), pp. 112–23.

Near Edinburg   [RGS]
April 11, 1862
Dear Mother,

Yours, Father's, Effie's, and Susie's were received yesterday, and are the first letters I have had since we left Strasburg. I wish you wouldn't make the other letters a reason for only writing me little notes, as you very often do.

We have heard of the capture of Island No. 10.[1] There are also rumours of a disaster of some kind at Corinth.[2] It seems time for us to have some reverse at the West. The people who talk of Western men fighting so well, don't consider that they are really Eastern men. In the Third Wisconsin Regiment, there are only nineteen men who were born in that State. The Major of the Eighth Ohio told me that all his men were either the sons of New-Yorkers and New-Englanders, or were born in the East themselves—and Ohio is one of the oldest of the Western States. The story of Captain Savage's capture is newspaper all over. It should have been Mudge and Cogswell; neither was thrown from his horse, and both rode into camp an hour after they went out, without any further accident.

We have been having very bad weather this week, until to-day. Nothing but rain, hail, and snow for four days. Our company was on outpost day before yesterday, and the men suffered more than at any time during the winter. The enemy's sentries and videttes are no longer in sight of ours, and it is my opinion that their principal force is far away by this time. The only sound I heard, all night, from the other side of the creek, was a man's voice saying: "That ain't the way, you d——d fool." From whom it proceeded, and to whom addressed, I don't know, for it was pitch dark. I didn't consider it sufficient reason for sending to rout General Banks out of bed, and get the Division under arms, though we have stood all night shivering in the road, many a time, for less.

The people about here are as *stuffy* as they can be about Secessionism, and I don't believe there is an *honest* Union man to be found. They are a nasty, dirty, ignorant race. A woman in Edinburg expressed great astonishment that Massachusetts men spoke the same language that she did. She called it the same, but I thank my stars I never learned such a *patois* as most of them speak.

Do you think there would be a chance of my getting a position with General Fremont, if I wanted to leave this regiment?[3] Tom Robeson, who was Commodore Goldsborough's signal-officer at Roanoke and Newbern, has come back.[4] He says the Commodore is a grouty old fellow, and won't let any one speak at table but himself.

Always your loving Son

1. Island No. 10 was a Confederate stronghold in a bend of the Mississippi River near New Madrid, Missouri. After a month-long defense against the land forces of Maj. Gen. John Pope and the river fleet of Adm. Andrew Hull Foote, Confederates surrendered the position on Apr. 7, 1862. Only Fort Pillow remained to defend the river above Memphis. Long, *Civil War Day By Day*, pp. 177, 196; Faust, *Encyclopedia*, p. 386.

2. The Battle of Shiloh (Pittsburg Landing), Tennessee, on Apr. 6–7, first seemed to be a victory for Confeder-

ate generals Albert Sidney Johnston and P. G. T. Beauregard. But Johnston fell dead, and Ulysses S. Grant used reinforcements to win the contest. Casualties at the Sunken Road, Hornet's Nest, and Peach Orchard stunned the nation. Union casualties totaled 13,047; Confederates lost 10,694. Foote, *Civil War*, vol. 1, pp. 343–51.

3. Francis Shaw and George Curtis knew Frémont and had campaigned for his presidential bid in 1856. Frémont attended the Staten Island wedding of Curtis to Anna Shaw in 1856. A posi-

tion on Frémont's staff could have been Shaw's for the asking.

4. First Lt. Thomas Rodman Robeson was in the class ahead of Shaw at Harvard. Still officially in the Second, Robeson served as a signal officer on the flagship of Commodore Louis

Malesherbes Goldsborough (1805–73), commander of the Atlantic Blockading Squadron, in Burnside's operations in Feb.–Apr. 1862. Higginson, *Harvard Memorial Biographies*, vol. 2, pp. 252–56; *Harper's Weekly*, Mar. 1, 1862, p. 7; Faust, *Encyclopedia*, p. 314.

Near Edenburg Va
April 16 1862
My dear Effie,

[HL]

Your last, I received yesterday. As you see from the date of this, we are still lying idle. When something will be done, nobody knows.

There is a rumour here, that Genl Banks is to go into the Cabinet, and that Genl Rosencrantz will have command of this Corps.[1] We have often had such reports before, and I suppose this one will prove to be unfounded, as former ones were. It would be a good thing if it should turn out to be true.

What I said about our volunteers should be modified somewhat, for I was only comparing them with private soldiers I have seen in European armies. Compared with these, they deserve all the praise I gave, but Joe C. was certainly right in saying that there are a great many thieves, & a great many more drunkards among them.[2] But they behave much worse here than they would at home, for, away from their families, there is no restraint upon them, but fear of punishment (which is very uncertain) and their own consciences, which latter article is more widely distributed among the men of our army than it ever was in any other, I think.

You are very much mistaken in thinking Frank Barlow's conduct as Officer of the Day was foolish.[3] It is his duty to have the Guard turned out *once* a day at least, and certainly oftener, if he thinks the officer of the guard allows the men to leave the Guard Tent or neglect their duty in any way. I don't believe there are 20 regiments in the Army of the Potomac in which Guard-duty is properly done. A great many of the officers are worthless & are therefore very angry when anyone tries to oblige them to do their duty. All you said about Frank, went to show that he was a better Field-Officer than 9 out of 10 in these two divisions, and from what I hear of the divisions about Washington they must be more poorly provided with good officers than we. Officers there, have been Court-Martialed for drawing the pay of deserters & dead men & appropriating it to their own use, and have brought up as defence, that it was a common thing in their regiments & considered proper. When such thieves & blacklegs are in command how can you expect to have good troops? The discipline which the papers talk of could all be put in a very small package. Many Officers wish to be popular with their men for political reasons, & others are afraid if the men don't like them, they will elect some one else over their heads. You know in most states, officers are elected by their men & not appointed by the Govr.

You would probably be very much shocked at the swearing & general profanity in our camps, if you should stay about here for a week. It is really extraordinary how many oaths a man can get into a sentence of 12 words. It seems to be a general habit among men from all parts of the country. In this regiment, I must confess, the officers have not done their duty in discouraging it; though it is not so bad now as it was some time ago. At one time, every one from the Col. to the smallest drummer indulged in the practice—but that was in August when we drilled four hours a day. The Chaplain, I [think] was an exception to the general rule, but I haven't the slightest doubt, that in his heart, he swore often & often.

Have you seen a picture of Capt Shriber of Genl Shields' Staff running a man through at the battle of Winchester? and have you read his report? [4] If you have, please bear in mind that the latter is all a lie, in so far as it concerns himself; also that he never ran a man through, but was seen to dip his sword in a puddle of blood after the fight was over. He was on General Banks' Staff until a day or two before the battle—and besides having borrowed money from all his brother officers, he has swindled nearly all his landlords, landladies, & other unsuspecting individuals who crossed his path. Paying his debts is not a part of his plan.

Yesterday we had a "scare" & got under arms in a great hurry at 3 P.M. It turned out to be nothing, so we sat down again.

I am much obliged to you, for wishing me a wound. Is there any other little favour I could do you?

Do tell me, or tell somebody else to tell me more about Mr. Dana's fall out with the Tribune and what occasioned it. [5] What is he doing now? If you want a paper with lots of news take the "Philadelphia Enquirer." There was a very interesting letter in it yesterday from a wounded rebel officer to a young lady in Philadelphia. He evidently has a "pongshong" for her. [6]

Is George at home? He will have to skip round and do a good deal of talking when the war is over, won't he? The real hard work will come then, and I hope there will be enough honest & able men to draw a "straight furrer" for us.

There are new charges against Fremont. I wonder how he will come out, this time. You can't realize how much the officers of the Regular Army hate him. From what I have heard some of them say, I believe they would stick at nothing to have him superseded again.

From what I can learn of the last battle, we didn't gain much of a victory there. Beauregard, it seems, was only driven back to his old position.[7] The victory at Island No. 10 was a great one though. We heard two days ago that the "Monitor" had sunk the "Merrimac" & there was great rejoicing in consequence—but it was all a humbug.[8]

I hope Susie is better than when she wrote to me. Her last was a long & interesting letter. I will answer it next time I write home.

Give my love to Mother, Father & all.
Always your afftc Brother,
Robert G. Shaw

1. Ohioan William Starke Rosencrans (1819–98) graduated from West Point in 1842. He resigned his commission in 1854 to enter business, but readily accepted a position as a brigadier general on May 16, 1861. He was promoted on June 11, 1862, to command the Union Army of the Mississippi. Faust, *Encyclopedia*, pp. 642–43.

2. Joseph Bridgham Curtis joined the Seventh New York Militia with Shaw in Apr. 1861. John R. Bartlett, *Memoirs of Rhode Island Officers who were Engaged in the Service of Their Country During the Great Rebellion in the South* (Providence, R.I.: S. S. Rider & Brother, 1867), pp. 226–40.

3. Francis Channing Barlow was the son of a Unitarian minister from Brooklyn, New York. Joining the army as a private on Apr. 19, 1861, Barlow rose in the ranks to be colonel of the Sixty-first New York Infantry on Apr. 14, 1862. Winslow Homer immortalized Barlow by using him as the model of the Union officer in his painting "Prisoners from

the Front" (1866), now hanging in the Metropolitan Museum of Art. Marc Simpson, *Winslow Homer: Paintings of the Civil War* (San Francisco: Bedford Arts, 1989), pp. 246–54.

4. Capt. Robert Charles Shriber, of the Thirteenth Massachusetts Infantry, served on Banks's staff, July 16–Oct. 22, 1861, before being transferred as acting inspector general on Shields's staff. Robert Charles Shriber file, CMSR; depiction of fight at Winchester in *Harper's Weekly*, Apr. 12, 1862, pp. 232–33, 235.

5. Charles A. Dana worked fifteen years for Greeley's *Tribune* and helped spread its fame. Then the Civil War exposed divergent views at the top of the editorial ladder. While Greeley wrote to let the South go in peace, Dana started the "Forward to Richmond!" fever. After Dana's editorials proposed the government take more aggressive steps to win the war, Greeley demanded his resignation. Dana quit, took six months severance pay, and landed on his feet in Washington as assistant secretary of war.

DAB, vol. 3, pp. 49–51.

6. The *Philadelphia Inquirer* of Apr. 11 (2:1), 1862, carried an "Interesting Letter From a Rebel Soldier." The soldier wrote his estranged lover that he knew she "scorned" him because he had joined the Rebel cause, but now that he was wounded, he implored, "a kind word from you would be treasured beyond price." Her answer was to ridicule him by making the letter public.

7. Louisianian Pierre Gustave Toutant Beauregard (1818–93) graduated from West Point in 1838, fought in the Mexican War, and superintended West Point in 1861. Before reassignment to the West, he commanded the attack on Fort Sumter, and led troops at First Manassas. After the Battle of Shiloh, Beauregard returned his army to the camp at Corinth. Boatner, *Dictionary*, p. 55.

8. The *Monitor* battled the *Merrimack* (CSS *Virginia*) near Hampton Roads, Virginia, on Mar. 9. A draw, the battle revolutionized naval warfare. Shaw had seen the steam frigate *Merrimack* in Boston harbor in 1857. When Confederates captured the Norfolk Navy Yard, they converted the ship into an ironclad and rechristened her. RGS to SBS, Apr. 22, 1857, *Letters: RGS* (1876), p. 122; *Harper's Weekly*, Mar. 29, 1862, pp. 11, 13; Apr. 12, 1862, pp. 12–13.

Near Newmarket, Va.   [RGS]
April 19, 1862
Dearest Mother,

The last time I wrote was from the other side of Edinburg, just before we started. The morning after that we turned out at 2 o'clock, and, at four, the whole Army Corps was on the road. That day our Brigade and one from Shields' Division were on foot eighteen or nineteen hours, for we were sent a long way off to the right to make a flank movement. The roads were like Staten Island roads in the worst season, and we had to ford several streams. At night we bivouacked in the woods, and started off again next morning. After a very warm march, we joined the main column again here. This was the first bad road we have been over this year. The turnpikes in Virginia are very fine, and we have not been off them before. We have been here now two nights, and it has been raining hard most of the time. You can't help wishing for tents in such weather, though they are a great encumbrance in marching. The worst nights we have had were at Charlestown and Strasburg, where it snowed, rained, and froze alternately, for several days; and being a good deal on outpost, we were often without fires. This sort of work is hard, but we get very little credit for it. I suppose we shall have our tents again some time, but they might as well be given up entirely, for we seldom see them.

Yesterday there came an order from the War Department, thanking General

Banks for operations of the 17th and 18th inst.—Mr. Stanton must be getting facetious.[1] Don't you think it a great pity that McClellan is being hampered so much by government? It seems now as if there were several heads pulling the army this way and that; whereas, while he was commander-in-chief, there was a settled plan. The army of Virginia, at any rate, ought to have one head. How can anything be accomplished, if all these generals work on their own hook? I don't believe Mr. Stanton, or any one else, can manage the War Department and command the army too.

General Grant's officers' report shows that the fight at Pittsburg Landing *was* a great victory after all.[2] Halleck and Burnside give McClellan the credit of everything that has been done in their departments.[3] Robeson says he heard Burnside say that he had done nothing but what McClellan had proposed, before the expedition sailed.

This valley, between Edinburg and Newmarket, is the most beautiful part of the country we have been in. There are a good many German names here, and that is, perhaps, one reason why the farms and villages are neater and better than those we have seen hitherto. We passed a good many fine places on the way, and there are farms of one thousand and sixteen hundred acres all along here. It is a grazing country, and would be just the place to divide among our soldiers after the war. If I could get hold of a lot of Confederate money, at a cheap rate, I would buy some land down here. The common people are as ignorant as they can be. They don't know what the war is about, and say they have heard all sorts of reasons.

A company of the Eighteenth Vermont Cavalry charged a whole squadron of Ashby's men, under a pretty heavy fire, and saved the bridge over the Shenandoah, yesterday.[4] They are finely mounted and men are good, but the field officers are not good. Excuse pencil, all my writing materials are somewhere behind. I hope you are all well, as I am. I have never told you that I read your Hymnbook a great deal. It is just a year since the Sixth Massachusetts went through Baltimore, and the Seventh New York left; what a time that was! I shall never forget it. What a blessing that we happened to be born in this century and country!

Has Father returned from Washington?

Your loving Son

1. Mercurial Edwin Masters Stanton (1814–69), of Ohio, served as U.S. secretary of war (1862–68). On Apr. 17 and 18, Banks occupied New Market, Virginia, as Jackson temporarily withdrew from the Shenandoah Valley. Long, *Civil War Day By Day*, pp. 200–201.

2. Grant's victory at Shiloh thrust

him into the public spotlight. He would soon climb to the top of Northern war heroship and to the presidency, even though Lincoln and Maj. Gen. Henry Halleck were appalled at his casualty rates. William S. McFeely, *Grant: A Biography* (New York: W. W. Norton, 1981), pp. 110–17.

3. Henry W. Halleck graduated West Point in 1839, fought in the Mexican War, served as secretary of state for California before the war, and accepted a commission from Lincoln as major general on Aug. 19, 1861. Halleck commanded the Department of Missouri after Lincoln removed Frémont from that position. Faust, *Encyclopedia*, p. 332.

4. The First Vermont Cavalry organized at Burlington on Nov. 19, 1861, and served under Banks in the Department of the Shenandoah in Apr. 1862. Dyer, *Compendium*, vol. 1, p. 233. Virginia planter and politician Turner Ashby (1828–62) served under Jackson as commander of all Confederate cavalry in the Shenandoah Valley until his death in action on June 6, 1862, near Harrisonburg, Virginia. Faust, *Encyclopedia*, p. 26; Boatner, *Dictionary*, p. 28.

Newmarket, Va.   [RGS]
May 9, 1862
Dear Mother,

As you will see from my date, we are back at Newmarket. Yesterday I wrote Father a note from camp in the mountains, about seven miles from here. On our arrival here, I found your letter beginning April 29, and three from Father, Effie and Susie, of about the same date. You can't think how pleasant it is to hear from you so often. I have heard more of what you are all doing lately, than I ever did before. Your first long "Diary Letter" I received last Sunday when I was on picket at Harrisonburg.

It was feared that Jackson was going to give us some trouble last night, but nothing happened.[1]

We (Company F) had hardly reached camp, however, and got a bath and some rest, when the long roll beat, and we had to tumble out again. We marched a short distance down the road towards Staunton, when it was discovered to be a false alarm, and we turned into a field by the road-side.[2] This has happened so often to our Brigade, that an alarm doesn't excite us in the least. It was a fine night, so we slept pretty comfortably for from four to five hours, and were up and on the road again at dawn, but with our faces turned in the opposite direction. The sun came up very hot, and we marched all day, over one of the dustiest roads I ever saw. It seemed as if we were a drove of bullocks going to Brighton. I used to see the poor beasts going through Cambridge, half hidden in a cloud of dust, and always thought that their destination, the slaughter-house, was preferable to what they were enduring then. We were cheered by the thought that we were retracing our steps, merely to get a good place to cross the mountains, and that we were to return to Strasburg.

We pitched tents here Monday night, expecting some rest, but hadn't been asleep two hours before we were aroused again, and marching up the side of the mountain. This would not have been so bad, if we hadn't known that we should have to return in a day or two. We reached the top just at sunrise, and the sight was worth the trouble. We could see for miles and miles down both valleys, East and West. The sun was shining brightly in one, and the other was gray, excepting the peaks of the distant mountains; I never saw anything so beautiful. We bivouacked a little way down on the other side, and lay there in the woods until Thursday noon, when it was found that General Sullivan didn't need our assistance, and we came back.[3]

Though we all growl terribly at our hard fortune in being left in this valley, I sometimes think, in my sanest moments, that the sight of our officers and men lying dead and wounded, like those we saw at Winchester and Ball's Bluff, would not be a cheering one; and that, after all, our desire to have a battle is a purely selfish feeling. In all probability, it will make no difference in the war, or to the country, if we never hear another shot, so we ought to be thankful to have all our men go home in safety to their families. As Colonel Gordon once said, we don't think, when we wish we were with Burnside or McClellan, how the number of orphans, widows, and childless people, is increased by the sending of one more regiment into a battle. For all this, though, he is as much disappointed as the rest of us, at being kept here doing nothing. We are going to make a great effort to be transferred to some other Division, after we get to Strasburg, and as that will probably fail, I hope Father, in the mean time, will try to get *me* into some better position, unless there is some way in which he can give the whole regiment a helping hand.

I have just been reading "The Idyls of the King," and as I haven't seen them since the summer we were at Naushon, where Edith Emerson read them aloud, it carried me back to that pleasant time.[4] That was before Ellen's death, and when they were as happy as a family could be, and long before any of us, who were there, thought we should now be scattered about in these Southern States.[5] I read Mr. Beecher's sermon which Susie sent; I wish I could have heard it from his own lips.[6] My stockings are getting worn out, and I wish you would send me a dozen woollen ones. Those you gave me at Camp Andrew have worn finely. I should like three or four flannel shirts with collars, too, as thin as you can find.

I don't believe Fremont will have much more to do than Banks, unless there is some change of plan, but it would be better to be on his staff, if it were only to know, and be with him, than to drill and go on guard, all through the hot summer; so do give me some encouragement in that hope.

Ask Effie to excuse me, if I don't fully understand everything she writes me. I will try to read up on "Plato" and "Socrates," when I have time, and can get the books; her last fairly floored me.

I hope my delay, in answering Susie's and hers, won't put a stop to their writing, though I fear every letter will be the last. It is the greatest pleasure to me to get all your letters. The paper you send is very useful, but I am out of stamps and envelopes.

Always, dear Mother,
Your loving Son

1. On May 8 Jackson defeated part of Frémont's army in the Battle of McDowell, Virginia. Jackson had won his first battle victory of this campaign and it emboldened him and frightened several Federal commanders. Foote, *Civil War*, vol. 1, pp. 423–26.

2. McDowell, Virginia, is twenty-five miles west of Staunton, across the Allegheny Mountains. Banks's Corps was nearly fifty-five miles by road from the battle.

3. Jeremiah Cutler Sullivan (1830–90) held a captaincy in the Sixth Indiana Infantry on Apr. 18, 1861. Promoted to brigadier general on Apr. 28, 1862, he commanded a brigade in Banks's V Corps. Boatner, *Dictionary*, p. 817.

4. Alfred Lord Tennyson (1809–92) published *Idylls of the King* in 1859. Edith Emerson (1841–?), daughter of Ralph Waldo Emerson.

5. Ellen R. Forbes, daughter of John Murray Forbes, was close friends with Edith Emerson and spent much time at the Forbes' vacation estate of Naushon Island. Ellen's brother, William Hathaway Forbes, married Edith in 1865.

6. Henry Ward Beecher (1813–87), pastor of Plymouth Congregationalist Church in Brooklyn, New York, came from a prominent antislavery family headed by his father, Lyman Beecher, and which included his sister, Harriet Beecher Stowe. Faust, *Encyclopedia*, p. 53.

CHAPTER 7

"A lull before the storm"

After a year of campaigning, Lieutenant Shaw had neither fired his pistol nor raised his sword against the enemy. Adept at drill, he still questioned his ability to fight and wanted a chance to test himself. He soon got his wish as Stonewall Jackson outmarched and outfought the three Federal armies in the Shenandoah. During the battle at Front Royal, Shaw's pocketwatch turned away what could have been a fatal bullet and left him only slightly bruised. Even though he was without his weapons—having left his pistol and sword in his luggage and using a "toy" sword borrowed from a drummer boy—Shaw had proven himself a capable officer in the circumstances of a wound, retreat, and battlefield defeat.

For the North, the buoyant hopes of spring turned gloomy with the military reversals of summer. The campaign for the valley transformed a "Stonewall" into a legend. The "Bold Dragoon"—cavalryman J. E. B. Stuart—humiliated his Federal opponents by riding completely around the Union position. Robert E. Lee pushed McClellan's massive army back from Richmond and had it huddled at Harrison's Ferry on the James River. McClellan and Lincoln bickered in public over tactics and responsibility.

In Washington, Lincoln signed an act that gave him the authority to use black men to help suppress the rebellion. Lincoln told his cabinet of his Emancipation Proclamation, something that would change the goal of the war from union to freedom. His cabinet told him to wait for a battlefield victory before reading it to the public. Shaw thought seriously about raising a black regiment but he would have to wait until the northern public would accept such a move. As the nation and Shaw watched the changing fortunes of war, they experienced "a lull before the storm."

Strasburg Va.   [HL]
May 13 1862
Dear Father,

Here we are again very near the camp which we left on the 1st of April.

We hear tonight that Richmond is in our possession. If so Virginia must be nearly cleaned out—though there are some idle rumours of the Rebel army having come up this way against McDowell.[1] They can't possibly be desperate enough to run into such a trap, with McClellan in their rear.

I wrote to Mr. Sumner today & asked him if there was any chance of my getting into the Regular Army.[2] Couldn't you or George give me some assistance by writing to him?[3] I think that the war is going to last some time yet and the regular service, I am convinced, is the one to be in. The fact of their retreating every where, shows that they are going to prolong the war as long as they can. If they get us down into the Southern States in the hot months we shall have a hard time.

Beauregard & Johnson joined together could make a strong stand somewhere—and then there is a chance of our having a row with France about Mexico.[4]

I told Mr. Sumner I wanted to get into the cavalry—but if that is not possible I shouldn't, of course, object to another branch, for there would be a chance of exchanging some time, probably. If a man were going to make it his profession it would be good to have been through all of them.

The two last days have been very hot & dusty. We have had Reveille at 1 1/2 A.M. getting underway at 2 1/2 or 3. So that each day a good part of the march was over before the hottest part of the day. Cavalry, Artillery, Infantry & Baggage Wagons together raise a dust, which at times was so thick that it was impossible to see half a company length.

Yesterday I received your letter from Washington. I haven't seen Capt Perkins but believe he was detained in Washington by illness.[5] Lieut. Tompkins of the 2d Cavalry has got the Colonelcy of the Vermont Cavalry.[6]

Isn't it queer to think of our having Norfolk & Richmond? The last ten days have been pretty successful for the Federal army & navy.[7]

Tell Nellie I got her letter yesterday. My mind is made up about the Regular Service so please do all you can for me. I haven't the same feeling about this regiment, as when Col. Gordon commanded it. There [are] not many Colonels like him.[8] The difference is perceptible in officers and men. This is private, you know.

May 14

We are having a heavy rainstorm today. Fortunately we have just got our tents again. Give my love to all.

Your afftc son
Robert G. Shaw

P.S. It seems that to have a staff appointment it is necessary to keep your regimental commission leaving the place unfilled. I shouldn't like to do that for it throws extra work on the other officers. Would it be a good thing to write to Mr. Hooper?[9] If so I wish you would. If I fail in getting this, for want of trying, I shall feel badly. Why did I take so little trouble about it last Spring?

1. Irvin McDowell (1818–85), career army officer, graduated from West Point in 1838, fought in the Mexican War, and became Lincoln's first commander of the Army of the Potomac. After Bull Run, Lincoln replaced him with McClellan. McDowell became a corps commander in the Department of the Rappahannock and had primary responsibility to protect Washington from Confederate armies. Foote, *Civil War*, vol. 1, pp. 405–6.

2. Charles Sumner was one of the most influential men in the U.S. Senate.

3. George William Curtis.

4. Confederate general Joseph Eggleston Johnston commanded the forces defending Richmond against McClellan's advance up the peninsula. France's Napoleon III hoped to capitalize on the Civil War by restoring French influence in the Western Hemisphere. French troops arrived in Mexico in 1862. After capturing Mexico City in June 1863 and setting up a monarchy under Ferdinand Maximilian in 1864, Napoleon III bowed to United States and European power diplomacy, removed his troops, and avoided war. McPherson, *Battle Cry*, pp. 683–84.

5. Captain Perkins.

6. Charles H. Tompkins (1830–?) of Virginia was commissioned a second lieutenant in the Second U.S. Cavalry on Mar. 23, 1861. He accepted a colonelcy and command of the 1st Vermont Cavalry on Apr. 24, 1862, only to resign command in Sept. 1862 to become a captain in the same unit. Boatner, *Dictionary*, p. 841.

7. Confederate major general Benjamin Huger abandoned Norfolk on May 9, 1862, to reinforce Richmond. Union troops occupied Norfolk the next day. *Harper's Weekly*, May 24, 1862, p. 1. Of course, Richmond did not fall until Apr. 3, 1865.

8. George Henry Gordon was promoted to brigadier general, effective June 9, 1862. Boatner, *Dictionary*, p. 348; for Gordon's account of his career and campaigns with the Second, see George H. Gordon, *Brook Farm to Cedar* *Mountain in the War of the Rebellion* (Boston: Osgood, 1883).

9. Samuel Hooper (1808–75), U.S. congressman from Massachusetts (1861–75). McGuiness and Sayers, *American Leaders*, p. 183.

Washington, D.C.   [RGS]
May 19, 1862
Dear Father,

You will be surprised to see that I am in Washington. I came down with Major Copeland to see if I could assist him at all, in a plan he has made for getting up a black regiment.[1] He says, very justly, that it would be much wiser to enlist men in the North, who have had the courage to run away, and have already suffered for their freedom, than to take them all from the contrabands at Port Royal and other places.[2] We were at Mr. Hooper's last evening. He said he had received your note, and that it was useless for me to try to get exchanged, so that matter seems settled. However, I shall ask Mr. Sumner to-day what he thinks. Copeland wants me to take hold of the black regiment with him, if he can get the permission to raise it, and offers me a major's commission in it.

They told us at the Sanitary Commission last night, that orders had come from Yorktown to prepare accommodation for six thousand men![3] It appears that the government has kept the details of the Williamsburg affair from the public, and that our troops were far from coming out of it first best.[4] This I heard as coming from Colonel —— of ——'s Brigade, who lost twenty-two officers and about three hundred men killed and wounded from his regiment alone. The Rebels are said to have retreated in good order, after having caused us immense loss. Our gunboats went up to within five miles of Richmond, but had to fall back, and the Galena got sixteen shot through her iron.[5] This is only gossip that I heard in the hotel last night, and you know Washington is the last place to get reliable news. It is also said that McClellan has called for sixteen thousand additional troops, and that they are to be taken from Banks and McDowell.[6] If so, we stand a small chance of going down there. I am very much obliged to you indeed for writing so soon to Messrs. Sumner and Wilson, and am disappointed at finding there is little or no chance.[7] Copeland thinks the raising [of] black regiments will be an era in our history, and the greatest thing that has been done for the negro race. He is very enthusiastic about it. I will write again before I leave here, which will be to-morrow or the next day.

Your loving son,
Robert G. Shaw

1. Apparently, R. Morris Copeland approached Shaw and James Savage with the plan to raise black troops. Both agreed to "go in" with Copeland if he could convince Lincoln and Stanton. Copeland used his position on Banks's staff to order leave for Shaw to accompany him to Washington. The plan was rejected. Shaw used the opportunity to travel to Staten Island for a two-day visit before rejoining his regiment on the 24th. Putnam, *Memoirs*, p. 24; note at bottom of page, RGS to FGS, May 19, 1862, *Letters: RGS* (1864), p. 153.

2. Gen. Benjamin F. Butler coined the term "contrabands" on May 23, 1861, when he refused to return fugitive slaves to their masters. Boatner, *Dictionary*, p. 172.

3. Composed of over seven thousand branches across the North, the U.S. Sanitary Commission had its headquarters in an old cane factory on North Capitol Street near the train station in Washington, D.C. Margaret Leech, *Reveille in Washington, 1860–1865* (New York: Harper, 1941), p. 214.

4. As Johnston retreated from Yorktown, James Longstreet, on May 5, protected his rear and clashed with McClellan's troops at Williamsburg. Longstreet had 1,700 casualties to the Union's 2,200. McPherson, *Battle Cry*, p. 427.

5. The ironclad USS *Galena* participated in James River operations against Fort Darling, seven miles south of Richmond. Eighteen of the twenty-eight shot that hit her from Confederate batteries penetrated her hull to kill thirteen and wound eleven. Faust, *Encyclopedia*, p. 296.

6. McClellan became infamous for overestimating his opponents. In this case, his army of 118,000 faced a foe less than half as large.

7. Henry Wilson (1812–75) served as U.S. senator from Massachusetts (1855–71) and later as vice president under Grant. A radical abolitionist, Wilson is best remembered for his three-volume work, *History of the Rise and Fall of the Slave Power in the United States* (Boston: Osgood, 1872–77).

Williamsport Md.   [HL]
May 27 1862
Dear Father,

My visit at home seemed hardly more real than a dream, when, little more than 24 hours after leaving Uncle Jim at Wallack's, I found myself on picket duty a little way out of Winchester.[1] The whole division, excepting those who were out off at Front Royal, had arrived there. The 2d Mass. covered the retreat from Strasburg on Saturday afternoon and from all accounts did good service.[2] Two Companies, Capt. Abbott & Cogswell, repulsed a body of cavalry, which would undoubtedly have thrown the rear of the column into confusion if they had got by.[3] As it was, a good many wagons were lost during the day.

As I said above I was on outpost Saturday night. We were firing at intervals all night long, and at daylight a large body of infantry approached and we were obliged to retire. The fight began immediately and continued for about two hours when we were ordered to retreat. The rebels had a much larger force and actually got into the town before we did. We lost a great many men in the streets of Winchester.[4] The inhabitants did their share from the windows—women as well as men. I hope that town will be destroyed when we go back there. We had time to burn part of it while the fight was going on.

Major Dwight is missing.[5] He was probably captured as he had dismounted for some reason—his horse got away. Capt. Mudge was wounded in the streets of the town.[6] Some way out of town I got him a horse & then left him. He is missing now though & I feel very anxious about him. He could ride perfectly well & the horse was a good one. It doesn't seem possible that he can have allowed himself to be caught. I am almost certain that he got to Harper's Ferry or some other points on the river—for some regiments went over in that direction. I telegraphed his Father that he had better come down here. It was real hard writing to them about it—for a wounded man may have a hard time among the Rebels.

Both our surgeons are taken. Leland stayed at Newtown with our wounded on Saturday & Stone was seized in the Winchester Hospital on Sunday.

All the men behaved well and obeyed all orders promptly. They began to straggle about two miles from the town. They were almost exhausted with the work of the day before, having got into camp at 1 A.M. Sunday. Nevertheless we managed to make 34 miles after the fight, though, to be sure, a good many stragglers were taken.[7]

I hope it will be understood that it was utterly impossible for Genl Banks to do anything with his small force. I believe I told you in my last that Genl Williams adjutant Genl & also our Signal Officers counted 28 Rebel Regiments.[8] It was a brilliant move on their part but unless they have a large force behind them they must be in a ticklish position. Mr. Stanton's work in this valley has been pretty unsuccessful & I hope it will all be put on his shoulders. The Baltimore & Ohio and the Manassas R.Rs. both destroyed & the valley of Virginia completely cleaned out—besides a panic in the North and the great encouragement to the Rebel cause.

Two regiments on our right did not stand steady. We were the third from the right & came near being thrown into confusion by them, when the retreat began. The men were so well in hand though, that Col. Andrews was able to halt us and form the regiment in the town & then start off again in good order.[9] Harry was guarding a bridge on the Manassas R.R. when Kenley was attacked on Friday—and on Saturday would have been caught if he hadn't made a very hard march to rejoin the regiment.[10] Saturday evening a company of the N.Y. Cavalry charged several of our companies by mistake & a horse tumbled on Harry's legs. They (the legs) troubled him very much on the retreat Sunday but he has got over it now.

It was hard to see our men tumbling over though it is not so horrid a sight as the battle-field & the wounded after the excitement is over.

It is strange that all the way from New York, as I was sitting alone in the cars, I kept thinking, more than I ever did before, of what my chances were of ever getting home, and how the last words Uncle Jim said were that he hoped to see me safe through it & soon in New York. So when I felt the blow on my side & found my watch had stopped the ball, the first thing I thought of was how you all would have felt if I had been left on that infernal pavement and it seemed as if I could see you all standing on the piazza just before I came away.[11]

Give my love to all of them.

Ever your loving son
Robert G. Shaw

It seems to us a perfect wonder that the army got away safely—marching about sixty miles—the rear skirmishing all the first day—all of them fighting hard the next morning & saving almost everything. Genl Banks certainly has reason to congratulate himself. The company I went on picket with had been in rear of the whole column skirmishing since 3 P.M., kept awake all night, retired firing the next morning, joined the regiment & was in the engagement with the rest. This was Capt. Cogswell's company & men.

1. James Sturgis lived in Boston. Sturgis, *Sturgis*, p. 53. "Wallack's" Theatre, owned by James W. Wallack was located on Broadway in NYC. Nevins, Allan, and Thomas, Milton H., eds., *The Diary of George Templeton Strong* (NY: Macmillan, 1952), vol. I, p. 125.

2. Stonewall Jackson defeated Federals at Front Royal on May 23, skirmished at Strasburg on the 24th, and narrowly failed to trap Banks's army before it could get to Winchester. On May 25, Jackson attacked and defeated Banks in the Battle of Winchester. Long, *Civil War Day By Day*, pp. 214–17.

3. Edward Gardner Abbott (1840–62), son of Judge Josiah Abbott of Lowell, Massachusetts, commanded Company A. Capt. William Cogswell of Salem commanded Company C. Bowen, *Massachusetts in the War*, p. 114.

4. Jackson employed 16,000 men

against 8,000 for Banks. Jackson lost 400 casualties to Banks's 2,019. Long, *Civil War Day By Day*, p. 216.

5. Wilder Dwight was captured and paroled. He returned to the regiment on June 2, 1862, and was promoted to lieutenant colonel on June 13. Higginson, *Harvard Memorial Biographies*, vol. 1, pp. 263–65.

6. Charles Redington Mudge.

7. Banks reported 1,714 men missing or captured. Long, *Civil War Day By Day*, p. 216.

8. Alpheus Starkey Williams (1810–78), a Connecticut lawyer, commanded Banks's First Division, Apr. 4–Sept. 4,

1862. After the war Williams served as U.S. Minister to El Salvador. Boatner, *Dictionary*, p. 927.

9. George L. Andrews.

10. Henry S. Russell. Colonel Kenley is unidentified.

11. Shaw's friend Charles Morse described this in a letter home: "Bob Shaw was struck by a minie ball, which passed through his coat and vest and dented into his watch, a very valuable gold one, shattering the works all to pieces, doing him no damage with the exception of a slight bruise; the watch saved his life. . . ." Morse, *Letters*, p. 66.

Williamsport, Md. [RGS]
June 6, 1862
My Dear Susie,

I have just received yours of 1st of June. Yesterday I had one from Effie. I believe I wrote last to her, so now I answer yours. You say at the top of your letter, "Nellie seventeen years old," 1st June, but I observe you say nothing of your birthday, the day before. As you see from the date of this, I can hardly be said to write from the seat of war. There are only four regiments on this side now. General Banks is at Winchester, and we are only waiting for clothes. The late rains have swollen the Potomac so that we shall have a good deal of difficulty in getting over if we go this week.

We had the same frightful accounts as Mrs. Gibbons, of the barbarity of the Rebels the first day after we arrived here, but since then it has turned out to be a mistake.[1] No doubt, in the heat of passion, a good many cruel things are done, but it is probably the same on every battle-field. A good many of our men were taken and subsequently escaped, and they were all treated well. Major Dwight and Dr. Stone met with nothing but kindness. A sergeant of my company died from wounds in the hospital there. General Jackson released a dozen non-commissioned officers and privates of this regiment for escort; furnished a coffin and ambulance, and they buried him with honours. All our wounded were left in the hospital at Winchester, and the Major says Jackson was very angry with one of his officers for wishing to carry some of them off, as he said it was inhuman. From all they tell us of Jackson, I should think he was a good man. He is certainly an able commander, for he has escaped everything, when it seemed almost impossible. Dwight says all the officers he saw seemed tired to death of the war, and the men still more so. Colonel Kenley, who was said to have been killed in an ambulance, is here with a slight wound in his head. A man at Harper's Ferry showed me a coffin, which he said contained Colonel Kenley's body; so much for rumours.

The papers say, that, for some unaccountable reason, the picket of the First Maryland, at Front Royal, gave no notice of the approach of the enemy.[2] It may seem unaccountable to some people, but it doesn't to me, for I was down there one day, and saw half of them asleep in the grass, and the rest fishing and bathing in the brook.

We have a beautiful camp here, and shall be sorry to leave it, though it looks bad to date our letters from Maryland. It is pleasant to see how differently the men feel towards their officers since we have been under fire together. They appreciate the advantages of strict discipline now. Quincy heard one say, "I notice we didn't shoot any of our officers."[3] "No," said another, "we need them to take care of us in a fight." Last winter a writer in the "Baltimore Clipper" said that we should all be killed by our own men in the first action. I believe I wrote home how six of our company took care of Captain Mudge, and really saved him from being captured. They carried him, and dragged him in a waggon, and dressed his wound. At Charlestown, they got hold of a Secession Doctor, and stood guard over him while he examined the Captain's leg. Harry sends his love.

Always your affectionate brother,
Robert G. Shaw

1. Abigail Hopper Gibbons (1801–93), abolitionist and women's rights advocate, whose husband, James Sloan Gibbons, was a New York banker and abolitionist. *DAB*, vol. 4, pp. 237–38.

Williamsport, Md.   [HL]
June 7, 1862
My dear Mary,[1]

Your letter enclosing the photograph reached me at Strasburg early last month when we thought we had settled down for a quiet summer.

So many things have happened since then that it seems a long while ago.

About the middle of the month I went with Copeland to Washington to see what assistance I could render him in getting permission to raise a black regiment in the North.

He was full of the idea, but the Secretary of War wouldn't allow it to be done. Of course you could better [recruit] soldiers among the Blacks of the North than among the poor contrabands at Port Royal who never had the pluck to run away. We left everything quiet behind us, and our regiment was scattered about in many places, some building fortifications & some guarding the rail-roads & bridges. Harry was all alone on the road to Front Royal and it was very fortunate he was not taken with his whole company, the day the retreat began. After getting through our business in Washington, we found we should have time to go home, and I had three pleasant days at Staten Island, which two lengthy visits to the dentist prevented from becoming monotonous.

Friday night the 23d about sunset I bid them all good-bye & started for Strasburg and the next evening hardly 24 hours later I was in the midst of Winchester. The road for miles was encumbered with the artillery, cavalry, infantry & the baggage trains, and as I gradually got towards the rear, where I was told the regiment was, the volleys of musketry & the bursting of shell got louder & louder. It didn't seem possible that so short a time before I had been standing on our quiet little lawn, at Staten Island.

I met the 2 Mass. some miles out of town at midnight & found they had been skirmishing all the afternoon & had lost a good many men. The enemy's fire had come down to an occasioned shot at our rearmost company by this time, and it was kept up all night at intervals, & answered by our sentinels after the picket was thrown out. They appeared with daylight, and the rattlety bing bang proceeded in fine style. You know the result of our mornings work and how we had a neck and neck race through Winchester. A heavy fire, from behind, is hard to bear—in advancing you hardly think of the bullets—but they seem relentless when you are running away from them. Then there was the certainty of being left if wounded & we all thought then, that that was equivalent to having our throats cut in cold blood for the amusement of Genl Jackson & friends. There has been no proof of any barbarity on the part of the Rebels this time, and it is pleasant to think that all the accounts have been exaggerated. Major Dwight & Dr. Stone were perfectly well-treated and had a pleasant time.

I write this to thank you for your photograph which I like very much indeed. I hope you are all well. Give my love to every one.

Yr afftc cousin,

Robert G. Shaw

I am on guard. It is 3 A.M. so excuse blots &c. My eyelids are heavy. Harry received a letter from your E. M [name unreadable] yesterday.

1. Mary A. Forbes, daughter of John
Murray Forbes.

Near Newtown, Va.   [RGS]
June 13, 1862
Dear Mother,

We arrived here last evening, after two and a half days' march from Williamsburg. We made nineteen miles yesterday, and a little more the day before, and as the weather has been very warm we came in very tired. I have written six times since we got to Williamsport, and hope you have received all my letters. We are encamped now, just on the spot where part of the regiment formed to receive the cavalry the night before the engagement. Abbott's company occupied the place where our messtable now is.

I have received your five and six; number four is still missing, but it can't have fallen into the enemy's hands, I think, because the mails always come up this valley, and would have gone back with us. We marched through Martinsburg and Winchester in close order, and band playing, so that there should be no chance of the men's falling out and committing any outrages. A house on the other side of Martinsburg was set on fire by some soldier, but, on the whole, our men show very little of the vices common in armies that have been some time in the field. They write so often to their families, and get so many letters from home, that it must have a good influence on them.

I am glad my watch arrived safely at home. You ask me to tell you how the blow felt. I hardly remember anything about it, for just at that moment we were busy with the men, as Colonel Andrews halted the regiment in the street and formed the line, so that every officer had his hands full keeping the men steady. The watch was in the pocket of my vest, though I almost always carry it in my fob. I felt a violent blow and a burning sensation in my side, and at the same moment a man by my side cried out, "O, my arm!" I had just time to wonder why I wasn't lying on the ground, when the order came, "Right face, double-quick, march," and off we went. A moment after this Captain Mudge was hit, and it seemed as if we couldn't possibly get him away, for there was a regiment of Rebels directly abreast with us in the parallel street. My sword and pistol were with the luggage, so I was without any weapon until some time after the fight began on Sunday, when I got a little sword from a drummer-boy. It was little better than a toy-sword, but you get so accustomed to having one in your hand when on duty, that until I got it I felt as if I had no right to give an order. At Williamsport I found my servant with all my traps, even the carpet-bag which I took home with me, and which one of the men had found and put into a waggon. We slept sound Sunday night, excepting four of our officers and the men of two companies, who went directly out on picket, and didn't take their clothes off, and hardly lay down until three days after. It was very hard for them.

In my company, out of fifty men who went into action on Sunday morning, there were one killed, eight wounded, and two taken prisoners and carried off by the Rebels when they retreated. Nine killed and wounded out of fifty, is a large proportion. Our wounded were all left at Winchester and paroled, and also several men who were acting as nurses in the hospitals. I hope they will soon be exchanged.

Fremont has been following Jackson up very energetically.[1] I saw Sigel yesterday; he is an insignificant looking man, at least at a little distance.[2] There are a great many troops in the valley now, but they are all raw, excepting Fremont's and ours. Where can Beauregard be?[3] I shouldn't wonder if he turned up unexpectedly, somewhere, and frightened the whole country into another militia fit.

Colonel Gordon's commission as Brigadier has been confirmed. We don't know yet what Brigade he will have. He told me he should be very sorry to have me leave the regiment, but said he would do what he could for me, either by letter or personal interview, if I were decided about wanting a commission in the regular army. I shall write a little note to Mr. Wilson, so as to keep myself in his mind's eye.

Love to all. I have Effie's letter of June 8.

Your loving son,
Robert G. Shaw

1. Shaw seems to have been cheerleading for Frémont. On June 8, 1862, part of Jackson's command under Richard Ewell defeated Frémont's much larger army at the Battle of Cross Keys. Then, leaving a small force to watch Frémont, Jack- son used Ewell's men to help him win the Battle of Port Republic on June 9 against General Shields. On June 11, Frémont pulled back further from Port Republic as Jackson confounded his opponents. Long, *Civil War Day By Day*,

pp. 224–25.

2. Franz Sigel (1824–1904) was born in Germany and fought in the German Revolution of 1848. Sigel immigrated to the United States in 1852. In May 1861, he organized and led the Third Missouri Infantry. As a brigadier general, Sigel helped Frémont win at Pea Ridge, Arkansas, on Mar. 8, 1862. He was promoted to major general on Mar. 21, 1862, and transferred to help

fight Jackson in the Shenandoah. In June, he became commander of I Corps in Pope's Army of Virginia. *DAB*, vol. 9, p. 153.

3. Beauregard had retreated from Corinth, Mississippi, and had his army around Tupelo. On June 17, Jefferson Davis replaced him with a more temerarious, if unpopular, commander, Braxton Bragg. Long, *Civil War Day By Day*, pp. 222, 227.

Near Front Royal, Va.   [RGS]
June 25, 1862
Dear Mother,

I wrote you last from our camp, near Newtown, and since then have received a note from Father, and one from Effie. We marched up from there yesterday, and what we are to do next, I don't know. Fremont and Sigel are in the valley, but Banks is reduced to his old Brigade, or rather to a part of it.

I was stationed with my company in Newtown the day before yesterday. Robeson and I got acquainted with some of the people there, and they treated us with great civility.[1] There was one exception, however, and the family is originally from Boston. The lady was a Barnard, and married a Dr. Davis. They have a fine place near Newtown, and Dr. Davis is in the Rebel service somewhere. I know the Barnard boys in Boston very well; so we thought we would walk in and look at the garden.[2] Some ladies who were sitting on the piazza got up, when they saw us coming, went into the house and slammed the door; and a little while after, we saw some of them peeking through the blinds.

We have a very pleasant feeling towards Rebel soldiers now, because our prisoners were treated so well by them, and because we have had very pleasant interviews with many of their officers and men, but the *citizens* of the towns we have passed through seem to hate us much more bitterly, as a general thing. I hope every Northern man in the Rebel service, like this Davis, will get his deserts some day.

General Gordon returned from Washington last week, but is gone again.[3] He finds there will be some difficulty in getting his old Brigade, and I am afraid he won't be back. He made a little speech to the regiment last Sunday, and a good many of the men cried. He, himself, was very much affected, and at first had some difficulty in speaking. I think he was pretty certain then that it was his farewell to us; indeed, he gave us that impression.

Don't things seem to be at a stand-still just now? Perhaps it is a lull before the storm. We are out of the valley of Virginia now, but the country here is even more beautiful than that. General Fremont is at Mount Jackson, and General Sigel at Middletown, half-way between us and the former, so that he can support either. I have had a good deal of writing to do, to the relatives of our wounded men, besides making out papers for them, so I have not written to you so often as usual.

I have had letters from four of the Mudge family, thanking me for my care of the Captain; and two from Miss Austin about one of our sergeants who was killed, who was a son of their coachman, so that I feel ashamed of having so many fine things said to me.[4] They all took me by surprise, *as I wasn't aware I was such a fine fellow*! Love to all.

Your affectionate son,
Robert G. Shaw

1. First Lt. Thomas Rodman Robeson.

2. The Barnards and Dr. Davis are unidentified.

3. George H. Gordon.

4. Miss Austin is unidentified.

Six Miles from Front Royal, Va.   [RGS]
June 29, 1862
Dear Father,

I must write to you in pencil to-day, as my company is seven or eight miles from camp, on outpost duty, and there are no pens or ink to be had. We came up here day before yesterday, and, with two other companies, are guarding three or four miles on the North Fork of the Shenandoah. We expect to be relieved to-morrow. You have probably heard that Pope is to have command in this department.[1] They say that Fremont and Sigel feel very much hurt at it, and I don't wonder. Fremont ranks next to McClellan, and it must be hard to have a Brigadier-General put over him.[2] Of course, I feel very sorry for him. I think, nevertheless, that it shows a great deal of determination in the President to do what he thinks best, in spite of all opposition. Fremont's party, will, of course, make a great row about it. What a hard time the poor General has had. After all, it may not be true, for I have it only from hearsay. I, myself, am a little perplexed as to what I had better do, for General Gordon has offered me a place as aide, on his staff. Not having heard from Mr. Gay

Massachusetts Governor John Albion Andrew. MOLLUS—Mass. Collection, USAMHI.

Frederick Douglass, recruiter for the Fifty-fourth Massachusetts Infantry.

Industrialist John Murray Forbes, adviser to Governor Andrew and member of the Fifty-fourth Massachusetts recruiting committee. Massachusetts Historical Society.

George Luther Stearns, head of the Fifty-fourth Massachusetts recruiting committee. Massachusetts Historical Society.

Sergeant-Major Lewis Douglass, Fifty-fourth
Massachusetts Infantry, 1863. Frederick
Douglass Collection, Box 28-10 Photo Album,
Moorland-Spingarn Research Center, Howard
University.

Sgt. Henry Stewart, Company E, Fifty-fourth
Massachusetts Infantry. Massachusetts
Historical Society.

Pvt. Abraham F. Brown, Company E, Fifty-fourth Massachusetts Infantry. Massachusetts Historical Society.

Peter Vogelsang, at age forty-six, the oldest man to join the Fifty-fourth Massachusetts. Vogelsang became one of the first black officers in the U.S. Army. MOLLUS—Mass. Collection, USAMHI.

Pvt. John W. M. Appleton, prior to recruiting for and serving in the Fifty-fourth Massachusetts Infantry. West Virginia and Regional History Collection, West Virginia University Library.

Lt. Col. Norwood Penrose Hallowell, Fifty-fourth Massachusetts Infantry. MOLLUS—Mass. Collection, USAMHI.

Lt. Garth Wilkinson James (younger brother of William James and Henry James, Jr.), Dr. Lincoln Ripley Stone (right), and an unknown soldier (left) of the Fifty-fourth Massachusetts at Camp Meigs, Readville, 1863. From the collection of, and by permission of, William Gladstone.

Lt. Cabot Jackson Russel, Fifty-fourth Massachusetts Infantry; killed at Fort Wagner, July 18, 1863. MOLLUS— Mass. Collection, USAMHI.

Maj. Edward Needles Hallowell, Fifty-fourth Massachusetts Infantry. MOLLUS—Mass. Collection, USAMHI.

Col. James M. Montgomery,
Second South Carolina Infantry.
Kansas State Historical Society,
Topeka, Kansas.

Former slaves, some wearing Union uniforms, harvesting sweet potatoes on Edisto Island, S.C., 1863. MOLLUS—Mass. Collection, USAMHI.

First day of freedom for contrabands of war at Hilton Head, S.C., aboard the U.S.S. *Vermont*. Montgomery's Second South Carolina Infantry was composed of contraband enlistees. MOLLUS—Mass. Collection, USAMHI.

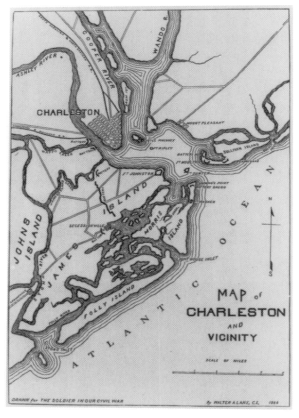

Map of Charleston, S.C., and vicinity. From *The Soldiers in Our Civil War* (1884). By permission of the New Bedford Whaling Museum.

Sketch of the Charleston Harbor defenses, 1863. Morris Island is in the lower left corner; Fort Wagner is in the middle of the island's sandy peninsula. *Harper's Weekly,* August 15, 1863.

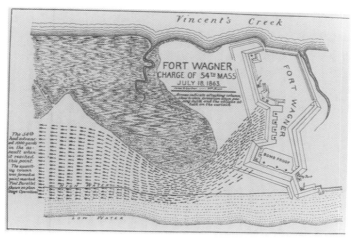

Charge of the Fifty-fourth Massachusetts at Fort Wagner, July 18, 1863. From Luis F. Emilio, *A Brave Black Regiment* (1891).

Drawing of Fort Wagner with annotations by John W. M. Appleton. West Virginia and Regional History Collection, West Virginia University Library.

Attack of the Fifty-fourth Massachusetts on Fort Wagner, July 18, 1863, by Thomas Nast. MOLLUS—Mass. Collection, USAMHI.

Battlefield sketch of Fort Wagner, July 19, 1863, by Frank Vizetelly. Inscribed on the sketch is the following description: "In the ditch, they lay piled, negroes & whites, four & five deep on each other, there could not have been less than 250 in the moat, some partially submerged. . . ." By permission of the Houghton Library, Harvard University.

Veterans of the Fifty-fourth Massachusetts at the dedication of the
Augustus Saint-Gaudens memorial to Shaw and the men of the Fifty-fourth
Massachusetts, May 31, 1897. The memorial is located on Boston Common.
Massachusetts Historical Society.

The Shaw memorial. Photograph by Clive Russ.

Robert Gould Shaw, circa 1841.
By permission of the Houghton
Library, Harvard University.

Robert Gould Shaw, 1859.
By permission of the Houghton
Library, Harvard University.

Shaw's father, Francis George Shaw, 1863.
Staten Island Institute of Arts and Sciences.

Shaw's mother, Sarah Blake Sturgis Shaw, with grandson Frankie Curtis, 1863.
Staten Island Institute of Arts and Sciences.

Shaw's sister Susanna. Staten Island Institute of Arts and Sciences.

Shaw's sister Ellen. Staten Island Institute of Arts and Sciences.

Shaw's sister Anna Shaw Curtis, wife of publisher George William Curtis, with daughter Sarah, circa 1863. Staten Island Institute of Arts and Sciences.

George William Curtis, 1863. Staten Island Institute of Arts and Sciences.

Shaw's sister Josephine with her fiancé, Charles Russell Lowell, Jr., circa 1863.

Robert Gould Shaw, Seventh New York State National Guard, 1861. Massachusetts Historical Society.

Col. Robert Gould Shaw, Fifty-fourth Massachusetts Infantry,
May 1863. Boston Athenaeum.

Shaw's wife, Annie Kneeland Haggerty Shaw, 1863.
Boston Athenaeum.

e came here —

We arrived at camp near
Mr. Butler's plantation
Tuesday evening — Today is
Saturday — and in the mean
time, we have been with
Montgomery on an expedition
up the Altamaha, and burned
the town of Darien — much
to my disgust — for we met
with no resistance & no
good reason can be given
for doing such a thing —

I have written Annie
an account of this, and
asked her to send it to
you, if she is not with
you, as I suppose she
may be, from what she

wrote —

Today I went over to Mr.
Butler's plantation & talked
with some of the old negroes—
There are about 10 left from
his great sale of three
years ago —

Though he had sold their
sons & daughters they said he
was a good master — Some
of them had lived there for
70 & 80 years —

I feel like writing you
a long account of things, as I have
to Annie, but it would be
only a repetition of that,
so I think it better to
employ the time with my
necessary correspondence

Portion of Shaw's June 13, 1863, letter to his mother. By permission of
the Houghton Library, Harvard University.

Departure of the Seventh New York State National Guard down
Broadway, April 19, 1861. Massachusetts Commandery Military Order
of the Loyal Legion and the U.S. Army Military History Institute
(MOLLUS—Mass. Collection, USAMHI).

Shaw (standing, left) in 1862 with fellow officers of the Second Massachusetts Infantry: (from left) James Savage, Jr., R. Morris Copeland, and Henry S. Russell. MOLLUS—Mass. Collection, USAMHI.

Departure of the Seventh New York State National Guard down
Broadway, April 19, 1861. Massachusetts Commandery Military Order
of the Loyal Legion and the U.S. Army Military History Institute
(MOLLUS—Mass. Collection, USAMHI).

Shaw (standing, left) in 1862 with fellow officers of the Second Massachusetts Infantry: (from left) James Savage, Jr., R. Morris Copeland, and Henry S. Russell. MOLLUS—Mass. Collection, USAMHI.

Some of Shaw's fellow officers of the Second Massachusetts Infantry at
Camp Andrew, Brook Farm, 1861: J. Parker Whitney, Francis H. Tucker,
Fletcher M. Abbott, William Cogswell, Thomas Rodman Robeson, James Francis,
Edwin R. Hill, Robert B. Brown, Rufus Choate, Richard Chapman Goodwin,
H. G. O. Weymouth, Samuel Miller Quincy, William Dwight Sedgwick.
MOLLUS—Mass. Collection, USAMHI.

Greely Stevenson Curtis, a captain in
the Second Massachusetts Infantry,
later a major in the First Regiment
Massachusetts Cavalry. MOLLUS—
Mass. Collection, USAMHI.

Charles Fessenden Morse, Second
Massachusetts Infantry. MOLLUS—
Mass. Collection, USAMHI.

NOW IN CAMP AT READVILLE!

54th REGIMENT!

MASS. VOLUNTEERS, composed of men of

AFRICAN DESCENT

Col. ROBERT G. SHAW.

 Colored Men, Rally 'Round the Flag of Freedom!

BOUNTY $100!

AT THE EXPIRATION OF THE TERM OF SERVICE.

Pay, $13 a Month!
Good Food & Clothing!
State Aid to Families!

RECRUITING OFFICE.

COR. CAMBRIDGE & NORTH RUSSELL STS.,
BOSTON.

Lieut. J. W. M. APPLETON, Recruiting Officer.

ZWELL & CO., Steam Job Printers, No. 47 Congress Street, Boston.

Recruiting poster, February 1863. Massachusetts Historical Society.

as to my prospects with General Fremont, I don't know what to expect from that quarter; and in the mean time, I run the risk of losing both.[3] I should like to stay here with General Gordon very much, both for the sake of the place itself, and to remain with the regiment, and I shouldn't feel the same compunction about keeping my commission, if I remain and make myself useful in the same Brigade. An officer who passed here to-day, told me there was talk of Fremont's resigning.[4] How sorry you will all feel about him! It seems as if he were being persecuted. Will you tell me what you advise me to do? Your reply will come more directly, if you address, Second Massachusetts Regiment, Gordon's Brigade, Banks' Army Corps, via Winchester.

Until yesterday, we have had three companies off on Provost Guard at Winchester, and two continually on picket. There have been so many officers off on different duties, that day before yesterday there were only three on dress-parade, for the five remaining companies. They are taken for Court Martial, Boards of Survey, &c., &c. Savage has received his major's commission, and Bangs will have his company.[5] You have probably read the many accounts of Ashby's career.[6] For my part, I can't understand where he got his reputation from, and am inclined to think there is a good deal of newspaper humbug about it. If he had half the energy that has been attributed to him, he might have made many an expedition into our lines, like that of Stewart at White House.[7] Our regiment has been in the advance a good deal, and yet we have not once been troubled by any of Ashby's men. When seen, they have always been out of rifle-range, and the few prisoners I have seen myself were wretched "white trash," poorly mounted. The cavalry that pursued us on the retreat was under the command of Colonel Lee. It used to be Stewart's regiment, I believe.[8] On our way down to Harrisonburg, I think General Banks himself might have been taken, by a body of good cavalry under a bold leader, and such a one might have alarmed us, and got us under arms, almost every night.

Give my love to Mother. Please write as soon as you can.

Always your affectionate son,
Robert G. Shaw

1. John Pope (1822–92), a career soldier from Kentucky, graduated from West Point in 1842, fought in Mexico, and was appointed a brigadier general in July 1861. His victory at Island No. 10 brought him fame and promotion to major general. With Jackson marching circles around three separate Union armies in the Shenandoah, Lincoln created a new Army of Virginia and named Pope to command it on June 26, 1862. Foote, *Civil War*, vol. 1, pp. 526–28.

2. Pope's new command placed him over three generals who had previously

outranked him, McDowell, Banks, and Frémont.

3. Sydney Howard Gay.

4. Frémont refused to serve under Pope, resigned (to Lincoln's great satisfaction), and was replaced by Franz Sigel.

5. James Savage and George P. Bangs were both promoted on June 13, 1862. Bowen, *Massachusetts in the War*, p. 28.

6. Brig. Gen. Turner Ashby, a romantic, impetuous officer died at Harrisonburg, Virginia, as he rallied his cavalry. According to legend, his last words implored, "Charge, men! For God's sake, charge!" Quoted in Foote, *Civil War*, vol. 1, p. 459.

7. Shaw's spelling here is problematic. Brig. Gen. G. H. Steuart commanded the Second Virginia Cavalry of Ewell's Division, Jackson's Corps. Shaw is prob-ably referring to the other "Stewart." Brig. Gen. James Ewell Brown Stuart (1833–64) was, according to Union general John Sedgwick, "The greatest cavalryman ever foaled in America." Stuart became widely recognized after he led twelve hundred men of the Army of Northern Virginia's cavalry on a reconnaissance completely around McClellan's army on June 12–15, 1862. White House is on the Pamunkey River forty miles east of Richmond. Emory Thomas, *Bold Dragoon: The Life of J. E. B. Stuart* (New York: Harper & Row, 1986), pp. 111–28, Sedgwick quote, p. 299.

8. Colonel Lee is unidentified. Robert E. Lee's son, William Henry Fitzhugh Lee (1837–91), and nephew, Fitzhugh Lee (1835–1905), rode with J. E. B. Stuart around McClellan in 1862. Ibid., p. 113.

Near Front Royal, Va. [RGS]
July 4, 1862
My Dear Mother,

I haven't had a letter from you or Father for a long time. Yesterday Effie's of June 29 came. Fremont's resignation has made me feel very badly. Every little while it comes over me like a disagreeable dream. It seems such a pity that his chance of making his worth felt all over the country is gone. Don't think it is any personal disappointment about his staff which makes me feel so, for when I heard he had seventeen aides, I wasn't very anxious to add to the number. The government seems to have made his staff a receptacle for all the Dutchmen who were floating about Washington.

I rode over to see Copeland yesterday. He says that when Fremont went away, he (C.) told him that if he were ever in a position where the services of one man could be of any use, he might count upon him. ——— thinks that there is a set of men in power who are bound to hunt down every prominent and popular antislavery man, and that Fremont's difficulties are to be attributed to them. All the Western men I see swear by him, and are in a great rage with government.

Copeland has been assigned to General Hunter as Assistant Adjutant-General.[1] He wants to take one of the new Massachusetts regiments. I don't know yet which he will do. He has offered me the majority if he takes the regiment. I think I should be tempted to take it, especially as it looks now as if the war would last some time.

How do you feel about the doings before Richmond? Pretty news for the 4th of July, isn't it?[2] Now we can look for something exciting from England and France, i.e. if we have suffered such a defeat as is at present supposed. My only prayer is, that our government won't be frightened into giving up. I hope they will begin to draft all over the country, and take every available man, and then fight until there is no one left. They ought to reduce our pay one half, I think, from Major-General to private. The new levy of 300,000 men will make nearly 1,000,000 men mustered into service within fourteen months.[3] A fourth of the 600,000 must now be at home or disabled, sick, wounded, making believe sick, or in their graves.

I hope you have an occasional talk with Mr. Beecher or some man of a sanguine temperament, otherwise you must be in rather bad spirits.[4] What sufferings the sick and wounded left by McClellan must have undergone! Their numbers would make it impossible they should be taken care of, if the Rebels had the best intentions. I trust our friends there are safe.

I have forgotten to tell you that I am now A. D. C. to General Gordon.[5] It will be very pleasant as a change, and perhaps in other respects. I slept through *reveille* this morning, for the first time since I joined the regiment, excepting the short time I was in Frederick, and the few days at home. We expect to move to-day or to-morrow; whither, no one knows; but probably *not* up the valley. Of course, this is only conjecture, but I shouldn't wonder if we went to Fortress Monroe, or in front of Washington.[6] I can see no use of our going towards Richmond on this side, for we have not a large enough force to do much. Copeland is very apt to look at things through a blue eye-glass; but it seems to me, that there is some truth in his idea, that the Republicans allow themselves to be wheedled and fooled, and that Democrats and old fogies have much more influence at Washington than they should. They have only to say they have changed their opinions, which is always a lie, and they are joyfully received. A few good lickings will perhaps, be beneficial. I hope General Fremont will offer his services again, even if they only give him a subordinate position, for the country needs every man who can come. What we *want*, is his "*d——n the expense*" spirit; don't you think so? If we only went in for sink or swim, we should finish the thing up; Stanton wants to be economical. It was for that he stopped recruiting at one time, without which an army in the field must dwindle to half its size in a short time. I don't mean that money should be wasted, but that there should be no economy which is sure to be waste in the end. Like buying bad boots, because they are cheap.

Love to all. I can't write any more now. If my grumblings make you feel gloomy, I will repress them in future. Do they? Harry sends love to all of you. The shirts and socks are very good. Ask Father to send me a good razor. I have bought a nice little mare.

Always, dearest Mother,
Your affectionate Son

1. David Hunter (1802–66) graduated from West Point in 1822, but resigned from the army in 1836 to go into business in Chicago. He donned his uniform again for the Mexican War and served in Kansas when the Civil War began. Commissioned a brigadier general at the beginning of the war, Hunter replaced Frémont in Missouri in 1861. After Mar. 1862, Hunter commanded the Department of the South. Copeland would have been happy to serve with Hunter, who believed that the Union should use black soldiers. Faust, *Encyclopedia*, p. 376.

2. On June 25, Robert E. Lee, now fortified with Jackson's Corps, began to attack McClellan's army in the Seven Days' Campaign. By June 27, McClellan had his huge army moving away from Richmond. The July 1 Battle of Malvern

Hill effectively ended the Peninsular Campaign. Total casualties for both sides during the Seven Days' probably influenced McClellan's decision: 5,025 killed, 23,971 wounded, and 6,999 missing. Long, *Civil War Day By Day*, pp. 230–36.

3. With June reverses in the Shenandoah Valley and on the peninsula before Richmond, Lincoln called for 300,000 more men. Foote, *Civil War*, vol. 1, p. 662.

4. Henry Ward Beecher.

5. "A. D. C." is the abbreviation for aide-de-camp.

6. Erected in the 1820s and 1830s of stone and brick, Fortress Monroe, located at the mouth of the Chesapeake Bay near Hampton Roads, was the country's largest fort. *Harper's Weekly*, Aug. 10, 1861, p. 11.

Washington, Va.   [RGS]
July 23, 1862
Dear Mother,

As I mentioned in a short note to Father day before yesterday, I have received several letters from home since we arrived here. Yesterday I got his of 18th July. I was very sorry to hear you had not been well. I hope you are careful about exposing yourself.

Now Congress has adjourned, perhaps the war will be more vigorously and systematically carried on, though I think we should do better still, if the President and his Cabinet would adjourn too. Our republican government never managed the country with a very firm hand, even in time of peace, and one year of war has shown pretty clearly that that is not its forte. We may finish the war, but it will certainly be with a much greater loss of time, life, and money than if we had had some men, any man almost, with a few common-sense military ideas, to manage matters, without being meddled with and badgered by a lot of men who show the greatest ignorance about the commonest things. Who but a crazy man could have stopped the enlisting, because there were 700,000 men mustered into the service?[1] Taking out of these the sick, the deserters, and those on detached service in hospitals, barracks, &c., we couldn't have more than 500,000 before the campaign began. All these were scattered about the country, and we had no reserve, or recruiting stations to draw from.

Banks' retreat would have been nothing at all, if there had been a large National Reserve, but as it was, every one was very naturally frightened, because if the enemy once get through our lines, there is nothing more to stop them.[2]

I see that the papers are all crying out and wondering because there are at least forty thousand men absent and unaccounted for, who should be with McClellan, or this army. What is the reason they can go off with impunity and be out of the way, just when they are wanted? Because when it was neccessary to shoot some men last winter for desertion, the President pardoned them, and every one thought it was too bad to punish our "brave Volunteers" for just going home to see their families for a little while, without permission.[3] They know now that nothing will be done to them, and many of them are deserting to enlist in the new regiments for $100 bounty.[4] The same policy has been followed with the army all along.

Senator Wilson makes a great fuss because some of his constituents are court-martialed and condemned to the Washington Penitentiary, for what he calls "trifling offences."[5] One "trifling offence" is leaving the ranks on the march. The regiment goes into a fight after four hours marching, and only two thirds or one half of the men are present. This may seem a "trifling offence" to some men, but it certainly is not. Men mustn't be severely punished for disobeying orders, for deserting, for insulting and even striking their officers and non-commissioned officers, and the result is that they do just about what they please. If the majority of them hadn't more intelligence and good sense than most members of Congress, the army would be in a very bad condition, or rather, much worse than it is now. I think this is partly due to the custom of allowing men to elect their own officers, who consequently have little control over them, and partly to the interference of government with our commanders in the management of their troops. Father thinks the temporizing commanders will be dropped by degrees. I don't think it looks much like it, if Halleck is to be our commander-in-chief, for he never would allow a fugitive slave inside his lines, and if he could, would have returned them all.[6]

There seem to be some singular ideas in the North about guarding Rebel property. I have never seen guards placed excepting to prevent plundering. If the soldiers were allowed to plunder indiscriminately, we should have an army of thieves and robbers that would be perfectly unmanageable. Blenker's Division were allowed a great deal of liberty, and they got to be a bad set.[7]

Captain Underwood of our regiment has been promoted to the rank of Major in one of the new Massachusetts regiments, and I shall soon have a captaincy, as I come next to Morse, who gets Underwood's company.[8] In my present position with General Gordon, my duties are very light; indeed, most of the time I have too little to do. When the Brigade is marching, I have to go round to the different regiments and batteries every morning, to see that they get under way at the proper time and in the proper order. After we get started, I ride at the head of the column with the General and the rest of the Staff. When we halt, I show each regiment to its camping-ground, and that is about all I have to do. In camp, I don't get up till breakfast time. After that, if there is anything to be looked after in the Brigade, I usually take a ride, and sometimes, when Scott is away, I have to write a few orders.[9]

Until lately, we have messed with Colonel Andrews and his Staff, but now we have a separate one. At first, we fared pretty badly, as it takes some time to get the cook and the caterer broken in. The mess consists of the General; Scott, Assistant Adjutant-General; Hawes, Quartermaster; Wheaton, Commissary; and myself.[10] We expect to have more aides before long. I don't know who they will be; they will probably come from home. On the whole, we have a very pleasant time. Our tents are always pitched pretty near the Second Massachusetts. I shall go back to the regiment again when I can get a captaincy; for if the war is to last a great while, rank may be a good thing. Harry is well, and sends his love to all. It is supposed that Fremont will have another command? I don't see how they can arrange it.

To-day I received a compliment which pleased me very much, as it was of a kind which is naturally more gratifying to an officer than any other. I will tell you what it was. Cogswell's First Sergeant told him, and he told me, that his men all thought I showed a great deal of courage and coolness that night before, and the morning of the fight at Winchester, when I was out with them.[11] You know I wrote you that I went on picket that night with Cogswell. It is so pleasant to know that your men have confidence in you, and to get a compliment that you know is genuine, I wanted to tell you of it, though I shouldn't any one else.

If we were sure of having a perfectly disinterested and patriotic man, what a good thing it would be to appoint a dictator in time of war. I begin to think I had rather have one at any rate, than see things go on as they do now. Love to Father and the girls. I can't conceive what delays my letters so long. You can do what you like with the clothes sent home in my trunk. The letters I should like to have you save. Don't you think it a great piece of folly to give so much money to the new volunteers? Also to enlist them for so short a time? They will not be fit for the field before half their term has run out. We have received about thirty new recruits. Our sutler has just arrived from New York, and brought me a letter from father. In future, if you have anything to send me, it had better be taken to the sutler's agent, as he is continually forwarding stores. Let me know whether you are entirely well again.

Your loving son,
Robert G. Shaw

1. Secretary of War Edwin M. Stanton.

2. Shaw is exaggerating the situation. McDowell's army still barred the way and part of McClellan's huge force could be rapidly moved to protect the capital.

3. What started as a trickle turned into a flood tide of desertion by 1863. During the conflict, 200,000 Union and 104,000 Confederate soldiers deserted their units; of those, 80,000 and 21,000, respectively, got caught and sent back to their armies. By mid 1863, both Union and Confederate commanders tightened discipline and began to severely punish or execute deserters and slackers. Enlistments had decreased, enrollment periods were ending, conscription had failed to bring in full quotas, and the war dragged on, killing men, and devastating entire units. Commanders could no longer tolerate deserters; hundreds were executed as object lessons for the rest. Gerald F.

Linderman, *Embattled Courage: The Experience of Combat in the American Civil War* (New York: Free Press, 1987), pp. 169–78.

4. In July 1861 Congress paid a bounty of $100 to each man who enlisted for three years. State and local bounties were also paid to encourage enlistment. Estimated bounties paid from all sources totalled $750 million for Northern soldiers. Some unscrupulous entrepreneurs made money by enlisting with one regiment, collecting the bounty, only to desert at the first opportunity to reenlist with another unit for another bounty. Many repeated this scam several times. Boatner, *Dictionary*, p. 74.

5. Henry Wilson of Massachusetts.

6. Lincoln named Maj. Gen. Henry Wager Halleck as general in chief of all Northern armies on July 16. Halleck took command on July 23. Aboli-

tionists loathed Halleck for his order while commanding the Department of the Mississippi that no fugitive slaves would be allowed in Union-held territory. Long, *Civil War Day By Day*, pp. 241, 243.

7. Louis Blenker (1812–63), a German immigrant and soldier of fortune, commanded a 10,000-man division of German and Eastern European immigrants.

8. Adin Ballou Underwood (1828–88), a Boston lawyer, had been a captain with the Second from its inception in 1861. Promoted to major on July 11,

1862, Underwood transferred to the Thirty-third Massachusetts Infantry. *Record of Mass. Vols.*, p. 28.

9. Capt. H. B. Scott. Report of Brig Gen George H. Gordon, August 11, 1862, *OR* I:12, pt. 2, p. 808.

10. First Lt. Marcus M. Hawes (1837–?), of Boston, became Gordon's Quartermaster on July 21, 1862. First Lt. Charles Wheaton, Jr. (1835–?), of Boston, served as an adjutant with the Second before Gordon made him the commissary officer on July 21, 1862. *Record of Mass. Vols.*, p. 28.

11. The first sergeant is unidentified.

Washington, Va.   [RGS]
July 28, 1862
Dear Mother,

Since I wrote last, I have yours of 20th and 24th July, the former enclosing Mr. Chandler's remarks to the Senate, and the latter, a note from Uncle Jim.[1] I have also had a letter from the faithful Effie at Nahant, full of abuse of ————————. It was something in the style of Secession ladies on the subject of Yankees.

Before I proceed, I must put your mind at rest about "Flannel Bandages." I kept three, and I believe four of them, and shall use them at the first sign of the approach of my last year's enemy. I don't wear them all the time, because the doctor and my own experience have told me, that after wearing them for some time, one gets so accustomed to them, that they do very little good. I have not had one on since December, and have never been in better health. I suppose none of us will be so liable to dysentery this year as last, as we have been sleeping on the ground, and in the open air so long.

Our baggage has been cut down to a very small valise. All the men's tents have been turned in, and each man carries a shelter (*tente d'abri*), which is about as big as a common shawl. Two buttoned together make a tent for two men. For line officers there is one wall tent to a company. Staff officers are two in a tent. Each regiment has only six or eight waggons, and these are filled principally with rations.

I wish I had seen the letter about Fremont from Memphis.[2] I am more and more sorry that he gave up his command here. It gives his enemies a good hold on him, and they say that he showed very little patriotism. You can't conceive how bitterly all army officers speak of him. I got so angry about it the other day, that if I hadn't merely confined myself to saying that I didn't believe their stories, I think I should have had a row. I don't know why I feel so about Fremont, but it always makes me wrathy to hear him abused, though I have managed to keep it to myself pretty well. Of course people have a right to say what they please about a public man's public character.

General Pope has just issued an order forbidding any commander to place a guard over private property in this department.[3] The soldiers will speedily make away with all food within ten or fifteen miles of the camps.

You don't say anything about your health. Is it better? Harry had a note from Alex. yesterday, announcing the birth of Annie's boy.[4] We were very glad to know that everything was going on well. That generation of the family is increasing fast, isn't it?

My relations with the General continue to be very pleasant, but the only thing I shall very much regret, when I go back to the regiment, will be marching on horseback. An *aide* has so little responsibility, and so little to do, that I feel as if I were nothing but an "orderly."

Perhaps you have seen some accounts of a young lady at Front Royal, named Belle Boyd.[5] There was quite a long and ridiculous letter about her copied into the "Evening Post" the other day. I have seen her several times, but never had any conversation with her. Other men who have talked with her, tell me that she never asked for any information about our army, or gave them the slightest reason to suppose her a spy; and they were probably as capable of judging as the correspondent who wrote about her. She gave Fred. d'Hauteville a very pretty Secession flag, which she said she carried when she went out to meet Jackson's troops coming into Front Royal.[6]

At one house there, I got quite intimate. Copeland and I stopped there on our way to Washington in May, and coming through this time, I made them a visit. I got there about an hour after tea, and they insisted upon getting up a second meal for me. Of course, I said I hoped they wouldn't, which was a great lie, as I was very hungry. They saw through it, and fed me to my heart's content on honey, bread and butter, apple-sauce, and tea; one of the young ladies sitting near, meanwhile, brushing away the flies with a broom made of peacock's feathers. They were the nicest people I have met in Virginia, and had a very prettily furnished house and good library. In the parlour, among other pictures, was the engraving of Evangeline, which you have in your room.[7] The family consisted of an old lady, two daughters, and a niece. They were Secessionists, but having no near relations in the army, they were rather mild than otherwise, besides being very good and religious. On the parlour-table were cards of Federal and Confederate officers, all mixed together.[8] Their town has been alternately in the United States and in the Confederate States, every three or four months.

We have had a good deal of fun at some of the farmer's houses where the General has had his head-quarters. Whenever he gets hold of a Virginian, he pitches into him. First he makes them say whether they voted for Secession; then he gets them to give their reasons, and usually winds up by calling them fools and asses, and worse slaves to Jeff Davis than any black man in the country, &c., &c. At one house, some time ago, just as we were about to start, he called for the owner and told him he must sign a *parole*. The man said he had rather not. "Guard," bawled the General, "carry this man off." After a good deal of talk the man finally signed, but said it was pretty hard after having all his corn and provisions eaten up, and his niggers encouraged to run off, to be treated in that manner. I should have pitied him, if he hadn't been a villanous looking wretch, who, without any doubt, had often been out bush-whacking. We don't find any able-bodied men in this valley, but there are a good many who are strong enough to go out with a gun. Six were caught near here yesterday, almost in the act of firing on some of our men.

What you say about —— ——'s opinion of McClellan makes me wonder whether the newspaper accounts of his army's enthusiasm are pure fabrication or not.

I had a letter from —— —— a short time since; he was in the fight on James Island, and was boiling with rage at having to retire from before Charleston.[9] He says another assault would have carried their works, but that Benham, after having got himself foolishly into a scrape, didn't have courage enough to carry the thing through.[10] To use his expression, "We are dying of the regular army." They have five generals down there, all regular army men, who, he thinks, have blundered very much.

Things look badly to us. Every one is ready and anxious to fight, where it will do any good, but few men care about going under fire, and losing their lives for experiments. There is not the same confidence in the government that there was. I must confess that my faith in Fremont has been somewhat shaken since his resignation. I am afraid he will never recover himself entirely. Tell Effie when you write, that I am well, and have received her letters.

With love to Susie and George and Anna.

Your affectionate son,
Robert G. Shaw

P.S.—Mr. Chandler says McClellan had as many troops as he wanted; but every one knows he didn't have them *when* he wanted them. They say, his idea was, if he had had as many men as he expected, to send a large force to West Point, and get in the enemy's rear, at the same time that he fought them at Yorktown.

1. Zachariah Chandler (1813–79), a former mayor of Detroit, sat in the U.S. Senate (1857–74) and served on the Committee on the Conduct of the War. An abolitionist, Chandler singled out McClellan for his soft stand on slavery and his poor generalship in the Peninsular Campaign. *NYDT*, July 21 (1:6, 2:1, 8:1), 1862; *Congressional Globe*, July 17, 1862, pp. 3386–89; Faust, *Encyclopedia*, p. 129.

2. The Memphis letter praised Frémont for his bold abolition stance and his 1861 proclamation, which initiated his troubles with Lincoln and led to his removal: "Politically he laid the ax at the root of the tree. He used no soft, obscure language; he did not talk of '*confiscation*' or '*system of labor*', but announced in plain Saxon, which rang through the land like a trumpet, 'The Slaves of Rebels are hereby declared Free Men!'" *NYDT*, July 23 (1:5), 1862.

3. Pope turned up the flame of war through a series of orders aimed at guerillas, private property, and traitors to the Union. He authorized his armies to execute any partisan rangers they captured, to appropriate private property without paying for it, and to evacuate forcefully all civilians not loyal to the Union. The only order enforced concerned the taking of private property. Historian James M. McPherson has discussed the "ideological dimension" of this destruction—meaning that Union soldiers could see no sense in protecting the property of the same men who were trying to kill them on the battlefields of the war. In 1862, the war moved a step closer to the total war that Sherman and Sheridan would employ. McPherson, *Battle Cry*, pp. 501–2.

4. Alexander and Annie Agassiz.

5. Belle Boyd (1843–1900), a resident of Front Royal, Virginia, used her many charms to mingle with Union officers. Her reports to Stonewall Jackson helped his Shenandoah Valley Campaign. McPherson, *Battle Cry*, p. 456.

6. Frederic Sears Grand d'Hauteville (1838–?) graduated from Harvard in 1859. After serving on Banks's staff in 1861 and 1862, Gordon appointed him as an assistant adjutant general on June 30, 1862. He married Hamilton Fish's daughter Bessie. Brown, "Roll of Students," p. 18; Smith, *Beacon Hill's*, p. 504.

7. Evangeline Bellefontaine, the heroine of Henry Wadsworth Longfellow's *Evangeline: A Tale of Acadie.*

8. During the Civil War, soldiers and civilians carried photographs of themselves to leave as remembrances with hosts. Standard *cartes de visite* were two and one-half by four inch cards. Faust, *Encyclopedia*, pp. 117–18.

9. Federal troops had been skirmishing on James Island, S.C., near Charles-

ton, on June 3–15. In the Battle of
Secessionville on June 16, 6,600 Union
troops under Gen. H. W. Benham attacked a Confederate force of 2,500 and
was repulsed with 683 casualties to 204.
Two weeks later, Union forces evacuated
James Island. It would be another year
before the Union would make a serious
attempt to control Charleston Harbor.

Long, *Civil War Day By Day*, pp. 221,
223, 227, 233.

10. Henry Washington Benham
(1813–84) was a career officer who
graduated from West Point in 1837 as an
engineer. He participated in the capture
of Fort Pulaski, near Savannah, Georgia, before his failure at James Island.
Boatner, *Dictionary*, pp. 58–59.

Washington, Va.   [RGS]
August 3, 1862
Dear Father,

Your letter of the 28th and 29th July from New York reached me day before
yesterday. The former enclosing note from Susie.

About having negroes in the present white regiments, I think the men
would object to it very strongly at first, but they would get accustomed to it
in time. I infer this from the fact that soldiers in our regiments, who are acting
as officer's servants, make no objection to living and sleeping in the same tent
with black servants. Still, there would undoubtedly be great dissatisfaction, if
we should enlist blacks and put them into the volunteer regiments now.

Your question about getting my captaincy in the regiment, and retaining
my position as aide, I think I have already answered, viz.: that I must give up
one or the other. An officer on a general's staff has many advantages that he
can't have in a regiment, and the life is so much easier that it is a very great
change from one to the other. On the staff, there are a great many opportunities for learning, and for getting acquainted with prominent men in the army.
Lately we have had a great many reviews, evolutions, &c.; so that it has been
a particularly fortunate time for me to be on General Gordon's staff.

One melancholy fact I have learned, which is, that a great part of this army
is composed of very poor troops. In one Brigade, there is only one regiment
which has more than two hundred men for duty; yet they have never been
in action, and have been in the field only since Banks' retreat. Some of these
regiments have been reduced by sickness, but most by desertion. Deserters
from the New York Ninth, now at Warrenton, go home and then write to
their friends in the regiment; yet no effort is made to take them.[1]

The recent orders of the President concerning deserters are a step in the
right direction, but I have no faith in the probability of their being strictly enforced: no orders ever have been.[2] Did you see the Rebels' opinion of General

Pope? It is just about the impression he has made on his own army. I think that he is bold and rapid, but likely to lay himself open. His proclamations and orders haven't done him much credit yet.[3] The remarks of newspaper correspondents about him seem very laughable to us. I mean about the enthusiasm and confidence of his troops. The American public are following their usual course of praising and expecting wonders of a man, before he has shown himself worthy of it, and if he fails in anything he undertakes, they will come down on him like an avalanche. That has been McClellan's fate, you know. Pope criticizes and abuses McClellan with a will, showing in a man in his position no better taste than appeared in his proclamation and some of his orders. His personal appearance is certainly not calculated to inspire confidence or liking. He looks just what we have always understood he was,— a great *blow-hard*, with no lack of confidence in his own powers. I hope he will be successful in his campaign, but if he is, I think he will owe it much to good fortune. When Fremont was superseded in the Western Department, Pope is said to have tried to stop all expressions of regret on the part of the troops, and to have been furious when they cheered Fremont. He hates him as much as he does McClellan. There is probably a great deal of jealousy in his composition.

For a long while, I never allowed myself to make any disparaging remarks concerning my superior officers, and now I am usually sorry when I have written a letter like this, but I may as well let it go this time. There is no doubt that good will ultimately come of this war; that slavery will disappear, and the country be eventually united; but I begin to doubt whether we shall accomplish it by force of arms.

General Gordon has had several Brigade drills lately. He has a great faculty for handling troops, and if they would let him drill the Division, he could do us lots of good. We are to have a large force here. One hundred thousand men I understand; there are at present hardly more than thirty thousand effective. Give my love to Mother. I have been expecting to hear from her for some time all about Sue's engagement. Love to George and the girls.

Your affectionate son,
R.G.S.

1. "Hawkins' Zouaves," the Ninth New York Infantry, organized in New York City in May 1861. Dyer, *Compendium*, vol. 1, p. 188.

2. On July 31, 1862, Lincoln revoked all furloughs and leaves, except those issued by the War Department, and ordered all officers and men to be at their posts as of Aug. 11, or face court martial. The *New York Times* reported

"not less than twenty-five thousand men" absent from duty and hailed this move to round up "these loiterers, carpet-knights, and bar-room heroes." *NYT*, August 3 (4:5), 1862.

3. Upon taking command, Pope, thinking he would inspire confidence in his men, made an infamous speech: "Let us understand each other. I have come to you from the West, where we have always seen the backs of our enemies." Contrary to its purpose, Pope's speech infuriated his men and McClellan, who took it to mean they were less brave than Western troops. Pope would get his due on Aug. 29–30, when his defeat at Second Bull Run prompted Lincoln to replace him with McClellan. Foote, *Civil War*, vol. 1, pp. 528–30.

CHAPTER 8

"*Metallic coffins*"

The "storm" blew its fury across the land in a wave of blood still unsurpassed on North American soil. The rainbow that followed promised liberty to millions of slaves. On a furious Wednesday along Antietam Creek, Maryland, Lee's army met McClellan's. When the fighting ended, 6,000 men lay dead or dying and 17,000 more were injured. Five days after the slaughter, Lincoln announced that as of January 1 next, all slaves held in areas "in rebellion against the United States, shall be then, thenceforward, and forever free."

Captain Shaw lived through the battle of Antietam even while receiving his second wound. This time, unlike the bullet that had struck with full velocity into his watch at Front Royal, the minie ball already spent its violence before careening into his neck and bouncing away. He was one of the lucky ones. In forty days the Second Massachusetts Infantry fought two battles and marched in support of two others. From the Cedar Mountain wheatfield on August 9 to the Antietam cornfield on September 17, Shaw watched his friends, fellow officers, and men, fall around him—243 casualties, 80 men killed, in two engagements.

The young man who marched off to war hoping for a chance to fight perhaps got more than he wanted. Shaw wrote his father that after the day at Antietam, "At last, night came on, and, with the exception of an occasional shot from the outposts, all was quiet. The crickets chirped, and the frogs croaked, just as if nothing unusual had happened all day long, and presently the stars came out bright, and we lay down among the dead, and slept soundly until daylight. There were twenty dead bodies within a rod of me."

Near Culpepper, Va.   [RGS]
August 11, 1862
Dear Father,

I telegraphed you yesterday and again to-day. Harry is in the hands of the enemy, and not wounded.[1] I telegraphed to that effect to Uncle Howland to-day.[2] There is some doubt about its going through safe, so I sent to both of you the second time.

We had a hard fight day before yesterday. Banks' Corps only was engaged, and was outnumbered as usual. We are driven back, though only a short distance.[3] Gordon's Brigade suffered severely; the Second Massachusetts more than the rest.[4] Captains Cary, Williams, Abbott, and Goodwin, and Lieutenant Perkins were killed.[5] Major Savage wounded and taken; Lieutenants Robeson, Oakey, Browning, and Grafton wounded, and sent to Alexandria.[6] Captains Russell and Quincy, and Lieutenant Miller, prisoners.[7] Surgeon Leland also wounded.[8] Of the wounds, Browning's only is serious.[9] Of the three prisoners, Harry only is not hurt. I ascertained that to-day myself, having been over to the Rebel lines, and talked with some Rebel officers. One of them saw twenty-five Federal officers, and heard Harry's name mentioned among them. They were all sent to Richmond yesterday. I shall try to send him a message, but I think it very doubtful whether it can get through. When I first telegraphed you, I was not at all certain about Harry's safety, but don't feel any doubt of it to-day. The loss from the Second Massachusetts is one hundred and ninety. Of these, one hundred and thirty or forty are known to be killed and wounded. Give my best love to Mother and the rest. I can't conceive how I could have got through without a scratch.[10]

In haste,
Your loving son

1. Capt. Henry Sturgis Russell was captured on Aug. 9, 1862, at the Battle of Cedar Mountain, Virginia. Russell file, CMSR.
2. Gardner Howland Shaw.
3. Nathaniel Banks's Corps of Pope's

Army of Virginia struck Jackson's Corps at Cedar Mountain. Banks successfully drove Jackson back until A. P. Hill's Division counterattacked and pushed Banks from the field. Banks had 2,403 casualties among his 8,000 men; Jackson lost 1,418 of 16,800. Robert C. Krick, *Stonewall Jackson at Cedar Mountain* (Chapel Hill: University of North Carolina Press, 1990), pp. 372–76.

4. In thirty minutes of fighting, Gordon's Brigade, numbering 1,500 men, lost 466 killed, wounded, and missing. The Second Massachusetts had 16 of its 23 officers killed or wounded, 49 enlisted men killed, 99 wounded, and 14 captured or missing. These numbers do not match exactly with those given by Shaw in his Aug. 12 letter to his mother. Report of Brig. Gen. Gordon, Aug. 11, 1862, *OR*, I:12, pt. 2, pp. 807–8; Bowen, *Mass. in the War*, p. 120.

5. Richard Cary (1836–62), William B. Williams (1830?–62), Edwin Gardner Abbott (1840–62), Richard Chapman Goodwin (1833–62), and Stephen George Perkins (1835–62).

Richard Cary file, CMSR; Higginson, *Harvard Memorial Biographies*, vol. 1, pp. 273–74, 349; *Rec. of Mass. Vols.*, p. 28.

6. James Savage, Thomas Rodman Robeson, Dan Oakey, George F. Browning, and J. Ingersoll Grafton. *Rec. of Mass. Vols.*, pp. 28–29.

7. Harry Russell, Samuel Miller Quincy, and Adam Miller (1840–?). Boatner, *Dictionary*, p. 676; *Rec. of Mass. Vols.*, p. 29.

8. Francis Leland resigned on Oct. 24, 1862. *Rec. of Mass. Vols.*, p. 28.

9. George Browning resigned on Dec. 22, 1862, due to disability. Ibid., p. 29.

10. General Gordon's official report of the battle cited Shaw and two others for "coolness under this terrific fire." Report of Brig Gen [George] Gordon, Aug. 11, 1862, *OR*, I:12, pt. 2, p. 808.

Near Culpepper Court-House, Va. [RGS]
August 12, 1862
Dearest Mother,

I hope my telegrams and my note to Father reached you, and relieved your anxiety about myself. We have had a hard time. We marched from Little Washington on the 7th inst. On the 9th we left Culpepper, and after a march of four or five miles Banks' Corps was formed in line of battle, Gordon's Brigade on the extreme right. The fight didn't begin until four o'clock, though all day there was some artillery firing. The infantry went forward on our left and centre, first.

We were posted on an eminence, and had a good view of everything. I don't know how the troops on the left behaved; they were all new troops, and I know that, after having once given way, they were not rallied again. Crawford's Brigade (in our Division), stationed in the centre, fought like tigers, and were dreadfully used up.[1] They advanced through a wood, emerged from it, and crossed an immense field under a very heavy fire from forces far superior in numbers. After they were cut to pieces, our Brigade was ordered up. We went through the same wood, but more to the right, and came out into the same broad field. I was with the Second Massachusetts, having been ordered to show Colonel Andrews where to go. The first thing I noticed upon coming out of the wood, was the immense number of bodies lying about the field, and then I saw a long line of Rebel battalions drawn up opposite, and almost concealed by the smoke from their pieces. The Second Massachusetts, the Third Wisconsin, and Twenty-seventh Indiana were placed on the edge of the wood, behind a snake-fence. The men were ordered to lie down until the enemy came nearer; almost all the officers kept on their feet, though.[2]

Just at this time I saw the last of Harry. I was about opposite to his company, a few paces in the rear, and he called out, "Hullo, Bob!" and came back to where I was. We talked a few minutes together about what was going on, and then he went back to his place and stood, pulling his moustache and looking over the field, the bullets whistling thick around him. He was perfectly quiet, but looked pretty fierce. I can't tell you how enraged I feel when I think of his being in Richmond. I have thought several times, when near the Rebel lines, of letting myself be captured too, but it would be wrong and foolish, because we have very few officers left, and I might never see Harry either. I never knew till now, how much his society had been to me this last year, nor how much I loved him. After he left me, I was in different parts of the field with General Gordon, who finally sent me back to get some artillery through the woods. It was impossible to do it, because the brush was so thick, and besides, I hadn't been gone five minutes, before the enemy got us under a cross fire, and our Brigade had to retreat. They advanced so close to the Second before the latter gave way, that it was easy to distinguish all their features. I think our regiment lost most at this time; they also inflicted a heavy loss on the regiments opposed to them. So, from what I can gather, I was saved from the hottest fire by being ordered to look for the artillery. There were four hundred and seventy-four enlisted men taken into action in the Second. Of these, one hundred and twenty were killed and wounded, and thirty-seven missing. They were not under fire more than thirty minutes. Twenty-two officers went in, and eight came out; five were killed, five wounded, four captured, three of whom are thought to be wounded. Harry is said now to have received a slight wound. It can't be much, for a private, who stayed hidden in the woods all night, saw him walking about under a guard, and getting assistance for Major Savage. I don't doubt he stayed to take care of the latter. The Major was wounded and taken prisoner. We have heard that he was in a house somewhere inside the Rebel lines, and Lieutenant Abbott sent him some money.[3] I wrote a short note to his Father to-day. We are very anxious about him, for he may be very uncomfortable, as Harry and Quincy are carried off to Richmond.

We hear to-day that the enemy have retired to some distance. If true, we may soon hear more of our missing. Goodwin, Cary, Choate, and Stephen Perkins were all quite ill, but would not stay away from the fight. Choate was the only one of the four not killed.[4] Goodwin couldn't keep up with the regiment, but I saw him toiling up the hill, at some distance behind, with the assistance of his servant. He hardly reached the front when he was killed. All our officers behaved nobly. Those who ought to have stayed away, didn't. It was splendid to see those sick fellows walk straight up into the shower of bullets, as if it were so much rain; men, who until this year, had lived lives of perfect ease and luxury. Oh! it is hard to believe that we shall never see them again, after having been constantly together for more than a year. I don't remember a single quarrel of any importance among our officers during all that time.

Yesterday I went over the battle-field with the General. The first man I recognized was Cary. He was lying on his back with his head on a piece of wood. He looked calm and peaceful, as if he were merely sleeping; his face was beautiful, and I could have stood and looked at it a long while. Captain Williams we found next. Then Goodwin, Abbott, and Perkins. They had all probably been killed instantly, while Cary lived until 2 o'clock P.M. of the next day.[5] His First Sergeant was shot in the leg, and lay by his side all the time. He says he was very quiet; spoke little, and didn't seem to suffer. We found a dipper with water, which some Rebel soldier had brought. They took everything from him after he died, but returned a ring and a locket with his wife's miniature to the Sergeant. His was the only dead body I have ever seen that it was pleasant to look at, and it was beautiful. I saw it again in Culpepper late that night. All these five were superior men; every one in the regiment was their friend. It was a sad day for us, when they were brought in dead, and they cannot be replaced.

The bodies were taken to town, and Lieutenant Francis and I had them packed in charcoal to go to Washington, where they will be put in metallic coffins.[6] I took a lock of hair from each one, to send to their friends. It took almost all night to get them ready for transportation.

I wrote Annie a short note to-day, and told her that Harry was reported slightly wounded.[7] I was going to write to Uncle George, but you had better send him this, for there is a great deal of work to be done, and I have been writing so much, that I have little time left.[8] I shall keep a sharp lookout all the time to get news of Harry, and will send him money whenever I can; $14 went yesterday, and I think it will reach him safely. I shall return to the regiment very soon now. Officers are very scarce there. I have just received a note from Susie, enclosing one for Harry from Emily.[9] The latter I will keep, and if another flag of truce goes over, will send it. It will be a consolation to him to hear from them. It makes me choke to think of him, especially since that inhuman order of Davis' concerning Pope's officers.[10] I don't think it will make a great deal of difference in the treatment of them; but it will be an excuse for neglect. I can't help wishing I were with him.

Gordon's Brigade was the only one that was kept together, and remained in position all night and the next day. The others scattered,—were collected the day after, and went into camp.

Banks had about seven thousand men, and was greatly outnumbered. We had a good many more in reserve, but they were not brought up for some reason. Whose mismanagement it was, I don't know. Opinions differ. Troops have been coming in pretty fast ever since, and we have a strong position. I have just heard decidedly that Harry was *not* hurt, and I believe it myself,— please let Annie know. I am sorry to send so many different accounts, but it is impossible to get at the truth immediately. Love to all, dear Mother, and God bless you!

Your ever loving son,
Robert G. Shaw

1. Brig. Gen. Samuel Wylie Crawford (1829–92) joined the army in 1851 as a surgeon, but made the transition to line officer in 1861. His First Brigade lost half its men at Cedar Mountain. Faust, *Encyclopedia*, p. 191.

2. These three regiments made up Gordon's Brigade. They met Jackson's men at the edge of a freshly mown wheat field, three hundred yards wide. Report of Brig Gen [George] Gordon, Aug. 11, 1862, *OR*, I:12, pt. 2, p. 808; Dyer, *Compendium*, pp. 135, 238.

3. First Lt. Fletcher M. Abbott of Lowell, Massachusetts. *Rec. of Mass. Vols.*, p. 29.

4. First Lt. Rufus Choate was pro-

moted to captain on Aug. 17, 1862. He resigned on Oct. 31, 1862, due to disability. Ibid., pp. 28–29.

5. Twenty-six-year-old Roland S. Willeston had been a corporal in Cary's company from May 25, 1861, until his promotion to first sergeant on May 10, 1862. Roland S. Williston file, CMSR; Morning Reports, Bound Record Books, Second Massachusetts Infantry, Records of the Adjutant General, Record Group 94, NA.

6. First Lt. James Francis was promoted to captain on Aug. 10, 1862. *Rec. of Mass. Vols.*, p. 29. The Adams Express Company had government and private business in transporting the Union dead.

At the beginning of the war, Adams allowed wooden coffins, but soon required metallic coffins to better handle hot weather and delays caused by thousands of casualties. Alvin F. Harlow, *Old Waybills: The Romance of the Express Companies* (New York: Appleton-Century, 1934), pp. 299–300.

7. Harry's sister Annie Agassiz.

8. George R. Russell, Harry's father.

9. Harry's sister Emily Russell. Smith, *Beacon Hill's*, p. 491.

10. In a preview of things to come, Lincoln and Pope escalated the war by ordering that the Union army would forage on the property of Rebel sympathizers without compensating the owners. Further, Pope ordered that any civilian who would not take an oath of allegiance to the United States be treated as a war criminal and arrested. Jefferson Davis retaliated by ordering that since Pope preyed upon innocents, Pope's officers were "not entitled to be considered as soldiers," and thus, "not entitled to parole as prisoners of war." *NYT*, Aug. 10 (4:2, 8:1), 1862.

Culpepper C. H.   [HL]
August 13, 1862
Dear Annie,

Yesterday I wrote you in a great hurry and told you that there was reason to suppose Harry had received a slight wound. I think now it was a mistake but men are constantly bringing so many contradictory reports that it is almost impossible to get the exact truth immediately.

The enemy have retired from their former position, and have left a good many of our wounded in the neighbouring farmhouses. I went out with a few men to see what information could be got about Harry, Savage & Quincy. There were several of our men there but no one had seen any of the three. They must, of course, have been carried away to Richmond.

Richard Cary's, Stephen Perkins', Goodwin's, William's, & Abbott's bodies have gone to Washington & from there will be sent to Boston. All were much disfigured excepting Cary—the heat was very great. Cary was lying near the position occupied by our regiment. He was on his back, his face turned to the right and his hands crossed over his chest. He looked as if he had just fallen asleep in a comfortable position. The expression of his face was as sweet and happy as an angel's and my first feeling was, that I wanted to stoop down & kiss him. There was a mug of water beside him, which one of the Rebel soldiers had left there. You have heard probably how his First Sergeant lay wounded beside him all the time, and didn't know he was dead until he spoke to him & received no answer.

This was the afternoon of the day following the battle. I think he must have died from internal bleeding. We couldn't get over there until the second day as the ground was in possession of the Rebels. They then sent a flag of truce to let us in—having removed most of their killed & wounded & withdrawn to a position somewhat farther off. The three other captains lay very near together, just where they stood before the regiment retreated—but Stephen Perkins was some distance to the rear, lying on his back with his face to the front as if he had turned round in the retreat.

I saw Harry once during the action and stood some time talking with him. After that I had to go to another part of the field with the General, and knew nothing of what had happened until it was all over. I think of him all the time, and miss him at every turn. It is as lonely for me as if there were no one here—and when I think how much he is probably in want of, and how much hardship & discomfort he may have to go through I feel very badly. Some months ago we agreed that neither of us would leave the regiment without the other, and little thought we should be separated in this way. I shall send home his things, for you will be able to communicate with him from there more easily than I shall. It is very difficult to get anything through these lines, as the regular route of communication is elsewhere. If you do have a chance to send him a bundle you had better put in it: 2 or 3 light flannel shirts & prs. of drawers, his toilet articles, his leather case containing knife, fork, cup &c. &c. inkstand, pens & paper & books. I wouldn't make a large bundle as it will not be likely to go through so safely. He has money with him, and our treasury notes are taken there, I believe, very readily. I sent him some gold too the other day which I hope he will get.

You probably have heard that Cary, Goodwin & Choate were all quite ill, and should have been off duty. They wouldn't stay away when there was any fighting.

I have not written to Uncle George because I should have had to send the letter to you first not knowing the address—so it is well to send them what news I have of Harry, through you. Please tell them that I have thought of them a great deal since that day.

Will you tell Richard Cary's wife the little I have written you about him. Shelton has probably sent them the particulars of his death, but I don't know.[1] Sergeant Willeston, who was near him, says he lay very quiet, speaking little, and apparently not suffering.[2] How sad it is, to think of his wife & little child. And there were hundreds of dead men about him, most of whom probably had wives & children. A battle-field, after all is over, brings the horrors of war forcibly to your mind.

The fact that many men get so accustomed to the thing, that they can step about among heaps of dead bodies, many of them their friends and acquaintances, without any particular emotion, is the worst of all. It is only at odd times that we realize what a fearful thing it is to see 100 or 200 men, whom we have lived in the midst of, for more than a year, killed in a few moments.

I long for the day when we shall attack the Rebels with an overwhelming force and annihilate them. May I live long enough to see them running before us hacked to little pieces.

Why doesn't every one come out to the army? If some want easy berths there are such to be had. A staff officer leads a luxurious life as a usual thing. Uncle Howland & Uncle Quin ought to go on some one's staff—and they would be of much more service than fifty per cent of the staff officers here.[3] And they could do more than in a regiment too, I think. I am going back to the regiment. Ask Uncle Quin if he doesn't want to come here.

I see some papers report Major Savage & Capt. Russell killed. It is entirely untrue & has no foundation at all. How terrible the news has been for you all in Boston this week. For 3 days after all was over we had hardly time to think of it, being up & waiting for another fight every instant. Harry will get word to us in some way where he is and then something can be sent him. Quincy is supposed to be with him. I can hear nothing about him, or I should have written to his Father. With love to Alex dear Annie

Yr afftc cousin

1. First Lt. Eugene E. Shelton of Boston. *Rec. of Mass. Vols.*, p. 29.

2. First Sgt. Roland S. Willeston died of his wounds on Aug. 18, 1862. Williston file, CMSR.

3. Quincy Adams Shaw (1825–1908) graduated from Harvard in 1845 and made about $30 million as president of the Calumet and Hecla Copper Mines. Alexander Agassiz also made a fortune with that company. On Dec. 30, 1860, Quincy married Alexander's sister, Pauline Agassiz (1841–1917). Smith, *Beacon Hill's*, pp. 30, 297; *DAB*, vol. 17, pp. 46–47.

Rappahannock River   [RGS]
August 19, 1862
Dearest Mother,

You are probably wondering at my long silence, but as Uncle Quin went home yesterday, and I have been quite busy, I thought I wouldn't write. Being back in the regiment, makes me think of our lost friends all the time, as they were all here when I left.

I received your letter yesterday, and all Father's have come to hand. Yesterday I sent Harry a short note and $25.00, and told him what you said; it went by a Rebel surgeon, and I think, from his looks, that if he possibly can, he will deliver it.

You see from my date, that we are no longer at Culpepper Court-House. The whole army has fallen back to the Rappahannock,—what for, I don't know,—whether from necessity, or whether it is "*a bit of a sthratagim*," as Shields says. I think of Harry all the time, as you do. Poor fellow; how lonely he must be in that filthy place![1] Thank God, he has a strong constitution, and courage to bear anything that man can. If the treatment of our prisoners depended on the officers and soldiers of the Rebel army, I think they would fare well, for those I have met seem to have no bitter feeling towards us. We can't help getting a feeling of respect for each other, after such a fight as the last.

The papers have made a great mistake about Jackson's flag of truce. It was sent in order that *we* might get our wounded and bury our dead; not to ask permission to do the same for his own. They had undisputed possession of the battle-field, and, unless done for some ulterior purpose, it was a very courteous act. They drew off their army that day, and may have sent the flag as a blind; probably did. Poor Copeland has had a hard time. I believe he is a great loss to us. I am afraid it is General ———'s doings. I shall write Copeland as soon as I can.[2]

Uncle Quin stayed with us two days, and lived in my tent; it was a great pleasure to have him here, for I was then in the most dismal state of mind. Please tell Minturn I received his note.[3] General Gordon asked me to tell Susie she ought to send him out here. Tell Uncle Jim not to think of coming out as a private, if he is drafted; it is terrible work, and he can get a commission.

Much as I long for the war to end, I can never think of our poor dead fellows, and of Harry, without longing for another battle. It gives us all a desire to fight them. There is no doubt that we fight better than they, and, with an even force, would come out best. Give my love to Father and all.

Always your loving Son

1. Harry Russell was confined in Libby Prison, the principal Confederate prison for Union officers, on the James River in Richmond. A paroled inmate described it as "a three story brick building, formerly the tobacco warehouse of Messrs. Libby & Sons, their quarters being on the third floor. . . . Upon entering the prison an officer takes the name of each prisoner, and his money, giving a receipt in exchange. . . . [Rations consist of] a small piece of bread and less than half a pound of salt beef, with an occassional taste of beans or rice. . . . The blankets were dreadfully filthy." *New Bedford Daily Mercury*, May 11 (2:3), 1862.

2. R. Morris Copeland had never

given up on his idea to raise a regiment of black soldiers. After Secretary of War Stanton met with Copeland and Shaw and refused to allow this, Copeland would not let the matter drop. He wrote an open letter to Stanton, published in Boston papers as an "Appeal to Massachusetts." Stanton, insulted and infuriated, revoked Copeland's commission and removed him from the army for a breach of military etiquette. Massachusetts governor John A. Andrew protested Stanton's action and demanded a Court of Inquiry be held. That never happened.

Schouler, *History of Mass. in the War*, vol. 1, pp. 405–6; John A. Andrew to Charles Sumner, Feb. 9, 1863, cited in Ira Berlin, ed., *The Black Military Experience* (Cambridge: Cambridge University Press, 1982), p. 337.

3. Robert Bowne Minturn, Jr. (1836–89) lived at 60 Fifth Avenue, New York City, and owned the shipping firm of Grinnell, Minturn & Company at 78 South Street. Shaw folder, SIHS; Leng and Davis, *Staten Island*, vol. 2, p. 929; *Trow's NYC Directory for 1863*, p. 611.

Near Manassas Junction

August 29 1862

Dear Father,

[HL]

My last letter was dated Aug 19 and I am afraid you have not received it even yet. General Halleck's order stopping all mails from this army was issued about that time.[1] When this will go it is impossible to conjecture. For the past ten days we have been hurrying alternately up & down the Rappahannock, remaining only on 2 or 3 occasions for a whole night in one place.

We have been drenched with rain & scorched by the Sun—have slept much of the time on the ground without blankets & have lived principally on green apples & corn. Sometimes really almost starving. We have not seen our wagons since we left Culpepper C.H. & for that reason have been short of rations. All this time there had been artillery firing going on about us & now & then some pretty heavy musketry, but we have not been in it once. We have been in constant expectation of a fight, having been roused at all hours of the day & night.

I have received all your letters since the Cedar Mt. battle [and] one from Mother of the 16th & from Effie of 17th. These are the latest.

Sept. 2 *Bull Run*

Since the above was written we have been wandering about as before and have now got on to the battle field of July 21/61. They say the rest of the army is about Centreville. We have not seen any of them for a week. They have been doing a good deal of fighting, for the enemy, as you perhaps know came down to Manassas Junction through Thoroughfare Gap.[2] I don't know which side has got the worst of it, but the Rebels have destroyed a great deal of Government property on the Rail Road. Yesterday we (Banks' Corps) were said to have been out off from the main army. We burnt a large train of cars full of Hospital & other stores & a good many wagons & made a forced march by a back road arriving here in the afternoon well tired out. Whether it was a false alarm or not I don't know. It is a fortnight today since we left Culpepper C. H. & I hope we shall get to some resting place before long. This is the hardest job we have ever had—and we have got through it with very little sickness. I myself have been perfectly well.

I heard from an officer of the 12th Mass (Dehon) that Harry had been heard from at home and I am very anxious to know what he wrote.[3] I hope it will turn out that they are not treated any worse than the other prisoners.[4] I have had two letters from Copeland and if you see or write to him please tell him why he has had nothing from me. I have thought of him a great deal. The whole proceeding seems to be the working of private malice. How can they refuse him a court of Inquiry? He says you have been very kind to him & I am very glad you happened to meet him & make his acquaintance when you did.

We have heard nothing of Savage or Quincy yet.[5] Mr. Quint, our Chaplain, went to Alexandria yesterday with Scott, who is ill, & promised to write you a note if it were possible to get one through.[6]

There will be a chance to send this today as far as Washington, but I am afraid it will stop there. This campaign began about the 1st of March. Now it is Septr and we are just where we started from. Just think of the Rebel Army being at Manassas again. We shall never do much until we get a very different army from what we have now. Until the Government finds that it is worth their while to get competent officers & attend themselves to the organization of the army & not allow it to be made a private speculation for Governors of States. There is a total want of discipline & system throughout. In every battle a part of the men skulk & after a day's march the roads are lined with stragglers. Williams Division is the best I have seen—not excepting any in the army of the Potomac.[7] I shouldn't say men skulked out of battle if I hadn't seen it myself. I had a fine chance to observe everything at Cedar Mt. There are cowards every where & there is probably very little difference between regiments in this respect. Their behavior depends almost entirely on the discipline. If the time could be properly employed, I should think we couldn't do better than to lay over until next Spring & move a good army. But this winter would be wasted probably, as last winter was.

The Confederates know a thing or two more than we do.

Give my love to Mother. I hope to hear from you soon. Be sure to tell me if you hear anything from Harry. We haven't fired a shot in this regiment since Cedar Mt. though the batteries of the Brigade have done a good deal & the enemy's shell have tumbled about us pretty freely sometimes.

Always your loving son
Robert G. Shaw

1. Sometimes the army temporarily stopped the mails in specific areas to limit information about movements and tactics.

2. The Battle of Second Bull Run (Second Manassas) on Aug. 29–30, 1862, pitted Pope's 75,000 men against Lee's 48,500. Total campaign casualties: Union, 16,054; Confederate, 9,197. Banks's Corps, still reeling from the carnage at Cedar Mountain, did not take an active part. Long, *Civil War Day By Day*, p. 258; Bowen, *Mass. in the War*, p. 121.

3. First Lt. Arthur Dehon (1841–62), of Boston, was a classmate of Shaw's at Harvard. Brown, "Roll of Students," p. 23; Higginson, *Harvard Memorial Biographies*, vol. 2, pp. 219–25.

4. In his first letter home, Harry wrote, "I am unhurt and well but a prisoner. I was taken while tying a hand-

kerchief around Jim Savage's leg." Two weeks later he wrote, "I am well and comfortably situated in the 'Tobacco Warehouse.' . . . we have plenty of air & room with enough to eat. . . . I am all right. Your brother, H. S. Russell." H. S. Russell to Alex [Agassiz], Aug. 11, 1862, and H. S. Russell to Annie [Russell Agassiz], Aug. 25, 1862, in Lyman Family Papers, 1785–1956, MHS.

5. Wounded and captured at Cedar Mountain, James Savage was in the Confederate Hospital at Charlottesville, Virginia. Sam Quincy roomed at Libby Prison, not far from Russell. James Savage, Jr. file, CMSR; Bowen, *Mass. in the War*, p. 972.

6. Alonzo H. Quint and H. B. Scott.

7. A. S. Williams commanded the 1st Division in Banks's Corps.

Maryland Heights   [RGS]
Sept. 21, 1862
Dear Father,

You will see, from the date of this, that we have returned after thirteen months to our old last year's camp. Yesterday I took dinner at the house where you found me, when you came down here a year and a month ago. I wrote you last, a day or two after we left Rockville, and when we came through Frederick, I asked Miss Goldsborough to write Mother a note, which she probably did.[1] I hope you also received Mr. Quint's telegram after the battle, giving the loss in this regiment.[2]

We left Frederick on the 14th inst., marched that day and the next to Boonsboro', passing through a gap in the mountain where Burnside had had a fight the day before. On the 16th, our Corps, then commanded by General Mansfield, took up a position in rear of Sumner's, and lay there all day.[3] The Massachusetts Cavalry was very near us. I went over and spent the evening with them, and had a long talk with Will. Forbes about home, and friends there.[4] I had just received two letters from Effie and Nellie, at Naushon, which I read to him, as he had heard nothing from there for a good while. We lay on his blanket before the fire, until nearly 10 o'clock, and then I left him, little realizing what a day the next was to be; though a battle was expected, and I thought, as I rode off, that perhaps we shouldn't see each other again. Fortunately, we have both got through safely so far. At about 11 P.M., Mansfield's Corps was moved two or three miles to the right. At one in the morning of the 17th, we rested in a wheat-field. Our pickets were firing all night, and at daylight we were waked up by the artillery; we were moved forward immediately, and went into action in about fifteen minutes. The Second Massachusetts was on the right of Gordon's Brigade, and the Third Wisconsin next; the latter was in a very exposed condition, and lost as many as two hundred killed and wounded in a short time. We were posted in a little orchard, and Colonel Andrews got a cross fire on that part of the enemy's line, which, as we soon discovered, did a great deal of execution, and saved the Third Wisconsin from being completely used up. It was the prettiest thing we have ever done, and our loss was small at that time; in half an hour, the Brigade advanced through a cornfield in front, which, until then, had been occupied by the enemy; it was full of their dead and wounded, and one of our sergeants took a regimental colour there, belonging to the Eleventh Mississippi.[5] Beyond the cornfield was a large open field, and such a mass of dead and wounded men, mostly Rebels, as were lying there, I never saw before; it was a terrible sight, and our men had to be very careful to avoid treading on them; many were mangled and torn to pieces by artillery, but most of them had been wounded by musketry fire. We halted right among them, and the men did everything they could for their comfort, giving them water from their canteens, and trying to place them in easy positions. There are so many young boys and old men among the Rebels, that it seems hardly possible that they can have come of their own accord to fight us, and it makes you pity them all the more, as they lie moaning on the field. We heard about this time that General Mansfield was mortally wounded. He had been with us only three days, but every one liked him; he took more personal interest in the comfort and welfare of the men than any commander the Corps has had. He has died since, to the great regret of all.[6]

The wounded Rebels were always as surprised and grateful as men could be at receiving attention from us, and many said that all they wanted was to get into our hospitals, and wished they had never fired a shot at us. One boy, seventeen or eighteen, told Morse he had only left North Carolina three weeks ago, and how his father and mother grieved at his going.

While we were halted in this field, Sumner's whole Corps swept across, close by us, and advanced into a wood on our right. It was a grand sight, and they looked as if they couldn't be repulsed; but they were received there with a most terrible musketry-fire, and finally had to fall back. In that wood, our dead and wounded outnumbered theirs, as much as they did us in the places mentioned above. Hooker had already been repulsed from the same wood, after driving the Rebels across the field in which our Brigade was halted.[7] All the time the artillery on both sides had been keeping up a steady fire, and I think it was in this arm that we had the advantage. Gordon's Brigade made another advance shortly after Sumner's but had to retire like the rest at this point. It was at this time that Lieutenant-Colonel Dwight and three other officers were hit.[8] Dwight was left on the field, and Dr. Stone very pluckily went back with a few men and got him; Stone's surgeon sash might have been some protection to him, but he didn't have it on. I lost one killed and five wounded from my company. The man who was killed belonged to Harry's company, but was with me. The enemy was not dislodged from that wood at all, but in other parts of the field we decidedly got the advantage of them, after a great deal of doubtful fighting all day. I was struck once by a spent ball in the neck, which bruised, but didn't break the skin.[9]

I suppose you know that poor Dwight is dead; he was very anxious to live until his Father and Mother could get here. He is a great loss to us, as well as to them; it will be a terrible blow to his Mother, as he was her favorite son, I have heard; he has three brothers in the army. Mills, Crowninshield, and Francis were wounded, but not dangerously.[10]

At last, night came on, and, with the exception of an occasional shot from the outposts, all was quiet. The crickets chirped, and the frogs croaked, just as if nothing unusual had happened all day long, and presently the stars came out bright, and we lay down among the dead, and slept soundly until daylight. There were twenty dead bodies within a rod of me. The next day, much to our surprise, all was quiet, and the burying and hospital parties worked hard, caring for the dead and wounded.[11]

The Second Massachusetts came to close quarters, i.e. within musket range, twice during the day, but we had several men wounded by shell, which were flying about loosely all day. It was the greatest fight of the war, and I wish

I could give you a satisfactory account of everything I saw, but there are so many things to tell, that it is impossible to do so without giving more time to it than I have, or being a better writer.[12] The enemy have started across the river, and McClellan will follow—I suppose. This Corps, under General Williams, was sent here, to Sandy Hook, yesterday. We have a fine view of the country from here. The regiment is on the summit of Maryland Heights, and we can see the Rebel camps. There was a sharp fight yesterday, but nothing to-day. Some citizens who have come down from Sharpsburg say McClellan has crossed there; the enthusiasm of the troops for him is great, and that they will fight under him better than under any one else, is proved by the difference between this battle and those about Manassas. In some places our artillery did great execution. Tompkin's Rhode Island Battery fired into a Rebel column with canister at sixty paces; they lay there the next morning as if the two front lines had dropped dead.[13] Some of our regiments suffered as badly; we counted seventy-two dead of the First Minnesota in a space of fifty to one hundred yards.[14] The proportion of wounded to killed is usually four to one, so you can imagine the loss of the First Minnesota. Major Sedgwick, formerly of our regiment, was wounded near us. I hope he will recover.[15]

I never felt, before, the excitement which makes a man want to rush into the fight, but I did that day. Every battle makes me wish more and more that the war was over. It seems almost as if nothing could justify a battle like that of the 17th, and the horrors inseparable from it.

I received your letter on the 18th, and one from Mother and Effie. I have just seen some letters from home to men who were killed the other day, begging them to write, and saying that "only one word after a battle is all they want." What a week for thousands of families throughout the country!

The result of the battle was, that we remained in possession of the field, and the enemy drew off undisturbed. Whether that is all we wanted, I don't know; but I should think not. The new troops did well in some instances, and badly in others.

Mother's letter, enclosing copies of two notes from Harry, is received. I was rejoiced to hear he was moderately comfortable. I wrote, and sent him more money through some friends in Frederick. We have good news from Savage. His brother-in-law, Professor Rogers, had a note from Mr. Randolph, saying he was as comfortable as they could make him. Mr. Rogers lived in Charlottesville a long time.[16]

Sept. 22d. We came down the mountain last night, and are pitching tents at last, after nearly six weeks' bivouacking. I have lots of work to do on company papers, &c.; so good bye for the present. Give my love to Mother, and ask her to write to me. Love to George and the girls. I am glad you are all so well. Good bye.

Your loving son,
Robert G. Shaw

1. Miss Goldsborough is unidentified.

2. In the Battle of Antietam (Sharpsburg), the Second Massachusetts lost fifteen killed and fifty wounded of the three hundred men it took into action. Bowen, *Mass. in the War*, p. 122.

3. On Sept. 12, 1862, Joseph King Fenno Mansfield (1803–62) replaced Banks, who became commander of the defenses around Washington. Edwin Vose Sumner (1797–1863), a career soldier from Boston who had been commissioned a second lieutenant in 1819, and was a brigadier general before Fort Sumter, had the distinction of being the oldest active corps commander in the Civil War. Faust, *Encyclopedia*, p. 473.

4. Shaw's cousin William H. Forbes (1840–97) served with the First Massachusetts Cavalry.

5. The Eleventh Mississippi Infantry made up part of Evander Law's Second Brigade, John Bell Hood's Division, Stonewall Jackson's Corps, Army of Northern Virginia. Law's brigade fought in the eastern half of the cornfield and shot an enfilading fire into Mansfield's brigade near the East Woods. Stephen Sears, *Landscape Turned Red: The Battle of Antietam* (New Haven: Ticknor & Fields, 1983), pp. 197–200.

6. Wounded on the 17th by Confederate fire from the cornfield, Mansfield died the next day. Faust, *Encyclopedia*, p. 473.

7. Joseph Hooker (1814–79) from Hadley, Massachusetts, graduated from West Point in 1837 and fought in the Seminole and Mexican wars before resigning in 1853. On May 17, 1861, he rejoined as a brigadier general and led the First Corps at Antietam. Hooker initially drove Jackson back, but Confederate reinforcements destroyed Hooker's Corps. McPherson, *Battle Cry*, p. 541; Faust, *Encyclopedia*, p. 370.

8. Wilder Dwight.

9. Charles Morse confirmed that Shaw had been hit. Morse added that after the battle, "our old crowd ate a nice dinner at Mrs. Buckles; it was very pleasant." Morse, *Letters*, pp. 89–90.

10. Writing to his wife on Sept. 23, Col. George Andrews called Dwight "faithful, brave, unselfish, and devoted" and fretted that the Second "is not the same regiment." George L. Andrews Papers, United States Military History Institute. Charles J. Mills joined the Second as a second lieutenant on Aug. 14, 1862, as part of the replacements for losses at Cedar Mountain. On Aug. 17, he was promoted to first lieutenant. Francis W. Crowninshield and James Francis. Order Book, Bound Record Books, Second Mass. Inf., Records of the Adjutant General's Office, Record Group 94, NA; *Rec. of Mass. Vols.*, p. 29.

11. Morse also described night on the battlefield: "We lay down that night about ten o'clock, glad enough to get a little rest. The dead and dying were all around us and in our midst. . . . I found that Bob Shaw and I had slept within

fifty feet of a pile of fourteen dead rebels, and in every direction about us they were lying thick." Morse, *Letters*, p. 89.

12. Sept. 17, 1862, has the dubious honor of being the bloodiest day of the Civil War. McClellan had stopped Lee's invasion of the North, but his failure to follow Lee's retreat probably prolonged the war and led Lincoln to remove McClellan for the last time. Lee lost 10,318 casualties out of 40,000 engaged; McClellan lost 12,401 of 75,000. Sears, *Landscape Turned Red*, pp. 294–96.

13. The First Regiment Light Artillery, Battery "A" organized in Providence on June 6, 1861. It saw heavy action with Banks's Corps at South Mountain and Antietam. Dyer, *Compendium*, vol. 1, p. 229, vol. 3, p. 1631.

14. The First Minnesota Infantry organized at Fort Snelling on Apr. 29, 1861. At Antietam, they were part of the First Brigade, Second Division, II Corps of the Army of the Potomac. Dyer, *Compendium*, vol. 1, p. 164.

15. William Dwight Sedgwick joined the Second as a first lieutenant on May 25, 1861. Four months later, Sedgwick was a major and assistant adjutant general of U.S. Volunteers. He died of his wounds. Higginson, *Harvard Memorial Biographies*, vol. 1, p. 167; Brown, "Roll of Students," p. 8.

16. Professor William B. Rogers taught at the University of Virginia before accepting a position at Harvard. Massachusetts Infantry, 2nd Regiment, Letters from the Army: A Scrapbook, BPL.

Maryland Heights [RGS]
Sept. 25, 1862
Dear Mother,

You have probably received my letter of 21st and 22d to Father. I heard that Mr. Quint's telegram, sent the day of the battle, did not get through, but hope it is a mistake, for it would have saved you a great deal of anxiety.

We are regularly encamped up here now, and hope to stay some time, for the army certainly needs rest; and Heaven preserve us from a winter campaign! If any newspaper talks of "On to Richmond" after the middle of November, let the editors come down and try it themselves; from what we experienced the first six weeks of this campaign, I am certain only about half the army would live through it; the wet and cold together are too much for men who can seldom change their shoes or clothing, and most of whom are without India-rubber blankets.[1] A wet overcoat, and woollen blanket in the same condition, are very small protection. We have four to six waggons per regiment now, so that no extra clothing can be carried. Our loss in the late battle is estimated at fourteen thousand; it seems a high figure to me.[2]

You have probably read Smalley's letter to the Tribune; he is by far the best correspondent out here; he is on Schurz's staff.[3] The wood he speaks of as being held all day by the enemy is the same one I mentioned as being on "our right," meaning the right of Gordon's Brigade.[4] It was the centre of the line. He also speaks of Sumner's and Smith's attack; you can't imagine a finer sight than those two bodies of troops; General Smith's was completely successful, and as the Rebels ran *pele mele* for the woods, the shells from our batteries fell fast among them.[5] The beauty of the battle was, that, wherever we had to give way, reinforcements would come pouring in, and regain the lost ground. Of course, there are mistakes made in every battle; that day we were the victims of one; for Gordon's Brigade was sent forward to support Sumner in a wood (*the* wood) which he had already been driven out of. Instead of finding friends there, we were met by a volley of musketry; we didn't return it for some time, thinking there was some mistake, and when we did fire, we did very little execution, and had to retire. Colonel Andrews saved us there, for if we had gone as far as we were ordered, we should probably have been overwhelmed. The rest of the Brigade followed him, and halted before getting into the wood. It is sometimes very hard to distinguish between friends and foes, when the fire (especially of artillery) is rapid, owing to smoke.

I saw part of one of my letters in the "Evening Post," after the Cedar Mountain battle.[6] It surprised me a good deal, as I thought you knew that was a thing I shouldn't like at all. Perhaps some one else did it, though, so I won't scold you before I know.

So the "Proclamation of Emancipation" has come at last, or rather, its forerunner.[7] I suppose you are all very much excited about it. For my part, I can't see what *practical* good it can do now. Wherever our army has been, there remain no slaves, and the Proclamation will not free them where we don't go. Jeff Davis will soon issue a proclamation threatening to hang every prisoner they take, and will make this a war of extermination. I would give anything to have had Harry free before Lincoln issued that; I am so afraid it will go hard with him. The condition of the slaves will not be ameliorated certainly, if they are suspected of plotting insurrection, or trying to run away; I don't mean to say that it is not the right thing to do, but that, as a war measure, the evil will overbalance the good for the *present*. Of course, after we have subdued them, it will be a great thing.

Won't you ask Mr. Gay or George, if either of them has the time, to write me their reasons for desiring emancipation as a war measure?[8]

I have just got a letter from Effie of 14th inst. She walks into McClellan for not following up the Rebels; but I don't sympathize with her a bit. If he is not a very great general, he is the best we have, I fully believe, and the same men who didn't behave well at Manassas, fought without faltering, the other day, under him. The men place the most implicit faith in him, and he never appears without being received with cheers.

Those who talk of rapid pursuit, don't know that there were, and are, about five thousand stragglers between here and Alexandria; a march made by easy stages. In my opinion, the individuals to be walked into are our rulers, who, after fifteen months' experience, continue a military system by which it is impossible to form a well-disciplined army, and on account of which thousands and thousands of lives have been thrown away. They not only continue the old system, but they neglect to fill up old regiments who have been through a long campaign, and have some *esprit de corps* and desire to distinguish themselves, and send out new ones which are perfectly unmanageable and useless. You can't find an old regiment with more than five hundred in it, and very few have more than three hundred and fifty; it is folly to say the new are as good as the old; I, myself, saw a regiment of two hundred and fifty stand under a sharp fire until ordered to retreat, when a new one of nine hundred men had broken ranks by its side, and left it alone. Marching is as important as fighting, but, if the sun is a little hot or we don't halt before dark, our new brethren in arms take matters into their own hands, halt at a convenient place, and go to housekeeping. I don't say they are not just as brave men, and I know they are physically far superior to the first levies, but there is no discipline, and without it a soldier is not a soldier. There is little enough of it in the old regiments, but they are inured to hardship, and accustomed to the sound of battle. Then they have learnt, in a great measure, that safety and honour depend on obedience to orders, and many come to it from their natural good sense. Recruits mixed in with old men do well; that's our experience.

This position on Maryland Heights seems almost impregnable from any side. Miles' surrender is incomprehensible; you know he left this, and crossed over to Harper's Ferry, leaving the bridge standing.[9] Harper's Ferry can be battered to pieces from four sides at once.

Love to Father and all. I wish he could come down here. I want to see some one from home very much. Uncle Quin's visit was a real comfort and consolation after the last battle. We are living very comfortably just at present; all are gradually recovering their natural expression of face, which has been lost for the last month in a dragged-out, wearied look. Rest and good food are great restoratives. We have been, and are, up to our ears in muster-rolls, recruits, and dead men's papers; having been so long without doing anything of the kind, all is behindhand. I am gradually working through, so I take time to write to you.

I wish we could both *feel* whenever we are thinking of each other; you don't know how often I have thought of you during those terrible days; almost as much as you have of me, I believe. The night of the battle, Charley Morse and I lay together, and talked about our homes, and those of the thousands of dead about us; and it seemed to me as if I could see the house and all of you there.[10] If this had been the last battle, what a blessing it would be.

Has Uncle Jim much to do now? Ask him to come down and call on me. All through Maryland the people received us with enthusiasm.

Sept. 26. We are all much afflicted at the news about Savage. We have thought that he was getting along well, and would recover.[11] I wrote to Professor Rogers the other day, to ask what had been heard of him.

Breck Parkman, of Savannah, was killed at Sharpsburg; on the other side, of course.[12]

Give my best love to all. I hope to hear from you soon.

Your loving son,
Robert G. Shaw

1. "On to Richmond" signified an impatience by the Northern public to end the war and led many Northern generals to make unwise attacks upon defensive positions. Half of all Union soldiers who were killed in the war died on the fields between Washington and Richmond. William Barney, *Battleground for the Union: The Era of the Civil War and Reconstruction, 1848–1877* (Englewood Cliffs, N.J.: Prentice-Hall, 1990), pp. 155–56.

2. Actual losses totaled 12,469.

3. George Washburn Smalley (1833–1916) graduated from Yale, then finished law school at Harvard in 1855 before becoming a lawyer in Boston. He became associated with William Lloyd Garrison and married Wendell Phillip's adopted daughter Phoebe Garnaut. Sydney Gay hired him as a war correspondent for the *New York Tribune* and sent him to Port Royal, S.C., then to the Shenandoah Valley; then, as Lee invaded Maryland, he reassigned him to follow McClellan.

His account of Antietam was the first complete account of the battle. *NYDT*, Sept. 20 (5:1), 1862; Faust, *Encyclopedia*, pp. 693–94. Carl Shurz (1829–1906) immigrated to the United States from Prussia in 1852. An abolitionist, he campaigned for Lincoln in 1860, became minister of Spain in 1861, and was commissioned a brigadier general in Apr. 1862. After the war, Schurz won election to the U.S. Senate from Missouri and served as secretary of the interior under Rutherford B. Hayes. Faust, *Encyclopedia*, p. 662.

4. This became known as the "West Woods," which were divided from the "East Woods" by the cornfield.

5. Maj. Gen. William Farrar Smith (1824–1903) of Vermont. Boatner, *Dictionary*, pp. 775–76.

6. Shaw's parents published his letter of Aug. 12, 1862, describing the beauty of death on the face of Richard Cary. *New York Evening Post*, undated, in Mass. Inf., 2nd Regt., Letters from the

Army, BPL.

7. On Sept. 22, 1862, after the Battle of Antietam, Lincoln issued the preliminary Emancipation Proclamation: "That on the first day of January next all persons held as slaves within any State, or designated part of a State, whose people shall be in rebellion against the United States, shall be thenceforward and forever free." The war was no longer just a war for Union, it had advanced to a war for freedom. *NYDT*, September 23 (4:2), 1862.

8. For the best discussion of the pros and cons of the Emancipation Proclamation among abolitionists and nonabolitionists, see James M. McPherson, *The Struggle for Equality: Abolitionists and the Negro in the Civil War and Reconstruction* (Princeton: Princeton University Press, 1964), pp. 99–133.

9. Col. Dixon S. Miles was in charge of defending Harper's Ferry. His command consisted of new recruits and his blunders cost him not only a defeat, but his life, as Jackson won another victory. Miles's failure to hold Jackson at Harper's Ferry cost McClellan dearly at Antietam as Stonewall's men arrived to save Lee's army. McPherson, *Battle Cry*, p. 538.

10. Capt. Charles F. Morse.

11. James Savage, Jr., wounded three times at Cedar Mountain, died on Sept. 22 after his leg was amputated at the Confederate hospital in Charlottesville, Virginia, where Savage was a prisoner of war. Higginson Scrapbook, "Soldier's Book," HL.

12. Lt. Samuel Breck Parkman (1836–62) graduated from Harvard in 1857 and worked as a lawyer in Savannah before the war. He served in Read's Georgia Battery. Brown, *Report of the Class of 1857*, p. 40.

Maryland Heights   [RGS]
Sept. 28, 1862
My Dear Sister,

Your welcome letter of Sept. 24th reached me yesterday. I am sorry General Gordon's message caused you any uncomfortable feeling; he meant it only for a joke. I always thought the idea, that every man should volunteer, absurd; I should be very sorry to have George or Uncle Jim do so and hope they will never persuade themselves that it is their duty; so don't imagine that the fact of R. M.'s staying at home will make any difference in my feelings towards him.[1]

To-day I read Harry's name in the list of paroled prisoners arrived within our lines; it has taken a load off my mind, and I thank God he is safe at last. I long to have a word from him, as it is not probable he will be exchanged very soon, I think. You will have him at your wedding, dear Sue, and I hope it will console you in some measure for my absence.[2] I want to be there, as much as you want me, but it would be unwise to indulge in any hope of getting a furlough; in fact, unless matters change very much, it will simply be impossible. While the fight was going on the other day, I thought that, if I should be wounded, it would take me home at just about the right time; but I am again one of the fortunate ones, without an injury. Some men *wish* for a wound, so as to have a chance to visit home, but it is not a safe thing to wish for, when half an inch, more or less, is of so much importance. I don't think I should ever run against a bullet on purpose.

As you say, Mother will miss you very much when you go, and you will miss her; and I don't wonder at your feeling depressed and sad about it, at times. You are not going very far, though; and if they go to town, you will see as much of them as ever. When I *do* sometimes think of the possibility of my getting away, the idea of coming back in a few days is so disagreeable, that it takes away all the pleasure of the prospect; but you may be sure if there is a chance, I shall seize it.

The enclosed letter I found on the breast of a dead Federal soldier, on the battle-field of Sharpsburg. There was a Bible beside or on it, which I have kept. It looked as if he had been reading them both before he died.

Poor Major Sedgwick gets along very slowly, and is not yet out of danger. He had the determination, while lying on the ground, to write two pages in his diary, addressed to his wife and family. He was shot through the body, and fully expected to die where he lay; he was in our regiment for some time, and I always liked him very much. The afternoon before the battle, he rode over to see us, and I talked with him for two hours; he was always an interesting talker; he went off finally merry and jolly, as usual, and about the same time next day we heard he was killed; but, fortunately, that has proved to be a mistake as yet. His wife was to leave Germany at about that time, and must arrive here shortly. His mother and sister are with him now.[3]

The photograph which you sent me is excellent, and I immediately tipped the old one out of its place in my book. M. Roulet's is perfect; I am very glad indeed to have it, and that you sent him mine. I wish you *would* copy his note for me; he wrote me a beautiful letter when I was at Camp Andrew, which I have often looked for since, to send to Mother, but it has disappeared. I shall try to write to him myself; but, in the mean time, when you do so, please thank him for the photograph, and for his kind message to me.

To-day I rode over to the Twentieth Massachusetts. They have dwindled down a good deal. Holmes, like Crowninshield of our regiment, has received his second ball.[4] Hallowell was badly hit in the arm; he is one of the No. 1 sort.[5]

One of the most noticeable things in a battle is the perfect calmness of the wounded men; they will lie in the most exposed positions, under fire from both sides, without apparently noticing it, and some have told me that, when once hit, they felt as if the thing were done, and they couldn't be touched again. I don't know whether Harry has gone home or not, but shall write to him there. If you know where he is, please write me of it. Give my love to all the family.

Always dear Sue,
Your loving Brother

1. Robert Bowne Minturn, Jr., was engaged to Susanna Shaw. Shaw folder, SIHS.

2. Susanna married Robert on Oct. 31, 1862. Sturgis, *Sturgis*, p. 58.

3. Maj. William Dwight Sedgwick. His mother, Elizabeth Buckminister Dwight Sedgwick (1804–64) operated a girls' school in Lenox, Massachusetts. Crawford, *Famous Families*, vol. 2, p. 289.

4. Francis Welch Crowninshield.

Oliver Wendell Holmes, Jr., had been wounded during Lee's counterattack from the West Woods on September 17. McPherson, *Battle Cry*, p. 541.

5. Norwood Penrose Hallowell, a fervent abolitionist, became the second-ranking officer of the Fifty-fourth Massachusetts in Feb. 1863. His Antietam wound never fully healed and forced him to resign in late 1863. *National Cyclopedia of American Biography*, vol. 17, p. 32.

CHAPTER 9

"Even more than mother"

In the aftermath of Antietam, McClellan failed to press Lee's weakened army. In fact, McClellan resisted moving the Army of the Potomac even after Lincoln visited camp and lived in a tent beside him. When he finally acted on October 26, it was too late. After midterm congressional elections indicated public dissatisfaction with the war, and frustrated with the slowness of McClellan, Lincoln ended the general's career by replacing him with Ambrose Burnside on November 5. Eleven weeks later, after Burnside's reckless assault at Fredericksburg and the infamous "mud march," Lincoln placed Joseph Hooker in his stead. The North's showcase army had changed commanders three times in three months.

Captain Shaw and the Second Massachusetts did not participate in the fight at Fredericksburg, but stayed in quarters at Sharpsburg, Maryland, and Fairfax Station, Virginia. Reflecting on the war, Shaw vascillated between ideas of a long struggle and a contest shortened by the "Peace Party." He thought the Emancipation Proclamation was morally correct and hoped that justice would prevail in the end. Shaw had inklings of joining the cavalry, but his loyalty to his unit nixed that move. News of the battle deaths of his first cousin Theodore Parkman and of George Curtis's brother Joe made him worry over his own future. Still, Shaw was determined to finish the contest and wrote: "I had rather stay here all my life . . . than give up to the South."

As his service passed its second Thanksgiving and Christmas, Shaw focused upon his dead and wounded comrades. He often retraced the events of Antietam by riding the battlefield to locate places where his friends had fallen. Living through the bitter cold winter of 1862–63, Shaw's thoughts carried him to the warmth of a woman, Annie Haggerty. He obtained a leave of absence to visit her and to see his family. Shaw wrote Annie that he loved her "even more than Mother," proposed marriage, and suffered through her uncertain answer.

Maryland Heights   [RGS]
Oct. 5, 1862
Dear Mother,

Your long letter of Sept. 30 reached me to-day, and I will try to answer some of your questions, or rather your objections to what I said in my last. I can't see any real solid reason for sending a private letter to a newspaper, unless there is something in it of personal interest to the families of soldiers, such as lists of wounded, &c., &c. I shouldn't object half so much if the extracts were practically anonymous; but it is always perfectly evident to all my acquaintance that I wrote them, and I am at this moment in a state of anxiety about what Father has had printed. It is the very last thing *he* would like, I know. The fact of it is, I *can't* write what I want to, if my letters are to be put in the papers.

Don't imagine, from what I said in my last, that I thought Mr. Lincoln's "Emancipation Proclamation" not right; as an act of justice, and to have real effect, it ought to have been done long ago. I believe, with you, that the closer we adhere to Right and Justice, the better it will be in the end, and that, if we want God on our side, we must be on His side; but still, as a *war-measure*, I don't see the immediate benefit of it, and I think much of the moral force of the act has been lost by our long delay in coming to it. Jefferson Davis will either take no notice of it, or he will threaten some frightful retaliation; and as the slaves are *sure* of being free at any rate, with or without an Emancipation Act, *le jeu ne vaut pas la chandelle*.[1] This is only how the thing looks to me now; I shall no doubt change my opinion.

I was very glad to get Harry's letter, and to know that he had time to go to the Island: I had already written to him. Charles Lowell came up to see me the other day, and I went to ride with him; he is a fascinating fellow to me.[2] General McClellan sent him to Washington to present the Rebel flags captured at Antietam; it was considered a good deal of an honour. Give my love to Father and all. I owe Effie and Nellie many letters.

I rode over to Sharpsburg this morning, and whom should I meet but old Tilden Auchmuty?[3] He looked just the same as ever. I didn't have time to talk with him for more than a minute, and I never asked him to come and see me, or even told him where I was to be found. If you see him, please excuse me to him, will you?

Your loving Son

1. Translated as: The game is not worth the candle.

2. Charles Russell Lowell of the Sixth U.S. Cavalry served on General McClellan's staff, July–Nov. 1862. Smith, *Beacon Hill's*, pp. 419–20.

3. Charles Morse wrote that he and Shaw took a "fine horseback ride of about twenty miles, visiting the vicinity

of Antietam." Morse, *Letters*, p. 99. Perhaps New York City architect Richard Tylden Auchmuty (1831–93), who served on the staff of Gen. George G. Meade during the war. After the war, Auchmuty moved to Lenox and built that town into a fashionable resort area. *Trow's NYC Directory for 1863*, p. 42; *NYT*, July 19 (4:5), 1893.

Maryland Heights   [RGS]
Oct. 14, 1862
Dear Mother,

I was very glad to get your long letter of Oct. 10, to-day. I have lately been reading "Gasparin's America before Europe," and your faith in truth and principles reminds me of much that he says on the same subject.[1] I agree with you perfectly in all this; but why do you think it necessary that a general, whose business it is to obey orders, and carry out plans, should be inspired with the same faith in principles that you have? It seems to me that if we have a man of military ability, we have what we need,—especially now that the government has a decided policy. Garibaldi, for instance, with all those noble qualities, is not necessarily a great general.[2] I believe that the Right will conquer in the end; but we ought not to forget that able generals, a well-disciplined army, and a powerful navy, are the means to reach our end in this case.

This raid of Rebel cavalry into Pennsylvania makes us feel pretty cheap; they must have had an exciting time of it; I wonder they didn't damage the railroads more.[3] Perhaps, if the war lasts long enough, we shall have some audacious cavalry officer too. I wish Greely Curtis had a Brigade.[4] He is the boldest man I know, and the most obstinate in carrying his undertakings through. There are no symptoms of movement here yet, though some of the papers think there are. Their correspondents, to be sure, may have better means of judging than I, as I don't leave camp oftener than twice a week.

You must have thought, from my late letters, that I was degenerating sadly from the principles in which I was brought up; but an ordinary mortal must be somewhat affected by his surroundings, and events which you look at in one way from a distance, often seem very different when you are in the midst of them. The man at a distance is more apt to be impartial.

What you wrote me about Garibaldi was very beautiful. I wonder how the government would receive him, if he should offer his services to us. In our army, as in all others, there is a jealousy of foreigners holding high positions. They think Garibaldi is a sort of a guerilla chieftain here.

Why do you say you hope I won't think your letter a silly one? I never read anything I like more than your letters. They are far from appearing "silly" to me. If there were a newspaper here, *I should have had some of them printed!* George's letter is very clear, and I am very curious to see whether the Proclamation will have the effect he thinks.[5] I am anxious you should understand that I never questioned the right of it.

How near Susie's wedding is getting! I have made all sorts of inquiries about my chances of getting away; but without success.

> Always, dear Mother,
> Your affectionate Son

1. Agenor Etienne Gasparin (1810–62), minister of the interior under Louis Phillipe, wrote *America Before Europe: Principles and Interests* (New York: Charles Scribner, 1862). *NYDT*, Sept. 20 (3:1), 24 (4:5), 1862.

2. Giuseppe Garibaldi (1807–82) was important as the ideological and nationalist leader of the Thousand Red Shirts in support of King Victor Emmanuel II and the unification of Italy. In 1851, Garibaldi lived on Staten Island making candles and brewing beer. Leng and Davis, *Staten Island*, pp. 255–56.

3. While the Union cavalry proved unable to stop or even to find him, J. E. B. Stuart and 1,800 men again rode completely around McClellan's army on October 8–12, 1862. Stuart seized about 1,200 horses and many supplies, then destroyed machine shops, arms, clothing, and boxcars loaded with military supplies in Chambersburg, Pennsylvania. Stuart accomplished this feat without the loss of a single man. Thomas, *Bold Dragoon*, pp. 163, 174–180.

4. Capt. Greely Stevenson Curtis left the Second Massachusetts in Nov. 1861 to accept a majority in the First Massachusetts Cavalry, then organizing at Camp Meigs, Readville. Greely S. Curtis file, CMSR.

5. While we do not know what George Curtis told Shaw, his letter to a friend delineated his thoughts on Lincoln's Proclamation. Curtis believed that the Emancipation Proclamation struck at the primary cause of the rebellion. Curtis wrote, "the contest becomes more vital. . . . Peace can be permanently

secured only by the absolute triumph of one of the contending principles." That principle was the supremacy of free labor over slave labor. Curtis also believed that the Proclamation would end "the supremacy of the Democratic party."

George W. Curtis to John E. Cairnes, Nov. 16, 1862, in Adelaide Weinberg, *John Elliot Cairnes and the American Civil War: A Study in Anglo-American Relations* (London: Kingswood Press, 1969), p. 53.

Near Sharpsburg, Md. [RGS]
Nov. 13, 1862
Dear Father,

The India-rubber blankets have arrived; they are of the greatest service to the men, as we have a hundred on picket every day, beside other guards, and the weather is stormy; I don't know anything you could have sent which would be more acceptable.

So General McClellan has been removed at last![1] I think every one in the army regrets it, excepting, perhaps, some envious major-generals. What Burnside has ever done to merit the position, I can't see. All is quiet here, and the weather *trying*; if the snow and cold continue, I think our army must stop operations; I am convinced nothing can be done in winter, both on account of the men's sufferings and Virginia roads.

Seymour's election has made us feel badly, and I suppose you are all blue enough; it is useless to talk about it, however.[2]

I think Professor Cairne's book is wonderful for its clearness and sagacity.[3] What a comfort it is to read of the crime of slavery as belonging entirely to another people, and to feel that there are some men in England who understand the matter.

Harry writes me that a new cavalry regiment is to be raised in Massachusetts, and wants to know what I think of going into it.

The First Massachusetts cavalry is near Hagerstown, and I have been up there twice since my return.[4] They have just received three or four hundred new horses, and are looking very well. I hope they will have a chance at Stuart's men, if they come over again, as many suppose they will. We had an alarm last night, but have heard nothing of it since. I am sitting on the bank of the river, where it is very wet and dark; but am fortunately under cover. Good night. With much love to Mother.

Your most affectionate son,
Robert G. Shaw

1. As the Democratic nominee for president in 1864, McClellan faced up to Lincoln one more time, and lost again. From 1878 to 1881, McClellan was governor of New Jersey. McGuiness and Sayers, *American Leaders*, p. 384.

2. Antiabolitionist Horatio Seymour (1810–86) had been governor of New York (1852–54). Campaigning for reelection in 1862, Seymour spoke out strongly against Lincoln's proposed emancipation plan as "a proposal for the butchery of women and children, for scenes of lust and rapine, of arson and murder unparalleled in the history of the world." While he won the election in 1862, he lost it in 1864. Seymour quoted in William Seraile, "The Struggle to Raise Black Regiments in New York, 1861–1864," *New York Historical Society Quarterly* 58 (Sept. 1974): 224; Faust, *Encyclopedia*, pp. 669–70, 795.

3. English abolitionist John Elliot

Cairnes (1823–75) wrote *The Slave Power: Its Character, Career, and Probable Designs: Being an Attempt to Explain the Real Issues in the American Contest* (London: Parker, Son & Bourn, 1862). Cairnes focused on slavery as the "cancer" that began the war and explained that the so-called Constitutional crisis, tariff, or states' rights arguments were secondary or superficial causes. George William Curtis and Sarah Shaw were the first two trans-Atlantic readers of Cairnes's book. Cairnes would become close friends with Sarah Shaw. Weinberg, *Cairnes*, pp. 11, 52, 131–60; *Dictionary of National Biography* (London: Oxford University Press, 1917), vol. 3, pp. 668–69.

4. Charles Morse also wrote of these visits with Shaw, after which he and Shaw ate roasted quail and smoked cigars. Morse, *Letters*, p. 104.

Camp near Sharpsburg   [RGS]
Nov. 17, 1862
Dear Mother,

Your note of the 10th came last night; just one week on the way. Nothing of interest has happened here yet, though we have occasional rumours of Rebel troops being in the vicinity, on the other side of the river. The pickets at Harper's Ferry were driven in to-day, and some cavalry have appeared opposite us. It would be rather startling to have them in Maryland, so near Pennsylvania again, with all our army away. Have you read the opinions of the Prince de Joinville on our army, and the campaign on the Peninsula?[1] His views of our organization and discipline are the most sensible I have ever seen in print. Everything he says about the extravagance, inefficiency, and almost total want of discipline inseparable from the volunteer system, is true. If we fail in this war from want of men and money, the most humiliating reflection will be, that with half the men, and half the money already expended, we might have been victorious, if we had gone properly to work, or had ever consented to learn by experience. If what he says of the management of the campaign is true, (and I can think of no reason why he should make false statements,) it proves more clearly than ever the impossibility of war being properly carried on by many heads. A military campaign is very different from a political one.

Cousin John Forbes wrote the other day, and asked me what I thought of the cavalry regiment.[2] I have not answered yet, because I am waiting until Harry comes, to know what his intentions about it are. I shan't accept any position below that of 4th Captain (the rank I hold here), and I can't believe they can guarantee that to me. I have felt very well contented here since my return. My company is an excellent one, and I am one of the oldest officers. In a new regiment, especially cavalry, I shouldn't find myself so pleasantly situated, as I should not start fair with those who have already served in that arm. Besides, the feeling all the old officers have for this regiment would make it a very melancholy affair to leave it. Nevertheless, when I have seen Harry, and heard more particulars of the other, I may decide for that. I have heard that Charles Lowell is to command the regiment, and Caspar Crowninshield to be Senior Major.[3] The fact of these two and Will. Forbes being in it, makes it very tempting to me. If Harry and Morse went too, I shouldn't want to stay here much. The latter wouldn't leave on any account, though, as he has an idea that it is his duty to stick by his men; and what he considers his duty, he does.[4]

The enclosed note is private for you and Father.[5] Please don't speak of it to any one else.

Your loving Son

1. François Ferdinand Philippe Louis Marie d'Orleans de Joinville (1818–1900) supported McClellan and believed the government lost the campaign by not sending the general enough troops. De Joinville cited the valor and cheerfulness of the Army of the Potomac while criticizing its slowness. *Harper's Weekly*, Nov. 22, 1862, p. 7.

2. John Murray Forbes.

3. Caspar Crowninshield had been Shaw's roommate at Harvard. He served in the Twentieth Massachusetts Infantry before transferring as a captain to the First Massachusetts Cavalry in Dec. 1861. The Second Massachusetts Cavalry began organizing in Jan. 1863 at Camp Meigs, Readville. Caspar Crowninshield file, CMSR.

4. Shaw shared Morse's loyalty. Morse mustered out of service with the Second on July 14, 1865, with the rank of colonel. *Rec. of Mass. Vols.*, p. 27.

5. The note Shaw enclosed is lost. It probably contained news that Shaw had proposed to Annie Kneeland Haggerty and that he awaited her answer. See RGS to FGS, Nov. 21, 1862, RGS to SBS, Nov. 21, 1862, included here.

Nov. 21, 1862

Dear Father,

Yours of Nov. 16th came to hand yesterday. In my last to Mother, I mentioned what I thought about the Second Cavalry. I also wrote to Cousin John yesterday, saying that I shouldn't take anything lower than the senior captaincy, and that I didn't care about making any application for it.[1] He is very kind indeed to take so much trouble about it, and I hope he won't feel as if I ought to accept the commission if offered, for I have never intimated that I would. Harry has arrived, and it is very pleasant to have him back; he is in excellent spirits, and it seems now as if he had never been away; he is doubtful about accepting the major's commission in the cavalry.[2] The principal charm for both of us would be the new experience. If we looked for a *safe* place, I think we should be more likely to find it in the cavalry than in any other arm of the service. It isn't so in all armies, but it certainly has been in ours, so far.

I don't see why you think Burnside has done anything to merit his position. I sincerely hope he will be successful now, and things certainly look promising, if this weather will only hold. South of the Rappahannock they will have nothing but dirt roads, and heavy rains or snow would make them almost impassable.[3] I observe by the papers that Mr. Lincoln has taken another "*stern resolve*" to stop abuses, punish deserters, and the like; also, that the government is now "*terribly in earnest*" again. I see, too, that a soldier condemned to death for striking a commissioned officer has been pardoned by Mr. Lincoln, because he was drunk. Drunkenness is always considered an aggravation of an offence by a court-martial, because, on that plea, almost all delinquents could escape punishment. We have been having slight rains and warm weather this week. The enclosed note to Mother is for you and her.

Always your affectionate son,
Robert G. Shaw

1. John Murray Forbes.

2. Harry Russell was paroled from Libby Prison on Sept. 28. Once an exchange had been made for a Confederate officer on Nov. 15, Captain Russell immediately rejoined his regiment. On Mar. 18, 1863, after Shaw had left the Second, Russell accepted a lieutenant colonelcy in the Second Massachusetts Cavalry. Fourteen months later, he helped to raise the Fifth Massachusetts Cavalry (Colored) and became Colonel Russell. Explaining why he had cast himself among black troopers, Russell said, "Bob [Shaw] would have liked to have me do it!" Russell file, CMSR; Putnam, *Memoirs of the War of '61*, p. 39.

3. Unknowingly, Shaw had forecast Burnside's infamous "mud march" of Jan. 1863.

Nov. 21, 1862   [RGS]

Dearest Mother,

I have received Annie's answer at last. She didn't say "Yes," outright, but it was enough to repay me for writing, and for the two weeks of anxious suspense. I feel, after reading her note, that it will come [out] all right in the end. If I ever get home, and do marry Annie, I hope you and Father will be pleased with it. Do tell me this when you write, for I should feel very badly if you were not. I would tell Susie of this, as she knew something of the matter before, but I don't think I have any right to tell any one but you. So please be very careful, as Annie would naturally be very much displeased to have anything said about it, while it is still so unsettled. It would be a hard blow for me to come home and find I had been too sanguine about this, and that what she wrote didn't authorize me to feel so sure. So if you should see her this winter, and should have a talk with her about it, won't you write me what you think? It would be the best thing you could do for me just now, dear Mother.

Your loving Son

Near Sharpsburg Md.   [HL, RGS]

Nov 21 1862

Dear Effie,

I have rec'd three of your notes during the last three days—Nov. 3, Nov. 8 & Nov 16—so it is time I wrote to you. In the first place I am sorry to disappoint you about the cavalry, but it is very unlikely that I shall take a commission in it. A man is or should be very loath to leave a regiment in which he has gone through as much as we have in this—especially when it is such a one as ours. I have had a great many discontented moments, when I have thought I wanted to change, but when it came to deciding, I never went—Excepting on to Gordon's staff & then I was delighted to get back. If you find yourself at Jamaica Plain and can conveniently call on Capt Morse's family, I wish you would. They must be people worth knowing, if he is a specimen of the family—and he has told me so much about them that I know they are. They live in the house next [to] Frank Parkman's on the Pond.[1] It *would* be pleasant, wouldn't it, to be at Readeville while you are at Milton? I wish it were to be so.

I don't care whether McClellan or Burnside commands the army, if the commander is only a capable man, but I still believe the former is the best general we have. No one has proved himself better yet. The newspapers and other jackasses can talk forever, but I shall still be persuaded that it is our Government that has failed and not our Generals. You would oblige me much, though, by not making any more remarks on the conduct of the War. Not that they are not very valuable (I wouldn't be so impolite as to hint it) but the subject is one, of which I am heartily sick.

I will give Harry your message.

We are to have a great race here tomorrow between Tom Robeson's & Dan Oakey's horses, ridden by the owners. It is expected to be a great thing—Oakey's horse "Burnside" stands about 10 hands & Robeson's "Little Mac" about 16. The latter is very lean too & shaky in the knees, having been deprived of half his daily food for a fortnight, by a mistake of a small nigger who takes care of him. Harry bets on Oakey & is trying to persuade him "to sweat himself down" to light weight during the night. We expect to do the thing up very brown. The horses will be led out heavily blanketed (which will astonish them, as I don't believe either ever heard of a blanket before) by the grooms, a chinaman & the 10 yr old nigger above mentioned. The two Gentlemen Riders will then arrive on the ground in a wagon—where after taking off 5 or 6 overcoats a piece they will mount & take a preliminary gallop. Capt Russell will then give the word to start & if neither tumbles off, their horses may be able to bear them three quarters of the way, when they will probably dismount & run the rest on foot. We tried to impress upon Dan

[last page missing; continued from RGS]

the propriety of appearing in a red cap, worsted-jacket, and red-flannel drawers, but I'm afraid he won't consent to it. If this race prove successful, there will probably be a foot-race between Captain Sawyer, height five feet six inches, weight two hundred and thirty pounds; and Captain Brown, height five feet five inches, weight one hundred and eighty pounds.[2] These figures are exact. We expect to have a good time Thanksgiving, and are getting dinner ready already. Excuse this writing. My hand runs away, and I have no control over it to-night. Give my love to Nellie.

Your loving Brother.

1. Francis Parkman (1823–93) became one of the nation's most famous historians. His grandfather and Francis Shaw's mother were siblings. Parkman often told stories to the young Robert Gould Shaw. His travels in the West and his life among the Sioux are documented in his first book, *The Oregon Trail* (1849). Hampton, *Staten Island's Claim to Fame*, pp. 58–62.

2. Probably Nathan D. A. Sawyer of Lowell, aged twenty-four, versus

Robert B. Brown of Salem, twenty-two. Another Captain Sawyer, Anson D., of Boston, joined the regiment on Nov. 9; he was twenty-eight. *Rec. of Mass. Vols.*, pp. 28–29.

Camp near Sharpsburg, Md. [RGS]
Nov. 23, 1862

Dear Annie,[1]

Your letter of Sunday the 16th was sent down to me last night on the river, where I was on picket. It was very cold, windy, and snowy down there; but it made me warm, and comfortable to hear from you again so soon. I was so glad you didn't think it necessary to wait until you got my answer to your first, before writing again.

Sergeant B. happened to be sergeant of the picket, so I handed him his mother's note on the spot.[2] I am afraid he is not a very affectionate son, and I shall tell him he ought to write to his mother oftener; which he will probably think is none of my business. . . .

I felt wicked when I told you I wanted to see you even more than Mother; for I have always loved her more than any one else in the world, and I think she has me, from the sacrifices she has made for me, and for which I can never repay her. But it was true, nevertheless, like every-thing I have written to you, and a great deal more besides, for my feelings to you have been almost the same since the first evening I saw you in New York; the evening I went with you and Susie to the opera.[3]

. . . .

If it is possible, I shall get a furlough. Our Corps seems destined to remain in this neighborhood all winter, so that may give me a chance.

I know how much you all think of Clem., and every one who sees her likes her.[4] I hope she will be at home with you again soon; and when she comes, give my love to her.

The Prince de Joinville's articles seem to me to be the clearest and most intelligent that have been written about this war, both as regards the Peninsular campaign, and the wretched organization of our army. It is almost an impossibility to enforce discipline in a volunteer army raised as ours is; but the government has shown itself too weak to do even what it had the power to do: desertion, straggling, and cowardice have gone unpunished; and in all cases of disaffection in the army, the government has yielded.

They have shown the same weakness in the matter of drafting; having ordered a draft, they were powerless, in most cases, to carry it out. In Pennsylvania the drafted men were ordered to be sent to the old regiments; but they refused to go, and the difficulty was "satisfactorily adjusted," as the papers say, by the government consenting to their demands to form new regiments, and elect their officers. So the old regiments, which it is of vital importance to fill up, have mostly only two to three hundred men apiece. A volunteer army is a miserable concern at the best, when the means of disciplining it, ready at hand, are not made use of. And the administration has been just as weak in its general plans as in the minor details. Burnside has an enormous army; and if they don't all straggle along the roadside, he ought to do something great. I hope he will, I am sure. Those who know him well don't seem to think him a man of very astounding ability; but the popular notion of a man is no criterion.

There is to be a new cavalry regiment raised in Massachusetts, in which I understand I can get a commission. If I take it, I shall be at home some time (i.e. in Boston), which would be better than having a short furlough, though I should be kept pretty busy. But it is very hard to decide to leave a regiment with which one has gone through so much danger and hardship as I have in this.

Now I think of it, all our applications for leave of absence have to go through Burnside's head-quarters, so it will be very difficult to get one, I am afraid. What do you think about it,—the cavalry?

Good night, dear Annie. Please write to me soon again.

How sad it is for a man, as he is growing old, to have so much sorrow as ——— has had! I should think some people, seeing others very happy, and themselves the reverse, would need an immense deal of faith to make them believe that Providence is not unjust.

Good night again.

Yours affectionately,
R.G.S.

1. Annie Kneeland Haggerty.   4. Clemence Haggerty, Annie's
2. Sergeant B. is unidentified.   sister.
3. Susanna Shaw.

Near Sharpsburg, Md.
Nov. 28, 1862

Dear Annie,

Your letter of the 16th instant was the last I got from you or any one else, so I am sadly in want of a mail. It is extraordinary how long our letters are on the road, almost never less than a week. Those directed to Sharpsburg come the soonest; those which go to Washington probably lie over two or three days, to be sorted from the rest of the army mail.

Yesterday was Thanksgiving, and we managed to have a very pleasant day. There would have been no drawback, if we hadn't missed from the table so many faces which were there last year at this time. This made the dinner a very quiet affair compared with most bachelor parties. Besides the seven officers killed last summer and this autumn, there are a good many at home wounded and ill; so that the society is materially changed since we came out.[1] It is very strange and unfortunate, that the officers that have been killed were the very best we had, both as comrades and as military men. No doubt, after a man is dead his virtues only are remembered, but in our case the dead ones really were the best.

Didn't I mention the new Massachusetts cavalry in my last, and that I might get a commission in it? I found, though, that the change would be no benefit in the way of rank, and this, with several other reasons, decided me to remain where I am.

Harry Russell and I have a very comfortable cubby-house together, with an open, brick fireplace, and all the modern conveniences. The house is only a pine box, 9 × 9, with a tent pitched over it for a roof; but it is very comfortable indeed. There is room in it for two berths, one above the other, a table, a bench, a washstand, and two valises. We hang all our clothes on a line which stretches from the front to the rear pole of the tent, and which is high enough over our heads to stand for an attic.

Poor Mr. Burnside is still lying idle.[2] Wouldn't it be a joke to have all the papers and other wise men begin to abuse him? I can't help thinking, though, that we *must* be successful this time. I am sure there must be a letter on the way to me from you, for you know what a pleasure it is to me to get them. So, be sure, Annie, whenever you feel an inclination to write, not to let it pass without doing so. If I had accepted the position in the cavalry, I shouldn't have had much pleasure from being at home, for I hear they have only enlisted about three men; so every officer would have to work like a Trojan at recruiting, and I shouldn't see anything of my friends after all.

Nothing came of the expected attack, of which I wrote to you, excepting a sleepless night for us.

The other day we sent a party over the river, and took twenty prisoners, among them three officers, and shot the leader of a guerilla band, for whose head $500 had been offered. One of our privates shot him as he tried to escape from a house; but I am afraid the man will never see the $500. It was all done at night, and those who went over found it very exciting work. The fact that several of the prisoners were only stragglers, who had domiciled themselves in Shepardstown, rather detracts from the glory of the exploit.

The other day I came across the grave of a man named Calvin Jones, from Pittsfield, Massachusetts, a private in some regular regiment.[3] Did you ever hear of any such individual? He was killed in a skirmish just after the battle of the Antietam. So the head-board says.

Our camp is close by the great battle-field, and our principal recreation has been to ride over it, and see the places where we fought, and where our men were killed. There is hardly a tree near without several bullets and cannon-balls in it, and some of the neighbouring buildings are perforated in every direction. The place is full of graves; thirty or forty men together in some of them, often without even a board to mark the place. In the village of Sharps-burg, the people all retreated to the cellars during the battle, and more than half the houses there have holes in them from solid shot and shell. The number of dead horses scattered about, for a distance of four miles, is enormous. One battery which was placed near us in line that day had sixteen horses killed.

A great many of the men's bodies have been taken up and carried home; but I should think the friends who see them would wish they had been left in their graves.

Good bye for the present.

Give my love to your mother, and write to me when you can.

Always affectionately yours,
Rob

1. Shaw is referring to those killed at Cedar Mountain and Antietam.

2. On Nov. 27, Burnside met with Lincoln to discuss tactics. Lincoln proposed a three-sided attack on Lee at Fredericksburg, but Burnside had already decided to strike Lee in one huge head-on assault. Shaw would not have long to wait for Burnside to move. Long, *Civil War Day By Day*, p. 290.

3. Calvin Jones is unidentified. Pittsfield is near Lenox, the summer home of the Haggertys.

Camp near Sharpsburg
Dec. 1, 1862

Dearest Mother,

Yours of the 26th November reached me this evening. You don't know how glad I am at what you say about Annie, for I was really uncertain how you would take it. Not that I thought you didn't like her, but that you might think that, under present circumstances (the war and my absence), I had better have waited. I wrote to her only because I couldn't help it, and with horrible misgivings. You wouldn't have thought I was very "BOLD," if you could have known my state of mind at the time. So far as I am concerned, I should like very much to tell Susie, Effie, and all of them about it, and I have asked Annie whether I can, but have not received an answer yet. Perhaps you may have asked when you wrote, and if she consents, you can tell them. I shall write to them myself, if she says so. As you say, I shall be a fortunate fellow to get her, and the thought of it makes me feel very happy; and I am happier still to hear that you and Father are so pleased with it in every way. The only drawback is, that it makes me want to get home very much; and if I thought my duties in the new cavalry would leave me any time to myself, I should feel very much like making the sacrifice of leaving this.

Father mentioned that you had written to Lenox, and I am very glad indeed that you did.[1] In fact, I thought you would. I suppose you didn't speak of the matter as entirely settled; for though what Annie has written makes me feel very easy, she has never said it in so many words.

In my last, I mentioned the reasons why we declined the commissions in the cavalry. In the extract from the Governor's letter which Father sent me, I was surprised to see that they didn't know exactly why we declined them. It was because the Majority was not enough to tempt Harry, and because I should be very foolish to accept one of the first *six* Captaincies in a new, untried, and unrecruited regiment, when I am now fourth Captain in one of the best volunteer regiments in the country. The work of helping to organize the regiment wouldn't frighten either of us much, as we never enjoyed ourselves more than at Camp Andrew.[2] For my part, I rather liked the idea of getting interested in a hard job, and having to work every day, and all day, at something of the kind. At this particular time, to be sure, I should like two or three weeks to myself.

We had a great race to-day. I rode a horse owned by Captain Cogswell, which has been the favorite all along.[3] I got myself up in the foxiest possible jockey style; was beaten very badly in two straight one-mile heats, and had my pretty clothes all covered with mud, from my collar down, besides getting my hair, eyes, nose, and mouth, full of the same article, from the heels of the winning horse, ridden by Mudge.[4] He came in perfectly clean, and his horse as fresh as a lark.

N.B. *I am disgusted with horse-racing, and think it is a very immoral practice, as well as ruinous to fine clothes.*

With love to all, dearest Mother,

Your loving Son

Thank you and Father again for your letters.

1. Lenox, Massachusetts.
2. The Second Massachusetts had organized at Camp Andrew, near

Boston.
3. William Cogswell.
4. Maj. Charles R. Mudge.

Fairfax Station, Va.   [RGS]
Dec. 18, 1862
Dear Father,

We came back here last night, by order of General Burnside, I believe; we had got almost to Dumfries; the roads are in a terrible state. To-day everything is frozen hard, so they are better than usual. Burnside's retreat is a nice discouraging affair. I have no doubt he was ordered to cross and attack, against his own wish.[1] Some one has seen Joe Curtis' name in the list of killed. Can it be true?[2] I hope not. Poor Mrs. Curtis and George will feel terribly. And for every other man killed, there are as many mourners as for Joe!

We have had some very hard weather since we left Sharpsburg, in the way of rain, snow, and cold,—all well still, though. The roads are frozen hard now, so that waggons can get along tolerably well; but three days ago they were all but impassable; we couldn't move faster than five or six miles a day, and this after only six hours' rain. We have six of your blankets fastened together, which make a good shelter for Harry, Morse, and me. The men say they are the most useful things they have. We lost from the Brigade two waggons, two men killed, and several taken prisoners by guerillas, near Leesburg. Among the prisoners were a sergeant, valuable mare, with overcoat, provisions, &c., belonging to Morse.

Your affectionate son,
Robert G. Shaw

1. At the Battle of Fredericksburg on Dec. 13, 1862, Burnside, with 121,402 men, attacked Lee's 78,511. In five assaults on the entrenched Confederate position on Marye's Heights, Burnside threw away men's lives. He wanted to

make another assault, but his aides dissuaded him. On Dec. 15, the Army of the Potomac withdrew back across the Rappahannock River. Press, politicians, civilians, soldiers, and generals questioned Burnside's sanity. The Union lost 12,653 casualties; the South lost 4,201. Foote, *Civil War*, vol. 2, pp. 20–44.

2. Lt. Col. Joseph Bridgham Curtis was killed at the Battle of Fredericksburg. Milne, *Curtis*, p. 118.

Fairfax Station, Va.   [RGS]
Dec. 18, 1862
Dear Annie,

It is a little over a week since I wrote to tell you we were going to leave Sharpsburg. Since then, we have been almost to Dumfries, and have returned here, on receipt of the news that Burnside had evacuated Fredericksburg. It is a terrible thing that so many lives should have been lost for nothing. It seems to be the prevailing opinion now, that nothing more will be attempted for a good while; and the roads are in such a condition, that it is next to impossible to move troops more than five or six miles a day. The first three days of our march were quite mild; the snow melted, and made the roads pretty bad; after that, we had a heavy rain, and now it is very cold. In the early morning the mud is half frozen, so that wagons stick fast at every step; and at noon it is soft enough for them to sink to the hubs of the wheels. An inch of snow would finish this business completely. We had a little snow-storm yesterday, on our way back here, and last night was the coldest we have had; it froze hard, and many of us had to get up and sit around the fires. It takes some time to accustom one's self to sleeping in the open air in winter.

Harry, Morse (one of our captains), and I, always turn in together, and the middle one is very comfortable. It was my turn to be in the middle last night, and I should have slept beautifully, if, in their efforts to keep warm, they had not squeezed me unmercifully between them. In washing this morning, I wet my head as usual, and when I went to comb my hair it was all frozen up.

The night it rained, we had a very funny time; for about 3 A.M. we all found ourselves lying in large puddles, and had to get up and sit in our India-rubber coats; those who hadn't any, got wet meal, as every plate and dish was full of water.

No one knows how long we may stay here. Part of the Corps will probably be left for the defence of the railroad.

I believe I never answered your question about my staying in the army after the war. I once thought of doing so, but have not for a good while. To judge from our lazy time in winter quarters, it must be a good-for-nothing sort of life in time of peace. When our three years are up, and this regiment is mustered out of service, I shall feel myself entitled to a vacation; but if the war goes on, there will be just as much reason for my doing my share in it as there was for coming out in the beginning. Don't you think so?

What you said about the new cavalry regiment was very true, for if I had gone into that, I shouldn't even have the chance of going home in eighteen months, which I have now.

We haven't had anything from home, even in the way of a newspaper, for more than ten days; and we don't expect a mail very soon, as everything has been ordered to Fredericksburg from the Sharpsburg post-office.

I wonder how people at home feel about Burnside's retrograde movement; they must begin to think that McClellan was not far wrong in thinking that little could be done in winter. We were almost twice as long going the distance we did, as we should have been in summer, and if Burnside expected us as reinforcements, he must have been disappointed. Such disappointments would be common over such roads as these. I am afraid our government will be persuaded to come to terms with the Rebels; I would rather stay here all my life than see that. Every reverse we have will make the "peace party" stronger, I should think, and foreign intervention more probable.[1]

I hope to hear from you again one of these days, but am afraid it will be a good while hence. Your last was of Dec. 1st.

> Sincerely and affectionately yours,
> Robert G. Shaw

1. Peace Democrats, known as "Copperheads," opposed Lincoln's policies on the war. Every Southern victory brought voters to their side; each Northern victory sent the voters back to the party of Lincoln.

Fairfax Station   [RGS]
Dec. 21, 1862
My Dear Annie,

Your letter of the 9th reached me yesterday. This is the first time I have heard from you since Dec. 1st, and your letter really gave me a great deal of pleasure. You mention another written on the 7th, which I have not yet received; it is probably at Sharpsburg, and will get to us in time.

As you say, snow is a very different thing to us from what it is to you, especially since our tents have been taken from us. We have nothing but the shelter-tents I told you about: mine is of India-rubber, so it keeps out the wet, and is also closed at one end by an India-rubber blanket; the other end is open, and has a large fire in front, which is very comfortable when the wind doesn't blow the smoke into the tent. We do not take the trouble to pitch the latter, unless it rains or we stay more than twenty-four hours in a place, for they are hardly high enough to sit up in.

In spite of all the discomforts, there are many charms about our life. I never had a pleasanter sensation than that of getting into bivouac after a hard march, having the blankets spread, a great fire built, a little supper, and a comfortable pipe. Then we lie looking at the stars through the trees, listening to the men singing,—which is often very good,—or talking about what we shall do when the war is over, and the scenes we have been through since it began. There are only a dozen of our old officers left, and I often wonder how many there will be when we go home.

When I read Irving's "Life of Washington," I thought it was as interesting as any novel.[1] I never knew before what a beautiful character he was.

You must excuse my writing to-day, Annie, for my fingers are perfectly stiff, and my ink freezes every little while. The last three days have been cold enough for any Northerner.

We don't know where we are going next. The useless battle at Fredericksburg seems to have thrown things into confusion. The papers say that Joe Curtis (George's brother) was killed, also Lieutenant Dehon, which I take to be Arthur.[2] Poor fellow! I saw him just after Antietam, and he was wondering why he never got hit. Did your Mother get my letter?

Give my love to her and to Clem.

Sincerely yours,
Robert G. Shaw

1. Washington Irving (1783–1859) wrote *Life of George Washington* (New York: G. P. Putnam, 1855–59).

2. Actually, Joe was George's half-brother, but he always referred to him as "brother." Arthur Dehon of the Twelfth Massachusetts Infantry. Arthur Dehon file, CMSR; Higginson, *Harvard Memorial Biographies*, vol. 2, pp. 219–25.

Fairfax Station   [RGS]
Dec. 23, 1862
Dear Mother,

I have both yours of Dec. 7th and 8th. I *did* have a very gloomy time on picket, that day and night I wrote you about. It was horrid weather, cold, cloudy, and smelling of coming snow. Until the receipt of that letter, I had been trying to make myself believe that everything was as jolly as possible, by reading the "Pickwick Papers."[1] It made me feel blue enough, dear Mother; but don't think I lay any blame to you, for it was evidently my indiscretion and carelessness in writing what would probably sound very differently if spoken.

Since we have been here, though, I have had several more letters, and I think, on the whole, the mistake has turned out favorably for me. I wrote to her in such a melancholy and humble vein, that she apparently felt worse than I did. So I am "fuss-rate" again.

From all I can hear, everything is in great confusion at Washington. Mr. Lincoln says he would rather be a private soldier than President.[2] Perhaps a good many people would rather have him in that position too. I have had no late letters from you, so I don't know what you and Father think of things. Oh! how blue they look! I have just finished Prince Joinville's pamphlet.[3] Some parts of it are excellent, I think; but, on the whole, it seems rather a Frenchy and varnished sort of tale.

We are encamped in a pine-wood, close to the railroad station; a fine, airy situation, nothing under us, and nothing over us, to speak of. The wind whistles through the pine-trees beautifully sometimes,—and about our ears too. Harry and I have just finished "Vanity Fair," which we have been reading aloud in our many bivouacs between Sharpsburg and Dumfries.[4] What a complete book it is! I have enjoyed it very much, though I have read it before.

Hoping to hear from you soon, and with love to Father, always, Dear Mother

Your affectionate Son

1. Shaw mentioned Mr. Pickwick in his letter of Sept. 11, 1861.

2. The *New York Times* reported Lincoln's comment: "Would that I had one of their places. There is not a man in the army with whom I would not willingly change places to-night." *NYT*, Dec. 21 (5:2), 1862. In the aftermath of Fredericksburg, Lincoln experienced the worst internal political crisis of his presidency. McPherson, *Battle Cry*, pp. 574–75.

3. Probably, Prince de Joinville, "The Army of the Potomac: Its Organization, Its Commander, Its Campaign" (New York: Randolph, 1862).

4. William Makepeace Thackeray, *Vanity Fair: A Novel Without a Hero* (New York: Harper, 1848).

Fairfax Station
Dec. 23, 1862
Dear Effie,

Your two letters of the 7th and 11th have reached me since we returned to this place. We have been here four days now; having been all the way to Dumfries and back, after the battle. Where we go next, no one seems to know; perhaps to Alexandria; perhaps to Harper's Ferry; perhaps to Fredericksburg; and—perhaps we stay here. I don't care much what we do, if it is only a change from our present position, one of perfect idleness in camp, and yet, with all the exposure and discomfort of active work; because, expecting to move every day, it is not worth while to make ourselves comfortable. Part of the time, the weather has been bitterly cold, and we have had some snow and rain. The men begin to feel the effects of it already; we are all in shelter-tents, excepting the field and staff officers. Morse, Harry, and I sleep together, and by means of buffalo-robes and blankets manage to keep pretty comfortable. Washing is a terrible ordeal, and it really requires some pluck to "come up to the scratch" every morning. To-day it is warm, and I seize the opportunity to finish up all my writing, which is an impossibility in ordinary weather.

I am glad the recruiting for the new regiment gets on tolerably well, and hope the regiment will be as good a one as the First Massachusetts.[1] That is the only good volunteer cavalry regiment I have seen. Most of them are so bad that we don't think much of them, excepting for the advantage they have in running away.

I have not heard from home since the Fredericksburg battle, so I don't know whether it is true that Joe Curtis was killed there. I hope it may turn out that he is only wounded. Poor Russell Sturgis must be in a sad state.[2] Do you know who will take the children while he is away?

So you and Nellie think it is "too foolish" for Father and Mother not to show you my letters lately. It is a good thing for you to curb your inquisitiveness now and then. I got up a secret especially for that purpose (your good).[3] There are some matters of state which can't be revealed to young women, even to those who know just how to put down the Rebellion, and conduct a war! But I don't want to chaff you, so I will stop this strain.

They say that "Uncle Abe" is on the verge of lunacy. I don't wonder at it. I am afraid now there is a danger of the government backing down. I had rather stay here all my life (though, in this case, I should pray for a short one) than give up to the South. The most satisfactory ending to me, would be to have them brought to their knees, and then kicked out, and allowed to set up for themselves within certain limits. I would have them hemmed in on all sides by free States, and not allowed a chance of extending.

Since we have been here, we get a mail almost every day, and it is a perfect blessing. Give my love to Nellie and Loulie.[4] I hope you will have a "Merry Christmas." If we had stayed in Sharpsburg, I should have tried to get to Frederick, where they always have pleasant times,—at least I do,—talking with Miss Goldsborough, and hearing Miss Shriver sing.[5]

The guerilla men lead the pleasantest life. They hung round us all the way down here, and carried off some one every day. Good bye for the present.

Your loving Brother

1. Shaw is referring to the Second Massachusetts Cavalry, being organized and commanded by Josephine's lover, Charles Russell Lowell.

2. Russell Sturgis was the eldest brother of Sarah Sturgis Shaw.

3. Shaw's engagement to Annie

Haggerty was a closely guarded secret.

4. Ellen Shaw and Shaw's first cousin Mary Louisa Shaw.

5. Miss Shriver is unidentified; she is probably the daughter of Gen. Edward Shriver, whom Shaw mentions in his letter to Josephine on Dec. 8, 1861.

Fairfax Station   [RGS]
Dec. 30, 1862
Dear Father,

Yours of the 22d reached me on Christmas day. I should have answered it before, but have been off towards Dumfries, to watch for some Rebel cavalry which you have perhaps heard came through here lately. I hope my long silence has not made you uneasy. Yours of the 26th, with the news of Theodore's death, I received this morning.[1] It took me entirely by surprise, and I think is the saddest death we have had yet. I don't know any one of all our friends and acquaintances, who have lost their sons, brothers, and husbands, who I think would feel it as much as Uncle John, Aunt Susan, and the girls.[2] How will they be able to bear it? Such a good son and brother as he was, and so loved and looked up to by them all. Last week Harry and I were saying, that we hoped that if any one in that regiment were killed, it wouldn't be Theodore; and this morning, ten minutes before I received your letter, I was lying on my blanket, thinking of a snipe-shooting excursion I made with him to Long Island one summer. I wish I had seen him after their return from Europe. I never knew a fellow like him for sticking to his principles. When we were in the Adirondack, it had rained so much that we had not had one shot, and when the sun shone for the first time it was Sunday, and we couldn't persuade Theodore to go out with us, although he probably cared more for the sport than any one of us.

The mail is going this moment, and I must close before I intended.

Affectionately,
R. G. S.

1. Shaw's first cousin Theodore Parkman (1837–62). Sturgis, *Sturgis*, p. 52.
2. Susan Parkman Sturgis (1810–69) married her first cousin John Parkman (?–1883) in 1835. They had one son and four daughters; two more children died in infancy. Theodore was the eldest child. Ibid., pp. 52–53.

Fairfax Station   [RGS]
Dec. 30, 1862
Dear Mother,

This morning I wrote a short note to Father, and having been "hauled up" very suddenly by departure of the mail, I didn't tell him that our sutler got the "Napier" and the cigars in Hagerstown, a few days ago.

I am very anxious to hear how Aunt Susan bears Theodore's death. What a terrible thing it must be for them! When I think what an affliction Susie's death was to her, it seems as if this would kill her.[1] Why should he be killed a month after leaving home, while I have been out for twenty months without a scratch? It must be all chance; for if he had lived, he would probably have done more good in the world than I ever shall.

The Rebel cavalry passed within three miles of here, while we were away, and we heard that all our luggage had been destroyed. They say that the Rebel commander telegraphed from the station below this to General Meigs, that *"The last lot of mules received from him wasn't quite up to the mark, and he would like to have him attend to it"*![2]

It was mild weather Christmas, so we could take our dinner out of doors without much discomfort. To-night it is cold and drizzly, but we have to take our supper out of doors just the same. We are fast putting up some log-huts, in which all hands will be comfortable, if we don't move before they are finished. One of our men has had his toes frostbitten, though we are in the "Sunny South."

Wasn't Burnside's report to the committee an honest account?[3] It doesn't give any one any great idea of his military ability, but he must be a real good man.

Isn't it strange that Joe and Theodore, both so near to us, should have been killed in battles in which the loss was so small compared to the numbers engaged?[4] At Fredericksburg there are so many slightly wounded, and so few killed, that I think the enemy must be reduced to buckshot. The proportion of killed to wounded is usually one to four. It was much less at Fredericksburg.

I suppose you saw Annie when she was in New York.[5] I have not heard from her for some time. Thank Susie for her comforting letter.[6]

Your loving Son

1. Shaw is probably referring to their third child Susan Parkman (1839–?). Sturgis, *Sturgis*, p. 52.

2. Montgomery Cunningham Meigs (1816–92) graduated from West Point in 1836. An engineer, Meigs supervised the building of the Washington, D.C., aqueduct, the wings and dome of the Capitol, and fortifications around Key West, Florida. On May 15, 1861, Lincoln commissioned Meigs a brigadier general to command the Union Quartermaster Corps, a position he held until 1882. *DAB*, vol. 6, pp. 507–8; Stewart Sifakis, *Who Was Who in the Civil War* (New York: Facts on File, 1988), pp. 442–43.

3. Five days after the Dec. 13 repulse at Fredericksburg, the Senate instructed the Committee on the Conduct of the War to investigate the action. Burnside testified on Dec. 23 that he had never believed himself competent to command so large an army but had obeyed orders after Lincoln and Stanton insisted he take the position. Burnside admitted that the attack had been ill-advised. *NYT*, Dec. 24 (1:1), 1862.

4. Joseph Bridgham Curtis and Theodore Parkman.

5. Annie Kneeland Haggerty.

6. Susanna Shaw was a close friend of Annie, who often stayed with her when she was in New York. Susie was in the position to inform Shaw of Annie's feelings toward acceptance or rejection.

Fairfax Station   [RGS]
Jan. 8, 1863
Dearest Mother,

On the outside of my last letter to you I mentioned having received yours enclosing one from Uncle Henry; we have had no letters for some time now; there is a hitch in the mail every little while.[1]

The other day I wrote to George, and spoke of what you wrote me about McClellan, in a way which I thought afterwards might look rude on paper. I didn't mean it so, and I wish you would tell him. It is astonishing how much the meaning of a sentence may be changed by the manner in which it is said, and consequently how a written sentence may be misunderstood.

We hear that Hooker will probably be made commander-in-chief before long. I believe he will be a failure too.[2] Though he got us so much glory at

Antietam, neither he nor his Corps were on the field after 8 1/2 A.M. We were under his command part of the time, or at least received orders from him, and they were thought to be pretty wild ones then. If we do change our commander again, and the new one doesn't do any better than his predecessors, I should think a crisis in our affairs might be expected. I hope the battle in the West may turn out to be as important as is supposed.[3]

We are all comfortably housed in log-huts, with brick fireplaces, and can laugh at the cold for the present. Harry and I are as cosey as possible in a house seven by six, with a tent for a roof. I feel almost as if I were at home, after the exposure and discomfort of the last three weeks. We may be ordered off at any moment though, so that we don't indulge in any hopes of escaping the frosts of January.

We have been reading "Bleak House," and I didn't remember how many beautiful things there were in it.[4] I am reading "Napier's Peninsular War" to myself, and it is really a classic work; I never knew before, either, what a man Sir John Moore was, nor was so impressed with Napoleon's military genius.[5] It is a great book, and a great many things in it apply to the conduct of our war. Speaking of one of Napoleon's letters to Joseph Bonaparte, he says: "Then followed an observation which may be studied with advantage by those authors who, unacquainted with the simplest rudiments of military science, censure the conduct of generals, and, from some obscure nook, are pleased to point out their errors to the world; authors who, profoundly ignorant of the numbers, situation, and resources of the opposing armies, pretend, nevertheless, to detail with great accuracy the right method of executing the most difficult and delicate operations of war."[6] The observation he refers to is: "But it is not permitted at the distance of three hundred leagues, without even a statement of the condition of the army, to direct what should be done." In another place, he says: "A ruinous defeat, the work of chance, often closes the career of the boldest and most sagacious of generals; and to judge of a commander's conduct by the event alone, is equally unjust and unphilosophical, a refuge for vanity and ignorance."

Did Father get my letter asking him to forward my coat lined with red flannel? If you have given it away, no matter. I can get along perfectly well without it, and if not, can get another from Baltimore. We have had some very warm woollen jackets issued to us lately, which are almost as good as an overcoat. Our men are all as well housed as the officers, each house having a fireplace in it. Give my love to Susie, and tell her not to nourish the hope that I can get away in February. I don't think there is any chance of it.

What a great year this is for the negroes and the country! I don't appreciate it at all times. If we get the Mississippi, it will make a great difference, I should think, in the spreading of the President's Proclamation. I read Mrs. Stowe's "Reply" in the January "Atlantic," and liked it very much.[7]

With love to Father, always your most

Affectionate Son

1. Henry Parkman Sturgis.

2. Lincoln replaced Burnside with Joseph Hooker on Jan. 26, 1863. Hooker would fail at Chancellorsville on May 1–3, 1863, and be replaced by George Gordon Meade just days before Gettysburg. Foote, *Civil War*, vol. 2, p. 131.

3. Shaw is probably either referring to the campaign to gain control of the Mississippi River or the recent battle in Tennessee. The armies of Braxton Bragg and William Rosecrans fought the Battle of Murfreesboro (Stone's River), Tennessee, on December 31–January 2, 1863. The battle was a draw, with each side losing nearly 12,000 casualties. Bragg

left the field first and Lincoln happily declared a victory. Ibid., pp. 79–103.

4. Charles Dickens's *Bleak House* (New York: Routledge, 1853).

5. Maj. Gen. Sir William F. P. Napier, *History of the War in the Peninsula and in the South of France from A.D. 1807 to A.D. 1814* (New York: W. J. Widdleton, 1862). British general Sir John Moore (1761–1809).

6. Joseph Bonaparte (1768–1844) was King of Naples and Spain.

7. Harriet Beecher Stowe, "Reply to the Address of the Women of England," *Atlantic Monthly* (Jan. 1863): 120–33.

Fairfax Station, Va.   [RGS]
Jan. 10, 1863
Dear Annie,

Your letter of the 5th inst., enclosing the vignette, came last night. At first I thought the latter was not good at all, but now I begin to like it, and am very glad indeed to have it. I have noticed that very often you must get acquainted with a portrait before you like it.

. . . .

I begin to think, Annie, that there will be enough fighting in the country to give us all plenty of occupation for the rest of our lives, even if they are not shortened by bullet or cannon-ball. If a peace is patched up with the South, I don't believe it can be a permanent one, and if the war goes on for another eighteen months, other nations are likely to be drawn into it. I hope I may be mistaken, for, though I don't think the soldiers are so much to be pitied as the fathers, mothers, wives, and sisters, who have to stay at home, there are few who are not heartily sick of the war. The anxiety some people must feel for their relatives in the army, is a great deal worse, I think, than anything we have to bear.

You asked me once if I knew why McClellan lay still after the battle of Antietam. We have never been able to discover why Lee was allowed to withdraw as he did. When we heard that he had gone, the day after the battle, we said it would ruin McClellan. After the Rebels got into Virginia, there were many good reasons given for not pursuing. We were not well supplied with ammunition (at least, I know that to have been the case in our Corps), our force was not so large as theirs, and our men were scattered by thousands from Frederick to Sharpsburg,—our troops always get scattered after a fight, and the new ones are much worse than the old. If a hard march precedes the battle, of course that adds to the number of stragglers. It may be true that McClellan is not rapid enough in carrying out his plans, but I wish he were in Halleck's place.[1]

I have read Cairne's book and Lecture. It is a pity they have not more such good and clear-headed men in England. I have just read "Gurowski's Diary."[2] It is very amusing, if no more, and no doubt there is much truth in it. The book I swear by now, is "Napier's Peninsular War." I have not read anything that has given me so much pleasure for a long while.

Did I tell you we were all comfortably hutted now? The men are all in log-shanties with fireplaces,—four men in a mess,—and the officers occupy palatial residences, seven or eight feet square, usually two in each. We can defy the weather, and if we are "let alone" for a time, we shall pass a comparatively pleasant winter.

I want to go home, I cannot tell you how much, in February, but I do not see any chance of it now.

Tell your mother not to trouble herself to answer my letter. I didn't expect an answer, as I knew she didn't write much.

Yours affectionately,
R. G. Shaw

P.S.—I wonder if you have received all my letters. Often I can only tell the date of yours by the postage-mark, for you give the day of the week merely.

1. General in Chief Henry W. Halleck.
2. Adam Gurowski (1805–66) immigrated to the United States from Poland and published a three-volume diary of his observations on American politics, personalities, and war tactics. Shaw read volume one, published in Boston by Lee and Shepard in 1862.

Washington, D.C.   [RGS]

Jan. 23, 1863

Dear Mother,

We arrived here at, or about 8 o'clock this morning, and find we can't get away until to-morrow morning.[1] We were an hour and a half too early last evening, as the train left at 7 1/2 instead of 6. It was provoking to find we might have spent the time at the house. If we had come in the 11 P.M. train, it would have been early enough, as we must remain here to-day.

What do you think was offered me this morning? A place as Aide on General Heintzleman's Staff, if I could get an order detailing me away from my Corps.[2] I don't know what I should do, if the order should make its appearance without any seeking; but I hate to take any steps to have myself detailed away from the regiment. I shouldn't think it wrong to do so, but a great many of our officers would; and it is very disagreeable to have men say that you are enjoying a pleasant position, by making their duty heavier. It would be a very pleasant change, and it is a very nice staff. Leo Hunt is Heintzleman's Assistant Adjutant-General; and Johnson, whom I knew very well in Boston, is one of his Aides.[3] It was the latter who made the proposal. I shall do nothing about it myself.

There are no sleeping cars from New York to Philadelphia; but I was so used up for want of rest, that I slept almost all the way. At Philadelphia we got a bunk, and I didn't wake up again until we arrived here.

If you have any talk with Annie, please find out whether she feels as I told you I thought she did, before you take anything for granted. This letter has been all about myself. Give my love to Father, Susie, and the girls, and tell George and Anna that I was very sorry not to see them and the babies again. With much love to yourself,

Your affectionate Son

1. Shaw split his ten-day furlough between Lenox and New York City. He departed New York on January 22. *Letters: RGS* (1864), p. 248.

2. Maj. Gen. Samuel Peter Heintzelman (1805–80), of Mannheim, Pennsylvania, a career soldier, succeeded Banks on Oct. 12, 1862, as commander of the defenses around Washington, D.C. Faust, *Encyclopedia*, p. 356.

3. Asst. Adj. Gen. Leo Hunt is otherwise unidentified. Johnson is unidentified.

Stafford C. H.   [RGS]
Jan. 25, 1863
Dear Annie,

I found your letter of the 14th here, last night, when we arrived. Please do not think of not sending me a letter, because you fancy it stupid; for they *always* give me a great deal of pleasure. Since I have been at home, I have begun to think that the war may very possibly come to a more sudden end than I have hitherto supposed, unless there is a great change in the feelings of the people. What I saw and heard in public conveyances and hotels surprised me very much; and one would think that the men who have remained quietly at their firesides were the principal sufferers, to judge from their complaints.

Morse and I left Washington yesterday morning, and came down to Aquia Landing by boat. There we took the train to Brooke's Station, which is three miles from here, and walked the rest of the way. The roads are in a condition which no one who has not seen them could imagine, and as it was quite dark we floundered about in the mud, in a very uncertain manner. We finally came across an officer, who directed us to our camp, and we got safely in about 8 P.M.

The corps had a very hard march down here;—while it was so cloudy and threatening at Lenox, it was raining hard here, and every one was soaked through and through for two or three days. The artillery had to throw away their ammunition, and the commissaries the rations, in order to get their waggons through the mud. As it was, many waggons were abandoned, and many mules were so hopelessly stuck in the mud, that they had to be left to end their days there. They sunk so deep in some places that only their heads could be seen,—so I am told, at least; but the story seems rather a startling one. The rate of marching was two to three miles a day; and the last day the men were without a morsel of food. You can imagine the difficulties of a winter campaign in Virginia.

In Washington, I heard, and you probably know by this time, that Burnside's move is entirely given up, the whole army having stuck in the mud.

Dear Annie, I have thought a great deal of you—indeed almost all the time since I left Lenox—and of my visit to you, especially the last part of it. O, dear! you don't know how much I should like to see you again!

Good night; with much love, your
Bob

Stafford CourtHouse Va.

January 25 1863

Dear Effie,

Your letter from Milton of Jan. 18 induces me to address myself to you this morning. I wrote to Father & Mother from Washington & hope they received my letters.

Morse & I left that town yesterday morning & came by boat to Aquia Cr. Landing. We arrived there about 1 P.M. and waited for a train until about 4— having got some bean (pebble) soup on board a canal boat for dinner. The cars took us to Brooke's Station about three miles from this camp, and from there we walked through the mud & darkness. After many inquiries & many unsatisfactory & often impertinent answers from individuals who had apparently been riled by having been asked similar questions from early dawn, we finally stumbled on C. Wheaton, Jr. the illustrious.[1] The sight of him calmed our ire, which was fast rising at hearing a man advise another (as we turned our backs) to tell the first person who asked him a question "to go to hell."

Wheaton directed us on our way and we soon arrived within sight of our camp-fires.

We find that we escaped the most miserable march the regiment ever made. The storm on Wednesday & Thursday was very severe and put the roads in such a condition that rations & ammunition had to be thrown away, many (even empty) wagons abandoned and mules left to die in mud holes. It rained hard for two days & on one of them the men went for nearly 24 hours without food. As I wrote Father, the movement of Burnside's Army has been entirely abandoned. They say the Rebels put out a large placard opposite Falmouth, saying: "Burnside stuck in the mud." "Shan't we come across & help you with your pontoons?" The letters were large enough to be easily read from our side.

I hope you wrote or will write to Annie H. as you intended to, and that you will get well acquainted with her when she comes down to stay with Susie. Tell her to stand straight. No you needn't say so from me. I don't feel certain that she considers the matter *entirely* settled.

They think here that the political troubles at home are going to finish the war before long. If we are not going to fight it out, the sooner it ends, the better. If we do make a peace now, we shall have to go at it again one of these days, I am sure, unless slavery dies out in the mean time.

The Paymaster came up with us, and we are going to receive four months' pay.

Did you go to tea at Col. Lowell's at last?

Give my love to Nellie. I am waiting to hear about the secret society.

Your loving brother
Rob

1. Charles Wheaton, Jr., the commissary officer of the Second Massachusetts Infantry.

CHAPTER 10

"I as a nigger colonel"

During the early months of 1863, with battlefield casualties rising, desertions increasing, and volunteering decreasing, Lincoln and Congress acted to secure men for the Union armies. On March 3, Congress passed the Enrollment Act, which authorized a draft of all men of ages twenty to forty-five to serve a three-year enlistment. That conscription act caused riots in Northern cities and was nearly as unpopular as the North's other new focus for soldier procurement.

In late January, Lincoln had authorized Secretary of War Edwin M. Stanton to enlist black men into volunteer regiments. Many people who supported the war for union lashed out at Lincoln for changing the goal of the war to one for freedom of the slaves. The idea of black men in uniforms with guns frightened some Northerners and most Southerners. Many white soldiers loathed the idea of serving with black soldiers. Nevertheless, Lincoln persisted with his plan. The first unit approved and organized in the North was the Fifty-fourth Massachusetts Volunteer Infantry. To command this vanguard regiment, Governor John A. Andrew handpicked a veteran soldier and son of a respected abolitionist family—Robert Gould Shaw.

Stafford Court-House, Va.

Feb. 4, 1863

My Dear Annie,

Your two letters, of the 25th and 29th of January, have reached me at last, and I was glad enough to get them. By this time you are on your way to New York, where you will find my last letter. I sent it to Father, thinking that you were going to Susie's.

I did not read General Hitchcock's testimony in McDowell's case.[1] Holt's summing up of the testimony for and against Porter, seemed to me very poor, for a man of his ability; and if I could persuade myself that the court (composed as it was, of officers of honourable standing) could be dishonest, I should think there had been foul play.[2] Several officers have been dismissed for uttering the like sentiments; so I think I had better keep my opinion to myself. I was much surprised to hear, the other day, from a regular officer in Porter's Corps, that, though they considered the latter a fine officer, he was not personally liked. I have hitherto heard just the contrary.

We are tolerably comfortable here now, as our log-huts are going up again, and we have come across a sutler who furnishes the officers with means to keep a very good mess.

Father has just left here. He came down yesterday, and brought me an offer from Governor Andrew of the Colonelcy of his new black regiment.[3] The Governor considers it a most important command; and I could not help feeling, from the tone of his letter, that he did me a great honour in offering it to me. My Father will tell you some of the reasons why I thought I ought not to accept it. If I had taken it, it would only have been from a sense of duty; for it would have been anything but an agreeable task. Please tell me, without reserve, what you think about it; for I am very anxious to know. I should have decided much sooner than I did, if I had known before. I am afraid Mother will think I am shirking my duty; but I had some good practical reasons for it, besides the desire to be at liberty to decide what to do when my three years have expired.[4]

You asked me in one of your letters whether I was a Unitarian. Since I have been old enough to think for myself, I have considered I had better not try to decide about sects. I always like to go to church, and I like to hear a good sermon, whether it is preached in an Episcopal or a Methodist church. The only Sunday school I ever went to, was Episcopal, and I have been to the Unitarian church less than to any other. While I am on this subject, I must remind you of the Bible you are going to send me.

I like the name Robert much better than Bob, and shall be very glad to have you call me so. Father, Mother, and Effie always call me "Rob," which slight change of a letter makes a great difference in the name.

There does not seem to be much enthusiasm for Hooker. The cry in the army is still for McClellan. I wonder whether he will ever get his old command again! I don't think he is doing himself any good by having public receptions in Boston.

The hills about Lenox would be a very welcome sight to me, whether they were covered with snow, with grass, or with nothing at all; though just now, I had rather be in New York. I want to see you *horribly* (that is the only word I can think of for it), but I have to console myself by looking at the vignette.

Did you manage to have some work done on the place before you left?

Our chaplain is an "Orthodox" clergyman, and is much superior to most in the army, I think, though he does get into very lazy habits.[5] Camp life gives no incentive to activity or energy.

I have about a dozen acquaintances in the South. Most of them classmates of mine, with a few of whom I was on most intimate terms. Two of them were captured in North Carolina by another classmate, a captain in the Forty-fourth Massachusetts. He invited them to dinner, and after having had a jolly time together, they were paroled and sent home. We heard, from some prisoners taken at Antietam, that some of our friends were in a regiment that was opposed to ours in that battle. I don't think I know any one in Richmond.

Being officer of the day, to-day, and having several little affairs to attend to in consequence, I must close. So good-bye, dear Annie, with a great deal of love.

Your affectionate Rob

P.S.—Do you know of a woman in Lenox named McDonald?[6] Whether she is very poor, or anything about her? Her son is in my company, and is always getting punished; but when the men's families are poor we do not like to cut down their pay, which is the most effectual punishment.

---

1. Gen. Ethan Allen Hitchcock (1798–1870) graduated from West Point in 1817 and resigned from the military to become a writer. In February 1862, Lincoln appointed Hitchcock as a major general and asked him to replace McClellan. Instead, Hitchcock accepted the post as director of prisoner exchange. After the defeat at Second Bull Run, army offi-cers pointed fingers blaming others for the loss. McClellan accused Pope of poor generalship, and rumors spread that McDowell was a traitor. In the forty-fifth day of inquiry into charges of treason against McDowell, Hitchcock testified on McDowell's behalf. McDowell was innocent of the charges against him, but Lincoln relieved him of command and

had him reassigned to California. Faust, *Encyclopedia*, p. 363; *NYT*, Jan. 20 (2:1), 1863; McPherson, *Battle Cry*, p. 532–33.

2. Joseph Holt (1807–94) was a Kentucky lawyer who became U.S. postmaster general and secretary of war under Buchanan. On Sept. 3, 1862, Lincoln appointed him judge advocate general of the army. His most famous case was the prosecution of Clement Vallandigham, a leading Copperhead. Gen. Fitz John Porter (1822–1901) graduated from West Point in 1845, served in the Mexican War, and became one of McClellan's closest friends and supporters. Porter disliked Pope, and vice versa. When Pope lost at Second Bull Run, he blamed Porter for not following orders and thus, causing the defeat. A court martial, with Holt prosecuting, found Porter guilty and revoked his commission on Jan. 21, 1863. Porter argued that he couldn't obey the order to strike Jackson's flank because Longstreet had moved into position next to Jackson

making no flank available. In 1886, a court of appeals reversed the decision against Porter. Faust, *Encyclopedia*, pp. 366, 594; McPherson, *Battle Cry*, p. 529.

3. John Albion Andrew (1818–67) was born in Maine, attended Bowdoin College, and set up a law practice in Boston. After Lincoln issued the Emancipation Proclamation, Andrew agitated until Edwin M. Stanton approved Andrew's requests to recruit a black regiment, the Fifty-fourth Massachusetts Infantry. The best source on Andrew is still Henry G. Pearson, *The Life of John A. Andrew, Governor of Massachusetts, 1861–1865* (Boston: Houghton Mifflin, 1904).

4. The Second Massachusetts Infantry was composed of three-year men. Those like Shaw who joined in May 1861 would complete their service obligation in May 1864.

5. Chaplain Alonzo H. Quint.

6. McDonald is unidentified.

Stafford C. H., Va.   [RGS]
Feb. 8, 1863
Dear Annie,

You know by this time, perhaps, that I have changed my mind about the black regiment. After Father left, I began to think I had made a mistake in refusing Governor Andrew's offer. Mother has telegraphed to me that you would not disapprove of it, and that makes me feel much more easy about having taken it. Going for another three years is not nearly so bad a thing for a colonel as a captain; as the former can much more easily get a furlough. Then, after I have undertaken this work, I shall feel that what I have to do is to prove that a negro can be made a good soldier, and, that being established, it will not be a point of honour with me to see the war through, unless I really occupied a position of importance in the army. Hundreds of men might leave the army, you know, without injuring the service in the slightest degree.

Last night I received your letter of last Sunday, February 1st. You must be at Susie's house now,—at least I judge so from Mother's telegram. As I may not receive my order to leave here for some days, do promise to stay there until I get to New York. You do not know how I shall feel if I find you are gone.

It is needless for me to overwhelm you with a quantity of arguments in favour of the negro troops; because you are with Mother, the warmest advocate the cause can have. I am inclined to think that the undertaking will not meet with so much opposition as was at first supposed. All sensible men in the army, of all parties, after a little thought, say that it is the best thing that can be done; and surely those at home, who are not brave or patriotic enough to enlist, should not ridicule, or throw obstacles in the way of men who are going to fight for them. There is a great prejudice against it; but now that it has become a government matter, that will probably wear away. At any rate, I shan't be frightened out of it by its unpopularity; and I hope you won't care if it is made fun of.

Dear Annie, the first thing I thought of, in connection with it, was how you would feel, and I trust, now I have taken hold of it, I shall find you agree with me and all of our family, in thinking I was right. You know how many eminent men consider a negro army of the greatest importance to our country at this time. If it turns out to be so, how fully repaid the pioneers in the movement will be, for what they may have to go through! And at any rate I feel convinced I shall never regret having taken this step, as far as I myself am concerned; for while I was undecided I felt ashamed of myself, as if I were cowardly.

Good bye, dear Annie. I hope that when I arrive at Sue's door you will not be very far off.

With a great deal of love, (more every day) your

Rob

Stafford Court-House, Va. [RGS]
Feb. 8, 1863
Dear Father,

Yours from Willard's, enclosing Mother's and Effie's, was received to-day.[1] Please tell Nellie I received hers of 17th January last night.

I telegraphed you yesterday that I couldn't get away from here without an order or furlough. It will have to come from Hooker or the War Department, and the Governor will have to get it for me. He knows what is needful, though, for he procured the necessary papers when Harry and I went home.

If I have to wait some time, don't let Annie go away until I get to New York, will you?[2]

Tell Mother I have not wavered at all, since my final decision. I feel that if we can get the men, all will go right.

With love to all,

Your affectionate son,
Robert G. Shaw

1. Willard's Hotel in Washington, D.C., located two blocks east of the White House, was the city's chief meeting and lobbying center. There the richest Americans mingled with the country's politicians and military leadership. Leech, *Reveille in Washington*, pp.

8–9.

2. A note at the bottom of the letter, edited in 1864, explained, "He reached New York on the 11th, and left for Boston on the 14th, to undertake the organization of the new regiment." *Letters: RGS* (1864), p. 259.

Boston   [RGS]
Feb. 16, 1863, Monday
Dearest Annie,

I arrived here yesterday morning, after a very uncomfortable night in the sleeping-car.

I have been at work all day, looking over papers with Hallowell, and talking with Governor Andrew.[1] We have decided to go into camp at Readville, and not at Worcester. It is near enough to Boston to make the transportation of supplies an easy matter, and we see no reason to apprehend any trouble from the white soldiers stationed there.[2]

Now that it is decided that coloured troops shall be raised, people seem to look upon it as a matter of course, and I have seen no one who has not expressed the kindest wishes for the success of the project.

Governor Andrew's ideas please me extremely, for he takes the most common-sense view of the thing. He seems inclined to have me do just what I please.

With much affection, your
Rob

P.S.—Our recruiting is getting along well.

1. Governor Andrew selected Capt. Norwood P. Hallowell of the Twentieth Massachusetts Infantry to be lieutenant

colonel and second in command of the Fifty-fourth Massachusetts.

2. The Second Massachusetts Cavalry,

under the command of Shaw's friend and future brother-in-law Charles Russell Lowell, was the only other regiment in camp at Camp Meigs, Readville.

Boston   [RGS]
Feb. 16, 1863
Dear Father,

I arrived here yesterday morning. Things are going along very well, and I think there is no doubt of our ultimate success.

I took a long drive with the Governor, and liked him very much. His views about the regiment are just what I should wish. We have decided to go into camp at Readville; as we think it best to plunge in without regard to outsiders. We shall have to do it some time, and it is best to begin immediately; I do not apprehend any trouble out there.

We have a great deal of work before us, but every one seems anxious to give us a helping hand, and applications for commissions come in, in shoals. The more money we can get, the better; the transportation of men from other States will cost a great deal.

I will write to Mother soon.

In haste,
Your affectionate Son

Boston   [RGS]
Feb. 18, 1863
Dear Father,

Will you please inquire of Judge Emerson where his son Charles is to be found, and whether he would take a First Lieutenancy in the coloured regiment.[1] I liked what I saw of him at college very much, and am very anxious to get hold of him. I am occupied all the time. Things look very encouraging.

Love to Mother.

Affectionately, your son,
Robert G. Shaw

1. Judge William Emerson (1801–68), the older brother of Ralph Waldo Emerson, lived on Staten Island for twenty-seven years, 1837–64. He served as county judge (1841–43). Milne, *Curtis*, p. 131; Leng and Davis, *Staten Island*, vol. 2, pp. 552, 810, 894. Charles Emerson, son of Judge Emerson, left Harvard in 1862 to drill with the Seventh New York Militia. Charles transferred

to the 174th New York Infantry (re-numbered the 162nd N.Y.) in Oct. 1862 and remained with it until his dis-charge on May 21, 1865. Brown, "Roll of Students," p. 28.

February 18, 1863   [RGS]
My Dear Annie,

Yours of Monday I received this morning. . . .

Last night I was at Milton Hill.[1] Miss Sedgwick (Aunt Kitty) came over.[2] She talked about you, and told me how much she loved your mother, and you and Clem.[3] I thought her a very charming person. Cousin Sarah was very kind and sympathizing; she wants to see you very much, and you will have to come here some time.[4] I have not seen Aunt Cora, as she was ill when I went there.[5]

Do write to me often, Annie dear, for I need a word occasionally from those whom I love, to keep up my courage. Whatever you write about, your letters always make me feel well; and I have enough discouraging work before me to make me feel gloomy.

Always, with great love,

Yours,
Rob

1. John Murray Forbes served on the governor's select committee, the Black committee, which sought money and re-cruits for the Fifty-fourth. Forbes named his home in Milton, "Milton Hill."

2. Miss Sedgwick is unidenti-fied, but she is most likely related to

Charles, Catherine, and Willie Sedgwick of Lenox.

3. Clemence Haggerty.

4. Sarah Forbes, wife of John Murray Forbes.

5. Aunt Cora is unidentified.

Boston   [HL, RGS]
Feby 20 1863
Dear Mother,

You have probably been looking for a letter from me for some days, but I have had so much to do that I couldn't write.

My interviews with the Govr have been very satisfactory—and we are get-ting along better than I expected we should.

Cousin John helps us along a great deal with his advice—he has thought of several men for officers who I think will be the best we shall get. After discussing their characters, he will say "now, does any one know whether he has enough nigger to him?" or "are his heels long eno' for this work?"[1] He is very funny.

Evening Your letter enclosing Mrs. Schuyler's & Mr. Ward's notes came this afternoon.[2] Please thank them both when you see them.

There was a meeting of the committee for the Col'd regt today and money was appropriated to aid enlistments in various places.[3] We have got the camp going and shall send some men out tomorrow.

At the meeting Richard Hallowell said it would please the coloured population to have some influential darkey on the committee—and Cousin John told him he would like to take in a nigger and turn him (H.) out, which naturally caused some merriment.[4] I didn't see the Governor's mouth twitch, and I like him more every day. He is not only a liberal minded philanthropist, but a man of real practical good-sense, I think—and as kind-hearted as he can be.

Some of the influential coloured men I have met please me very much. They are really so gentlemanlike & dignified.[5]

Please tell Father that I have been requested by the committee to ask him to find some responsible & respectable coloured men, who can help enlistments in New York & Brooklyn.[6] As soon as he will notify me of his having met some such person or persons I will send him some tickets for their transportation to Massachusetts. They should be ascertained to be physically sound before being sent—and there should be no noise made about it, as N.Y. authorities might object to our taking them from there. No recruiting office should be opened.

I shall write to you as often as ever dearest Mother, as I don't intend to abandon you entirely for Annie, as you seem to think. Just now while I am so much engaged, my letters may be a little less frequent.

Ever your loving son,
Robert G. Shaw

Said nothing to C.S.[7] The passage of the conscription act makes the raising of coloured troops less important, I think.[8] I have received many notes of congratulation both on my engagement & my having taken the Regt. I have just been reading all the letters rec'd by Jim Savage's family concerning him, and my head is full of those Cedar Mt. & Rappahannock days. Sad ones they were.

[from RGS; but not in HL]

I spent last evening with Aunt Susan and family.[9] It was very sad; they talked of Theodore a great deal, and seemed to find great comfort in it.[10] They all bear the loss like true Christians; and when I think what a terrible blow it is to them, I cannot admire them sufficiently. The girls seemed lovely in their gentleness, and sweet way of speaking of Theodore. Uncle John is cheerful too; probably from feeling how much Aunt Susan has need of all the consolation he can give her. It is an immense comfort to them to talk of and remember Theodore's beautiful and pure character. I shall go there again soon. They thought I had done a great thing in taking the Fifty-fourth Massachusetts. About this, I have had only good words from friends and foes of the project. As you say, the result is sure to be good when a man takes a firm stand for what he thinks is the right. Annie Agassiz, the Professor, and all the family, as well as many others, made the most complimentary remarks.[11] I have spoken so much of this, not from egotism, but because the kindness of every one I have met, has made a great impression upon me. Tell Father, Homans has a Second Lieutenancy in my regiment.[12]

Your loving son

1. Historian Joseph Glatthaar found that even the most sympathetic whites made racist jokes stereotyping the physical differences of the races. Glatthaar, *Forged in Battle*, pp. 86–87.

2. The Schuylers and Wards lived on Staten Island near the Shaws.

3. Originally made up of ten prominent men, the Black committee soon expanded to include over one hundred members. It raised $100,000 and advertised for recruits in over a hundred Northern papers. Unfortunately, the papers of this committee were destroyed in a Boston fire. Smith, *Beacon Hill's*, pp. 397–400.

4. Richard Price Hallowell (1835–1904), brother of Norwood P. Hallowell, was a Philadelphia Quaker and Boston wool merchant. He married the granddaughter of James and Lucretia Mott, the famous antislavery advocates. After John Brown's execution, Hallowell went to Virginia and took Brown's body North. He served as treasurer for the black committee. After the war, Hallowell donated time and money to help educate blacks. *DAB*, vol. 4, p. 160.

5. It is important for Shaw's development to notice his word selection. Here he calls black leaders "gentlemanlike"; but he has yet to admit that they are men, gentlemen. Until February 1863, Shaw had never associated with black people and he still had prejudices against them.

6. Francis George Shaw oversaw black committee affairs in New York.

7. C. S. is unidentified.

8. By the date of this letter, only the Senate had passed the Conscription Act. Enacted on March 3, the Conscription Act seemed the only way to replenish the army with bodies. Volunteering was at a standstill and besides those men lost in battle, many soldiers's terms would soon expire. Refusing to lose the war due to lack of men, the government instituted a draft of men aged twenty to forty-five. To protect those of its own class, Congress allowed the wealthy to pay a fee to avoid the draft; or a man could hire a substitute to serve for him. Shaw's prediction that this act would

solve the North's manpower problem proved wrong. Lincoln used the act four times to call for troops—in all, 776,000 men. But with many fleeing to Canada to avoid the call, with others gaining exemptions for physical disabilities or hardship, and with many more paying a commutation fee or hiring a substitute, only six percent of draftees actually went into the army. Still, we do not know how many men enlisted to avoid being drafted. Shaw's appraisal that the draft now made it less important to raise black regiments indicates how far apart he stood from committed egalitarians. Frederick Douglass and others knew that the way to citizenship and freedom lay through putting black men in blue uniforms and having them spill red blood for their country. Shaw never seemed to understand that or never cared to. McPherson, *Battle Cry*, pp. 600–604.

9. Susan and John Parkman.

10. Theodore Parkman.

11. Annie Russell Agassiz and her father-in-law Professor Louis Agassiz.

12. William Henry Homans (1840–93), a clerk from Augusta, Maine, joined the First Massachusetts Infantry as a corporal on May 24, 1861. He transferred to the Fifty-fourth on Feb. 19, 1863. Emilio, *A Brave Black Regiment*, pp. 332–33.

Boston   [LYM]
February 20, 1863
Dear Mimi,[1]

You will be astonished to hear, I suppose, (unless some one has mentioned it already) that I am engaged to Miss Annie Haggerty. Perhaps you remember that two years ago I told you she would be my "young woman" some time.

Harry and I keep along pretty well together, don't we?[2] And we are both so unfortunate, as to have the prospect of being dragged off again to the tented field, when we want most horribly to stay at home. We are at home now together, he as Lieut. Col. of the 2d Mass. Cavalry, and I as a Nigger Col., for Gov. Andrew has given me the command of his black regiment.

The conscription bill has passed so I advise Theodore not to come home, lest he be drafted.[3] Tell him I will give him a position as chaplain if he would like to go into a good nigger concern.

I hope, dear Mimi, you and he and the baby are well, and are having a pleasant time. It seems as if we were to have continual war in this country. I pray God it may not be so, for there has been enough blood shed to atone for a great many sins.

Since I have been at home the misery and unhappiness caused by this war have struck me more forcibly than ever—for in active service one gets accustomed to think very lightly of such things. Last evening I went to see the

Parkmans, and the way in which they bear Theodore's loss is beautiful. You know how devoted they all were to him, and what a terrible blow his death must have been—and there are thousands of such cases on both sides.

Give my love to Theodore. I hope we shall see you safe at home before long—before Harry and I go off again. All are well here.

Always your affectionate Cousin,
Robert G. Shaw

1. Elizabeth Russell Lyman.
2. Mimi's brother, Harry S. Russell.
3. Mimi's husband, Theodore Lyman.

Boston   [MHS]
February 21, 1863
My dear Charley,[1]

Your letter with enclosures reached me yesterday. I am much obliged to you for attending to those matters. Do I owe you anything? Please let me know as soon as possible. I think Johnson's bill was a little more than I supposed.[2]

Perhaps you know by this time, that my engagement is out. I had a nice time for four days in New York as Miss H. was staying at my sister's.[3]

Harry Russell looks more cheerful & happy than I ever saw him—and Miss Forbes likewise. They are about as devoted a couple as I ever saw.[4]

The darky concern is getting along very well. We are going into camp at Readeville. Sent 25 men out this morning & hope soon to have things entrain. The State House people give us every assistance in their power. The Somerset Club crowd are down on us, but nevertheless I had an invitation to go there whenever I wished.[5] I hear there was a little row about it at first.

Please ask Coughlin, when he goes to Washington to get a package from Adams for me, and send it to 44 Beacon St., Boston.[6] It is something which I should be very sorry to lose.

Henry Higginson has been here for a week.[7] Give my love to Greely & if you see B. Adams tell him that I received his letter and that it gave me a great deal of pleasure.[8]

I suppose Brown & Fox are back by this time.[9] Give my love to Tom Robeson & Grafton.[10] Charley Horton & I dine with Bangs today en famille.[11]

Good-bye my dear Charley. I hope you will enjoy your Provost Martial duties.

Affectionately Yours,
Robert G. Shaw

1. Charles Fessenden Morse.

2. Johnson is unidentified.

3. Annie Haggerty often stayed with Susie Shaw Minturn.

4. Harry Russell was engaged to Mary Hathaway Forbes, daughter of John M. Forbes. After the war, Harry became a partner in J. M. Forbes and Company, China merchants. *Harvard College: Report of the Class of 1860*, pp. 44–45.

5. The Somerset Club, one of Boston's most exclusive clubs, became a haven for Democrats during the war who were among the most influential voices against black troops. Many members disagreed with club leadership and walked out to join the rival Union Club.

6. Coughlin is unidentified. The Adams Express Company. Shaw's aunt, Mary Louisa Sturgis Shaw, and her daughter Louisa lived at 44 Beacon Street.

7. Henry Lee Higginson had been a lieutenant in the Second Massachusetts, May–Oct. 1861, when he transferred to a captaincy in the First Massachusetts Cavalry. *Rec. of Mass. Vols.*, pp. 28, 29.

8. Lt. Col. Greely S. Curtis of the First Massachusetts Cavalry. B. Adams is unidentified.

9. Probably Capt. Robert B. Brown and either Thomas B. Fox or John A. Fox of the Second Massachusetts Infantry. *Rec. of Mass. Vols.*, p. 28.

10. Capt. Thomas Rodman Robeson and Capt. James Ingersoll Grafton (1841–65) of Boston, both of the Second Massachusetts Infantry. Higginson, *Harvard Memorial Biographies*, vol. 2, pp. 270–74.

11. Capt. Charles P. Horton (1836–?) and Capt. George P. Bangs, both of Boston and the Second Massachusetts Infantry. *Rec. of Mass. Vols.*, pp. 28, 29.

CHAPTER 11

"The camp at Readville"

Oh! Standing on this desecrated mould,
Methinks that I behold,
Lifting her bloody daisies up to God,
Spring kneeling on the sod,

And calling with the voice of all her rills
Upon the ancient hills,
To fall and crush the tyrants and the slaves
Who turn her meads to graves.
—Henry Timrod, "Spring," 1863

The war was moving in slow motion as armies on both sides readied themselves for the spring campaigns. During the war, springtime forsook its normal meaning as a time of rejoicing, new birth, and life to become a time of fear, sorrow, and dying. Meadows became battlefields; streams and woods swallowed up soldiers and became gravesites. But in late winter 1863 in Massachusetts, a regiment trained that promised to turn springtime back into a time of new birth. Black "boys" were going to have the chance to prove themselves "men" by donning blue uniforms and fighting Confederates.

Boston

Feb. 23, (Monday) 1863

Dearest Annie,

We have opened the camp at Readville, got the barracks in good order, and sent twenty-seven men out there. I have a good quartermaster, who has got all the necessary stores out there, and seems to be attending to his business in the most satisfactory manner.[1]

Captain Edward Hallowell, a brother of the Lieutenant-Colonel, is in command of the camp.[2] Day before yesterday he had the men all washed and uniformed, which pleased them amazingly. They are being drilled as much as is possible in-doors, for it is too cold out there to keep them in the open air for any length of time. These twenty-seven men are all from Philadelphia and Boston.

From other recruiting-offices we hear very good accounts, and the men seem to be enlisting quite fast.[3] Governor Sprague has authorized a recruiting-office to be opened in Providence for this regiment.[4] We have an officer at Fortress Monroe, but he has to be very secret about his work; and to-day three men are going on a campaign into Canada.[5] By these different means we expect, or rather hope, to fill our ranks pretty rapidly. We are getting men from Pennsylvania, New York, Maine, Rhode Island, and Connecticut. So far, they are not of the best class, because the good ones are loath to leave their families, while there is a hope of getting a bounty later. Now, they receive only the $100 from the Federal government at the expiration of their term of enlistment.

Hallowell and I get along together in the pleasantest way.[6]

I like Governor Andrew more and more every day. As Charles Lowell says: "It was worth while to come home, if it were only to get acquainted with him."

. . . All my mornings are spent in the State-House; and as in-door, furnace-heated work does not agree with me, I shall get out to Readville as soon as possible.

Good bye for the present, my darling.

Always your loving Rob

1. First Lt. John Ritchie (1836–1919), of Boston and the Harvard class of 1861, joined the Fifty-fourth on Feb. 19, 1863. Shaw appointed him quartermaster the next day. Emilio, *A Brave Black Regiment*, p. 330; *Rec. of Mass. Vols.*, p. 847.

2. Edward Needles Hallowell (1837–71) served as an aide-de-camp to General Frémont in Missouri in 1861 and was a first lieutenant in the Twentieth Massachusetts before accepting Governor Andrew's invitation to join the Fifty-

fourth. Boatner, *Dictionary*, p. 367.

3. Camp opened at Readville for the Fifty-fourth on Feb. 21. By the end of the first week, seventy-two men were in camp. For the eighty days until May 12, when the regiment had its one thousand men, an average of twelve men a day re-

moved their civilian clothes for the blue uniforms of the Union. Schouler, *Report of the Adjutant General*, pp. 899–900.

4. William Sprague.

5. The officer at Fortress Monroe is unidentified.

6. Norwood Penrose Hallowell.

Boston   [MHS]
February 24, 1863
My dear Charley,

I thought I would write to you again this morning to tell you what Lowell says of the battle of Antietam. Hooker's & Mansfield's attack on the right was intended only for a feint—and Burnside's was to have been the true attack— which would have cut off their retreat to the Fords & driven them into the river or obliged them to make a flank march by the Hagerstown road in the face of Hooker's & Mansfield's Corps.[1]

Hooker got so sharply engaged that Sumner had to be sent to his support, instead of being held for a grand attack on the centre—and Burnside, as you know, did not do his work. This gives me a different idea of the battle from what I had before, and explains its plan.

Perhaps you already knew these facts. I was at a small party last night, where I saw Henry Hig.[2] He goes away today and is very melancholy at the idea.

Charley Horton is still on the town—but goes in a few days.[3] I saw him yesterday on his way to a reception at Mrs. H. G. Otis', with sash & belt & head well over to the right.[4]

We have got 30 men out at Readeville—all washed & uniformed. They feel as big as all creation—and really look very well. We expect a good many from New York & Philadelphia, and shall know soon how many we can expect from Canada & Fortress Monroe.

The thing is getting along very nicely. With [love] to the fellows.

Your affectionate friend,
Robert G. Shaw

1. Lowell seems to be mistaken. Actually, Burnside had the secondary role of creating a diversion on the left while the main attack came on the right. Mansfield, Hooker, and Sumner, in

uncoordinated assaults, hit Lee's army before Burnside could get across a bridge—later called Burnside Bridge. Lee skillfully shifted his men and awaited the arrival of A. P. Hill's division to force an inconclusive result at Antietam. McPherson, *Battle Cry*, p. 539.

2. Maj. Henry Lee Higginson of the First Massachusetts Cavalry.

3. Charles P. Horton.

4. Eliza Henderson Boardman Otis was one of Boston's leading philanthropists.

Boston   [RGS]
Feb. 24, 1863
Dear Father,

The regimental committee here have engaged a coloured man, named W. Wells Brown, to go to New York and help along the enlistments there.[1] He will call at your office immediately after his arrival. Mr. Hallowell thinks that he and Givens had better enroll as many men as they can, and that you had better buy tickets in New York for their transportation.[2] The only bounty they will receive is $100 from the United States at the expiration of their time of service. The pay is $13 per month, the same our white soldiers receive.

You can probably make an arrangement with the Stonington Line to pay the men's passage to Readville, and let them out there.[3] Mr. Hallowell wants you to pay everything, and send the accounts to him for reimbursement. Can't you engage some surgeon to examine them before they start, so that we need not be under the necessity of sending any back? Telegraph to Mr. Hallowell, 98 Federal Street, when a squad is shipped, the time of their departure, and their number. I suppose it had better be done as quietly as possible. Our agents start for Canada to-morrow.

The want of State aid for the men's families will be a great drawback to their enlistment in other States. Only Massachusetts men can get it.[4] Mr. Hallowell will answer your letter to him. I have not received the one you mention having written to me.

Love to Mother and the girls.

Your affectionate son,
Robert G. Shaw

1. William Wells Brown (1814–84) escaped from slavery in 1834, settled in Ohio, and became one of the most active abolitionists. After the war, Brown became a physician and wrote a dozen books, including *The Negro in the American Rebellion: His Heroism and His Fidelity* (Boston: Lee & Shepard, 1867).

Unfortunately, Brown's account tells little of what recruiting entailed. Logan and Winston, *Dictionary of American Negro Biography*, pp. 71–73.

2. Richard Price Hallowell. Givens, a black recruiter, is unidentified.

3. The Stonington Line Railroad connected New York City to Boston

through Providence, Rhode Island. The first track connecting Stonington to the existing Providence-Boston line was completed in 1837. Balthasar H. Meyer, *History of Transportation in the United States before 1860* (Cambridge: Peter Smith, 1948), pp. 323, 577.

4. While no state bounty was offered to get men to enlist, after the regiment filled, the Massachusetts legislature voted a bounty of $50 to be paid to each enlistee. Few cities paid bounties, even though local citizens often formed soldier's fund committees to help spur recruiting and to help families left behind. In New Bedford, volunteers who passed a medical inspection got a $10 bounty; by Feb. 16, thirty-five had been enrolled and paid. Massachusetts did provide aid for families of married men from the state, once those men were mustered into a unit. Again, some localities also gave aid to families. New Bedford soldiers' dependents received one dollar a week apiece, limited to a total of $12 per month per soldier. Schouler, *Report of the Adjutant General*, p. 900; Scrapbook of Congdon, Soldier's Fund Committee, NBFPL.

Readville   [RGS]
Feb. 25, 1863
Dear Effie,

I got your Sunday's letter last night. I have not seen Colonel Lowell since, but will deliver your message at first opportunity.

We have forty Darks out here now, and expect some more from New York and New Bedford in a day or two. When I hear from Providence, Fortress Monroe, and Canada, I shall be able to tell how rapidly the regiment will be likely to fill up. I am not staying out here yet, but shall probably take up my quarters here, in ten days or a fortnight.

Loulie has shown me several of Nellie's letters.[1] What good ones she writes.

I am sorry you don't see anything of Annie. I shall try to go on to New York on the 6th of March, and spend Saturday and Sunday at Susie's.

I spent last Sunday at Milton Hill with Henry Higginson and Charles Lowell. Monday evening, there was a small party at Clover Hooper's, where I had a very pleasant time indeed, with Miss Ida, Miss Heath, &c.[2]

To-morrow evening, I am going to see old Mr. Quincy; he sent me word he should like to see me; the next evening, to the Sedgwicks in Cambridge.[3] I have been somewhere almost every night.

Love to all.

Your loving Brother

1. Mary Louisa Shaw.
2. Marian "Clover" Hooper
(1843–85), one of Shaw's cousins, married Henry Adams in 1872. Ward

Thoron, ed., *The Letters of Mrs. Henry Adams, 1865–1883* (Boston: Little, Brown, 1936), pp. xiii, 465. Ida Agassiz, daughter of Professor Louis Agassiz, married Henry Lee Higginson on Dec. 5, 1863. Crawford, *Famous Families*, vol. 1, pp. 219, 225, 254. Miss Heath is unidentified.

3. Josiah Quincy (1772–1864) was a former mayor of Boston (1823–28) and president of Harvard (1829–45). *DAB*, vol. 8, pp. 308–11. Perhaps Shaw is referring to the home of Henry Dwight Sedgwick, a prominent Boston abolitionist. Crawford, *Famous Families*, vol. 2, pp. 288–89.

Readville   [HL]
Feb. 25 1863
Dear Father,

I forgot to mention yesterday that a man is entitled to $2.00 per head for sound recruits sent to camp.[1]

We have got our barracks all in order here, and can accommodate all the men that come now. I hope you will be able to send us some, before many days.

We have 40 here already and they look remarkably well in their uniforms. They are not of the best class of nigs—and if it weren't for the want of state aid we should be able to get a much better set from the other states.[2]

If you have any difficulty about making the arrangements I spoke of in my yesterday's note, I wish you would let me know. Perhaps you can find a better man than Givens to do the work, and I think it would be well to get some white man who would interest himself in superintending the recruiting & take it off your hands. Doesn't Mr. Gay know some one who would like a commission in the Regt & would be a good man to look after matters in N.Y.[3]

Your loving son
R. G. S.

1. Massachusetts paid recruiting officers two dollars for each recruit mustered into a Massachusetts unit. This incentive caused many recruiters to beat the bushes for volunteers, sometimes going to extremes to sign up any and every available body. While payment depended upon the recruit's passing a physical inspection, recruiters sent along anyone who could walk and

thus caused the state excessive costs in transporting unacceptable individuals to and from camps. R. P. Hallowell to James Bunker Congdon, Mar. 3, 1863, Congdon Scrapbook, NBFPL.

2. In *Letters: RGS* (1864), an editor, probably Shaw's mother, made two important deletions to what Shaw had written. This sentence about the men not being "the best class of nigs" is impor-

tant for understanding Shaw's mindset at the beginning of camp. Two sentences later, where Shaw wrote "get some white man," his 1864 editor left out the words "white man" and inserted the word

"one." Givens's name is also deleted from the printed version. *Letters: RGS* (1864), p. 267.

3. Sydney Howard Gay.

Boston [RGS]
March 3, 1863
My Dearest Annie,

To-day I received your letter of the 1st of March, from Astoria, and was delighted to hear you were having such a nice, quiet time.

It hardly seems possible that those three weeks are nearly over, which we, or I, looked forward to with dread.[1]

Next Saturday morning I shall find you at Susie's, and I hope with your mind at ease, and all your business wound up; for if you have a hundred people to see, and fifty errands to do, I shall be very much "aggrawated."

Did I tell you that Uncle William Greene had given me silver eagles for my shoulder-straps?[2] He gave them to me, on condition that, when I needed them no longer, I should give you one, and Pauline (Uncle Quin's wife) the other, for shawl-pins.[3] So I shall have your names engraved on them, and I don't think I could carry two better girls on my shoulders.

. . . Good bye until next Saturday—No, I shall write once more.

With love,
Your Rob

1. Annie probably took a three-week trip to prepare for the wedding and to allow Shaw to concentrate on the regiment.

2. Minister William Batchelder

Greene rose to the rank of general during the Civil War. Smith, *Beacon Hill's*, p. 491.

3. Quincy Adams Shaw and Pauline Agassiz Shaw.

Boston [HL]
March 3 1863
My dear Effie,

Yours of last Sunday, reached me today. Next Sunday you must write something in your own room & send it down to the parlour as I shall be there.

We have some more engagements here—Greely Curtis to Miss Hatty Appleton—Dr. Stone to Miss Hodges of Salem—and as you have, no doubt, heard, Fred. d'Hauteville to Miss Bessie Fish.[1] It has become so entirely the fashion that all the fellows who have come home since I have been here have either *been* engaged or tried to be. Of the latter class I know two or three—who poor devils have returned to their regiments in a very melancholy condition.

The other day, I went to call on Greely Curtis' Mother. I rang the bell with great calmness, when the door was thrown eagerly open, some one cried "Come in Mickey" and I saw two ladies, strangers to me, just on the point of throwing their arms about my innocent neck. The change which came over their faces was very laughable, and I have no doubt I looked as funny as they, for my eyes and mouth were both as wide open as they could comfortably be. I mentioned my name in rather an agitated voice, and they then told me they had been expecting Greely all day, & seeing a uniform at the door thought it must be he.

I must tell you another frightful scrape I got into this afternoon. At 2 P.M. I was informed I must meet and confer with a committee of ladies, who wished to do something to assist the 54th Mass. At 4 P.M. I proceeded, with a light heart & jaunty step, to 44 Bowdoin St. where the 4 females composing the committee were supposed to be in session. I rang the bell, the door opened, I hung up my coat in the entry, and stepping to the parlour, a fearful sight met my terrified gaze. There sat what seemed to me, about 17000 ladies & two men. The ladies were of all ages, but the majority were on the down side.

If I could possibly have bolted, I should have made the attempt, but it was useless. I was brought forward, as to the slaughter, in a terrible perspiration, and if I had not been able to recover myself, while I was being introduced to the audience, I don't know that I should have pulled through. As it was I managed to give an account of what progress had been made in my regiment & what articles the men were in need of. If I am ever caught in that way again, I hope I shall at least know it beforehand.

Friday I am invited to attend a meeting in commemoration of the death of Crispus Attucks, but I shall have Hallowell go instead, as he is a very good speaker—and has already begun in that line, since we have been here.[2]

Next Saturday morning, I shall be at Susie's door-step again, and hope you will all be at home.

Give my love to Mother & Nellie & Sue. I am going out to camp tomorrow. We expect to have 200 men there by the end of the week.

Your loving brother

1. Hatty Appleton (1842–1923) was the daughter of Harriet Coffin Sumner

Appleton and Nathan Appleton (1779–1861). Nathan Appleton, along with

Francis Lowell and Benjamin Ward, established the first power-loom textile factory in Lowell, Massachusetts. Robert Winthrop, *Memoir of the Hon. Nathan Appleton* (Boston: Wilson & Son, 1861; reprint ed., New York: Greenwood Press, 1969), p. 143; Crawford, *Famous Families*, vol. 2, p. 171. Dr. Lincoln Ripley Stone of Salem had been the surgeon of the Second Massachusetts before transferring with Shaw to the Fifty-fourth. Miss Hodges is unidentified.

2. Little is known about the background of Crispus Attucks (1750?–70). He was probably an escaped slave who worked in the whaling industry around Boston. He gained fame by being the first man killed during the Boston Massacre, Mar. 5, 1770. Logan and Winston, *Dictionary of American Negro Biography*, pp. 18–19.

Readville   [RGS]
March 4, 1863
Dear Father,

I have just received yours of the 3d inst. Governor Andrew says that all Colonel Higginson's men, and the Colonel himself, wish to get into the regular United States uniform; and strongly advises our sticking to it.[1] We are getting men very fast. There has been a hitch in the Rhode Island recruiting, but we hope to get it going in a day or two.

I trust ———— will do something more practical than having meetings, and will manage to send some recruits.[2] What do you think? Had we better send an officer on there to work?

Your loving Son

P.S.—Enclosed is another private letter for Mother.

1. Thomas Wentworth Higginson, a Unitarian minister from Worcester, Massachusetts, had long worked for abolition. Believing militancy the only way to force society to reform, Higginson attempted a rescue of captured fugitive slave, Anthony Burns, in 1854, sent guns to Kansas free-soilers in 1856, and aided John Brown's raid on Harpers Ferry. In Nov. 1862, Gen. Rufus Saxton, commander of the Department of the South, chose Higginson to recruit and lead the First South Carolina Volunteers, a regiment to be formed from slaves freed by Union army occupation of Beaufort, S.C.

2. Perhaps Shaw is referring to the New York recruiter named Givens.

March 4, 1863

My dear Charley,

Your letter of the 23d Feb. reached me today. In future address to 44 Beacon St. Though I shall be in camp after this I can get my letters sooner there.

I got yours just as I returned from visiting your Mother & sister at Jamaica Plain. I should have gone there long ago, if I could have found time—and shall certainly make them another visit as soon as I can. Greely Curtis is at home as you know, and his engagement is all right.

I had an invitation to visit the Somerset Club whenever I wished, and the other evening I went there. A great many of them are "bloody Copperheads" but no one made any disagreeable remarks while I was there. It would be a good thing for Greely to go in and give some of them a soaping down.

My regiment is making pretty good headway. We have nearly 150 men in camp, and they come in pretty fast. There are several among them, who have been well drilled, & who are acting sergeants. They drill their squads with a great deal of snap, and I think we shall have some good soldiers. Thirty four came up from New Bedford this afternoon, and marched with a drum & fife creating the greatest enthusiasm among the rest. We have them examined, sworn in, washed & uniformed as soon as they arrive—and when they get into their buttons they feel about as good as a man can. It is very laughable to hear the sergeants explain the drill to the men, as they use words long enough for a Doctor of Divinity or anything else.

The heel question is not a fabulous one—for some of them are wonder-ful in that line. One man has them so long that they actually prevent him from making the facings properly.[1] Since you were here, I think there has come a change over the public mind, in regard to the war. That feeling which we noticed, was a sort of reaction from the early enthusiasm, and I believe it is fast passing.

The conscription act has encouraged me very much, and must show the Rebels and European Powers, that we have no thought of giving in. If it is enforced we are safe, but if the Government gives in to rebellious demonstrations in the North, it is lost, because that will be a test of its power—don't you think so?[2] I hope the 2d New Hampshire is only one of many old regiments coming home, to enforce conscription.[3] It can never be done, I think, in many states without military aid. But the talk of resistance *may* turn out to be mere bluster after all.

I came out to Readeville yesterday for good—and it seems like Camp

Andrew over again. Everything topsy turvy. Nothing to eat and the coldest possible barracks.

George Bangs is in a state of despondency difficult to describe or even imagine.[4] He says he thinks sometimes that he is going to become insane—and if he doesn't take up another train of thought, I think there is some danger in it.

I saw Sam Quincy on Monday, just before he left.[5] He may be able to keep the field, but he will need a great deal of pluck to do it. Charley Mudge seems very ill indeed.[6] Between the two, you and Bangs stand a good chance of being Field officers. I hope to hear of your promotion before long, and in the mean time it is good you are in such comfortable quarters & pleasant company.

It has been a subject of wonder to me that the nigger concern meets with so little opposition here. Almost everyone, even those who do not favour it, says that it is a good thing to try. Even such fellows as Bill Horton, now they see that we are not tabooed, by what he considers respectable society, talk of wanting to go into it.[7]

Perhaps though, there may be something rough for us to go through yet, in the way of abuse. It is a matter of chance, which way the public sentiment may take a turn—Especially in the army.

I have been to a dinner or small party almost every day since I got to Boston, and have enjoyed myself amazingly—though my mind wanders sometimes to a certain person in N. Y.

Powdered hair is coming in again. The gayety in N. Y. & Boston is greater than ever.

Postman waits. Good bye & God bless you my dear fellow.

Always afftcly yours,
R. G. S.

1. During the Civil War scientists and pseudoscientists, following Darwin, attempted to reinforce an ideology that elevated the white race. Shaw's friend and Harvard professor Louis Agassiz lent his name and talents to this movement. One of the anthropometric theories held that blacks had longer heels than whites. To many this helped prove a difference and thus a superior-inferior relationship. John S. Haller, Jr., *Outcasts from Evolution: Scientific Attitudes of Racial Inferiority, 1859–1900* (Urbana: University of Illinois Press, 1971), pp. 19–34.

2. There were major riots in the North against the Conscription Act. The largest was in New York City, where Irish immigrants went on a four-day spree against draft officials, abolitionists, and blacks. Irish laborers were angry that pay had not increased with industry profits, that the wealthy were able to hire substitutes, and that the Emancipation

Proclamation would free blacks to compete with them for jobs. The government did not "give in" to draft riots, but sent in federal troops to restore order. For the best study on the New York riot, see Iver Bernstein, *The New York City Draft Riots: Their Significance for American Society and Politics in the Age of Civil War* (New York: Oxford University Press, 1990).

3. The Second New Hampshire Infantry organized at Portsmouth in June 1861. Dyer, *Compendium*, vol. 1, p. 176.

4. George P. Bangs.

5. Col. Samuel M. Quincy, of the powerful Boston family, was second in command of the Second Massachusetts. Quincy resigned from his position on June 2, 1863, to lead a regiment of U.S. Colored Troops. *Rec. of Mass. Vols.*, p. 27.

6. Maj. Charles Redington Mudge (1839–63) had been wounded on May 23, 1862, at Winchester, Virginia. He recovered, fought at Chancellorsville, and made lieutenant colonel on June 6, 1863. *Harvard College: Report of the Class of 1860*, pp. 34–35.

7. Bill Horton is unidentified.

Boston   [MHS]
March 12, 1863
My dear Charley,

I received your note enclosing Brangle's bill & send you now (8) Eight dolls.[1]

We are getting on swimmingly, having near 250 men in camp. My Officers too are pretty good, some of them excellent.

I came down from Lenox last night, where I have been having rather a comfortable time for a few days. On the train I met Sergt. Griswold, looking a little peaked still, but intending to rejoin the regt soon.[2]

I think of you very often and I wish we could be together again. Perhaps some day it may be our luck to fall in with each other somewhere. I find my feeling for old class-mates is weak compared with friendships formed in the 2d—like yours & mine. I have not seen Harry for a week—as I have been away 4 days.

I read Hooker's order with exultation when I found the name of our sturdy old regt among the favoured ones. The order will do more, I should think, towards creating a spirit of emulation in the army than any that has been issued since we entered the service. Indeed no other General ever attempted anything of the sort.[3]

My third sister (Effie) is engaged to Charley Lowell.[4] It is a very satisfactory affair for us all & especially for me—as I like him very much, and she and I have always been together, more than any other two of the family.

I telegraphed to John Fox today, to know whether they had been notified of the extension of my leave—as I am in continual dread of seeing my name among the Absent without Authority.[5]

There seem to be shoals of men from the 2d in Boston. I suppose in a month or six weeks from this you will all be at work again.

It is the luckiest thing in the world that Slocum has taken a fancy to our regiment.[6]

I have not seen any of your family since I wrote last.

Hoping to hear from you soon, and regularly, I am always

> Your sincerely attached friend,
> Robert G. Shaw

If you hear of anything going wrong regarding my leave, I wish you would let me know—as soon as possible.

1. Brangle is unidentified.

2. The Second Massachusetts had two Griswolds, Alonzo and Dwight F., both from Boston, who joined the regiment as sergeants on May 25, 1861. Alonzo's military service record states little more than his induction date and age, twenty-four. Dwight's records show him reduced to private in Sept. 1861, discharged and reenrolled on Oct. 27, 1862. Dwight was killed at Chancellorsville on May 3, 1863. Alonzo Griswold and Dwight F. Griswold files, CMSR.

3. Hooker wanted to create esprit d'corps by emphasizing unit pride and healthy competition. He improved living conditions, and approved insignia badges for the different corps. He rewarded "model" regiments by granting them increased furloughs. Hooker's first "models" included three Massachusetts units, the First, Second, and Twentieth. McPherson, Battle Cry, p. 585. Robert Garth Scott, ed., Fallen Leaves: The Civil War Letters of Major Henry Livermore Abbott (Kent, Ohio: Kent State University Press, 1991), p. 169.

4. Josephine Shaw married Charles Russell Lowell, Jr., on Oct. 31, 1863. Henry Lee Higginson heard of the engagement and wrote to Effie, "One might almost have forseen that Charley, from liking Bob so much, would inevitably fall in love with his sister who so resembled him." Stewart, Philanthropic Works, pp. 38, 45; H. L. Higginson to Effie Shaw, Mar. 15, 1863, James Russell Lowell Papers, 1842–1924, MHS.

5. First Lt. John A. Fox of Dorchester, Massachusetts, an officer in the Second Massachusetts. Rec. of Mass. Vols., p. 29.

6. Henry Warner Slocum (1827–94), of New York, graduated West Point in 1852, fought in the Seminole War, and became a lawyer. At the beginning of the war he was appointed colonel of the Twenty-seventh New York Infantry. From Sept. 1862 to Apr. 1864, Slocum commanded the XII Corps of the Army of the Potomac. Faust, Encyclopedia, p. 692; Boatner, Dictionary, p. 765.

Boston
March 14, 1863
My Dear Annie,

Your yesterday's letters reached me this morning, and gave me more pleasure than I can tell you.

I find that Mother is not coming to Boston in a fortnight; so please don't
change your mind, but come on the 21st. I will go up and meet you at Springfield. Aunt Mary wanted you to come here, even if Mother and Effie were
here too. When the snow is gone, we can have some nice rides together. . . .

I went out to Readville yesterday morning, and have just come in. Everything out there is going on prosperously. The officers and men are very satisfactory. When Clem. comes, she mustn't compare my men with French
soldiers, but with American *volunteers*.

From what I have seen of them, they will be more soldierly than the latter,
because it is so easy to control and discipline them. The company from New
Bedford are a very fine body of men, and out of forty, only two cannot read
and write.[1] Their barracks are in better order, and more cleanly, than the
quarters of any volunteer regiment I have seen in this country. . . .

Excuse a short note, dear Annie, and, with love, believe me,

> Always yours,
> Rob

P.S.—. . . Last night I went to call on Lucy Codman.[2] Do you know her? She
is a cousin of ours, whom Mother had the care of for a good while, when
Lucy was a little girl. She is a very lovely person, and we are all very much
attached to her.

1. The New Bedford Company, Company C, included William H. Carney,
the nation's first black medal of honor
recipient.

2. Lucy Codman lived in West
Roxbury.

Readville
March 17, 1863
Dearest Mother,

Your note of Sunday reached me to-day. I am sorry it was a mistake about
your visit to Boston, though I was astonished at there being any thought of
your leaving Anna just now.

I had a pleasant time at Lenox. Annie and I went to see Mrs. Charles and

Willie Sedgwick.[1] The day before the battle of Antietam her husband spent with us, and I had a great deal to tell them about him.[2] His little girl wanted to hear all about her father. His mother is one of the most patriotic women I have seen, and seemed to feel proud that her son had died for his country.

The regiment continues to flourish. Men come in every day. Mr. Stearns, who is at home for a few days from Canada, says we can get more men than we want from there.[3] The Governor thinks of getting authority to raise some more coloured regiments. If he does, I hope Frank Barlow can get the command.[4] He is just the man for it, and I should like to be under him. Yesterday we had several officers out to take a look at the men; they all went away very much pleased. Some were very sceptical about it before, but say, now, that they shall have no more doubts of negroes making good soldiers. The Massachusetts Legislature has passed a bill appropriating $75,000 for each new regiment, ours included. The men will receive $50 bounty, and the rest will be used for recruiting purposes.

Love to Father and Susie,

Your loving son,
Rob

1. Elizabeth Sedgwick was the sister-in-law of Lenox author Catharine Maria Sedgwick (1789–1867), to whom Fanny Kemble dedicated her book in 1863. Mrs. William Sedgwick's given name is unidentified.

2. Maj. William Dwight Sedgwick.

3. George Luther Stearns (1809–67). On June 13, 1863, Stearns became the War Department's chief of recruiting for regiments composing the U.S. Colored Troops. Emilio, *A Brave Black Regiment*, p. 12; Mary Frances Berry, *Military Necessity and Civil Rights Policy: Black Citizenship and the Constitution, 1861–1868* (Port Washington, N.Y.: Kennikat Press, 1977), p. 63.

4. Francis Channing Barlow.

Readville [RGS]
March 17, 1863
My Dear Annie,

Your note of Monday reached me to-day. If I hadn't written you such a very contemptible one yesterday, I should have thought yours was altogether too short.

To-night we received quite a large squad of men from Pittsfield. They seem to be very patriotic up there. We are beginning to get our men from Western New York and Canada now. Our recruiting agent up there says he can get enough to make two or three regiments, if the Governor is authorized to raise them; at any rate, we can fill ours up.[1]

Effie will be here to-morrow, and I wish, dear Annie, you were coming too. However, a week is not a very long time. If you put off coming I shall begin to feel very melancholy. . . .

The other day I dined at H. Mason's with seventeen officers, four of whom had to have their food cut up for them, being badly wounded in the arm, and several others had wounds in other parts.[2] We had a very interesting time in talking over events of the past year. I have got the pup which Captain Scott brought me from Virginia, out here, and if he grows up to be a nice dog, I will leave him with you when I go off.[3] Yesterday I bought a full-bred English terrier, which is a beauty. . . .

There is a blue-eyed, yellow-haired, white-skinned, black preacher out here, who has great influence among the blacks. He wants to go as chaplain, and I think I shall take him; he looks so much like a white man, that I don't believe there would be much prejudice against it.[4] I think I should care very little for public opinion, if it did no harm to the regiment. It would be out of the question to have any black, field or line, officers at present, because of public sentiment.[5] It ruined the efficiency of the Louisiana coloured regiments. . . .[6]

Good night, dearest Annie.

Always,
your affectionate Rob

Our men are to have $50 bounty from the State, according to a bill which has just passed the Legislature.

1. Recruiting agent George L. Stearns.

2. Capt. Herbert C. Mason of the Twentieth Massachusetts was wounded less than four months later at the battle of Gettysburg. Henry L. Abbott to J. G. Abbott, July 6, 1863, in Scott, *Fallen Leaves*, pp. 88, 186.

3. Capt. H. B. Scott.

4. Shaw is referring to either William Jackson or William Grimes, both preachers from New Bedford who ministered to the Fifty-fourth. *New Bedford Mercury*, Apr. 6 (2:3), 1863; John A. Andrew to RGS, May 14, 1863, in Miscellaneous

Bound, MHS; newspaper clipping, *New Bedford Mercury*, Mar. 30, 1863, in Congdon Scrapbook, NBFPL.

5. It had been an uphill battle to get black men enlisted as privates. One Democratic congressman who opposed recruiting black soldiers summed up the beliefs of many Americans, Republicans and Democrats alike: "This is a government of white men, made by white men for white men, to be administered, protected, defended, and maintained by white men." The white nation was not yet ready to see black men in positions of leadership as officers. Democrat quoted

in James M. McPherson, *Ordeal by Fire: The Civil War and Reconstruction* (New York: Knopf, 1982), p. 349.

6. In summer 1862, Gen. Benjamin Butler allowed black Louisiana militia units to be officered by seventy-five black captains and lieutenants. Stanton replaced Butler with Gen. N. P. Banks, who quickly dismissed the black officers and put white ones in their places. Banks believed that the sight of black officers demoralized white troops. Glatthaar, *Forged in Battle*, pp. 176–77.

Readville [HL]

March 21 1863

Dear Father,

Yours of the 18th Inst is received. I don't think there is any chance for Mr. Wingate in my regiment.[1] We have filled the list of Officers already. There will probably be some vacancies before we leave, but I don't want to take any one whom I don't know myself, and the Governor is averse to any but Massachusetts men, as there are a great many applications from his regiments.

Please tell Mother I received her note and will take her advice about Aunt Mary's house. Charley and Effie arrived safely night before last. The latter found some beautiful bouquets awaiting her, and yesterday received a swarm of visitors.

We have received a large number of men lately from New York State & Pennsylvania. Mr. Stearns' recruits are beginning to come in too. We are picking them carefully & shall have a very sound set. I expect to have, at least 450 in camp before the middle of next week.

Don't you think Brown had better give up his office in New York?[2] We get finer men from the country, and there is no doubt of our filling up pretty rapidly.[3]

Annie isn't coming until next Wednesday and I am afraid she will put off her visit even longer than that, from what she writes me of her mother's health.

I suppose you are at the Island again by this time. Give my best love to George & Anna. I hope they are both well.

The snow here is still deep, and is making a good layer of mud for us. We can't drill out of doors which is a great disadvantage as the barracks are crowded.

Give my love to Mother. I hope Nellie is having a pleasant time in Philadelphia. I suppose it is pretty gay there.

> Your loving son
> Robert G. Shaw

1. Mr. Wingate is unidentified.

2. William Wells Brown.

3. It is difficult to assess Shaw's claim about country versus city men. Col. T. W. Higginson recalled that

Colonel Hallowell once told him that the Fifty-fourth had in its ranks "some of the worst reprobates of Northern cities." Higginson, *Army Life in a Black Regiment*, p. 232.

Readeville   [MHS]
March 23, 1863
My dear Charley,

I received yours of the 19th today, and was very glad to hear your account of the review of 12th Corps, by Hooker. I have been expecting it for some time, as you said in your last, that it was going to take place.

I can imagine your feelings very easily, when the old regiment was complimented by the General, for I felt just so when Pope reviewed us at Little Washington, and I was on Gordon's Staff. It sent a thrill through me to see their steady marching & well closed ranks.

It is very encouraging to hear your favourable account of Hooker.[1] It really seems as if he *must* do something this Spring. The army will start, at any rate, in better condition and spirits than ever before. Oh, how I wish I were going to be with you! I should like to make one successful & brilliant campaign with the 2d and the Army of the Potomac.

I don't think the conscription will stop the raising of negro regiments, for every one seems to go in for having them drafted too. And then they are destined for a peculiar service, I think, that of drawing off the blacks from the plantations, and making the Proclamation of Emancipation a reality. People lately from England say the change of feeling there, is a wonder—and they attribute it almost entirely to the Proclamation.

I have been meaning to write to you, for the last week, especially to urge you, if you are offered a position on Slocum's, or any other good man's Staff not to refuse it out of feeling for the regiment. You must reflect that this war may last a long time, and that you owe it to yourself and to your friends & relatives to get the best rank and position you honourably can. If you get on a good Staff, you will be sure to rise, and if a military man doesn't continually look for promotion, what interest can he have in his profession?

We have 350 men in camp today and expect to get 100 or more during the week. I think we shall be full in a month—unless something occurs to stop the recruiting. That is not likely though, as $50 bounty has just been offered, while hitherto we have had none.

Let me hear from you regularly, my dear Charley, as I depend upon it. Tom Robeson & Grafton are here, but I have not seen them yet.[2]

Miss Haggerty is coming to Boston to stay with one of my Aunts, so that my prospects for the next few weeks is pleasant.

Your sincere friend,
Robert G. Shaw

P.S. I saw Miss Nellie Low today & had a walk & a talk with her.[3] She asked after you with much interest.

1. Hooker instilled McClellan-like discipline on the Army of the Potomac, which had slipped under the commands of Pope and Burnside. Hooker demanded and got better food, allowed a liberal furlough system, and held grand parades to keep his men busy and believing in themselves. The men and officers cheered Hooker like they had cheered McClellan. Foote, *Civil War*, vol. 2, pp. 232–33.

2. Thomas R. Robeson and James I. Grafton.

3. Nellie Low is unidentified.

Readville   [HL]
March 25 1863
Dear Mother,

I have received two notes from you, one about our course of conduct at Aunt Mary's, and the other about shirts. I agree with you entirely about what you said in the first, and shall do as you suggest. I burned the note, as you requested, and will not say anything to Aunt Mary about it. I have bought the shirts but will pay the bill myself, as I shall be happy to make Howard a present of the others.[1]

If the success of the 54 Mass. gives you so much pleasure, I shall have no difficulty in giving you good news of it, whenever I write.

Everything goes on prosperously. The intelligence of the men is a great surprise to me. They learn all the details of guard duty and Camp service, infinitely more readily than the Irish I have had under my command.

There is not the least doubt, that we shall leave the state, with as good a regiment, as any that has marched.

One trouble, which I anticipated, has begun-viz: complaints from outsiders of undue severity. But I shall continue to do, what I know is right in that particular, and you may be perfectly certain, that any reports of cruelty, ar entirely untrue. I have treated them much more mildly, than we did the m of the 2d.[2]

Tell Father I received his note, and would like very much to have him me the horse he speaks of, if he is satisfied with him. I want as handsome a horse as I can get & need it as soon as possible.

I am going up to Lenox tonight, to come down with Annie tomorrow.

I found I should have to be away just as long, if I only went to Springfield. Love George, Anna & Susie.

Your loving son

1. Howard is unidentified.

2. Not only outsiders criticized the severity of Shaw's camp. Shaw's officers admitted that Shaw used "coercion" and strict discipline. Camp Meigs commander Gen. Richard Peirce had to order Shaw to stop "severe and unusual punishments" of his men; he did not specify what those punishments entailed. Newspaper clipping in Hallowell Papers, MHS; Hallowell, *Negro as a Soldier*, p. 9; Order of General Peirce, Camp Meigs Papers, NBFPL.

Readville   [RGS]
March 27, 1863
Dear Mother,

Annie and I got to Boston last evening. Will you please tell me *exactly* what you think of our being married before I go away? I want to have your opinion about it, and Father's too. Please ask him to write me what he thinks of it; and make a point of it yourself, will you?

We received thirty men yesterday and to-day. The snow has almost disappeared, and the camp is fast getting dry. I am sorry I wrote you what I did about punishments in my regiment, and it may have seemed to you more important than it really is; what made me speak of it was a letter from the Surgeon-General of the State, asking what punishments were inflicted, and I thought some one had been complaining; but I can't find that such is the fact, though.[1]

Your loving Son

1. William Johnson Dale (1815–?), from Gloucester, Massachusetts, graduated from Harvard Medical School in ... opened an office in Boston. In ... Governor Andrew appointed him to be surgeon general of Massachusetts, with the rank of colonel. *Appleton's Cyclopedia of American Biography* (New York: Appleton, 1887), vol. 2, p. 57.

CHAPTER 12

"*So fine a set of men*"

The armies of the North had begun the spring offensives that might end the war. In the West, Ulysses S. Grant advanced upon Vicksburg, the strongest Confederate position on the Mississippi River. In Virginia, the Army of the Potomac under "Fighting Joe" Hooker tried to outflank Robert E. Lee. But Lee frightened Hooker into taking the defensive when he moved out of Fredericksburg and met the Yankees near Chancellorsville. In the face of the 70,000-man enemy, Stonewall Jackson took 25,000 of Lee's 47,000 Rebels around Hooker's right and struck the Union army at dusk on May 1. Jackson was fatally wounded, but Lee won the battle and made plans for another invasion of the North. Grant's assaults on Vicksburg failed and he settled into siege operations.

On May 13 at the Camp Meigs training facility near Boston, Shaw pinned on the silver eagles denoting his promotion to colonel. For ninety days he had busily instructed his men, met with hundreds of visitors who came to see the North's first black regiment, and spent what spare time he had courting fiancée Annie Haggerty. Shaw took pains to ensure the fitness of his men, the approval of the visitors, and his marriage to Annie. The last he arranged only after his and Annie's parents backed away from their original objections.

On May 2, with the regiment fully manned at one thousand volunteers, Shaw exchanged vows with Annie and traveled by train to honeymoon at the Lenox cottage of her parents. Five days later he received a telegram that brought him back to Boston sooner than he wanted. The regiment had received orders to depart for the South.

Readville   [RGS]
March 30, 1863
Dear Father,

Caraway should not have received a pass. He was away on leave, and should have paid his own expenses.[1] We have had four companies mustered in to-day. There is another one half full, and sixty men on their way from Buffalo. In a month I think we shall be full.

Thank you for your answer to my question about our being married. There is no reason why it should interfere with my duties as an officer.

I hope all the coloured people will be as sensible as Downing; I didn't know he had been here.[2] The mustering-officer, who was here to-day, is a Virginian, and has always thought it was a great joke to try to make soldiers of "*niggers*"; but he told me to-day, that he had never mustered in so fine a set of men, though about twenty thousand had passed through his hands since September last. The sceptics need only come out here now, to be converted.

I hope to find a letter from Mother when I go in town to-morrow afternoon. Give my love to her. Annie has not been well since she came here. In one way it has been very fortunate, for we have had several quiet evenings together. I don't know what her Mother will say to our plan of being married before I go, but I hope she will come into it.

Your loving son,
Robert G. Shaw

1. Caraway is unidentified.
2. Probably George Thomas Downing (1819–1903), a prominent abolitionist who graduated from Hamilton College and worked hard to help fugitive slaves ride the Underground Railroad. He owned a successful catering business in New York City before moving it to

Newport, Rhode Island. For a decade, from 1856 to 1866, he advocated the integration of Rhode Island's segregated public-school system, something that happened in 1866. Logan and Winston, *Dictionary of American Negro Biography*, p. 187.

April 1, 1863

Dear Mother,

I received your letter last evening, and you must excuse me for saying, I didn't think your arguments very powerful. If I thought that being married were going to make me neglect my duty, I should think it much better never to have been engaged. As for Annie's going out with me, I don't think such a thing would ever enter my head. It is the last thing I should desire, as I have seen the evil consequences of it very often. The chances of my coming home in six months are very small; for, if we are put on the service we expect, we shall get into the interior before long. Indeed, one reason for my wishing to be married is, that we are going to undertake a very dangerous piece of work, and I feel that there are more chances than ever of my not getting back. I know I should go away more happy and contented if we were married. I showed Annie your letter, and she wants to show it to Aunt Anna; to which I suppose you have no objection.[1]

We have had another snow-storm, which makes drilling very uncomfortable, as there is little room in the barracks. Tell Father that Dr. Stone has gone to Buffalo to examine a hundred men there, so that his man Jackson cannot be put through immediately.[2] As soon as he is, I will let him know.

Your loving Son

1. Aunt Anna is unidentified.

2. Lincoln Ripley Stone was on detached duty to the Fifty-fourth Massachusetts from the time of its organization in Feb. 1863; the transfer became permanent on Apr. 2, 1863. At times, Stone would travel to make his medical examinations of recruits before they arrived in camp. In so doing Stone saved the black committee a lot of money in roundtrip transportation costs for unsuitable recruits. Lincoln R. Stone file, CMSR. Seventeen Jacksons had enlisted into the regiment by Apr. 9; Shaw is probably referring to Moses Jackson, 24, a barber from Galt, Canada. Emilio, *A Brave Black Regiment*, p. 361.

April 2/63

Dear George,

Your letter of the 31 March reached me yesterday. I have already seen Mr. Guerrier several times.[1] I liked him very well, but didn't think him one of the best on our list of applicants. Now, we are absolutely full, but I may have a 2d Lieut.'s vacancy, before we start. There are other men from my own regiment though, whom I want to take very much, and whom I am *sure* of, as regards qualifications.

I wish I could serve Mr. Ricketson, but see very little chance of it, now.[2] I am sorry that your only recommendation should not have met with more success. I didn't think Mr. Phillips particularly well qualified to give an opinion as to the merits of an officer.[3]

A great many men have come with such recommendations & with papers from the Common Councilmen of their towns, but I never pay any attention to such, & call for recommendations from their superior officers, if they have been in service.

The other day I called on Mr. Josiah Quincy Seniorissimo, and had a very interesting visit.[4] He told me to say to you, that he often heard of you in Boston, but hadn't seen you lately and that if you didn't go to see him the next time you came, he should drop you from his books. His memory is evidently failing him, and he talked principally of events which happened in the last century, which of course I was delighted to hear about. He had an engraving of Uncle Sam hanging at the head of his bed, and referred to him continually during my visit.[5] He seemed to recollect him with a sort of veneration. He said "I shook hands with him last, on the wharf, when he sailed for China, in 17 hundred & something."

What a beautiful head & face Mr. Quincy has! I sat & looked at him in perfect wonder, as I thought of the men he had known & the events he had an active part in.

They showed me some of the most interesting relics I ever saw. Some of Washington's hair, letters, gloves & documents & letters from hosts of celebrated men & women. They have a metal plate like this [drawing included here] which Washington wore, with the arms of Virginia engraved on it & with the ribbon with which he hung it round his neck.

Give my best love to dear Anna. God bless you both, and may you get happily through this month.

I see Annie every evening almost, and feel more & more satisfied every day, as I learn to know her better. Effie & Charley are well & enjoying each other.

Goodbye dear George & believe me,

Always your loving brother

1. George P. Guerrier, an Englishman, who had been with the Twenty-second Massachusetts Infantry for over a year, earnestly sought a position with the Fifty-fourth. Staunch Quaker abolitionist Joseph Ricketson and his brother, Daniel, lobbied heavily for Guerrier through their friends, Governor Andrew,

Wendell Phillips, George William Curtis, and General Peirce. Joe Ricketson wrote to Peirce that Guerrier "entered the Army with the highest and purest motives to fight for Liberty, and is a good sound Antislavery man." When Shaw could not or would not make a place for Guerrier, Governor Andrew obtained a second lieutenancy for him with Col. E. A. Wild's black regiment being raised in North Carolina. Joseph Ricketson to Gen [R. A.] Peirce, Apr. 1, 1863, May 13 and 15, 1863, Camp Meigs Papers, NBFPL; *New Bedford Mercury*, May 8 (2:2), 1863.

2. Joseph Ricketson of New Bedford.

3. Wendell Phillips (1811–84), Harvard graduate, Boston lawyer, and one of the earliest and most visible abolitionists.

Because of his oratorical ability, Phillips is remembered as "the golden trumpet of abolition." *DAB*, vol. 7, pp. 546–47.

4. Josiah Quincy was a prominent Boston politician and educator.

5. Shaw's great-grandfather's brother, Maj. Samuel Shaw (1754–94) grew up in Boston in North Square, one house away from the home of Paul Revere. During the American Revolution, Major Shaw served on the staff of Gen. Henry Knox. When Knox became the new nation's first secretary of war, Shaw served briefly in the War Department before President Washington named him as counsel to Canton—therein began a tie to China that the Shaws would exploit for their China trading business. Smith, *Beacon Hill's*, pp. 62, 490–91.

Readville

April 2 1863

Dear Father,

[HL]

Jackson has been examined & passed by the Surgeon. Yours of 31st ulto. received. I hardly think that a man of 46 would pass.[1] Still if he were perfectly sound in *every* other respect he might. In my opinion Dr. Stone is not too strict in his examinations.[2] In fact I have continually urged him to be particular—and the committee here have complained of it very much, because the expense of sending men home is so great. The consequence is that we have an empty hospital, while that of the cavalry opposite, is full—though they have only 60 or 70 men in camp.[3] To accept a man who is doubtful, is, in my opinion, cheating the Government, wronging the man, & harming the regiment. The standard of most surgeons is very low, because it has been so difficult lately to fill the town quotas—and in consequence our regiments dwindle away very fast, and the Govt hospitals are full of men who never did a day's duty. In the 2d, I have seen several recruits die from mere fatigue & exposure.

Stone has gone to Buffalo to examine a large squad, & set the Surgeon there on the right track. He will afterwards probably go to Philadelphia. We have another man who comes out from Boston every day.

Edward Hallowell will undoubtedly be major.[4] The Govr promised me as much day before yesterday. I myself shall be mustered in a major this week in order to leave a vacancy in the 2d.[5] My name ought to be Sam for a little while.[6]

The Governor has written to the Secretary of War, asking to have my regt sent to Newbern, to form the nucleus of a brigade—also recommending Barlow, very strongly, for the command.[7] The latter wants it, and I have done all I could to get him for a commander. Charley Lowell too has been writing & talking to a great many people, for the same object. I think if the thing works we can do a good work in that way.

Give my love to Mother & Susie.

Your loving son

P.S. We have accepted men over age, but they were physically perfect. Col. Frank Lee says a brigade of coloured men could be easily raised in North Carolina.[8] The country there is more easy to operate in, than South Carolina.

1. At least thirty-eight men over forty years of age joined the Fifty-fourth. The oldest man in the regiment was Peter Vogelsang, who joined at age forty-seven. Emilio, *A Brave Black Regiment*, pp. 328–88.

2. Stone ran a very strict physical examination and turned away one man out of every three sent to Camp Meigs. *Annual Report of the Adjutant-General of the Commonwealth of Massachusetts . . . for the Year Ending December 31, 1863* (Boston: Wright & Potter, 1864), p. 13.

3. Charles Lowell's Second Massachusetts Cavalry. Most of this unit was raised in California among former residents of Massachusetts. Schouler, *History of Mass. in the War*, vol. 1, pp. 393–94.

4. Edward Hallowell became a captain on Mar. 30, a major on May 13, a lieutenant colonel on July 1, and a colonel on Sept. 1. Boatner, *Dictionary*, p. 367.

5. Shaw was mustered a major on Apr. 11, 1863. He would finally pin on his colonel's eagles on May 13. Robert Gould Shaw file, CMSR.

6. Maj. Samuel Shaw.

7. Governor Andrew and Secretary of War Stanton raised the Fifty-fourth with the idea of sending them to New Bern, North Carolina, as part of a brigade forming there. The regiment would cooperate with Colonel Wild's just-formed regiment of Southern freedmen. Andrew had urged Stanton to make Wild a brigadier general and send him to North Carolina to raise troops; Stanton had done so on Apr. 24, 1863. Later, in June, Andrew supported Barlow to become a brigade commander over black troops in South Carolina and Georgia. Richard Reid, "General Edward A. Wild and Civil War Discrimination," *Historical Journal of Massachusetts* 13 (Jan. 1985): 14–16; *OR*, III:3, p. 423.

8. Commissioned a colonel on Aug. 26, 1862, Francis L. Lee commanded the Forty-fourth Massachusetts Infantry at New Bern, North Carolina. Francis L. Lee file, CMSR.

April 3, 1863
Dear Father,

I received yours of 1st to-day. As regards our being married, Mr. and Mrs. Haggerty seem as much opposed to it as Mother.[1] The reason I should like to have it, is the very one that Mother gives for opposing it; namely, that I am going away. I can't help feeling that, if we are not married before I go, I shall feel very much dissatisfied and discontented. For the sake of Annie's and my own peace of mind, I want it.

> Your loving son,
> Robert G. Shaw

1. Ogden and Elizabeth Kneeland Haggerty.

April 7 1863
Dearest Mother,

I didn't mean to worry you by what I said of our being sent away suddenly. I really thought you knew the officers of coloured regiments were supposed to be in rather a ticklish situation, if caught by the Rebels—and it was not any feeling of annoyance at your letter which made me speak of it.[1]

The Governor has permission to organize a brigade at Newbern, and wants to start our four companies off immediately. So that I am just now in the midst of much correspondence on the subject. If they do Edward Hallowell will be in command of them.

I hope that they will be left though, unless there is some great benefit to be gained by sending them away, as I want to march & arrive at our destination, with a full & well organized regiment. At Newbern they would serve as a nucleus for the Brigade, which might then be started a little sooner.

Love to Susie. In haste

> Your loving son

Col. Wild of the 35 Mass. will probably command the Brigade, though I want Barlow very much.[2]

1. On Dec. 23, 1862, Jefferson Davis proclaimed that if caught, white officers of black units would be executed or otherwise harshly dealt with. By May 1863, the Confederate Congress resolved that any white officer of black

units would be hanged and any black soldier would be returned to slavery. Glatthaar, *Forged in Battle*, p. 201; Brainard Dyer, "The Treatment of Colored Union Troops by the Confederates, 1861–1865," *Journal of Negro History* 20 (July 1935): 273–86; *NYT*, Dec. 29 (3:4–5), 1862.

2. Edward Augustus Wild (1825–91) of Brookline, Massachusetts, graduated from Harvard in 1844 and served as a doctor with the Turkish Army in the Crimean War. As colonel of the Thirty-fifth Massachusetts Infantry, Wild was wounded at Antietam and had to have his left arm amputated. He helped re- cruit for the Fifty-fourth before being promoted to brigadier general and sent to North Carolina to raise black troops for the government. In New Bern, Wild quickly raised two regiments from among the 7,500 refugees congregating there. The First and Second regiments of the North Carolina Colored Volunteers made up what would come to be called Wild's African Brigade. Reid, "General Edward A. Wild," pp. 14–29; Edward Longacre, "Brave Radical Wild: The Contentious Career of Brigadier Edward A. Wild," *Civil War Times Illustrated* 19 (June 1980): 8–11.

Boston [RGS]
April 8, 1863
Dearest Mother,

Your note, enclosing Uncle George's, arrived to-day.[1] I hope you will get over your idea that I was so annoyed with your letter. I knew very well that you would not be in favour of our marrying now, and was not disappointed or annoyed. I assure you that's the truth.

The Governor is very anxious to get us away in a month. He has given up the notion of sending off part of the regiment; and Stanton telegraphed yesterday, that he should by no means do anything that would injure the progress or completion of the regiment.

Mr. and Mrs. Haggerty seem to have changed their mind about the marriage. I really should feel very much dissatisfied, if I went away for an indefinitely long time—as I shall—without having it all settled. Don't feel uneasy about its keeping me from my work, dear Mother; I am sure it will not. Annie wants us to go to New York and be married in church, and very privately. Do you know if there is any publishing of banns (or whatever you call them) required by law in New York?[2]

Your loving Son

P.S.—The Governor says General Wool wants us to go through New York, and promised to have all the troops in the harbour up, if there were danger of any row.[3] I told him (the Governor) that if they would warn innocent people to stay at home, we should be happy to handle any New York mob without assistance, whereat he laughed very much. I don't think I ever heard a jollier laugh than his. He is in New York now, and I hope you will see him.

1. George Russell.

2. A bann is a church proclamation of intended marriages.

3. John Ellis Wool (1784–1869), a career soldier from Newburg, New York, who fought in the War of 1812

and the Mexican War. In 1861, Wool was the nation's senior brigadier general. *The National Cyclopedia of American Biography* (New York: James T. White, 1897), vol. 4, p. 282.

Readville
[HL]
April 14 1863

Dearest Mother,

Annie received your note this morning, and showed it to me. I am very glad, of course, that you feel perfectly satisfied about our marriage. She and I agree that it is much better to have it as quiet as possible. If it were to be a Show Wedding, I should wear my uniform, as you wish, but under the circumstances it would be very inconvenient, as I should have to change it before we went away. You don't seem to appreciate how unpleasant it is to wear a uniform in public. If I were not on duty here, I shouldn't wear one in Boston, ever.

Everything, as regards the regiment, is going on swimmingly, as usual. We have 630 men, and shall probably have over 700 before the week is out. I don't remember whether I told you that Col. Wild has been ordered to raise, and take command of a brigade of coloured troops at Newbern. He is an excellent man. He lost his arm at Antietam and, I am afraid, may not be able to remain in active service, though he is determined to try it.

We have decided to have the wedding on Saturday 2d of May—and I think, by that time, there will be no objection to my taking a week's vacation.

Edward Hallowell, who has just returned from Philadelphia, says he heard Susie was at Uncle Robert's.[1] Is it so?

I suppose Robert M. will be home before long.[2]

Mrs. Haggerty and Clem are here, and the change of air is doing them a great deal of good. I am getting very fond of them.

When we come back from Lenox, I hope Uncle Henry Grew, will invite Annie to stay at his house a little while, as it is close to my camp.[3]

Ever your loving son,
Robert G. Shaw

P.S. Tell Father I bought a good horse today for $300. The reason I have drawn so much money is because I have had to pay several times for the regt.

1. Robert Shaw Sturgis lived in Philadelphia.
2. Robert Bowne Minturn, Jr.
3. Henry Grew (?–1892) was married to Sarah Shaw's sister Elizabeth Perkins Sturgis Grew (1809–48). Sturgis, *Sturgis*, p. 52.

Readville   [HL]
April 17 1863
Dearest Mother,

About half a mile from here I have discovered a very nice house kept by a lady who takes boarders. So, if I find it best to return here immediately after our marriage, Annie will come & live there. Both she & I want you to come too, for I don't want to go away without seeing something more of you than I have. I shall ask Clem to come too. Annie will come there, at any rate, after we leave Lenox—and if you refuse this invitation I shall begin to think you don't want to see me.

It is a very pretty place, and you can have a private table & parlour & everything else.

I saw Effie at Milton Hill last night. She looks a little tired, but otherwise well.

Your loving son,
Robert G. Shaw

Readville   [HL]
April 17 1863
Dear Father,

I received yours of the 14 inst. enclosing recommendation from citizens of Haverhill, for Wingate.[1] I will hand it to the Governor today. The others he already has.

The only notice he ever takes of such papers is to hand them to me. Every officer who has been appointed since I arrived, has been chosen by me, and I like to see them before I take them. Couldn't Wingate come on here?

There may be more vacancies than I expected, if Genl Foster doesn't come out safe—and John White, whom I expected, can't come.[2] I showed Charles Lowell your letter in Effie's presence & I think she read it herself.

Your loving son

I hope you will come to Boston before I go.

1. Wingate is unidentified.

2. Maj. Gen. John Gray Foster (1823–74), of New Hampshire, graduated from West Point in 1846 and made a career in the army. Foster commanded a brigade at Roanoke Island and New Bern in 1861. From July to November 1863, Foster commanded the Department of North Carolina. *Harper's Weekly*, Mar. 1, 1862, p. 7; Faust, *Encyclopedia*, p. 282. John White is unidentified.

Readville   [HL]
April 24 1863

Dear Father,

I ought to have written you long ago, that your man Vogelsang was accepted, and is a Sergeant in one of the new companies. He is very efficient.[1]

Mr. Wingate has probably told you the result of his visit. He didn't like to accept the position of Second Lieutenant, which was the only one I could offer him. I told him, I would write him, if there was a chance of a higher rank for him, in my regiment. I liked his looks very much. Col. Wild has his name on his list.

You will see me in New York a week from today—and the day after that is the Wedding.

Everything continues to progress favourably with the 54th. We have now about 730 men. They are beginning to desert.[2] There are 17–20 absent without leave. None caught yet. I shall set a detective at work tomorrow.[3]

Please honour a draft from Thos. B. Fox to the amount of $230.[4] It is the Company fund sent you by Uzias[?] Goodwin, and which I have never paid to them.[5] I don't know that he will draw it now. My business correspondence is getting larger and larger, and tonight I have written six letters—some of them long.

All our ordinance has come from Washington. I expect to get it out here tomorrow. We have Enfield Rifles.[6]

The Ladies' committee have agreed to pay an instructor for a band, so I shall have one going before long.[7]

Effie is well. She and Mrs. Lowell came out here today.[8]

The house is a very pleasant one. When Annie & I come back & Mother & Nellie come on, Mrs. L will go home, which will leave room for all of us.

There are three flag committees entrain for this regiment. One white and two black. They are all quarreling together, and are distracted by internal dissension at the same time. I wrote one of them today that if they didn't settle their difficulties I should probably not accept a flag from either of them.

Love to Mother & Nellie

Your loving son

1. Peter Vogelsang (1815–87) was married and working as a clerk in Brooklyn, New York, when he heard that the government had authorized the formation of a black regiment. Mustered on Apr. 17 as a sergeant in Company H, Vogelsang became company sergeant, then regimental quartermaster sergeant in Nov. 1863. He distinguished himself by rallying and leading a group of men at James Island on July 16, 1863. Vogelsang was one of three black soldiers in the Fifty-fourth to advance to officer's rank, being promoted to first lieutenant and regimental quartermaster in mid-July 1865. Emilio, *A Brave Black Regiment*, pp. 58, 315–17, 330, 339; Peter Vogelsang file, CMSR.

2. Desertion was a fact of life for Civil War armies, and the desertion rate for black soldiers mirrored that of their white counterparts. But for black soldiers to desert meant that white racists could giggle and laugh and say "I told you so." The prevailing opinion among white Americans held that blacks would not fight, or not fight well, and would thus demoralize white troops. Shaw knew that the Fifty-fourth must disprove this notion. Deserters would not help the cause. Glatthaar, *Forged in Battle*, p. 165.

3. The printed version, *Letters: RGS* (1864), omits the four sentences about black deserters. Shaw's mother was much too proud that the Fifty-fourth had shown that blacks could fight to

allow these sentences to stand.

4. First Lt. Thomas Bayley Fox (1839–63) of Newburyport, Massachusetts, a Harvard classmate of Shaw's who joined the Second Massachusetts in Aug. 1862, died at Gettysburg on July 3. Shaw requested that Fox be given a majority in the Fifty-fourth, but before Governor Andrew acted, Fox was dead. Higginson, *Harvard Memorial Biographies*, vol. 2, pp. 115–23.

5. Goodwin is unidentified.

6. Enfield rifles fired a .577 caliber minie ball accurately over several hundred yards. Made in London and Birmingham, England, the Enfield was used by nearly 800,000 soldiers on both sides during the war. Faust, *Encyclopedia*, pp. 243–44.

7. The ladies' committee is unidentified. Commonly, mothers, wives, sisters, girlfriends, and friends of a regiment's soldiers formed a committee to coordinate news, special supplies, and comfort to the men. Naturally, the committee also served as a support group for the women.

8. Anna Cabot Jackson Lowell, mother of Charles Russell Lowell, Jr., and James Jackson Lowell, married cousin Charles Russell Lowell (1807–70) in 1832. Mrs. Lowell founded and conducted a preparatory school for girls in Cambridge. She lost both sons to the war. Greenslet, *Lowells and Their Seven Worlds*, pp. 239, 424–25.

Lenox, Mass.
May 3, 1863
My dear Charley,

I can only guess at your whereabouts. The papers tell us that you are once more at work in good earnest. How I wish I were to take my share in this campaign, and that my future fighting were to be (if there is any in store for me) might be done alongside of my old companions. Think of me when you come into camp of a night, and lie down on your blanket, before a rail fire (the rails must be scarce in that neighbourhood though.)

Just now I am very differently occupied, for I was married yesterday and have just come up here to spend a week.[1]

The country is just beginning to look green & the weather is perfect. We are living at Pa Haggerty's place, which is a remarkably pretty one, & I expect to have as nice a time as any one in the same circumstances ever did.[2] Saddle horses & a light wagon are at hand, when we want to ride or drive, and a nice garden & pine grove near, to furnish pleasant walks.

I feel very humble when I think of you fellows out there, but shan't fret much, as I expect to be off myself in less than 30 days. I have got my minimum of enlisted men & received my Col's commission.[3]

Harry follows suit, & will be married next Wednesday, after asserting for six weeks that he should wait until he returned home again.[4]

I dined at your Father's Sunday before last, and passed a most pleasant afternoon on the border of the pond.[5] It made me think of your many adventures in the neighbourhood.

I saw Miss Goreham and couldn't but admire your brother's good taste. Your Mother, I only saw for a moment, as some indisposition prevented her from coming down to dinner.[6]

I don't think I ever saw a sweeter face than your sister's, and if her lameness has had anything to do with forming such a beautiful character as she must have, it is not a dear price to pay for it.

I hope this will find you alive & well.

Please hand the enclosed slip to Tom Fox at earliest opportunity.[7]

Write me what is going on when you have a chance. Bangs is engaged to Miss Laura Pell—a very handsome young lady, and one of the best amateur performers on the [one word illegible] in N. Y.[8] I didn't send cards to the fellows in the regt because it didn't seem worth while. If any one speaks of it please excuse me to them.

                                        Your afftc friend,
                                        Bob

1. Shaw married Annie Kneeland Haggerty in the Church of the Ascension, a Protestant Episcopal Church on Fifth Avenue in New York City. Teamoh, *Sketch of Shaw*, p. 19; *Trow's NYC Directory for 1863*, p. 14.

2. Ogden Haggerty.

3. Shaw was commissioned a colonel on Apr. 17, 1863, and mustered as a colonel on May 13. MS. L. Robert Gould Shaw, MHS; Robert Gould Shaw

file, CMSR.

4. Harry Russell married Mary Forbes on May 6, 1863. Hughes, ed., *Forbes*, vol. 2, p. 4.

5. Charles Morse's father is unidentified.

6. Morses's mother and sister and Miss Goreham are unidentified.

7. Thomas B. Fox.

8. George P. Bangs. Laura Pell is unidentified.

Lenox   [RGS]
May 6, 1863
My Dear Effie,

Annie and I shall be in Boston on Monday. Will you please tell Mrs. Crehore to expect us on Tuesday?[1] No matter whether she wants us or not, we are coming. I was very glad to hear from Mother that Charley ("*Katie*") had got to New York after all.[2] Harry and Mary are married by this time; I wish I could have been at the wedding; what a pity the weather is so bad; it has been beautiful up here until now. I have been in quite an angelic mood ever since we got here,—as is becoming,—and haven't felt envious of any one. Excuse this short note, for I am *dreadfully* busy.

Annie sends love to you and Charley. We haven't seen a single soul until today, and we've only been off the place twice. We began to read "The Mill on the Floss," but have only finished three or four chapters. We read it three years ago together, when I was here on a visit. Our own ideas are more interesting to us just now, than Miss Evans'.[3]

Always your loving Brotherum

1. Mrs. Crehore ran a boarding house where the Shaws, Haggertys, and Lowells stayed while visiting Camp Meigs, one-half mile away. Shaw and Lowell boarded there while their men stayed in camp.

2. Charles Russell Lowell, Jr.

3. Author Mary Ann Evans (1819–80) took the pen name George Eliot, and published *The Mill on the Floss* (New York: Harper, 1860) and many other fictional works.

Lenox   [RGS]
May 7, 1863
Dear Sue,

I have just received a telegram from Hallowell, saying that the Governor is going to send us off on the 20th. Please drop a line to Mother, and tell her this. We go down Saturday instead of Monday. O, how glum I feel! Colonel Hallowell remains at Readville to start the Fifty-fifth.[1] If I lose the Major too, I don't know what I *shall* do.[2]

Give my love to Robert, and tell him his cigars are splendid.[3] Annie sends her best love. I shall send this to Father, so you needn't write to Mother.

Always dear Susie,
Your loving Brother

1. The recruiters for the Fifty-fourth had been so successful and so many black Northerners wanted to fight for the Union and for themselves that the overflow of volunteers formed into a new regiment, the Fifty-fifth Massachusetts. Governor Andrew had only to look as far as Norwood Hallowell for its commander. Hallowell, who wanted to stay with the regiment he had been instrumental in forming, could not refuse the governor's order to take charge of the new regiment. He was commissioned a

colonel on June 24, 1863. Charles B. Fox, *Record of the Service of the Fifty-Fifth Regiment of Massachusetts Volunteer Infantry* (Cambridge, Mass.: John Wilson, 1868).

2. Edward Needles Hallowell was promoted to the lieutenant colonelcy vacated by his brother. He would always be called "the Major" by his men. Upon Shaw's death, the wounded Hallowell was promoted to colonel. Emilio, *A Brave Black Regiment*, p. 328.

3. Robert Bowne Minturn, Jr.

Readville   [RGS]
May 11, 1863
Dear Father,

I received your note, acknowledging my last from Lenox, this morning.

Annie and I got to Boston, Saturday evening; coming the last part of the way with Mrs. Haggerty and Clem., having met them at Springfield. I found the regiment looking remarkably well; there are already one hundred men for the Fifty-fifth. Both the Hallowells refused the Colonelcy of it; but the Governor says Norwood must stay and help organize it, whether he wishes to or not; so he will be detailed by the War Department. I hope Mother and you will come on very soon. We shall get away next week without a doubt, if nothing unexpected turns up. General Wilde goes to New York Wednesday, and sails for Newbern on Friday.[1]

We are settled at Mrs. Crehore's, and ready to receive you whenever you can come. By this time, there *must* be some news from the coming baby.[2] Love to Mother and Nellie. I received Mother's note at Lenox.

Your loving Son

1. Edward Augustus Wild.
2. Shaw's sister Anna Curtis would deliver her third child, Sarah Shaw Curtis, on May 17. Sturgis, *Sturgis*, p. 57.

CHAPTER 13

"*The burning of Darien*"

The gray line moved north, the blue line stayed put, and the black line went south. On June 3, Lee began his second invasion of the North, pulled along unknowingly by the magnet that became Gettysburg. At Brandy Station on June 6, twenty thousand horsemen under J. E. B. Stuart and Alfred Pleasanton charged and recharged each other for nearly twelve hours in the greatest cavalry clash of the war. All the while, Grant continued to squeeze Vicksburg. The same day that Lee started north from Fredericksburg, the Fifty-fourth Massachusetts Infantry reported for duty at Port Royal, South Carolina.

A week before, on May 28, to an astonishing fanfare of support unseen since the first days of the war, Shaw had departed Boston with his regiment. Abolitionist supporters and Democratic detractors watched the Fifty-fourth carefully to see if blacks would fight. Fourteen days later, the regiment saw its first action, burning the undefended town of Darien on the banks of the Altamaha River in Georgia. Opponents of black troops screamed "I told you so; savages!" Blacks could burn defenseless buildings, but what would happen when they formed into line of battle against white men? The Darien affair had hurt this most watched of all regiments. With a sense of duty to his men and supporters, Shaw spent the next—and last—month of his life trying to put Darien behind him and rekindle the kind of glory and pride he felt while in the Second Massachusetts.

Readville [HL]
May 17 1863
Dear Mother,

We were very sorry not to find you in the train last night, and to hear that you were ill.

Nellie arrived safely and is at present domiciled with Effie & us at Mrs. Crehore's.

Tomorrow, if it is not stormy, there are to be four banners presented to the 54th.[1] I have persuaded all the donors to have them presented together by the Govr so that the whole affair will not occupy more than 1/2 hour.

The War Department has been notified that we shall be ready to go on the 20th Inst. but we have heard nothing from them yet, so that I can't tell when we shall go.

I will telegraph to you when I find out. Do try to come if you can.

Give my love to Father, Anna, & George. I wish I had something more to write you but I haven't, because I am so sleepy and stupid. Goodnight dearest Mother. Annie sends you & Father her best love.

Always your loving son

1. On May 18, a tremendous crowd made an excursion to Readville to see the regiment and watch Governor Andrew present the flags. The four flags were the Stars and Stripes, the state flag, a white silk flag with the goddess of Liberty and the motto: "Liberty, Loyalty, and Unity," and a blue flag with a cross to symbolize Christ's mission. Emilio, *A Brave Black Regiment*, pp. 24–30.

Readville [RGS]
May 18, 1863
Dearest Mother,

I am so sorry you were not here to-day. The presentation went off finely. The Governor made a beautiful speech.[1] My response was *small potatoes*.[2] The day has been beautiful; and on the whole it was a success. After the ceremony, we had a Battalion drill, and then refreshments for guests at my head-quarters. The Governor handed me a telegram from the Secretary of War, saying, "*The Fifty-fourth Massachusetts will report to General Hunter; make requisitions for transportation, so that they may go at once.*"[3]

As soon as the transports are ready, we shall be off; that may not be for a week, though. I shall find out to-morrow, if possible, and telegraph Father; if I don't see you and Father before I go, I shall be terribly disappointed. Effie and Nellie are at Milton Hill to tea this evening.[4] Cabot Russel and Wilkie James hired a large "carryall," and drove them over.[5] They thought the carryall more in accordance with your ideas of propriety, than separate buggies.

You will wonder, no doubt, at our being taken from General Wilde.[6] General Hunter wanted us, and I told the Governor I thought the men would have a better chance for work than with Foster.[7] The latter, as likely as not, would make us do all the digging of the department.[8]

Always, dearest Mother,
Your loving Son

1. Governor Andrew cast his speech in terms of the vindication of a race. He told the Fifty-fourth that the world would be watching their actions for proof of "character, the manly character, the zeal, the manly zeal, of the colored citizens" of America. He told the black men "to strike a blow" and to uphold the flag, "*their* country's flag, now as well as ours." The Stars and Stripes had never before flown for blacks, now the Fifty-fourth could envelop themselves in it and make it stand for something higher. For the full text of Governor Andrew's speech, see Emilio, *A Brave Black Regiment*, pp. 25–30.

2. In a response only six sentences long, Shaw thanked the governor for the flags, thanked the friends of the regiment and the soldiers of the Fifty-fourth for their devotion to the cause, and in the one sentence that counted, said, "May we have an opportunity to show that you have not made a mistake in intrusting the honor of the State to a colored regiment,—the first State that has sent one to the war." Ibid., pp. 30–31.

3. Maj. Gen. David Hunter, comman-der of the Department of the South, headquartered at Hilton Head, South Carolina.

4. Josephine and Ellen went to the Forbes's home, Milton Hill.

5. Cabot Jackson Russel (1844–63), of New York City, left Harvard in January of his freshman year, 1862, to join the Forty-fourth Massachusetts Infantry as a sergeant. He saw the war as one for emancipation. In 1859, after Virginians executed John Brown, Russel put a picture of Brown over his bed, where it remained throughout his life. Once the government began to enroll black troops, Russel sought and got a transfer to the Fifty-fourth to accept a lieutenancy, then captaincy. Eighteen-year-old Cabot Russel died on the ramparts at Fort Wagner on July 18, 1863. Higginson, *Harvard Memorial Biographies*, vol. 2, pp. 457–66; Putnam, *Memoirs of the War of '61*, pp. 54–56; Cabot Jackson Russel file, CMSR. Garth Wilkinson James (1845–83), brother of William and Henry James, left college to join the Forty-fourth Massachusetts, then, with Cabot Russel, transferred from the

Forty-fourth to the Fifty-fourth. James was wounded at Fort Wagner and spent a long convalescence before resigning due to his wounds. Writing to his son Henry while James recovered from his wounds, James's father said that James was "vastly attached to the negro-soldier cause; believes (I think) that the world has existed for it; and is sure that enormous results to civilisation are coming out of it." James's father also wrote that "Cabot Russel, Wilky's dearest friend, is, we fear, a prisoner and wounded. . . . Poor Wilky cries aloud for his friends gone and missing." Emilio, *A Brave Black Regiment*, pp. 333–34; James's letter cited in Henry James, *Notes of a Son and Builder* (New York: Charles Scribner's Sons, 1914), pp. 241–42.

6. Edward Augustus Wild.

7. Maj. Gen. John Gray Foster never felt the need to raise black troops, whom he thought would not enlist anyway. Reid, "General E. A. Wild," pp. 15–16.

8. During the war, Union and Confederate commanders often employed or forced blacks to dig fortifications, work as cooks and servants, fill in latrines, drive wagons, and do a vast amount of the manual labor for white soldiers. When black regiments joined white regiments in the field, many Union commanders disproportionately allocated most of the disagreeable jobs to the black men. Shaw was aware of this. He knew the Fifty-fourth had to fight, not dig, to prove themselves men.

Steamer De Molay   [RGS]
June 1, 1863, Off Cape Hatteras
Dearest Annie,

We have got thus far on our voyage without accident, excepting the loss of Major Hallowell's mare, which died this morning, and was consigned to the sea.

We left the wharf at 4 P.M., having been detained nearly two hours in packing the arms.[1] That night, and the next day, the sea was very smooth, but Friday evening the wind rose, and before long we had a very sea-sick cargo. Since then, we have been rolling and pitching very steadily. I myself have not been ill at all, so I have done nothing but think over the events of the last three months; which has given me so much occupation, that I have hardly read anything. It is only three months and a half since I got to New York, and Nellie called to you to come down and see me. I hope I shall never forget the happy days we have passed together since then, and that I shall always look back on them with the same pleasure as now. It may be a long time before we find ourselves driving about Berkshire together again; but I do hope that some day we can live over those days at Lenox once more; or even Mrs. Crehore's, with a regiment close by to worry us, would not be very bad.

. . . The more I think of the passage of the Fifty-fourth through Boston, the more wonderful it seems to me. Just remember our own doubts and fears, and other people's sneering and pitying remarks, when we began last winter, and then look at the perfect triumph of last Thursday. We have gone quietly along, forming the regiment, and at last left Boston amidst a greater enthusiasm than has been seen since the first three-months troops left for the war. Every one I saw, from the Governor's staff (who have always given us rather the cold shoulder) down, had nothing but words of praise for us. Truly, I ought to be thankful for all my happiness, and my success in life so far; and if the raising of coloured troops prove such a benefit to the country, and to the blacks, as many people think it will, I shall thank God a thousand times that I was led to take my share in it.

This steamer is a very slow one, but fortunately perfectly clean, and well-ventilated. She is entirely free from all disagreeable odours; and the cabin is as comfortable as possible. The weather to-day is perfectly clear, and the sun is getting hot. We have a fine large awning over the quarter-deck, so that we can sit there very pleasantly. You would hardly believe that we have very little trouble in keeping the men's quarters clean, and that the air there is perfectly good. The men behave very well; in fact, they have so much animal spirits, that nothing can depress them for any length of time. I heard one man saying, *"I felt sick, but I jes' kep' a ramblin' round, and now I'm right well."* My three horses are perfectly well, though thin.

I wonder where you now are; whether on the way to Lenox, or already there. Remember that the vessel is rolling and pitching in the most persevering manner, and don't criticise my calligraphy too severely. . . .

June 3d, 10 A.M.—We passed the blockading fleet off Charleston at seven this morning, and saw the top of Fort Sumter, and the turrets of the iron-clads, or at any rate, something that looked like them. We expect to reach Hilton Head at about three this afternoon. O dear! I wish you were with us.

. . . Did any one tell you that, after bidding you and Mother and the girls good bye so stoically, Harry and I had to retire into the back parlour, and have a regular girl's cry? It was like putting the last feather on the camel's back; I had as much as I could carry before. It was a great relief, though.

Give my dearest love to your Mother and to Clem. I hope they are well, though I suppose you don't know much about the latter, as she is not with you. How nice and cool and pleasant it must be at Lenox now. The air is pretty hot here, even at sea, but it is not close or oppressive. Remember me to "Mammy Did."[2] I thought yesterday at dinner that I should like some of her soup. Some day we will make that journey we used to talk of, from Lenox through Springfield and Northampton.

I will add a P. S. to this after we get safely established on dry land. Until then, good bye, darling Annie. I hope you have recovered your spirits, got over your cold, and are feeling happy. Remember all your promises to me; go to bed early, and take as much exercise as you can, without getting fatigued. . . .

Your ever loving Husband

1. The regiment departed Boston from Battery Wharf on May 28.
2. "Mammy Did" is unidentified, but is, most likely, the Haggertys' cook in Lenox.

Steamer De Molay   [RGS]
June 3, 1863, Off Charleston
Dearest Mother,

Here we are near the end of our voyage. Everything has prospered thus far. We have had no illness on board, with the exception of a little "*heebin*" (heaving), as the men call it. I have had no sea-sickness at all myself.

The more I think of last Thursday, the more complete a triumph it seems to me. You know from the first day the regiment was organized, no one connected with it has talked extravagantly, or boasted about it in any way; we went on quietly with our work, letting outsiders say what they chose, and wound up with what you saw, as we passed through Boston. That was the greatest day for us all that we ever passed, and I only hope it was of corresponding importance to the cause.

We saw the blockading fleet, and the top of Fort Sumter, off Charleston this morning. We expect to get in this afternoon. I shall go on shore immediately, and report to General Hunter, and if we can find a good camping-ground, shall land the regiment this evening.

Your loving Son

June 3/63   [HL]
Dear Father,

My note to Mother will tell you of our prosperous voyage. My horses are all doing well fortunately. Major Hallowell's died the 3d day out.[1]

I told Annie that if she needed any more money than her allowance, towards the end of the year, to write to you for it. I shall soon be sending you home plenty.

Will you please send an account of how much I have drawn, since I went home, and how much property I own now in the bank & in treasury notes. I shall send Annie's letters to her Father's care, unless she is staying at the Island, as I think that is the quickest way.

I enclose a note for Anna Curtis.[2] Call and Tuttle are making me a flannel suit, which I ordered to be sent to you.[3] Please put in the bundle a good stock of stationery and waste paper—and a supply of quinine, in pills & powder—and some postage stamps.

Your loving son

P.S. I enclose draft of R. P. Hallowell for $137.00.[4]

Hilton Head—

Arrived safe at 2 1/2. We go to camp at Beaufort up the bay. Montgomery has just ret. from an expedition with 725 blacks from plantations.[5]

1. An editor of *Letters: RGS* (1864) substantially cut this letter without using ellipses. Paragraphs two through four were deleted in their entirety, with the exception of the sentence that tells of enclosing a note to Anna.

2. Anna Shaw Curtis.

3. John M. Call and Thomas W. Tuttle operated a mercantile tailor's store at 182 Washington Street, Boston. *Boston City Directory, 1863* (Boston: Adams, Sampson, 1863), pp. 61, 357.

4. Richard Price Hallowell.

5. On Jan. 13, 1863, Col. James Montgomery (1814–71) used his strong connections with George Stearns to obtain permission to raise a black regiment, the Second South Carolina Infantry. Montgomery arrived at Port Royal on Feb. 24 and began recruiting from among the contrabands. He adapted the tactics he had learned while fighting for Kansas free-soldiers, including retaliatory burnings, to the South. Col. Thomas W. Higginson of the First South Carolina recorded that Montgomery was "splen-did, but impulsive and changeable; never plans far ahead, and goes off at a tangent." Of his return from the Combahee raid on the same day Shaw and the Fifty-fourth arrived, Higginson wrote in his journal, "Montgomery's raid was a most brilliant success, though I don't believe in burning private houses, as he does. Nearly eight hundred contrabands!" Harriet Tubman led the Combahee raid and worked spying and scouting for Montgomery. Frank P. Stearns, *The Life and Public Services of George Luther Stearns* (Philadelphia: J. B. Lippincott, 1907), pp. 226, 286; AAG Thomas M. Vincent to Col. James Montgomery, Jan. 13, 1863, in "The Negro in the Military Service of the United States, 1607–1889," M-858, Roll 2, p. 1067, NA; Mary T. Higginson, ed., *Letters and Journals of Thomas Wentworth Higginson, 1846–1906* (Boston: Houghton Mifflin, 1921), pp. 185–86, 188, 207; Dorothy Sterling, ed., *Black Women in the Nineteenth Century* (New York: W. W. Norton, 1984), p. 259.

Str. De Molay, Off Hilton Head, S.C.
June 3, 1863
Dear Cousin John,[1]

Here we are (the 54th Mass. Vols. (coloured) close to our Department, and in a very different condition from that in which you left us.

Our recruiting system did not get well under weigh, until sometime after you went, and then we filled up very rapidly. The Governor gave Ned Hallowell the Majority without any difficulty, and soon after Norwood was ordered to take the 55th which was started about the 10th of May. He refused the Colonelcy for some time, but has finally decided to take it, as the Governor wouldn't let him come with us, at any rate.

The 54th has been a success from beginning to end. The drill & discipline are all that anyone could expect.

Crowds of people came to our battalion drills & dress parades every afternoon, and we have heard nothing but words of praise & astonishment from friend & foe—from hunkers & fogeys, old and young.

The camp was crowded on the day of our banner presentation—and the Governor made an excellent speech. Last Thursday, 28 May, we left Readville at 7 A.M. & went by rail to Boston. We marched from the Providence Depot through Essex, Federal, Franklin, School Sts., Pemberton Square, Beacon St. to the Common—then by Tremont & State Sts. to Battery Wharf where we embarked.

The streets were crowded, & I have not seen such enthusiasm since the first troops left for the war.

On the Common the regiment was received

[rest of letter missing]

1. John Murray Forbes.

Beaufort, S.C.
June 5 1863
Dear Father,

We came down from Hilton Head day before yesterday. I saw Col. Montgomery, who was about to embark for an expedition to Georgia. I immediately requested permission to go with him but was too late, and shall probably follow tomorrow or day after. I thought it best to get my men at work as soon as possible.

We shall, I think, not return here, but have our camp at St. Simon's Island. If you don't hear from me to the contrary, address letters &c to Hilton Head—from there they will be forwarded to wherever we are.

Montgomery is a good man to begin under—as he is a guerrilla-man by profession, you know. We are all very much refreshed by two days on shore.

Tell Mother that from all I can ascertain, there is very little danger in this sort of work. Col. Montgomery says he never was in a fight in his life, where he lost more than 2 men killed. He is an Indian in his mode of warfare, and though I am glad to see something of it, I can't say I admire it. It isn't like a fair stand up such as our Potomac Army is accustomed to.

A telegram just received for Genl Hunter informs me that we must wait for other transports as our steamer must go North.

Love all at home.

Your loving son

Beaufort [HL]
June 6 1863
Dear Mother,

The mail which was to have gone last night is still here, so I can send you a few lines.

Col. Montgomery sailed yesterday, and we shall go after him before long, I suppose.

This is an odd sort of place. All the original inhabitants are gone—and the houses are occupied by Northerners & a few Florida refugees.[1]

The Northern ladies here are a fearful crowd—ungrammatical and nasal. I had a taste of them the first evening we arrived, having unawares booked into a house where 8 or 10 teachers live.[2] Ned Hooper extracted me by taking me to tea to his house, and I have not ventured in town, on foot, since.[3]

Col. Higginson came over to see us, day before yesterday.[4] I never saw any one who put his whole soul into his work as he does. I was very much impressed with his open-heartedness & purity of character. He is encamped about 10 miles from here.

The bush-whacker Montgomery is a strange compound. He allows no swearing or drinking in his regiment & is anti tobacco—But he burns & destroys wherever he goes with great gusto, & looks as if he had quite a taste for hanging people & throat-cutting whenever a suitable subject offers.

All our stores are very acceptable now, and the Hungarian wine Father sent us is excellent.

Genl Hunter doesn't impress me as being a great man. There is some talk of his being relieved. If we could have Fremont in his place, wouldn't it be fine?

Mr. Eustis was over here yesterday.[5] Tomorrow the Major & I ride over to his plantation.

I hope you will send me all the papers containing accounts of our passage through Boston.

It is impossible to keep clean here for two hours—the fine sand covers everything. Every one here has received us very kindly; though there are a great many opposers among the officers they show no signs of it to us.

Love to the girls & yourself dearest Mother.

Your loving son

Dear Father,

Please send the enclosed to Annie. Put a stamp on it & drop it in the box—so it will get there later than another I addressed to her Father's care yesterday.

1. The Union forces under Adm. Samuel Francis du Pont had established a beachhead at Port Royal in November 1861 that was expanded to a full-scale military base by mid-summer 1862. Those planters who had time gathered up their household belongings and slaves and moved to the interior, away from Federal forces. Those slaves who could, escaped, hid out, and waited until Union armies had cleared the land of their old masters before they returned for the protection of blue-clad men. Rose, *Rehearsal for Reconstruction*, especially pp. 11–79.

2. Northern missionaries, many of them schoolteachers, flocked into Port Royal to educate, assimilate, and help the freed slaves build lives on the sandy soil that had been confiscated for them.

3. Edward William Hooper (1839–1901), of Boston, graduated Harvard Law School in 1861 and volunteered to go to Port Royal with a band of reform-ers, "Gideon's Band," led by Edward Pierce, a firm antislavery reformer and friend of Charles Sumner. Hooper be-came a captain on Brig. Gen. Rufus Saxton's staff on June 28, 1862, and he helped Saxton take charge of the freed-men and settle them on land confiscated from Rebels. Rose, *Rehearsal*, pp. 21–50; Brown, *Harvard University in the War*, p. 127.

4. Higginson remembered meeting Shaw in Beaufort on June 4 and talk-ing about whether blacks would fight. Higginson recalled Shaw proposing that "it would always be possible to put another line of soldiers behind a black regiment, so as to present equal danger in either direction." Higginson, *Army Life in a Black Regiment*, p. 216; Thomas W. Higginson, *Cheerful Yester-days* (1899; reprint ed., New York: Arno Press, 1968), p. 257.

5. Mr. Eustis is unidentified.

June 8 1863

Dear Father,

We got aboard this vessel again this morning and came up from Beaufort. I shall go ashore here in a little while & get my orders from Genl Hunter. We go probably to St. Simon's Island, as I told you in my last. No mail has gone, I believe, since the first night we arrived, and we have received nothing since we left Boston.

I am not very anxious to have my large horse sold, unless he will bring a good price. When he gets well, perhaps Uncle Jim would like to take him & use him.[1] He would make an excellent carryall horse & is steadier in harness than in the saddle. The three horses I have here are all good. The small black one I shall probably sell to Major Hallowell.

Please send me the price of the mess-chests so that I can divide among the officers of my mess.

Enclosed is a note for Annie. Love to Mother & all.

Always your loving son

P.S. Hilton Head. We *are* going to St. Simon's & shall get away immediately. R. G. S.

1. James Sturgis of Boston.

St. Simon's Island, Ga.   [RGS]
Tuesday, June 9, 1863

My Dearest Annie,

We arrived at the southern point of this island at six this morning. I went ashore to report to Colonel Montgomery, and was ordered to proceed with my regiment to a place called "Pike's Bluff," on the inner coast of the island, and encamp.[1] We came up here in another steamer, the "Sentinel," as the "De Molay" is too large for the inner waters,—and took possession to-day of a plantation formerly owned by Mr. Gould.[2] We have a very nice camping-ground for the regiment, and I have my quarters in "*the house*"; very pleasantly situated, and surrounded by fine large trees. The island is beautiful, as far as I have seen it. You would be enchanted with the scenery here; the foliage is wonderfully thick, and the trees covered with hanging moss, making beautiful avenues wherever there is a road or path; it is more like the tropics than anything I have seen. Mr. Butler King's plantation, where I first went ashore, must have been a beautiful place, and well kept.[3] It is entirely neglected now, of course; and as the growth is very rapid, two years' neglect almost covers all traces of former care.

12th.—If I could have gone on describing to you the beauties of this region, who knows but I might have made a fine addition to the literature of our age? But since I wrote the above, I have been looking at something very different.

On Wednesday, a steamboat appeared off our wharf, and Colonel Montgomery hailed me from the deck with, "How soon can you get ready to start on an expedition?" I said, "In half an hour," and it was not long before we were on board with eight companies, leaving two for camp-guard.

We steamed down by his camp, where two other steamers with five companies from his regiment, and two sections of Rhode Island artillery, joined us.[4] A little below there we ran aground, and had to wait until midnight for flood-tide, when we got away once more.

At 8 A.M., we were at the mouth of the Altamaha River, and immediately made for Darien. We wound in and out through the creeks, twisting and turning continually, often heading in directly the opposite direction from that which we intended to go, and often running aground, thereby losing much time. Besides our three vessels, we were followed by the gunboat "Paul Jones."

On the way up, Montgomery threw several shells among the plantation buildings, in what seemed to me a very brutal way; for he didn't know how many women and children there might be.

About noon we came in sight of Darien, a beautiful little town. Our artillery peppered it a little, as we came up, and then our three boats made fast to the wharves, and we landed the troops. The town was deserted, with the exception of two white women and two negroes.

Montgomery ordered all the furniture and movable property to be taken on board the boats.[5] This occupied some time; and after the town was pretty thoroughly disembowelled, he said to me, "I shall burn this town." He speaks always in a very low tone, and has quite a sweet smile when addressing you. I told him, "I did not want the responsibility of it," and he was only too happy to take it all on his shoulders; so the pretty little place was burnt to the ground, and not a shed remains standing; Montgomery firing the last buildings with his own hand.[6] One of my companies assisted in it, because he ordered them out, and I had to obey. You must bear in mind, that not a shot had been fired at us from this place, and that there were evidently very few men left in it. All the inhabitants (principally women and children) had fled on our approach, ınd were no doubt watching the scene from a distance. Some of our grape-hot tore the skirt of one of the women whom I saw. Montgomery told her hat her house and property should be spared; but it went down with the rest.

The reasons he gave me for destroying Darien were, that the Southerners nust be made to feel that this was a real war, and that they were to be swept away by the hand of God, like the Jews of old. In theory it may seem all right to some, but when it comes to being made the instrument of the Lord's vengeance, I myself don't like it. Then he says, "We are outlawed, and therefore not bound by the rules of regular warfare"; but that makes it none the less revolting to wreak our vengeance on the innocent and defenceless.[7]

By the time we had finished this dirty piece of business, it was too dark to go far down the narrow river, where our boat sometimes touched both banks at once; so we lay at anchor until daylight, occasionally dropping a shell at a stray house. The "Paul Jones" fired a few guns as well as we.

I reached camp at about 2 P.M. to-day, after as abominable a job as I ever had a share in.

We found a mail waiting for us, and I received your dear letter, and several from Father, Mother, Effie, and some business correspondence. This is the first news we have had since our departure, and I rather regained my good spirits.

Now, dear Annie, remember not to breathe a word of what I have written about this raid, to any one out of our two families, for I have not yet made up my mind what I ought to do. Besides my own distaste for this barbarous sort of warfare, I am not sure that it will not harm very much the reputation of black troops and of those connected with them. For myself, I have gone through the war so far without dishonour, and I do not like to degenerate into a plunderer and robber,—and the same applies to every officer in my regiment. There was not a deed performed, from beginning to end, which required any pluck or courage. If we had fought for possession of the place, and it had been found necessary to hold or destroy it, or if the inhabitants had done anything which deserved such punishment, or if it were a place of refuge for the enemy, there might have been some reason for Montgomery's acting as he did; but as the case stands, I can't see any justification. If it were the order of our government to overrun the South with fire and sword, I might look at it in a different light; for then we should be carrying out what had been decided upon as a necessary policy. As the case stands, we are no better than "Semmes," who attacks and destroys defenceless vessels, and haven't even the poor excuse of gaining anything by it; for the property is of no use to us, excepting that we can now sit on chairs instead of camp-stools.[8]

But all I complain of, is wanton destruction. After going through the hard campaigning and hard fighting in Virginia, this makes me very much ashamed of myself.

Montgomery, from what I have seen of him, is a conscientious man, and really believes what he says,—"that he is doing his duty to the best of his knowledge and ability."

. . . There are two courses only for me to pursue: to obey orders and say nothing; or to refuse to go on any more such expeditions, and be put under arrest, probably court-martialled, which is a serious thing.

June 13th.—This letter I am afraid will be behindhand, for a boat went to Hilton Head this morning from the lower end of the island, and I knew nothing about it. Colonel Montgomery has gone up himself, and will not be back until Tuesday probably.

. . . To-day I rode over to Pierce Butler's plantation.[9] It is an immense place, and parts of it very beautiful. The house is small, and badly built, like almost all I have seen here. There are about ten of his slaves left there, all of them sixty or seventy years old. He sold three hundred slaves about three years ago.[10]

I talked with some, whose children and grandchildren were sold then, and though they said that was a "weeping day," they maintained that "Massa Butler was a good massa," and they would give anything to see him again. When I told them I had known Miss Fanny, they looked very much pleased, and one named John wanted me to tell her I had seen him.[11] They said all the house-servants had been taken inland by the overseer at the beginning of the war; and they asked if we couldn't get their children back to the island again. These were all born and bred on the place, and even selling away their families could not entirely efface their love for their master. Isn't it horrible to think of a man being able to treat such faithful creatures in such a manner?

The island is traversed from end to end by what they call a shell-road; which is hard and flat, excellent for driving. On each side there are either very large and overhanging trees, with thick underbrush, or open country covered with sago-palm, the sharp-pointed leaves making the country impassable. Occasionally we meet with a few fields of very poor grass; when there is no swamp, the soil is very sandy.

There are a good many of these oyster-shell roads, for in many places there are great beds of them, deposited nobody knows when, I suppose. The walls of many of the buildings are built of cement mixed with oyster-shells, which make it very durable.[12]

I forgot to tell you that the negroes at Mr. Butler's remembered Mrs. Kemble very well, and said she was a very fine lady. They hadn't seen her since the young ladies were very small, they said.[13] My visit there was very interesting and touching.

A deserted homestead is always a sad sight, but here in the South we must look a little deeper than the surface, and then we see that every such over-grown plantation, and empty house, is a harbinger of freedom to the slaves, and every lover of his country, even if he have no feeling for the slaves them-selves, should rejoice.

Next to Mr. Butler's is the house of Mr. James E. Cooper.[14] It must have been a lovely spot; the garden is well laid out, and the perfume of the flowers is delicious. The house is the finest on the island. The men from our gunboats have been there, and all the floors are strewed with books and magazines of every kind. There is no furniture in any of these houses.

Please send this to Father, for I want him and Mother to read it, and I don't care about writing it over.

Colonel Montgomery's original plan, on this last expedition, was to land about fifteen miles above Darien, and march down on two different roads to the town, taking all the negroes to be found, and burning every planter's house on the passage. I should have commanded our detachment, in that case. The above are the orders he gave me.

Good bye for to-day, dearest Annie.

Your loving Rob

9 P.M. June 13th . . . To-morrow is Sunday, and perhaps you will be at Staten Island; at any rate, I suppose, not at Lenox; but wherever you are, I wish I could go to church with you, and saunter about in some pretty garden afterwards.

. . . There is a beautiful little church near here, almost buried in trees and moss. I have had it put to rights (it was damaged by some sailors and soldiers), and the Chaplain of the Second South Carolina Regiment is to preach there for us to-morrow.

I shall always have a service of some kind on Sunday; and if we can't always get a chaplain, I shall have one of the officers officiate. I don't feel good enough myself to undertake to teach others, as you suggest. Perhaps I shall some time. I have read some of Robertson's sermons, and think them very beautiful.[15]

. . . I shall never let Mr. Ritchie go, if I can prevent it.[16] He is a perfect jewel, and has been of incalculable service to us, in managing the regimental quartermaster's department. . . .

Your loving Husband

1. Pike's Bluff Plantation was located seven miles south-southeast of Darien, Georgia, on Buttermilk Sound on the western side of St. Simons Island.

2. James Gould (1773–1852) of Granville, Massachusetts, moved to St. Simon's in 1794 to enter the timber business. In 1807, he won the bid to erect and tend the government lighthouse. Soon thereafter, Gould bought slaves, planted cotton, and built two houses, "Rosemount" and "Black Banks," on his 1,500-acre plantation. With his death, the plantation passed to his children. Gould's eldest daughter Mary and son Horace evacuated the island in 1861 to protect their movable property and slaves from Union naval raids. When Horace returned to St. Simon's in 1865, he found "Rosemount" burned down. U.S. Census, Seventh Census, 1850, Population Schedules, Georgia, Glynn County, p. 39; Burnette Vanstory, *Georgia's Land of the Golden Isles* (Athens: University of Georgia Press, 1956), pp. 194–99.

3. Thomas Butler King (1800–64), a Massachusetts-born lawyer, married Matilda Page, daughter of a rich St. Simons cotton planter. King served four years in the Georgia Senate and two terms as a U.S. congressman (1839–43). After the death of his father-in-law, William Page, King owned and operated Retreat Plantation on the southernmost tip of St. Simons. Malcolm Bell, Jr., *Major Butler's Legacy: Five Generations of a Slaveholding Family* (Athens: University of Georgia Press, 1987), pp. 109, 342, 539; *DAB*, vol. 5, p. 403.

4. Third Rhode Island Artillery. Burchard, *One Gallant Rush*, p. 105.

5. Montgomery, with Shaw in agreement, let his men take whatever might be useful for camp. One officer described the scene: "The men began to come in by twos, threes, and dozens, loaded with every species and all sorts and quantities of furniture, stores, trinkets, etc., till one would be tired enumerating. We had sofas, tables, pianos, chairs, mirrors, carpets, beds, bedsteads, carpenter's tools, cooper's tools, books, law-books, account-books in unlimited supply, china sets, tinware, earthenware, Confederate shinplasters, old letters, papers, etc. A private would come along with a slate, yard-stick, and a brace of chickens in one hand, and in the other hand a rope with a cow attached." Officer quoted in Smith, *Beacon Hill's*, pp. 435–36.

6. Even though Shaw did not want to burn the town, he was blamed for what happened because one of his men scribbled Shaw's name in a book, which townspeople later found. In 1870, Shaw's family sought to overturn this "conviction" by publishing letters that Shaw wrote at the time in which he expressed his disgust at what had happened. Shaw's parents sent money to Darien after the war to rebuild a church that had been burned in June 1863. *Harper's Weekly*, Sept. 3, 1870, p. 3.

7. In 1858, John Brown labeled Montgomery a "lover of freedom," and stated matter of factly, "Captain Montgomery is the only soldier I have met among the prominent Kansas men. He understands my system of warfare exactly. He is a natural chieftan, and knows how to lead." Historian Dudley T. Cornish evaluated Montgomery's style as unbound by Harvard notions of fair-

ness and romantic ideas of war fought by defined rules. In Cornish's words, "Higginson the romantic, had raised money to send Sharp's rifles to Kansas in the fifties. Montgomery, the realist, had used them." Now, it was the same in Georgia, as Montgomery understood total war against civilians and Shaw wanted a limited war. Brown quoted in Du Bois, *John Brown*, pp. 190, 254; Oates, *To Purge This Land With Blood*, p. 254; Cornish, *The Sable Arm*, p. 150.

8. Raphael Semmes (1809–77), of Maryland, was commissioned a commander in the Confederate navy in 1861 and became an advocate for, and chief enforcer of, using commerce raiders to hurt Northern trade. He commanded the *Sumter*, then the more famous *Alabama*, with which he destroyed seventy-two U.S. merchant ships. Northerners thought him a pirate. For Semmes's side, see his *Memoirs of Service Afloat During the War Between the States* (Baltimore: Kelly, Piet, 1869). Faust, *Encyclopedia*, p. 666.

9. Pierce Butler (1807–67) was the richest slaveowner along Georgia's rice coast. His Hampton Plantation, on the island's north end, was described by Fanny Kemble in her *Journal of the Residence on a Georgian Plantation, 1828–9*. For the best study of Butler, see Bell, *Major Butler's Legacy*.

10. In February 1859, Butler sold 429 men, women, and children in the largest single sale of human beings in American history. Butler gave each slave four quarters to remember him by. Buyers paid Butler $303,850 for his slaves. J. C. Furnas, *Fanny Kemble: Leading Lady of the Nineteenth-Century Stage* (New York:

Dial Press, 1982), pp. 374–75; Bell, *Major Butler's Legacy*, pp. 311–40.

11. Slave John was still living at Hampton Plantation in 1873. Bell, *Major Butler's Legacy*, p. 559.

12. Oyster shells mixed with lime and sand makes a very durable concrete known as "tabby." Tabby-walled slave cabins can still be found along the Georgia coast.

13. Fanny Kemble left Hampton Plantation in 1839, never to return. She divorced Pierce Butler in 1849 and bought a cottage in Lenox, Massachusetts, near the Haggerty's summer home. Fanny's *Journal* was published in May 1863; she assigned the American copyright to Francis Shaw, who published an American edition on July 16, 1863. George William Curtis reviewed the book in *Atlantic Monthly* (August 1863): 260–63. Frances A. Kemble, *Journal of a Residence* (New York: Harper, 1863; reprint, Athens: University of Georgia Press, 1984), pp. xliii, l.

14. James Hamilton Couper (1794–1866) owned Cannon's Plantation, located just east of Butler's plantation and separated from it by a finger of the Hampton River. Couper also owned Hopeton Plantation, located nearby Butler's Island Plantation in the Altamaha River below Darien. Two of his sons died in Virginia fighting for the Confederacy and their future in holding slaves. Bell, *Major Butler's Legacy*, pp. 515–16.

15. Robertson is unidentified.

16. Quartermaster and First Lt. John Ritchie, of Boston, one of the first officers selected for the regiment. Emilio, *A Brave Black Regiment*, p. 330.

St. Simon's Island   [HL]
June 13 1863
Dearest Mother,

Last evening I received your two letters of the 31st May, & 1st June—one from Annie, two from Father & one from Effie.

This is the first news I have had since I left home. I hope you have received all mine. This should have gone this morning, but the steamer went off before her time, and my letter will consequently reach you a few days later. I am very sorry about it, as you have had nothing from me since we came here.

We arrived at camp near Mr. Pierce Butler's plantation Tuesday evening. Today is Saturday—and in the mean time, we have been with Montgomery on an expedition up the Altamaha, and burned the town of Darien—much to my disgust—for we met with no resistance & no good reason can be given for doing such a thing. I have written Annie an account of this, and asked her to send it to you, if she is not with you, as I suppose she may be, from what she wrote.

Today I went over to Mr. Butler's plantation & talked with some of the old negroes. There are about 10 left from his great sale of three years ago.

Though he had sold their sons & daughters they said he was a good Marst'r. Some of them had lived there for 70 & 80 years.

I feel like writing you a long account of our doings as I have to Annie, but it would be only a repetition of that, so I think it better to employ the time with my necessary correspondence with Gov. Andrew & other great men.

I couldn't help thinking today, at Mr. Butler's of Mrs. Kemble that summer at Sorrento, & what she told you of the paying the houseservants wages. I little thought then, I should ever visit the place under such circumstances. In regard to the burning of Darien, I am going to write to Genl Hunter's A.A.G. for unless Montgomery has orders from headquarters to lay the country in ruins, I am determined to refuse to obey his orders in that respect.[1] You will see from my letter to Annie, how I feel about it. Montgomery told me he did it because he thought it his duty. I asked him if it wasn't partly from pure hatred of everything Southern. He said no—& that he only hated them as being enemies of liberty & he had good reason to hate every enemy of liberty.

I can't help feeling a great respect for him. He is quiet, gentlemanly, full of determination, but convinced that the South should be devastated with fire & sword. His perfect calmness at all times is very impressive. My objection is to firing into houses occupied by noncombatants, & burning down dwellings which shelter only women & children. It is most barbarous—more so than would be the hanging of every man we take in arms.

This strikes one very forcibly, when one is engaged in it, propria persona.

June 14

I find a steamer is going this morning quite unexpectedly & send this without finishing it.

Your loving son

1. Shaw wrote Hunter's assistant adjutant general, Lt. Col. Charles G. Halpine (1829–68), on June 14, 1863. Calling the burning of Darien "barbarous" and "distasteful," Shaw asked, "Has Colonel Montgomery orders from General Hunter to burn and destroy all towns and dwellings he may capture?" There is no record of Halpine's reply. Halpine served on Hunter's staff from November 8, 1862 to July 1, 1863. Shaw's letter quoted in *Harper's Weekly*, Sept. 3, 1870, p. 3.

St. Simon's Island   [RGS]
June 15, 1863
My Dear Effie,

I received yours of 31 May, day before yesterday. Before you receive this, you will know, from my letters to Mother and Father, our doings since we left Boston.

We are very pleasantly situated here; the island is beautiful, and my house is a very comfortable one for the climate. Fortunately, there is an excellent camping-ground for the regiment close to it; otherwise I shouldn't have taken it. The Major and I might have half our two families here without inconvenience.[1] The only objection is, that Montgomery never lies quiet for more than four days at a time, so we are likely to be constantly on the go, and may leave the place at any time.

In front of us is St. Simon's River, full of alligators, and behind, a thick wood full of insects and snakes. The former make such a noise at night, that I, at first, thought it was a vessel blowing off steam. The house had a few chairs and tables left when we got here, and our late expedition supplied all deficiencies. Our most respectable acquisitions are a table-cloth, and two large maps of the United States and Georgia, which latter, hung up in the hall, give an air of solidity to the entrance.

The only troops on the island are Montgomery's regiment and the Fifty-fourth. Montgomery being absent, I am in command of the post. Imagine me governor of an island fifteen miles long and six or seven broad. It is all that "Sancho Panza" could desire.[2]

Yesterday afternoon, in the course of a ride, the Major, Dr. Stone, and I came across a herd of cattle, and drove them in; so now we have fresh milk and meat in plenty. Some of them are very fine, and must have been the fancy stock of the former owners of the island. I am afraid we shan't long have the island to ourselves, as there is some intention of sending more troops here, I believe.

What you say about Annie gives me a great deal of pleasure, as of course I like to hear her praised. Give my love to Charley, if you happen to be writing one of these days, and thank him for his letter to me.[3] I shall write to him myself before long. I had a nice note from Alice Forbes yesterday. As I have several letters to write, I must leave you here.

Ever your loving brother,
Rob

1. Edward Needles Hallowell.   3. Charles Russell Lowell, Jr.
2. Sancho Panza was Don Quixote's
sidekick.

St. Simon's Island, Ga.   [RGS]
June 17, 1863
My Dear Clem.,[1]

You have probably heard from Annie of our adventures since we left Boston; that is, if my many letters reached her. We are entirely isolated here, and know nothing of what has been going on in other parts of the country for the last two weeks. We have only just heard that General Hunter, in our own Department, was relieved.[2] It is such a short time since you and I have been so nearly related, that I hardly realize it as yet; and now I am back in the old track, and routine of camp-life again, the three months at home, with their great pleasures and little troubles, seem to have been passed in dream-land. I don't believe I think much more of Annie than I used to, but the great difference in our relation to each other seems very strange.

Now that General Hunter is relieved, I may say, without danger of being overhauled for it, that I am very glad. He does not impress one as being a man of power. General Gillmore, I hear, is not a friend to black troops, but I don't mind that, for as long as there are so few regiments of them here, they may as well lie quiet as not.[3] These little miserable expeditions are of no account at all; that is, as regards their effect on the war; but they serve to keep up the spirits of our men, and when successful, do a good deal towards weakening the prejudice against black troops, especially in this department, where, hitherto, absolutely nothing has been done.

. . . I read Mr. Ward's present (Thiers' Waterloo) very carefully, on the way down, and found it very interesting.[4] Since I came here I have been reading "The Campaigns of 1862 and 1863," by Emil Schalk.[5] He shows what he thinks are the mistakes that have been made, and lays out an imaginary campaign, which he thinks ought to be successful. It is a good thing to read, but I don't know how much humbug or how much solid stuff it contains. A former book of his—"Summary of the Art of War"—is quite interesting.[6] There, he makes several prophecies that have been fulfilled. I wish some one like Napier could give us his opinion of the war.[7]

You can't imagine what a spooney, home-sick set we are here, after our pleasant times at Readville. Major Hallowell lies on his back singing,—

> "No one to love, none to caress,
>
> None to respond to this heart's wretchedness";

and we all feel just so. It is very demoralizing to be at home for so long a time.

I felt quite sorry to deprive you of my old sword, but I wanted my Mother to have it, as I hadn't given her any of my discarded shoulder-straps, sashes, &c., &c. I think of you every morning and evening when I put on my slippers; they are a great comfort. When you see your father, please give him my regards. I was sorry not to see him before I came away.

With much love to your Mother, and yourself, I am, dear Clem.,

your affectionate Brother

P.S.—If you read Thiers' Waterloo, I advise you to get Jomini's also, and compare them.[8] The former is infinitely superior, I think, so much more clear and exact; there is something of the romance about it, though, which you never find in Napier. The latter seems to be the perfect historian.

1. Shaw's sister-in-law Clemence Haggerty.

2. Lincoln replaced Hunter on June 12, 1863, with Brig. Gen. Quincy Adams Gillmore. Long, *Civil War Day By Day*, p. 365.

3. Quincy Adams Gillmore (1825–88), of Ohio, graduated from West Point in 1849 as an engineer and fort builder. Gillmore became recognized for his ability as an artillerist when he forced the surrender of Fort Pulaski, near Savan-

nah, in 1862. Promoted to major general on July 10, 1862, Gillmore was to turn his bombardment skills onto the forts surrounding Charleston Harbor. Faust, *Encyclopedia*, pp. 310–11.

4. Adolphe Thiers (1797–1877), *Waterloo* (Paris: Lheureux, 1862).

5. Emil Schalk (1834–?), *The Campaigns of 1862 and 1863, Illustrating the Principles of Strategy* (Philadelphia: J. B. Lippincott, 1863).

6. *Summary of the Art of War: Written Expressly for and Dedicated to the U.S. Volunteer Army* (Philadelphia: J. B. Lippincott, 1862).

7. British general Sir William Francis Patrick Napier (1785–1869) wrote *History of the War in the Peninsula and in the South of France from the year 1807 to the year 1814*. This popular book on the war with Napoleon had many different publishers and publication dates, 1828–63. *Dictionary of National Biography*, vol. 14, pp. 82–85.

8. Henri Jomini (1779–1869), *The Art of War* (Philadelphia: J. B. Lippincott, 1862).

CHAPTER 14

"*M*ontgomery the Kansas man"

During his third month at war, Shaw, in Virginia, had visited the site of John Brown's 1859 raid on Harper's Ferry and his jail cell in Charlestown. Now in his third year of war, Shaw, in South Carolina, became enamored with James Montgomery, who had been Brown's most able lieutenant from the days when Kansas bled. Shaw admired Montgomery's attractive looks, past work, dedication to abolition, and adherence to discipline.

When he wasn't talking with or writing about Montgomery, Shaw spent his time visiting plantations, conversing with former slaves, drilling the regiment, and missing his old friends and new wife. On July 3, Shaw wrote to Maj. Charles F. Morse and told him that he "longed" to campaign with him again in the Second Massachusetts, and asked, "I wonder where the deuce you are." Morse was fighting in the battle of Gettysburg.

St. Simon's Island   [HL]
June 18 1863
Dearest Mother,

We have received nothing since our first mail, which I mentioned in my last to you. Captain Rand arrived at Beaufort after we had left there, and your second note arrived at the same time with the first.[1]

I am very glad you feel so happy and contented about my course in taking the black regiment and besides that cause for satisfaction—I have never had to regret it, for material reasons.

There is no doubt that all the black troops in the country should be gathered into one or two armies—as in small bodies they can never make themselves felt much. It was quite astonishing to be received as we were at Beaufort.[2] The Commander of the Post, there, Col. Davis, is almost a Copperhead—as well as a good many of his subordinates—and I was told, at Hilton Head, that they might not be very cordial.[3] But, on the contrary, they treated me with the greatest consideration and there was no end to the offers of services from all the Colonels, Quartermasters & Commissaries of the place.

Some, who had been very violent in their opposition to the enlistment of negroes, seemed glad of this chance to back out, by degrees, and say there was a vast difference between contrabands & free negroes &c, &c.

I am placed in a position where, if I were a man of real strength and ability, I might do a great deal, but where, under present circumstances, I am afraid I shall show that I am not of much account. Ned Hooper at Beaufort is the head of the whole Contraband Department.[4] Every one there has the highest opinion of him. I should like to have stayed where I could see him every day.

Annie has sent you, I hope, my letter about the Darien expedition. I have not yet discovered if Col. Montgomery has Hunter's orders to burn every thing, but expect to hear soon from Hilton Head. M. has not yet returned from there, so I remain still in command here.[5] I have no doubt you may think at home that Col. M's action is perfectly proper, but you would change your mind if you had to assist in it.

Frank Barlow still wishes to get command of a coloured Brigade, and I think it would be a great piece of good fortune for us if we could get him—& for the cause, as well. If Father can do anything towards it, I wish he would.

Always dear Mother,

Your loving son

P.S. If we remain here for long we could entertain any number of visitors on our plantation, after the hot weather is over, & I hope Father & you & some of the girls can come down & bring Annie for a [one word illegible] while I have no doubt some of the Hallowells may be persuaded to come.

---

1. Captain Rand is unidentified.

2. The arrival of the Fifty-fourth in Beaufort on June 3 started a gala celebration. Several bands played and

hundreds of people turned out to see the famous black regiment from the North. Historian Willie Lee Rose noted that Beaufort, at that time, proportionately, had more abolitionists than did Boston. Rose, *Rehearsal for Reconstruction*, p. 248.

3. William Watts Hart Davis, of Pennsylvania, served in the X Corps, Department of the South, at Port Royal, Folly and Morris islands before com-manding the District of Hilton Head, South Carolina. Boatner, *Dictionary*, p. 226.

4. Edward William Hooper.

5. James Montgomery.

St. Simon's Island, Ga. [NYPL]
June 20, 1863
My dear Charley,[1]

I received your kind letter before I left Readville—and beg you will excuse my long delay in answering you.

Besides other matters to occupy my attention, you will appreciate the fact of my having a more voluminous private correspondence than ever before.

You may have heard from Effie of our doings, since we left Boston—though, to be sure, I don't know how many of my letters have reached home. We have only heard from there once.

I am totally in the dark as to what has been going on in other parts of the country for two weeks past. The last paper I saw, was of June 6.

I should like to ask your opinion on a subject, which has troubled me a little lately. On a late expedition we made with Montgomery—he burnt the town of Darien about 20 miles from here. We had met with no resistance there & the only men to be seen were some horsemen at a great distance. There were a few women & darkeys in the place and a great many more had gone off in vehicles on our approach. It was never known to be a refuge for guerillas, and our gunboats have been in the habit of running by it at will & without opposition.

Don't you think that unless it is a settled policy of the Government to destroy all the property in rebeldom, the destruction of a defenceless town, containing only a few non-combatants, is unjustifiable, and contrary to all rules of warfare?

Harry writes me that you have been transferred to Heintzelman, so I suppose there is a good chance of your remaining for some time, near Washington.[2] Good, for Effie.

Now you are so near Headquarters, can't you do something towards getting Barlow for us? I have just heard from him under date of May 21. He says he had just received yours of March 20 & regrets very much not having got it before. He still wishes to command a colored Brigade & I have no doubt we should do something under him.

Montgomery who seems the only active man in this Department, is enormously energetic, and devoted to the cause, but he is a bush-whacker—in his fighting, and a perfect fanatic in other respects. He never drinks, smokes or swears, & considers that praying, shooting, burning & hanging are the true means to put down the Rebellion. If he had been educated as a military man in rather a different school, I think he would accomplish a great deal, & he may yet in a certain way.

He is very prompt & active, never lying idle, if he can help it, for more than three days at a time. When delayed and disappointed, he is wonderfully patient & calm, never letting a word escape him & putting through what he undertakes in spite of everything. I never met a man who impressed me as being more conscientious.

Isn't it strange, being back at the old work again under such different circumstances. I shan't realize until about two years after the war is over, that I am married.

I have often thought since I left, of our meetings at Harper's Ferry, and how little I supposed then that we should be so intimately connected.[3]

I hope this war will not finish one or both of us, and that we shall live to know each other well. I had a note from Effie a week ago. I remember, at Susie's, just after you were engaged you said to me: "Am not I a lucky fellow?" And I must say, I think you are. There are not many girls like Effie; though she is my sister, I may say it. Hoping to hear from you occasionally, believe me, dear Charley.

Your afftc brother,
R. G. S.

1. Charles Russell Lowell.
2. Samuel Peter Heintzelman.
3. Shaw first met Lowell in Oct. 1862,

at Harper's Ferry. See RGS to SBS, Oct. 5, 1862, included herein.

St. Simon's Island   [HL]
June 22 1863
Dear Father,

We got a small mail today, but there was nothing for me. I was very much disappointed, the latest date from you, being 3d Inst. & from Annie 31 Ulto.

Col. Montgomery returned from Hilton Head, this morning, bringing us news of the capture of the Ram "Fingal."[1]

He found General Gilmor[e] very friendly and anxious to second him in every way, with the exception of the burning business—so that is satisfactorily settled.[2] Montgomery tells me he acted entirely under orders from Hunter, and was at first very much opposed to them himself, but finally changed his mind.

I like him very much. He is not what one would call a "Kansas Ruffian"— being very quiet and reserved, & rather consumptive-looking. His language is very good & always grammatical. He is very religious & always has services in his regiment, before starting on an expedition.

Please don't wait for the sailing of the "Arago" to mail my letters. Gunboats and transports come here (to Hilton Head) every week from Boston, New York & Philadelphia, and usually bring a mail.

We are waiting here for coal for our transports; as soon as it arrives, we shall probably be off again, for a little while.

They think at the "Head" that there will soon be another attempt made on Savannah or Charleston.[3] Gilmor is certainly much more active and energetic than Hunter.

Give my love to Mother and the girls. I am impatient to hear whether the Russells arrived safely and well.

The "Nelly Baker is expected from Hilton Head" tomorrow, and I hope she will bring us some letters. I sent her up there, day before yesterday.

Your loving son

1. Built in Scotland in 1861 for the Confederacy to use as a blockade runner, the *Fingal* was converted to an ironclad and rechristened the *Atlanta*. The most powerful ship in the Confederate navy, at 204 feet long and 41 feet wide, with a power plant that pushed her at a faster speed than other rams, the *Atlanta* ran aground on June 16, 1863, near Wassaw Sound, Georgia, where the Union monitor *Weehawken* captured her. *Harper's Weekly*, July 11, 1863, pp. 8, 11; *OR*, I:28, pt. 1, pp. 189–92; Faust, *Encyclopedia*, p. 28.

2. Quincy A. Gillmore.

3. Hilton Head.

St. Simon's Island   [HL]
June 24 1863
Dear Father,

Yours of the 9th came to hand last evening. At the same time we received news of the Rebel incursion into the Northern [North] and orders to embark at once for Port Royal.[1] We are now waiting for a transport, which will hold the regiment.

The news from the North is very exciting but not entirely unexpected, for Morse wrote me, that Lee wouldn't leave the Potomac army quiet very long.[2] Then my theory has always been that the North must feel the war much more than they have, before it is ended.

I don't know why we are ordered to return to Beaufort, unless the troops there are going North, or another attack is to be made on Charleston or Savannah.

I thank you a thousand times for your generosity to me in money affairs, dear Father; I never imagined you were going to assume so many of my debts.

If Rice has not paid you, what he owes, I wish you would take it out of my funds.[3] I enclose to you some bills which I had in Boston, lest they should be sent to you. I also enclose the following promissory notes:

Lincoln R. Stone	—	$115
John Ritchie	—	115
G. W. James	—	115
C. B. Bridgham	—	96

I will notify you as soon as they are paid.[4]

I send this off immediately as Col. Montgomery's boats which will get away before we do, will probably catch the "Arago."

Love to all,
Your loving son

Please drop Annie a line saying we return to Beaufort lest my letter to her should not be ready.

1. On June 3, 1863, Robert E. Lee began to move his army west and north for an invasion of the North. By June 16, Lee's army began to cross the Potomac into Maryland, and Joe Hooker and the Army of the Potomac groped to find the Confederates. On June 24, Longstreet and Hill's corps crossed the Potomac to join Ewell's corps. The invasion would end when Pickett's charge failed at

Gettysburg on July 3. Long, *Civil War Day By Day*, pp. 361, 367, 370.

2. Charles F. Morse.

3. Rice is unidentified.

4. First Lt. Charles Burr Bridgham (1841–?), a student from Buckfield, Maine, joined the Fifty-fourth as an assistant surgeon on May 1, 1863. Emilio, *A Brave Black Regiment*, p. 330.

Steamer, off Hilton Head
June 25, 1863
Dear Mother,

I wrote Father yesterday that we were to return here. We sailed this morning at six, having been up all night loading the ship. I don't know where we are to be sent now; it is supposed that Gillmore is going to make an attack on Morris Island and Fort Sumter, from Folly Island. Whether we go with him, or into garrison at Beaufort, or on some detached expedition, I can't say; as soon as I find out, I will write. We have had a good deal of moving about, for so young a regiment.

The captain of this ship says there is a large mail on shore; so I shall perhaps find a good many letters from home. You must be back in New York by this time. I have written to Uncle George and Aunt Sarah.[1] I wish I could see them. Love to Father and the girls, and believe me,

Your ever loving son,
Rob

I enclose a note to Annie.

1. George Robert Russell and Sarah Parkman Russell.

St. Helena's Island
June 26, 1863
Dearest Annie,

At Hilton Head we found our letters waiting, and I got two from you, of June 12th, and June 17th and 18th. As I have had nothing from May 31st to June 12th, I infer that one or more of yours have been lost. This is very disappointing, but I hope they will turn up finally. I was thankful to hear from you at all. Thank Clem. for hers; mine crossed hers on the way.

You will have got my account of Mr. Butler's plantation by this time, and from what you say, I see that it will have interested you. He has another large place, a rice plantation, opposite where Darien once was; but that I only saw from a distance.[1]

The only persons responsible for the depravity of the negroes are their scoundrelly owners, who are, nevertheless, not ashamed to talk of the Christianizing influence of slavery.[2] Whatever the condition of the slaves may be, it does not degrade them, as a bad life does most people, for their faces are generally good. I suppose this is owing to their utter ignorance, and innocence of evil.

. . . We landed on this island last night, and to-day are bringing everything to our camp, a mile from the landing, by hand. Having a great many stores, it is a long job. I am sitting on a box in the middle of a field of sand, under a tent-fly, and writing on my knee.

I have not yet heard what is to be done with the forces here. General Strong tells me that Admiral Foote's illness may interfere with their plans very much. . . .[3]

June 27, 8 A.M.—General Strong (formerly of Butler's staff), who commands on this island, I like very much; he came over to see me yesterday, and I must return his call to-morrow.[4] The papers say there are about twenty thousand coloured troops in the service now. Just think what a change from six months since! . . .

10 P.M.—To-day I have been watching and talking with a good many of the negroes about here. Whatever their habits of life may be, they certainly are not bad or vicious; they are perfectly childlike, it seems to me, and are no more responsible for their actions than so many puppies.

Sunday, June 28—We have just had a two hours' thunder-storm, with such a wind that a good many of our tents were blown away, and the occupants of the rest sat in them in fear and trepidation.

I think it is better, as you say, not to build too many *Chateaux en Espagne*, for they are sure to blow away (like our tents).[5] For that reason, I am more uneasy in camp than ever before, and always wishing for a move and something to occupy my mind, in spite of myself. When we lie idle, as at present, I do nothing but think and think, until I am pretty *home*-sick.

. . . Shall we ever have a home of our own, do you suppose? I can't help looking forward to that time, though I should not; for when there is so much for every man in the country to do, we ought hardly to long for ease and comfort. I wish I could do my share; i.e. that I had as much talent and ability to give to it as I want. . . .

Good bye for the present, my dearest.

Your faithful and affectionate Husband

P.S.—Now that the conflagration policy is settled, I don't mind your speaking of what I wrote about it.[6] Though I would never justify such acts for a moment, there is a spark of truth in the reasoning that, if we are to be treated as brigands, if captured, we are not bound to observe the laws of war. But I think now, as I did at the time, that it is cruel, barbarous, impolitic, and degrading to ourselves and to our men; and I shall always rejoice that I expressed myself so at the time of the destruction of Darien.

It is rather hard that my men, officers, and myself should have to bear part of the abuse for the destruction of Darien, isn't it?—when they (at least the officers) all felt just as I did about it.[7]

You see, darling, from our wanderings so far, that it is impossible to make any plans for the winter; so don't set your heart upon it.

1. Butler's Island consisted of 1,490 acres and was located south across General's Island from Darien and ten miles west of Hampton Plantation on St. Simons. Butler established a complex system of canals and irrigation ditches and earth-banked rice, cotton, and sugarcane fields where he worked hundreds of slaves. Bell, *Major Butler's Legacy*, pp. 117–25.

2. Southern slaveowners often tried to justify holding human beings in bondage by stressing the African background as "savage," and the "positive good" that slavery and Christianity brought to civilizing black people.

3. George Crockett Strong (1833–63), of Stockridge, Vermont, graduated West Point in 1857 and served with McClellan and others during the war. Appointed a brigadier general on Mar. 23, 1863, Strong commanded the Second Brigade, Second Division, X Corps, under General Gillmore. *New York Tribune*, July 31 (5:3), 1863; Boatner, *Dictionary*, p. 811; Faust, *Encyclopedia*, p. 727. Adm. Andrew Hull Foote (1806–63), of Connecticut, joined the navy in 1822, graduated Annapolis, and won battles on the Mississippi River at forts Henry and Donelson and at

Island No. 10. Wounded at Donelson, Foote was named commander of the South Atlantic Blockading Squadron on June 4, 1863, to succeed Adm. Samuel du Pont. Foote died on June 26, 1863, on the way to assume that command. *DAB*, vol. 3, pp. 499–501.

4. Benjamin Franklin Butler.

5. The proverb *chateaux en Espagne* (castles in Spain) is a derivative of the more known "castles in the air." In the eleventh century, a French knight, Henry of Burgundy, crossed the Pyrenees to help the Christian king, Alfonso of Castile, free Spain from Moorish rule. As reward for his services, he received a royal bride, Theresa, and a kingdom, which became Portugal. Thereafter, soldiers of wars dreamed of winning land and love in foreign lands. Shaw seems to be referring to the more common metaphor of "castles in the air." William S. Walsh, *Handy-Book of Literary Curiosities* (Philadelphia: J. B. Lippincott, 1966), p. 140.

6. Shaw means that since the burning of Darien was Hunter's responsibility and now Hunter had been replaced, it would be all right to let his own opposition to the policy be known. The Union would turn again to this scorched-earth

policy under Sherman and Sheridan in 1864.

7. Newspapers, North and South, carried lengthy stories about the burning of Darien by the black soldiers of the Fifty-fourth Massachusetts and the Second South Carolina. Southern papers and Northern Copperhead journals accused the Lincoln government of turning black savages in blue uniforms loose on a defenseless white population of women and children. These papers basically wrote, "I told you so," and "what did you expect?" Northern papers rallied to defend the regiment but added that perhaps black soldiers were in a position too touchy to allow them to apply the torch to property. Some of these papers argued that it was all right to burn, but that white soldiers should do it. *Savannah Morning News*, June 16, 1863, quoted from *Commonwealth*, July 3 (4:3), 1863; *Commonwealth*, July 3 (2:3), 1863; *New Bedford Mercury*, July 8, 1863, in Scrapbook, NBFPL.

St. Helena's Island, S.C.
June 28 1863

Dearest Mother,

Your note of the 20th came to me on board the "Benj. DeFord" just after I had sent my last ashore—also letters from Father of the 10, 13, 15, 18, 19 Inst. & others from Annie, Effie & Harry. Some of Annie's have been lost, however.

We did not land at Hilton Head but were ordered to this Island that same afternoon. We landed and bivouacked for the night—and since then have been engaged in transporting our stores by hand from the landing, more than a mile.

Our whole experience, so far, has been in loading & discharging vessels.

There is nothing said about future plans. General Strong tells me that Admiral Foote's illness will interfere materially with them. I hope and pray that we may go to Charleston. Strong, who was one of Butler's staff officers, is very desirous to have the negro troops take their part in whatever is done.[1]

Montgomery did a characteristic thing this morning. His men being near their homes have deserted rapidly since we returned from St. Simon's. He sent word by their wives & others to the deserters that those who returned of their own free will should be pardoned—that those, whom he caught, he would shoot. This morning one of my sergeants captured one. At 8 o'cl. Col. Montgomery called him up & said: "Is there any reason why you should not be shot?" "No, Sir." "Then, be ready to die at 9:30." At 9:15 the man sent to ask permission to see the Colonel, but it was refused, and at 9:30 he was taken out and shot.[2] There was no Court-Martial—and the case was not referred to a superior officer. Montgomery, who just told me the story, in his low voice, but with an occasional glare in his eye (which by the bye, is very extraordinary) thinks that this prompt action was the only way to stop desertion, and it only remains to be seen whether he will be pulled up for it. I wish you could see him. You would think at first sight that he was a school-master or parson. The only thing that shows the man, is that very queer roll or glare in his eye— and a contraction of the eyebrows every now & then, which gives him rather a fierce expression.[3] He says he never had a fight until he went to Kansas, and was a very harmless creature formerly, though never a non-resistant.

June 29—To continue the subject of Col. Montgomery, I went over last evening, after writing the above, & sat two hours with him. He gave me his whole history, which interested me very much. I wish I could tell you all he said of his life during the last ten years. He has been in such a state of excitement all that time that he says it seems as if the whole were compressed into a few days—and he could hardly help crying when he talked of the state of utter desperation & hopelessness in which they began their fight against the Border Ruffians, and compared it with present times which seem to him bright & cheerful.[4] He believes that nothing happens by chance & is full of faith in Providence. His account of the abject manner in which he had seen some Missourians whom he had taken prisoners, beg for their lives was very interesting. He says that without exception, under such circumstances, their manhood forsook them completely—& he compared their conduct with that of the negro, who was shot yesterday, and who never flinched from it.

I said above that M. looked like a schoolmaster, & he says he did teach school in Kentucky for many years, and learnt more about managing men there, than at any other time.

He strikes me as being a very simple-minded man—and seems to be pleased at any little attention—perhaps because he has been so much abused. You will see that he is very attractive to me, and indeed I have taken a great fancy to him.

Evening—

I have just got your letter of the 21 Inst. & Father's of 23d—his other two written after receipt of mine from St. Simon's have not yet come to hand. What you say of Montgomery's wife amused me very much, after hearing his account of it last evening. He said his wife saw an article in the paper stating what you say, and that all the punishment he ever wishes the writer to receive, is to come within reach of her broom-stick. Then he laughed very loud &

long. Besides this, he assured me that no property of his was ever touched by a Border-Ruffian, being protected by his pro-slavery neighbours, whom he held responsible for it. He also said "To give the Devil his due" that he never, during his whole experience in Kansas heard of a well-authenticated case of a Border Ruffian having offered violence to a white woman, in any way—and he thinks that courtesy towards women is characteristic of the Southerners, good & bad.[5] His wife is the daughter of a Kentucky Slave-holder.

I see by the papers, what is thought of the destruction of Darien, and it provokes me to have it laid on Montgomery's shoulders, when he acted under orders from Hunter. I, myself, saw Hunter's letters referring to it.[6] I am sorry if it is going to harm the negro troops, but I think myself it will soon be forgotten.

The two boxes Father sent arrived tonight. Mr. Pierce has been up here today.[7] I hope Father wrote to Gov. Andrew, after receiving my late letters, about Darien, & told him that Hunter, only, was to blame.

I was so sorry & provoked at getting no word from Annie tonight, that I didn't know what to do. I have only heard from her 3 times & the latest date is the 18th. After the number of letters I have written her, I thought it was pretty "steep."

Uncle George has sent me an English sword, & a flask, knife, fork, spoon &c. They have not yet come.[8]

My warmest love to Father & the girls.

Always dearest Mother,
your loving son

P.S. I suppose Annie is with you by this time. If so give my love to her.

1. Edward L. Pierce remembered that at St. Helena, Shaw "contracted there a friendship for General Strong. . . ." That friendship would be important for getting the Fifty-fourth into combat alongside white troops on July 18, 1863. Edward L. Pierce to FGS and SBS, July 22, 1863, quoted in *Memorial: RGS*, p. 53.

2. Montgomery used a twenty-four-man firing squad to execute the deserter. Colonel Higginson complained in his journal that Montgomery was in step only with uncivilized warfare.

Commonwealth, July 24 (3:2–3), 1863; *National Anti-Slavery Standard*, July 18 (3:4), 1863; Higginson, ed., *Letters and Journals*, p. 209.

3. Beaufort schoolteacher Charlotte Forten described Montgomery as "tall, muscular, with a shrewd face, brown and wrinkled." She liked "his look of quiet determination." Capt. J. W. M. Appleton of the Fifty-fourth best described the Kansas hero as "a tall thin man, his eyes are grey, his nose like a bird's beak, deep lines graven all over his face, bushy whiskers at the sides. His shoulders are

sloping and he stoops. He is awkward in his movements and unsoldierlike in appearance but he believes that a soldier's use is to fight, and [he] is terribly in earnest." Billington, ed., *Journal of Charlotte L. Forten*, p. 180; J. W. M. Appleton Papers, WVU.

4. Border Ruffians were proslavery men from Missouri, who used fraud, intimidation, and violence against the free-soil settlers of Kansas.

5. Perhaps Shaw is referring to the gossip-mill account that once, in Kansas, Border Ruffians tied Montgomery to a tree and raped his wife in front of him. Lydia Maria Child to Mary Stearns, Jan. 20, 1862, in Milton Meltzer and Patricia Holland, eds., *Lydia Maria Child: Selected Letters, 1817–1880* (Amherst: University of Massachusetts Press, 1982), p. 405.

6. On May 22, 1863, Hunter wrote Lincoln and suggested that Hunter's army should not be used against strongholds like Charleston, but should go into the heart of Georgia to wreak "a total destruction of their resources." Hunter argued that that would force the Confederates to defend every town, thus dividing their forces, which the Federal army could then defeat piecemeal. Ten days later, after Montgomery returned with 725 contrabands, Hunter wrote Stanton that Montgomery would continue raids "injuring the enemy all he can. . . ." Lincoln removed Hunter from command, even as Hunter was issuing orders to Montgomery to "avoid any devastation which does not strike immediately at the resources or material of the armed insurrection. . . . All household furniture, libraries, churchs, and hospitals you will of course spare." That letter was too late to save Hunter or Darien. David Hunter to A. Lincoln, May 22, 1863, "The Negro in the Military Service of the United States, 1607–1889," Record Group 94, NA, #1258; MajGen [David] Hunter to E. M. Stanton, June 3, 1863, and MajGen [David] Hunter to James Montgomery, June 9, 1863, *OR*, 1:14, pp. 463, 464, 466.

7. Edward Lillie Pierce (1829–97), Boston abolitionist and lawyer, graduated from Harvard Law School in 1852 and studied law in the Cincinnati office of Salmon P. Chase. When the war started, Pierce enlisted in the Third Massachusetts Infantry. General Butler placed him in command of contrabands at Fortress Monroe. Later Pierce would be very influential in the rehearsal for Reconstruction at Port Royal. *DAB*, vol. 7, pp. 575–76.

8. George Robert Russell.

St. Helena Island S.C.

July 1 1863

Dear Father,

In my last to Mother, I mentioned receipt of all your letters, and yesterday, your other two of the 22d ulto. came to hand, having gone first to Beaufort.

The two boxes which, I heard, were at Hilton Head, did come in the

"Arago" but are still enroute, on board of some brig.[1] A box of Uncle George's containing a beautiful English sword came all right.

Do you ever write to Dr. Bowditch?[2] If so, I wish, you would mention to him that Lieutenant Reid (whom he recommended) is an excellent officer.[3]

Do you know [four words crossed out and illegible] very well? He doesn't strike me as being a very straightforward man.

You may have perhaps heard that the coloured troops are to receive $10 instead [of] $13 per mo. It is not yet decided that this regt comes under the order. If it does I shall refuse to allow them to be paid until I hear from Gov. Andrew. The regt ought, in that case, to be mustered out of service, as they were enlisted on the understanding that they were to be on the same footing as other Mass. Vols.[4]

Another plan is to arm the negroes with pikes.[5] I shall escape that, but Montgomery & Higginson, I am afraid, will have to come to it, unless the plan is given up. Of course, it will be the ruin of all spirit & courage in their men.

Everyone who has been in any of our battles should know that Pikes against Minie balls is not fair play—especially in the hands of negroes whose great pride lies in being a soldier like white men. One of Col. Montgomery's remarks is that it is folly to suppose that a race, which has been in bondage for 200 years can be as brave as freemen, and that all our energies must be devoted to making the most of them.

You will see from my letter to Mother that there is a good deal of exaggeration in the stories of Montgomery's experience in Kansas. At any rate he says so himself.

Whom did you give those last letters (22 June) to? They had no post-mark & were sent to Beaufort.

Love to all,
Your most loving son

1. The *Arago* was a transatlantic mail ship owned by the New York and Havre Steam Navigation Company. *NYT*, July 27 (1:1), 1863.

2. Henry Ingersoll Bowditch (1808–92) was an abolitionist and prominent physician in Boston. He served as a medical examiner in Boston for men trying to enroll in the army. Frederick Douglass claimed of Bowditch: "he first treated me as if I were a man." Later a professor at Harvard Medical School, Bowditch helped to establish the Massachusetts State Board of Health in 1869. Crawford, *Famous Families*, vol. 2, p. 337; Douglass quoted from Lader, *Bold Brahmins*, pp. 73–74.

3. First Lt. David Reid (1829–64) was married and worked as a bookkeeper in Boston when he joined the Eleventh

Massachusetts Infantry on Sept. 9, 1861, as a commissary sergeant. Reid transferred to the Fifty-fourth and became a second lieutenant on Apr. 17, 1863. He was promoted to first lieutenant the day after the assault on Fort Wagner and he died in action on Nov. 30, 1864. Emilio, *A Brave Black Regiment*, p. 335; David Reid file, CMSR.

4. The newspaper advertisements, broadsides, and friends of the Fifty-fourth recruited volunteers with the promise of equal pay with the white soldiers. The government had been paying the black militia and contraband regiments ten dollars per month as authorized by the Militia Act of July 17, 1862. On June 4, 1863, Stanton ordered black soldiers to be paid ten dollars a month, of which three dollars could be appropriated for clothing. Shaw wrote Governor Andrew, called the pay cut "a great piece of injustice," and told the governor to muster them out or pay them equally. The governor agreed with Shaw and began to write Lincoln and Stanton telling them to make things right. Corp. James H. Gooding of New Bedford wrote to Abraham Lincoln and asked, "Now the main question is, Are we *soldiers*, or are we *Labourers*?" Most men of the regiment refused to accept the lesser pay; many held out until Sept. 29, 1864, when, after Congress had agreed to equalize their pay with white soldiers, the regiment got paid. The men sent most of their long-awaited compensation home to families who had suffered severely while waiting for the paychecks. *OR*, 3 : 5, pp. 632–33; Emilio, *A Brave Black Regiment*, pp. 130, 227–28; RGS to Governor [John A.] Andrew, July 2, 1863, pp. 47–48; Governor Andrew to RGS, July 11, 1863, in "Negro in Military Service of U.S.," pp. 1384–1405; James H. Gooding to Abraham Lincoln, Sept. 28, 1863, in Berlin, *Black Military Experience*, pp. 385–86; Gov. [John A.] Andrew to James B. Congdon, Dec. 28, 1863, in Scrapbook of Congdon, NBFPL.

5. This plan to arm blacks with pikes has shades of John Brown all over it. The plan, if there ever truly was one, came to nothing.

St. Helena's Island, S.C.   [RGS]
July 1, 1863
My dear Clem.,

Yours of the 23d reached me day before yesterday, and I read it with a great deal of pleasure. I anticipated your and Annie's indignation at the vandal policy of Hunter. (Please always remember that Hunter began it). . . .

General Gillmore and General Strong (the latter our immediate commander) are both excellent men, I should think. The former I have not seen, but judge from what I hear.

There is a late-order from Washington, cutting down the pay of coloured troops from $13 to $10 per month. They have not yet decided here whether we come under the order or not. If we do, I shall refuse to have the regiment paid off, until I hear from Governor Andrew.

Another bit of insanity is a proposition to arm the negroes with pikes instead of muskets. They might as well go back eighteen centuries as three, and give us bows and arrows.

General Strong says the regiment shall retain their rifles; but Montgomery and Higginson are in a great stew about it; and, indeed, such an act would take all the spirit and pluck out of their men, and show them that the government didn't consider them fit to be trusted with fire-arms; they would be ridiculed by the white soldiers, and made to feel their inferiority in every respect. The folly of some of our leaders is wonder-ful! I can't imagine who started the idea. I hope the gentleman has a book of drill for the pike all ready.

There is some movement on foot in this Department. We do not know exactly what will be done yet. I don't believe Charleston will be taken without some hard knocks.

Give my best love and a kiss to the mamma from me. I imagine you will all soon be at Lenox again, among the cool mountains. I always think of Lenox as in a haze, for during my visits there I was in a haze myself.

> Always, dear Clem., most affectionately,
> your Brother

St. Helena's Island, S. C.   [MHS]

July 3, 1863

My dear Charley,

Before I proceed to any other subject, let me ask you, if I ever sent you the $5.00 which you paid Brangle for me, & if you know of any other debts of mine in the Second.[1] I don't remember when I last wrote to you, but think it was just after I took dinner at your Father's.

Since then I have seen your letters to your Brother describing the Chancellorsville fights, which I read with a great deal of interest.[2] Harry and I couldn't help feeling blue, when we heard the 2d was at work again, and we away from our old posts. I was very glad to hear that you liked Slocum so much, & had such confidence in him.[3] It will, no doubt, be one of the Division or Corps Generals who will be the great man of the war.

I wish I knew where you were now; we have had no late news from the North, and what we have had, has served mostly to confuse my mind very decidedly, as to the whereabouts of the two armies.[4]

So the 1st Mass. Cavalry has had a regular shindy at last. I was glad to hear that Henry Hig's wounds were not dangerous.[5] What a bloody-looking boy he must be, with a scar across his face.

Remember me to Curtis, if you see or write to him.[6]

You may have heard that the passage of the 54th Mass through Boston was a great success. I never saw such a heavy turn-out there before. We came down to Hilton Head in a very nice Steamer, though a slow one, for we were six days en route.

We landed at Beaufort, and went into camp there. Hearing that Col. Montgomery the Kansas man, was going farther South, I asked permission to join him. So we remained only two days at Beaufort, and then sailed for St. Simon's Island, on the coast of Georgia. The day after we arrived there, Montgomery started us off, up the Altamaha River, and after capturing a little schooner full of cotton & burning the town of Darien, we returned to the Island, having been absent two days.

The destruction of Darien disgusted me very much, and as soon as Montgomery told me he was going to burn it, I said I didn't want to have anything to do with [it] and he was glad to take the responsibility. It was done by Genl Hunter's order, however. We remained at St. Simon's for about ten days after this.

I had a large plantation to myself & lived very comfortably in the former owner's house—the regt being encamped in an adjacent field.

The island is very beautiful, and [is] traversed in all directions by excellent roads. We had splendid rides every day & explored the place from one end to the other. It has been uninhabited for so long, that it is completely full of birds of all kinds, and on the neighbouring Islands, there is good deer-shooting. There were a great many fine plantations & country seats there, and the people must have had a very jolly time. We found the records of a Yacht Race Club—and other signs of fun. Fanny Kemble's husband, Pierce Butler, has a very large place, six or seven miles long, there, and another near Darien. We left St. Simon's on the 25th & ret'd here by order of General Gillmore.

Montgomery is a strange sort of man. At first sight one would think him a parson or a school-master. He is a very quiet gentlemanlike sort of person—very careful to speak grammatically & not in the least like a Western man. He is religious, & never drinks, smokes, chews or swears. He shoots his men with perfect looseness, for a slight disobedience of orders, but is very kind & indulgent to those who behave themselves properly. The other night on board the steamer, he shot at and wounded a man for talking after taps, when he had twice ordered him to be quiet. He told me that he had intended to kill him & throw him overboard, & was much astonished at having missed his aim.

Last Sunday he caught a deserter—and had him executed without trial by Court Martial, or referring the case to any one (Strange to say the General has not taken any notice of it). Montgomery says he doesn't like the red-tape way of doing things.

He is a very attractive man, and it is very interesting to sit & hear him relate his experiences.

Everything here indicates that there is to be another attack on Charleston. I trust we shall have a share in it—and indeed, we have been given to understand, that we should go with the army, wherever it went.

I want to hear from you, very much, Charley. Tell me as much as you can of your movements since you left Stafford C. H. this last time—and how the old regt is. I have been expecting to hear of your promotion. Good-bye, my dear fellow, for the present. I often long to be with you fellows. When you & Harry & I bunked together, from Sharpsburg to Fairfax, we hardly expected to be so far separated as we are now. I wonder where the deuce you are. Give my love to Tom R, Jim Francis, Brown, the Foxes & Mudge.[7]

Always your affectionate friend,
Robert G. Shaw

1. See Shaw's letter to Charley [Morse], Mar. 12, 1863, included here.

2. On Apr. 27–May 4, 1863, Hooker tried to flank Lee at Fredericksburg, but Lee met him in the underbrush near Chancellorsville. Surprised, Hooker lost faith in himself. Lee divided his army and sent Jackson to flank Hooker's right, which he did to great effect. The Union lost 17,287; of the Confederate's 12,764 casualties, the biggest loss was that of Stonewall Jackson. Faust, *Encyclopedia*, p. 126.

3. Henry Warner Slocum.

4. On July 3, Maj. Charles Morse stood with the Second Massachusetts at Gettysburg. He was promoted to lieutenant colonel the next day. *Rec. of Mass. Vols.*, p. 28.

5. Henry Lee Higginson was wounded in three places during the cavalry battle at Aldie, Virginia, on June 17, 1863. A Confederate sabre cut him from right ear to right cheek. Benjamin W. Crowninshield, *A History of the First Regiment of Massachusetts Cavalry Volunteers* (Boston: Houghton Mifflin, 1891), p. 145.

6. Greely Curtis.

7. Capt. Thomas Rodman Robeson and Maj. Charles Redington Mudge were killed at Gettysburg on July 3. Capt. Thomas B. Fox, wounded at Gettysburg, died of his wounds on July 25. Capt. James Francis, Capt. Robert B. Brown and First Lt. John A. Fox survived the battle. *Rec. of Mass. Vols.*, pp. 28, 29.

CHAPTER 15

"God isn't very far off"

The war sped on, but the beginning of the end had come. On successive July days, Lee lost at Gettysburg and Grant walked into Vicksburg. Shaw missed his old regiment, and news of the victory in Pennsylvania and the deaths of more of his friends caused him to regret that he was so far away. He was a bit consoled by his proximity to Charleston. He believed that his commanding general, Quincy A. Gillmore, would soon capture the city that started the rebellion. Shaw longed for the opportunity to put the Fifty-fourth—and himself—into the fight, to win victory over this most defiant Southern city.

Lincoln and his generals had hoped that Charleston could be taken by water. On Apr. 7, 1863, Admiral Samuel du Pont led nine ironclads into the harbor and tried to destroy Fort Sumter. When he withdrew, five monitors were disabled as Confederate cannon fired 2,209 shells against 154 thrown by du Pont's fleet. New plans combined a naval operation with a land assault against the defenses ringing the harbor.

Morris Island held formidable Battery Wagner, which guarded one of the Confederate's key artillery positions protecting Charleston Harbor. For an attack upon Sumter to succeed, Gillmore first had to eliminate Wagner. Gillmore landed troops on Morris Island and, on July 11, made a frontal assault that failed. He determined to try again in a week after a tremendous naval bombardment softened up the defense.

While Shaw waited and hoped for the call to bring up his men, he enjoyed the pleasant company of schoolteacher Charlotte Forten, who accompanied him to a praise meeting and Independence Day celebration. Montgomery was still on his mind. But more than anything else, Shaw fretted that he might not get a chance to get his men alongside white troops in the "grand attack on Charleston."

Then it came. On July 8, Shaw received orders to take his regiment to James Island. Three days later the regiment landed and took up its position beside white troops. This was not exactly what Shaw wanted, but it was a start. From a housetop on James Island, he looked upon Fort Sumter and the church spires in Charleston and prayed for battle.

July 3 1863   [HL]
Dearest Mother,

You will have been sometime without letters from me, when you receive this, as the "Arago" was not allowed to take a mail last week, I understand, because of the late movement on Charleston. Last night, I went over to tea at a plantation 4 or 5 miles from here where some of the teachers, four ladies and the same number of gentlemen live. The interesting member of the family is Miss Lottie Forten, from Philadelphia, a niece of Mr. Purvis, and a quadroon.[1] She is quite pretty, remarkably well educated, and a very interesting woman. She is decidedly the belle here, and the officers, both of the army & navy, seem to think her society far preferable to that of the other ladies.

After tea we went to what the negroes call a praise-meeting, which was very interesting.[2] The praying was done by an old blind fellow, who made believe, all the time, that he was reading out of a book.[3] He was also the leader in the singing, and seemed to throw his whole soul into it. After the meeting they had a shout, which is a most extraordinary performance. They all walk & shuffle round in a ring, singing & chanting, while 3 or 4 stand in a corner and clap their hands to mark the time. At certain parts of the chorus, they all give a duck, the effect of which is very peculiar. The shuffling is what they call shouting. They some times keep it up all night, and only church members are allowed to join in it.

Their singing, when there are a great many voices, is fine, but otherwise I don't like it at all. The women's voices are so shrill, that I can't listen to them with comfort.

I met Mr. Arthur Turner, a brother of Ned Turner's, over there, and today he came to see me. He has been teaching here some time.[4]

The licentiousness among the negroes is very great, but they say that the improvement in that respect, is very encouraging. They feel no shame about it at all, and hardly understand that it is wrong. As a general thing the men seem to me to have better faces than the women.[5]

July 4

Today there has been a great meeting for the coloured people, at the Baptist Church 6 or 7 miles from camp. I rode down there, and heard a speech from a coloured preacher of Baltimore, named Lynch, & another from Mr. [one word crossed out and illegible] which latter was very bad. It may have seemed so to me, because [two words illegible] very much. (This is private).[6]

Mr. Lynch was very eloquent. Can you imagine anything more wonderful than a coloured-Abolitionist meeting on a South Carolina plantation? Here were collected all the freed slaves on this Island listening to the most ultra abolition speeches, that could be made; while two years ago, their masters were still here, the lords of the soil & of them. Now they all own a little themselves, go to school, to church, and work for wages. It is the most extraordinary change. Such things oblige a man to believe that God isn't very far off.

A little black boy read the Declaration of Independence, and then, they all sang some of their hymns. The effect was grand. I would have given anything to have had you there. I thought of you all the time. The day was beautiful and the crowd was collected in the churchyard under some magnificent old oaks, covered with the long, hanging, grey moss, which grows on the trees here. The gay dresses & turbans of the women made the sight very brilliant.

Miss Forten promised to write me out the words of some of the hymns they sang, which I will send to you.[7]

July 6

Yesterday I went to church at the same place, where the meeting was held on the 4th. The preaching was very bad, being full of "hell & damnation" but administered in such a dull way, that sleep soon overcame most of the Congregation & we counted fifty darkeys fast in arms of Murphy. After the sermon the preacher said "Those who wish to be married can come forward." Some one then punched a stout young fellow, in white gloves, near me, and as soon as he could be roused, and made to understand that the hour was come, he walked up to the altar. A young woman, still stouter, & broader shouldered, than the bride groom, advanced from the women's side of the church, accompanied by a friend, and they both stood by his side—so that it looked as if he were being married to both of them. However they got through it all right, as he evidently knew which was which, and they both said "Yes sir" in answer to all the preacher asked them. They were both coal black. I couldn't find out if the bride had been snoring, during the sermon, as well as the groom.

At the church they sing our hymns, and make a sad mess of them, but they do justice to their own at their praise meetings.

9 P.M.

We have just had Miss Forten & two other ladies to tea, and entertained them afterwards with some singing from the men.[8] It made us all think of those latter evenings at Readville, which were so pleasant. If there were any certainty of our being permanently here you & Annie (if Father or some other protector would accompany you) could come down & spend a month without the least difficulty. You would enjoy it immensely. There is enough here to interest you for months.

As you may suppose, I was bitterly disappointed at being left behind, but nothing has been done at Charleston yet, and we may still have a chance.

Today I went on board the Monitor "Montauk" & the Rebel ram "Fingal." The latter is very strong and very powerfully armed—but the work is rough, and looks as if they wanted money & workmen to finish it properly.

We don't know with any certainty, what is going on in the North, but can't believe Lee will get far into Pennsylvania.[9] I suppose it is not sure that he will not get Washington this time. My feeling towards the Government is one of pity—as if they were a poor weak creature goaded & tormented on every side, not knowing which way to turn.

No matter if the Rebels get to New York, I shall never lose my faith in our ultimate success. We are not yet ready for peace—and want a good deal of purging still. I got a letter from Annie this afternoon, but no others. What lively times they have been having at Portland. I wrote to General Strong this afternoon, & expressed my wish to be in his Brigade. Though I like Montgomery, I want to get my men alongside of white troops, and into a good fight if there is to be one. The General sent me word, before he went away, that he was very much disappointed at being ordered to leave us so I thought it well to put it into his head, to try to get us back.

Working independently, the coloured troops come only under the eyes of their own officers and to have their worth properly acknowledged, they should be with other troops in action. It is an incentive to them too to do their best.

There is some rumour tonight of our being ordered to James Island, and put under Genl Terry's command. I should be satisfied with that.[10]

I shall write to Effie & Susie tomorrow if nothing happens to prevent it. Please tell them, so, if they don't hear from me, for we may have to leave this, at any moment. Indeed I have been expecting it, every day.

Goodnight darling Mother. Give my love to Father & the girls. I hope you are all well. I had a note from Cousin John today enclosing an ivy leaf from the wall at Hugomount, Waterloo.[11]

If the Rebels get near New York, do go to Massachusetts. I shall be so anxious, if you don't. Lenox would be a safe place.

Your ever loving son

Will you send this to Annie?

1. Robert Purvis (1810–98) was a free-born black abolitionist and Philadelphia merchant. A good friend of Sydney Howard Gay, Purvis headed the American Anti-Slavery Society and actively worked on the "Underground Railroad." William Wells Brown, *The Black Man, His Antecedents, His Genius, and His Accomplishments* (Philadelphia: J. B. Lippincott, 1863), pp. 253–56; Hine and Davis, *Legends*, p. 65. Charlotte L. Forten (1837–1914), of Salem, Massachusetts, worked as a missionary teaching in Beaufort. Lydia Maria Child described her as "queenly enough for a model of Cleopatra." Edward Pierce wrote of her as "a young woman of African descent, of olive complexion, finely cultured, and attuned to all the beautiful sympathies, of gentle address. . . . She had read the best books. . . ." It is little wonder that she became the "belle" of the area. Lydia Maria Child to William P. Cutler, July 10, 1862, in Meltzer and Holland, *Lydia Maria Child*, p. 414; Edward L. Pierce, "The Freedmen at Port Royal," *Atlantic Monthly*

12 (Sept. 1863): 305; see also Charlotte Forten, "Life on the Sea Islands," *Atlantic Monthly* 13 (May 1864): 587–96, and 13 (June 1864): 666–76.

2. A praise meeting consists of prayers and singing. Forten, "Life on the Sea Islands," p. 672.

3. Maurice, the blind man, lost his sight when an overseer or master hit him in the head with a loaded whip. Ibid.

4. The Turners are unidentified. This paragraph was deleted from *Letters: RGS* (1864), p. 316.

5. Shaw's mother also deleted this paragraph. Ibid.

6. The sentences of this paragraph after "named Lynch" are absent from the printed letters in 1864. Ibid. Sarah Shaw released this letter for print after Robert's death. The newspaper account was full and revealed that Edward L. Pierce gave the bad speech. *National Anti-Slavery Standard*, Aug. 22 (3:6), 1863. James Lynch grew up in Baltimore, was educated at Dartmouth College, participated in the Negro Convention Movement, and followed

his father's path to the pulpit. Leroy Graham, *Baltimore: The Nineteenth Century Black Capital* (Washington, D.C.: University Press of America, 1982), pp. 137–38.

7. Charlotte Forten copied and mailed the hymns to Shaw's mother six weeks later. Charlotte Forten to SBS, August 16, 1863, in *Memorial: RGS*, p. 145.

8. Miss Forten mentions her fondness for taking tea with Shaw and his officers. Forten, "Life on the Sea Islands," p. 675.

9. In the greatest battle of the war, Gettysburg, the Army of the Potomac turned back the Army of Northern Virginia on July 1–3, 1863. On July 4 and 5, Lee ordered his army to retreat to Virginia.

10. Alfred Howe Terry (1827–90) was a Connecticut lawyer appointed to command the Second Connecticut in May 1861. One year later, Terry, as a brigadier general, commanded forces at Hilton Head Island. Boatner, *Dictionary*, p. 831.

11. John Murray Forbes.

St. Helena I.   [HL]
July 4, 1863
Dear Father,

All the troops, excepting the coloured Regiments, are ordered to Folly Island. There will be a grand attack on Charleston, I suppose.

I feel very much disappointed at being left behind, especially after Montgomery was promised by Genl Gilmore that we should have our share in it.

I write you this lest you should see mention of the movement in the papers, & think we were in it.

I have not time to write to Annie, as the mail goes directly. Please send her this, or write to her.

Your loving Son

P.S. I sent you a box with some clothes & my old sword. Enclosed is receipt.

St. Helena's Island   [RGS]
July 6, 1863
My Own Darling Wife,

As I wrote you last week, your long letter of June 5th to 10th came at last, and to-day I got that of the 23d to 26th. I am so sorry you have been worrying yourself about Montgomery and my connection with him, and I hope that my later letters have put your mind at rest. . . .

When you get this, you will have been a good while without news from me, as the last mail was not allowed to go, on account of the military movements in this Department. I wrote to Father the other day that we were left here, and most of the other troops had gone to Folly Island,—at least we suppose that was their destination. There is no knowing how soon, or in what direction, we may get orders to move. It is my great desire to join the main army, and General Strong was so sorry to leave this regiment, that I think there may be a chance of his getting hold of us again.

. . . To-day I went on board the "Montauk," a Monitor lying in the harbour. I met there an officer named Cushman, who took me all over the vessel, and explained everything.[1] In port the cabins are tolerably well ventilated, though very dark; but at sea everything is closed, and in action also; so that the air in the men's quarters becomes so foul that the lights can hardly be kept going. Forty per cent of their men are on the sick-list, and they have to send some of them home every day. Such a hideous place to live in I never saw.

The officers of the navy have by no means as much confidence in the Monitors as the public at large, and say they can be of service only against other iron-clads, or wooden vessels, and *brick-and-mortar walls*. Forts of other descriptions, such as field-works and sand-batteries, they think would get the better of them. It has been necessary to make a great many changes and improvements in them to render them fit for active service; and as this has been done by officers of the navy, they all seem very indignant that Ericsson should have all the credit.[2] They say that, as he turned them over to the navy, they would have been useless. The officers also affirm that the Monitor class or iron-clads was invented by a New York man named Pimbey, four years before Ericsson's was presented, and that the latter now pays him $30,000 for every Monitor he turns out.[3] In short, they pitch into Ericsson energetically, and think he has appropriated other men's work and inventions unsparingly. They showed us all the places where the "Montauk" was struck at Charleston, and explained how several of the vessels were disabled by one plate or bolt being forced out of place. The 11-inch gun can be fired once in 2.30 minutes, and the 15-inch not so often. This is very slow. Nevertheless, they are terrible engines, and wonderful in their strength.

I afterwards visited the "Atlanta," or "Fingal," the Rebel ram lately captured. She is very powerful, but roughly finished. She had four pieces; two 7–inch and two 6½–inch rifles, marked "Tredegar Foundry."[4] They were roughly finished on the outside, but terrible-looking guns. This craft would have made great havoc in our blockading fleet, if she had got out, and it was by a piece of good fortune that we captured her. . . .

July 7th—Good morning. You will see in my letter to Mother what I said about your and her coming down here. Of course it depends entirely upon what we do. The last two weeks would have been delightful for you.

I have got you some of the moss, and send you as much as I can in a large envelope,—enough to hang over a small picture.

On Sunday, I rode six miles to the Episcopal church, but it was closed, the clergyman being ill, and I went to the Baptist. . . .

The gentleness and respect for civilized usages in this war have been wonderful, and for that reason Montgomery's doings seem very horrible. I am not excusing them, but merely giving another side of the picture. He is not the only man who has done so. Foster destroyed three towns in North Carolina without reason, and Blufftown, in this Department, was burnt the other day by white troops.[5] Montgomery's previous reputation has been such that he attracts attention. Many people here blame him for having had one of his men shot without trial. According to Regulations, it was wrong; but the court-martial in this case would have been a technicality, for the man's guilt was unquestionable, and before he could have been tried Montgomery's regiment would have been dissolved. He had lost seventy men by desertion, in two days. Since the execution not one has gone, but thirty or forty have secretly returned in the night. Of course such a power cannot be allowed to a Colonel, as there would be murders without number under the name of execution; and I do not believe Montgomery has heard the last of it. Nevertheless, as to the right and wrong of the matter, he only violated a clause of the Regulations, and the result is extremely beneficial. I think that a Brigadier-General should have power to approve a sentence of death given by a court; but now it has to go to the Department commander.

Colonel Montgomery has told me some fearful stories of his life in Kansas. I will send you one, in order that you may know what a life he has led for ten years past. He had captured five men who had been committing depredations,—shooting men from behind, and taking their scalps. He intended to kill them, but they begged for life so hard, that he let them go, on condition they would not come into Kansas again. Instead of keeping their word, they began their old occupation again, and having captured some of his men, killed them, and took their scalps away with them. Some time after Montgomery took the same five again. This time there was no chance for them. Their courage forsook them entirely, so that they absolutely fell to the earth with fright, and begged and prayed for their lives, and said they should go to Hell, if he killed them.

When they were being taken out to be shot, seeing him somewhat moved by their entreaties, they clung to his knees and his garments, and it required the strength of three men to drag one of them away. At the first fire three were killed, and the other two only mortally wounded; these last kept on moaning, and begging in a weak voice to be allowed to live; but the sergeant in command of the squad of executioners drew his revolver, and blew their brains out!

Scenes like this were common occurences in Kansas at that time, and I wonder that Montgomery has not become a *wild beast* instead of a reasonable man. He commands the respect of all his superiors, and is undoubtedly a man gifted with some great qualities. You cannot talk with him long without discovering that he is in reality a tender-hearted man. This assertion would probably amuse most people, who only know him by reputation.

Don't think I am humbugged by Montgomery. I am not often enthusiastic, and what I say of him is not of that kind. . . .

With all the love that I have,
Your attached Husband

1. Cushman is unidentified.

2. John Ericsson (1803–89), a naval engineer who emigrated from Sweden, signed a government contract on Sept. 15, 1861, to build an ironclad. He built and launched the ironclad *Monitor* from Greenpoint, Long Island, on Jan. 30, 1862. *Harper's Weekly*, Mar. 22, 1862, pp. 1, 7; Mar. 29, 1862, pp. 11, 13; Faust, *Encyclopedia*, p. 246.

3. Pimbey is unidentified and this story is unverified.

4. Joseph R. Anderson's Tredegar Iron Works in Richmond, the South's only major ironworks, provided siege guns, rifled cannon, and iron plates for the Confederacy. Faust, *Encyclopedia*,

p. 762.

5. In Nov. 1862, John Gray Foster led five thousand men on a raid into the interior of North Carolina. Foster's men broke into homes and took everything of value. One soldier remembered that "everything that could not be taken was destroyed." The men set fire to most of the homes in Williamston and Hamilton. Besides the amount of private property put to the torch and the large number of slaves freed from their plantations, the raid accomplished little of military value. John G. Barrett, *The Civil War in North Carolina* (Chapel Hill: University of North Carolina Press, 1963), pp. 137–39. The Blufftown burning is unidentified.

Stono River, S.C.   [RGS]
July 9, 1863 (James' Island)
My Darling Annie,

Just after closing my last, on the envelope of which I said we were ordered away from St. Helena's Island, we embarked on board the "Chasseur." We sailed at about 3 P.M., without anything but India-rubber blankets and a little hardbread, and arrived off Stono Inlet, near Charleston Harbour, at about one o'clock this morning. We lay off the bar until 1 P.M. waiting for the flood-tide. The sea was running very high all the time, so that the men were very sea-sick, and we had a decidedly uncomfortable day. In the night it rained hard, and we all got a good soaking, as it was too hot to stay below. At about 2 P.M. we came to an anchor at the southern point of Folly Island, and Colonel Montgomery reported to General Terry. We then steamed up the Stono River, in company with the Monitor "Nantucket," the gunboat "Pawnee," two other little gunboats, and seven transports containing General Terry's Division.[1]

We now lie off the place where General Hunter's troops landed last year in the attack on Charleston.[2] The sail up the river was beautiful, the sun just sinking as we reached our anchorage.

July 10th—Still on board our transport. Last night, two regiments landed, but encountered nothing but a few outposts. General Terry's part is only to make a feint, the real attack being on Morris Island from Folly. That began this morning, and the news from there is, that General Gillmore has got all his troops on Morris Island, and has possession of nearly half of it.[3]

This afternoon I went inland about two miles, and from a housetop saw Fort Sumter, our Monitors, and the spires of Charleston. Just now the news of the fall of Vicksburg, and of Lee's defeat has reached us. What an excitement there must be through the North![4]

For my part, though, I do not believe the end is coming yet, and the next mail will probably tell us that Lee has got away with a good part of his army; there is too much danger of our government making a compromise, for peace to be entirely welcome now. I am very glad that McClellan was not restored to command, for such vacillation in the government would have been too contemptible. Every one can rejoice at Meade's success, as he is as yet identified with no party.[5] I hope the prisoners will not be paroled, for they will be in the army again in a month, if they are.

I found a classmate, to-day, on board the "Nantucket," surgeon there, and George Lawrence, of the class above me, paymaster on board the "Pawnee."[6] They are both very nice fellows; particularly so, because they have invited me to dinner; having had hardly anything but hard-bread and salt-junk since we left camp, a good dinner is to be desired.[7]

July 11th—This morning I got a paper from General Terry of July 7th, giving an incomplete list of the killed and wounded in the Second and Twentieth Massachusetts Regiments at Gettysburg.[8] Poor Mudge is dead, I see.[9] It will be a terrible blow to his family. You know he was my captain when we first went out. But every one must expect to lose their friends and relatives, and consider themselves as particularly favoured by Providence if they do not.

General Gillmore made an attack on Ft. Wagner this morning, and was repulsed.[10] He will probably begin a regular siege now. Fort Wagner is half-way down Morris Island.

Saturday evening—We landed at noon to-day, and are now about two miles inland. There are two Brigades in line in advance of us. I don't think anything will be done on this side.

13th—Yesterday I dined with Lawrence on board the "Pawnee," and met some very pleasant men among the officers. It has been very fortunate for me to have found so many old acquaintances here, as it has been the means of my meeting a great many people who would have otherwise been disinclined to make the acquaintance of an officer commanding a black regiment.

Our men are out on picket with the white regiments, and have no trouble with them. One of my companies was driven in by a small force of Rebels last night, and behaved very well indeed. The Rebel pickets call to us, that they will give us three days to clear out.

. . . There is a letter from Father a month old at Beaufort, and perhaps your missing ones are there. I shall send this to Father, as our conveniences for writing are very few, and I cannot write another letter in time for this mail.

We have not had our clothes off since we left St. Helena, and have absolutely nothing but an India-rubber blanket apiece. Officers and men are in the same boat. I sent down to-day to get a clean shirt and a horse. They will not allow any accumulation of luggage here.

The general feeling is that Gillmore will get Charleston at last. . . .

Governor Andrew writes that he has urged the Secretary of War to send General Barlow here to take command of the black troops.[11] This is what I have been asking him to do for some time.

We got some ham for dinner to-day, which is an improvement on salt-junk. I hope the mail will be allowed to go this time.

Good bye, dearest Annie.

Your loving Rob

1. Brig. Gen. Alfred H. Terry commanded the First Division of Gillmore's X Corps. Boatner, *Dictionary*, p. 831.

2. On June 16, 1862, Hunter lost the Battle of Secessionville. Long, *Civil War Day By Day*, p. 227.

3. Gillmore planned to attack Morris Island and reduce Battery Wagner, one of the strongest forts defending Charleston Harbor. As the support fleet of Admiral Dahlgren pounded the earthworks of Wagner, he moved part of his army from Folly Island to Morris Island in preparation for an infantry assault upon the battery. Emilio, *A Brave Black Regiment*, pp. 51–52. For day-to-day operations by Gillmore on Morris Island, see *OR*, I:28, pt. 1, entire.

4. In a one-two punch that foreshadowed the end of the Confederacy, Lee lost at Gettysburg on July 3 and Vicksburg surrendered on July 4.

5. Maj. Gen. George Gordon Meade (1815–72) was born in Spain. A career soldier, he graduated from West Point in 1835 and fought in the Seminole and Mexican wars. On June 28, Lincoln appointed him to relieve Hooker in pursuit of Lee's army toward Gettysburg. Faust, *Encyclopedia*, p. 482.

6. Francis Minot Weld served as an assistant surgeon in the U.S. Naval Hospital in Boston from June 1862 until his reassignment aboard the ironclad *Nantucket* on Jan. 14, 1863. Weld resigned in Dec. 1863 only to reenlist as a surgeon with the U.S. Colored Troops in Apr. 1864. George Lawrence joined the navy as an assistant paymaster on Aug. 31, 1861, and became paymaster on the *Pawnee* on Feb. 6, 1862. Brown, *Harvard*

University in the War, pp. 129, 152–53.

7. Salt junk, also known as salt horse, is salted beef. Daily, the ration of salt junk for each Union soldier was twenty ounces. Faust, *Encyclopedia*, p. 654.

8. The *New York Tribune* of July 7 (8:3–4), 1863, listed the partial, first-reported casualties of Twentieth and Second Massachusetts at Gettysburg.

9. Maj. Charles Redington Mudge.

10. In the assault against Fort Wagner on July 11, 1863, Gillmore's forces lost 49 killed, 123 wounded, and 167 captured or missing. *OR*, I:28, pt. 1, pp. 210–11, 363–64, 367–71.

11. Governor Andrew recommended Francis Channing Barlow to Secretary of War Edwin M. Stanton on June 29, 1863. Andrew supported Barlow over Thomas W. Higginson, who "has never seen much service," and James Montgomery, who is "very useful as a good bushwacker. . . ." Still supporting the Fifty-fourth, Andrew told Stanton that he wanted a brigade commander who would do the regiment "justice" and no harm. Barlow was severely wounded at Gettysburg on July 1. He remained a prisoner of war in a Confederate hospital until exchanged in Mar. 1864. He did not command a black brigade. John A. Andrew to E. M. Stanton, June 29, 1863, *OR*, III:3, p. 423; *DAB*, vol. 1, pp. 608–9.

July 13, 1863   [RGS]

My Dearest Annie,

I sent the family letter to Father, to this date, and you will get it very soon after this. You will see from it what we have been doing lately.

I should have been Major of the Second now if I had remained there, and lived through the battles. As regards my own pleasure, I had rather have that place than any other in the army. It would have been fine to go home, a field-officer in that regiment. Poor fellows, how they have been slaughtered! Our mail came to-night, but was taken away by mistake.

My warmest love to Mamma and Clem. . . . That country place of ours is often before my eyes in the dim future. . . .

[fragment printed]

CHAPTER 16

"Nothing but praise"

A living cloud of mingled hue
Across the sand impetuous came,
Into a fiery whirlwind grew
And dashed against the fort in flame.
—George William Curtis, June 1865

On the early morning of July 16, the soldiers of the Fifty-fourth Massachusetts Infantry stood strong. They were on picket duty when a Confederate force screamed the Rebel yell and slammed into them. Forced to retreat, the regiment fought a delaying action that prevented the enemy from routing it and a white regiment, the Tenth Connecticut. The tough resistance by the black soldiers convinced the Confederates not to press the attack later in the day.

Receiving praise from General Gillmore and from white soldiers, Shaw wrote Annie that "to-day wipes out the remembrance of the Darien affair. . . ." Black soldiers had proven they would fight well on the defensive. Two days later, on July 18, they led an assault that demonstrated forever that black Americans could attack fortified positions, kill, and die like whites. Knowing the question many whites still held, Shaw had admonished them to "prove yourselves men." Their charge into the guns of Wagner gave their answers.

James' Island, S.C.   [RGS]
July 15, 1863

My Dearest Annie,

Your letters of June 3d, 14th, and 28th, and July 3d, 4th, and 5th, came to-day, and I felt horridly ashamed of myself for having blamed you for not taking care to post your letters. Do excuse it. It will show you how much I value your dear letters.

You don't know what a fortunate day this has been for me and for us all, excepting some poor fellows who were killed and wounded. We have at last fought alongside of white troops. Two hundred of my men on picket this morning were attacked by five regiments of infantry, some cavalry, and a battery of artillery.[1] The Tenth Connecticut (of Stevenson's Brigade) were on their left, and say they should have had a bad time, if the Fifty-fourth men had not stood so well.[2] The whole Division was under arms in fifteen minutes, and after coming up close in front of us, the enemy, finding us so strong, fell back. The other regiments lost in all, three men wounded. We lost seven killed, twenty-one wounded, six missing, supposed killed, and nine unaccounted for. These last are probably killed or captured.[3] All these belonged to the four companies which were on picket. The main body, excepting artillery, was not engaged at all.

General Terry sent me word he was highly gratified with the behavior of my men, and the officers and privates of other regiments praise us very much.[4] All this is very gratifying to us personally, and a fine thing for the coloured troops. It is the first time they have been associated with white soldiers, this side of the Mississippi.

To make my happiness and satisfaction complete, the afternoon brought your and Mother's letters. . . .

I have just come in from the front with my regiment, where we were sent as soon as the Rebels retired. This shows that the events of the morning did not destroy the General's confidence in us.

We found some of our wounded, who say the Rebels treated them kindly. Other men report that some prisoners were shot. It is very common for frightened men to tell fearful stories of what they have seen; the first report comes from the wounded men themselves; the second from the stragglers. . . .[5]

Good bye, darling, for the night. I know this letter will give you pleasure, because what we have done to-day wipes out the remembrance of the Darien affair, which you could not but grieve over, though we were innocent participators. You will have some satisfaction in telling it to your father, your Uncle Charles, and Aunt Fanny, to all of whom please give my sincere regards.[6] Whenever you see your grandfather and grandmother, do not forget to give them my respects. To our Mamma, and Clem. I needn't say I send my warmest love. I got my horse, India-rubber tube, and some clean clothes to-day.

Your most loving Husband

Cole's Island (opposite Folly Island)   [RGS]
July 17th, 4 P.M.

James Island was evacuated last night by our forces. My regiment started first, at 9 1/2 P.M. Not a thing was moved until after dark, and the Rebels must have been astonished this morning. Terry went there originally only to create a diversion from Morris Island, and it was useless to stay and risk being driven off, after Morris was taken. It thundered and lightened, and rained hard all night, and it took us from 10 P.M. to 5 A.M. to come four miles. Most of the way we had to march in single file along the narrow paths through the swamps. For nearly half a mile we had to pass over a bridge of one, and in some places, two planks wide, without a railing, and slippery with rain,—mud and water below several feet deep,—and then over a narrow dike so slippery as to make it almost impossible to keep one's feet. It took my regiment alone nearly two hours to pass the bridge and dike. By the time we got over, it was nearly daylight, and the Brigade behind us had a pretty easy time. I never had such an extraordinary walk.

We are now lying on the beach opposite the southern point of Folly Island, and have been here since five this morning. When they can get boats, they will set us across, I suppose.

There is hardly any water to be got here, and the sun and sand are dazzling and roasting us. I shouldn't like you to see me as I am now; I haven't washed my face since day before yesterday. My conscience is perfectly easy about it, though, for it was an impossibility, and every one is in the same condition. Open air dirt, i.e. mud, &c is not like the indoor article.

. . . I have had nothing but crackers and coffee these two days. It seems like old times in the army of the Potomac.

Good bye again, darling Annie.

Rob

July 18th. Morris Island—We are in General Strong's Brigade, and have left Montgomery, I hope for good. We came up here last night, and were out again all night in a very heavy rain. Fort Wagner is being very heavily bombarded.[7] We are not far from it.

1. This letter is misdated. Shaw wrote the letter after the attack on July 16. Either he mistakenly dated it or the editor of his *Letters: RGS* (1864) made an error. Princeton graduate Alfred H. Colquitt, later a Georgia governor and senator, led the attack on the Union forces. Emilio, *A Brave Black Regiment*, pp. 57–63.

2. The Tenth Connecticut Infantry organized at Hartford on Oct. 22, 1861. In July 1863, it was part of the First Brigade, First Division, X Corps. Dyer, *Compendium*, vol. 1, p. 115; Thomas Greely Stevenson (1836–64), of Boston, joined the army as a colonel just after the beginning of the war. Stevenson opposed using blacks as Union soldiers. He died at Spotsylvania in 1864. Boatner, *Dictionary*, p. 798.

3. The day after the battle, Capt. Cabot Russel wrote his father that "my men were slaughtered but fought like demons." He added, "my men did nobly." The Fifty-fourth lost 14 killed, 18 wounded, and 13 missing. Capt. Russel to Father, July 17, 1863, quoted in *Memorial: RGS*, pp. 44–45; Bowen, *Mass. in the War*, p. 674.

4. Capt. J. W. M. Appleton remembered that fight on James Island: "In this first fight with the enemy, their [the men of the regiment] stubborn courage filled the officers with joy." J. W. M. Appleton, "That Night at Fort Wagner," *Putnam's Magazine* 19 (July 1869): 9–11.

5. A few prisoners may have been shot by the rebels if the following story has any truth in it. The *Charleston Daily Courier*, reflecting white Southern attitudes toward black soldiers, printed a story from a Confederate soldier who disagreed with how well the Fifty-fourth had done: "We encountered the principal line of the Abolitionists. . . . One rascal, running up with his musket, exclaimed—'Here mossa, nebber shoot him off—tak him'—but unfortunately somebody's gun went off about the same time, and the fellow was killed. They received no tender treatment during the skirmish. . . . The prisoners believe they are to be hung, and gave as a reason for fighting as well as they did, that they would rather die of bullet than rope." *Charleston Daily Courier*, July 17 (1:4), 1863.

6. Perhaps Charles is William C. Haggerty of New York City. *Trow's NYC Directory for 1863*, p. 358. Aunt Fanny is unidentified.

7. The bombardment began about 12:30 P.M. with fire and shot blazing from five monitors, two ships, six mortar boats, and Gillmore's land batteries. The shelling stopped at about 7:00 P.M. after about nine thousand rounds had struck Fort Wagner. Johnson Hagood, *Memoirs of the War of Secession* (Columbia, S.C.: The State, 1910), p. 141.

Morris Island   [RGS]
July 18, 1863
Dear Father,

I enclose this letter for Annie, which I didn't intend to send you, because it is impossible to tell whether I can write again by this mail. If I do, please send this to Annie without taking it home, and tell her why it didn't go direct.

We hear nothing but praise of the Fifty-fourth on all hands. Montgomery is under Stevenson. I wish I were. He is a good soldier. Strong I like too. Love to Mother and the girls.

Rob

Epilogue

The survivors of the Fifty-Fourth struggled through the sand away from the assault on Fort Wagner, found friends, and reformed at the southern end of Morris Island where the sand dunes played out onto the flat beach near the Atlantic Ocean. Luis Emilio, the only officer above the rank of captain not wounded or killed in the attack, commanded the regiment. Men hugged one another, thanked God for their safety, and wept over the dead. They worried what the Confederates might do to their captured comrades, and prayed that Shaw had somehow survived his wounds and would be returned by prisoner exchange. Since the fight on James Island on the sixteenth, the men had been in motion. Now they rested, but only for one day.

Many wrote hurried notes telling loved ones that no matter what the papers reported, they were alive. In a letter to his fiancée two days after the assault, Sgt.-Maj. Lewis Douglass "snatched a moment to write." He knew they had passed the test and cast off the burden of proving themselves capable of fighting like white men. Rightfully proud that the Fifty-Fourth had "established its reputation as a fighting regiment," Douglas told her, "not a man flinched." He understood the futility of the assault even as he wanted more: "Men fell all around me. A shell would explode and clear a space of twenty feet, our men would close up again, but it was no use we had to retreat.... How I got out of that fight alive I cannot tell, but I am here.... Remember if I die I die in a good cause. I wish we had a hundred thousand colored troops we would put an end to this war."[1]

Inside and outside of the hospital tents, Dr. Ripley Stone treated the injured, sending the more seriously wounded to the better-staffed medical facilities near Beaufort. There, Charlotte Forten left her schoolhouse duties to help nurse the men. When news of the battle reached her, Forten put her thoughts in her journal: "It is too terrible, too terrible to write. We only hope it may not all be true. That our noble, beautiful young Colonel is killed and the reg[iment] cut to pieces! I cannot, cannot believe it.... But oh, I am stunned, sick at heart. I can scarcely write.... And oh, I still must hope that our colonel, *ours* especially he seems to me, is not killed." Forten bolstered the wounded men's morale and her own by repeating the rumor—or hope— that Shaw "was not dead, but had been taken prisoner by the rebels." With that news, Forten recorded, "How joyfully their wan faces lighted up!" A few days later, after receiving definite news of Shaw's fate, she confided to her journal that it "makes me sad, sad at heart.... I know it was a glorious death." Forten also grieved for Shaw's "young wife" and mother.[2]

On July 20, those who had not been wounded were at work again, co-operating with white regiments on guard duty and in digging the siege trenches that would zig and zag the Union line forward toward Fort Wagner and beyond, to Charleston. After three full days of scooping sand, the men closed the 1350-yard separation to 400 yards. The day before Forten knew, confirmation of Shaw's death and burial reached the regiment as well as word that no black prisoners would be exhanged. Colonel M. S. Littlefield of the Fourth South Carolina (Colored) Infantry assumed temporary command of the regiment. Toward the end of the month, Norwood Hallowell arrived with the Fifty-Fifth Massachusetts, camped on Folly Island, and undoubtedly raised spirits with news from home, consolations, and praise. At the same time, Brig.-Gen. Edward Wild's First North Carolina Colored Infantry increased spirits by bringing more black fighting men into position against the Charleston defenses.[3]

Still, the birthplace of the rebellion would not yield to Union pressure until February 1865, even though the siege against Wagner brought the fort's evacuation on September 7. By that time, fifty-eight days after the assault, the daily bombardment by Union monitors and land batteries had raised, in the words of a Confederate defender, "an intolerable stench from the unearthed dead." The Confederates climbed aboard boats and left Fort Wagner to Union troops.[4]

The men of the Fifty-Fourth walked into this ground hallowed by their comrades' lives and by their efforts to gain respect as men of war. Perhaps expressing best what most believed, Lt. Wilkie James, twice wounded in the assault, wrote that Wagner "was the culmination of our hopes and our toils, the point above all other points to which we had been climbing from the moment the negro soldier at Readville took the musket in his hand." While proud, the men worried over what the Confederates might do to those who had been captured. They took some solace in Lincoln's order to protect African-American captives: "for every soldier of the United States killed in violation of the laws of war, a rebel soldier shall be executed, and for every one enslaved by the enemy or sold into slavery, a rebel soldier shall be placed at hard labor on the public works." There is no proof that Confederates killed or enslaved any Fifty-Fourth prisoners except for those who died from wanting for provisions and attention at Andersonville and other prisons.[5]

The regiment occupied the fort until January 1864 and regained strength as men arrived from Boston to refill the ranks. Edward Hallowell, healed of his three wounds and promoted to colonel, took command of the men. For the next eighteen months the unit would fight in the Department of the South, most notably at the battles of Olustee, James Island, and Honey Hill. In early 1865, the regiment pulled garrison duty in Savannah. Later, in Charleston, the men quartered in the Citadel. The Fifty-Fourth celebrated Independence day in the city that most symbolized resistance to their freedom with a reading of the Emancipation Proclamation as a corrective and addition to the Declaration of Independence.[6]

On August 20 the regiment was officially mustered out of service. Within twenty-four hours the men boarded a transport for Boston. Six days later, Brevet Brig.-Gen. Hallowell and half the regiment arrived at Gallop's Island in Boston Harbor. The rest of the men joined them on August 29.

On September 2, after being ferried to Commercial Wharf, the Fifty-Fourth formed into ranks and marched toward the State House and Boston Common. Completing the circle of service, this parade was most unlike the one in May 1863 when everything stood in the balance, when they had yet to grieve for Shaw and the others, when "boys" had not proven themselves men, when the war had not turned.

Edward Hallowell was at the front of the regiment. He had been just a length behind Shaw on that recent yet long ago May, but unlike Shaw, he led not enthusiastic, untried, and nervous men, but, in Emilio's words, men who marched "with the swing . . . and the bearing of seasoned soldiers." No dissenters booed or yelled racial epithets this time; no one dared do such a thing. These were the men who for eighteen months had refused to accept lesser pay than Congress gave to its white soldiers. Congress finally agreed that fighting men—black and white—deserved equal compensation. The Fifty-Fourth had forced parity by its courage on the sloping sand of Wagner and by proven dedication to the Union in the face of appalling discrimination.[7]

Conspicuous in the regimental ranks marched Sgt. William H. Carney, whose deeds at Wagner would garner the Medal of Honor. 1st Lt. Stephen A. Swails, the first African-American to be commissioned an officer in the army, was the pride of his company. Peter Vogelsang and Frank Welch, also lieutenants and also black, marched alongside their men. They strode into the Common and stopped to perform the manual of arms for themselves and for the crowd. After a short speech in which he thanked them and hoped for their future as citizens in every state, Hallowell led his men to a feast of celebration at the Charles Street Mall where he disbanded them for the last time.[8]

Shaw's family carried on with life even while grieving over their loss. The Haggertys protected Annie from the early newspaper accounts and telegrams of Shaw's death until they confirmed the report. Nine months later Annie became a vivid symbol of her sacrifice and Shaw's when she reviewed the departure of New York's first black regiment. Until her death in 1907, Annie lived primarily in Switzerland and France, never remarried, and kept up a sporadic correspondence with Josephine Shaw Lowell.[9]

In the months following her brother's death, Josephine must have recalled her diary entries of 1862 when she had yet to be touched by personal tragedy: "delight fills my soul when I think of the noble fellows advancing, retreating, charging and dying." Josephine wrote once that Shaw told her he "expected to be 'slaughtered before it was over.'" Another entry announced that "martyrs are not to be pitied." In October 1864, Josephine, who had been married just twelve months and was eight months pregnant, learned that her husband Charles Russell Lowell had been killed in a cavalry charge at Cedar Creek. Earlier in the month he had written her worrying, "'I don't want to be shot till I've had a chance to come home. I have no idea that I shall be hit, but . . . it frightens me." As strong and determined as her mother, Josephine devoted herself to public service, worked for the New York State Board of Charities and Women's Municipal League, and wrote over fifty pamphlets to bring such issues as pauperism, asylums, unemployment, and children's and workers' rights before the public.[10]

Shaw's other sisters, Anna, Susanna, and Ellen, filled their lives with marriage and children. Susanna named her first son, born one month after Shaw's death, Robert Shaw Minturn. Anna stayed close to home while her husband, George Curtis, continued to write for *Harper's Weekly* and threw himself into the political questions of the day. After the war, Ellen married her brother's old tutor, Maj.-Gen. Francis C. Barlow and worked for Civil Service reform, African-American education and prison reform. Barlow became attorney general of New York and achieved fame when Winslow Homer used him as the model for the Union officer in "Prisoners at the Front."[11]

Sarah and Francis Shaw were consoled by their son's bravery to a cause they had long advanced. They understood the symbolism in ensuring that his grave be undisturbed, allowing him to remain forevermore in a foreign soil. His burial tied up the idea of martyrdom they so respected in John Brown and now in their son. But the reality of losing a child coiled deeply within the mother. Sarah wrote to a longtime abolitionist and friend to tell him of the "treasure God had called upon us to lay upon His Altar—a treasure indeed it was, our only son. . . . I fully recognize that the cause for which he died is sacred to God & Humanity . . . [yet now] the cup of life for me is poisoned. The same sun no longer shines for me." Perhaps Sarah regretted that she had ever pushed him to do his duty as she believed it to be. Still she must have been comforted by the praise that others heaped upon her son's act and she would allow no one to second guess his devotion to his men.[12]

Further to tie up the wounds of war and to erase any stain from their son's name, the Shaws sent one thousand dollars to rebuild the Episcopal Church in Darien, Georgia, which had been destroyed along with the rest of the town when Colonel James Montgomery ordered Shaw to help him burn away the sins of the slaveholding South. Sarah wrote the church's pastor, Reverend Robert F. Clute, pled for her son's innocence in the sack of Darien, and lamented, "Were I able I would rebuild the whole pretty town in his memory."[13]

Sarah continued to be the active matriarch of an ever-larger family that included fourteen grandchildren. Francis served as President of the National Freedmen's Relief Association, an organization which raised money and sent teachers to educate ex-slaves. He joined with Levi Coffin and others successfully to lobby Congress for the establishment of a Freedmen's Bureau. The Shaws remained philanthropists and spokespersons for progressive reform.[14]

Few acts have been more right for memorial than Shaw's death and burial at Wagner. Hundreds gave money to build a monument to honor him. In

1863, the men and friends of the regiment in South Carolina contributed nearly three thousand dollars to build a memorial on Morris Island. But instead of a monument, the money was used to help finance a more useable remembrance, the Shaw School for black children in Charleston.[15]

Still, the colonel has traditional memorials. A granite column stands as a tombstone would in the Moravian Cemetery plot on Staten Island. Shaw's likeness and name appear alongside others in the wall to the alumni dead in Memorial Hall at Harvard University. More than forty poems have been written to recall his deeds. The movie *Glory* resurrected Shaw for a public who cannot seem to learn enough about the sacrifices of his time. And then, of course, there is the masterpiece by Augustus Saint-Gaudens that stands facing the Old State House from Boston Common. The sculptor labored fourteen years designing and molding into bas-relief what Robert Lowell reinterpretd as "For the Union Dead."[16]

Dedicated on May 31, 1897, thirty-four years after the grand march from Boston, Shaw was again leading his men toward recognition and glory. In 1897, sixty-five officers and men, most in their old uniforms, listened to the band play "John Brown's Body," heard William James and Booker T. Washington talk about sacrifice, and saluted the memorial, their fallen comrades, and each other. Most had read Luis Emilio's three-year-old history, *A Brave Black Regiment*, to which they had contributed their memories and anecdotes. Of the 1354 men who served in the Fifty-Fourth, one hundred died of battle wounds, nineteen perished in prison camps, ninety-four succumbed to disease or accident, and fifty-seven were considered missing in action, probably dead.[17]

Fort Wagner has since been reclaimed by the sea and the grave of Shaw and his men lie undisturbed from the footfalls of tourists. In this sense they belong to the world and are washed by the same waters that link the Americas to Africa and Europe. The ocean is such a powerful metaphor for life and equality that no better resting place can be conceived. That they died for each other, and that Saint-Gaudens could build the magnificent monument to their triumph over inequality is just and proper.

In 1897, Booker T. Washington told the assembled crowd that the "full measure of the fruit of Fort Wagner and all that this monument stands for will not be realized until every man covered by a black skin" has the unrestricted opportunity to succeed. That we have yet to enjoy the fruit of the lessons they tried to teach us is disheartening, but their sacrifice should not be seen as in vain. For as we strive to learn, Shaw and his men continue to march forward from Boston Common toward equality.[18]

1. Lewis [Douglass] to Amelia [Loguen], 20 July 1863, Carter Woodson Papers, LC.

2. Ray Allen Billington, ed., *The Journal of Charlotte L. Forten* (New York: Dryden, 1953), pp. 213–17.

3. Luis F. Emilio, *A Brave Black Regiment: History of the Fifty-Fourth Regiment of Massachuetts Volunteer Infantry, 1863–1865* (Boston: Boston Book Co., 1891; reprint, New York: Arno Press, 1969), pp. 106–108.

4. Ibid., p. 120.

5. Ibid., pp. 279, 393–433; Garth W. James, "The Assault Upon Fort Wagner," *War Papers Read before the Commandery of the State of Wisconsin, Military Order of the Loyal Legion of the U.S.* (Milwaukee: Burdick, Armitage & Allen, 1891), pp. 23, 27; General Order No. 252, July 31, 1863, OR II, vol. 6, p. 163.

6. Emilio, *Brave Black Regiment*, pp. 148–216, 277–88, 310–14.

7. Ibid., pp. 227–28, 317–20.

8. Ibid., pp. 330, 336; Joseph T. Glatthaar, *Forged in Battle: The Civil War Alliance of Black Soldiers and White Officers* (New York: Free Press, 1990), pp. 140, 152, 179.

9. See Ogden [Haggerty] to Charles P. Haggerty, July 24, 1863, in Robert Gould Shaw: Military and Personal Telegrams, New York Historical Society; Peter Burchard, *One Gallant Rush: Robert Gould Shaw and His Brave Black Regiment* (New York: St. Martin's, 1965), p. 147; and "Topics of the Time," *Century Magazine* 54 (June 1897): 312.

10. William R. Stewart, *The Philanthropic Works of Josephine Shaw Lowell* (New York: Macmillan, 1911), pp. 28, 30, 37; *In Memorium: Josephine Shaw Lowell* (New York: Charity Organization of New York, 1905), pp. 43–101; James B. Lane, "Jacob A. Riis and Scientific Philanthropy During the Progressive Era," *Social Science Review* 47 (March 1973): 32–48; Lowell's letter quoted in Ferris Greenslet, *The Lowells and Their Seven Worlds* (Boston: Houghton Mifflin, 1946), p. 294.

11. Notes on the Barlow family by Louisa Barlow Jay, Houghton Library, Harvard University.

12. Sarah Shaw to John E. Cairnes, November 2, 1863, quoted in Adelaide Weinberg, *John Elliot Cairnes and the American Civil War: A Study in Anglo-American Relations* (London: Kingswood Press, 1969), p. 167.

13. Sarah Shaw to Rev. [Robert] Clute, August 29 and September 24, 1870, quoted from Buddy Sullivan, *Early Days on the Georgia Tidewater: The Story of McIntosh County and Sapelo* (Darien, GA: Darien News, 1990), pp. 305–6.

14. Francis Shaw to Edwin M. Stanton, 6 October 1863, Records of the Office of the Secretary of War, RG 107, Micro. 221, Roll 240, Letter S-1361, National Archives; James M. McPherson, *The Struggle For Equality: Abolitionists and the Negro in the Civil War and Reconstruction* (Princeton: Princeton University Press, 1964), p. 189.

15. Emilio, *Brave Black Regiment*, p. 229; E. N. Hallowell to Rufus Saxton, October 7, 1864, N. P. Hallowell Papers, MHS; Laura Towne, *Letters and Diary of Laura M. Towne: Written from the Sea Islands of South Carolina,*

1862–1884 (1912; reprint, New York: Negro Universities Press, 1969), p. 116.

16. For the best look at Saint-Gaudens and the poems to Shaw, see Homer Saint-Gaudens, ed., *The Reminiscences of Augustus Saint-Gaudens* (New York: Century, 1913); Steven G. Axelrod, "Colonel Shaw in American Poetry: 'For the Union Dead and Its Precursors,'" *American Quarterly* 24 (October 1972): 523–37; and Robert Lowell, *Life Studies and For the Union Dead* (New York: Noonday Press, 1971).

17. Emilio, *Brave Black Regiment*, p. 391.

18. Speech of Booker T. Washington at Shaw Memorial, May 31, 1897, quoted from Richard Benson, *Lay This Laurel* (New York: Eakins, 1973), no page numbers.

Letters Not Included in This Volume

Date		Recipient	Collection	Date		Recipient	Collection
1861				Sept.	12	SBS	[RGS]
April	18	FGS	[RGS]		?	FGS	[RGS]
	19	George Curtis	[HL]	Oct.	14	SBS	[RGS]
	20	SBS	[RGS]		17	SBS	[RGS]
	25	FGS	[HL]		21	FGS	[RGS]
	28	Susanna Shaw	[RGS]		21	FGS	[RGS]
	28	FGS	[RGS]		23	SBS	[RGS]
May	3	SBS	[HL]		28	SBS	[RGS]
	6	SBS	[HL]		31	SBS	[HL]
	7	FGS	[HL]	Nov.	2	SBS	[RGS]
	19	FGS	[HL]		11	Josephine Shaw	[HL]
	22	FGS	[RGS]		15	FGS	[RGS]
	31	SBS	[HL]	Dec.	1	Josephine Shaw	[HL]
June	4	FGS	[HL]		5	FGS	[RGS]
	7	FGS	[RGS]		8	FGS	[RGS]
	13	FGS	[RGS]				
	14	FGS	[HL]	**1862**			
	?	SBS	[HL]	Jan.	13	SBS	[RGS]
July	5	SBS	[RGS]		16	Susanna Shaw	[RGS]
	24	SBS	[HL]		22	SBS	[RGS]
	25	FGS	[RGS]		24	FGS	[HL]
	27	FGS	[RGS]		31	FGS	[RGS]
	30	SBS	[RGS]	Feb.	2	SBS	[RGS]
Aug.	2	FGS	[RGS]		6	SBS	[RGS]
	6	SBS	[RGS]		24	SBS	[RGS]
	12	FGS	[HL]		28	SBS	[HL]
	14	FGS	[RGS]	Mar.	19	SBS	[RGS]
	15	FGS	[RGS]		22	Susanna Shaw	[RGS]
	17	FGS	[RGS]	April	24	FGS	[RGS]
	19	SBS	[RGS]		30	SBS	[RGS]
	24	SBS	[RGS]	May	1	FGS	[RGS]
	27	FGS	[HL]		8	FGS	[RGS]
	27	SBS	[RGS]		26	FGS	[RGS]
					31	SBS	[RGS]

Date		Recipient	Collection	Date		Recipient	Collection
June	25	Josephine Shaw	[HL]		30	Annie Haggerty	[RGS]
July	9	SBS	[RGS]		30	SBS	[RGS]
	12	FGS	[RGS]		31	Josephine Shaw	[RGS]
	20	SBS	[RGS]	1863			
Sept.	4	SBS	[RGS]	Jan.	1	George Curtis	[HL]
	10	FGS	[RGS]		5	Annie Haggerty	[RGS]
	30	FGS	[RGS]		12	FGS	[RGS]
Oct.	8	FGS	[RGS]		16	Annie Haggerty	[RGS]
	13	Josephine Shaw	[NYPL]		23	Annie Haggerty	[RGS]
	23	FGS	[RGS]		23	FGS	[RGS]
	24	SBS	[RGS]		29	SBS	[RGS]
Nov.	3	SBS	[HL]	Mar.	12	SBS	[RGS]
	25	SBS	[RGS]		12	Annie Haggerty	[RGS]
	29	FGS	[RGS]	April	27	SBS	[HL]
Dec.	2	FGS	[RGS]	May	22	FGS	[RGS]
	9	SBS	[RGS]	June	3	Anna Shaw Curtis	[HL]
	10	FGS	[RGS]	July	4	FGS	[HL]
	15	SBS	[RGS]		8	Josephine Shaw	[HL]
	19	Susanna Shaw	[RGS]				

SELECTED BIBLIOGRAPHY

PRIMARY SOURCES

Manuscripts:
Boston Public Library
  Lydia Maria Child Papers.
  William Lloyd Garrison Papers.
  Thomas W. Higginson Papers.
  Massachusetts Infantry, 2nd Regiment. Letters from the Army: A Scrapbook.
  Weston Sisters Papers.
Gettysburg College Library
  Albanus S. Fisher Papers.
Houghton Library, Harvard University
  George William Curtis. Papers, 1842–1892.
  Henry Lee Higginson scrapbook: "The Soldier's Book."
  Louisa Barlow Jay Collection.
  Amos Adams Lawrence Papers.
  Francis George Shaw Letters.
  Robert Gould Shaw Collection.
  Sarah Blake Sturgis Shaw Papers.
  Frank Vizetelly. Sketches.
Massachusetts Historical Society
  John Albion Andrew Papers.
  Nathan Bowditch. CDV album: "Our Martyr Soldiers of the Great Rebellion."
  Broadsides—L.(1863).
  Carte-de-Visite Album, Civil War, 54th Massachusetts.
  Richard Cary Papers.
  Crowninshield-Magnus Papers, 1834–1965.
  Dana Collection: Letter, Francis G. Shaw to George Ripley, Feb. 1845.
  Fifty-fourth Massachusetts Infantry Regiment Papers.
  Norwood P. Hallowell Papers and Scrapbooks, 1764–1914.
  A. A. Lawrence Collection.
  Lee Family Papers.
  James Russell Lowell Papers, 1842–1924.
  T. Lyman III Collection.
  Lyman Family Papers, 1785–1956.
  Miscellaneous Bound.
  Photographic Collection.
  MS. L. Robert Gould Shaw.
  R. G. Shaw II Collection.

National Archives
   Record Group 94. Records of the Adjutant General's Office.
      Bound Record Books. 2nd Massachusetts Infantry.
      Bound Record Books. 54th Massachusetts Infantry (Colored).
      Colored Troops Division, 1863–1889.
      Compiled Military Service Records.
      "The Negro in the Military Service of the United States, 1607–1889."
      Pension Files.
   Record Group 107. Records of the Office of the Secretary of War.
      Letters Received.
   Record Group 393. Department of the South.
      Letters Received.
      Registers of Letters Sent.
      Special Orders.
New Bedford Free Public Library
   Camp Meigs Papers.
   Soldier's Fund Committee. Scrapbook of James Bunker Congdon.
New York Historical Society
   Major Philip Schuyler. Roll of Co. 6, 7th Regiment National Guard, N.Y.
   Petition for Raising a Colored Regiment, October 1862.
   Philip Schuyler. Letters to His Parents, 1863–1864.
   Robert Gould Shaw. Military and Personal Telegrams.
   Shaw folder. Photograph of Robert Gould Shaw.
New York Public Library, Rare Books and Manuscripts Division
   Cabot Jackson Russel. Papers, 1859–1865.
   Shaw Family Letters, 1862–1876.
Staten Island Historical Society
   George William Curtis clippings.
   R. B. Minturn House photograph.
   Shaw family folder.
   F. G. Shaw House photograph.
Staten Island Institute of Arts and Sciences
   George William Curtis Collection.
   F. G. Shaw, biographical notes.
United States Army Military History Institute at Carlisle Barracks
   George L. Andrews Papers.
   Massachusetts-MOLLUS Collection.
West Virginia University Library
   John W. M. Appleton Papers, 1861–1916. Letterbook.

Newspapers and Periodicals:
Atlantic Monthly.
(Boston) Commonwealth.
Boston Daily Journal.
Boston Herald.

Charleston Daily Courier.
Douglass' Monthly.
Frank Leslie's Illustrated Newspaper.
Harper's Weekly.
The Illustrated London News.
National Anti-Slavery Standard.
New Bedford Daily Mercury.
New Bedford Standard.
New York Daily Tribune.
New York Times.
Punch.
Richmond County (N.Y.) Gazette.
Savannah Morning News.

Books and Articles:

Adams, Virginia M., ed. *On the Altar of Freedom: A Black Soldier's Civil War Letters from the Front.* Amherst: University of Massachusetts Press, 1991.

Agassiz, George R., ed. *Meade's Headquarters, 1863–1865.* Boston: Atlantic Monthly Press, 1922.

Annual Report of the Adjutant-General of the Commonwealth of Massachusetts . . . for the Year Ending December 31, 1863. Boston: Wright & Potter, 1864.

Appleton, J. W. M. "That Night at Fort Wagner." *Putnam's Magazine* 19 (July 1869): 9–16.

Aptheker, Herbert, ed. *A Documentary History of the Negro People of the United States.* 2 volumes. New York: Citadel Press, 1951.

Basler, Roy P., ed. *The Collected Works of Abraham Lincoln.* 9 volumes. New Brunswick, N.J.: Rutgers University Press, 1952–55.

Berlin, Ira, Joseph P. Reidy, and Leslie S. Rowland, eds. *Freedom: A Documentary History of Emancipation, 1861–1867.* Series II. *The Black Military Experience.* Cambridge: Cambridge University Press, 1982.

Berlin, Ira, et al. *Freedom: A Documentary History of Emancipation, 1861–1867.* Series I. *The Destruction of Slavery.* Cambridge: Cambridge University Press, 1985.

Billington, Ray Allen, ed. *The Journal of Charlotte L. Forten.* New York: Dryden Press, 1953.

Blassingame, John W., ed. *The Frederick Douglass Papers.* 3 volumes. New Haven: Yale University Press, 1979–85.

Boston City Directory. Boston: Adams, Sampson, 1861–63.

Bowditch, Vincent Y. *Life and Correspondence of Henry I. Bowditch.* Boston: Houghton Mifflin, 1902.

Butler, Benjamin F. *Private and Official Correspondence of General Benjamin F. Butler.* 5 volumes. Norwood, Mass.: Plimpton Press, 1917.

Cairnes, John E. *The Slave Power: Its Character, Career, and Probable Designs; Being an Attempt to Explain the Real Issues Involved in the American Contest.* New York: Carleton, 1862.

Casey, Silas. *Infantry Tactics.* 3 volumes. New York: D. Van Nostrand, 1862.

"A Catalogue of the Officers and Students of Harvard University for the Academical Year 1856–57 . . . 1858–59." 6 pamphlets. Cambridge, Mass.: John Bartlett, 1856–1858.

Child, Lydia Maria. "Correspondence between Lydia Child and Gov. Wise and Mrs. Mason of Virginia," pp. 1–28, in *Anti-Slavery Tracts*. Boston: American Anti-Slavery Society, 1860; reprint, Westport: Negro Universities Press, 1970.

———. *Letters of Lydia Maria Child*. Boston: Houghton Mifflin, 1882.

Crowninshield, Benjamin W. *A History of the First Regiment of Massachusetts Cavalry Volunteers*. Boston: Houghton Mifflin, 1891.

Curtis, George William. *From the Easy Chair*. 3 volumes. New York: Harper, 1892.

Dwight, Elizabeth, ed. *Life and Letters of Wilder Dwight, Lieut-Col. 2nd Massachusetts Infantry Volunteers*. Boston: Ticknor & Fields, 1868.

Emerson, Edward W. *Life and Letters of Charles Russell Lowell, Captain Sixth United States Cavalry, Colonel 2nd Massachusetts Cavalry, Brigadier General United States Volunteers*. Boston: Houghton Mifflin, 1907.

Emilio, Luis F. *A Brave Black Regiment: History of the Fifty-Fourth Regiment of Massachusetts Volunteer Infantry, 1863–1865*. Boston: Boston Book Co., 1891; reprint, New York: Arno Press, 1969.

———. "The Assault on Fort Wagner." Boston: Rand Avery, 1887.

Forten, Charlotte. "Life on the Sea Islands." *Atlantic Monthly* 13 (May 1864): 587–96, 13 (June 1864): 666–76.

Garrison, W. P. and F. J. Garrison. *William Lloyd Garrison, 1805–1879: The Story of His Life*. 4 volumes. New York: Century, 1889.

Gordon, George H. *Brook Farm to Cedar Mountain in the War of the Great Rebellion, 1861–1862*. Boston: Osgood, 1883.

———. *History of the Second Massachusetts Regiment of Infantry*. Boston: Alfred Mudge & Son, 1874.

Hallowell, Norwood P. *Selected Letters and Papers of N. P. Hallowell*. Peterborough, N.H.: Richard R. Smith Co., 1963.

———. *The Negro as a Soldier in the War of the Rebellion*. Boston: Little, Brown, 1897.

Harlan, Louis R., ed. *The Booker T. Washington Papers*. 13 volumes. Urbana: University of Illinois Press, 1972–84.

Harvard College. *Report of the Class of 1860: 1860–1866*. Cambridge, Mass.: Wilson & Sons, 1866.

Higginson, Henry Lee. *Four Addresses*. Boston: Merrymount Press, 1902.

Higginson, Mary T., ed. *Letters and Journals of Thomas Wentworth Higginson, 1846–1906*. Boston: Houghton Mifflin, 1921.

Higginson, Thomas W. *Army Life in a Black Regiment*. 1869; reprint, New York: W. W. Norton, 1984.

———. *Cheerful Yesterdays*. 1899; reprint, New York: Arno Press, 1968.

———. *Harvard Memorial Biographies*. 2 volumes. Cambridge, Mass.: Sever & Francis, 1867.

Hough, Franklin B., comp. *Census of the State of New York for 1855*. Albany: Van Benthysen, 1857.

————. *Census of the State of New York for 1865.* 2 volumes. Albany: Van Benthysen, 1867.

Howe, Mark DeWolfe, ed. *Touched With Fire: Civil War Letters and Diary of Oliver Wendell Holmes, Jr., 1861–1864.* Cambridge, Mass.: Harvard University Press, 1946.

Hughes, Sarah Forbes, ed. *Letters and Recollections of John Murray Forbes.* 2 volumes. Boston: Houghton Mifflin, 1899.

In Memoriam: Josephine Shaw Lowell. New York: Charity Organization of New York, 1905.

James, Garth W. "The Assault Upon Fort Wagner," *War Papers Read before the Commandery of the State of Wisconsin, Military Order of the Loyal Legion of the U.S.* Milwaukee: Burdick, Armitage & Allen, 1891.

Johnson R. V., and C. C. Buel, eds. *Battles and Leaders of the Civil War.* New York: Century, 1888.

Kemble, Frances Anne, *Journal of a Residence on a Georgian Plantation in 1838–9.* Edited, with an introduction by John A. Scott. New York: A. A. Knopf, 1961; also Brown Thrasher edition, Athens: University of Georgia Press, 1984.

Langston, John M. *From the Virginia Plantation to the National Capitol.* Hartford: American Publishing Co., 1894; reprint, New York: Johnson Reprint Corp., 1968.

Massachusetts Soldiers, Sailors, and Marines in the Civil War. 8 volumes. Norwood, Mass.: Norwood Press, 1931.

Meagher, Walter, ed. *A Proper Bostonian, Priest, Jesuit: Diary of Fr. Joseph Coolidge Shaw,* S.J. Boston: Published by the author, 1965.

Meltzer, Milton, ed. *The Black Americans: A History in Their Own Words, 1619–1983.* New York: Harper & Row, 1964

Meltzer, Milton, and Patricia Holland, eds. *Lydia Maria Child: Selected Letters, 1817–1880.* Amherst: University of Massachusetts Press, 1982.

Memorial: RGS. Cambridge, Mass.: Harvard University Press, 1864.

Merrill, Walter M., and Louis Ruchames, eds. *The Letters of William Lloyd Garrison.* 7 volumes. Cambridge, Mass.: Harvard University Press, 1979.

Montgomery, Horace, ed. "A Union Officer's Recollections of the Negro as a Soldier." *Pennsylvania History* 28 (April 1961): 156–86.

Morse, Charles F. "From Second Bull Run to Antietam," *War Papers and Personal Reminiscences,* 1861–1865. St. Louis: Becktold, 1892.

————. *Letters Written During the Civil War, 1861–1865.* Boston: Privately printed, 1898.

Nalty, Bernard C., and Morris J. MacGregor. *Blacks in the Military: Essential Documents.* Wilmington: Scholarly Resources, Inc., 1981.

Nevins, Allan, and Milton Thomas, eds. *The Diary of George Templeton Strong.* 4 volumes, New York: Macmillan, 1952.

Norton, Charles E., ed. *Letters of James Russell Lowell.* 2 volumes. New York: Harper, 1893–94.

Oakey, Daniel. "History of the Second Massachusetts Regiment of Infantry: Beverly Ford, June 9, 1863." Boston: George H. Ellis, 1884.

Parker, Theodore. *the Slave Power.* Edited by James K. Hosmer. Boston: American Unitarian Association, 1916; reprint, New York: Arno Press, 1969.

Pattison, Everett W. "Some Reminiscences of Army Life," *War Papers and Personal Reminiscences, 1861–1865*. St. Louis: Becktold, 1892.

Pearson, Elizabeth W., ed. *Letters From Port Royal, 1862–1868*. New York: Arno Press, 1969.

Perry, Bliss, ed. *Life and Letters of Henry Lee Higginson*. Boston: Atlantic Monthly Press, 1921.

Pickard, John B., ed. *The Letters of John Greenleaf Whittier*. 3 volumes. Cambridge, Mass.: Harvard University Press, 1975.

Pierce, Edward L., ed. *Memoir and Letters of Charles Sumner*. 4 volumes. Boston: Roberts Brothers, 1877–93.

Putnam, Elizabeth C., comp. *Memoirs of the War of '61: Colonel Charles Russell Lowell, Friends and Cousins*. Boston: G. H. Ellis, 1920.

Quincy, Samuel M. "History of the Second Massachusetts Regiment of Infantry: A Prisoner's Diary." Boston: George H. Ellis, 1882.

Quint, Alonzo Hall. *Record of the 2nd Massachusetts Infantry*. Boston: James P. Walker, 1867.

Record of the Massachusetts Volunteers, 1861–1865. 2 volumes. Boston: Wright & Potter, 1870.

Record of the Service of the Fifty-Fifth Regiment of Massachusetts Volunteer Infantry. 2 volumes. Cambridge, Mass.: John Wilson & Son, 1868.

"The Report of the Secretary of the Class of 1855 of Harvard College." Boston: Alfred Mudge & Son, 1865.

Richards, Laura E., ed. *Letters and Journals of Samuel Gridley Howe*. 2 volumes. Boston: D. Estes, 1909.

Saint-Gaudens, Homer, ed. *The Reminiscences of Augustus Saint-Gaudens*. 2 volumes. New York: Century, 1913.

Sanborn, F. B. *Recollections of Seventy Years*. 2 volumes. Boston: Gorham Press, 1909.

Schouler, William. *A History of Massachusetts in the Civil War*. 2 volumes. Boston: E.P. Dutton, 1868.

Scott, Robert Garth, ed. *Fallen Leaves: The Civil War Letters of Major Henry Livermore Abbott*. Kent: Kent State University Press, 1991.

Shaw, Robert Gould. *Letters: RGS*. Cambridge, Mass.: Harvard University Press, 1864.

———. *Letters: RGS*. New York: Collins & Brother, 1876.

Simmons, William J., ed. *Men of Mark: Eminent, Progressive and Rising*. 1887; reprint, New York: Arno Press, 1968.

"Souvenir of the Massachusetts Fifty-Fourth (Colored) Regiment." Boston: 1863.

Sterling, Dorothy, ed. *We Are Your Sisters: Black Women in the Nineteenth Century*. New York: W. W. Norton, 1984.

Stowe, Harriet Beecher. *The Key to Uncle Tom's Cabin*. Boston: Jewett, 1854; reprint, New York: Arno Press, 1968.

"Topics of the Time." *Century Magazine* 54 (June 1897): 312–14.

Towne, Laura. *Letters and Diary of Laura M. Towne: Written from the Sea Islands of South Carolina, 1862–1884*. 1912; reprint, New York: Negro Universities Press, 1969.

Trow's New York City Directory for the Year ending May 1, 1860 [1861–1863]. New York: John F. Trow, 1859 [1860–1862].

Twiggs, Hanaford D. D. "Defence of Battery Wagner, July 18, 1863." Augusta, Ga: Chronicle Publishing Co., 1892.

United States Census. Eighth Census. 1860. New York, Richmond County.

The War of the Rebellion: A Compilation of the Official Records of the Union and Confederate Armies. 128 volumes. Washington, D.C.: U.S. Government Printing Office, 1880–1901.

Warbutton, A. F., comp. "Commemoration by the Loyal League of Union Citizens, Madison Square, April 20, 1863." New York: George F. Nesbitt, 1863.

Whitman, Robert Shaw Sturgis. "The 'Glory' Letters," *Berkshire* (Mass.) *Eagle*, Feb. 2 (6:2), 1990.

Wilson's New York City Copartnership Directory for 1861–1862. New York: John F. Trow, 1861.

Woodson, Thomas, Neal Smith, and Norman H. Pearson, eds. *Nathaniel Hawthorne: The Letters, 1843–1853.* Columbus: Ohio State University Press, 1985.

Zilversmit, Arthur, ed. *Lincoln on Black and White: A Documentary History.* Belmont, Cal.: Wadsworth, 1971.

SECONDARY SOURCES

Books and Pamphlets:

Amory, Cleveland. *The Proper Bostonians.* New York: E. P. Dutton, 1947.

Andrews, J. Cutler. *The South Reports the Civil War.* Princeton: Princeton University Press, 1970.

Appleton's Cyclopedia of American Biography. New York: Appleton, 1887.

Aptheker, Herbert. *The Negro in the Civil War.* New York: International Publishers, 1938.

Barney, William L. *Battleground for the Union: The Era of the Civil War and Reconstruction, 1848–1877.* Englewood Cliffs, N.J.: Prentice-Hall, 1990.

Barrett, Walter. *The Old Merchants of New York City.* 3 volumes. New York: M. Doolady, 1865.

Bartlett, Samuel R. "The Charge of the Fifty-Fourth." Chicago: Church, Goodman & Donnelly, 1869.

Bayles, Richard M., ed. *History of Richmond County (Staten Island) New York From Its Discovery to the Present Time.* New York: L. E. Preston, 1887.

Benson, Richard. *Lay This Laurel: An Album on the Saint-Gaudens Memorial on Boston Common Honoring Black and White Men Together Who Served the Union Cause with Robert Gould Shaw and Died With Him July 18, 1863.* New York: Eakins, 1973.

Bell, Malcolm, Jr. *Major Butler's Legacy: Five Generations of a Slaveholding Family.* Athens: University of Georgia Press, 1987.

Berry, Mary Frances. *Military Necessity and Civil Rights Policy: Black Citizenship and the Constitution, 1861–1868.* Port Washington: Kennikat Press, 1977.

Binkin, Martin and Mark J. Eitelberg. *Blacks and the Military.* Washington, D.C.: Brookings Institution, 1982.

Blight, David W. *Frederick Douglass' Civil War: Keeping Faith in Jubilee*. Baton Rouge: Louisiana State University Press, 1989.

———. *When This Cruel War is Over: The Civil War Letters of Charles Harvey Brewster*. Amherst: University of Massachusetts Press, 1992.

Boatner, Mark M., III. *The Civil War Dictionary*. New York: David McKay, 1959.

Bowen, James L. *Massachusetts in the War, 1861–1865*. Springfield, Mass.: Bryan, 1889.

Bowman, John S., ed. *The Civil War Almanac*. New York: Bison Books, 1983.

Brown, Francis Henry. "First Report of the Class of 1857 in Harvard College." Cambridge, Mass.: John Wilson & Sons, 1866.

———. *Harvard University in the War of 1861–65*. Boston: Cupples, 1886.

———. *Report of the Class of 1857 in Harvard College*. Cambridge, Mass.: John Wilson, 1893.

———. "Roll of Students of Harvard University who served in the Army or Navy of the United States During the War of the Rebellion." Cambridge: Welch, Bigelow, 1866.

Brown, William Wells. *The Negro in the American Rebellion: His Heroism and His Fidelity*. New York: Lee & Shepard, 1867.

Browne, Albert G. *Sketch of the Official Life of Governor Andrew*. New York: Hurd & Houghton, 1868.

Bruce, George A. *The Twentieth Regiment of Massachusetts Volunteer Infantry, 1861–1865*. Boston: Houghton Mifflin, 1906.

Burchard, Peter. *One Gallant Rush: Robert Gould Shaw and His Brave Black Regiment*. New York: St. Martin's Press, 1965.

Burton, E. Milby. *The Siege of Charleston, 1861–1865*. Columbia: University of South Carolina Press, 1970.

Cary, Edward. *George William Curtis*. Boston: Houghton Mifflin, 1894.

Clark, Emmons. *History of the Seventh Regiment of New York, 1806–1889*. 2 volumes. New York: Published by the author, 1890.

Clute, J. J. *Annals of Staten Island, From Its Discovery to the Present Time*. New York: Charles Vogt, 1877.

Cook, Adrian. *The Armies of the Streets: The New York Draft Riots of 1863*. Lexington: University of Kentucky Press, 1974.

Cooke, George W. *Unitarianism in America: A History of Its Origin and Development*. Boston: American Unitarian Association, 1902.

Cornish, Dudley T. *The Sable Arm: Negro Troops in the Union Army, 1861–1865*. New York: Longmans, 1956.

Crawford, Mary C. *Famous Families of Massachusetts*. 2 volumes. Boston: Little, Brown, 1930.

Crowninshield, Benjamin W. *A History of the First Regiment of Massachusetts Cavalry Volunteers*. Boston: Houghton Mifflin, 1891.

Cudahy, Brian J. *Over and Back: The History of Ferryboats in New York Harbor*. New York: Fordham University Press, 1990.

Dalzell, Robert. *Enterprising Elite: The Boston Associates and the World They Made*. Cambridge, Mass.: Harvard University Press, 1987.

Dictionary of American Biography. 10 volumes and 8 supplements. New York: Charles Scribner's Sons, 1927–88.

Duberman, Martin B. *James Russell Lowell*. Boston: Houghton Mifflin, 1966.

Duberman, Martin B., ed. *The Antislavery Vanguard: New Essays on the Abolitionists*. Princeton: Princeton University Press, 1965.

Du Bois, W. E. B. *Black Reconstruction: An Essay Toward the History of the Part which Black Folk Played in the Reconstruction of America*. New York: Harcourt, Brace, 1935.

———. *John Brown*. Philadelphia: Jacobs, 1909; reprint, New York: International Publishers, 1962.

Dumond, Dwight L. *Antislavery: The Crusade for Freedom in America*. Ann Arbor: University of Michigan Press, 1961.

Dyer, Frederick H. *Compendium of the War of the Rebellion*. 3 volumes. Des Moines: 1908; reprint, New York: T. Yoseloff, 1959.

Farrison, William E. *William Wells Brown: Author and Reformer*. Chicago: University of Chicago Press, 1969.

Faust, Patricia L., ed. *Historical Times Illustrated Encyclopedia of the Civil War*. New York: Harper & Row, 1986.

Foner, Eric. *Free Labor, Free Soil, Free Men: The Ideology of the Republican Party before the Civil War*. New York: Oxford University Press, 1970.

———. *Politics and Ideology in the Age of the Civil War*. New York: Oxford University Press, 1980.

Foner, Jack D. *Blacks and the Military in American History: A New Perspective*. New York: Praeger Publishers, 1974.

Foote, Shelby. *The Civil War: A Narrative*. New York: Random House, 1958–1974.

Forbes, Abner, and J. W. Greene. *The Rich Men of Massachusetts*. Boston: Fetridge, 1852.

Fox, William F. *Regimental Losses in the American Civil War, 1861–1865*. Albany, N.Y.: Albany Publishing Co., 1889.

Frederickson, George M. *The Black Image in the White Mind: The Debate on Afro-American Character and Destiny, 1817–1914*. New York: Harper & Row, 1971.

———. *The Inner Civil War: Northern Intellectuals and the Crisis of the Union*. New York: Harper & Row, 1965.

Furnas, J. C. *Fanny Kemble: Leading Lady of the Nineteenth-Century Stage*. New York: Dial Press, 1982.

Gerteis, Louis S. *From Contraband to Freedman: Federal Policy Toward Southern Blacks, 1861–1865*. Westport, Conn.: Greenwood Press, 1973.

Gilchrist, Robert C. *The Confederate Defence of Morris Island, Charleston Harbor*. Charleston, S.C.: News & Courier, 1884.

Gladstone, William A. *United States Colored Troops, 1863–1867*. Gettysburg, Pa.: Thomas Publishers, 1990.

Glatthaar, Joseph T. *Forged in Battle: The Civil War Alliance of Black Soldiers and White Officers*. New York: Free Press, 1990.

Gray, J. Glenn. *The Warriors: Reflections of Men in Battle*. New York: Harper & Row, 1959.

Greenslet, Ferris. *The Lowells and Their Seven Worlds*. Boston: Houghton Mifflin, 1946.

Guthrie, James M. *Camp Fires of the Afro-American*. Philadelphia: American Publishing Co., 1899; reprint, New York: Johnson Reprint Co., 1970.

Hampton, Vernon B. *Staten Island's Claim to Fame*. Staten Island, N.Y.: Richmond Borough, 1925.

Hargrove, Hondon B. *Black Union Soldiers in the Civil War*. Jefferson, N.C.: McFarland, 1988.

Hart, Albert B., ed. *Commonwealth History of Massachusetts*. New York: States History Co., 1930.

Headley, Phineas C. *Massachusetts in the Rebellion*. Boston: Walker, Fuller, 1866.

Higginson, Thomas W. *Massachusetts in the Army and Navy During the War of 1861–65*. 2 volumes. Boston: Wright & Potter, 1896.

Hine, Charles G., and William T. Davis. *Legends, Stories and Folklore of Old Staten Island*. New York: Staten Island Historical Society, 1925.

History of Berkshire County, Massachusetts. 2 volumes. New York: J. B. Beers, 1885.

Horton, James O., and Lois E. Horton. *Black Bostonians: Family Life and Community Struggle in the Antebellum North*. New York: Holmes & Meier, 1979.

Kaplan, Sidney. *American Studies in Black and White*. Amherst: University of Massachusetts Press, 1990.

King, Spencer B., Jr. *Darien: The Death and Rebirth of a Southern Town*. Macon, Ga.: Mercer University Press, 1981.

Krick, Robert C. *Stonewall Jackson at Cedar Mountain*. Chapel Hill: University of North Carolina Press, 1990.

Lader, Lawrence. *The Bold Brahmins: New England's War Against Slavery, 1831–1863*. New York: E. P. Dutton, 1961.

Leech, Margaret. *Reveille in Washington, 1860–1865*. New York: Harper, 1941.

Leng, Charles W., and William T. Davis. *Staten Island and Its People: A History, 1609–1929*. 2 volumes. New York: Lewis Publishing Co., 1929–30.

Linderman, Gerald F. *Embattled Courage: The Experience of Combat in the American Civil War*. New York: Free Press, 1987.

Litwack, Leon F. *Been in the Storm So Long: The Aftermath of Slavery*. New York: A. A. Knopf, 1979.

Litwack, Leon F., and August Meier, eds. *Black Leaders of the Nineteenth Century*. Urbana: University of Illinois Press, 1988.

Logan, Rayford W., and Michael R. Winston, eds. *Dictionary of American Negro Biography*. New York: W. W. Norton, 1982.

Long, E. B., and Barbara Long. *The Civil War Day by Day: An Almanac, 1861–1865. Garden City, N.Y.*: Doubleday, 1971.

Lowell, Robert. *Life Studies and For the Union Dead*. New York: Noonday Press, 1971.

McFeely, William S. *Frederick Douglass*. New York: W. W. Norton, 1991.

———. *Grant: A Biography*. New York: W. W. Norton, 1981.

McGuiness, Colleen, and Maria J. Sayers, eds. *American Leaders, 1789–1987: A Biographical Summary*. Washington, D.C.: Congressional Quarterly, 1987.

McKay, Ernest A. *The Civil War and New York City*. Syracuse University Press, 1990.

McKay, Martha N. *When the Tide Turned in the Civil War*. Indianapolis: Hollenbeck Press, 1929.

McKinsey, Folger. *History of Frederick County Maryland*. 2 volumes. Baltimore: L. R. Titsworth, 1910.

McPherson, James M. *Abraham Lincoln and the Second American Revolution*. New York: Oxford University Press, 1991.

———. *Battle Cry of Freedom: The Civil War Era*. New York: Oxford University Press, 1988.

———. *The Negro's Civil War: How American Negroes Felt and Acted During the War for the Union*. New York: Pantheon, 1965.

———. *The Struggle for Equality: Abolitionists and the Negro in the Civil War and Reconstruction*. Princeton: Princeton University Press, 1964.

Mays, Joe H. *Black Americans and Their Contributions Toward Union Victory in the American Civil War, 1861–1865*. Latham, Md.: University Press of America, 1984.

Milne, Gordon. *George William Curtis and the Genteel Tradition*. Bloomington: Indiana University Press, 1956.

The Monument to Robert Gould Shaw: Its Inception, Completion and Unveiling, 1865–1897. Boston: Houghton Mifflin, 1897.

Moore, Frank, ed. *Heroes and Martyrs: Notable Men of the Time*. New York: G. P. Putnam, 1861.

Morris, Ida K. *Morris's Memorial History of Staten Island, NY*. 2 volumes. Staten Island: Published by the author, 1900.

Nalty, Bernard C. *Strength for the Fight: A History of Black Americans in the Military*. New York: Free Press, 1986.

National Cyclopedia of American Biography. New York: James T. White, 1897–1972.

Neely, Mark E. *The Abraham Lincoln Encyclopedia*. New York: McGraw-Hill, 1982.

Nevins, Allan. *Frémont: The West's Greatest Adventurer*. 2 volumes. New York: Harper, 1928.

Oates, Stephen B. *To Purge This Land With Blood: A Biography of John Brown*. New York: Harper & Row, 1970.

Paludan, Phillip S. *"A People's Contest": The Union and the Civil War, 1861–1865*. New York: Harper & Row, 1988.

Pearson, Henry G. *An American Railroad Builder: John Murray Forbes*. Boston: Houghton Mifflin, 1911.

———. *The Life of John A. Andrew, Governor of Massachusetts, 1861–1865*. 2 volumes. Boston: Houghton Mifflin, 1904.

Phisterer, Frederick, comp. *New York in the War of the Rebellion, 1861 to 1865*. Albany: Weed, Parsons, 1890.

Quarles, Benjamin. *The Negro in the Civil War*. Boston: Little, Brown, 1953; reprint, New York: Da Capo, 1989.

Roehrenbeck, William J. *The Regiment That Saved the Capital*. New York: A. S. Barnes, 1961.

Rose, Willie Lee. *Rehearsal for Reconstruction: The Port Royal Experiment*. London & New York: Oxford University Press, 1964.

Royster, Charles. *The Destructive War: William Tecumseh Sherman, Stonewall Jackson and the Americans.* New York: A. A. Knopf, 1991.

Sears, Stephen. *Landscape Turned Red: The Battle of Antietam.* New Haven: Ticknor & Fields, 1983.

Shaw, Frances George. "A Piece of Land." In Henry George, *Social Problems.* New York: J. W. Lovell, 1883, pp. 298–304.

————, trans. *The Children of the Phalanstary: A Familiar Dialogue on Education,* by F. Cantagrel. New York: W. H. Graham, 1848.

Sifakis, Stewart. *Who Was Who in the Civil War.* New York: Facts on File, 1988.

Simpson, Marc. *Winslow Homer: Paintings of the Civil War.* San Francisco: Bedford Arts, 1989.

Smith, Marion W. *Beacon Hill's Colonel Robert Gould Shaw.* New York: Carlton Press, 1986.

Sorin, Gerald. *The New York Abolitionists: A Case Study of Political Radicalism.* Westport, Conn.: Greenwood Press, 1971.

Spalding, Walter R. *Music at Harvard: A Historical Review of Men and Events.* New York: Coward-McCann, 1935.

Stearns, Frank P. *The Life and Public Services of George Luther Stearns.* Philadelphia: J. B. Lippincott, 1907.

Stewart, James Brewer. *Holy Warriors: The Abolitionists and American Slavery.* New York: Hill & Wang, 1976.

Stewart, William R. *The Philanthropic Works of Josephine Shaw Lowell.* New York: Macmillan, 1911.

Sturgis, Roger Faxton, ed. *Edward Sturgis of Yarmouth, Mass., 1613–1695, and His Descendants.* Boston: Stanhope, 1914.

Swift, Lindsay. *Brook Farm: Its Members, Scholars, and Visitors.* New York: Macmillan, 1900.

Swinton, William. *History of the Seventh Regiment National Guard, State of New York During the War of the Rebellion.* New York: Dillingham, 1886.

Teamoh, Robert T. *Sketch of the Life and Death of Colonel Robert Gould Shaw.* Boston: Boston Globe, 1904.

Thomas, Emory M. *Bold Dragoon: The Life of J.E.B. Stuart.* New York: Harper & Row, 1986.

Uglow, Jennifer S., ed. *The International Dictionary of Women's Biography.* New York: Continuum, 1982.

Ullman, Victor. *Martin R. Delany: The Beginnings of Black Nationalism.* Boston: Beacon Press, 1971.

Wakelyn, Jon L. *Biographical Dictionary of the Confederacy.* Westport, Conn.: Greenwood Press, 1977.

Ware, Edith E. *Political Opinion in Massachusetts During the Civil War and Reconstruction.* New York: Columbia University Press, 1916.

Weinberg, Adelaide. *John Elliot Cairnes and the American Civil War: A Study in Anglo-American Relations.* London: Kingswood Press, 1969.

Wells, Anna Mary. *Dear Preceptor: The Life and Times of Thomas Wentworth Higginson.* Boston: Houghton Mifflin, 1963.

Werstein, Irving. *The Storming of Fort Wagner: Black Valor in the Civil War*. New York: Scholastic Books, 1970.

Whitehall, Walter M. *Boston and the Civil War*. Boston: Boston Athenaeum, 1963.

Wiley, Bell I. *The Life of Billy Yank: The Common Soldier of the Union*. Baton Rouge: Louisiana State University Press, 1952.

Williams, George W. *A History of Negro Troops in the War of the Rebellion, 1861–1865*. New York: Harper, 1888; reprint, New York: Greenwood Press, 1969.

Williams, T. J. C., and Folger McKinsey. *History of Frederick County, Maryland*. 2 volumes. Baltimore: Regional Publishing Co., 1967.

Wilson, Joseph T. *The Black Phalanx: A History of the Negro Soldiers of the United States in the Wars of 1775–1812, 1861–'65*. Hartford: American Publishing Co., 1888; reprint, New York: Arno Press, 1968.

Winthrop, Robert C. *Memoir of the Hon. Nathan Appleton*. Boston: Wilson & Son, 1861; reprint, New York: Greenwood Press, 1969.

Periodicals:

Abbott, Mabel. "Some Faded Pages of Local History." *New Bulletin* (December 1965): 23–31.

Abbott, Richard H. "Massachusetts and the Recruitment of Southern Negroes, 1863–1865." *Civil War History* 14 (September 1968): 197–210.

Axelrod, Steven G. "Colonel Shaw in American Poetry: 'For the Union Dead' and Its Precursors." *American Quarterly* 24 (October 1972): 523–37.

Belz, Herman. "Law, Politics and Race in the Struggle for Equal Pay During the Civil War." *Civil War History* 22 (September 1976): 197–213.

Cornish, Dudley T. "To Be Recognized as Men: The Practical Utility of History." *Military Review* 58 (February 1978): 40–55.

Coulter, E. Merton. "Robert Gould Shaw and the Burning of Darien, Georgia." *Civil War History* 5 (Fall 1959): 363–73.

Duberman, Martin B., ed. "A New England Soldier's Last Letter." *Civil War History* 9 (September 1963): 325–27.

Dyer, Brainard. "The Treatment of Colored Union Troops by the Confederates, 1861–1865." *Journal of Negro History* 20 (July 1935): 273–86.

Fincher, Jack. "The Hard Fight Was Getting Into the Fight At All." *Smithsonian* (October 1990): 46–61.

Flint, Allen. "Black Responses to Colonel Shaw." *Phylon* 45 (Fall 1984): 210–19.

Hansen, Chadwick. "The 54th Massachusetts Volunteer Black Infantry as a Subject for American Artists." *Massachusetts Review* 16 (Autumn 1975): 745–59.

Heller, Charles E. "The 54th Massachusetts." *Civil War Times Illustrated* 11 (April 1972): 32–41.

————. "George Luther Stearns." *Civil War Times Illustrated* 13 (July 1974): 20–28.

Hess, Earl J. "Northern Responses to the Ironclad: A Prospect for the Study of Military Technology." *Civil War History* 31 (June 1985): 126–43.

Higginson, Thomas W. "The Shaw Memorial and the Sculptor St. Gaudens." *Century Magazine* 54 (June 1897): 176–200.

Lane, James B. "Jacob A. Riis and Scientific Philanthropy During the Progressive Era." *Social Science Review* 47 (March 1973): 32–48.

Longacre, Edward. "Brave Radical Wild: The Contentious Career of Brigadier Edward A. Wild." *Civil War Times Illustrated* 19 (June 1980): 8–19.

Redding, Saunders. "Tonight For Freedom." *American Heritage* 9 (June 1958): 52–55, 90.

Redkey, Edwin S. "Black Chaplains in the Union Army." *Civil War History* 33 (December 1987): 331–50.

Reid, Richard. "General Edward A. Wild and Civil War Discrimination." *Historical Journal of Massachusetts* 13 (January 1985): 14–29.

Riley, Stephen T. "A Monument to Colonel Robert Gould Shaw." *Proceedings of the Massachusetts Historical Society* 75 (1963): 27–38.

Roper, Laura Wood. "Frederick Law Olmsted in the 'Literary Republic.'" *Journal of American History* 39 (December 1952): 459–82.

Scharnhorst, Gary. "From Soldier to Saint: Robert Gould Shaw and the Rhetoric of Racial Justice." *Civil War History* 34 (December 1988): 308–22.

Seraile, William. "The Struggle to Raise Black Regiments in New York, 1861–1864." *New York Historical Society Quarterly* 58 (August 1974): 215–33.

Shannon, Fred A. "The Federal Government and the Negro Soldier, 1861–1865." *Journal of Negro History* 11 (October 1926): 563–83.

Westwood, Horace C. "Captive Black Soldiers in Charleston—What to Do?" *Civil War History* 28 (March 1982): 28–44.

———. "The Cause and Consequence of a Union Black Soldier's Mutiny and Execution." *Civil War History* 31 (September 1985): 222–36.

———. "Generals David Hunter and Rufus Saxton and Black Soldiers." *South Carolina Historical Magazine* 86 (Summer 1985): 165–81.

Zettl, Herbert. "Garibaldi and the American Civil War." *Civil War History* 22 (March 1976): 70–76.

Joy Street Baptist Church, 26